ENVIRONMENTAL STATUTES

1983 Edition

- Clean Air Act
- Federal Insecticide, Fungicide and Rodenticide Act (FIFRA)
- Federal Water Pollution Control Act (Clean Water Act)
- Marine Sanctuaries Act
- National Environmental Policy Act
- Noise Control Act
- Occupational Safety and Health Act
- Resource Conservation and Recovery Act or Solid Waste Disposal Act
- Safe Drinking Water Act
- Superfund or Comprehensive Environmental Response, Compensation, and Liability Act of 1980 (CERCLA)
- Toxic Substances Control Act
- Used Oil Recycling Act of 1980

Government Institutes, Inc.

PUBLISHER'S NOTE

This book is designed to provide accurate and authoritative information on the subject matter. It is sold with the understanding that the publisher is not engaged in rendering legal, accounting or other professional services. If legal advice or other expert assistance is needed, the services of a competent professional should be sought. (From the Declaration of Principles adopted jointly by a committee of the American Bar Association and a committee of publishers.)

DISCLAIMER

Some of the statutes have been revised regularly with the result that there is considerable confusion as to what is officially contained in these statutes at any one time. Also, amendments are contemplated to some of these statutes, so the reader should use care in relying on what is the actual statute at any point in time.

July 1983

Published by
Government Institutes, Inc.
966 Hungerford Drive, #24
Rockville, MD 20850
U.S.A.

ISBN: 0-86587-114-0 (softcover)
ISBN: 0-86587-113-2 (hardcover)
Printed and bound in the United States of America

GENERAL TABLE OF CONTENTS

DETAILED TABLE OF CONTENTS

THE CLEAN AIR ACT

TITLE I – Air Pollution Prevention And Control

Part A – Air Quality And Emission Limitations

Part B – Ozone Protection

TABLE OF CONTENTS

Part C – Prevention of Significant Deterioration of Air Quality

Subpart 1

Subpart 2

Part D – Plan Requirements for Nonattainment Areas

TITLE II – Emission Standards for Moving Sources

Part A – Motor Vehicle Emission and Fuel Standards

Part B – Aircraft Emission Standards

TABLE OF CONTENTS

TITLE III - General

APPENDIX - Provisions of the Clean Air Act Amendments of 1977 (Public Law 95-95) Which did not Amend the Clean Air Act

TABLE OF CONTENTS

THE FEDERAL INSECTICIDE, FUNGICIDE AND RODENTICIDE ACT

Section:

FEDERAL WATER POLLUTION CONTROL ACT
as amended by the CLEAN WATER ACT OF 1977

TITLE 1 - Research and Related Programs

Section:

TABLE OF CONTENTS

TABLE OF CONTENTS

TITLE V - General Provisions

MARINE PROTECTION, RESEARCH, AND SANCTUARIES ACT OF 1972

TITLE I - Ocean Dumping

NATIONAL ENVIRONMENTAL POLICY ACT OF 1969
as amended through August 1975

TITLE I - Declaration of National Environmental Policy

TABLE OF CONTENTS

TABLE OF CONTENTS

RESOURCE CONSERVATION AND RECOVERY ACT OF 1976

Section:

TITLE II - Solid Waste Disposal

Subtitle A - General Provisions

Section:

Subtitle B - Office of Solid Waste: Authorities of the Administrator

Section:

Subtitle C - Hazardous Waste Management

Section:

TABLE OF CONTENTS

TABLE OF CONTENTS

TABLE OF CONTENTS

TABLE OF CONTENTS

TITLE III - Miscellaneous Provisions

TOXIC SUBSTANCES CONTROL ACT

ENVIRONMENTAL STATUTES

1983 Edition

THE CLEAN AIR ACT

as amended[1]

TITLE I—AIR POLLUTION PREVENTION AND CONTROL

PART A—AIR QUALITY AND EMISSION LIMITATIONS

FINDINGS AND PURPOSES

SEC. 101. (a) The Congress finds—

(1) that the predominant part of the Nation's population is located in its rapidly expanding metropolitan and other urban areas, which generally cross the boundary lines of local jurisdictions and often extend into two or more States;

(2) that the growth in the amount and complexity of air pollution brought about by urbanization, industrial development, and the increasing use of motor vehicles, has resulted in mounting dangers to the public health and welfare, including injury to agricultural crops and livestock, damage to and the deterioration of property, and hazards to air and ground transportation;

(3) that the prevention and control of air pollution at its source is the primary responsibility of States and local governments; and

(4) that Federal financial assistance and leadership is essential for the development of cooperative Federal, State, regional, and local programs to prevent and control air pollution.

(b) The purposes of this title are—

(1) to protect and enhance the quality of the Nation's air resources so as to promote the public health and welfare and the productive capacity of its population;

(2) to initiate and accelerate a national research and development program to achieve the prevention and control of air pollution;

(3) to provide technical and financial assistance to State and local governments in connection with the development and execution of their air pollution prevention and control programs; and

(4) to encourage and assist the development and operation of regional air pollution control programs.

---

[1]Clean Air Act (42 U.S.C. 1857 et seq.) includes the Clean Air Act of 1963, PL 88-206 and amendments made by the Motor Vehicle Air Pollution Control Act , PL 89-272, October 20, 1965, the Clean Air Act Amendments of 1966, PL 89-675, October 15, 1966, The Air Quality Act of 1967, PL 90-148, November 21, 1967; the Clean Air Amendments of 1970, PL 91-604, December 31, 1970; the Comprehensive Health Manpower Training Act of 1971, PL 92-157, November 18, 1971; the Energy Supply and Environmental Coordination Act of 1974, PL 93-319, June 22, 1974, Clean Air Act Amendments of 1977, PL 95-95, August 7, 1977; Safe Drinking Water Act of 1977, PL 95-190, November 16, 1977; Public Law 96-300, July 2, 1980, and Public Law 97-23, July 17, 1981. Amendments made by the 1981 amendments (PL 97-23), are shown as follows: language to be omitted is struck through; new language is printed in italic.

COOPERATIVE ACTIVITIES AND UNIFORM LAWS

SEC. 102. (a) The Administrator shall encourage cooperative activities by the States and local governments for the prevention and control of air pollution; encourage the enactment of improved and, so far as practicable in the light of varying conditions and needs, uniform State and local laws relating to the prevention and control of air pollution; and encourage the making of agreements and compacts between States for the prevention and control of air pollution.

(b) The Administrator shall cooperate with and encourage cooperative activities by all Federal departments and agencies having functions relating to the prevention and control of air pollution, so as to assure the utilization in the Federal air pollution control program of all appropriate and available facilities and resources within the Federal Government.

(c) The consent of the Congress is hereby given to two or more States to negotiate and enter into agreements or compacts, not in conflict with any law or treaty of the United States, for (1) cooperative effort and mutual assistance for the prevention and control of air pollution and the enforcement of their respective laws relating thereto, and (2) the establishment of such agencies, joint or otherwise, as they may deem desirable for making effective such agreements or compacts. No such agreement or compact shall be binding or obligatory upon any State a party thereto unless and until it has been approved by Congress. It is the intent of Congress that no agreement or compact entered into between States after the date of enactment of the Air Quality Act of 1967, which relates to the control and abatement of air pollution in an air quality control region, shall provide for participation by a State which is not included (in whole or in part) in such air quality control region.

RESEARCH, INVESTIGATION, TRAINING, AND OTHER ACTIVITIES

SEC. 103. (a) The Administrator shall establish a national research and development program for the prevention and control of air pollution and as part of such program shall—

(1) conduct, and promote the coordination and acceleration of, research, investigations, experiments, demonstrations, surveys, and studies relating to the causes, effects, extent, prevention, and control of air pollution;

(2) encourage, cooperate with, and render technical services and provide financial assistance to air pollution control agencies and other appropriate

public or private agencies, institutions, and organizations, and individuals in the conduct of such activities;

(3) conduct investigations and research and make surveys concerning any specific problem of air pollution in cooperation with any air pollution control agency with a view to recommending a solution of such problem, if he is requested to do so by such agency or if, in his judgment, such problem may affect any community or communities in a State other than that in which the source of the matter causing or contributing to the pollution is located;

(4) establish technical advisory committees composed of recognized experts in various aspects of air pollution to assist in the examination and evaluation of research progress and proposals and to avoid duplication of research; and

(5) conduct and promote coordination and acceleration of training for individuals relating to the causes, effects, extent, prevention, and control of air pollution.

(b) In carrying out the provisions of the preceding subsection the Administrator is authorized to—

(1) collect and make available, through publications and other appropriate means, the results of and other information, including appropriate recommendations by him in connection therewith, pertaining to such research and other activities;

(2) cooperate with other Federal departments and agencies, with air pollution control agencies, with other public and private agencies, institutions, and organizations, and with any industries involved, in the preparation and conduct of such research and other activities;

(3) make grants to air pollution control agencies, to other public or nonprofit private agencies, institutions, and organizations, and to individuals, for purposes stated in subsection (a) (1) of this section;

(4) contract with public or private agencies, institutions, and organizations, and with individuals, without regard to sections 3648 and 3709 of the Revised Statutes (31 U.S.C. 529; 41 U.S.C. 5);

(5) establish and maintain research fellowships, in the Environmental Protection Agency and at public or nonprofit private educational institutions or research organizations;

(6) collect and disseminate, in cooperation with other Federal departments and agencies, and with other public or private agencies, institutions, and organizations having related responsibilities, basic data on chemical, physical, and biological effects of varying air quality and other information pertaining to air pollution and the prevention and control thereof; and

(7) develop effective and practical processes, methods, and prototype devices for the prevention or control of air pollution.

In carrying out the provisions of subsection (a), the Administrator shall provide training for, and make training grants to, personnel of air pollution control agencies and other persons with suitable qualifications and make grants to such agencies, to other public or nonprofit private agencies, institutions, and organizations for the purposes stated in subsection (a)(5). Reasonable fees may be charged for such training provided to persons other than personnel of air pollution control agencies but such training shall be provided to such personnel of air pollution control agencies without charge.

(c) In carrying out the provisions of subsection (a) of this section the Administration shall conduct research on, and survey the results of other scientific studies on, the harmful effects on the health or welfare of persons by the various known air pollutants.

(d) The Administrator is authorized to construct such facilities and staff and equip them as he determines to be necessary to carry out his functions under this Act.

(e) If, in the judgment of the Administrator, an air pollution problem of substantial significance may result from discharge or discharges into the atmosphere, he may call a conference concerning this potential air pollution problem to be held in or near one or more of the places where such discharge or discharges are occurring or will occur. All interested persons shall be given an opportunity to be heard at such conference, either orally or in writing, and shall be permitted to appear in person or by representative in accordance with procedures prescribed by the Administrator. If the Administrator finds, on the basis of evidence presented at such conference, that the discharge or discharges if permitted to take place or continue are likely to cause or contribute to air pollution subject to abatement under section 115, he shall send such findings, together with recommendations concerning the measures which he finds reasonable and suitable to prevent such pollution, to the person or persons whose actions will result in the discharge or discharges involved; to air pollution agencies of the State or States and of the municipality or municipalities where such discharge or discharges will originate; and to the interstate air pollution control agency, if any, in the jurisdictional area of which any such municipality is located. Such findings and recommendations shall be advisory only, but shall be admitted together with the record of the conference, as part of the proceedings under subsections (b), (c), (d), (e), and (f) of section 115.

(f)(1) In carrying out research pursuant to this Act, the Administrator shall give special emphasis to research on the short- and long-term effects of air pollutants on public health and welfare. In the furtherance of such research, he shall conduct an accelerated research program—

(A) to improve knowledge of the contribution of air pollutants to the occurrence of adverse effects on health, including, but not limited to, behavioral physiological, toxicological, and biochemical effects; and

(B) to improve knowledge of the short- and long-term effects of air pollutants on welfare.

(2) In carrying out the provisions of this subsection the Administrator may—

(A) conduct epidemiological studies of the effects of air pollutants on mortality and morbidity;

(B) conduct clinical and laboratory studies on the immunologic, biochemical, physiological, and the toxicological effects including carcinogenic, teratogenic, and mutagenic effects of air pollutants;

(C) utilize, on a reimbursable basis, the facilities of existing Federal scientific laboratories and research centers;

(D) utilize the authority contained in paragraphs (1) through (4) of subsection (b); and

(E) consult with other appropriate Federal agencies to assure that research of studies conducted pursuant to this subsection will be coordinated with research and studies of such other Federal agencies.

(3) In entering into contracts under this subsection, the Administrator is authorized to contract for a term not to exceed 10 years in duration. For the purposes of this paragraph, there are authorized to be appropriated $15,000,000. Such amounts as are appropriated shall remain available until expended and shall be in addition to any other appropriations under this Act.

RESEARCH RELATING TO FUELS AND VEHICLES

SEC. 104 (a) The Administrator shall give special emphasis to research and development into new and improved methods, having industrywide application, for the prevention and control of air pollution resulting from the combustion of fuels. In furtherance of such research and development he shall—

(1) conduct and accelerate research programs directed toward development of improved, low-cost techniques for—

(A) control of combustion byproducts of fuels,

(B) removal of potential air pollutants from fuels prior to combustion,

(C) control of emissions from the evaporation of fuels,

(D) improving the efficiency of fuels combustion so as to decrease atmospheric emissions, and

(E) producing synthetic or new fuels which,

when used, result in decreased atmospheric emissions.

(2) provide for Federal grants to public or nonprofit agencies, institutions, and organizations and to individuals, and contracts with public or private agencies, institutions or persons, for payment of (A) part of the cost of acquiring, constructing, or otherwise securing for research and development purposes, new or improved devices or methods having industrywide application of preventing or controlling discharges into the air of various types of pollutants; (B) part of the cost of programs to develop low emission alternatives to the present internal combustion engine; (C) the cost to purchase vehicles and vehicle engines, or portions thereof, for research, development, and testing purposes; and (D) carrying out the other provisions of this section, without regard to sections 3648 and 3709 of the Revised Statutes (31 U.S.C. 529; 41 U.S.C. 5): *Provided*, That research or demonstration contracts awarded pursuant to this subsection or demonstration contracts awarded pursuant to this subsection (including contracts for construction) may be made in accordance with, and subject to the limitations provided with respect to research contracts of the military departments in, section 2353 of title 10, United States Code, except that the determination, approval, and certification required thereby shall be made by the Administrator: *Provided further*, That no grant may be made under this paragraph in excess of $1,500,000;

(3) determine, by laboratory and pilot plant testing, the results of air pollution research and studies in order to develop new or improved processes and plant designs to the point where they can be demonstrated on a large and practical scale;

(4) construct, operate, and maintain, or assist in meeting the cost of the construction, operation, and maintenance of new or improved demonstration plants or processes which have promise of accomplishing the purposes of this Act;

(5) study new or improved methods for the recovery and marketing of commercially valuable byproducts resulting from the removal of pollutants.

(b) In carrying out the provisions of this section, the Administrator may—

(1) conduct and accelerate research and development of low-cost instrumentation techniques to facilitate determination of quantity and quality of air pollutant emissions, including, but not limited to, automotive emissions;

(2) utilize, on a reimbursable basis, the facilities of existing Federal scientific laboratories;

(3) establish and operate necessary facilities and test sites at which to carry on the research, testing, development, and programing necessary to effectuate the purposes of this section;

(4) acquire secret processes, technical data, inventions, patent applications, patents, licenses, and an interest in lands, plants, and facilities, and other property or rights by purchase, license, lease, or donation; and

(5) cause on-site inspections to be made of promising domestic and foreign projects, and cooperate and participate in their development in instances in which the purposes of the Act will be served thereby.

(c) For the purposes of this section there are authorized to be appropriated $75,000,000 for the fiscal year ending June 30, 1971, $125,000,000 for the fiscal year ending June 30, 1972, and $150,000,000 for the fiscal year ending June 30, 1973, $150,000,000 for the fiscal year ending June 30, 1974, and $150,000,000 for the fiscal year ending June 30, 1975. Amounts appropriated pursuant to this subsection shall remain available until expended.

GRANTS FOR SUPPORT OF AIR POLLUTION PLANNING AND CONTROL PROGRAMS

SEC. 105. (a)(1)(A) The Administrator may make grants to air pollution control agencies in an amount up to two-thirds of the cost of planning, developing, establishing, or improving, and up to one-half of the cost of maintaining, programs for the prevention and control of air pollution or implementation of national primary and secondary ambient air quality standards.

(B) Subject to subparagraph (C), the Administrator may make grants to air pollution control agencies within the meaning of paragraph (1), (2), or (4) of section 302(b) in an amount up to three-fourths of the cost of planning, developing, establishing, or improving, and up to three-fifths of the cost of maintaining, any program for the prevention and control of air pollution or implementation of national primary and secondary ambient air quality standards in an area that includes two or more municipalities, whether in the same or different States.

(C) With respect to any air quality control region or portion thereof for which there is an applicable implementation plan under section 110, grants under subparagraph (B) may be made only to air pollution control agencies which have substantial responsibilities for carrying out such applicable implementation plan.

(2) Before approving any grant under this subsection to any air pollution control agency within the meaning of sections 302(b)(2) and 302(b)(4) the Administrator shall receive assurances that such agency provides for

adequate representation of appropriate State, interstate, local, and (when appropriate) international, interests in the air quality control region.

(3) Before approving any planning grant under this subsection to any air pollution control agency within the meaning of sections 302(b)(2) and 302(b)(4), the Administrator shall receive assurances that such agency has the capability of developing a comprehensive air quality plan for the air quality control region, which plan shall include (when appropriate) a recommended system of alerts to avert and reduce the risk of situations in which there may be imminent and serious danger to the public health or welfare from air pollutants and the various aspects relevant to the establishment of air quality standards for such air quality control region, including the concentration of industries, other commercial establishments, population and naturally occurring factors which shall affect such standards.

(b) From the sums available for the purposes of subsection (a) of this section for any fiscal year, the Administrator shall from time to time make grants to air pollution control agencies upon such terms and conditions as the Administrator may find necessary to carry out the purpose of this section. In establishing regulations for the granting of such funds the Administrator shall, so far as practicable, give due consideration to (1) the population, (2) the extent of the actual or potential air pollution problem, and (3) the financial need of the respective agencies. No agency shall receive any grant under this section during any fiscal year when its expenditures of non-Federal funds for other than nonrecurrent expenditures for air pollution control programs will be less than its expenditures were for such programs during the preceding fiscal year, unless the Administrator, after notice and opportunity for public hearing, determines that a reduction in expenditures is attributable to a nonselective reduction in expenditures in the programs of all executive branch agencies of the applicable unit of Government; and no agency shall receive any grant under this section with respect to the maintenance of a program for the prevention and control of air pollution unless the Administrator is satisfied that such grant will be so used to supplement and, to the extent practicable, increase the level of State, local, or other non-Federal funds that would in the absence of such grant be made available for the maintenance of such program, and will in no event supplant such State, local, or other non-Federal funds. No grant shall be made under this section until the Administrator has consulted with the appropriate official as designated by the Governor or Governors of the State or States affected.

(c) Not more than 10 per centum of the total of funds appropriated or allocated for the purposes of subsection

(a) of this section shall be granted for air pollution control programs in any one State. In the case of a grant for a program in an area crossing State boundaries, the Administrator shall determine the portion of such grant that is chargeable to the percentage limitation under this subsection for each State into which such area extends. In fiscal year 1978 and subsequent fiscal years, subject to the provisions of subsection (b) of this section, no State shall receive less than one-half of 1 per centum of the annual appropriation for grants under this section for grants to agencies within such State.

(d) The Administrator, with the concurrence of any recipient of a grant under this section may reduce the payments to such recipient by the amount of the pay, allowances, traveling expenses, and any other costs in connection with the detail of any officer or employee to the recipient under section 301 of this Act, when such detail is for the convenience of, and at the request of, such recipient and for the purpose of carrying out the provisions of this Act. The amount by which such payments have been reduced shall be available for payment of such costs by the Administrator, but shall, for the purpose of determining the amount of any grant to a recipient under subsection (a) of this section, be deemed to have been paid to such agency.

(e) No application by a State for a grant under this section may be disapproved by the Administrator without prior notice and opportunity for a public hearing in the affected State, and no commitment or obligation of any funds under any such grant may be revoked or reduced without prior notice and opportunity for a public hearing in the affected State (or in one of the affected States if more than one State is affected).

INTERSTATE AIR QUALITY AGENCIES OR COMMISSIONS

SEC. 106. For the purpose of developing implementation plans for any interstate air quality control region designated pursuant to section 107, the Administrator is authorized to pay, for two years, up to 100 per centum of the air quality planning program costs of any agency designated by the Governors of the affected States, which agency shall be capable of recommending to the Governors plans for implementation of national primary and secondary ambient air quality standards and shall include representation from the States and appropriate political subdivisions within the air quality control region. After the initial two-year period the Administrator is authorized to make grants to such agency in an amount up to three-fourths of the air quality planning program costs of such agency.

AIR QUALITY CONTROL REGIONS

SEC. 107. (a) Each State shall have the primary responsibility for assuring air quality within the entire geographic area comprising such State by submitting an implementation plan for such State which will specify the manner in which national primary and secondary ambient air quality standards will be achieved and maintained within each air quality control region in such State.

(b) For purposes of developing and carrying out implementation plans under section 110—

(1) an air quality control region designated under this section before the date of enactment of the Clean Air Amendments of 1970, or a region designated after such date under subsection (c), shall be an air quality control region; and

(2) the portion of such State which is not part of any such designated region shall be an air quality control region, but such portion may be subdivided by the State into two or more air quality control regions with the approval of the Administrator.

(c) The Administrator shall, within 90 days after the date of enactment of the Clean Air Amendments of 1970, after consultation with appropriate State and local authorities, designate as an air quality control region any interstate area or major intrastate area which he deems necessary or appropriate for the attainment and maintenance of ambient air quality standards. The Administrator shall immediately notify the Governors of the affected States of any designation made under this subsection.

(d) (1) For the purpose of transportation control planning, part D (relating to nonattainment), part C (relating to prevention of significant deterioration of air quality), and for other purposes, each State, within one hundred and twenty days after the date of enactment of the Clean Air Act Amendments of 1977, shall submit to the Administrator a list, together with a summary of the available information, identifying those air quality control regions, or portions thereof, established purusant to this section in such State which on the date of enactment of the Clean Air Act Amendments of 1977—

(A) do not meet a national primary ambient air quality standard for any air pollutant other than sulfur dioxide or particulate matter;

(B) do not meet, or in the judgment of the State may not in the time period required by an applicable implementation plan attain or maintain, any national primary ambient air quality standard for sulfur dioxide or particulate matter;

(C) do not meet a national secondary ambient air quality standard;

(D) cannot be classified under subparagraph (B) or (C) of this paragraph on the basis of available information, for ambient air quality levels for sulfur oxides or particulate matter; or

(E) have ambient air quality levels better than any national primary or secondary air quality standard other than for sulfur dioxide or particulate matter, or for which there is not sufficient data to be classified under subparagraph (A) or (C) of this paragraph.

(2) Not later than sixty days after submittal of the list under paragraph (1) of this subsection the Administrator shall promulgate each such list with such modifications as he deems necessary. Whenever the Administrator proposes to modify a list submitted by a State, he shall notify the State and request all available data relating to such region or portion, and provide such State with an opportunity to demonstrate why any proposed modification is inappropriate.

(4) Any region or portion thereof which is not classified under subparagraph (B) or (C) of paragraph (1) of this subsection for sulfur dioxide or particulate matter within one hundred and eighty days after enactment of the Clean Air Act Amendments of 1977 shall be deemed to be a region classified under subparagraph (D) of paragraph (1) of this subsection.[2]

(5) A State may from time to time review, and as appropriate revise and resubmit, the list required under this subsection. The Administrator shall consider and promulgate such revised list in accordance with this subsection.

(e) (1) Except as otherwise provided in paragraph (2), the Governor of each State is authorized, with the approval of the Administrator, to redesignate from time to time the air quality control regions within such State for purposes of efficient and effective air quality management. Upon such redesignation, the list under subsection (d) shall be modified accordingly.

(2) In the case of an air quality control region in a State, or part of such region, which the Administrator finds may significantly affect air pollution concentrations in another State, the Governor of the State in which such region, or part of a region, is located may redesignate from time to time the boundaries of so much of such air quality control region as is located within such State only with the approval of the Administrator and with the consent of all Governors of all States which the Administrator determines may be significantly affected.

(3) No compliance date extension granted under section 113(d)(5) (relating to coal conversion) shall cease to be effective by reason of the regional limitation pro-

---

[2] This paragraph was apparently intended to be numbered paragraph (3). See section 103 of Public Law 95–95.

vided in section 113(d)(5) if the violation of such limitation is due solely to a redesignation of a region under this subsection.

AIR QUALITY CRITERIA AND CONTROL TECHNIQUES

SEC. 108. (a)(1) For the purpose of establishing national primary and secondary ambient air quality standards, the Administrator shall within 30 days after the date of enactment of the Clean Air Amendments of 1970 publish, and shall from time to time thereafter revise, a list which includes each air pollutant—

(A) emissions of which, in his judgment, cause or contribute to air pollution which may reasonably be anticipated to endanger public health or welfare;

(B) the presence of which in the ambient air results from numerous or diverse mobile or stationary sources; and

(C) for which air quality criteria had not been issued before the date of enactment of the Clean Air Amendments of 1970, but for which he plans to issue air quality criteria under this section.

(2) The Administrator shall issue air quality criteria for an air pollutant within 12 months after he has included such pollutant in a list under paragraph (1). Air quality criteria for an air pollutant shall accurately reflect the latest scientific knowledge useful in indicating the kind and extent of all identifiable effects on public health or welfare which may be expected from the presence of such pollutant in the ambient air, in varying quantities. The criteria for an air pollutant, to the extent practicable, shall include information on—

(A) those variable factors (including atmospheric conditions) which of themselves or in combination with other factors may alter the effects on public health or welfare of such air pollutant;

(B) the types of air pollutants which, when present in the atmosphere, may interact with such pollutant to produce an adverse effect on public health or welfare; and

(C) any known or anticipated adverse effects on welfare.

(b)(1) Simultaneously with the issuance of criteria under subsection (a), the Administrator shall, after consultation with appropriate advisory committees and Federal departments and agencies, issue to the States and appropriate air pollution control agencies information on air pollution control techniques, which information shall include data relating to the cost of installation and operation, energy requirements, emission reduction benefits, and environmental impact of the emission control technology. Such information shall include such data as are available on available technology and alternative methods of prevention and control of air pollution. Such information shall also include data on alternative fuels, processes, and operating methods which will result in elimination or significant reduction of emissions.

(2) In order to assist in the development of information on pollution control techniques, the Administrator may establish a standing consulting committee for each air pollutant included in a list published pursuant to subsection (a)(1), which shall be comprised of technically qualified individuals representative of State and local governments, industry, and the economic community. Each such committee shall submit, as appropriate, to the Administrator information related to that required by paragraph (1).

(c) The Administrator shall from time to time review, and, as appropriate, modify, and reissue any criteria or information on control techniques issued pursuant to this section. Not later than six months after the date of the enactment of the Clean Air Act Amendments of 1977, the Administrator shall revise and reissue criteria relating to concentrations of NO_2 over such period (not more than three hours) as he deems appropriate. Such criteria shall include a discussion of nitric and nitrous acids, nitrites, nitrates, notrosamines, and other carcinogenic and potentially carcinogenic derivatives of oxides of nitrogen.

(d) The issuance of air quality criteria and information on air pollution control techniques shall be announced in the Federal Register and copies shall be made available to the general public.

(e) The Administrator shall, after consultation with the Secretary of Transportation and the Secretary of Housing and Urban Development and State and local officials and within 180 days after the enactment of this subsection, and from time to time thereafter, publish guidelines on the basic program elements for the planning process assisted under section 175 of part D. Such guidelines shall include information on—

(1) methods to identify and evaluate alternative planning and control activities;

(2) methods of reviewing plans on a regular basis as conditions change or new information is presented;

(3) identification of funds and other resources necessary to implement the plan, including interagency agreements on providing such funds and resources;

(4) methods to assure participation by the public in all phases of the planning process; and

(5) such other methods as the Administrator determines necessary to carry out a continuous planning process.

(f)(1) The Administrator shall publish and make available to appropriate Federal agencies, States, and air pollution control agencies, including agencies assisted under section 175 within 6 months after enactment of this subsection for clauses (i), (ii), (iii), and (iv) of subparagraph (A) and within one year after the enactment of this subsection for the balance of this subsection (and from time to time thereafter),

(A) information, prepared, as appropriate, in cooperation with the Secretary of Transportation, regarding processes, procedures, and methods to reduce or control each such pollutant, including but not limited to—

(i) motor vehicle emission inspection and maintenance programs;

(ii) programs to control vapor emissions from fuel transfer and storage operations and operations using solvents;

(iii) programs for improved public transit;

(iv) programs to establish exclusive bus and carpool lanes and areawide carpool programs;

(v) programs to limit portions of road surfaces or certain sections of the metropolitan areas to the use of common carriers, both as to time and place;

(vi) programs for long-range transit improvements involving new transportation policies and transportation facilities or major changes in existing facilities;

(vii) programs to control on-street parking;

(viii) programs to construct new parking facilities and operate existing parking facilities for the purpose of park and ride lots and fringe parking;

(ix) programs to limit portions of road surfaces or certain sections of the metropolitan area to the use of nonmotorized vehicles or pedestrian use, both as to time and place;

(x) provisions for employer participation in programs to encourage carpooling, vanpooling, mass transit, bicycling, and walking;

(xi) programs for secure bicycle storage facilities and other facilities, including bicycle lanes, for the convenience and protection of bicyclists, in both public and private areas;

(xii) programs of staggered hours of work;

(xiii) programs to institute road user charges, tolls, or differential rates to discourage single occupancy automobile trips;

(xiv) programs to control extended idling of vehicles;

(xv) programs to reduce emissions by improvements in traffic flow;

(xvi) programs for the conversion of fleet vehicles to cleaner engines or fuels, or to otherwise control fleet vehicle operations;

(xvii) programs for retrofit of emission devices or controls on vehicles and engines, other than light duty vehicles, not subject to regulations under section 202 of title II of this Act; and

(xviii) programs to reduce motor vehicle emissions which are caused by extreme cold start conditions;

(B) information on additional methods or strategies that will contribute to the reduction of mobile source related pollutants during periods in which any primary ambient air quality standard will be exceeded and during episodes for which an air pollution alert, warning, or emergency has been declared;

(C) information on other measures which may be employed to reduce the impact on public health or protect the health of sensitive or susceptible individuals or groups; and

(D) information on the extent to which any process, procedure, or method to reduce or control such air pollutant may cause an increase in the emissions or formation of any other pollutant.

(2) In publishing such information the Administrator shall also include an assessment of—

(A) the relative effectiveness of such processes, procedures, and methods;

(B) the potential effect of such processes, procedures, and methods on transportation system and the provision of transportation services; and

(C) the environmental, energy, and economic impact of such processes, procedures, and methods.

NATIONAL AMBIENT AIR QUALITY STANDARDS

SEC. 109. (a)(1) The Administrator—

(A) within 30 days after the date of enactment of the Clean Air Amendments of 1970, shall publish proposed regulations prescribing a national primary ambient air quality standard and a national secondary ambient air quality standard for each air pollutant for which air quality criteria have been issued prior to such date of enactment; and

(B) after a reasonable time for interested persons to submit written comments thereon (but no later than 90 days after the initial publication of such proposed standards) shall by regulation promulgate such proposed national primary and secondary ambient air quality standards with such modifications as he deems appropriate.

(2) With respect to any air pollutant for which air quality criteria are issued after the date of enactment of the Clean Air Amendments of 1970, the Administrator shall publish, simultaneously with the issuance of such criteria and information, proposed national primary and secondary ambient air quality standards for any such pollutant. The procedure provided for in paragraph (1)(B) of this subsection shall apply to the promulgation of such standards.

(b)(1) National primary ambient air quality standards, prescribed, under subsection (a) shall be ambient air quality standards the attainment and maintenance of which in the judgment of the Administrator, based on such criteria and allowing an adequate margin of safety, are requisite to protect the public health. Such primary standards may be revised in the same manner as promulgated.

(2) Any national secondary ambient air quality standard prescribed, under subsection (a) shall specify a level of air quality the attainment and maintenance of which in the judgment of the Administrator, based on such criteria, is requisite to protect the public welfare from any known or anticipated adverse effects associated with the presence of such air pollutant in the ambient air. Such secondary standards may be revised in the same manner as promulgated.

(c) The Administrator shall, not later than one year after the date of the enactment of the Clean Air Act Amendments of 1977, promulgate a national primary ambient air quality standard for NO_2 concentrations over a period of not more than 3 hours unless, based on the criteria issued under section 108(c), he finds that there is no significant evidence that such a standard for such a period is requisite to protect public health.

(d)(1) Not later than December 31, 1980, and at five-year intervals thereafter, the Administrator shall complete a thorough review of the criteria published under section 108 and the national ambient air quality standards promulgated under this section and shall make such revisions in such criteria and standards and promulgate such new standards as may be appropriate in accordance with section 108 and subsection (b) of this section. The Administrator may review and revise criteria or promulgate new standards earlier or more frequently than required under this paragraph.

(2)(A) The Administrator shall appoint an independent scientific review committee composed of seven members including at least one member of the National Academy of Sciences, one physician, and one person representing State air pollution control agencies.

(B) Not later than January 1, 1980, and at five-year intervals thereafter, the committee referred to in subparagraph (A) shall complete a review of the criteria published under section 108 and the national primary and secondary ambient air quality standards promulgated under this section and shall recommend to the Administrator any new national ambient air quality standards and revisions of existing criteria and standards as may be appropriate under section 108 and subsection (b) of this section.

(C) Such committee shall also (i) advise the Administrator of areas in which additional knowledge is required to appraise the adequacy and basis of existing, new, or revised national ambient air quality standards, (ii) describe the research efforts necessary to provide the required information, (iii) advise the Administrator on the relative contribution to air pollution concentrations of natural as well as anthropogenic activity, and (iv) advise the Administrator of any adverse public health, welfare, social, economic, or energy effects which may result from various strategies for attainment and maintenance of such national ambient air quality standards.

IMPLEMENTATION PLANS

SEC. 110. (a)(1) Each State shall, after reasonable notice and public hearings, adopt and submit to the Administrator, within nine months after the promulgation of a national primary ambient air quality standard (or any revision thereof) under section 109 for any air pollutant, a plan which provides for implementation, maintenance, and enforcement of such primary standard in each air quality control region (or portion thereof) within such State. In addition, such State shall adopt and submit to the Administrator (either as a part of a plan submitted under the preceding sentence or separately) within nine months after the promulgation of a national ambient air quality secondary standard (or revision thereof), a plan which provides for implementation, maintenance, and enforcement of such secondary standard in each air quality control region (or portion thereof) within such State. Unless a separate public hearing is provided, each State shall consider its plan implementing such secondary standard at the hearing required by the first sentence of this paragraph.

(2) The Administrator shall, within four months after the date required for submission of a plan under paragraph (1), approve or disapprove such plan for each portion thereof. The Administrator shall approve such plan, or any portion thereof, if he determines that it was adopted after reasonable notice and hearing and that—

(A) except as may be provided in subparagraph (I)(i) in the case of a plan implementing a national primary ambient air quality standard, it provides for the attainment of such primary standard as expeditiously as practicable but (subject to subsection (e)) in no case later than three years from the date of approval of such plan (or any revision thereof to take account of a revised primary standard); and (ii) in the case of a plan implementing a national secondary ambient air quality standard, it specifies a reasonable time at which such secondary standard will be attained;

(B) it includes emission limitations, schedules, and timetables for compliance with such limitations, and such other measures as may be necessary to insure attainment and maintenance of such primary or secondary standard, including, but not limited to transportation controls, air quality maintenance plans, and preconstruction review of direct sources of air pollution as provided in subparagraph (D);

(C) it includes provision for establishment and operation of appropriate devices, methods, systems, and procedures necessary to (i) monitor, compile, and analyze data on ambient air quality and, (ii) upon request, make such data available to the Administrator;

(D) it includes a program to provide for the enforcement of emission limitations and regulation of the modification, construction, and operation of any stationary source, including a permit program as required in parts C and D and a permit or equivalent program for any major emitting facility, within such region as necessary to assure (i) that national ambient air quality standards are achieved and maintained, and (ii) a procedure, meeting the requirements of paragraph (4), for review (prior to construction or modification) of the location of new sources to which a standard of performance will apply;

(E) it contains adequate provisions (i) prohibiting any stationary source within the State from emitting any air pollutant in amounts which will (I) prevent attainment or maintenance by any other State of any such national primary or secondary ambient air quality standard, or (II) interfere with measures required to be included in the applicable implementation plan for any other State under part C to prevent significant deterioration of air quality or to protect visibility, and (ii) insuring compliance with the requirements of section 126, relating to interstate pollution abatement;

(F) it provides (i) necessary assurances that the State will have adequate personnel, funding, and authority to carry out such implementation plan, (ii) requirements for installation of equipment by owners or operators of stationary sources to monitor emissions from such sources, (iii) for periodic reports on the nature and amounts of such emissions; (iv) that such reports shall be correlated by the State agency with any emission limitations or standards established pursuant to this Act, which reports shall be available at reasonable times for public inspection; (v) for authority comparable to that in section 303, and adequate contingency plans to implement such authority; and (vi) requirements that the State comply with the requirements respecting State boards under section 128;

(G) it provides, to the extent necessary and practicable, for periodic inspection and testing of motor vehicles to enforce compliance with applicable emission standards;

(H) it provides for revision, after public hearing, of such plan (i) from time to time as may be necessary to take account of revisions of such national primary or secondary ambient air quality standard or the availability of improved or more expeditious methods of achieving such primary or secondary standard; or (ii) except as provided in paragraph (3)(C), whenever the Administrator finds on the basis of information available to him that the plan is substantially inadequate to achieve the national ambient air quality primary or secondary standard which it implements or to otherwise comply with any additional requirements established under the Clean Air Act Amendments of 1977;

(I) it provides that after June 30, 1979, no major stationary source shall be constructed or modified in any nonattainment area (as defined in section 171 (2)) to which such plan applies, if the emissions from such facility will cause or contribute to concentrations of any pollutant for which a national ambient air quality standard is exceeded in such area, unless, as of the time of application for a permit for such construction or modification, such plan meets the requirements of part D (relating to nonattainment areas);

(J) it meets the requirements of section 121 (relating to consultation), section 127 (relating to public notification), part C (relating to prevention of significant deterioration of air quality and visability protection); and

(K) it requires the owner or operator of each major stationary source to pay to the permitting authority as a condition of any permit required under this Act a fee sufficient to cover—

(i) the reasonable costs of reviewing and acting upon any application for such a permit, and

(ii) if the owner or operator receives a permit for such source, whether before or after the date of enactment of this subparagraph, the reasonable costs (incurred after such date of enactment) of implementing and enforcing the terms and conditions of any such permit (not including any court costs or other costs associated with any enforcement action).

(3)(A) The Administrator shall approve revision of any implementation plan applicable to an air quality control region if he determines that it meets the requirements of paragraph (2) and has been adopted by the State after reasonable notice and public hearings.

(B) As soon as practicable, the Administrator shall, consistent with the purposes of this Act and the Energy Supply and Environmental Coordination Act of 1974, review each State's applicable implementation plans and report to the State on whether such plans can be revised in relation to fuel burning stationary sources (or persons supplying fuel to such sources) without interfering with the attainment and maintenance of any national ambient air quality standard within the period permitted in this section. It the Administrator determines that any such plan can be revised, he shall notify the State that a plan revision may be submitted by the State. Any plan revision which is submitted by the State shall, after public notice and opportunity for public hearing, be approved by the Administrator if the revision relates only to fuel burning stationary sources (or persons supplying fuel to such sources), and the plan as revised complies with paragraph (2) of this subsection. The Administrator shall approve or disapprove any revision no later than three months after its submission.

~~(C) Neither the State, in the case of a plan (or portion thereof) approved under this subsection, nor the Administrator in the case of a plan (or portion thereof) promulgated under subsection (c), shall be required to revise an applicable implementation plan because one or more exemptions under section 118 (relating to Federal facilities), enforcement orders under section 113(d), suspensions under section 110(f) or (g) (relating to temporary energy or economic authority) or orders under section 119 (relating to primary nonferrous smelters) have been granted, if such plan would have met the requirements of this section if no such exemptions, orders, extension, or variances had been granted.~~

(C) Neither the State, in the case of a plan (or portion thereof) approved under this subsection, nor the Administrator, in the case of a plan (or portion thereof) promulgated under subsection (c), shall be required to revise an applicable implementation plan because one or more exemptions under section 118 (relating to Federal facilities), enforcement orders under section 113(d), suspensions under section 110 (f) or (g) (relating to

temporary energy or economic authority), orders under section 119 (relating to primary nonferrous smelters), or extensions of compliance in decrees entered under section 113(e) (relating to iron- and steel-producing operations) have been granted, if such plan would have met the requirements of this section if no such exemptions, orders, or extensions had been granted.

(D) Any applicable implementation plan for which an attainment date later than December 31, 1982, is provided pursuant to section 172(a)(2) shall be revised by July 1, 1979, to include the comprehensive measures and requirements referred to in subsection (c)(5)(B).

(4) The procedure referred to in paragraph (2)(D) for review, prior to construction or modification, of the location of new sources shall (A) provide for adequate authority to prevent the construction or modification of any new source to which a standard of performance under section 111 will apply at any location which the State determines will prevent the attainment or maintenance within any air quality control region (or portion thereof) within such State of a national ambient air quality primary or secondary standard, and (B) require that prior to commencing construction or modification of any such source, the owner or operator thereof shall submit to such State such information as may be necessary to permit the State to make a determination under clause (A).

(5)(A)(i) Any State may include in a State implementation plan, but the Administrator may not require as a condition of approval of such plan under this section, any indirect source review program. The Administrator may approve and enforce, as part of an applicable implementation plan, an indirect source review program which the State chooses to adopt and submit as part of its plan.

(ii) Except as provided in subparagraph (B), no plan promulgated by the Administrator shall include any indirect source review program for any air quality control region, or portion thereof.

(iii) Any State may revise an applicable implementation plan approved under section 110(a) to suspend or revoke any such program included in such plan, provided that such plan meets the requirements of this section.

(B) The Administrator shall have the authority to promulgate, implement and enforce regulations under section 110(c) respecting indirect source review programs which apply only to federally assisted highways, airports, and other major federally assisted indirect sources and federally owned or operated indirect sources.

(C) For purposes of this paragraph, the term "indirect source" means a facility, building, structure, installation, real property, road, or highway which attracts, or may attract, mobile sources of pollution. Such term includes parking lots, parking garages, and other facilities subject to any measure for management of parking supply (within the meaning of section 110(c)(2)(D)(ii)), including regulation of existing off-street parking but such term does not include new or existing on-street parking. Direct emissions sources or facilities at, within, or associated with, any indirect source shall not be deemed indirect sources for the purpose of this paragraph.

(D) For purposes of this paragraph the term "indirect source review program" means the facility-by-facility review of indirect sources of air pollution, including such measures as are necessary to assure, or assist in assuring, that a new or modified indirect source will not attract mobile sources of air pollution, the emissions from which would cause or contribute to air pollution concentrations—

(i) exceeding any national primary ambient air quality standard for a mobile source-related air pollutant after the primary standard attainment date, or

(ii) preventing maintenance of any such standard after such date.

(E) For purposes of this paragraph and paragraph (2)(B), the term "transportation control measure" does not include any measure which is an "indirect source review program."

(6) No State plan shall be treated as meeting the requirements of this section unless such plan provides that in the case of any source which uses a supplemental, or intermittent control system for purposes of meeting the requirements of an order under section 113(d) or section 119 (relating to primary nonferrous smelter orders), the owner or operator of such source may not temporarily reduce the pay of any employee by reason of the use of such supplemental or intermittent or other dispersion dependent control system.

(b) The Administrator may, wherever he determines necessary, extend the period for submission of any plan or portion thereof which implements a national secondary ambient air-quality standard for a period not to exceed eighteen months from the date otherwise required for submission of such plan.

(c)(1) The Administrator shall, after consideration of any State hearing record, promptly prepare and publish proposed regulations setting forth an implementation plan, or portion thereof, for a State if—

(A) the State fails to submit an implementation plan which meets the requirements of this section,

(B) the plan, or any portion thereof, submitted for such State is determined by the Administrator not to be in accordance with the requirements of this section, or

(C) the State fails, within 60 days after notification by the Administrator or such longer period as he may prescribe, to revise an implementation plan as required pursuant to a provision of its plan referred to in subsection (a)(2)(H).

If such State held no public hearing associated with respect to such plan (or revision thereof), the Administrator shall provide opportunity for such hearing within such State on any proposed regulation. The Administrator shall, within six months after the date required for submission of such plan (or revision thereof), promulgate any such regulations unless, prior to such promulgation, such State has adopted and submitted a plan (or revision) which the Administrator determines to be in accordance with the requirements of this section. Notwithstanding the preceding sentence, any portion of a plan relating to any measure described in the first sentence of section 121 (relating to consultation) or the consultation process required under such section 121 shall not be required to be promulgated before the date eight months after such date required for submission.

(2)(A) The Administrator shall conduct a study and shall submit a report to the Committee on Interstate and Foreign Commerce of the United States House of Representatives and the Committee on Public Works of the United States Senate not later than three months after date of enactment of this paragraph on the necessity of parking surcharge, management of parking supply, and preferential bus/carpool lane regulations as part of the applicable implementation plans required under this section to achieve and maintain national primary ambient air quality standards. The study shall include an assessment of the economic impact of such regulations, consideration of alternative means of reducing total vehicle miles traveled, and an assessment of the impact of such regulations on other Federal and State programs dealing with energy or transportation. In the course of such study, the Administrator shall consult with other Federal officials including, but not limited to, the Secretary of Transportation, the Federal Energy Administrator, and the Chairman of the Council on Environmental Quality.

(B) No parking surcharge regulation may be required by the Administrator under paragraph (1) of this subsection as a part of an applicable implementation plan. All parking surcharge regulations previously required by the Administrator shall be void upon the date of enactment of this subparagraph. This subparagraph shall not prevent the Administrator from approving parking surcharges if they are adopted and submitted by a State as part of an applicable implementation plan. The Administrator may not condition approval of any implementation plan submitted by a State on such plan's including a parking surcharge regulation.

(C) The Administrator is authorized to suspend until January 1, 1975, the effective date or applicability of any regulations for the management of parking supply or any requirement that such regulations be a part of an applicable implementation plan approved or promulgated under this section. The exercise of the authority under this subparagraph shall not prevent the Administrator from approving such regulations if they are adopted and submitted by a State as part of an applicable implementation plan. If the Administrator exercises the authority under this subparagraph, regulations requiring a review or analysis of the impact of proposed parking facilities before construction which take effect on or after January 1, 1975, shall not apply to parking facilities on which construction has been initiated before January 1, 1975.

(D) For purposes of this pargaraph—

(i) The term "parking surcharge regulation" means a regulation imposing or requiring the imposition of any tax, surcharge, fee, or other charge on parking spaces, or any other area used for the temporary storage of motor vehicles.

(ii) The term "management of parking supply" shall include any requirement providing that any new facility containing a given number of parking spaces shall receive a permit or other prior approval, issuance of which is to be conditioned on air quality considerations.

(iii) The term "preferential bus/carpool lane" shall include any requirement for the setting aside of one or more lanes of a street or highway on a permanent or temporary basis for the exclusive use of buses or carpools, or both.

(E) No standard, plan, or requirement, relating to management of parking supply or preferential bus/carpool lanes shall be promulgated after the date of enactment of this paragraph by the Administrator pursuant to this section, unless such promulgation has been subjected to at least one public hearing which has been held in the area affected and for which reasonable notice has been given in such area. If substantial changes are made following public hearings, one or more additional hearings shall be held in such area after such notice.

(3) Upon application of the chief executive officer of any general purpose unit of local government, if the Administrator determines that such unit has adequate authority under State or local law, the Administrator may delegate to such unit the authority to implement and enforce within the jurisdiction of such unit any part of a plan promulgated under this subsection. Nothing in this paragraph shall prevent the Administrator from implementing or enforcing any applicable provision of a plan promulgated under this subsection.

(4) In the case of any applicable implementation plan containing measures requiring—

(A) retrofits on other than commercially owned in-use vehicles,

(B) gas rationing which the Administrator finds would have seriously disruptive and widespread economic or social effects, or

(C) the reduction of the supply of on-street parking spaces,

the Governor of the State may, after notice and opportunity for public hearing, temporarily suspend such measures notwithstanding the requirements of this section until January 1, 1979, or the date on which a plan revision under section 110(a)(2)(I) is submitted, whichever is earlier. No such suspension shall be granted unless the State agrees to prepare, adopt, and submit such plan revision as determined by the Administrator.

(5) (A) Any measure in an applicable implementation plan which requires a toll or other charge for the use of a bridge located entirely within one city shall be eliminated from such plan by the Administrator upon application by the Governor of the State, which application shall include a certification by the Governor that he will revise such plan in accordance with subparagraph (B).

(B) In the case of any applicable implementation plan with respect to which a measure has been eliminated under subparagraph (A), such plan shall, not later than one year after the date of the enactment of this subparagraph, be revised to include comprehensive measures (including the written evidence required by part D), to:

(i) establish, expand, or improve public transportation measures to meet basic transportation needs, as expeditiously as is practicable; and

(ii) implement transportation control measures necessary to attain and maintain national ambient air quality standards,

and such revised plan shall, for the purpose of implementing such comprehensive public transportation measures, include requirements to use (insofar as is necessary) Federal grants, State or local funds, or any combination of such grants and funds as may be consistent with the terms of the legislation providing such grants and funds. Such measures shall, as a substitute for the tolls or charges eliminated under subparagraph (A), provide for emissions reductions equivalent to the reductions which may reasonably be expected to be achieved through the use of the tolls or charges eliminated.

(C) Any revision of any implementation plan for purposes of meeting the requirements of subparagraph (B) shall be submitted in coordination with any plan revision required under part D.

(d) For purposes of this Act, an applicable implementation plan is the implementation plan, or most recent revision thereof, which has been approved under subsection (a) or promulgated under subsection (c) and which implements the requirements of this section.

(e)(1) Upon application of a Governor of a State at the time of submission of any plan implementing a national ambient air quality primary standard, the Administrator may (subject to paragraph (2)) extend the three-year period referred to in subsection (a)(2)(A)(i) for not more than two years for an air quality control region if after review of such plan the Administrator determines that—

(A) one or more emission sources (or classes of moving sources) are unable to comply with the requirements of such plan which implement such primary standard because the necessary technology or other alternatives are not available or will not be available soon enough to permit compliance within such three-year period, and

(B) the State has considered and applied as a part of its plan reasonably available alternative means of attaining such primary standard and has justifiably concluded that attainment of such primary standard within the three years cannot be achieved.

(2) The Administrator may grant an extension under paragraph (1) only if he determines that the State plan provides for—

(A) application of the requirements of the plan which implement such primary standard to all emission sources in such region other than the sources (or classes) described in paragraph (1)(A) within the three-year period, and

(B) such interim measures of control of the sources (or classes) described in paragraph (1)(A) as the Administrator determines to be reasonable under the circumstances.

(f)(1) Upon application by the owner or operator of a fuel burning stationary source, and after notice and opportunity for public hearing, the Governor of the State in which such source is located may petition the President to determine that a national or regional energy emergency exists of such severity that—

(A) a temporary suspension of any part of the applicable implementation plan may be necessary, and

(B) other means of responding to the energy emergency may be inadequate.

Such determination shall not be delegable by the President to any other person. If the President determines that a national or regional energy emergency of such severity exists, a temporary emergency suspension of any part of an applicable implementation plan adopted by the State may be issued by the Governor of any State covered by the President's determination under the condition specified in paragraph (2) and may take effect immediately.

(2) A temporary emergency suspension under this subsection shall be issued to a source only if the Governor of such State finds that—

(A) there exists in the vicinity of such source a temporary energy emergency involving high levels of unemployment or loss of necessary energy supplies for residential dwellings; and

(B) such unemployment or loss can be totally or partially alleviated by such emergency suspension.

Not more than one such suspension may be issued for any source on the basis of the same set of circumstances or on the basis of the same emergency.

(3) A temporary emergency suspension issued by a Governor under this subsection shall remain in effect for a maximum of four months or such lesser period as may be specified in a disapproval order of the Administrator, if any. The Administrator may disapprove such suspension if he determines that it does not meet the requirements of paragraph (2).

(4) This subsection shall not apply in the case of a plan provision or requirement promulgated by the Administrator under subsection (c) of this section, but in any such case the President may grant a temporary emergency suspension for a four month period of any such provision or requirement if he makes the determinations and findings specified in paragraphs (1) and (2).

(5) The Governor may include in any temporary emergency suspension issued under this subsection a provision delaying for a period identical to the period of such suspension any compliance schedule (or increment of progress) to which such source is subject under section 119, as in effect before the date of the enactment of this paragraph or section 113(d) of this Act, upon a finding that such source is unable to comply with such schedule (or increment) solely because of the conditions on the basis of which a suspension was issued under this subsection.

(g) (1) In the case of any State which has adopted and submitted to the Administrator a proposed plan revision which the State determines—

(A) meets the requirements of this section, and

(B) is necessary (i) to prevent the closing for one year or more of any source of air pollution, and (ii) to prevent substantial increases in unemployment which would result from such closing, and

which the Administrator has not approved or disapproved under this section within the required four month period, the Governor may issue a temporary emergency suspension of the part of the applicable implementation plan for such State which is proposed to be revised with respect to such source. The determination under subparagraph (B) may not be made with respect to a source which would close without regard whether or not the proposed plan revision is approved.

(2) A temporary emergency suspension issued by a Governor under this subsection shall remain in effect for a maximum of four months or such lesser period as may be specified in a disapproval order of the Administrator. The Administrator may disapprove such suspension if he determines that it does not meet the requirements of this subsection.

(3) The Governor may include in any temporary emergency suspension issued under this subsection a provision delaying for a period identical to the period of such suspension any compliance schedule (or increment of progress) to which such source is subject under section 119 as in effect before the date of the enactment of this paragraph, or under section 113(d) upon a finding that such source is unable to comply with such schedule (or increment) solely because of the conditions on the basis of which a suspension was issued under this subsection.

(h)(1) Not later than one year after the date of enactment of the Clean Air Act Amendments of 1977 and annually thereafter, the Administrator shall assemble and publish a comprehensive document for each State setting forth all requirements of the applicable implementation plan for such State and shall publish notice in the Federal Register of the availability of such documents. Each such document shall be revised as frequently as practicable but not less often than annually.

(2) The Administrator may promulgate such regulations as may be reasonably necessary to carry out the purpose of this subsection.

(i) Except for a primary nonferrous smelter order under section 119, a suspension under section 110 (f) or (g) (relating to emergency suspensions), an exemption under section 118 (relating to certain Federal facilities), an order under section 113(d) (relating to compliance orders), a plan promulgation under section 110(c), or a plan revision under section 110(a)(3), no order, suspension, plan revision, or other action modifying any requirement of an applicable implementation plan may be taken with respect to any stationary source by the State or by the Administrator.

(j) As a condition for issuance of any permit required under this title, the owner or operator of each new or modified stationary source which is required to obtain such a permit must show to the satisfaction of the permitting authority that the technological system of continuous emission reduction which is to be used will enable such source to comply with the standards of performance which are to apply to such source and that the construction or modification and operation of such source will be in compliance with all other requirements of this Act.

STANDARDS OF PERFORMANCE FOR NEW STATIONARY SOURCES

SEC. 111. (a) For purposes of this section:

(1) The term "standard of performance" means—

(A) with respect to any air pollutant emitted from a category of fossil fuel fired stationary sources to which subsection (b) applies, a standard—

(i) establishing allowable emission limitations for such category of sources, and

(ii) requiring the achievement of a percentage reduction in the emissions from such category of sources from the emissions which would have resulted from the use of fuels which are not subject to treatment prior to combustion,

(B) with respect to any air pollutant emitted from a category of stationary sources (other than fossil fuel fired sources) to which subsection (b) applies, a standard such as that referred to in subparagraph (A) (i); and

(C) with respect to any air pollutant emitted from a particular source to which subsection (d) applies, a standard which the State (or the Administrator under the conditions specified in subsection (d) (2)) determines is applicable to that source and which reflects the degree of emission reduction achievable through the application of the best system of continuous emission reduction which (taking into consideration the cost of achieving such emission reduction, and any nonair quality health and environmental impact and energy requirements) the Administrator determines has been adequately demonstrated for that category of sources.

For the purpose of subparagraphs (A) (i) and (ii) and (B), a standard of performance shall reflect the degree of emission limitation and the percentage reduction achievable through application of the best technological system of continuous emission reduction which (taking into consideration the cost of achieving such emission reduction, any nonair quality health and environmental impact and energy requirements) the Administrator determines has been adequately demonstrated. For the purpose of subparagraph (1) (A) (ii), any cleaning of the fuel or reduction in the pollution characteristics of the fuel after extraction and prior to combustion may be credited, as determined under regulations promulgated by the Administrator, to a source which burns such fuel.

(2) The term "new source" means any stationary source, the construction or modification of which is

commenced after the publication of regulations (or, if earlier, proposed regulations) prescribing a standard of performance under this section which will be applicable to such source.

(3) The term "stationary source" means any building, structure, facility, or installation which emits or may emit any air pollutant.

(4) The term "modification" means any physical change in, or change in the method of operation of, a stationary source which increases the amount of any air pollutant emitted by such source or which results in the emission of any air pollutant not previously emitted.

(5) The term "owner or operator" means any person who owns, leases, operates, controls, or supervises a stationary source.

(6) The term "existing source" means any stationary source other than a new source.

(7) The term "technological system of continuous emission reduction" means—

(A) a technological process for production or operation by any source which is inherently low-polluting or nonpolluting, or

(B) a technological system for continuous reduction of the pollution generated by a source before such pollution is emitted into the ambient air, including precombustion cleaning or treatment of fuels.

(8) A conversion to coal (A) by reason of an order under section 2(a) of the Energy Supply and Environmental Coordination Act of 1974 or any amendment thereto, or any subsequent enactment which supersedes such Act, or (B) which qualifies under section 113(d)(5)(A)(ii) of this Act, shall not be deemed to be a modification for purposes of paragraphs (2) and (4) of this subsection.

(b)(1)(A) The Administrator shall, within 90 days after the date of enactment of the Clean Air Amendments of 1970, publish (and from time to time thereafter shall revise) a list of categories of stationary sources. He shall include a category of sources in such list if in his judgment it causes, or contributes significantly to, air pollution which may reasonably be anticipated to endanger public health or welfare.

(B) Within 120 days after the inclusion of a category of stationary sources in a list under subparagraph (A), the Administrator shall publish proposed regulations, establishing Federal standards of performance for new sources within such category. The Administrator shall afford interested persons an opportunity for written comment on such proposed regulations. After considering such comments, he shall promulgate, within 90 days after such publication, such standards with such modifications as he deems appropriate. The Administrator shall, at least every four years, review and, if appropriate, revise such standards following the procedure required by this subsection for promulgation of such standards. Standards of performance or revisions thereof shall become effective upon promulgation.

(2) The Administrator may distinguish among classes, types, and sizes within categories of new sources for the purpose of establishing such standards.

(3) The Administrator shall, from time to time, issue information on pollution control techniques for categories of new sources and air pollutants subject to the provisions of this section.

(4) The provisions of this section shall apply to any new source owned or operated by the United States.

(5) Except as otherwise authorized under subsection (h), nothing in this section shall be construed to require, or to authorize the Administrator to require, any new or modified source to install and operate any particular technological system of continuous emission reduction to comply with any new source standard of performance.

(6) The revised standards of performance required by enactment of subsection (a)(1)(A) (i) and (ii) shall be promulgated not later than one year after enactment of this paragraph. Any new or modified fossil fuel fired stationary source which commences construction prior to the date of publication of the proposed revised standards shall not be required to comply with such revised standards.

(c)(1) Each State may develop and submit to the Administrator a procedure for implementing and enforcing standards of performance for new sources located in such State. If the Administrator finds the State procedure is adequate, he shall delegate to such State any authority he has under this Act to implement and enforce such standards.

(2) Nothing in this subsection shall prohibit the Administrator from enforcing any applicable standard of performance under this section.

(d)(1) The Administrator shall prescribe regulations which shall establish a procedure similar to that provided by section 110 under which each State shall submit to the Administrator a plan which (A) establishes standards of performance for any existing source for any air pollutant (i) for which air quality criteria have not been issued or which is not included on a list published under section 108(a) or 112(b)(1)(A) but (ii) to which a standard of performance under subsection (b) would apply if such existing source were a new source, and (B) provides for the implementation and enforcement of such standards of performance. Regulations of the Administrator under this paragraph shall permit the

State in applying a standard of performance to any particular source under a plan submitted under this paragraph to take into consideration, among other factors, the remaining useful life of the existing source to which such standard applies.

(2) The Administrator shall have the same authority—

(A) to prescribe a plan for a State in cases where the State fails to submit a satisfactory plan as he would have under section 110(c) in the case of failure to submit an implementation plan, and

(B) to enforce the provisions of such plan in cases where the State fails to enforce them as he would have under sections 113 and 114 with respect to an implementation plan. In promulgating a standard of performance under a plan prescribed under this paragraph, the Administrator shall take into consideration, among other factors, remaining useful lives of the sources in the category of sources to which such standard applies.

(e) After the effective date of standards of performance promulgated under this section, it shall be unlawful for any owner or operator of any new source to operate such source in violation of any standard of performance applicable to such source.

(f) (1) Not later than one year after the date of enactment of this subsection, the Administrator shall promulgate regulations listing under subsection (b) (1) (A) the categories of major stationary sources which are not on the date of the enactment of this subsection included on the list required under subsection (b) (1) (A). The Administrator shall promulgate regulations establishing standards of performance for the percentage of such categories of sources set forth in the following table before the expiration of the corresponding period set forth in such table:

Percentage of source categories required to be listed for which standards must be established:	Period by which standards must be promulgated after date list is required to be promulgated:
25	2 years.
75	3 years.
100	4 years.

(2) In determining priorities for promulgating standards for categories of major stationary sources for the purpose of paragraph (1), the Administrator shall consider—

(A) the quantity of air pollutant emissions which each such category will emit, or will be designed to emit;

(B) the extent to which each such pollutant may reasonably be anticipated to endanger public health or welfare; and

(C) the mobility and competitive nature of each such category of sources and the consequent need for nationally applicable new source standards of performance.

(3) Before promulgating any regulations under this subsection or listing any category of major stationary sources as required under this subsection, the Administrator shall consult with appropriate representatives of the Governors and of State air pollution control agencies.

(g)(1) Upon application by the Governor of a State showing that the Administrator has failed to specify in regulations under subsection (f)(1) any category of major stationary sources required to be specified under such regulations, the Administrator shall revise such regulations, to specify any such category.

(2) Upon application of the Governor of a State, showing that any category of stationary sources which is not included in the list under subsection (b)(1)(A) contributes significantly to air pollution which may reasonably be anticipated to endanger public health or welfare (notwithstanding that such category is not a category of major stationary sources), the Administrator shall revise such regulations to specify such category of stationary sources.

(3) Upon application of the Governor of a State showing that the Administrator has failed to apply properly the criteria required to be considered under subsection (f)(2), the Administrator shall revise the list under subsection (b)(1)(A) to apply properly such criteria.

(4) Upon application of the Governor of a State showing that—

(A) a new, innovative, or improved technology or process which achieves greater continuous emission reduction has been adequately demonstrated for any category of stationary sources, and

(B) as a result of such technology or process, the new source standard of performance in effect under subsection (b) for such category no longer reflects the greatest degree of emission limitation achievable through application of the best technological system of continuous emission reduction which (taking into consideration the cost of achieving such emission reduction, and any non-air quality health and environmental impact and energy requirements) has been adequately demonstrated,

the Administrator shall revise such standard of performance for such category accordingly.

(5) Upon application by the Governor of a State showing that the Administrator has failed to list any air pollutant which causes, or contributes to, air pollution which

may reasonably be anticipated to result in an increase in mortality or an increase in serious irreversible, or incapacitating reversible, illness as a hazardous air pollutant under section 112, the Administrator shall revise the list of hazardous air pollutants under such section to include such pollutant.

(6) Upon application by the Governor of a State showing that any category of stationary sources of a hazardous air pollutant listed under section 112 is not subject to emission standards under such section, the Administrator shall propose and promulgate such emission standards applicable to such category of sources.

(7) Unless later deadlines for action of the Administrator are otherwise prescribed under this section or section 112, the Administrator shall, not later than three months following the date of receipt of any application by a Governor of a State, either—

(A) find that such application does not contain the requisite showing and deny such application, or

(B) grant such application and take the action required under this subsection.

(8) Before taking any action required by subsection (f) or by this subsection, the Administrator shall provide notice and opportunity for public hearing.

(h)(1) For purposes of this section, if in the judgment of the Administrator, it is not feasible to prescribe or enforce a standard of performance, he may instead promulgate a design, equipment, work practice, or operational standard, or combination thereof, which reflects the best technological system of continuous emission reduction which (taking into consideration the cost of achieving such emission reduction, and any non-air quality health and environmental impact and energy requirements) the Administrator determines has been adequately demonstrated. In the event the Administrator promulgates a design or equipment standard under this subsection, he shall include as part of such standard such requirements as will assure the proper operation and maintenance of any such element of design or equipment.

(2) For the purpose of this subsection, the phrase "not feasible to prescribe or enforce a standard of performance" means any situation in which the Administrator determines that (A) a pollutant or pollutants cannot be emitted through a conveyance designed and constructed to emit or capture such pollutant, or that any requirement for, or use of, such a conveyance would be inconsistent with any Federal, State, or local law, or (B) the application of measurement methodology to a particular class of sources is not practicable due to technological or economic limitations.

(3) If after notice and opportunity for public hearing, any person establishes to the satisfaction of the Adminis-

trator that an alternative means of emission limitation will achieve a reduction in emissions of any air pollutant at least equivalent to the reduction in emissions of such air pollutant achieved under the requirements of paragraph (1), the Administrator shall permit the use of such alternative by the source for purposes of compliance with this section with respect to such pollutant.

(4) Any standard promulgated under paragraph (1) shall be promulgated in terms of standard of performance whenever it becomes feasible to promulgate and enforce such standard in such terms.

(i) Any regulations promulgated by the Administrator under this section applicable to grain elevators shall not apply to country elevators (as defined by the Administrator) which have a storage capacity of less than two million five hundred thousand bushels.

(j) (1) (A) Any person proposing to own or operate a new source may request the Administrator for one or more waivers from the requirements of this section for such source or any portion thereof with respect to any air pollutant to encourage the use of an innovative technological system or systems of continuous emission reduction. The Administrator may, with the consent of the Governor of the State in which the source is to be located, grant a waiver under this paragraph, if the Administrator determines after notice and opportunity for public hearing, that—

(i) the proposed system or systems have not been adequately demonstrated,

(ii) the proposed system or systems will operate effectively and there is a substantial likelihood that such system or systems will achieve greater continuous emission reduction than that required to be achieved under the standards of performance which would otherwise apply, or achieve at least an equivalent reduction at lower cost in terms of energy, economic, or nonair quality environmental impact,

(iii) the owner or operator of the proposed source has demonstrated to the satisfaction of the Administrator that the proposed system will not cause or contribute to an unreasonable risk to public health, welfare, or safety in its operation, function, or malfunction, and

(iv) the granting of such waiver is consistent with the requirements of subparagraph (C).

In making any determination under clause (ii), the Administrator shall take into account any previous failure of such system or systems to operate effectively or to meet any requirement of the new source performance standards. In determining whether an unreasonable risk exists under clause (iii), the Administrator shall consider, among other factors, whether and to what extent the use of the proposed technological system will cause, increase, reduce, or eliminate emissions of any unregulated pollutants; available methods for reducing or eliminating any risk to public health, welfare, or safety which may be associated with the use of such system; and the availability of other technological systems which may be used to conform to standards under subsection (b) of this section without causing or contributing to such unreasonable risk. The Administrator may conduct such tests and may require the owner or operator of the proposed source to conduct such tests and provide such information as is necessary to carry out clause (iii) of this subparagraph. Such requirements shall include a requirement for prompt reporting of the emission of any unregulated pollutant from a system if such pollutant was not emitted, or was emitted in significantly lesser amounts without use of such system.

(B) A waiver under this paragraph shall be granted on such terms and conditions as the Administrator determines to be necessary to assure—

(i) emissions from the source will not prevent attainment and maintenance of any national ambient air quality standards, and

(ii) proper functioning of the technological system or systems authorized.

Any such term or condition shall be treated as a standard of performance for the purposes of subsection (e) of this section and section 113.

(C) The number of waivers granted under this paragraph with respect to a proposed technological system of continuous emission reduction shall not exceed such number as the Administrator finds necessary to ascertain whether or not such system will achieve the conditions specified in clauses (ii) and (iii) of subparagraph (A).

(D) A waiver under this paragraph shall extend to the sooner of—

(i) the date determined by the Administrator, after consultation with the owner or operator of the source, taking into consideration the design, installation, and capital cost of the technological system or systems being used, or

(ii) the date on which the Administrator determines that such system has failed to—

(I) achieve at least an equivalent continuous emission reduction to that required to be achieved under the standards of performance which would otherwise apply, or

(II) comply with the condition specified in paragraph (1)(A)(iii),

and that such failure cannot be corrected.

(E) In carrying out subparagraph (D)(i), the Administrator shall not permit any waiver for a source or portion thereof to extend beyond the date—

(i) seven years after the date on which any waiver is granted to such source or portion thereof, or

(ii) four years after the date on which such source or portion thereof commences operation,

whichever is earlier.

(F) No waiver under this subsection shall apply to any portion of a source other than the portion on which the innovative technological system or systems of continuous emission reduction is used.

(2)(A) If a waiver under paragraph (1) is terminated under clause (ii) of paragraph (1)(D), the Administrator shall grant an extension of the requirements of this section for such source for such minimum period as may be necessary to comply with the applicable standard of performance under subsection (b) of this section. Such period shall not extend beyond the date three years from the time such waiver is terminated.

(B) An extension granted under this paragraph shall set forth emission limits and a compliance schedule containing increments of progress which require compliance with the applicable standards of performance as expeditiously as practicable and include such measures as are necessary and practicable in the interim to minimize emissions. Such schedule shall be treated as a standard of performance for purposes of subsection (e) of this section and section 113.

NATIONAL EMISSION STANDARDS FOR HAZARDOUS AIR POLLUTANTS

SEC. 112. (a) For purposes of this section—

(1) The term "hazardous air pollutant" means an air pollutant to which no ambient air quality standard is applicable and which in the judgment of the Administrator causes, or contributes to, air pollution which may reasonably be anticipated to result in an increase in mortality or an increase in serious irreversible, or incapacitating reversible, illness.

(2) The term "new source" means a stationary source the construction or modification of which is commenced after the Administrator proposes regulations under this section establishing an emission standard which will be applicable to such source.

(3) The terms "stationary source," "modification," "owner or operator" and "existing source" shall have the same meaning as such terms have under section 111(a).

(b)(1)(A) The Administrator shall, within 90 days after the date of enactment of the Clean Air Amendments of 1970, publish (and shall from time to time thereafter revise) a list which includes each hazardous air pollutant for which he intends to establish an emission standard under this section.

(B) Within 180 days after the inclusion of any air pollutant in such list, the Administrator shall publish proposed regulations establishing emission standards for such pollutant together with a notice of a public hearing within thirty days. Not later than 180 days after such publication, the Administrator shall prescribe an emission standard for such pollutant, unless he finds, on the basis of information presented at such hearings, that such pollutant clearly is not a hazardous air pollutant. The Administrator shall establish any such standard at the level which in his judgment provides an ample margin of safety to protect the public health from such hazardous air pollutant.

(C) Any emission standard established pursuant to this section shall become effective upon promulgation.

(2) The Administrator shall, from time to time, issue information on pollution control techniques for air pollutants subject to the provisions of this section.

(c) (1) After the effective date of any emission standard under this section—

(A) no person may construct any new source or modify any existing source which, in the Administrator's judgment, will emit an air pollutant to which such standard applies unless the Administrator finds that such source if properly operated will not cause emissions in violation of such standard, and

(B) no air pollutant to which such standard applies may be emitted from any stationary source in violation of such standard, except that in the case of an existing source—

(i) such standard shall not apply until 90 days after its effective date, and

(ii) the Administrator may grant a waiver permitting such source a period of up to two years after the effective date of a standard to comply with the standard, if he finds that such period is necessary for the installation of controls and that steps will be taken during the period of the waiver to assure that the health of persons will be protected from imminent endangerment.

(2) The President may exempt any stationary source from compliance with paragraph (1) for a period of not more than two years if he finds that the technology to implement such standards is not available and the operation of such source is required for reasons of national security. An exemption under this paragraph may be extended for one or more additional periods, each period not to exceed two years. The President shall make a report to Congress with respect to each exemption (or extension thereof) made under this paragraph.

(d)(1) Each State may develop and submit to the Administrator a procedure for implementing and enforcing emission standards for hazardous air pollutants for stationary sources located in such State. If the Administrator finds the State procedure is adequate, he shall delegate to such State any authority he has under this Act to implement and enforce such standards.

(2) Nothing in this subsection shall prohibit the Administrator from enforcing any applicable emission standard under this section.

(e)(1) For purposes of this section, if in the judgment of the Administrator, it is not feasible to prescribe or enforce an emission standard for control of a hazardous air pollutant or pollutants, he may instead promulgate a design, equipment, work practice, or operational standard, or combination thereof, which in his judgment is adequate to protect the public health from such pollutant or pollutants with an ample margin of safety. In the event the Administrator promulgates a design or equipment standard under this subsection, he shall include as part of such standard such requirements as will assure the proper operation and maintenance of any such element of design or equipment.

(2) For the purpose of this subsection, the phrase "not feasible to prescribe or enforce an emission standard" means any situation in which the Administrator determines that (A) a hazardous pollutant or pollutants cannot be emitted through a conveyance designed and constructed to emit or capture such pollutant, or that any requirement for, or use of, such a conveyance would be inconsistent with any Federal, State, or local law, or (B) the application of measurement methodology to a particular class of sources is not practicable due to technological or economic limitations.

(3) If after notice and opportunity for public hearing, any person establishes to the satisfaction of the Administrator that an alternative means of emission limitation will achieve a reduction in emissions of any air pollutant at least equivalent to the reduction in emissions of such air pollutant achieved under the requirements of paragraph (1), the Administrator shall permit the use of such alternative by the source for purposes of compliance with this section with respect to such pollutant.

(4) Any standard promulgated under paragraph (1) shall be promulgated in terms of an emission standard whenever it becomes feasible to promulgate and enforce such standard in such terms.

FEDERAL ENFORCEMENT

SEC. 113. (a)(1) Whenever, on the basis of any information available to him, the Administrator finds that any person is in violation of any requirement of an applicable implementation plan, the Administrator shall notify the person in violation of the plan and the State in which the plan applies of such finding. If such violation extends beyond the 30th day after the date of the Administrator's notification, the Administrator may issue an order requiring such person to comply with the requirements of such plan or he may bring a civil action in accordance with subsection (b).

(2) Whenever, on the basis of information available to him, the Administrator finds that violations of an applicable implementation plan are so widespread that such violations appear to result from a failure of the State in which the plan applies to enforce the plan effectively, he shall so notify the State. If the Administrator finds such failure extends beyond the thirtieth day after such notice, he shall give public notice of such finding. During the period beginning with such public notice and ending when such State satisfies the Administrator that it will enforce such plan (hereafter referred to in this section as "period of federally assumed enforcement"), the Administrator may enforce any requirement of such plan with respect to any person—

(A) by issuing an order to comply with such requirement, or

(B) by bringing a civil action under subsection (b).

(3) Whenever, on the basis of any information available to him, the Administrator finds that any person is in violation of section 111(e) (relating to new source performance standards), 112(c) (relating to standards for hazardous emissions), or 119(g) (relating to energy-related authorities), or is in violation of any requirement of section 114 (relating to inspections, etc.), he may issue an order requiring such person to comply with such section or requirement, or he may bring a civil action in accordance with subsection (b).

(4) An order issued under this subsection (other than an order relating to a violation of section 112) shall not take effect until the person to whom it is issued has had an opportunity to confer with the Administrator concerning the alleged violation. A copy of any order issued under this subsection shall be sent to the State air pollution control agency of any State in which the violation occurs. Any order issued under this subsection shall state with reasonable specificity the nature of the violation, specify a time for compliance which the Administrator determines is reasonable, taking into account the seriousness of the violation and any good faith efforts to comply with applicable requirements. In any case in which an order under this subsection (or notice to a violator under paragraph (1)) is issued to a corporation, a copy of such order (or notice) shall be issued to appropriate corporate officers.

(5) Whenever, on the basis of information available to him, the Administrator finds that a State is not acting in compliance with any requirement of the regulation referred to in section 129(a)(1) of the Clean Air Act Amendments of 1977 (relating to certain interpretative regulations) or any plan provisions required under section 110(a)(2)(I) and part D, he may issue an order prohibiting the construction or modification of any major stationary source in any area to which such provisions apply or he may bring a civil action under subsection (b)(5).

(b) The Administrator shall in the case of any person which is the owner or operator of a major stationary source, and may, in the case of any other person, commence a civil action for a permanent or temporary injunction, or to assess and recover a civil penalty of not more than $25,000 per day of violation, or both, whenever such person—

(1) violates or fails or refuses to comply with any order issued under subsection (a); or

(2) violates any requirement of an applicable implementation plan (A) during any period of Federally assumed enforcement, or (B) more than 30 days after having been notified by the Administration under subsection (a)(1) that such person is violating such requirement; or

(3) violates section 111(e),[3] 112(c), section 119(g) (as in effect before the date of the enactment of the Clean Air Act Amendments of 1977), subsection (d)(5) (relating to coal conversion), section 320 (relating to cost of certain vapor recovery), section 119 (relating to smelter orders), or any regulation under part B (relating to ozone); or

(4) fails or refuses to comply with any requirement of section 114 or subsection (d) of this section; or

(5) attempts to construct or modify a major stationary source in any area with respect to which a finding under subsection (a)(5) has been made.

The Administrator may commence a civil action for recovery of any noncompliance penalty under section 120 or for recovery of any nonpayment penalty for which any person is liable under section 120 or for both. Any action under this subsection may be brought in the district court of the United States for the district in which the violation occurred or in which the defendant resides or has his principal place of business, and such court shall have jurisdiction to restrain such violation, to require compliance, to assess such civil penalty and to collect any noncompliance penalty (and nonpayment penalty) owed under section 120. In determining the amount of any civil penalty to be assessed under this subsection, the court

[3] The word "section" was apparently omitted following the comma.

shall take into consideration (in addition to other factors) the size of the business, the economic impact of the penalty on the business, and the seriousness of the violation. Notice of the commencement of such action shall be given to the appropriate State air pollution control agency. In the case of any action brought by the Administrator under this subsection, the court may award costs of litigation (including reasonable attorney and expert witness fees) to the party or parties against whom such action was brought in any case where the court finds that such action was unreasonable.

(c) (1) Any person who knowingly—

(A) violates any requirement of an applicable implementation plan (i) during any period of Federally assumed enforcement, or (ii) more than 30 days after having been notified by the Administration under subsection (a) (1) that such person is violating such requirement, or

(B) violates or fails or refuses to comply with any order under section 119 or under subsection (a) or (d) of this section, or

(C) violates section 111(e), section 112(c), or

(D) violates any requirement of section 119(g) (as in effect before the date of the enactment of this Act, subsection (b) (7) or (d) (5) of section 120 (relating to noncompliance penalties), or any requirement of part B (relating to ozone),

shall be punished by a fine of not more than $25,000 per day of violation, or by imprisonment for not more than one year, or by both. If the conviction is for a violation committed after the first conviction of such person under this paragraph, punishment shall be by a fine of not more than $50,000 per day of violation, or by imprisonment for not more than two years, or by both.

(2) Any person who knowingly makes any false statement, representation, or certification in any application, record, report, plan, or other document filed or required to be maintained under this Act or who falsifies, tampers with, or knowingly renders inaccurate any monitoring device or method required to be maintained under this Act, shall upon conviction, be punished by a fine of not more than $10,000, or by imprisonment for not more than six months, or by both.

(3) For the purpose of this subsection, the term "person" includes, in addition to the entities referred to in section 302(e), any responsible corporate officer.

(d) (1) A State (or, after thirty days notice to the State, the Administrator) may issue to any stationary source which is unable to comply with any requirement of an applicable implementation plan an order which specifies a date for final compliance with such requirement later than the date for attainment of any national ambient air quality standard specified in such plan if—

(A) such order is issued after notice to the public (and, as appropriate, to the Administrator) containing the content of the proposed order and opportunity for public hearing;

(B) the order contains a schedule and timetable for compliance;

(C) the order requires compliance with applicable interim requirements as provided in paragraph (5)(B) (relating to sources converting to coal), and paragraphs (6) and (7) (relating to all sources receiving such orders) and requires the emission monitoring and reporting by the source authorized to be required under sections 110(a)(2)(F) and 114(a)(1);

(D) the order provides for final compliance with the requirement of the applicable implementation plan as expeditiously as practicable, but (except as provided in paragraph (4) or (5)) in no event later than July 1, 1979, or three years after the date for final compliance with such requirement specified in such plan, whichever is later; and

(E) in the case of a major stationary source, the order notifies the source that, unless exempted under section 120(a)(2) (B) or (C), it will be required to pay a noncompliance penalty effective July 1, 1979, as provided under section 120 or by such later date as is set forth in the order in accordance with section 120 (b)(3) or (g), in the event such source fails to achieve final compliance by July 1, 1976.

(2) In the case of any major stationary source, no such order issued by the State shall take effect until the Administrator determines that such order has been issued in accordance with the requirements of this Act. The Administrator shall determine, not later than 90 days after receipt of notice of the issuance of an order under this subsection with respect to any major stationary source, whether or not any State order under this subsection is in accordance with the requirements of this Act. In the case of any source other than a major stationary source, such order issued by the State shall cease to be effective upon a determination by the Administrator that it was not issued in accordance with the requirements of this Act. If the Administrator so objects, he shall simultaneously proceed to issue an enforcement order in accordance with subsection (a) or an order under this subsection. Nothing in this section shall be construed as limiting the authority of a State or political subdivision to adopt and enforce a more stringent emission limitation or more expeditious schedule or timetable for compliance than that contained in an order by the Administrator.

(3) If any source not in compliance with any requirement of an applicable implementation plan gives written notification to the State (or the Administrator) that such source intends to comply by means of replacement of the

facility, a complete change in production process or a termination of operation, the State (or the Administrator) may issue an order under paragraph (1) of this subsection permitting the source to operate until July 1, 1979, without any interim schedule of compliance: *Provided*, That as a condition of the issuance of any such order, the owner or operator of such source shall post a bond or other surety in an amount equal to the cost of actual compliance by such facility and any economic value which may accrue to the owner or operator of such source by reason of the failure to comply. If a source for which the bond or other surety required by this paragraph has been posted fails to replace the facility, change the production process, or terminate the operations as specified in the order by the required date, the owner or operator shall immediately forefit on the bond or other surety and the State (or the Administrator) shall have no discretion to modify the order under this paragraph or to compromise the bond or other surety.

(4) An order under paragraph (1) of this subsection may be issued to an existing stationary source if—

(A) the source will expeditiously use new means of emission limitation which the Administrator determines is likely to be adequately demonstrated (within the meaning of section 111(a)(1)) upon expiration of the order,

(B) such new means of emission limitation is not likely to be used by such source unless an order is granted under this subsection,

(C) such new means of emission limitation is determined by the Administrator to have a substantial likelihood of—

(i) achieving greater continuous emission reduction than the means of emission limitation which, but for such order, would be required; or

(ii) achieving an equivalent continuous reduction at lower cost in terms of energy, economic, or nonair quality environmental impact; and

(D) compliance by the source with the requirement of the applicable implementation plan would be impracticable prior to, or during, the installation of such new means.

Such an order shall provide for final compliance with the requirement in the applicable implementation plan as expeditiously as practicable, but in no event later than five years after the date on which the source would otherwise be required to be in full compliance with the requirement.

[4](5)(A) In the case of a major stationary source which is burning petroleum products or natural gas, or both and which—

(i) is prohibited from doing so under an order pursuant to the provisions of section 2(a) of the Energy Supply and Environmental Coordination Act of 1974 or any amendment thereto, or any subsequent enactment which supersedes such provisions, or

(ii) within one year after enactment of the Clean Air Act Amendments of 1977 gives notice of intent to convert to coal as its primary energy source because of actual or anticipated curtailment of natural gas supplies under any curtailment plan or schedule approved by the Federal Power Commission (or, in the case of intrastate natural gas supplies, approved by the appropriate State regulatory commission),

and which thereby would no longer be in compliance with any requirement under an applicable implementation plan, an order may be issued by the Administrator under paragraph (1) of this subsection for such source which specifies a date for final compliance with such requirement as expeditiously as practicable, but not later than December 31, 1980. The Administrator may issue an additional order under paragraph (1) of this subsection for such source providing an additional period for such source to come into compliance with the requirement in the applicable implementation plan, which shall be as expeditiously as practicable, but in no event later than five years after the date required for compliance under the preceding sentence.

(B) In issuing an order pursuant to subparagraph (A), the Administrator shall prescribe (and may from time to time modify) emission limitations, requirements respecting pollution characteristics of coal, or other enforceable measures for control of emissions for each source to which such an order applies. Such limitations, requirements, and measures shall be those which the Administrator determines must be complied with by the source in order to assure (throughout the period before the date for final compliance established in the order) that the burning of coal by such source will not result in emissions which cause or contribute to concentrations of any air pollutant in excess of any national primary ambient air quality standard for such pollutant.

(C) The Administrator may, by regulation, establish priorities under which manufacturers of continuous emission reduction systems necessary to carry out this paragraph shall provide such systems to users thereof, if he finds, after consultation with the States, that priorities must be imposed in order to assure that such systems are first provided to sources subject to orders under this paragraph in air quality control regions in which national primary ambient air quality standards have not been achieved. No regulation under this subparagraph may impair the obligation of any contract entered into before the date of enactment of the Clean Air Act Amendments of 1977.

(D) No order issued to a source under this paragraph with respect to an air pollutant shall be effective if the national primary ambient air quality standard with respect to such pollutant is being exceeded at any time in the air quality control region in which such source is located. The preceding sentence shall not apply to a source if, upon submission by any person of evidence satisfactory to the Administrator, the Administrator determines (after notice and public hearing)—

(i) that emissions of such air pollutant from such source will affect only infrequently the air quality concentrations of such pollutant in each portion of the region where such standard is being exceeded at any time;

(ii) that emissions of such air pollutant from such source will have only insignificant effect on the air quality concentration of such pollutant in each portion of the region where such standard is being exceeded at any time; and

(iii) with reasonable statistical assurance that emissions of such air pollutant from such source will not cause or contribute to air quality concentrations of such pollutant in excess of the national primary ambient air quality standard for such pollutant.

(6) An order issued to a source under this subsection shall set forth compliance schedules containing increments of progress which require compliance with the requirement postponed as expeditiously as practicable.

(7) A source to which an order is issued under paragraph (1), (3), (4), or (5) of this subsection shall use the best practicable system or systems of emission reduction (as determined by the Administrator taking into account the requirement with which the source must ultimately comply) for the period during which such order is in effect and shall comply with such interim requirements as the Administrator determines are reasonable and practicable. Such interim requirements shall include—

(A) such measures as the Administrator determines are necessary to avoid an imminent and substantial endangerment to health of persons, and

(B) a requirement that the source comply with the requirements of the applicable implementation plan during any such period insofar as such source is able to do so (as determined by the Administrator).

(8) Any order under paragraph (1) of this subection shall be terminated if the Administrator determines on the record, after notice and hearing, that the inability of the source to comply no longer exists. If the owner or operator of the source to which the order is issued demon-

strates that prompt termination of such order would result in undue hardship, the termination shall become effective at the earliest practicable date on which such undue hardship would not result, but in no event later than the date required under this subsection.

(9) If the Administrator determines that a source to which an order is issued under this subsection is in violation of any requirement of this subsection, he shall—

(A) enforce such requirement under subsections (a), (b), or (c) of this section,

(B) (after notice and opportunity for public hearing) revoke such order and enforce compliance with the requirement with respect to which such order was granted,

(C) give notice of noncompliance and commence action under section 120, or

(D) take any appropriate combination of such actions.

(10) During the period of the order in effect under this subsection and where the owner or operator is in compliance with the terms of such order, no Federal enforcement action pursuant to this section and no action under section 304 of this Act shall be pursued against such owner or operator based upon noncompliance during the period the order is in effect with the requirement for the source covered by such order.

(11) For the purposes of sections 110, 304, and 307 of this Act, any order issued by the State and in effect pursuant to this subsection shall become part of the applicable implementation plan.

(12) Any enforcement order issued under subsection (a) of this section or any consent decree in an enforcement action which is in effect on the day of enactment of the Clean Air Act Amendments of 1977 shall remain in effect to the extent that such order or consent decree is (A) not inconsistent with the requirements of this subsection and section 119 or (B) the administrative orders on consent issued by the Administrator on November 5, 1975 and February 26, 1976 and requiring compliance with sulfur dioxide emission limitations or standards at least as stringent as those promulgated under section 111. Any such enforcement order issued under subsection (a) of this section or consent decree which provides for an extension beyond July 1, 1979, except such administrative orders on consent, is void unless modified under this subsection within one year after the enactment of the Clean Air Act Amendments of 1977 to comply with the requirements of this subsection.

(e) (1) The Administrator may, in his discretion, in the case of any person which is the owner or operator of a stationary source in an iron- and steel-producing operation not in compliance with the emission limitation requirements of an applicable implementation plan, consent to entry of a Federal judicial decree, or to the modification of an existing Federal judicial decree, with such person establishing a schedule for compliance for such source extending beyond December 31, 1982, but ending not later than December 31, 1985, on the following conditions:

(A) the Administrator finds, on the basis of information submitted by the applicant and other information available to him, that such extension of compliance is necessary to allow such person to make capital investments in its iron- and steel-producing operations to improve their efficiency and productivity;

(B) the Administrator finds, on the basis of information submitted by the applicant and other information available to him, that an amount equal to the funds the expenditure of which would have been required to comply by December 31, 1982, with those requirements of an applicable implementation plan for which such extensions of compliance are granted and whose expenditure for such purposes are being deferred until after December 31, 1982, pursuant to such extensions will be invested prior to two years from the date of enactment of this subsection in additional capital investments in the iron- and steel-producing operations owned or operated by such person, and located in communities which already contain iron- and steel-producing operations, to improve their efficiency and productivity;

(C) the Administrator and such person consent to entry of Federal judicial decree(s) establishing a phased program of compliance to bring each stationary source at all of such person's iron- and steel-producing operations into compliance with the emission limitation requirements of applicable implementation plans (or, with respect to existing stationary sources located in any nonattainment area for which no implementation plan has been approved as meeting the requirements of part D and subject to implementation plan(s) which do not require compliance with emission limitations which represent at least reasonably available control technology, compliance with emission limitations which represent reasonably available control technology) as expeditiously as practicable but no later than December 31, 1982, or in the case of sources for which extensions of compliance have been granted, no later than December 31, 1985; such decree(s) shall also

contain, at a minimum, (i) requirements for interim controls (which may include operation and maintenance procedures); (ii) increments of compliance sufficient to assure compliance by the final compliance deadlines; (iii) requirement(s) that the amount referred to in subpapragraph (B) above, is to be invested in projects representing additional capital investments in the iron- and steel-producing operations owned or operated by such person for the purposes specified in such subparagraph and shall contain schedule(s) specifying when each such project (or specified alternative project) is to be commenced and completed, as well as increments of progress toward completion; (iv) stipulated monetary penalties covering completion of the air pollution control projects required by the decree, the projects referred to under (iii) above, and such other items as appropriate; (v) monitoring requirements; (iv) reporting requirements (including provision for periodic reports to be filed with the court); and (vii) provisions for preventing increases of emissions from each stationary source;

(D) the Administrator finds, on the basis of information submitted by the applicant and other information available to him, that such person will have sufficient funds to comply with all applicable requirements by the times set forth in the judicial decree(s) entered into pursuant to subparagraph (C) of this subsection;

(E) the Administrator finds, on the basis of information submitted by the applicant and other information available to him, that the applicant is in compliance with existing Federal judicial decrees (if any) entered under section 113 of this Act applicable to its iron- and steel-producing operations or that any violations of such decrees are de minimus in nature: and

(F) the Administrator finds, on the basis of information submitted by the appplicant and other information available to him, that any extension of compliance granted pursuant to this subsection will not result in degradation of air quality during the term of the extension.

(2) For the purpose of this subsection, "iron- and steel-producing operations" include production facilities for iron and steel, as well as associated processing, coke making and sintering facilities. For the purpose of this subsection, "phased program of compliance" means a program assuring, to the extent possible, that capital expenditures for achieving compliance at all sources owned or operated by such person in iron- and steel-producing

operations must be made during the second and each succeeding year of the period covered by the decree(s) in an amount such that at the end of each such year the cumulative expenditures under the decree(s) will be at least equal to the amount which would have been spent if the total expenditures to be made under the decree(s) were made in equal increments during each year of the decree(s). For the purpose of this subsection, "additional capital investments in iron- and steel-producing operations" means investments which the Administrator finds would not be made during the same time period if extension(s) of time for compliance with clean air requirements were not granted under this subsection. The decree entered into pursuant to subparagraph (C) of paragraph (1) of this subsection shall specify the projects which represent additional capital investment in iron- and steel-producing operations, but may also contain specified alternative projects. The decree may also be modified to substitute equivalent projects for those specified. The owner or operator of iron- and steel-producing operations seeking an extension of compliance under this subsection has the burden of satisfying the Administrator with regard to the findings required in paragraphs (A), (B), (D), (E), and (F). A person which is subject to a judicial decree entered or modified pursuant to this subsection shall not be assessed a noncompliance penalty under section 120 of the Act for any source with an extension of compliance under such decree for the period of time covered by the decree only if such source remains in compliance with all provisions and requirements of such decree.

(3) Any records, reports, or information obtained by the Administrator under this subsection shall be available to the public, except that upon a showing satisfactory to the Administrator by any person that records, reports, or information, or particular part thereof (other than emission data) to which the Administrator has access under this section if made public, is likely to cause substantial harm to the person's competitive position, the Administrator shall consider such record, report, or information or particular portion thereof confidential in accordance with the purposes of section 1905 of title 18 of the United States Code, except that such record, report, or information may be disclosed to other officers, employees, or authorized representatives of the United States concerned with carrying out this Act or when relevant in any proceeding under this Act. Any regulations promulgated under section 114 of this Act apply with equal force to this subsection, subject, however, to any changes that the Administrator shall determine are necessary. This paragraph does not constitute authority to withhold records, reports, or information from the Congress.

(4) Nothing in this subsection shall preclude or deny the right of any State or political subdivision to enforce any air pollution requirements in any State judicial or administrative forum.

(5) The provisions of this subsection shall be self-executing, and no implementing regulations shall be required.

(6) Upon receipt of an application for an extension of time under this subsection with respect to any stationary source the Administrator shall promptly—

(i) publish notice of such receipt in the Federal Register;

(ii) notify the Governor of the State in which the stationary source is located; and

(iii) notify the chief elected official of the political subdivision in which the source is located.

(7)(A) The Administrator shall publish in the Federal Register notice of any finding made, or other action taken, by him in connection with the entry of any consent decree or modification of an existing consent decree pursuant to this subsection or in connection with the Administrator's failure or refusal to consent to such a decree.

(B)(i) Except as provided in clause (ii), any finding or other action of the Administrator under this subsection with respect to any stationary source, and any failure or refusal of the Administrator to make any such finding or to take any such action under this subsection, shall be reviewable only by a court in which a civil action under section 113 of this Act is brought against the owner or operator of such stationary source.

(ii) Where, before the date of the enactment of the Steel Industry Compliance Extension Act of 1981, a civil action was brought under this Act against the owner or operator of such stationary source, any finding or other action of the Administrator under this subsection with respect to such stationary source, and any failure or refusal of the Administrator to make any such finding or to take any such action under this subsection, shall be reviewable only by the court in which the civil action was brought.

(8) The provisions of section 304(b)(1)(B) of this Act shall be applicable to this subsection.

(9) For a source which receives an extension under this subsection, air pollution requirements specified in Federal judicial decrees entered into or modified under this subsection that involves such source may not be modified to extend beyond December 31, 1985.

INSPECTIONS, MONITORING, AND ENTRY

SEC. 114. (a) For the purpose (i) of developing or assisting in the development of any implementation plan under section 110 or 111(d), any standard of performance under section 111, or any emission standard under section 112 [4] (ii) of determining whether any person is in violation of any such standard or any requirement of such a plan, or (iii) carrying out any provision of this Act (except a provision of title II with respect to a manufacturer of new motor vehicles or new motor vehicle engines) —

(1) the Administrator may require any person who owns or operates any emission source or who is subject to any requirement of this Act (other than a manufacturer subject to the provisions of section 206(c) or 208) with respect to a provision of title II to (A) establish and maintain such records, (B) make such reports, (C) install, use, and maintain such monitoring equipment or methods, (D) sample such emissions (in accordance with such methods, at such locations, at such intervals, and in such manner as the Administrator shall prescribe), and (E) provide such other information, as he may reasonably require; and

(2) the Administrator or his authorized representative, upon presentation of his credentials—

(A) shall have a right of entry to, upon, or through any premises of such person or in which any records required to be maintained under paragraph (1) of this section are located, and

(B) may at reasonable times have access to and copy any records, inspect any monitoring equipment and method required under paragraph (1), and sample any emissions which such person is required to sample under paragraph (1).

(b) (1) Each State may develop and submit to the Administrator a procedure for carrying out this section in such State. If the Administrator finds the State procedure is adequate, he may delegate to such State any authority he has to carry out this section.

(2) Nothing in this subsection shall prohibit the Administrator from carrying out this section in a State.

(c) Any records, reports, or information obtained under subsection (a) shall be available to the public, except that upon a showing satisfactory to the Administrator by any person that records, reports, or information, or particular part thereof, (other than emission data) to which the Administrator has access under this section if made public, would divulge methods or processes entitled to protection as trade secrets of such person, the Administrator shall consider such record, report, or in-

---

[4] A comma was apparently omitted following "section 112."

formation or particular portion thereof confidential in accordance with the purposes of section 1905 of title 18 of the United States Code, except that such record, report, or information may be disclosed to other officers, employees, or authorized representatives of the United States concerned with carrying out this Act or when relevant in any proceeding under this Act.

(d) (1) In the case of any emission standard or limitation or other requirement which is adopted by a State, as part of an applicable implementation plan or as part of an order under section 113(d), before carrying out an entry, inspection, or monitoring under paragraph (2) of subsection (a) with respect to such standard, limitation, or other requirement, the Administrator (or his representatives) shall provide the State air pollution control agency with reasonable prior notice of such action, indicating the purpose of such action. No State agency which receives notice under this paragraph of an action proposed to be taken may use the information contained in the notice to inform the person whose property is proposed to be affected of the proposed action. If the Administrator has reasonable basis for believing that a State agency is so using or will so use such information, notice to the agency under this paragraph is not required until such time as the Administrator determines the agency will no longer so use information contained in a notice under this paragraph. Nothing in this section shall be construed to require notification to any State agency of any action taken by the Administrator with respect to any standard, limitation, or other requirement which is not part of an applicable implementation plan or which was promulgated by the Administrator under section 110(c).

(2) Nothing in paragraph (1) shall be construed to provide that any failure of the Administrator to comply with the requirements of such paragraph shall be a defense in any enforcement action brought by the Administrator or shall make inadmissible as evidence in any such action any information or material obtained notwithstanding such failure to comply with such requirements.

INTERNATIONAL AIR POLLUTION

SEC. 115. (a) Whenever the Administrator, upon receipt of reports, surveys or studies from any duly constituted international agency has reason to believe that any air pollutant or pollutants emitted in the United States cause or contribute to air pollution which may reasonably be anticipated to endanger public health or welfare in a foreign country or whenever the Secretary of State requests him to do so with respect to such pollution which the Secretary of State alleges is of such a nature, the Administrator shall give formal notification thereof to the Governor of the State in which such emissions originate.

(b) The notice of the Administrator shall be deemed to be a finding under section 110(a)(2)(H)(ii) which requires a plan revision with respect to so much of the applicable implementation plan as is inadequate to prevent or eliminate the endangerment referred to in subsection (a). Any foreign country so affected by such emission of pollutant or pollutants shall be invited to appear at any public hearing associated with any revision of the appropriate portion of the applicable implementation plan.

(c) This section shall apply only to a foreign country which the Administrator determines has given the United States essentially the same rights with respect to the prevention or control of air pollution occurring in that country as is given that country by this section.

(d) Recommendations issued following any abatement conference conducted prior to the enactment of the Clean Air Act Amendments of 1977 shall remain in effect with respect to any pollutant for which no national ambient air quality standard has been established under section 109 of this Act unless the Administrator, after consultation with all agencies which were party to the conference, rescinds any such recommendation on grounds of obsolescence.

RETENTION OF STATE AUTHORITY

SEC. 116. Except as otherwise provided in sections 119 (c), (e), and (f) (as in effect before the date of the enactment of the Clean Air Act Amendments of 1977), 209, 211(c)(4), and 233 (preempting certain State regulation of moving sources) nothing in this Act shall preclude or deny the right of any State or political subdivision thereof to adopt or enforce (1) any standard or limitation respecting emissions of air pollutants or (2) any requirement respecting control or abatement of air pollution; except that if an emission standard or limitation is in effect under an applicable implementation plan or under section 111 or 112, such State or political subdivision may not adopt or enforce any emission standard or limitation which is less stringent than the standard or limitation under such plan or section.

PRESIDENT'S AIR QUALITY ADVISORY BOARD AND ADVISORY COMMITTEES

SEC. 117. (a) In order to obtain assistance in the development and implementation of the purposes of this Act including air quality criteria, recommended control techniques, standards, research and development, and to encourage the continued efforts on the part of industry to improve air quality and to develop economically feasible methods for the control and abatement of air pollution, the Administrator shall from time to time establish advisory committees. Committee members shall include, but not be limited to, persons who are knowledgeable concerning air quality from the standpoint of health, welfare, economics, or technology.

(b) The members of any other advisory committees appointed pursuant to this Act who are not officers or employees of the United States while attending conferences or meetings or while otherwise serving at the request of the Administrator, shall be entitled to receive compensation at a rate to be fixed by the Administrator, but not exceeding $100 per diem, including traveltime, and while away from their homes or regular places of business they may be allowed travel expenses, including per diem in lieu of subsistence, as authorized by section 5703 of title 5 of the United States Code for persons in the Government service employed intermittently.

(c) Prior to—

(1) issuing criteria for an air pollutant under section 108(a)(2),

(2) publishing any list under section 111(b)(1)(A) or 112(b)(1)(A),

(3) publishing any standard under section 111(b)(1)(B) or section 112(b)(1)(B), or

(4) publishing any regulation under section 202(a),

the Administrator shall, to the maximum extent practicable within the time provided, consult with appropriate advisory committees, independent experts, and Federal departments and agencies.

CONTROL OF POLLUTION FROM FEDERAL FACILITIES

SEC. 118. (a) Each department, agency, and instrumentality of executive, legislative, and judicial branches of the Federal Government (1) having jurisdiction over any property or facility, or (2) engaged in any activity resulting, or which may result, in the discharge of air pollutants, and each officer, agent, or employee thereof, shall be subject to, and comply with, all Federal, State, interstate, and local requirements, administrative authority, and process and sanctions respecting the control and abatement of air pollution in the same manner, and to the same extent as any nongovernmental entity. The preceding sentence shall apply (A) to any requirement whether substantive or procedural (including any recordkeeping or reporting requirement, any requirement respecting permits and any other requirement whatsoever), (B) to the exercise of any Federal, State, or local administrative authority, and (C) to any process and sanction, whether enforced in Federal, State, or local courts or in any other manner. This subsection shall apply notwithstanding any immunity of such agencies, officers, agents, or employees under any law or rule of law. No officer, agent, or employee of the United States shall be personally liable for any civil penalty for which he is not otherwise liable.

(b) The President, may exempt any emission source of any department, agency, or instrumentality in the executive branch from compliance with such a requirement if he determines it to be in the paramount interest of the United States to do so, except that no exemption may be granted from section 111, and an exemption from section 112 may be granted only in accordance with section 112(c). No such exemption shall be granted due to lack of appropriation unless the President shall have specifically requested such appropriation as a part of the budgetary process and the Congress shall have failed to make available such requested appropriation. Any exemption shall be for a period not in excess of one year, but additional exemptions may be granted for periods of not to exceed one year upon the President's making a new determination. In addition to any such exemption of a particular emission source, the President may, if he determines it to be in the paramount interest of the United States to do so, issue regulations exempting from compliance with the requirements of this section any weaponry, equipment, aircraft, vehicles, or other classes or categories of property which are owned or operated by the Armed Forces of the United States (including the Coast Guard) or by the National Guard of any State and which are uniquely military in nature. The President shall reconsider the need for such regulations at three-year intervals. The President shall report each January to the Congress all exemptions from the requirements of this section granted during the preceding calendar year, together with his reason for granting each such exemption.

PRIMARY NONFERROUS SMELTER ORDERS

SEC. 119. (a)(1) Upon application by the owner or operator of a primary nonferrous smelter, a primary nonferrous smelter order under subsection (b) may be issued—

(A) by the Adminstrator, after thirty days' notice to the State, or

(B) by the State in which such source is located, but no such order issued by the State shall take effect until the Administrator determines that such order has been issued in accordance with the requirements of this Act.

Not later than ninety days after submission by the State to the Administrator of notice of the issuance of a primary nonferrous smelter order under this section, the Administrator shall determine whether or not such order has been issued by the State in accordance with the requirements of this Act. If the Administrator determines that such order has not been issued in accordance with such requirements, he shall conduct a hearing respecting the reasonably available control technology for primary nonferrous smelters.

(2)(A) An order issued under this section to a primary nonferrous smelter shall be referred to as a "primary nonferrous smelter order". No primary nonferrous smelter may receive both an enforcement order under section 113(d) and a primary nonferrous smelter order under this section.

(B) Before any hearing conducted under this section, in the case of an application made by the owner or operator of a primary nonferrous smelter for a second order under this section, the applicant shall furnish the Administrator (or the State as the case may be) with a statement of the grounds on which such application is based (including all supporting documents and information). The statement of the grounds for the proposed order shall be provided by the Administrator or the State in any case in which such State or Administrator is acting on its own initiative. Such statement (including such documents and information) shall be made available to the public for a thirty-day period before such hearing and shall be considered as part of such hearing. No primary nonferrous smelter order may be granted unless the applicant establishes that he meets the conditions required for the issuance of such order (or the Administrator or State establishes the meeting of such conditions when acting on their own initiative).

(C) Any decision with respect to the issuance of a primary nonferrous smelter order shall be accompanied by a concise statement of the findings and of the basis of such findings.

(3) For the purposes of section [5] 110, 304, and 307 of this Act, any order issued by the State and in effect pursuant to this subsection shall become part of the applicable implementation plan.

(b) A primary nonferrous smelter order under this section may be issued to a primary nonferrous smelter if—

(1) such smelter is in existence on the date of the enactment of this section;

(2) the requirement of the applicable implementation plan with respect to which the order is issued is an emission limitation or standard for sulfur

[5] The word "section" is apparently intended to mean "sections".

oxides which is necessary and intended to be itself sufficient to enable attainment and maintenance of national primary and secondary ambient air quality standards for sulfur oxides; and

(3) such smelter is unable to comply with such requirement by the applicable date for compliance because no means of emission limitation applicable to such smelter which will enable it to achieve compliance with such requirement has been adequately demonstrated to be reasonably available (as determined by the Administrator, taking into account the cost of compliance, nonair quality health and environmental impact, and energy consideration).

(c)(1) A second order issued to a smelter under this section shall set forth compliance schedules containing increments of progress which require compliance with the requirement postponed as expeditiously as practicable. The increments of progress shall be limited to requiring compliance with subsection (d) and, in the case of a second order, to procuring, installing, and operating the necessary means of emission limitation as expeditiously as practicable after the Administrator determines such means have been adequately demonstrated to be reasonably available within the meaning of subsection (b)(3).

(2) Not in excess of two primary nonferrous smelter orders may be issued under this section to any primary nonferrous smelter. The first such order issued to a smelter shall not result in the postponement of the requirement with respect to which such order is issued beyond January 1, 1983. The second such order shall not result in the postponement of such requirement beyond January 1, 1988.

(d)(1)(A) Each primary nonferrous smelter to which an order is issued under this section shall be required to use such interim measures for the period during which such order is in effect as may be necessary in the judgment of the Administrator to assure attainment and maintenance of the national primary and secondary ambient air quality standards during such period, taking into account the aggregate effect on air quality of such order together with all variances, extensions, waivers, enforcement orders, delayed compliance orders and primary nonferrous smelter orders previously issued under this Act.

(B) Such interim requirements shall include—

(i) a requirement that the source to which the order applies comply with such reporting requirements and conduct such monitoring as the Administrator determines may be necessary, and

(ii) such measures as the Administrator determines are necessary to avoid an imminent and substantial endangerment to health of persons.

(C) Such interim measures shall also, except as provided in paragraph (2), include continuous emission reduction technology. The Administrator shall condition the use of any such interim measures upon the agreement of the owner or operator of the smelter—

(i) to comply with such conditions as the Administrator determines are necessary to maximize the reliability and enforceability of such interim measures, as applied to the smelter, in attaining and maintaining the national ambient air quality standards to which the order relates, and

(ii) to commit reasonable resources to research and development of appropriate emission control technology.

(2) The requirement of paragraph (1) for the use of continuous emission reduction technology may be waived with respect to a particular smelter by the State or the Administrator, after notice and a hearing on the record, and upon a showing by the owner or operator of the smelter that such requirement would be so costly as to necessitate permanent or prolonged temporary cessation of operations of the smelter. Upon application for such waiver, the Administrator shall be notified and shall, within ninety days, hold a hearing on the record in accordance with section 554 of title 5 of the United States Code. At such hearing the Administrator shall require the smelter involved to present information relating to any alleged cessation of operations and the detailed reasons or justifications therefor. On the basis of such hearing the Administrator shall make findings of fact as to the effect of such requirement and on the alleged cessation of operations and shall make such recommendations as he deems appropriate. Such report, findings, and recommendations shall be available to the public, and shall be taken into account by the State or the Administrator in making the decision whether or not to grant such waiver.

(3) In order to obtain information for purposes of a waiver under paragraph (2), the Administrator may, on his own motion, conduct an investigation and use the authority of section 321.

(4) In the case of any smelter which on the date of enactment of this section uses continuous emission reduction technology and supplemental controls and which receives an initial primary nonferrous smelter order under this section, no additional continuous emission reduction technology shall be required as a condition of such order unless the Administrator determines, at any time, after notice and public hearing, that such additional continuous emission reduction technology is adequately demonstrated to be reasonably available for the primary nonferrous smelter industry.

(e) At any time during which an order under this section applies, the Administration may enter upon a public hearing respecting the availability of technology. Any order under this section shall be terminated if the Administrator determines on the record, after notice and public hearing, that the conditions upon which the order was based no longer exist. If the owner or operator of the smelter to which the order is issued demonstrates that prompt termination of such order would result in undue hardship, the termination shall become effective at the earliest practicable date on which such undue hardship would not result, but in no event later than the date required under subsection (c).

(f) If the Administrator determines that a smelter to which an order is issued under this section is in violation of any requirement of subsection (c) or (d), he shall—

(1) enforce such requirement under section 113,

(2) (after notice and opportunity for public hearing) revoke such order and enforce compliance with the requirement with respect to which such order was granted.

(3) give notice of noncompliance and commence action under section 120, or

(4) take any appropriate combination of such actions.

NONCOMPLIANCE PENALTY

SEC. 120. (a)(1)(A) Not later than 6 months after the date of enactment of this section, and after notice and opportunity for a public hearing, the Administrator shall promulgate regulations requiring the assessment and collection of a noncompliance penalty against persons referred to in paragraph (2)(A).

(B)(i) Each State may develop and submit to the Administrator a plan for carrying out this section in such State. If the Administrator finds that the State plan meets the requirements of this section, he may delegate to such State any authority he has to carry out this action.

(ii) Notwithstanding a delegation to a State under clause (i), the Administrator may carry out this section in such State under the circumstances described in subsection (b)(2)(B).

(2)(A) Except as provided in subparagraph (B) or (C) of this paragraph, the State or the Administrator shall assess and collect a noncompliance penalty against every person who owns or operates—

(i) a major stationary source (other than a primary nonferrous smelter which has received a primary nonferrous smelter order under section 119) which is not in compliance with any emission limitation, emission standard or compliance schedule under any applicable implementation plan (whether or not such source is subject to a Federal or State consent decree), or

(ii) a stationary source which is not in compliance with an emission limitation, emission standard, standard of performance, or other requirement established under section 111 or 112 of this Act, or

(iii) any source referred to in clause (i) or (ii) (for which an extension, order, or suspension referred to in subparagraph (B), or Federal or State consent decree is in effect), or a primary nonferrous smelter which has received a primary nonferrous smelter order under section 119 which is not in compliance with any interim emission control requirement or schedule of compliance under such extension, order, suspension, or consent decree.

For purposes of subsection (d)(2), in the case of a penalty assessed with respect to a source referred to in clause (iii) of this subparagraph, the costs referred to in such subsection (d)(2) shall be the economic value of noncompliance with the interim emission control requirement or the remaining steps in the schedule of compliance referred to in such clause.

(B) Notwithstanding the requirements of subparagraph (A)(i) and (ii), the owner or operator of any source shall be exempted from the duty to pay a noncompliance penalty under such requirements with respect to that source if, in accordance with the procedures in subsection (b)(5), the owner or operator demonstrates that the failure of such source to comply with any such requirement is due solely to—

(i) a conversion by such source from the burning of petroleum products or natural gas, or both, as the permanent primary energy source to the burning of coal pursuant to an order under section 113(d)(5) or section 119 (as in effect before the date of the enactment of the Clean Air Act Amendments of 1977);

(ii) in the case of a coal-burning source granted an extension under the second sentence of section 119(c)(1) (as in effect before the date of the enactment of the Clean Air Act Amendments of 1977), a prohibition from using petroleum products or natural gas or both, by reason of an order under the provisions of section 2 (a) and (b) of the Energy Supply and Environmental Coordination Act of 1974 or under any legislation which amends or supersedes such provisions;

(iii) the use of innovative technology sanctioned by an enforcement order under section 113(d)(4);

(iv) an inability to comply with any such requirement, for which inability the source has received an order under section 113(d) (or an order under section 113 issued before the date of enactment of this section) which has the effect of permitting a delay or violation of any requirement of this Act (including a requirement of an applicable implementation plan) which inability results from reasons entirely beyond the control of the owner or operator of such source or of any entity controlling, controlled by, or under common control with the owner or operator of such source; or

(v) the conditions by reason of which a temporary emergency suspension is authorized under section 110 (f) or (g).

An exemption under this subparagraph shall cease to be effective if the source fails to comply with the interim emission control requirements or schedules of compliance (including increments of progress) under any such extension, order, or suspension.

(C) The Administrator may, after notice and opportunity for public hearing, exempt any source from the requirements of this section with respect to a particular instance of noncompliance if he finds that such instance of noncompliance is de minimis in nature and in duration.

(b) Regulations under subsection (a) shall—

(1) permit the assessment and collection of such penalty by the State if the State has a delegation of authority in effect under subsection (a)(1)(B)(i);

(2) provide for the assessment and collection of such penalty by the Administrator, if—

(A) the State does not have a delegation of authority in effect under subsection (a)(1)(B)(i), or

(B) the State has such a delegation in effect but fails with respect to any particular person or source to assess or collect the penalty in accordance with the requirements of this section;

(3) require the States, or in the event the States fail to do so, the Administrator, to give a brief but reasonably specific notice of noncompliance under this section to each person referred to in subsection (a)(2)(A) with respect to each source owned or operated by such person which is not in compliance as provided in such subsection, not later than July 1, 1979, or thirty days after the discovery of such noncompliance, whichever is later;

(4) require each person to whom notice is given under paragraph (3) to—

(A) calculate the amount of the penalty owed (determined in accordance with subsection (d)(2) and the schedule of payments (determined in accordance with subsection (d)(3)) for each such source and, within forty-five days after the issuance of such notice or after the denial of a petition under subparagraph (B), to submit that calculation and proposed schedule, together with the information necessary for an independent verification thereof, to the State and to the Administrator, or

(B) submit a petition, within forty-five days after the issuance of such notice, challenging such notice of noncompliance or alleging entitlement to an exemption under subsection (a)(2)(B) with respect to a particular source;

(5) require the Administrator to provide a hearing on the record (within the meaning of subchapter II of chapter 5 of title 5, United States Code) and to make a decision on such petition (including findings of fact and conclusions of law) not later than ninety days after the receipt of any petition under paragraph (4)(B), unless the State agrees to provide a hearing which is sustantially similar to such a hearing on the record and to make a decision on such petition (including such findings and conclusions) within such ninety day period;

(6)(A) authorize the Administrator on his own initiative to review the decision of the State under paragraph (5) and disapprove it if it is not in accordance with the requirements of this section, and (B) require the Administrator to do so not later than sixty days after receipt of a petition under this subparagraph, notice, and public hearing and a showing by such petitioner that the State decision under paragraph (5) is not in accordance with the requirements of this section;

(7) require payment, in accordance with subsection (d), of the penalty by each person to whom notice of noncompliance is given under paragraph (3) with respect to each noncomplying source for which such notice is given unless there has been a final determination granting a petition under paragraph (4)(B) with respect to such source;

(8) authorize the State or the Administrator to adjust (and from time to time to readjust) the amount of the penalty assessment calculated or the payment schedule proposed by such owner or operator under paragraph (4), if the Administrator finds after notice and opportunity for a hearing on the record that the penalty or schedule does not meet the requirements of this section; and

(9) require a final adjustment of the penalty within 180 days after such source comes into compliance in accordance with subsection (d)(4).

In any case in which the State establishes a noncompliance penalty under this section, the State shall provide notice thereof to the Administrator. A noncompliance penalty established by a State under this section shall apply unless the Administrator, within ninety days after the date of receipt of notice of the State penalty assessment under this section, objects in writing to the amount of the penalty as less than would be required to comply with guidelines established by the Administrator. If the Administrator objects, he shall immediately establish a substitute noncompliance penalty applicable to such source.

(c) If the owner or operator of any stationary source to whom a notice is issued under subsection (b)(3)—

(1) does not submit a timely petition under subsection (b)(4)(B), or

(2) submits a petition under subsection (b)(4)(B) which is denied, and

fails to submit a calculation of the penalty assessment, a schedule for payment, and the information necessary for independent verification thereof, the State (or the Administrator, as the case may be) may enter into a contract with any person who has no financial interest in the owner or operator of the source (or in any person controlling, controlled by or under common control with such source) to assist in determining the amount of the penalty assessment or payment schedule with respect to such source. The cost of carrying out such contract may be added to the penalty to be assessed against the owner or operator of such source.

(d)(1) All penalties assessed by the Administrator under this section shall be paid to the United States Treasury. All penalties assessed by the State under this section shall be paid to such State.

(2) The amount of the penalty which shall be assessed and collected with respect to any source under this section shall be equal to—

(A) the amount determined in accordance with regulations promulgated by the Administrator under subsection (a), which is no less than the economic value which a delay in compliance beyond July 1, 1979, may have for the owner of such source, including the quarterly equivalent of the capital costs of compliance and debt service over a normal amortization period, not to exceed ten years, operation and maintenance costs foregone as a result of noncompliance, and any additional economic value which such a delay may have for the owner or operator of such source, minus

(B) the amount of any expenditure made by the owner or operator of that source during any such quarter for the purpose of bringing that source into, and maintaining compliance with, such requirement, to the extent that such expenditures have not been taken into account in the calculation of the penalty under subparagraph (A).

To the extent that any expenditure under subparagraph (B) made during any quarter is not subtracted for such quarter from the costs under subparagraph (A), such expenditure may be subtracted for any subsequent quarter from such costs. In no event shall the amount paid be less than the quarterly payment minus the amount attributed to actual cost of construction.

(3)(A) The assessed penalty required under this section shall be paid in quarterly installments for the period of covered noncompliance. All quarterly payments (determined without regard to any adjustment or any subtraction under paragraph (2)(B)) after the first payment shall be equal.

(B) The first payment shall be due on the date six months after the date of issuance of the notice of noncompliance under subsection (b)(3) with respect to any source or on January 1, 1980, whichever is later. Such first payment shall be in the amount of the quarterly installment for the upcoming quarter, plus the amount owed for any preceding period within the period of covered noncompliance for such source.

(C) For the purpose of this section, the term "period of covered noncompliance" means the period which begins—

(i) two years after the date of enactment of this section, in the case of a source for which notice of noncompliance under subsection (b)(3) is issued on or before the date two years after such date of enactment, or

(ii) on the date of issuance of the notice of noncompliance under subsection (b)(3), in the case of a source for which such notice is issued after July 1, 1979,

and ending on the date on which such source comes into (or for the purpose of establishing the schedule of payments, is estimated to come into) compliance with such requirement.

(4) Upon making a determination that a source with respect to which a penalty has been paid under this section is in compliance and is maintaining compliance with the applicable requirement, the State (or the Administrator as the case may be) shall review the actual expenditures made by the owner or operator of such source for the purpose of attaining and maintaining compliance, and shall within 180 days after such source comes into compliance—

(A) provide reimbursement with interest (to be paid by the State or Secretary of the Treasury, as the case may be) at appropriate prevailing rates (as determined by the Secretary of the Treasury) for any overpayment by such person, or

(B) assess and collect an additional payment with interest at appropriate prevailing rates (as determined by the Secretary of the Treasury) for any underpayment by such person.

(5) Any person who fails to pay the amount of any penalty with respect to any source under this section on a timely basis shall be required to pay in addition a quarterly nonpayment penalty for each quarter during which such failure to pay persists. Such nonpayment penalty shall be in an amount equal to 20 percent of the aggregate amount of such person's penalties and nonpayment penalties with respect to such source which are unpaid as of the beginning of such quarter.

(e) Any action pursuant to this section, including any objection of the Administrator under the last sentence of subsection (b), shall be considered a final action for purposes of judicial review of any penalty under section 307 of this Act.

(f) Any orders, payments, sanctions, or other requirements under this section shall be in addition to any other permits, orders, payments, sanctions, or other requirements established under this Act, and shall in no way affect any civil or criminal enforcement proceedings brought under any provisions of this Act or State or local law.

(g) In the case of any emission limitation or other requirement approved or promulgated by the Administrator under this Act after the enactment of the Clean Air Act Amendments of 1977 which is more stringent than the emission limitation or requirement for the source in effect prior to such approval or promulgation, if any, or where there was no emission limitation or requirement approved or promulgated before enactment of the Clean Air Act Amendments of 1977, the date for imposition of the non-compliance penalty under this section, shall be either July 1, 1979, or the date on which the source is required to be in full compliance with such emission limitation or requirement, whichever is later, but in no event later than three years after the approval or promulgation of such emission limitation or requirement.

CONSULTATION

SEC. 121. In carrying out the requirements of this Act requiring applicable implementation plans to contain—

(1) any transportation controls, air quality maintenance plan requirements or preconstruction review of direct sources of air pollution, or

(2) any measure referred to—

(A) in part D (pertaining to nonattainment requirements), or

(B) in part C (pertaining to prevention of significant deterioration),

and in carrying out the requirements of section 113(d) (relating to certain enforcement orders), the State shall provide a satisfactory process of consultation with general purpose local governments, designated organizations of elected officials of local governments and any Federal land manager having authority over Federal land to which the State plan applies, effective with respect to any such requirement which is adopted more than one year after the date of enactment of the Clean Air Act Amendments of 1977 as part of such plan. Such process shall be in accordance with regulations promulgated by the Administrator to assure adequate consultation. Such regulations shall be promulgated after notice and opportunity for public hearing and not later than 6 months after the date of enactment of the Clean Air Act Amendments of 1977. Only a general purpose unit of local government, regional agency, or council of governments adversely affected by action of the Administrator approving any portion of a plan referred to in this subsection may petition for judicial review of such action on the basis of a violation of the requirements of this section.

LISTING OF CERTAIN UNREGULATED POLLUTANTS

SEC. 122. (a) Not later than one year after date of enactment of this section (two years for radioactive pollutants) and after notice and opportunity for public hearing, the Administrator shall review all available relevant information and determine whether or not emissions of radioactive pollutants (including source material, special nuclear material, and byproduct material), cadmium, arsenic and polycyclic organic matter into the ambient air will cause, or contribute to, air pollution which may reasonably be anticipated to endanger public health. If the Administrator makes an affirmative determination with respect to any such substance, he shall simultaneously with such determination include such substance in the list published under section 108(a)(1) or 112(b)(1)(A) (in the case of a substance which, in the judgment of the Administrator, causes, or contributes to, air pollution which may reasonably be anticipated to result in an increase in mortality or an increase in serious irreversible, or incapacitating reversible, illness), or shall include each category of stationary sources emitting such substance in significant amounts in the list published under section 111(b)(1)(A), or take any combination of such actions.

(b) Nothing in subsection (a) shall be construed to affect the authority of the Administrator to revise any list referred to in subsection (a) with respect to any substance (whether or not enumerated in subsection (a)).

(c) (1) Before listing any source material, special nuclear, or byproduct material (or component or derivative thereof) as provided in subsection (a), the Administrator shall consult with the Nuclear Regulatory Commission.

(2) Not later than six months after listing any such material (or component or derivative thereof) the Administrator and the Nuclear Regulatory Commission shall enter into an interagency agreement with respect to those sources or facilities which are under the jurisdiction of the Commission. This agreement shall, to the maximum extent practicable consistent with this Act, minimize duplication of effort and conserve administrative resources in the establishment, implementation, and enforcement of emission limitations, standards of performance, and other requirements and authorities (substantive and procedural) under this Act respecting the emission of such material (or component or derivative thereof) from such sources or facilities.

(3) In case of any standard or emission limitation promulgated by the Administrator, under this Act or by any State (or the Administrator) under any applicable implementation plan under this Act, if the Nuclear Regulatory Commission determines, after notice and opportunity for public hearing that the application of such standard or limitation to a source or facility within the jurisdiction of the Commission would endanger public health or safety, such standard or limitation shall not apply to such facilities or sources unless the President determines otherwise within ninety days from the date of such finding.

STACK HEIGHTS

SEC. 123. (a) The degree of emission limitation required for control of any air pollutant under an applicable implementation plan under this title shall not be affected in any manner by—

(1) so much of the stack height of any source as exceeds good engineering practice (as determined under regulations promulgated by the Administrator), or

(2) any other dispersion technique.

The preceding sentence shall not apply with respect to stack heights in existence before the date of enactment of the Clean Air Amendments of 1970 or dispersion techniques implemented before such date. In establishing an emission limitation for coal-fired steam electric generating units which are subject to the provisions of section 118 and which commenced operation before July 1, 1957, the effect of the entire stack height of stacks for which a construction contract was awarded before February 8, 1974, may be taken into account.

(b) For the purpose of this section, the term "dispersion technique" includes any intermittent or supplemental control of air pollutants varying with atmospheric conditions.

(c) Not later than six months after the date of enactment of this section, the Administrator, shall after notice and opportunity for public hearing, promulgate regulations to carry out this section. For purposes of this section, good engineering practice means, with respect to stack heights, the height necessary to insure that emissions from the stack do not result in excessive concentrations of any air pollutant in the immediate vicinity of the source as a result of atmospheric downwash, eddies and wakes which may be created by the source itself, nearby structures or nearby terrain obstacles (as determined by the Administrator). For purposes of this section such height shall not exceed two and a half times the height of such source unless the owner or operator of the source demonstrates, after notice and opportunity for public hearing, to the satisfaction of the Administrator, that a greater height is necessary as provided under the preceding sentence. In no event may the Administrator prohibit any increase in any stack height or restrict in any manner the stack height of any source.

ASSURANCE OF ADEQUACY OF STATE PLANS

SEC. 124. (a) As expeditiously as practicable but not later than one year after date of enactment of this section, each State shall review the provisions of its implementation plan which relate to major fuel burning sources and shall determine—

(1) the extent to which compliance with requirements of such plan is dependent upon the use by major fuel burning stationary sources of petroleum products or natural gas,

(2) the extent to which such plan may reasonably be anticipated to be inadequate to meet the requirements of this Act in such State on a reliable and long-term basis by reason of its dependence upon the use of such fuels, and

(3) the extent to which compliance with the requirements of such plan is dependent upon use of coal or coal derivatives which is not locally or regionally available.

Each State shall submit the results of its review and its determination under this paragraph to the Administrator promptly upon completion thereof.

(b)(1) Not later than eighteen months after the date of enactment of this section, the Administrator shall review the submissions of the States under subsection (a) and shall require each State to revise its plan if, in the judgment of the Administrator, such plan revision is necessary to assure that such plan will be adequate to assure compliance with the requirements of this Act in such State on a reliable and long-term basis, taking into account the actual or potential prohibitions on use of petroleum products or natural gas, or both, under any other authority of law.

(2) Before requiring a plan revision under this subsection, with respect to any State the Administrator shall take into account the report of the review conducted by such State under paragraph (1) and shall consult with the Governor of the State respecting such required revision.

MEASURES TO PREVENT ECONOMIC DISRUPTION OR UNEMPLOYMENT

SEC. 125. (a) After notice and opportunity for a public hearing—

(1) the Governor of any State in which a major fuel burning stationary source referred to in this subsection (or class or category thereof) is located,

(2) the Administrator, or

(3) the President (or his designee),

may determine that action under subsection (b) is necessary to prevent or minimize significant local or regional economic disruption or unemployment which would otherwise result from use by such source (or class or category) of—

(A) coal or coal derivatives other than locally or regionally available coal,

(B) petroleum products,

(C) natural gas, or

(D) any combination of fuels referred to in subparagraphs (A) through (C),

to comply with the requirements of a State implementation plan.

(b) Upon a determination under subsection (a)—

(1) such Governor, with the written consent of the President or his designee,

(2) the President's designee with the written consent of such Governor, or

(3) the President

may by rule or order prohibit any such major fuel burning stationary source (or class or category thereof) from using fuels other than locally or regionally available coal or coal derivatives to comply with implementation plan requirements. In taking any action under this subsection, the Governor, the President, or the President's designee as the case may be, shall take into account, the final cost to the consumer of such an action.

(c) The Governor, in the case of action under subsection (b)(1), or the Administrator, in the case of an action under subsection (b) (2) or (3) shall, by rule or order, require each source to which such action applies to—

(1) enter into long-term contracts of at least ten years in duration (except as the President or his designee may otherwise permit or require by rule or order for good cause) for supplies of regionally available coal or coal derivatives,

(2) enter into contracts to acquire any additional means of emission limitation which the Administrator or the State determines may be necessary to comply with the requirements of this Act while using such coal or coal derivatives as fuel, and

(3) comply with such schedules (including increments of progress), timetables and other requirements as may be necessary to assure compliance with the requirements of this Act.

Requirements under this subsection shall be established simultaneously with, and as a condition of, any action under subsection (b).

(d) This section applies only to existing or new major fuel burning stationary sources—

(1) which have the design capacity to produce 250,000,000 Btu's per hour (or its equivalent), as determined by the Administrator, and

(2) which are not in compliance with the requirements of an applicable implementation plan or which are prohibited from burning oil or natural gas, or both, under any other authority of law.

(e) Except as may otherwise be provided by rule by the State or the Administrator for good cause, any action required to be taken by a major fuel burning stationary source under this section shall not be deemed to constitute a modification for purposes of section 111(a) (2) and (4) of this Act.

(f) For purposes of sections 113 and 120 a prohibition under subsection (b), and a corresponding rule or order under subsection (c), shall be treated as a requirement of section 113. For purposes of any plan (or portion thereof) promulgated under section 110(c), any rule or order under subsection (c) corresponding to a prohibition under subsection (b), shall be treated as a part of such plan. For purposes of section 113, a prohibition under subsection (b), applicable to any source, and a corresponding rule or order under subsection (c), shall be treated as part of the applicable implementation plan for the State in which subject source is located.

(g) The President may delegate his authority under this section to an officer or employee of the United States designated by him on a case-by-case basis or in any other manner he deems suitable.

(h) For the purpose of this section the term "locally or regionally available coal or coal derivatives" means coal or coal derivatives which is, or can in the judgment of the State or the Administrator feasibly be, mined or produced in the local or regional area (as determined by the Administrator) in which the major fuel burning stationary source is located.

INTERSTATE POLLUTION ABATEMENT

SEC. 126. (a) Each applicable implementation plan shall—

(1) require each major proposed new (or modified) source—

(A) subject to part C (relating to significant deterioration of air quality) or

(B) which may significantly contribute to levels of air pollution in excess of the national ambient air quality standards in any air quality control region outside the State in which such source intends to locate (or make such modification),

to provide written notice to all nearby States the air pollution levels of which may be affected by such source at least sixty days prior to the date on which commencement of construction is to be permitted by the State providing notice, and

(2) identify all major existing stationary sources which may have the impact described in paragraph (1) with respect to new or modified sources and provide notice to all nearby States of the identity of such sources not later than three months after the date of enactment of the Clean Air Act Amendments of 1977.

(b) Any State or political subdivision may petition the Administrator for a finding that any major source emits or would emit any air pollutant in violation of the prohibition of section 110(a)(2)(E)(i). Within 60 days after receipt of any petition under this subsection and after public hearing, the Administrator shall make such a finding or deny the petition.

(c) Notwithstanding any permit which may have been granted by the State in which the source is located (or intends to locate), it shall be a violation of the applicable implementation plan in such State—

(1) for any major proposed new (or modified) source with respect to which a finding has been made under subsection (b) to be constructed or to operate in violation of the prohibition of section 110(a)(2)(E)(i), or

(2) for any major existing source to operate more than three months after such finding has been made with respect to it.

The Administrator may permit the continued operation of a source referred to in paragraph (2) beyond the expiration of such three-month period if such source complies with such emission limitations and compliance schedules (containing increments of progress) as may be provided by the Administrator to bring about compliance with the requirements contained in section 110(a)(2)(E)(i) as expeditiously as practicable, but in no case later than three years after the date of such finding. Nothing in the preceding sentence shall be construed to preclude any such source from being eligible for an enforcement order under section 113(d) after the expiration of such period during which the Administrator has permitted continuous operation.

SEC. 127. (a) Each State plan shall contain measures which will be effective to notify the public during any calendar year on a regular basis of instances or areas in which any national primary ambient air quality standard is exceeded or was exceeded during any portion of the preceding calendar year to advise the public of the health hazards associated with such pollution, and to enhance public awareness of the measures which can be taken to prevent such standards from being exceeded and the ways in which the public can participate in regulatory and other efforts to improve air quality. Such measures may include the posting of warning signs on interstate highway access points to metropolitan areas or television, radio, or press notices or information.

(b) The Administrator is authorized to make grants to States to assist in carrying out the requirements of subsection (a).

STATE BOARDS

SEC. 128. (a) Not later than the date one year after the date of the enactment of this section, each applicable implementation plan shall contain requirements that—

(1) any board or body which approves permits or enforcement orders under this Act shall have at least a majority of members who represent the public interest and do not derive any significant portion of their income from persons subject to permits or enforcement orders under this Act, and

(2) any potential conflicts of interest by members of such board or body or the head of an executive agency with similar powers be adequately disclosed.

A State may adopt any requirements respecting conflicts of interest for such boards or bodies or heads of executive agencies, or any other entities which are more stringent than the requirements of paragraph (1) and (2), and the Administrator shall approve any such more stringent requirements submitted as part of an implementation plan.

PART B—OZONE PROTECTION

PURPOSES

SEC. 150. The purposes of this part are (1) to provide for a better understanding of the effects of human actions on the stratosphere, especially the ozone in the stratosphere, (2) to provide for a better understanding of the effects of changes in the stratosphere, especially the ozone in the stratosphere on the public health and welfare, (3) to provide information on the progress of regulation of activities which may reasonably be anticipated to affect the ozone in the stratosphere in such a way as to cause or contribute to endangerment of the public health or welfare, and (4) to provide information on the need for additional legislation in this area, if any.

FINDINGS AND DEFINITIONS

SEC. 151. (a) The Congress finds, on the basis of presently available information, that—

(1) halocarbon compounds introduced into the environment potentially threaten to reduce the concentration of ozone in the stratosphere;

(2) ozone reduction will lead to increased incidence of solar ultraviolet radiation at the surface of the Earth;

(3) increased incidence of solar ultraviolet radiation is likely to cause increased rates of disease in humans (including increased rates of skin cancer), threaten food crops, and otherwise damage the natural environment;

(4) other substances, practices, processes, and activities may affect the ozone in the stratosphere, and should be investigated to give early warning of any potential problem and to develop the basis for possible future regulatory action; and

(5) there is some authority under existing law, to regulate certain substances, practices, processes, and activities which may affect the ozone in the stratosphere.

DEFINITIONS

SEC. 152. For the purposes of this subtitle—

(1) the term "halocarbon" means the chemical compounds $CFCl_3$ and CF_2Cl_2 and such other halogenated compounds as the Administrator determines may reasonably be anticipated to contribute to reductions in the concentration of ozone in the stratosphere;

(2) the term "stratosphere" means that part of the atmosphere above the tropopause.

STUDIES BY ENVIRONMENTAL PROTECTION AGENCY

SEC. 153. (a) The Administrator shall conduct a study of the cumulative effect of all substances, practices, processes, and activities which may affect the stratosphere, especially ozone in the stratosphere. The study shall include an analysis of the independent effects on the stratosphere especially such ozone in the stratosphere of—

(1) the release into the ambient air of halocarbons,

(2) the release into the ambient air of other sources of chlorine,

(3) the uses of bromine compounds, and

(4) emissions of aircraft and aircraft propulsion systems employed by operational and experimental aircraft.

The study shall also include such physical, chemical, atmospheric, biomedical, or other research and monitoring as may be necessary to ascertain (A) any direct or indirect effects upon the public health and welfare of changes in the stratosphere, especially ozone in the stratosphere, and (B) the probable causes of changes in the stratosphere, especially the ozone in the stratosphere.

(b) The Administrator shall undertake research on—

(1) methods to recover and recycle substances which directly or indirectly affect the stratosphere, especially ozone in the stratosphere,

(2) methods of preventing the escape of such substances,

(3) safe substitutes for such substances, and

(4) other methods to regulate substances, practices, processes, and activities which may reasonably be anticipated to affect the stratosphere, especially ozone in the stratosphere.

(c)(1) The studies and research conducted under this section may be undertaken with such cooperation and assistance from universities and private industry as may be available. Each department, agency, and instrumentality of the United States having the capability to do so is authorized and encouraged to provide assistance to the Administrator in carrying out the requirements of this section, including (notwithstanding any other provision of law) any services which such department, agency, or instrumentality may have the capability to render or obtain by contract with third parties.

(2) The Administrator shall encourage the cooperation and assistance of other nations in carrying out the studies and research under this section. The Administrator is authorized to cooperate with and support similar research efforts of other nations.

(d)(1) The Administrator shall undertake to contract with the National Academy of Sciences to study the state of knowledge and the adequacy of research efforts to understand (A) the effects of all substances, practices, processes, and activities which may affect the stratosphere, especially ozone in the stratosphere; (B) the health and welfare effects of modifications of the stratosphere, especially ozone in the stratosphere; and (C) methods of control of such substances, practices, processes, and activities including alternatives, costs, feasibility, and timing. The Academy shall make a report of its findings by January 1, 1978.

(2) The Administrator shall make available to the Academy such information in the Administrator's possession as is needed for the purposes of the study provided for in this subsection.

(e) The Secretary of Labor shall study and transmit a report to the Administrator and the Congress not later than six months after date of enactment, with respect to the losses and gains to industry and employment which could result from the elimination of the use of halocarbons in aerosol containers and for other purposes. Such report shall include recommended means of alleviating unemployment or other undesirable economic impact, if any, resulting therefrom.

(f) (1) The Administrator shall establish and act as Chairman of a Coordinating Committee for the purpose of insuring coordination of the efforts of other Federal agencies carrying out research and studies related to or supportive of the research provided for in subsections (a) and (b) and section 154.

(2) Members of the Coordinating Committee shall include the appropriate official responsible for the relevant research efforts of each of the following agencies:

(A) the National Oceanic and Atmospheric Administration,

(B) the National Aeronautics and Space Administration,

(C) the Federal Aviation Administration,

(D) the Department of Agriculture.

(E) the National Cancer Institute,

(F) the National Institute of Environmental Health Sciences,

(G) the National Science Foundation, and the appropriate officials responsible for the relevant research efforts of such other agencies carrying out related efforts as the Chairman shall designate. A representative of the Department of State shall sit on the Coordinating Committee to encourage and facilitate international coordination.

(3) The Coordinating Committee shall review and comment on plans for, and the execution and results of, pertinent research and studies. For this purpose, the agencies named in or designated under paragraph (2) of this subsection shall make appropriate and timely reports to the Coordinating Committee on plans for and the execution and results of such research and studies.

(4) The Chairman may request a report from any Federal Agency for the purpose of determining if that agency should sit on the Coordinating Committee.

(g) Not later than January 1, 1978, and biennially thereafter, the Administrator shall report to the appropriate committees of the House and the Senate, the results of the studies and research conducted under this section and the results of related research and studies conducted by other Federal agencies.

RESEARCH AND MONITORING BY OTHER AGENCIES

SEC. 154. (a) The Administrator of the National Oceanic and Atmospheric Administration shall establish a continuing program of research and monitoring of the stratosphere for the purpose of early detection of changes in the stratosphere and climatic effects of such changes. Such Administrator shall on or before January 1, 1978, and biennially thereafter, transmit such report to the Administrator and the Congress on the findings of such research and monitoring. Such report shall contain any appropriate recommendations for legislation or regulation (or both).

(b) The National Aeronautics and Space Administration shall, pursuant to its authority under title IV of the National Aeronautics and Space Act of 1958, continue programs of research, technology, and monitoring of the stratosphere for the purpose of understanding the physics and chemistry of the stratosphere and for the early detection of potentially harmful changes in the ozone in the stratosphere. Such Administration shall transmit reports by January 1, 1978, and biennially thereafter to the Administrator and the Congress on the results of the programs authorized in this subsection, together with any appropriate recommendations for legislation or regulation (or both).

(c) The Director of the National Science Foundation shall encourage and support ongoing stratospheric research programs and continuing research programs that will increase scientific knowledge of the effects of changes in the ozone layer in the stratosphere upon living organisms and ecosystems. Such Director shall transmit reports by January 1, 1978, and biennially thereafter to the Administrator and the Congress on the results of such programs, together with any appropriate recommendations for legislation or regulation (or both).

(d) The Secretary of Agriculture shall encourage and support continuing research programs that will increase scientific knowledge of the effects of changes in the ozone in the stratosphere upon animals, crops, and other plant life. Such Secretary shall transmit reports by January 1, 1978, and biennially thereafter to the Administrator and the Congress on the results of such programs together with any appropriate recommendations for legislation or regulation (or both).

(e) The Secretary of Health, Education, and Welfare shall encourage and support continuing research programs that will increase scientific knowledge of the effects of changes in the ozone in the stratosphere upon human health. Such Secretary shall transmit reports by January 1, 1978, and biennially thereafter, to the Administrator and the Congress on the results of such programs, together with any appropriate recommendations for legislation or regulation (or both).

(f) In carrying out subsections (a) through (e) of this section, the agencies involved (1) shall enlist and encourage cooperation and assistance from other Federal agencies, universities, and private industry, and (2) shall solicit the views of the Administrator with regard to plans for the research involved so that any such research will, if regulatory action by the Administrator is indicated, provide the preliminary information base for such action.

PROGRESS OF REGULATION

SEC. 155. The Administrator shall provide an interim report to the Congress by January 1, 1978, shall provide a final report within two years after date of enactment, and shall provide follow-up reports anually thereafter on the actions taken by the Environmental Protection Agency and all other Federal agencies to regulate sources of halocarbon emissions, the results of such regulations in protecting the ozone layers, and the need for additional regulatory action, if any. The reports under this section shall also include recommendations for the control of substances, practices, processes, and activities other than those involving halocarbons, which are found to affect the ozone in the stratosphere and which may cause or contribute to harmful effects on public health or welfare.

INTERNATIONAL COOPERATION

SEC. 156. The President shall undertake to enter into international agreements to foster cooperative research which complements studies and research authorized by this part, and to develop standards and regulations which protect the stratosphere consistent with regulations applicable within the United States. For these purposes the President through the Secretary of State and the Assistant Secretary of State for Oceans and International Environmental and Scientific Affairs, shall negotiate multilateral treaties, conventions, resolutions, or other agreements, and formulate, present, or support proposals at the United Nations and other appropriate international forums and shall report to the Congress periodically on efforts to arrive at such agreements.

REGULATIONS

SEC. 157. (a) If at any time prior to the submission of the final report referred to in section 155 in the Administrator's judgment, any substance, practice, process, or activity may reasonably be anticipated to affect the stratosphere, especially ozone in the stratosphere, and such effect may reasonably be anticipated to endanger public health or welfare, the Administrator shall promptly promulgate regulations respecting the control of such substance, practice, process, or activity, and shall simultaneously submit notice of the promulgation of such regulation to the Congress.

(b) Upon submission of the final report referred to in section 155, and after consideration of the research and study under sections 153 and 154 and, consultation with appropriate Federal agencies and scientific entities, the Administrator shall propose regulations for the control of any substance, practice, process, or activity (or any combination thereof) which in his judgment may reasonably be anticipated to affect the stratosphere, especially ozone in the stratosphere, if such effect in the stratosphere may reasonably be anticipated to endanger public health or welfare. Such regulations shall take into account the feasibility and the costs of achieving such control. Such regulations may exempt medical use products for which the Administrator determines there is no suitable substitute. Not later than three months after proposal of such regulations the Administrator shall promulgate such regulations in final form. From time to time, and under the same procedures, the Administrator may revise any of the regulations submitted under this subsection.

OTHER PROVISIONS UNAFFECTED

SEC. 158. Nothing in this part shall be construed to alter or affect the authority of the Administrator under section 303 (relating to emergency powers), under section 231 (relating to aircraft emission standards), or under any other provision of this Act or to affect the authority of any other department, agency, or instrumentality of the United States under any other provision of law to promulgate or enforce any requirement respecting the control of any substance, practice, process, or activity for purposes of protecting the stratosphere or ozone in the stratosphere. In the case of any proposed rule respecting ozone in the stratosphere which has been published under the Toxic Substances Control Act prior to the date of enactment of this Act notwithstanding section 9(b) of such Act, nothing in this part shall be construed to prohibit or restrict the Administrator from taking any action under the Toxic Substances Control Act respecting the promulgation or enforcement of such rule.

STATE AUTHORITY

SEC. 159. (a) Nothing in this part shall preclude or deny any State or political subdivision thereof from adopting or enforcing any requirement respecting the control of any substance, practice, process, or activity for purposes of protecting the stratosphere or ozone in the stratosphere except as otherwise provided in subsection (b).

(b) If a regulation of any substance, practice, process, or activity is in effect under this part in order to prevent or abate any risk to the stratosphere, or ozone in the stratosphere, no State or political subdivision thereof may adopt or attempt to enforce any requirement respecting the control of any such substance, practice, process, or activity to prevent or abate such risk, unless the requirement of the State or political subdivision is identical to the requirement of such regulation. The preceding sentence shall not apply with respect to any law or regulation of any State or political subdivision controlling the use of halocarbons as propellants in aerosol spray containers.

PART C—PREVENTION OF SIGNIFICANT DETERIORATION OF AIR QUALITY

SUBPART 1

PURPOSES

SEC. 160. The purposes of this part are as follows:

(1) to protect public health and welfare from any actual or potential adverse effect which in the Administrator's judgment may reasonably be anticipated to occur from air pollution or from exposures to pollutants in other media, which pollutants originate as emissions to the ambient air), notwithstanding attainment and maintenance of all national ambient air quality standards;

(2) to preserve, protect, and enhance the air quality in national parks, national wilderness areas, national monuments, national seashores, and other areas of special national or regional natural, recreational, scenic, or historic value;

(3) to insure that economic growth will occur in a manner consistent with the preservation of existing clean air resources;

(4) to assure that emissions from any source in any State will not interfere with any portion of the applicable implementation plan to prevent significant deterioration of air quality for any other State; and

(5) to assure that any decision to permit increased air pollution in any area to which this section applies is made only after careful evaluation of all the consequences of such a decision and after adequate procedural opportunities for informed public participation in the decisionmaking process.

PLAN REQUIREMENTS

SEC. 161. In accordance with the policy of section 101 (b)(1), each applicable implementation plan shall contain emission limitations and such other measures as may be necessary, as determined under regulations promulgated under this part, to prevent significant deterioration of air quality in each region (or portion thereof) identified pursuant to section 107(d)(1) (D) or (E).

INITIAL CLASSIFICATIONS

SEC. 162. (a) Upon the enactment of this part, all—

(1) international parks,

(2) national wilderness areas which exceed 5,000 acres in size,

(3) national memorial parks which exceed 5,000 acres in size, and

(4) national parks which exceed six thousand acres in size, and which are in existence on the date of enactment of the Clean Air Act Amendments of 1977 shall be class I areas and may not be redesignated. All areas which were redesignated as class I under regulations promulgated before such date of enactment shall be class I areas which may be redesignated as provided in this part.

(b) All areas in such State identified pursuant to section 107(d)(1)(D) or (E) which are not established as class I under subsection (a) shall be class II areas unless redesignated under section 164.

INCREMENTS AND CEILINGS

SEC. 163. (a) In the case of sulfur oxide and particulate matter, each applicable implementation plan shall contain measures assuring that maximum allowable increases over baseline concentrations of, and maximum allowable concentrations of, such pollutant shall not be exceeded. In the case of any maximum allowable increase (except an allowable increase specified under section 165(d)(2)(C)(iv)) for a pollutant based on concentrations permitted under national ambient air quality standards for any period other than an annual period, such regulations shall permit such maximum allowable increase to be exceeded during one such period per year.

(b)(1) For any class I area, the maximum allowable increase in concentrations of sulfur dioxide and particulate matter over the baseline concentration of such pollutants shall not exceed the following amounts:

Pollutant	*Maximum allowable increase (micrograms per cubic meter)*
Particulate matter:	
Annual geometric mean	5
Twenty-four-hour maximum	10
Sulfur dioxide:	
Annual arithmetic mean	2
Twenty-four-hour maximum	5
Three-hour maximum	25

(2) For any class II area, the maximum allowable increase in concentrations of sulfur dioxide and particulate matter over the baseline concentration of such pollutants shall not exceed the following amounts:

Pollutant	*Maximum allowable increase (micrograms per cubic meter)*
Particulate matter:	
Annual geometric mean	19
Twenty-four-hour maximum	37
Sulfur dioxide:	
Annual arithmetic mean	20
Twenty-four-hour maximum	91
Three-hour maximum	512

(3) For any class III area, the maximum allowable increase in concentrations of sulfur dioxide and particulate matter over the baseline concentration of such pollutants shall not exceed the following amounts:

Pollutant	*Maximum allowable increase (micrograms per cubic meter)*
Particulate matter:	
Annual geometric mean	37
Twenty-four-hour maximum	75
Sulfur dioxide:	
Annual arithmetic mean	40
Twenty-four-hour maximum	182
Three-hour maximum	700

(4) The maximum allowable concentration of any air pollutant in any area to which this part applies shall not exceed a concentration for such pollutant for each period of exposure equal to—

(A) the concentration permitted under the national secondary ambient air quality standard, or

(B) the concentration permitted under the national primary ambient air quality standard,

whichever concentration is lowest for such pollutant for such period of exposure.

(c)(1) In the case of any State which has a plan approved by the Administrator for purposes of carrying out this part, the Governor of such State may, after notice and opportunity for public hearing, issue orders or promulgate rules providing that for purposes of determining compliance with the maximum allowable increases in ambient concentrations of an air pollutant, the following concentrations of such pollutant shall not be taken into account:

(A) concentrations of such pollutant attributable to the increase in emissions from stationary sources which have converted from the use of petroleum products, or natural gas, or both, by reason of an order which is in effect under the provisions of sections 2 (a) and (b) of the Energy Supply and Environmental Coordination Act of 1974 (or any subsequent legislation which supersedes such provisions) over the emissions from such sources before the effective date of such order.

(B) the concentrations of such pollutant attributable to the increase in emissions from stationary sources which have converted from using natural gas by reason of a natural gas curtailment pursuant to a natural gas curtailment plan in effect pursuant to the Federal Power Act over the emissions from such sources before the effective date of such plan.

(C) concentrations of particulate matter attributable to the increase in emissions from construction or other temporary emission-related activities, and

(D) the increase in concentrations attributable to new sources outside the United States over the concentrations attributable to existing sources which are included in the baseline concentration determined in accordance with section 169(4).

(2) No action taken with respect to a source under paragraph (1)(A) or (1)(B) shall apply more than five years after the effective date of the order referred to in paragraph (1)(A) or the plan referred to in paragraph (1)(B), whichever is applicable. If both such order and plan are applicable, no such action shall apply more than five years after the later of such effective dates.

(3) No action under this subsection shall take effect unless the Governor submits the order or rule providing for such exclusion to the Administrator and the Administrator determines that such order or rule is in compliance with the provisions of this subsection.

AREA REDESIGNATION

SEC. 164. (a) Except as otherwise provided under subsection (c), a State may redesignate such areas as it deems appropriate as class I areas. The following areas may be redesignated only as class I or II:

(1) an area which exceeds ten thousand acres in size and is a national monument, a national primitive area, a national preserve, a national recreation area, a national wild and scenic river, a national wildlife refuge, a national lakeshore or seashore, and

(2) a national park or national wilderness area es-

tablished after the date of enactment of this Act which exceeds ten thousand acres in size.

Any area (other than an area referred to in paragraph (1) or (2) or an area established as class I under the first sentence of section 162(a)) may be redesignated by the State as class III if—

(A) such redesignation has been specifically approved by the Governor of the State, after consultation with the appropriate Committees of the legislature if it is in session or with the leadership of the legislature if it is not in session (unless State law provides that such redesignation must be specifically approved by State legislation) and if general purpose units of local government representing a majority of the residents of the area so redesignated enact legislation (including for such units of local government resolutions where appropriate) concurring in the State's redesignation;

(B) such redesignation will not cause, or contribute to, concentrations of any air pollutant which exceed any maximum allowable increase or maximum allowable concentration permitted under the classification of any other area; and

(C) such redesignation otherwise meets the requirements of this part.

Subparagraph (A) of this paragraph shall not apply to area redesignations by Indian tribes.

(b)(1)(A) Prior to redesignation of any area under this part, notice shall be afforded and public hearings shall be conducted in areas proposed to be redesignated and in areas which may be affected by the proposed redesignation. Prior to any such public hearing a satisfactory description and analysis of the health, environmental, economic, social, and energy effects of the proposed redesignation shall be prepared and made available for public inspection and prior to any such redesignation, the description and analysis of such effects shall be reviewed and examined by the redesignating authorities.

(B) Prior to the issuance of notice under subparagraph (A) respecting the redesignation of any area under this subsection, if such area includes any Federal lands, the State shall provide written notice to the appropriate Federal land manager and afford adequate opportunity (but not in excess of 60 days) to confer with the State respecting the intended notice of redesignation and to submit written comments and recommendations with respect to such intended notice of redesignation. In redesignating any area under this section with respect to which any Federal land manager has submitted written comments and recommendations, the State shall publish a list of any inconsistency between such redesignation and such recommendations and an explanation of such inconsistency (together with the reasons for making such redesignation against the recommendation of the Federal land manager).

(C) The Administrator shall promulgate regulations not later than six months after date of enactment of this part, to assure, insofar as practicable, that prior to any public hearing on redesignation of any area, there shall be available for public inspection any specific plans for any new or modified major emitting facility which may be permitted to be constructed and operated only if the area in question is designated or redesignated as class III.

(2) The Administrator may disapprove the redesignation of any area only if he finds, after notice and opportunity for public hearing, that such redesignation does not meet the procedural requirements of this section or is inconsistent with the requirements of section 162(a) or of subsection (a) of this section. If any such disapproval occurs, the classification of the area shall be that which was in effect prior to the redesignation which was disapproved.

(c) Lands within the exterior boundaries of reservations of federally recognized Indian tribes may be redesignated only by the appropriate Indian governing body. Such Indian governing body shall be subject in all respect to the provisions of subsection (e).

(d) The Federal Land Manager shall review all national monuments, primitive areas, and national preserves, and shall recommend any appropriate areas for redesignation as class I where air quality related values are important attributes of the area. The Federal Land Manager shall report such recommendations, within supporting analysis, to the Congress and the affected States within one year after enactment of this section. The Federal Land Manager shall consult with the appropriate States before making such recommendations.

(e) If any State affected by the redesignation of an area by an Indian tribe or any Indian tribe affected by the redesignation of an area by a State disagrees with such redesignation of any area, or if a permit is proposed to be issued for any new major emitting facility proposed for construction in any State which the Governor of an affected State or governing body of an affected Indian tribe determines will cause or contribute to a cumulative change in air quality in excess of that allowed in this part within the affected State or tribal reservation, the Governor or Indian ruling body may request the Administrator to enter into negotiations with the parties involved to resolve such dispute. If requested by any State or Indian tribe involved, the Administrator shall make a recommendation to resolve the dispute and protect the air quality related values of the lands involved. If the parties involved do not reach agreement, the Administrator shall resolve the dispute and his determination, or the results of agreements reached through other means, shall become part of the applicable plan and shall be enforceable as part of such plan. In resolving such disputes relating to area redesignation, the Administrator shall consider the extent to which the lands involved are of sufficient size to allow effective air quality management or have air quality related values of such an area.

PRECONSTRUCTION REQUIREMENTS

SEC. 165. (a) No major emitting facility on which construction is commenced after the date of the enactment of this part, may be constructed in any area to which this part applies unless—

(1) a permit has been issued for such proposed facility in accordance with this part setting forth emission limitations for such facility which conform to the requirements of this part;

(2) the proposed permit has been subject to a review in accordance with this section, the required analysis has been conducted in accordance with regulations promulgated by the Administrator, and a public hearing has been held with opportunity for interested persons including representatives of the Administrator to appear and submit written or oral presentations on the air quality impact of such source, alternatives thereto, control technology requirements, and other appropriate considerations;

(3) the owner or operator of such facility demonstrates, as required pursuant to section 110(j), that emissions from construction or operation of such facility will not cause, or contribute to, air pollution in excess of any (A) maximum allowable increase or maximum allowable concentration for any pollutant in any area to which this part applies more than one time per year, (B) national ambient air quality standard in any air quality control region, or (C) any other applicable emission standard or standard of performance under this Act;

(4) the proposed facility is subject to the best available control technology for each pollutant subject to regulation under this Act emitted from, or which results from, such facility;

(5) the provisions of subsection (d) with respect to protection of class I areas have been complied with for such facility;

(6) there has been an analysis of any air quality impacts projected for the area as a result of growth associated with such facility;

(7) the person who owns or operates, or proposes to own or operate, a major emitting facility for

which a permit is required under this part agrees to conduct such monitoring as may be necessary to determine the effect which emissions from any such facility may have, or is having, on air quality in any area which may be affected by emissions from such source; and

(8) in the case of a source which proposes to construct in a class III area, emissions from which would cause or contribute to exceeding the maximum allowable increments applicable in a class II area and where no standard under section 111 of this Act has been promulgated subsequent to enactment of the Clean Air Act Amendments of 1977, for such source category, the Administrator has approved the determination of best available technology as set forth in the permit.

(b) The demonstration pertaining to maximum allowable increases required under subsection (a)(3) shall not apply to maximum allowable increases for class II areas in the case of an expansion or modification of a major emitting facility which is in existence on the date of enactment of the Clean Air Act Amendments of 1977, whose allowable emissions of air pollutants, after compliance with subsection (a)(4), will be less than fifty tons per year and for which the owner or operator of such facility demonstrates that emissions of particulate matter and sulfur oxides will not cause or contribute to ambient air quality levels in excess of the national secondary ambient air quality standard for either of such pollutants.

(c) Any completed permit application under section 110 for a major emitting facility in any area to which this part applies shall be granted or denied not later than one year after the date of filing of such completed application.

(d)(1) Each State shall transmit to the Administrator a copy of each permit application relating to a major emitting facility received by such State and provide notice to the Administrator of every action related to the consideration of such permit.

(2)(A) The Administrator shall provide notice of the permit application to the Federal Land Manager and the Federal official charged with direct responsibility for management of any lands within a class I area which may be affected by emissions from the proposed facility.

(B) The Federal Land Manager and the Federal official charged with direct responsibility for management of such lands shall have an affirmative responsibility to protect the air quality related values (including visibility) of any such lands within a class I area and to consider, in consultation with the Administrator, whether a proposed major emitting facility will have an adverse impact on such values.

(C)(i) In any case where the Federal official charged with direct responsibility for management of any lands within a class I area or the Federal Land Manager of such lands, or the Administrator, or the Governor of an adjacent State containing such a class I area files a notice alleging that emissions from a proposed major emitting facility may cause or contribute to a change in the air quality in such area and identifying the potential adverse impact of such change, a permit shall not be issued unless the owner or operator of such facility demonstrates that emissions of particulate matter and sulfur dioxide will not cause or contribute to concentrations which exceed the maximum allowable increases for a class I area.

(ii) In any case where the Federal Land Manager demonstrates to the satisfaction of the State that the emissions from such facility will have an adverse impact on the air quality-related values (including visibility) of such lands, notwithstanding the fact that the change in air quality resulting from emissions from such facility will not cause or contribute to concentrations which exceed the maximum allowable increases for a class I area, a permit shall not be issued.

(iii) In any case where the owner or operator of such facility demonstrates to the satisfaction of the Federal Land Manager, and the Federal Land Manager so certifies, that the emissions from such facility will have no adverse impact on the air quality-related values of such lands (including visibility) notwithstanding the fact that the change in air quality resulting from emissions from such facility will cause or contribute to concentrations which exceed the maximum allowable increases for class I areas, the State may issue a permit.

(iv) In the case of a permit issued pursuant to clause (iii), such facility shall comply with such emission limitations under such permit as may be necessary to assure that emissions of sulfur oxides and particulates from such facility, will not cause or contribute to concentrations of such pollutant which exceed the following maximum allowable increases over the baseline concentration for such pollutants:

	Maximum allowable increase (micrograms per cubic meter)
Particulate matter:	
Annual geometric mean	19
Twenty-four-hour maximum	37
Sulfur dioxide:	
Annual arithmetic mean	20
Twenty-four-hour maximum	91
Three-hour maximum	325

(D)(i) In any case where the owner or operator of a proposed major emitting facility who has been denied a certification under subparagraph (C)(iii) demonstrates to the satisfaction of the Governor, after notice and public hearing, and the Governor finds, that the facility cannot be constructed by reason of any maximum allowable increase for sulfur dioxide for periods of twenty-four hours or less applicable to any class I area and, in the case of Federal mandatory class I areas, that a variance under this clause will not adversely affect the air quality related values of the area (including visibility), the Governor, after consideration of the Federal Land Manager's recommendation (if any) and subject to his concurrence, may grant a variance from such maximum allowable increase. If such variance is granted, a permit may be issued to such source pursuant to the requirements of this subparagraph.

(ii) In any case in which the Governor recommends a variance under this subparagraph in which the Federal Land Manager does not concur, the recommendations of the Governor and the Federal Land Manager shall be transmitted to the President. The President may approve the Governor's recommendation if he finds that such variance is in the national interest. No Presidential finding shall be reviewable in any court. The variance shall take effect if the President approves the Governor's recommendations. The President shall approve or disapprove such recommendation within ninety days after his receipt of the recommendations of the Governor and the Federal Land Manager.

(iii) In the case of a permit issued pursuant to this subparagraph, such facility shall comply with such emission limitations under such permit as may be necessary to assure that emissions of sulfur oxides from such facility will not (during any day on which the otherwise applicable maximum allowable increases are exceeded) cause or contribute to concentrations which exceed the following maximum allowable increases for such areas over the baseline concentration for such pollutant and to assure that such emissions will not cause or contribute to concentrations which exceed the otherwise applicable maximum allowable increases for periods of exposure of 24 hours or less on more than 18 days during any annual period:

Maximum allowable increase

Period of exposure:	*Micrograms per cubic meter*
Low terrain areas:	
24-hr maximum	36
3-hr maximum	130
High terrain areas:	
24-hr maximum	62
3-hr maximum	221

(iv) For purposes of clause (iii), the term "high terrain area" means with respect to any facility, any area having an elevation of 900 feet or more above the base of the stack of such facility, and the term "low terrain area" means any area other than a high terrain area.

(e)(1) The review provided for in subsection (a) shall be preceded by an analysis in accordance with regulations of the Administrator, promulgated under this subsection, which may be conducted by the State (or any general purpose unit of local government) or by the major emitting facility applying for such permit, of the ambient air quality at the proposed site and in areas which may be affected by emissions from such facility for each pollutant subject to regulation under this Act which will be emitted from such facility.

(2) Effective one year after date of enactment of this part, the analysis required by this subsection shall include continuous air quality monitoring data gathered for purposes of determining whether emissions from such facility will exceed the maximum allowable increases or the maximum allowable concentration permitted under this part. Such data shall be gathered over a period of one calendar year preceding the date of application for a permit under this part unless the State, in accordance with regulations promulgated by the Administrator, determines that a complete and adequate analysis for such purposes may be accomplished in a shorter period. The results of such analysis shall be available at the time of the public hearing on the application for such permit.

(3) The Administrator shall within six months after the date of enactment of this part promulgate regulations respecting the analysis required under this subsection which regulations—

(A) shall not require the use of any automatic or uniform buffer zone or zones,

(B) shall require an analysis of the ambient air quality, climate and meteorology, terrain, soils and vegetation, and visibility at the site of the proposed major emitting facility and in the area potentially affected by the emissions from such facility for each pollutant regulated under this Act which will be emitted from, or which results from the construction or operation of, such facility, the size and nature of the proposed facility, the degree of continuous emission reduction which could be achieved by such facility, and such other factors as may be relevant in determining the effect of emissions from a proposed facility on any air quality control region,

(C) shall require the results of such analysis shall be available at the time of the public hearing on the application for such permit, and

(D) shall specify with reasonable particularity each air quality model or models to be used under specified sets of conditions for purposes of this part.

Any model or models designated under such regulations may be adjusted upon a determination, after notice and opportunity for public hearing, by the Administrator that such adjustment is necessary to take into account unique terrain or meteorological characteristics of an area potentially affected by emissions from a source applying for a permit required under this part.

OTHER POLLUTANTS

SEC. 166. (a) In the case of the pollutants hydrocarbons, carbon monoxide, photochemical oxidants, and nitrogen oxides, the Administrator shall conduct a study and not later than two years after the date of enactment of this part, promulgate regulations to prevent the significant deterioration of air quality which would result from the emissions of such pollutants. In the case of pollutants for which national ambient air quality standards are promulgated after the date of the enactment of this part, he shall promulgate such regulations not more than 2 years after the date of promulgation of such standards.

(b) Regulations referred to in subsection (a) shall become effective one year after the date of promulgation. Within 21 months after such date of promulgation such plan revision shall be submitted to the Administrator who shall approve or disapprove the plan within 25 months after such date or promulgation in the same manner as required under section 110.

(c) Such regulations shall provide specific numerical measures against which permit applications may be evaluated, a framework for stimulating improved control technology, protection of air quality values, and fulfill the goals and purposes set forth in section 101 and section 160.

(d) The regulations of the Administrator under subsection (a) shall provide specific measures at least as effective as the increments established in section 163 to fulfill such goals and purposes, and may contain air quality increments, emission density requirements, or other measures.

(e) With respect to any air pollutant for which a national ambient air quality standard is established other than sulfur oxides or particulate matter, an area classification plan shall not be required under this section if the implementation plan adopted by the State and submitted for the Administrator's approval or promulgated by the Administrator under section 110(c) contains other provisions which when considered as a whole, the Administrator finds will carry out the purposes in section 160 at least as effectively as an area classification plan for such pollutant. Such other provisions referred to in the preceding sentence need not require the establishment of maximum allowable increases with respect to such pollutant for any area to which this section applies.

ENFORCEMENT

SEC. 167. The Administrator shall, and a State may, take such measures, including issuance of an order, or seeking injunctive relief, as necessary to prevent the construction of a major emitting facility which does not conform to the requirements of this part, or which is proposed to be constructed in any area included in the list promulgated pursuant to paragraph (1)(D) or (E) of subsection (d) of section 107 of this Act and which is not subject to an implementation plan which meets the requirements of this part.

PERIOD BEFORE PLAN APPROVAL

SEC. 168. (a) Until such time as an applicable implementation plan is in effect for any area, which plan meets the requirements of this part to prevent significant deterioration of air quality with respect to any air pollutant, applicable regulations under this Act prior to enactment of this part shall remain in effect to prevent significant deterioration of air quality in any such area for any such pollutant except as otherwise provided in subsection (b).

(b) If any regulation in effect prior to enactment of this part to prevent significant deterioration of air quality would be inconsistent with the requirements of section 162(a), section 163(b) or section 164(a), then such regulations shall be deemed amended so as to conform with such requirements. In the case of a facility on which construction was commenced (in accordance with this definition of "commenced" in section 169(2)) after June 1, 1975, and prior to the enactment of the Clean Air Act Amendments of 1977, the review and permitting of such facility shall be in accordance with the regulations for the prevention of significant deterioration in effect prior to the enactment of the Clean Air Act Amendments of 1977.

DEFINITIONS

SEC. 169. For purposes of this part—

(1) The term "major emitting facility" means any of the following stationary sources of air pollutants which emit, or have the potential to emit, one hundred tons per year or more of any air pollutant from the following types of stationary sources: fossil-fuel fired steam electric plants of more than two hundred and fifty million British thermal units per hour heat input, coal cleaning plants (thermal dryers), kraft pulp mills, Portland Cement plants, primary zinc smelters, iron and steel mill plants, primary aluminum ore reduction plants, primary copper smelters, municipal incinerators capable of

charging more than two hundred and fifty tons of refuse per day, hydrofluoric, sulfuric, and nitric acid plants, petroleum refineries, lime plants, phosphate rock processing plants, coke oven batteries, sulfur recovery plants, carbon black plants (furnace process) primary lead smelters, fuel conversion plants, sintering plants, secondary metal production facilities, chemical process plants, fossil-fuel boilers of more than two hundred and fifty million British thermal units per hour heat input, petroleum storage and transfer facilities with a capacity exceeding three hundred thousand barrels, taconite ore processing facilities, glass fiber processing plants, charcoal production facilities. Such term also includes any other source with the potential to emit two hundred and fifty tons per year or more of any air pollutant. This term shall not include new or modified facilities which are nonprofit health or education institutions which have been exempted by the State.

(2)(A) The term "commenced" as applied to construction of a major emitting facility means that the owner or operator has obtained all necessary preconstruction approvals or permits required by Federal, State, or local air pollution emissions and air quality laws or regulations and either has (i) begun, or caused to begin, a continuous program of physical on-site construction of the facility or (ii) entered into binding agreements or contractual obligations, which cannot be canceled or modified without substantial loss to the owner or operator, to undertake a program of construction of the facility to be completed within a reasonable time.

(B) The term "necessary preconstruction approvals or permits" means those permits or approvals required by the permitting authority as a precondition to undertaking any activity under clauses (i) or (ii) of subparagraph (A) of this paragraph.

(C) The term "construction" when used in connection with any source or facility, includes the modification (as defined in section 111(a)) of any source or facility.

(3) The term "best available control technology" means an emission limitation based on the maximum degree of reduction of each pollutant subject to regulation under this Act emitted from or which results from any major emitting facility, which the permitting authority, on a case-by-case basis, taking into account energy, environmental, and economic impacts and other costs, determines is achievable for such facility through application of production processes and available methods, systems, and techniques, including fuel cleaning or treatment or

innovative fuel combustion techniques for control of each such pollutant. In no event shall application of "best available control technology" result in emissions of any pollutants which will exceed the emissions allowed by any applicable standard established pursuant to section 111 or 112 of this Act.

(4) The term "baseline concentration" means, with respect to a pollutant, the ambient concentration levels which exist at the time of the first application for a permit in an area subject to this part, based on air quality data available in the Environmental Protection Agency or a State air pollution control agency and on such monitoring data as the permit applicant is required to submit. Such ambient concentration levels shall take into account all projected emissions in, or which may affect, such area from any major emitting facility on which construction commenced prior to January 6, 1975, but which has not begun operation by the date of the baseline air quality concentration determination. Emissions of sulfur oxides and particulate matter from any major emitting facility on which construction commenced after January 6, 1975, shall not be included in the baseline and shall be counted against the maximum allowable increases in pollutant concentrations established under this part.

SUBPART 2

VISIBILITY PROTECTION FOR FEDERAL CLASS I AREAS

SEC. 169A. (a)(1) Congress hereby declares as a national goal the prevention of any future, and the remedying of any existing, impairment of visibility in mandatory class I Federal areas which impairment results from manmade air pollution.

(2) Not later than six months after the date of the enactment of this section, the Secretary of the Interior in consultation with other Federal land managers shall review all mandatory class I Federal areas and identify those where visibility is an important value of the area. From time to time the Secretary of the Interior may revise such identifications. Not later than one year after such date of enactment, the Administrator shall, after consultation with the Secretary of the Interior, promulgate a list of mandatory class I Federal areas in which he determines visibility is an important value.

(3) Not later than eighteen months after the date of enactment of this section, the Administrator shall complete a study and report to Congress on available methods for implementing the national goal set forth in paragraph (1). Such report shall include recommendations for—

(A) methods for identifying, characterizing, determining, quantifying, and measuring visibility impairment in Federal areas referred to in paragraph (1), and

(B) modeling techniques (or other methods) for determining the extent to which manmade air pollution may reasonably be anticipated to cause or contribute to such impairment, and

(C) methods for preventing and remedying such manmade air pollution and resulting visibility impairment.

Such report shall also identify the classes or categories of sources and the types of air pollutants which, alone or in conjunction with other sources or pollutants, may reasonably be anticipated to cause or contribute significantly to impairment of visibility.

(4) Not later than twenty-four months after the date of enactment of this section, and after notice and public hearing, the Administrator shall promulgate regulations to assure (A) reasonable progress toward meeting the national goal specified in paragraph (1), and (B) compliance with the requirements of this section.

(b) Regulations under subsection (a)(4) shall—

(1) provide guidelines to the States, taking into account the recommendations under subsection (a)(3) on appropriate techniques and methods for implementing this section (as provided in subparagraphs (A) through (C) of such subsection (a)(3)), and

(2) require each applicable implementation plan for a State in which any area listed by the Administrator under subsection (a)(2) is located (or for a State the emissions from which may reasonably be anticipated to cause or contribute to any impairment of visibility in any such area) to contain such emission limits, schedules of compliance and other measures as may be necessary to make reasonable progress toward meeting the national goal specified in subsection (a), including—

(A) except as otherwise provided pursuant to subsection (c), a requirement that each major stationary source which is in existence on the date of enactment of this section, but which has not been in operation for more than fifteen years as of such date, and which, as determined by the State (or the Administrator in the case of a plan promulgated under section 110(c)) emits any air pollutant which may reasonably be anticipated to cause or contribute to any impairment of visibility in any such area, shall procure, install, and operate, as expeditiously as practicable (and maintain thereafter) the best available retrofit technology, as determined by the State (or the Administrator in the case of a plan promulgated under section 110(c)) for controlling emissions from such source for the purpose of eliminating or reducing any such impairment, and

(B) a long-term (ten to fifteen years) strategy for making reasonable progress toward meeting the national goal specified in subsection (a).

In the case of a fossil-fuel fired generating powerplant having a total generating capacity in excess of 750 megawatts, the emission limitations required under this paragraph shall be determined pursuant to guidelines, promulgated by the Administrator under paragraph (1).

(c) (1) The Administrator may, by rule, after notice and opportunity for public hearing, exempt any major stationary source from the requirement of subsection (b) (2) (A), upon his determination that such source does not or will not, by itself or in combination with other sources, emit any air pollutant which may reasonably be anticipated to cause or contribute to a significant impairment of visibility in any mandatory class I Federal area.

(2) Paragraph (1) of this subsection shall not be applicable to any fossil-fuel fired powerplant with total design capacity of 750 megawatts or more, unless the owner or operator of any such plant demonstrates to the satisfaction of the Administrator that such powerplant is located at such distance from all areas listed by the Administrator under subsection (a) (2) that such powerplant does not or will not, by itself or in combination with other sources, emit any air pollutant which may reasonably be anticipated to cause or contribute to significant impairment of visibility in any such area.

(3) An exemption under this subsection shall be effective only upon concurrence by the appropriate Federal land manager or managers with the Administrator's determination under this subsection.

(d) Before holding the public hearing on the proposed revision of an applicable implementation plan to meet the requirements of this section, the State (or the Administrator, in the case of a plan promulgated under section 110(c)) shall consult in person with the appropriate Federal land manager or managers and shall include a summary of the conclusions and recommendations of the Federal land managers in the notice to the public.

(e) In promulgating regulations under this section, the Administrator shall not require the use of any automatic or uniform buffer zone or zones.

(f) For purposes of section 304(a)(2), the meeting of the national goal specified in subsection (a)(1) by any specific date or dates shall not be considered a "nondiscretionary duty" of the Administrator.

(g) For the purpose of this section—

(1) in determining reasonable progress there shall be taken into consideration the costs of compliance, the time necessary for compliance, and the energy and nonair quality environmental impacts of compliance, and the remaining useful life of any existing source subject to such requirements;

(2) in determining best available retrofit technology the State (or the Administrator in determining emission limitations which reflect such technology) shall take into consideration the costs of compliance, the energy and nonair quality environmental impacts of compliance, any existing pollution control technology in use at the source, the remaining useful life of the source, and the degree of improvement in visibility which may reasonably be anticipated to result from the use of such technology;

(3) the term "manmade air pollution" means air pollution which results directly or indirectly from human activities;

(4) the term "as expeditiously as practicable" means as expeditiously as practicable but in no event later than five years after the date of approval of a plan revision under this section (or the date of promulgation of such a plan revision in the case of action by the Administrator under section 110(c) for purposes of this section);

(5) the term "mandatory class I Federal areas" means Federal areas which may not be designated as other than class I under this part;

(6) the terms "visibility impairment" and "impairment of visibility" shall include reduction in visual range and atmospheric discoloration; and

(7) the term "major stationary source" means the following types of stationary sources with the potential to emit 250 tons or more of any pollutant; fossil-fuel fired steam electric plants of more than 250 million British thermal units per hour heat input, coal cleaning plants (thermal dryers), kraft pulp mills, Portland Cement plants, primary zinc smelters, iron and steel mill plants, primary aluminum ore reduction plants, primary copper smelters, municipal incinerators capable of charging more than 250 tons of refuse per day, hydrofluoric, sulfuric, and nitric acid plants, petroleum refineries, lime plants, phosphate rock processing plants, coke oven batteries, sulfur recovery plants, carbon black

plants (furnace process), primary lead smelters, fuel conversion plants, sintering plants, secondary metal production facilities, chemical process plants, fossil-fuel boilers of more than 250 million British thermal units per hour heat input, petroleum storage and transfer facilities with a capacity exceeding 300,000 barrels, taconite ore processing facilities, glass fiber processing plants, charcoal production facilities.

Part D—Plan Requirements for Nonattainment Areas

DEFINITIONS

Sec. 171. For the purpose of this part and section 110(a)(2)(I)—

(1) The term "reasonable further progress" means annual incremental reductions in emissions of the applicable air pollutant (including substantial reductions in the early years following approval or promulgation of plan provisions under this part and section 110(a)(2)(I) and regular reductions thereafter) which are sufficient in the judgment of the Administrator, to provide for attainment of the applicable national ambient air quality standard by the date required in section 172(a).

(2) The term "nonattainment area" means, for any air pollutant an area which is shown by monitored data or which is calculated by air quality modeling (or other methods determined by the Administrator to be reliable) to exceed any national ambient air quality standard for such pollutant. Such term includes any area identified under subparagraphs (A) through (C) of section 107(d)(1).

(3) The term "lowest achievable emission rate" means for any source, that rate of emissions which reflects—

(A) the most stringent emission limitation which is contained in the implementation plan of any State for such class or category of source, unless the owner or operator of the proposed source demonstartes that such limitations are not achievable, or

(B) the most stringent emission limitation which is achieved in practice by such class or category of source, whichever is more stringent.

In no event shall the application of this term permit a proposed new or modified source to emit any pollutant in excess of the amount allowable under applicable new source standards of performance.

(4) The terms "modifications" and "modified" mean the same as the term "modification" as used in section 111(a)(4) of this Act.

NONATTAINMENT PLAN PROVISIONS

SEC. 172. (a)(1) The provisions of an applicable implementation plan for a State relating to attainment and maintenance of national ambient air quality standards in any nonattainment area which are required by section 110(a)(2)(I) as precondition for the construction or modification of any major stationary source in any such area on or after July 1, 1979, shall provide for attainment of each such national ambient air quality standard in each such area as expeditiously as practicable, but, in the case of national primary ambient air quality standards, not later than December 31, 1982.

(2) In the case of the national primary ambient air quality standard for photochemical oxidants or carbon monoxide (or both) if the State demonstrates to the satisfaction of the Administrator (on or before the time required for submission of such plan) that such attainment is not possible in an area with respect to either or both of such pollutants within the period prior to December 31, 1982, despite the implementation of all reasonably available measures, such provisions shall provide for the attainment of the national primary standard for the pollutant (or pollutants) with respect to which such demonstration is made, as expeditiously as practicable but not later than December 31, 1987.

(b) The plan provisions required by subsection (a) shall—

(1) be adopted by the State (or promulgated by the Administrator under section 110(c)) after reasonable notice and public hearing;

(2) provide for the implementation of all reasonably available control measures as expeditiously as practicable;

(3) require, in the interim, reasonable further progress (as defined in section 171(1)) including such reduction in emissions from existing sources in the area as may be obtained through the adoption, at a minimum, of reasonably available control technology;

(4) include a comprehensive, accurate, current inventory of actual emissions from all sources (as provided by rule of the Administrator) of each such pollutant for each such area which is revised and resubmitted as frequently as may be necessary to assure that the requirements of paragraph (3) are met and to assess the need for additional reductions to assure attainment of each standard by the date required under subsection (a);

(5) expressly identify and quantify the emissions, if any, of any such pollutant which will be allowed to result from the construction and operation of major new or modified stationary sources for each such area:

(6) require permits for the construction and operation of new or modified major stationary sources in accordance with section 173 (relating to permit requirements);

(7) identify and commit the financial and manpower resources necessary to carry out the plan provisions required by this subsection;

(8) contain emission limitations, schedules of compliance and such other measures as may be necessary to meet the requirements of this section;

(9) evidence public, local government, and State legislative involvement and consultation in accordance with section 174 (relating to planning procedures) and include (A) an identification and analysis of the air quality, health, welfare, economic, energy, and social effects of the plan provisions required by this subsection and of the alternatives considered by the State, and (B) a summary of the public comment on such analysis;

(10) include written evidence that the State, the general purpose local government or governments, or a regional agency designated by general purpose local governments for such purpose, have adopted by statute, regulation, ordinance, or other legally enforceable document, the necessary requirements and schedules and timetables for compliance, and are committed to implement and enforce the appropriate elements of the plan;

(11) in the case of plans which make a demonstration pursuant to paragraph (2) of subsection (a)—

(A) establish a program which requires, prior to issuance of any permit for construction or modification of a major emitting facility, an analysis of alternative sites, sizes, production processes, and environmental control techniques for such proposed source which demonstrates that benefits of the proposed source significantly outweigh the environmental and social costs imposed as a result of its location, construction, or modification;

(B) establish a specific schedule for implementation of a vehicle emission control inspection and maintenance program; and

(C) identify other measures necessary to provide for attainment of the applicable national ambient air quality standard not later than December 31, 1987.

(c) In the case of a State plan revision required under the Clean Air Act Amendments of 1977 to be submitted before July 1, 1982, by reason of a demonstration under subsection (a)(2), effective on such date such plan shall contain enforceable measures to assure attainment of the applicable standard not later than December 31, 1987.

PERMIT REQUIREMENTS

SEC. 173. The permit program required by section 172(b)(6) shall provide that permits to construct and operate may be issued if—

(1) the permitting agency determines that—

(A) by the time the source is to commence operation, total allowable emissions from existing sources in the region, from new or modified sources which are not major emitting facilities, and from the proposed source will be sufficiently less than total emissions from existing sources allowed under the applicable implementation plan prior to the application for such permit to construct or modify so as to represent (when considered together with the plan provisions required under section 172) reasonable further progress (as defined in section 171); or

(B) that emissions of such pollutant resulting from the proposed new or modified major stationary source will not cause or contribute to emissions levels which exceed the allowance permitted for such pollutant for such area from new or modified major stationary sources under section 172(b);

(2) the proposed source is required to comply with the lowest achievable emission rate;

(3) the owner or operator of the proposed new or modified source has demonstrated that all major stationary sources owned or operated by such person (or by any entity controlling, controlled by, or under common control with such person) in such State are subject to emission limitations and are in compliance, or on a schedule for compliance, with all applicable emission limitations and standards under this Act; and

(4) the applicable implementation plan is being carried out for the nonattainment area in which the proposed source is to be constructed or modified in accordance with the requirements of this part.

Any emission reductions required as a precondition of the issuance of a permit under paragraph (1)(A) shall be legally binding before such permit may be issued.

PLANNING PROCEDURES

SEC. 174. (a) Within six months after the enactment of the Clean Air Act Amendments of 1977, for each region in which the national primary ambient air quality standard for carbon monoxide or photochemical oxidants will not be attained by July 1, 1979, the State and elected officials of affected local governments shall jointly determine which elements of a revised implementation plan will be planned for and implemented or enforced by the State and which such elements will be planned for and implemented or enforced by local governments or regional agencies, or any combination of local governments, regional agencies, or the State. Where possible within the time required under this subsection, the implementation plan required by this part shall be prepared by an organization of elected officials of local governments designated by agreement of the local governments in an affected area, and certified by the State for this purpose. Where such an organization has not been designated by agreement within six months after the enactment of the Clean Air Act Amendments of 1977, the Governor (or, in the case of an interstate area, Governors), after consultation with elected officials of local governments, and in accordance with the determination under the first sentence of this subparagraph, shall designate an organization of elected officials of local governments in the affected area or a State agency to prepare such plan. Where feasible, such organization shall be the metropolitan planning organization designated to conduct the continuing, cooperative and comprehensive transportation planning process for the area under section 134 of title 23, United States Code, or the organization responsible for the air quality maintenance planning process under regulations implementing this section, or the organization with both responsibilities.

(b) The preparation of implementation plan provisions under this part shall be coordinated with the continuing, cooperative, and comprehensive transportation planning process required under section 134 of title 23, United States Code, and the air quality maintenance planning process required under section 110, and such planning processes shall take into account the requirements of this part.

ENVIRONMENTAL PROTECTION AGENCY GRANTS

SEC. 175. (a) The Administrator shall make grants to any organization of local elected officials with transportation or air quality maintenance planning responsibilities recognized by the State under section 174(a) for payment of the reasonable costs of developing a plan revision under this part.

(b) The amount granted to any organization under subsection (a) shall be 100 percent of any additional costs of developing a plan revision under this part for the first two fiscal years following receipt of the grant under this paragraph, and shall supplement any funds available under Federal law to such organization for transportation or air quality maintenance planning.

Grants under this section shall not be used for construction.

LIMITATIONS ON CERTAIN FEDERAL ASSISTANCE

SEC. 176. (a) The Administrator shall not approve any projects or award any grants authorized by this Act and the Secretary of Transportation shall not approve any projects or award any grants under title 23, United States Code, other than for safety, mass transit, or transportation improvement projects related to air quality improvement or maintenance, in any air quality control region—

(1) in which any national primary ambient air quality standard has not been attained,

(2) where transportation control measures are necessary for the attainment of such standard, and

(3) where the Administrator finds after July 1, 1979, that the Governor has not submitted an implementation plan which considers each of the elements required by section 172 or that reasonable efforts toward submitting such an implementation plan are not being made (or, after July 1, 1982, in the case of an implementation plan revision required under section 172 to be submitted before July 1, 1982).

(b) In any area in which the State or, as the case may be, the general purpose local government or governments or any regional agency designated by such general purpose local governments for such purpose, is not implementing any requirement of an approved or promulgated plan under section 110, including any requirement for a revised implementation plan under this part, the Administrator shall not make any grants under this Act.

(c) No department, agency, or instrumentality of the Federal Government shall (1) engage in, (2) support in any way or provide financial assistance for, (3) license or permit, or (4) approve, any activity which does not conform to a plan after it has been approved or promulgated under section 110. No metropolitan planning organization designated under section 134 of title 23, United States Code, shall give its approval to any project, program, or plan which does not conform to a plan approved or promulgated under section 110. The assurance of conformity to such a plan shall be an affirmative responsibility of the head of such department, agency, or instrumentality.

(d) Each department, agency, or instrumentality of the Federal Government having authority to conduct or support any program with air-quality related transportation consequences shall give priority in the exercise of such authority, consistent with statutory requirements for allocation among States or other jurisdictions, to the implementation of those portions of plans prepared under this section to achieve and maintain the national primary ambient air quality standard. This paragraph extends to, but is not limited to, authority exercised under the Urban Mass Transportation Act, title 23 of the United States Code, and the Housing and Urban Development Act.

NEW MOTOR VEHICLE EMISSION STANDARDS IN NONATTAINMENT AREAS

SEC. 177. Notwithstanding section 209(a), any State which has plan provisions approved under this part may adopt and enforce for any model year standards relating to control of emissions from new motor vehicles or new motor vehicle engines and take such other actions as are referred to in section 209(a) respecting such vehicles if—

(1) such standards are identical to the California standards for which a waiver has been granted for such model year, and

(2) California and such State adopt such standards at least two years before commencement of such model year (as determined by regulations of the Administrator).

GUIDANCE DOCUMENTS

SEC. 178. The Administrator shall issue guidance documents under section 108 for purposes of assisting States in implementing requirements of this part respecting the lowest achievable emission rate. Such a document shall be published not later than nine months after the date of enactment of this part and shall be revised at least every two years thereafter.

TITLE II—EMISSION STANDARDS FOR MOVING SOURCES

SHORT TITLE

SEC. 201. This title may be cited as the "National Emission Standards Act."

PART A—MOTOR VEHICLE EMISSION AND FUEL STANDARDS

ESTABLISHMENT OF STANDARDS

SEC. 202. (a) Except as otherwise provided in subsection (b)—

(1) The Administrator shall by regulation prescribe (and from time to time revise) in accordance with the provisions of this section, standards applicable to the emission of any air pollutant from any

class or classes of new motor vehicles or new motor vehicle engines, which in his judgment cause, or contribute to, air pollution which may reasonably be anticipated to endanger public health or welfare. Such standards shall be applicable to such vehicles and engines for their useful life (as determined under subsection (d), relating to useful life of vehicles for purposes of certification), whether such vehicles and engines are designed as complete systems or incorporate devices to prevent or control such pollution.

(2) Any regulation prescribed under paragraph (1) of this subsection (and any revision thereof) shall take effect after such period as the Administrator finds necessary to permit the development and application of the requisite technology, giving appropriate consideration to the cost of compliance within such period.

(3) (A) (i) The Administrator shall prescribe regulations under paragraph (1) of this subsection applicable to emissions of carbon monoxide, hydrocarbons, and oxides of nitrogen from classes or categories of heavy-duty vehicles or engines manufactured during and after model year 1979. Such regulations applicable to such pollutants from such classes or categories of vehicles or engines manufactured during model years 1979 through 1982 shall contain standards which reflect the greatest degree of emission reduction achievable through the application of technology which the Administrator determines will be available for the model year to which such standards apply, giving appropriate consideration to the cost of applying such technology within the period of time available to manufacturers and to noise, energy, and safety factors associated with the application of such technology.

(ii) Unless a different standard is temporarily promulgated as provided in subparagraph (B) or unless the standard is changed as provided in subparagraph (E), regulations under paragraph (1) of this subsection applicable to emissions from vehicles or engines manufactured during and after model year—

(I) 1983, in the case of hydrocarbons and carbon monoxide, shall contain standards which require a reduction of at least 90 per cent, and

(II) 1985, in the case of oxides of nitrogen, shall contain standards which require a reduction of at least 75 per cent,

from the average of the actually measured emissions from heavy-duty gasoline-fueled vehicles or engines, or any class or category thereof, manufactured during the baseline model year.

(iii) The Administrator shall prescribe regulations under paragraph (1) of this subsection applicable to emissions of particulate matter from classes or categories of vehicles manufactured during and after model year 1981 (or during any earlier model year, if practicable). Such regulations shall contain standards which reflect the greatest degree of emission reduction achievable through the application of technology which the Administrator determines will be available for the model year to which such standards apply, giving appropriate consideration to the cost of applying such technology within the period of time available to manufacturers and to noise, energy, and safety factors associated with the application of such technology. Such standards shall be promulgated and shall take effect as expeditiously as practicable taking into account the period necessary for compliance.

(iv) In establishing classes or categories of vehicles or engines for purposes of regulations under this paragraph, the Administrator may base such classes or categories on gross vehicle weight, horsepower, or such other factors as may be appropriate.

(v) For the purpose of this paragraph, the term "baseline model year" means, with respect to any pollutant emitted from any vehicle or engine, or class or category thereof, the model year immediately preceding the model year in which Federal standards applicable to such vehicle or engine, or class or category thereof, first applied with respect to such pollutant.

(B) During the period of June 1 through December 31, 1978, in the case of hydrocarbons and carbon monoxide, or during the period of June 1 through December 31, 1980, in the case of oxides of nitrogen, and during each period of June 1 through December 31 of each third year thereafter, the Administrator may, after notice and opportunity for a public hearing promulgate regulations revising any standard prescribed as provided in subparagraph (A) (ii) for any class or category of heavy-duty vehicles or engines. Such standard shall apply only for the period of three model years beginning four model years after the model year in which such revised standard is promulgated. In revising any standard under this subparagraph for any such three model year period, the Administrator shall determine the maximum degree of emission reduction which can be achieved by means reasonably expected to be available for production of such period and shall prescribe a revised emission standard in accordance with such determination. Such revised standard shall require a reduction of emissions from any standard which applies in the previous model year.

(C) Action revising any standard for any period may be taken by the Administrator under subparagraph (B) only if he finds—

(i) that compliance with the emission standards otherwise applicable for such model year cannot be achieved by technology, processes, operating methods, or other alternatives reasonably expected to be available for production for such model year without increasing cost or decreasing fuel economy to an excessive and unreasonable degree; and

(ii) the National Academy of Sciences has not, pursuant to its study and investigation under subsection (c) issued a report substantially contrary to the findings of the Administrator under clause (i).

(D) A report shall be made to the Congress with respect to any standard revised under subparagraph (B) which shall contain—

(i) a summary of the health effects found, or believed to be associated with, the pollutant covered by such standard,

(ii) an analysis of the cost-effectiveness of other strategies for attaining and maintaining national ambient air quality standards and carrying out regulations under part C of title I (relating to significant deterioration) in relation to the cost-effectiveness for such purposes of standards which, but for such revision, would apply.

(iii) a summary of the research and development efforts and progress being made by each manufacturer for purposes of meeting the standards promulgated as provided in subparagraph (A)(ii) or, if applicable, subparagraph (E), and

(iv) specific findings as to the relative costs of compliance, and relative fuel economy, which may be expected to result from the application for any model year of such revised standard and the application for such model year of the standard, which, but for such revisions, would apply.

(E)(i) The Administrator shall conduct a continuing pollutant specific study concerning the effects of each air pollutant emitted from heavy-duty vehicles or engines and from other sources of mobile source related pollutants on the public health and welfare. The results of such study shall be published in the Federal Register and reported to the Congress not later than June 1, 1978, in the case of hydrocarbons and carbon monoxide, and June 1, 1980, in the case of oxides of nitrogen, and before June 1 of each third year thereafter.

(ii) On the basis of such study and such other information as available to him (including the studies under section 214), the Administrator may, after notice and opportunity for a public hearing, promulgate regulations under paragraph (1) of this subsection changing any standard prescribed in subparagraph (A)(ii) (or revised under subparagraph (B) or previously changed under this subparagraph). No such changed standard shall apply for any model year before the model year four years after the model year during which regulations containing such changed standard are promulgated.

(F) For purposes of this paragraph, motorcycles and motorcycle engines shall be treated in the same manner as heavy-duty vehicles and engines (except as otherwise permitted under section 206(f)(1)) unless the the Administrator promulgates a rule reclassifying motorcycles as light-duty vehicles within the meaning of this section or unless the Administrator promulgates regulations under subsection (a) applying standards applicable to the emission of air pollutants from motorcycles as a separate class or category. In any case in which such standards are promulgated for such emissions from motorcycles as a separate class or category, the Administrator, in promulgating such standards, shall consider the need to achieve equivalency of emission reductions between motorcycles and other motor vehicles to the maximum extent practicable.

(4)(A) Effective with respect to vehicles and engines manufactured after model year 1978, no emission control device, system, or element of design shall be used in a new motor vehicle or new motor vehicle engine for purposes of complying with standards prescribed under this subsection if such device, system, or element of design will cause or contribute to an unreasonable risk to public health, welfare, or safety in its operation or function.

(B) In determining whether an unreasonable risk exists under subparagraph (A), the Administrator shall consider, among other factors, (i) whether and to what extent the use of any device, system, or element of design causes, increases, reduces, or eliminates emissions of any unregulated pollutants; (ii) available methods for reducing or eliminating any risk to public health, welfare, or safety which may be associated with the use of such device, system, or element of design, and (iii) the availability of other devices, systems, or elements of design which may be used to conform to standards prescribed under this subsection without causing or contributing to such unreasonable risk. The Administrator shall include in the consideration required by this paragraph all relevant information developed pursuant to section 214.

(5)(A) If the Administrator promulgates final regulations which define the degree of control required and the test procedures by which compliance could be determined for gasoline vapor recovery of uncontrolled emissions from the fueling of motor vehicles, the Administrator shall, after consultation with the Secretary of Transportation with respect to motor vehicle safety, prescribe, by regulation, fill pipe standards for new motor vehicles in order to insure effective connection between such fill pipe and any vapor recovery system which the Administrator determines may be required to comply with such vapor recovery regulations. In promulgating such standards the Administrator shall take into consideration limits on fill pipe diameter, minimum design criteria for nozzle retainer lips, limits on the location of the unleaded fuel restrictors, a minimum access zone surrounding a fill pipe, a minimum pipe or nozzle insertion angle, and such other factors as he deems pertinent.

(B) Regulations prescribing standards under subparagraph (A) shall not become effective until the introduction of the model year for which it would be feasible to implement such standards, taking into consideration the restraints of an adequate leadtime for design and production.

(C) Nothing in subparagraph (A) shall (i) prevent the Administrator from specifying different nozzle and fill neck sizes for gasoline with additives and gasoline without additives or (ii) permit the Administrator to require a specific location, configuration, modeling, or styling of the motor vehicle body with respect to the fuel tank fill neck or fill nozzle clearance envelope.

(D) For the purpose of this paragarph, the term "fill pipe" shall include the fuel tank fill pipe, fill neck, fill inlet, and closure.

(6) The Administrator shall determine the feasibility and desirability of requiring new motor vehicles to utilize onboard hydrocarbon control technology which would avoid the necessity of gasoline vapor recovery of uncontrolled emissions emanating from the fueling of motor vehicles. The Administrator shall compare the costs and effectiveness of such technology to that of implementing and maintaining

vapor recovery systems (taking into consideration such factors as fuel economy, economic costs of such technology, administrative burdens, and equitable distribution of costs). If the Administrator finds that it is feasible and desirable to employ such technology, he shall, after consultation with the Secretary of Transportation with respect to motor vehicle safety, prescribe, by regulation, standards requiring the use of onboard hydrocarbon technology which shall not become effective until the introduction to the model year for which it would be feasible to implement such standards, taking into consideration compliance costs and the restraints of an adequate lead time for design and production.

(b)(1)(A) The regulations under subsection (a) applicable to emissions of carbon monoxide and hydrocarbons from light-duty vehicles and engines manufactured during model years 1977 through 1979 shall contain standards which provide that such emissions from such vehicles and engines may not exceed 1.5 grams per vehicle mile of hydrocarbons and 15.0 grams per vehicle mile of carbon monoxide. The regulations under subsection (a) applicable to emissions of carbon monoxide from light-duty vehicles and engines manufactured during the model year 1980 shall contain standards which provide that such emissions may not exceed 7.0 grams per vehicle mile: The regulations under subsection (a) applicable to emissions of hydrocarbons from light-duty vehicles and engines manufactured during or after model year 1980 shall contain standards which require a reduction of at least 90 percent from emissions of such pollutant allowable under the standards under this section applicable to light-duty vehicles and engines manufactured in model year 1970. Unless waived as provided in paragraph (5), regulations under subsection (a) applicable to emissions of carbon monoxide from light-duty vehicles and engines manufactured during or after the model year 1981 shall contain standards which require a reduction of at least 90 percent from emissions of such pollutant allowable under the standards under this section applicable to light-duty vehicles and engines manufactured in model year 1970.

(B) The regulations under subsection (a) applicable to emissions of oxides of nitrogen from light-duty vehicles and engines manufactured during model years 1977 through 1980 shall contain standards which provide that such emissions from such vehicles and engines may not exceed 2.0 grams per vehicle mile. The regulations under subsection (a) applicable to emissions of oxides of nitrogen from light-duty vehicles and engines manufactured during the model year 1981 and thereafter shall contain standards which provide that such emissions from such vehicles and engines may not exceed 1.0 gram per vehicle mile. The Administrator shall prescribe standards in lieu of those required by the preceding sentence which provide that emissions of oxides of nitrogen may not exceed 2.0 grams per vehicle mile for any light-duty vehicle manufactured during model years 1981 and 1982 by any manufacturer whose production, by corporate identity, for calendar year 1976 was less than three hundred thousand light-duty motor vehicles worldwide if the Administrator determines that—

(i) the ability of such manufacturer to meet emission standards in the 1975 and subsequent model years was, and is, primarily dependent upon technology developed by other manufacturers and purchased from such manufacturers; and

(ii) such manufacturer lacks the financial resources and technological ability to develop such technology.

(C) Effective with respect to vehicles and engines manufactured after model year 1978 (or in the case of heavy-duty vehicles or engines, such later model year as the Administrator determines is the earliest feasible model year), the test procedure promulgated under paragraph (2) for measurement of evaporative emissions of hydrocarbons shall require that such emissions be measured from the vehicle or engine as a whole. Regulations to carry out this subparagraph shall be promulgated not later than two hundred and seventy days after date of enactment of this subparagraph.

(2) Emission standards under paragraph (1), and measurement techniques on which such standards are based (if not promulgated prior to the date of enactment of the Clear Air Amendments of 1970), shall be prescribed by regulation within 180 days after such date.

(3) For purposes of this part—

(A)(i) The term "model year" with reference to any specific calendar year means the manufacturer's annual production period (as determined by the Administrator) which includes January 1 of such calendar year. If the manufacturer has no annual production period, the term "model year" shall mean the calendar year.

(ii) For the purpose of assuring that vehicles and engines manufactured before the beginning of a model year were not manufactured for purposes of circumventing the effective date of a standard required to be prescribed by subsection (b), the Administrator may prescribe regulations defining "model year" otherwise than as provided in clause (i).

(B) The term "light duty vehicles and engines" means new light duty motor vehicles and new light duty motor vehicle engines, as determined under regulations of the Administrator.

(C) The term "heavy duty vehicle" means a truck, bus, or other vehicle manufactured primarily for use on the public streets, roads, and highways (not including any vehicle operated exclusively on a rail or rails) which has a gross vehicle weight (as determined under regulations promulgated by the Administrator) in excess of six thousand pounds. Such term includes any such vehicle which has special features enabling off-street or off-highway operation and use.

(4) On July 1 of 1971, and of each year thereafter, the Administrator shall report to the Congress with respect to the development of systems necessary to implement the emission standards established pursuant to this section. Such reports shall include information regarding the continuing effects of such air pollutants subject to standards under this section on the public health and welfare, the extent and progress of efforts being made to develop the necessary systems, the costs associated with development and application of such systems, and following such hearings as he may deem advisable, any recommendations for additional congressional action necessary to achieve the purposes of this Act. In gathering information for the purposes of this paragraph and in connection with any hearing, the provisions of section 307(a) (relating to subpenas) shall apply.

(5)(A) At any time after August 31, 1978, any manufacturer may file an application requesting the waiver for model years 1981 and 1982 of the effective date of the emission standard required by paragraph (1)(A) for carbon monoxide applicable to any model (as determined by the Administration) of light-duty motor vehicles and engines manufactured in such model years. The Administrator shall make his determination with respect to any such application within sixty days after such application is filed with respect to such model. If he determines, in accordance with the provisions of this paragraph, that such waiver should be granted, he shall simultaneously with such determination prescribe by regulation emission standards which shall apply (in lieu of the standards required to be prescribed by paragraph (1)(A) of this subsection) to emissions of carbon monoxide from such model of vehicles or engines manufactured during model years 1981 and 1982.

(B) Any standards prescribed under this paragraph shall not permit emissions of carbon monoixde from vehicles and engines to which such waiver applies to exceed 7.0 grams per vehicle per mile.

(C) Within sixty days after receipt of the application for any such waiver and after public hearing, the Administrator shall issue a decision granting or refusing such waiver. The Administrator may grant such waiver if he finds that protection of the public health does not require attainment of such 90 percent reduction for carbon monoxide for the model years to which such waiver applies in the case of such vehicles and engines and if he determines that—

(i) such waiver is essential to the public interest or the public health and welfare of the United States;

(ii) all good faith efforts have been made to meet the standards established by this subsection;

(iii) the applicant has established that effective control technology, processes, operating methods, or other alternatives are not available or have not been available with respect to the model in question for a sufficient period of time to achieve compliance prior to the effective date of such standards, taking into consideration costs, driveability, and fuel economy; and

(iv) studies and investigations of the National Academy of Sciences conducted pursuant to subsection (c) and other information available to him has not indicated that technology, processes, or other alternatives are available (within the meaning of clause (iii)) to meet such standards.

(6)(A) Upon the petition of any manufacturer, the Administrator, after notice and opportunity for public hearing, may waive the standard required under subparagraph (B) of paragraph (1) to not exceed 1.5 grams of oxides of nitrogen per vehicle mile for any class or category of light-duty vehicles or engines manufactured by such manufacturer during any period of up to four model years beginning after the model year 1980 if the manufacturer demonstrates that such waiver is necessary to permit the use of an innovative power train technology, or innovative emission control device or system, in such class or category of vehicles or engines and that such technology or system was not utilized by more than 1 percent of the light-duty vehicles sold in the United States in the 1975 model year. Such waiver may be granted only if the Administrator determines—

(i) that such waiver would not endanger public health,

(ii) that there is a substantial likelihood that the vehicles or engines will be able to comply with the applicable standard under this section at the expiration of the waiver, and

(iii) that the technology or system has a potential for long-term air quality benefit and has the potential to meet or exceed the average fuel economy standard applicable under the Energy Policy and Conservation Act upon the expiration of the waiver.

No waiver under this subparagraph granted to any manufacturer shall apply to more than 5 percent of such manufacturer's production or more than fifty thousand vehicles or engines, whichever is greater.

(B) Upon the petition of any manufacturer, the Administrator, after notice and opportunity for public hearing, may waive the standard required under subparagraph (B) of paragraph (1) to not to exceed 1.5 grams of oxides of nitrogen per vehicle mile for any class or category of light-duty vehicles and engines manufactured by such manufacturer during the four model year period beginning with the model year 1981 if the manufacturer can show that such waiver is necessary to permit the use of diesel engine technology in such class or category of vehicles or engines. Such waiver may be granted if the Administrator determines—

(i) that such waiver will not endanger public health,

(ii) that such waiver will result in significant fuel savings at least equal to the fuel economy standard applicable in each year under the Energy Policy and Conservation Act, and

(iii) that the technology has a potential for long-term air quality benefit and has the potential to meet or exceed the average fuel economy standard applicable under the Energy Policy and Conservation Act at the expiration of the waiver.

(7) The Congress hereby declares and establishes as a research objective, the development of propulsion systems and emission control technology to achieve standards which represent a reduction of at least 90 per centum from the average emissions of oxides of nitrogen actually measured from light-duty motor vehicles manufactured in model year 1971 not subject to any Federal or State emission standard for oxides of nitrogen. The Administrator shall, by regulations promulgated within one hundred and eighty days after enactment of the Clean Air Act Amendments of 1977, require each manufacturer whose sales represent at least 0.5 per centum of light-duty motor vehicle sales in the United States, to build and, on a regular basis, demonstrate the operation of light-duty motor vehicles that meet this research objective, in addition to any other applicable standards or requirements for other pollutants under this Act. Such demonstration vehicles shall be submitted to the Administrator no later than model year 1979 and in each model year thereafter. Such demonstration shall, in accordance with applicable regulations, to the greatest extent possible. (A) be designed to encourage the development of new powerplant and emission control technologies that are fuel efficient, (B) assure that the demonstration vehicles are or could reasonably be expected to be within the productive capability of the manufacturers, and (C) assure the utilization of optimum engine, fuel, and emission control systems.

(c)(1) The Administrator shall undertake to enter into appropriate arrangements with the National Academy of Sciences to conduct a comprehensive study and investigation of the technological feasibility of meeting the emissions standards required to be prescribed by the Administrator by subsection (b) of this section.

(2) Of the funds authorized to be appropriated to the Administrator by this Act, such amounts as are required shall be available to carry out the study and investigation authorized by paragraph (1) of this subsection.

(3) In entering into any arrangement with the National Academy of Sciences for conducting the study and investigation authorized by paragraph (1) of this subsection, the Administrator shall request the National Academy of Sciences to submit semiannual reports on the progress of its study and investigation to the Administrator and the Congress, beginning not later than July 1, 1971, and continuing until such study and investigation is completed.

(4) The Administrator shall furnish to such Academy at its request any information which the Academy deems necessary for the purpose of conducting the investigation and study authorized by paragraph (1) of this subsection. For the purpose of furnishing such information, the Administrator may use any authority he has under this Act (A) to obtain information from any person, and (B) to require such person to conduct such tests, keep such records, and make such reports respecting research or other activities conducted by such person as may be reasonably necessary to carry out this subsection.

(d) The Administrator shall prescribe regulations under which the useful life of vehicles and engines shall be determined for purposes of subsection (a)(1) of this section and section 207. Such regulations shall provide that useful life shall—

(1) in the case of light duty vehicles and light duty vehicle engines, be a period of use of five years or of fifty thousand miles (or the equivalent), whichever first occurs;

(2) in the case of any other motor vehicle or motor vehicle engine (other than motorcycles or motorcycle engines) be a period of use set forth in paragraph (1) unless the Administrator determines that a period of use of greater duration or mileage is appropriate; and

(3) in the case of any motorcycle or motorcycle engine, be a period of use the Administrator shall determine.

(e) In the event a new power source or propulsion system for new motor vehicles or new motor vehicle engines is submitted for certification pursuant to section 206(a), the Administrator may postpone certification until he has prescribed standards for any air pollutants emitted by such vehicle or engine which in his judgment cause or contribute to, air pollution which may reasonably be anticipated to endanger the public health or welfare but for which standards have not been prescribed under subsection (a).

(f) (1) The high altitude regulation in effect with respect to model year 1977 motor vehicles shall not apply to the manufacture, distribution, or sale of 1978 and later model year motor vehicles. Any future regulation affecting the sale or distribution of motor vehicles or engines manufactured before the model year 1984 in high altitude areas of the country shall take effect no earlier than model year 1981.

(2) Any such future regulation applicable to high altitude vehicles or engines shall not require a percentage of reduction in the emissions of such vehicles which is greater than the required percentage of reduction in emissions from motor vehicles as set forth in section 202(b). This percentage reduction shall be determined by comparing any proposed high altitude emission standards to high altitude emissions from vehicles manufactured during model year 1970. In no event shall regulations applicable to high altitude vehicles manufactured before the model year 1984 established a numerical standard which is more stringent than that applicable to vehicles certified under non-high altitude conditions.

(3) Section 307(d) shall apply to any high altitude regulation referred to in paragraph (2) and before promulgating any such regulation, the Administrator shall consider and make a finding with respect to—

(A) the economic impact upon consumers, individual high altitude dealers, and the automobile industry of any such regulation, including the economic impact which was experienced as a result of the regulation imposed during model year 1977 with respect to high altitude certification requirements;

(B) the present and future availability of emission control technology capable of meeting the applicable vehicle and engine emission requirements without reducing model availability; and

(C) the likelihood that the adoption of such a high altitude regulation will result in any significant improvement in air quality in any area to which it shall apply.

PROHIBITED ACTS

SEC. 203. (a) The following acts and the causing thereof are prohibited—

(1) in the case of a manufacturer of new motor vehicles or new motor vehicle engines for distribution in commerce, the sale, or the offering for sale, or the introduction, or delivery for introduction, into

commerce, or (in the case of any person, except as provided by regulation of the Administrator), the importation into the United States, of any new motor vehicle or new motor vehicle engine, manufactured after the effective date of regulations under this part which are applicable to such vehicle or engine unless such vehicle or engine is covered by a certificate of conformity issued (and in effect) under regulations prescribed under this part (except as provided in subsection (b));

(2) for any person to fail or refuse to permit access to or copying of records or to fail to make reports or provide information, required under section 208 or for any person to fail or refuse to permit entry, testing, or inspection authorized under section 206(c);

(3)(A) for any person to remove or render inoperative any device or element of design installed on or in a motor vehicle or motor vehicle engine in compliance with regulations under this title prior to its sale and delivery to the ultimate purchaser, or for any manufacturer or dealer knowingly to remove or render inoperative any such device or element of design after such sale and delivery to the ultimate purchaser; or

(B) for any person engaged in the business of repairing, servicing, selling, leasing, or trading motor vehicles or motor vehicle engines, or who operates a fleet of motor vehicles, knowingly to remove or render inoperative any device or element of design installed on or in a motor vehicle or motor vehicle engine in compliance with regulations under this title following its sale and delivery to the ultimate purchaser; or

(4) for any manufacturer of a new motor vehicle or new motor vehicle engine subject to standards prescribed under section 202—

(A) to sell or lease any such vehicle or engine unless such manufacturer has complied with the requirements of section 207 (a) and (b) with respect to such vehicle or engine, and unless a label or tag is affixed to such vehicle or engine in accordance with section 207(c)(3),

(B) to fail or refuse to comply with the requirements of section 207 (c) or (e),

(C) except as provided in subsection (c)(3) of section 207, to provide directly or indirectly in any communication to the ultimate purchaser or any subsequent purchaser that the coverage of any warranty under this Act is conditioned upon use of any part, component, or system manufactured by such manufacturer or any person acting for such manufacturer or under his control, or conditioned upon service performed by any such person, or

(D) to fail or refuse to comply with the terms and conditions of the warranty under section 207(a) or (b) with respect to any vehicle.

No action with respect to any element of design referred to in paragraph (3) (including any adjustment or alteration of such element) shall be treated as a prohibited Act under such paragraph (3) if such action is in accordance with section 215. Nothing in paragraph (3) shall be construed to require the use of manufacturer parts in maintaining or repairing any motor vehicle or motor vehicle engine. For the purposes of the preceding sentence, the term "manufacturer parts" means, with respect to a motor vehicle engine, parts produced or sold by the manufacturer of the motor vehicle or motor vehicle engine.

(b) (1) The Administrator may exempt any new motor vehicle or new motor vehicle engine from subsection (a), upon such terms and conditions as he may find necessary for the purpose of research, investigations, studies, demonstrations, or training, or for reasons of national security.

(2) A new motor vehicle or new motor vehicle engine offered for importation or imported by any person in violation of subsection (a) shall be refused admission into the United States, but the Secretary of the Treasury and the Administrator may, by joint regulation, provide for deferring final determination as to admission and authorizing the delivery of such a motor vehicle or engine offered for import to the owner or consignee thereof upon such terms and conditions (including the furnishing of a bond) as may appear to them appropriate to insure that any such motor vehicle or engine will be brought into conformity with the standards, requirements, and limitations applicable to it under this part. The Secretary of the Treasury shall, if a motor vehicle or engine is finally refused admission under this paragraph, cause disposition thereof in accordance with the customs laws unless it is exported, under regulations prescribed by such Secretary, within ninety days of the date of notice of such refusal or such additional time as may be permitted pursuant to such regulations, except that disposition in accordance with the customs laws may not be made in such manner as may result, directly or indirectly, in the sale, to the ultimate consumer, of a new motor vehicle or new motor vehicle engine that fails to comply with applicable standards of the Administrator under this part.

(3) A new motor vehicle or new motor vehicle engine intended solely for export, and so labeled or tagged on the outside of the container and on the vehicle or engine itself, shall be subject to the provisions of subsection (a),

except that if the country which is to receive such vehicle or engine has emission standards which differ from the standards prescribed under section 202, then such vehicle or engine shall comply with the standards of such country which is to receive such vehicle or engine.

(c) Upon application therefor, the Administrator may exempt from section 203(a)(3) any vehicles (or class thereof) manufactured before the 1974 model year from section 203(a)(3)[6] for the purpose of permitting modifications to the emission control device or system of such vehicle in order to use fuels other than those specified in certification testing under section 206(a)(1), if the Administrator, on the basis of information submitted by the applicant, finds that such modification will not result in such vehicle or engine not complying with standards under section 202 applicable to such vehicle or engine. Any such exemption shall identify (1) the vehicle or vehicles so exempted, (2) the specific nature of the modification, and (3) the person or class of persons to whom the exemption shall apply.

INJUNCTION PROCEEDINGS

SEC. 204. (a) The district courts of the United States shall have jurisdiction to restrain violations of section 203(a).

(b) Actions to restrain such violations shall be brought by and in the name of the United States. In any such action, subpenas for witnesses who are required to attend a district court in any district may run into any other district.

PENALTIES

SEC. 205. Any person who violates paragraph (1), (2), or (4) of section 203(a) or any manufacturer, dealer, or other person who violates paragraph (3)(A) of section 203(a) shall be subject to a civil penalty of not more than $10,000. Any person who violates paragraph (3)(B) of such section 203(a) shall be subject to a civil penalty of not more than $2,500. Any such violation with respect to paragraph (1), (3), or (4) of section 203(a) shall constitute a separate offense with respect to each motor vehicle or motor vehicle engine.

MOTOR VEHICLE AND MOTOR VEHICLE ENGINE COMPLIANCE TESTING AND CERTIFICATION

SEC. 206. (a)(1) The Administrator shall test, or require to be tested in such manner as he deems appropriate, any new motor vehicle or new motor vehicle engine submitted by a manufacturer to determine whether such vehicle or engine conforms with the regula-

[6] The words "from section 203(a)(3)" are apparently redundant in this sentence.

tions prescribed under section 202 of this Act. If such vehicle or engine conforms to such regulations, the Administrator shall issue a certificate of conformity upon such terms, and for such period (not in excess of one year) as he may prescribe. In the case of any manufacturer of vehicles or vehicle engines whose projected sales in the United States for any model year (as determined by the Administrator) will not exceed three hundred, the regulations prescribed by the Administrator concerning testing by the manufacturer for purposes of determining compliance with regulations under section 202 for the useful life of the vehicle or engine shall not require operation of any vehicle or engine manufactured during such model year for more than five thousand miles or one hundred and sixty hours, respectively, but the Administrator shall apply such adjustment factors as he deems appropriate to assure that each such vehicle or engine will comply during its useful life (as determined under section 202(d)) with the regulations prescribed under section 202 of this Act.

(2) The Administrator shall test any emission control system incorporated in a motor vehicle or motor vehicle engine submitted to him by any person, in order to determine whether such system enables such vehicle or engine to conform to the standards required to be prescribed under section 202(b) of this Act. If the Administrator finds on the basis of such tests that such vehicle or engine conforms to such standards, the Administrator shall issue a verification of compliance with emission standards for such system when incorporated in vehicles of a class of which the tested vehicle is representative. He shall inform manufacturers and the National Academy of Sciences, and make available to the public, the results of such tests. Tests under this paragraph shall be conducted under such terms and conditions (including requirements for preliminary testing by qualified independent laboratories) as the Administrator may prescribe by regulations.

(3)(A) A certificate of conformity may be issued under this section only if the Administrator determines that the manufacturer (or in the case of a vehicle or engine for import, any person) has established to the satisfaction of the Administrator that any emission control device, system, or element of design installed on, or incorporated in, such vehicle or engine conforms to applicable requirements of section 202(a)(4).

(B) The Administrator may conduct such tests and may require the manufacturer (or any such person) to conduct such tests and provide such information as is necessary to carry out subparagraph (A) of this paragraph. Such requirements shall include a requirement for prompt reporting of the emission of any unregulated pollutant from a system, device, or element of design if such pollutant was not emitted, or was emitted in significantly lesser amounts, from the vehicle or engine without use of the system, device, or element of design.

(b)(1) In order to determine whether new motor vehicles or new motor vehicle engines being manufactured by a manufacturer do in fact conform with the regulations with respect to which the certificate of conformity was issued, the Administrator is authorized to test such vehicles or engines. Such tests may be conducted by the Administrator directly or, in accordance with conditions specified by the Administrator, by the manufacturer.

(2)(A)(i) If, based on tests conducted under paragraph (1) on a sample of new vehicles or engines covered by a certificate of conformity, the Administrator determines that all or part of the vehicles or engines so covered do not conform with the regulations with respect to which the certificate of conformity was issued and with the requirements of section 202(a)(4), he may suspend or revoke such certificate in whole or in part, and shall so notify the manufacturer. Such suspension or revocation shall apply in the case of any new motor vehicles or new motor vehicle engines manufactured after the date of such notification (or manufactured before such date if still in the hands of the manufacturer), and shall apply until such time as the Administrator finds that vehicles and engines manufactured by the manufacturer do conform to such regulations and requirements. If, during any period of suspension or revocation, the Administrator finds that a vehicle or engine actually conforms to such regulations and requirements, he shall issue a certificate of conformity applicable to such vehicle or engine.

(ii) If, based on tests conducted under paragraph (1) on any new vehicle or engine, the Administrator determines that such vehicle or engine does not conform with such regulations, he may suspend or revoke such certificate insofar as it applies to such vehicle or engine until such time as he finds such vehicle or engine actually so conforms with such regulations, and he shall so notify the manufacturer.

(B)(i) At the request of any manufacturer the Administrator shall grant such manufacturer a hearing as to whether the tests have been properly conducted or any sampling methods have been properly applied, and make a determination on the record with respect to any suspension or revocation under subparagraph (A); but suspension or revocation under subparagraph (A) shall not be stayed by reason of such hearing.

(ii) In any case of actual controversy as to the validity of any determination under clause (i), the manufacturer may at any time prior to the 60th day after such determination is made file a petition with the United States court of appeals for the circuit wherein such manufacturer resides or has his principal place of business for a judicial review of such determination. A copy of the petition shall be forthwith transmitted by the clerk of the court to the Administrator or other officer designated by him for that purpose. The Administrator thereupon shall file in the court the record of the proceedings on which the Administrator based his determination, as provided in section 2112 of title 28 of the United States Code.

(iii) If the petitioner applies to the court for leave to adduce additional evidence, and shows to the satisfaction of the court that such additional evidence is material and that there were reasonable grounds for the failure to adduce such evidence in the proceeding before the Administrator, the court may order such additional evidence (and evidence in rebuttal thereof) to be taken before the Administrator, in such manner and upon such terms and conditions as the court may deem proper. The Administrator may modify his findings as to the facts, or make new findings, by reason of the additional evidence so taken and he shall file such modified or new findings, and his recommendation, if any, for the modification or setting aside of his original determination, with the return of such additional evidence.

(iv) Upon the filing of the petition referred to in clause (ii), the court shall have jurisdiction to review the order in accordance with chapter 7 of title 5, United States Code, and to grant appropriate relief as provided in such chapter.

(c) For purposes of enforcement of this section, officers or employees duly designated by the Administrator, upon presenting appropriate credentials to the manufacturer or person in charge, are authorized (1) to enter, at reasonable times, any plant or other establishment of such manufacturers, for the purpose of conducting tests of vehicles of engines in the hands of the manufacturer, or (2) to inspect at reasonable times, records, files, papers, processes, controls, and facilities used by such manufacturer in conducting tests under regulations of the Administrator. Each such inspection shall be commenced and completed with reasonable promptness.

(d) The Administrator shall by regulation establish methods and procedures for making tests under this section.

(e) The Administrator shall announce in the Federal Register and make available to the public the results of his tests of any motor vehicle or motor vehicle engine submitted by a manufacturer under subsection (a) as promptly as possible after the enactment of the Clean Air Amendments of 1970 and at the beginning of each model year which begins thereafter. Such results shall be described in such nontechnical manner as will reasonably disclose to prospective ultimate purchasers of new motor vehicles and new motor vehicle engines the comparative performance of the vehicles and engines tested in meeting the standards prescribed under section 202 of this Act.

(f)(1) All light duty vehicles and engines manufactured during or after model year 1984 shall comply with the requirements of section 202 of this Act regardless of the altitude at which they are sold.

(2) By October 1, 1978, the Administrator shall report to the Congress on the economic impact and technological feasibility of the requirements found in subparagraph (1) of this subsection. The report is also to evaluate the technological feasibility and the health consequences of separate proportional emission standards for light duty vehicles and engines in high altitude areas that would reflect a comparable percentage of reduction in emissions to that achieved by light duty vehicles and engines in low altitude areas.

(g)(1) In the case of any class or category of heavy-duty vehicles or engines to which a standard promulgated under section 202(a) of this Act applies, except as provided in paragraph (2), a certificate of conformity shall be issued under subsection (a) and shall not be suspended or revoked under subsection (b) for such vehicles or engines manufactured by a manufacturer notwithstanding the failure of such vehicles or engines to meet such standard if such manufacturer pays a nonconformance penalty as provided under regulations promulgated by the Administrator after notice and opportunity for public hearing. In the case of motorcycles to which such a standard applies, such a certificate may be issued notwithstanding such failure if the manufacturer pays such a penalty.

(2) No certificate of conformity may be issued under paragraph (1) with respect to any class or category of vehicle or engine if the degree by which the manufacturer fails to meet any standard promulgated under section 202(a) with respect to such class or category exceeds the percentage determined under regulations promulgated by the Administrator to be practicable. Such regulations shall require such testing of vehicle or engines being produced as may be necessary to determine the percentage of the classes or categories of vehicles or engines which are not in compliance with the regulations with respect to which a certificate of conformity was issued and shall be promulgated not later than one year after the date of enactment of the Clean Air Act Amendments of 1977.

(3) The regulations promulgated under paragraph (1) shall, not later than one year after the date of enactment of the Clean Air Act Amendments of 1977, provide for nonconformance penalties in amounts determined under a formula established by the Administrator. Such penalties under such formula—

(A) may vary from pollutant-to-pollutant;

(B) may vary by class or category or vehicle or engine;

(C) shall take into account the extent to which actual emissions of any air pollutant exceed allowable emissions under the standards promulgated under section 202;

(D) shall be increased periodically in order to create incentives for the development of production vehicles or engines which achieve the required degree of emission reduction; and

(E) shall remove any competitive disadvantage to manufacturers whose engines or vehicles achieve the required degree of emission reduction (including any such disadvantage arising from the application of paragraph (4)).

(4) In any case in which a certificate of conformity has been issued under this subsection, any warranty required under section 207(b)(2) and any action under section 207(c) shall be required to be effective only for the emission levels which the Administrator determines that such certificate was issued and not for the emission levels required under the applicable standard.

(5) The authorities of section 208(a) shall apply, subject to the conditions of section 208(b), for purposes of this subsection.

COMPLIANCE BY VEHICLES AND ENGINES IN ACTUAL USE

SEC. 207. (a)(1) Effective with respect to vehicles and engines manufactured in model years beginning more than 60 days after the date of the enactment of the Clean Air Amendments of 1970, the manufacturer of each new motor vehicle and new motor vehicle engine shall warrant to the ultimate purchaser and each subsequent purchaser that such vehicle or engine is (A) designed, built, and equipped so as to conform at the time of sale with applicable regulations under section 202, and (B) free from defects in materials and workmanship which cause such vehicle or engine to fail to conform with applicable regulations for its useful life (as determined under sec. 202(d)).

(2) In the case of a motor vehicle part or motor vehicle engine part, the manufacturer or rebuilder of such part may certify that use of such part will not result in a failure of the vehicle or engine to comply with emission standards promulgated under section 202. Such certification shall be made only under such regulations as may be promulgated by the Administrator to carry out the purposes of subsection (b). The Administrator shall promulgate such regulations no later than two years following the date of the enactment of this paragraph.

(3) The cost of any part, device, or component of any light-duty vehicle that is designed for emission control and which in the instructions issued pursuant to subsection (c)(3) of this section is scheduled for replacement during the useful life of the vehicle in order to maintain compliance with reglations under section 202 of this Act, the failure of which shall not interfere with the normal performance of the vehicle, and the expected retail price of which, including installation costs, is greater than 2 percent of the suggested retail price of such vehicle, shall be borne or reimbursed at the time of replacement by the vehicle manufacturer and such replacement shall be provided without cost to the ultimate purchaser, subsequent purchaser, or dealer. The term "designed for emission control" as used in the preceding sentence means a catalytic converter, thermal reactor, or other component installed on or in a vehicle for the sole or primary purpose of reducing vehicle emissions (not including those vehicle components which were in general use prior to model year 1968 and the primary function of which is not related to emission control).

(b) If the Administrator determines that (i) there are available testing methods and procedures to ascertain whether, when in actual use throughout its useful life (as determined under section 202(d)), each vehicle and engine to which regulations under section 202 apply complies with the emission standards of such regulations, (ii) such methods and procedures are in accordance with good engineering practices, and (iii) such methods and procedures are reasonably capable of being correlated with tests conducted under section 206(a)(1), then—

(1) he shall establish such methods and procedures by regulation, and

(2) at such time as he determines that inspection facilities or equipment are available for purposes of carrying out testing methods and procedures established under paragraph (1), he shall prescribe regulations which shall require manufacturers to warrant the emission control device or system of each new motor vehicle or new motor vehicle engine to which a regulation under section 202 applies and which is manufactured in a model year beginning after the Administrator first prescribes warranty regulations under this paragraph. The warranty under such regulations shall run to the ultimate purchaser and each subsequent purchaser and shall provide that if—

(A) the vehicle or engine is maintained and operated in accordance with instructions under subsection (c)(3),

(B) it fails to conform at any time during its useful life (as determined under section

202(d)) to the regulations prescribed under section 202, and

(C) such nonconformity results in the ultimate purchaser (or any subsequent purchaser) of such vehicle or engine having to bear any penalty or other sanction (including the denial of the right to use such vehicle or engine) under State or Federal law,

then such manufacturer shall remedy such nonconformity under such warranty with the cost thereof to be borne by the manufacturer. No such warranty shall be invalid on the basis of any part used in the maintenance or repair of a vehicle or engine if such part was certified as provided under subsection (a)(2). For purposes of the warranty under this subsection, for the period after twenty-four months or twenty-four thousand miles (whichever first occurs) the term "emission control device or system" means a catalytic converter, thermal reactor, or other component installed on or in a vehicle for the sole or primary purpose of reducing vehicle emissions. Such terms shall not include those vehicle components which were in general use prior to model year 1968.

(c) Effective with respect to vehicles and engines manufactured during model years beginning more than 60 days after the date of enactment of the Clean Air Amendments of 1970—

(1) If the Administrator determines that a substantial number of any class or category of vehicles or engines, although properly maintained and used, do not conform to the regulations prescribed under section 202, when in actual use throughout their useful life (as determined under section 202(d)), he shall immediately notify the manufacturer thereof of such nonconformity, and he shall require the manufacturer to submit a plan for remedying the nonconformity of the vehicles or engines with respect to which such notification is given. The plan shall provide that the nonconformity of any such vehicles or engines which are properly used and maintained will be remedied at the expense of the manufacturer. If the manufacturer disagrees with such determination of nonconformity and so advises the Administrator, the Administrator shall afford the manufacturer and other interested persons an opportunity to present their views and evidence in support thereof at a public hearing. Unless, as a result of such hearing the Administrator withdraws such determination of nonconformity, he shall, within 60 days after the completion of such hearing, order the manufacturer to provide prompt notification of such nonconformity in accordance with paragraph (2).

(2) Any notification required by paragraph (1) with respect to any class or category of vehicles or engines shall be given to dealers, ultimate purchasers, and subsequent purchasers (if known) in such manner and containing such information as the Administrator may be regulations require.

(3) (A) The manufacturer shall furnish with each new motor vehicle or motor vehicle engine written instructions for the proper maintenance and use of the vehicle or engine by the ultimate purchaser and such instructions shall correspond to regulations which the Administrator shall promulgate. The manufacturer shall provide in boldface type on the first page of the written maintenance instructions notice that maintenance, replacement, or repair of the emission control devices and systems may be performed by any automotive repair establishment or individual using any automotive part which has been certified as provided in subsection (a) (2).

(B) The instruction under subparagraph (A) of this paragraph shall not include any condition on the ultimate purchaser's using, in connection with such vehicle or engine, any component or service (other than a component or service provided without charge under the terms of the purchase agreement) which is identified by brand, trade, or corporate name; or directly or indirectly distinguishing between service performed by the franchised dealers of such manufacturer or any other service establishments with which such manufacturer has a commercial relationship, and service performed by independent automotive repair facilities with which such manufacturer has no commercial relationship; except that the prohibition of this subsection may be waived by the Administrator if—

(i) the manufacturer satisfies the Administrator that the vehicle or engine will function properly only if the component or service so identified is used in connection with such vehicle or engine, and

(ii) the Administrator finds that such a waiver is in the public interest.

(C) In addition, the manufacturer shall indicate by means of a label or tag permanently affixed to such vehicle or engine that such vehicle or engine is covered by a certificate of conformity issued for the purpose of assuring achievement of emissions standards prescribed under section 202 of this Act. Such label or tag shall contain such other information relating to control of motor vehicle emissions as the Administrator shall prescribe by regulation.

(d) Any cost obligation of any dealer incurred as a result of any requirement imposed by subsection (a), (b), or (c) shall be borne by the manufacturer. The transfer of any such cost obligation from a manufacturer to any dealer through franchise or other agreement is prohibited.

(e) If a manufacturer includes in any advertisement a statement respecting the cost or value of emission control devices or systems, such manufacturer shall set forth in such statement the cost or value attributed to such devices or systems by the Secretary of Labor (through the Bureau of Labor Statistics). The Secretary of Labor, and his representatives, shall have the same access for this purpose to the books, documents, papers, and records of a manufacturer as the Comptroller General has to those of a recipient of assistance for purposes of section 311.

(f) Any inspection of a motor vehicle or a motor vehicle engine for purposes of subsection (c)(1), after its sale to the ultimate purchaser, shall be made only if the owner of such vehicle or engine voluntarily permits such inspection to be made, except as may be provided by any State or local inspection program.

(g) For the purposes of this section, the owner of any motor vehicle or motor vehicle engine warranted under this section is responsible in the proper maintenance of such vehicle or engine to replace and to maintain, at his expense at any service establishment or facility of his choosing, such items as spark plugs, points, condensers, and any other part, item, or device related to emission control (but not designed for emission control under the terms of the last three sentences of section 207(a)(1), unless such part, item, or device is covered by any warranty not mandated by this Act.

(h)(1) Upon the sale of each new light-duty motor vehicle by a dealer, the dealer shall furnish to the purchaser a certificate that such motor vehicle conforms to the applicable regulations under section 202, including notice of the purchaser's rights under paragraph (2).

(2) If at any time during the period for which the warranty applies under subsection (b), a motor vehicle fails to conform to the applicable regulations under section 202 as determined under subsection (b) of this section such nonconformity shall be remedied by the manufacturer at the cost of the manufacturer pursuant to such warranty as provided in section 207(b)(2) (without regard to subparagraph (C) thereof).

(3) Nothing in section 209(a) shall be construed to prohibit a State from testing, or requiring testing of, a motor vehicle after the date of sale of such vehicle to the ultimate purchaser (except that no new motor vehicle manufacturer or dealer may be required to conduct testing under this paragraph).

RECORDS AND REPORTS

SEC. 208. (a) Every manufacturer shall establish and maintain such records, make such reports, and provide such information as the Administrator may reasonably require to enable him to determine whether such manufacturer has acted or is acting in compliance with this part and regulations thereunder and shall, upon request of an officer or employee duly designated by the Administrator, permit such officer or employee at reasonable times to have access to and copy such records.

(b) Any records, reports or information obtained under subsection (a) shall be available to the public, except that upon a showing satisfactory to the Administrator by any person that records, reports, or information, or particular part thereof (other than emission data), to which the Administrator has access under this section if made public, would divulge methods or processes entitled to protection as trade secrets of such person, the Administrator shall consider such record, report, or information or particular portion thereof confidential in accordance with the purposes of section 1905 of title 18 of the United States Code, except that such record, report, or information may be disclosed to other officers, employees, or authorized representatives of the United States concerned with carrying out this Act or when relevant in any proceeding under this Act. Nothing in this section shall authorize the withholding of information by the Administrator or any officer or employee under his control from the duly authorized committees of the Congress.

STATE STANDARDS

SEC. 209. (a) No State or any political subdivision thereof shall adopt or attempt to enforce any standard relating to the control of emissions from new motor vehicles or new motor vehicle engines subject to this part. No State shall require certification, inspection, or any other approval relating to the control of emissions from any new motor vehicle or new motor vehicle engine as condition precedent to the initial retail sale, titling (if any), or registration of such motor vehicle, motor vehicle engine, or equipment.

(b)(1) The Administrator shall, after notice and opportunity for public hearing, waive application of this section to any State which has adopted standards (other than crankcase emission standards) for the control of emissions from new motor vehicles or new motor vehicle engines prior to March 30, 1966, if the State determines that the State standards will be, in the aggregate, at least as protective of public health and welfare as applicable Federal standards. No such waiver shall be granted if the Administrator finds that—

(A) the determination of the State is arbitrary and capricious,

(B) such State does not need such State standards to meet compelling and extraordinary conditions, or

(C) such State standards and accompanying enforcement procedures are not consistent with section 202(a) of this part.

(2) If each State standard is at least as stringent as the comparable applicable Federal standard, such State standard shall be deemed to be at least as protective of health and welfare as such Federal standards for purposes of paragraph (1).

(3) in the case of any new motor vehicle or new motor vehicle engine to which State standards apply pursuant to a waiver granted under paragraph (1), compliance with such State standards shall be treated as compliance with applicable Federal standards for purposes of this title.

(c) Whenever a regulation with respect to any motor vehicle part or motor vehicle engine part is in effect under section 207(a)(2), no State or political subdivision thereof shall adopt or attempt to enforce any standard or any requirement of certification, inspection, or approval which relates to motor vehicle emissions and is applicable to the same aspect of such part. The preceding sentence shall not apply in the case of a State with respect to which a waiver is in effect under subsection (b).

(d) Nothing in this part shall preclude or deny to any State or political subdivision thereof the right otherwise to control, regulate, or restrict the use, operation, or movement of registered or licensed motor vehicles.

STATE GRANTS

SEC. 210. The Administrator is authorized to make grants to appropriate State agencies in an amount up to two-thirds of the cost of developing and maintaining effective vehicle emission devices and systems inspection and emission testing and control programs, except that—

(1) no such grant shall be made for any part of any State vehicle inspection program which does not directly relate to the cost of the air pollution control aspects of such a program;

(2) no such grant shall be made unless the Secretary of Transportation has certified to the Administrator that such program is consistent with any highway safety program developed pursuant to section 402 of title 23 of the United States Code; and

(3) no such grant shall be made unless the program includes provisions designed to insure that emission control devices and systems on vehicles in actual use have not been discontinued or rendered inoperative. Grants may be made under this section by way of reimbursement in any case in which amounts have been expended by the State before the date on which any such grant was made.

REGULATION OF FUELS

SEC. 211. (a) The Administrator may by regulation designate any fuel or fuel additive and, after such date or dates as may be prescribed by him, no manufacturer or processor of any such fuel or additive may sell, offer for sale, or introduce into commerce such fuel or additive unless the Administrator has registered such fuel or additive in accordance with subsection (b) of this section.

(b)(1) For the purpose of registration of fuels and fuel additives, the Administrator shall require—

(A) the manufacturer of any fuel to notify him as to the commercial identifying name and manufacturer of any additive contained in such fuel; the range of concentration of any additive in the fuel; and the purpose-in-use of any such additive; and

(B) the manufacturer of any additive to notify him as to the chemical composition of such additive.

(2) For the purpose of registration of fuels and fuel additives, the Administrator may also require the manufacturer of any fuel or fuel additive—

(A) to conduct tests to determine potential public health effects of such fuel or additive (including, but not limited to, carcinogenic, teratogenic, or mutagenic effects), and

(B) to furnish the description of any analytical technique that can be used to detect and measure any additive in such fuel, the recommended range of concentration of such additive, and the recommended purpose-in-use of such additive, and such other information as is reasonable and necessary to determine the emissions resulting from the use of the fuel or additive contained in such fuel, the effect of such fuel or additive on the emission control performance of any vehicle or vehicle engine, or the extent to which such emissions affect the public health or welfare.

Tests under subparagraph (A) shall be conducted in conformity with test procedures and protocols established by the Administrator. The results of such tests shall not be considered confidential.

(3) Upon compliance with the provisions of this subsection, including assurances that the Administrator will receive changes in the information required, the Administrator shall register such fuel or fuel additive.

(c)(1) The Administrator may, from time to time on the basis of information obtained under subsection (b) of this section or other information available to him, by regulation, control or prohibit the manufacture, introduction into commerce, offering for sale, or sale of any fuel or fuel additive for use in a motor vehicle or motor vehicle engine (A) if in the judgment of the Administrator any emission product of such fuel or fuel additive causes, or contributes, to air pollution which may reasonably be anticipated to endanger the public health or welfare, or (B) if emission products of such fuel or fuel additive will impair to a significant degree the performance of any emission control device or system which is in general use, or which the Administrator finds has been developed to a point where in a reasonable time it would be in general use were such regulation to be promulgated.

(2) (A) No fuel, class of fuels, or fuel additive may be controlled or prohibited by the Administrator pursuant to clause (A) of paragraph (1) except after consideration of all relevant medical and scientific evidence available to him, including consideration of other technologically or economically feasible means of achieving emission standards under section 202.

(B) No fuel or fuel additive may be controlled or prohibited by the Administrator pursuant to clause (B) of paragraph (1) except after consideration of available scientific and economic data, including a cost benefit analysis comparing emission control devices or systems which are or will be in general use and require the proposed control or prohibition with emission control devices or systems which are or will be in general use and do not require the proposed control or prohibition. On request of a manufacturer of motor vehicles, motor vehicle engines, fuels, or fuel additives submitted within 10 days of notice of proposed rulemaking, the Administrator shall hold a public hearing and publish findings with respect to any matter he is required to consider under this subparagraph. Such findings shall be published at the time of promulgation of final regulations.

(C) No fuel or fuel additive may be prohibited by the Administrator under paragraph (1) unless he finds, and publishes such finding, that in his judgment such prohibition will not cause the use of any other fuel or fuel additive which will produce emissions which will endanger the public health or welfare to the same or greater degree than the use of the fuel or fuel additive proposed to be prohibited.

(3) (A) For the purpose of obtaining evidence and data to carry out paragraph (2), the Administrator may require the manufacturer of any motor vehicle or motor vehicle engine to furnish any information which has been developed concerning the emissions from motor vehicles resulting from the use of any fuel or fuel additive, or the effect of such use on the performance of any emission control device or system.

(B) In obtaining information under subparagraph (A), section 307 (a) (relating to subpenas) shall be applicable.

(4) (A) Except as otherwise provided in subparagraph (B) or (C), no State (or political subdivision thereof) may prescribe or attempt to enforce, for the purposes of motor vehicle emission control, any control or prohibition respecting use of a fuel or fuel additive in a motor vehicle or motor vehicle engine—

(i) if the Administrator has found that no control or prohibition under paragraph (1) is necessary and has published his finding in the Federal Register, or

(ii) if the Administrator has prescribed under paragraph (1) a control or prohibition applicable to such fuel or fuel additive, unless State prohibition or control is identical to the prohibition or control prescribed by the Administrator.

(B) Any State for which application of section 209(a) has at any time been waived under section 209(b) may at any time prescribe and enforce, for the purpose of motor vehicle emission control, a control or prohibition respecting any fuel or fuel additive.

(C) A State may prescribe and enforce, for purposes of motor vehicle emission control, a control or prohibition respecting the use of a fuel or fuel additive in a motor vehicle or motor vehicle engine if an applicable implementation plan for such State under section 110 so provides. The Administrator may approve such provision in an implementation plan, or promulgate an implementation plan containing such a provision, only if he finds that the State control or prohibition is necessary to achieve the national primary or secondary ambient air quality standard which the plan implements.

(d) Any person who violates subsection (a) or (f) or the regulations prescribed under subsection (c) or who fails to furnish any information required by the Administrator under subsection (b) shall forfeit and pay to the United States a civil penalty of $10,000 for each and every day of the continuance of such violation, which shall accrue to the United States and be recovered in a civil suit in the name of the United States, brought in the district where such person has his principal office or in any district in which he does business. The Administrator may, upon application therefor, remit or mitigate any forfeiture provided for in this subsection and he shall have authority to determine the facts upon all such applications.

(e) (1) Not later than one year after the date of enactment of this subsection and after notice and opportunity for a public hearing, the Administrator shall promulgate regulations which implement the authority under subsection (b) (2) (A) and (B) with respect to each fuel or fuel additive which is registered on the date of promulgation of such regulations and with respect to each fuel or fuel additive for which an application for registration is filed thereafter.

(2) Regulations under subsection (b) to carry out this subsection shall require that the requisite information be provided to the Administrator by each such manufacturer—

(A) prior to registration, in the case of any fuel or fuel additive which is not registered on the date of promulgation of such regulations; or

(B) not later than three years after the date of promulgation of such regulations, in the case of any fuel or fuel additive which is registered on such date.

(3) In promulgating such regulations, the Administrator may—

(A) exempt any small business (as defined in such regulations) from or defer or modify the requirements of, such regulations with respect to any such small business;

(B) provide for cost-sharing with respect to the testing of any fuel or fuel additive which is manufactured or processed by two or more persons or otherwise provide for shared responsibility to meet the requirements of this section without duplication; or

(C) exempt any person from such regulations with respect to a particular fuel or fuel additive upon a finding that any additional testing of such fuel or fuel additive would be duplicative of adequate existing testing.

(f)(1) Effective upon March 31, 1977, it shall be unlawful for any manufacturer of any fuel or fuel additive to first introduce into commerce, or to increase the concentration in use of, any fuel or fuel additive for general use in light duty motor vehicles manufactured after model year 1974 which is not substantially similar to any fuel or fuel additive utilized in the certification of any model year 1975, or subsequent model year, vehicle or engine under section 206.

(2) Effective November 30, 1977, it shall be unlawful for any manufacturer of any fuel to introduce into commerce any gasoline which contains a concentration of manganese in excess of .0625 grams per gallon of fuel, except as otherwise provided pursuant to a waiver under paragraph (4).

(3) Any manufacturer of any fuel or fuel additive which prior to March 31, 1977, and after January 1, 1974, first introduced into commerce or increased the concentration in use of a fuel or fuel additive that would otherwise have been prohibited under paragraph (1) if introduced on or after March 31, 1977, shall, not later than September 15, 1978, cease to distribute such fuel or fuel additive in commerce. During the period beginning 180 days after the date of the enactment of this subsection

and before September 15, 1978, the Administrator shall prohibit, or restrict the concentration of any fuel additive which he determines will cause or contribute to the failure of an emission control device or system (over the useful life of any vehicle in which such device or system is used) to achieve compliance by the vehicle with the emission standards with respect to which it has been certified under section 206.

(4) The Administrator, upon application of any manufacturer of any fuel or fuel additive, may waive the prohibitions established under paragraph (1) or (3) of this subsection or the limitation specified in paragraph (2) of this subsection, if he determines that the applicant has established that such fuel or fuel additive or a specified concentration thereof, and the emission products of such fuel or additive or specified concentration thereof, will not cause or contribute to a failure of any emission control device or system (over the useful life of any vehicle in which such device or system is used) to achieve compliance by the vehicle with the emission standards with respect to which it has been certified pursuant to section 206. If the Administrator has not acted to grant or deny an application under this paragraph within one hundred and eighty days of receipt of such application, the waiver authorized by this paragraph shall be treated as granted.

(5) No action of the Administrator under this section may be stayed by any court pending judicial review of such action.

(g) (1) For the purposes of this subsection:

(A) The terms "gasoline" and "refinery" have the meaning provided under regulations of the Administrator promulgated under this section.

(B) The term "small refinery" means a refinery or a portion of refinery producing gasoline—

(i) the gasoline producing capacity of which was in operation or under construction at any time during the one-year period immediately preceding October 1, 1976, and

(ii) which has a crude oil or bona fide feed stock capacity (as determined by the Administrator) of 50,000 barrels per day or less, and

(iii) which is owned or controlled by a refiner with a total combined crude oil or bona fide feed stock capacity (as determined by the Administrator) of 137,500 barrels per day or less.

(2) No regulations of the Administrator under this section (or any amendment or revision thereof) respecting the control or prohibition of lead additives in gasoline shall require a small refinery prior to October 1, 1982, to reduce the average lead content per gallon of

gasoline refined at such refinery below the applicable amount specified in the table below:

If the average gasoline production of the small refinery for the immediately preceding calendar year (or, in the case of refineries under construction, half the designed crude oil capacity) was (in barrels per day):

	The applicable amount (in grams per gallon)
5,000 or under	2.65.
5,001 to 10,000	2.15.
10,001 to 15,000	1.65.
15,001 to 20,000	1.30.
20,001 to 25,000	.80.
25,001 or over	As prescribed by the Administrator, but not greater than 0.80.

The Administrator may promulgate such regulations as he deems appropriate with respect to the reduction of the average lead content of gasoline refined by small refineries on and after October 1, 1982, taking into account the experience under the preceding provisions of this paragraph.

(3) Effective on the date of the enactment of this subsection, the regulations of the Administrator under this section respecting fuel additives (40 CFR part 80) shall be deemed amended to comply with the requirement contained in paragraph (2).

(4) Nothing in this section shall be construed to preempt the right of any State to take action as permitted by section 211(c)(4) of this Act.

DEVELOPMENT OF LOW-EMISSION VEHICLES

SEC. 212. (a) For the purpose of this section—

(1) The term "Board" means the Low-Emission Vehicle Certification Board.

(2) The term "Federal Government" includes the legislative, executive, and judicial branches of the Government of the United States, and the government of the District of Columbia.

(3) The term "motor vehicle" means any self-propelled vehicle designed for use in the United States on the highways, other than a vehicle designed or used for military field training, combat, or tactical purposes.

(4) The term "low-emission vehicle" means any motor vehicle which—

(A) emits any air pollutant in amounts significantly below new motor vehicle standards applicable under section 202 at the time of procurement to that type of vehicle; and

(B) with respect to all other air pollutants meets the new motor vehicle standards applicable under section 202 at the time of procurement to that type of vehicle.

(5) The term "retail price" means (A) the maximum statutory price applicable to any class or model of motor vehicle; or (B) in any case where there is no applicable maximum statutory price, the most recent procurement price paid for any class or model of motor vehicle.

(b)(1) There is established a Low-Emission Vehicle Certification Board to be composed of the Administrator or his designee, the Secretary of Transportation or his designee, the Chairman of the Council on Enivornmental Quality or his designee, the Director of the National Highway Safety Bureau in the Department of Transportation, the Administrator of General Services, and two members appointed by the President. The President shall designate one member of the Board as Chairman.

(2) Any member of the Board not employed by the United States may receive compensation at the rate of $125 for each day such member is engaged upon work of the Board. Each member of the Board shall be reimbursed for travel expenses, including per diem in lieu of subsistence as authorized by section 5703 of title 5, United States Code, for persons in the Government service employed intermittently.

(3)(A) The Chairman, with the concurrence of the members of the Board, may employ and fix the compensation of such additional personnel as may be necessary to carry out the functions of the Board, but no individual so appointed shall receive compensation in excess of the rate authorized for GS–18 by section 5332 of title 5, United States Code.

(B) The Chairman may fix the time and place of such meetings as may be required, but a meeting of the Board shall be called whenever a majority of its members so requests.

(C) The Board is granted all other powers necessary for meeting its responsibilities under this section.

(c) The Administrator shall determine which models or classes of motor vehicles qualify as low-emission vehicles in accordance with the provisions of this section.

(d)(1) The Board shall certify any class or model of motor vehicles—

(A) for which a certification application has been filed in accordance with paragraph (3) of this subsection;

(B) which is a low-emission vehicle as determined by the Administrator; and

(C) which it determines is suitable for use as a substitute for a class or model of vehicles at that time in use by agencies of the Federal Government.

The Board shall specify with particularity the class or model of vehicles for which the class or model of vehicles described in the application is a suitable substitute. In making the determination under this subsection the Board shall consider the following criteria:

(i) the safety of the vehicle;

(ii) its performance characteristics;

(iii) its reliability potential;

(iv) its serviceability;

(v) its fuel availability;

(vi) its noise level; and

(vii) its maintenance costs as compared with the class or model of motor vehicle for which it may be a suitable substitute.

(2) Certification under this section shall be effective for a period of one year from the date of issuance.

(3) (A) Any party seeking to have a class or model of vehicle certified under this section shall file a certification application in accordance with regulations prescribed by the Board.

(B) The Board shall publish a notice of each application received in the Federal Register.

(C) The Administrator and the Board shall make determinations for the purpose of this section in accordance with procedures prescribed by regulation by the Administrator and the Board, respectively.

(D) The Administrator and the Board shall conduct whatever investigation is necessary, including actual inspection of the vehicle at a place designated in regulations prescribed under subparagraph (A).

(E) The Board shall receive and evaluate written comments and documents from interested parties in support of, or in opposition to, certification of the class or model of vehicle under consideration.

(F) Within ninety days after the receipt of a properly filed certification application, the Administrator shall determine whether such class or model of vehicles is a low-emission vehicle, and within 180 days of such determination, the Board shall reach a decision by majority vote as to whether such class or model of vehicle, having been determined to be a low-emission vehicle, is a suitable substitute for any class or classes of vehicles presently being purchased by the Federal Government for use by its agencies.

(G) Immediately upon making any determination or decision under subparagraph (F), the Administrator and the Board shall each publish in the Federal Register notice of such determination or decision, including reasons therefor and in the case of the Board any dissenting views.

(e) (1) Certified low-emission vehicles shall be acquired by purchase or lease by the Federal Government for use by the Federal Government in lieu of other vehicles if the Administrator of General Services determines that such certified vehicles have procurement costs which are no more than 150 per centum of the retail price of the least expensive class or model of motor vehicle for which they are certified substitutes.

(2) In order to encourage development of inherently low-polluting propulsion technology, the Board may, at its discretion, raise the premium set forth in paragraph (1) of this subsection to 200 per centum of the retail price of any class or model of motor vehicle for which a certified low-emission vehicle is a certified substitute, if the Board determines that the certified low-emission vehicle is powered by an inherently low-polluting propulsion system.

(3) Data relied upon by the Board and the Administrator in determining that a vehicle is a certified low-emission vehicle shall be incorporated in any contract for the procurement of such vehicle.

(f) The procuring agency shall be required to purchase available certified low-emission vehicles which are eligible for purchase to the extent they are available before purchasing any other vehicles for which any low-emission vehicle is a certified substitute. In making purchasing selections between competing eligible certified low-emission vehicles, the procuring agency shall give priority to (1) any class or model which does not require extensive periodic maintenance to retain its low-polluting qualities or which does not require the use of fuels which are more expensive than those of the classes or models of vehicles for which it is a certified substitute; and (2) passenger vehicles other than buses.

(g) For the purpose of procuring certified low-emission vehicles any statutory price limitations shall be waived.

(h) The Administrator shall, from time to time as the Board deems appropriate, test the emissions from certified low-emission vehicles purchased by the Federal Government. If at any time he finds that the emission rates exceed the rates on which certification under this section was based, the Administrator shall notify the Board. Thereupon the Board shall give the supplier of such vehicles written notice of this finding, issue public notice of it, and give the supplier an opportunity to make necessary repairs, adjustment, or replacements. If no such repairs, adjustments, or replacements are made within a period to be set by the Board, the Board may order the supplier to show cause why the vehicle involved should be eligible for recertification.

(i) There are authorized to be appropriated for paying additional amounts for motor vehicles pursuant to, and for carrying out the provisions of, this section, $5,-

000,000 for the fiscal year ending June 30, 1971, and $25,000,000 for each of the two succeeding fiscal years.

(j) The Board shall promulgate the procedures required to implement this section within one hundred and eighty days after the date of enactment of the Clean Air Amendments of 1970.

FUEL ECONOMY IMPROVEMENT FROM NEW MOTOR VEHICLES

SEC. 213. (a)(1) The Administrator and the Secretary of Transportation shall conduct a joint study, and shall report to the Committee on Interstate and Foreign Commerce of the United States House of Representatives and the Committees on Public Works and Commerce of the United States Senate within one hundred and twenty days following the date of enactment of this section, concerning the practicability of establishing a fuel economy improvement standard of 20 per centum for new motor vehicles manufactured during and after model year 1980. Such study and report shall include, but not be limited to, the technological problems of meeting any such standard, including the leadtime involved; the test procedures required to determine compliance; the economic costs associated with such standard, including any beneficial economic impact; the various means of enforcing such standard; the effect on consumption of natural resources, including energy consumed; and the impact of applicable safety and emission standards. In the course of performing such study, the Administrator and the Secretary of Transportation shall utilize the research previously performed in the Department of Transportation, and the Administrator and the Secretary shall consult with the Federal Energy Administrator, the Chairman of the Council on Environmental Quality, and the Secretary of the Treasury. The Office of Management and Budget may review such report before its submission to such committees of the Congress, but such Office may not revise the report or delay its submission beyond the date prescribed for its submission, and may submit to Congress its comments respecting such report. In connection with such study, the Administrator may utilize the authority provided in section 307(a) of this Act to obtain necessary information.

(2) For the purpose of this section, the term "fuel economy improvement standard" means a requirement of a percentage increase in the number of miles of transportation provided by a manufacturer's entire annual production of new motor vehicles per unit of fuel consumed, as determined for each manufacturer in accordance with test procedures established by the Administrator pursuant to this Act. Such term shall not include any requirement for any design standard or any other requirement specifying or otherwise limiting the manu-

facturer's discretion in deciding how to comply with the fuel economy improvement standard by any lawful means.

STUDY OF PARTICULATE EMISSIONS FROM MOTOR VEHICLES

SEC. 214. (a)(1) The Administrator shall conduct a study concerning the effects on health and welfare of particulate emissions from motor vehicles or motor vehicle engines to which section 202 applies. Such study shall characterize and quantify such emissions and analyze the relationship of such emissions to various fuels and fuel additives.

(2) The study shall also include an analysis of particulate emissions from mobile sources which are not related to engine emissions (including, but not limited to tire debris, and asbestos from brake lining).

(b) The Administrator shall report to the Congress the findings and results of the study conducted under subsection (a) not later than two years after the date of the enactment of the Clean Air Act Amendments of 1977. Such report shall also include recommendations for standards or methods to regulate particulate emissions described in paragraph (2) of subsection (a).

HIGH ALTITUDE PERFORMANCE ADJUSTMENTS

SEC. 215. (a)(1) Any action taken with respect to any element of design installed on or in a motor vehicle or motor vehicle engine in compliance with regulations under this title (including any alteration or adjustment of such element), shall be treated as not in violation of section 203(a) if such action is performed in accordance with high altitude adjustment instructions provided by the manufacturer under subsection (b) and approved by the Administrator.

(2) If the Administrator finds that adjustments or modifications made pursuant to instructions of the manufacturer under paragraph (1) will not insure emission control performance with respect to each standard under section 202 at least equivalent to that which would result if no such adjustments or modifications were made, he shall disapprove such instructions. Such findings shall be based upon minimum engineering evaluations consistent with good engineering practice.

(b)(1) Instructions respecting each class or category of vehicles or engines to which this title applies providing for such vehicle and engine adjustments and modifications as may be necessary to insure emission control performance at different altitudes shall be submitted by the manufacturer to the Administrator pursuant to regulations promulgated by the Administrator.

(2) Any knowing violation by a manufacturer of requirements of the Administrator under paragraph (1) shall be treated as a violation by such manufacturer of section 203(a)(3) for purposes of the penalties contained in section 205.

(3) Such instruction shall provide, in addition to other adjustments, for adjustments for vehicles moving from high altitude areas to low altitude areas after the initial registration of such vehicles.

(c) No instructions under this section respecting adjustments or modifications may require the use of any manufacturer parts (as defined in section 203(a)) unless the manufacturer demonstrates to the satisfaction of the Administrator that the use of such manufacturer parts is necessary to insure emission control performance.

(d) Before January 1, 1981 the authority provided by this section shall be available in any high altitude State (as determined under regulations of the Administrator under regulations promulgated before the date of the enactment of this Act) but after December 31, 1980, such authority shall be available only in any such State in which an inspection and maintenance program for the testing of motor vehicle emissions has been instituted for the portions of the State where any national ambient air quality standard for auto-related pollutants has not been attained.

DEFINITIONS FOR PART A

SEC. 216. As used in this part—

(1) The term "manufacturer" as used in sections 202, 203, 206, 207, and 208 means any person engaged in the manufacturing or assembling of new motor vehicles or new motor vehicle engines, or importing such vehicles or engines for resale, or who acts for and is under the control of any such person in connection with the distribution of new motor vehicles or new motor vehicle engines, but shall not include any dealer with respect to new motor vehicles or new motor vehicle engines received by him in commerce.

(2) The term "motor vehicle" means any self-propelled vehicle designed for transporting persons or property on a street or highway.

(3) Except with respect to vehicles or engines imported or offered for importation, the term "new motor vehicle" means a motor vehicle the equitable or legal title to which has never been transferred to an ultimate purchaser; and the term "new motor vehicle engine" means an engine in a new motor vehicle or a motor vehicle engine the equitable or legal title to which has never been transferred to the ultimate purchaser; and with respect to imported vehicles or engines, such terms mean a motor vehicle and engine, respectively, manufactured after the effective date of

a regulation issued under section 202 which is applicable to such vehicle or engine (or which would be applicable to such vehicle or engine had it been manufactured for importation into the United States).

(4) The term "dealer" means any person who is engaged in the sale or the distribution of new motor vehicles or new motor vehicle engines to the ultimate purchaser.

(5) The term "ultimate purchaser" means, with respect to any new motor vehicle or new motor vehicle engine, the first person who in good faith purchases such new motor vehicle or new engine for purposes other than resale.

(6) The term "commerce" means (A) commence between any place in any State and any place outside thereof; and (B) commerce wholly within the District of Columbia.

Part B—Aircraft Emission Standards

ESTABLISHMENT OF STANDARDS

Sec. 231. (a)(1) Within 90 days after the date of enactment of the Clean Air Amendments of 1970, the Administrator shall commence a study and investigation of emissions of air pollutants from aircraft in order to determine—

(A) the extent to which such emissions affect air quality in air quality control regions throughout the United States, and

(B) the technological feasibility of controlling such emissions.

(2) The Administrator shall, from time to time, issue proposed emission standards applicable to the emission of any air pollutant from any class or classes of aircraft engines which in his judgment causes, or contributes to, air pollution which may reasonably be anticipated to endanger public health or welfare.

(3) The administrator shall hold public hearings with respect to such proposed standards. Such hearings shall, to the extent practicable, be held in air quality control regions which are most seriously affected by aircraft emissions. Within 90 days after the issuance of such proposed regulations, he shall issue such regulation with such modifications as he deems appropriate. Such regulations may be revised from time to time.

(b) Any regulation prescribed under this section (and any revision thereof) shall take effect after such period as the Administrator finds necessary (after consultation with the Secretary of Transportation) to permit the development and application of the requisite technology, giving appropriate consideration to the cost of compliance within such period.

(c) Any regulations in effect under this section on date of enactment of the Clean Air Act Amendments of 1977 or proposed or promulgated thereafter, or amendments thereto, with respect to aircraft shall not apply if disapproved by the President, after notice and opportunity for public hearing, on the basis of a finding by the Secretary of Transportation that any such regulation would create a hazard to aircraft safety. Any such finding shall include a reasonably specific statement of the basis upon which the finding was made.

ENFORCEMENT OF STANDARDS

SEC. 232. (a) The Secretary of Transportation, after consultation with the Administrator, shall prescribe regulations to insure compliance with all standards prescribed under section 231 by the Administrator. The regulations of the Secretary of Transportation shall include provisions making such standards applicable in the issuance, amendment, modification, suspension, or revocation of any certificate authorized by the Federal Aviation Act or the Department of Transportation Act. Such Secretary shall insure that all necessary inspections are accomplished, and, may execute any power or duty vested in him by any other provision of law in the execution of all powers and duties vested in him under this section.

(b) In any action to amend, modify, suspend, or revoke a certificate in which violation of an emission standard prescribed under section 231 or of a regulation prescribed under subsection (a) is at issue, the certificate holder shall have the same notice and appeal rights as are prescribed for such holders in the Federal Aviation Act of 1958 or the Department of Transportation Act, except that in any appeal to the National Transportation Safety Board, the Board may amend, modify, or revoke the order of the Secretary of Transportation only if it finds no violation of such standard or regulation and that such amendment, modification, or revocation is consistent with safety in air transportation.

STATE STANDARDS AND CONTROLS

SEC. 233. No State or political subdivision thereof may adopt or attempt to enforce any standard respecting emissions of any air pollutant from any aircraft or engine thereof unless such standard is identical to a standard applicable to such aircraft under this part.

DEFINITIONS

SEC. 234. Terms used in this part (other than Administrator) shall have the same meaning as such terms have under section 101 of the Federal Aviation Act of 1958.

TITLE III—GENERAL

ADMINISTRATION

SEC. 301. (a)(1) The Administrator is authorized to prescribe such regulations as are necessary to carry out his functions under this Act. The Administrator may delegate to any officer or employee of the Environmental Protection Agency such of his powers and duties under this Act, except the making of regulations, as he may deem necessary or expedient.

(2) Not later than one year after the date of enactment of this paragraph, the Administrator shall promulgate regulations establishing general applicable procedures and policies for regional officers and employees (including the Regional Administrator) to follow in carrying out a delegation under paragraph (1), if any. Such regulations shall be designed—

(A) to assure fairness and uniformity in the criteria, procedures, and policies applied by the various regions in implementing and enforcing the Act;

(B) to assure at least an adequate quality audit of each State's performance and adherence to the requirements of this Act in implementing and enforcing the Act, particularly in the review of new sources and in enforcement of the Act; and

(C) to provide a mechanism for identifying and standardizing inconsistent or varying criteria, procedures, and policies being employed by such officers and employees in implementing and enforcing the Act.

(b) Upon the request of an air pollution control agency, personnel of the Environmental Protection Agency may be detailed to such agency for the purpose of carrying out the provisions of this Act.

(c) Payments under grants made under this Act may be made in installments, and in advance or by way of reimbursement, as may be determined by the Administrator.

DEFINITIONS

SEC. 302. When used in this Act—

(a) The term "Administrator" means the Administrator of the Environmental Protection Agency.

(b) The term "air pollution control agency" means any of the following:

(1) A single State agency designated by the Governor of that State as the official State air pollution control agency for purposes of this Act;

(2) An agency established by two or more States and having substantial powers or duties pertaining to the prevention and control of air pollution;

(3) A city, county, or other local government health authority, or, in the case of any city, county, or other local government in which there is an agency other than the health authority charged with responsibility for enforcing ordinances or laws relating to the prevention and control of air pollution, such other agency; or

(4) An agency of two or more municipalities located in the same State or in different States and having substantial powers or duties pertaining to the prevention and control of air pollution.

(c) The term "interstate air pollution control agency" means—

(1) an air pollution control agency established by two or more States, or

(2) an air pollution control agency of two or more municipalities located in different States.

(d) The term "State" means a State, the District of Columbia, the Commonwealth of Puerto Rico, the Virgin Islands, Guam, and American Samoa and includes the Commonwealth of the Northern Mariana Islands.

(e) The term "person" includes an individual, corporation, partnership, association, State, municipality, political subdivision of a State, and any agency, department, or instrumentality of the United States and any officer, agent, or employee thereof.

(f) The term "municipality" means a city, town, borough, county, parish, district, or other public body created by or pursuant to State law.

(g) The term "air pollutant" means any air pollution agent or combination of such agents, including any physical, chemical, biological, radioactive (including source material, special nuclear material, and byproduct material) substance or matter which is emitted into or otherwise enters the ambient air.

(h) All language referring to effects on welfare includes, but is not limited to, effects on soils, water, crops, vegetation, man-made materials, animals, wildlife, weather, visibility, and climate, damage to and deterioration of property, and hazards to transportation, as well as effects on economic values and on personal comfort and well-being.

(i) The term "Federal land manager" means, with respect to any lands in the United States, the Secretary of the department with authority over such lands.

(j) Except as otherwise expressly provided, the terms "major stationary source" and "major emitting facility" mean any stationary facility or source of air pollutants which directly emits, or has the potential to emit, one hundred tons per year or more of any air pollutant (including any major emitting facility or source of fugitive emissions of any such pollutant, as determined by rule by the Administrator).

(k) The terms "emission limitation" and "emission standard" mean a requirement established by the State or the Administrator which limits the quantity, rate, or concentration of emissions of air pollutants on a continuous basis, including any requirement relating to the operation or maintenance of a source to assure continuous emission reduction.

(l) The term "standard of performance" means a requirement of continuous emission reduction, including any requirement relating to the operation or maintenance of a source to assure continuous emission reduction.

(m) The term "means of emission limitation" means a system of continuous emission reduction (including the use of specific technology or fuels with specified pollution characteristics).

(n) The term "primary standard attainment date" means the date specified in the applicable implementation plan for the attainment of a national primary ambient air quality standard for any air pollutant.

(o) The term "delayed compliance order" means an order issued by the State or by the Administrator to an existing stationary source, postponing the date required under an applicable implementation plan for compliance by such source with any requirement of such plan.

(p) The term "schedule and timetable of compliance" means a schedule of required measures including an enforceable sequence of actions or operations leading to compliance with an emission limitation, other limitation, prohibition, or standard.

EMERGENCY POWERS

SEC. 303. (a) Notwithstanding any other provisions of this Act, the Administrator upon receipt of evidence that a pollution source or combination of sources (including moving sources) is presenting an imminent and substantial endangerment to the health of persons, and that appropriate State or local authorities have not acted to abate such sources, may bring suit on behalf of the United States in the appropriate United States district court to immediately restrain any person causing or contributing to the alleged pollution to stop the emission of air pollutants causing or contributing to such pollution or to take such other action as may be necessary. If it is not practicable to assure prompt protection of the health of persons solely by commencement of such a civil action, the Administrator may issue such orders as may be necessary to protect the health of persons who are, or may be, affected by such pollution source (or sources). Prior to taking any action under this section, the Administrator shall consult with the State and local authorities in order to confirm the correctness of the information on which the action proposed to be taken is based and to ascertain the action which such authorities are, or will be, taking. Such order shall be effective for a period of not more than twenty-four hours unless the Administrator brings an action under the first sentence of this subsection before the expiration of such period. Whenever the Administrator brings such an action within such period, such order shall be effective for a period of forty-eight hours or such longer period as may be authorized by the court pending litigation or thereafter.

(b) Any person who willfully violates, or fails or refuses to comply with, any order issued by the Administrator under subsection (a) may, in an action brought in the appropriate United States district court to enforce such order, be fined not more than $5,000 for each day during which such violation occurs or failure to comply continues.

CITIZEN SUITS

SEC. 304. (a) Except as provided in subsection (b), any person may commence a civil action on his own behalf—

(1) against any person (including (i) the United States, and (ii) any other governmental instrumentality or agency to the extent permitted by the Eleventh Amendment to the Constitution) who is alleged to be in violation of (A) an emission standard or limitation under this Act or (B) an order issued by the Administrator or a State with respect to such a standard or limitation,

(2) against the Administrator where there is alleged a failure of the Administrator to perform any act or duty under this Act which is not discretionary with the Administrator, or

(3) against any person who proposes to construct or constructs any new or modified major emitting facility without a permit required under part C of title I (relating to significant deterioration of air quality) or part D of title I (relating to nonattainment) or who is alleged to be in violation of any condition of such permit.

The district courts shall have jurisdistion, without regard to the amount in controversy or the citizenship of the parties, to enforce such an emission standard or limitation, or such an order, or to order the Administrator to perform such act or duty, as the case may be.

(b) No action may be commenced—

(1) under subsection (a)(1)—

(A) prior to 60 days after the plaintiff has given notice of the violation (i) to the Administrator, (ii) to the State in which the violation occurs, and (iii) to any alleged violator of the standard, limitation, or order, or

(B) if the Administrator or State has commenced and is diligently prosecuting a civil action in a court of the United States or a State to require compliance with the standard, limitation, or order, but in any such action in a court of the United States any person may intervene as a matter of right.

(2) under subsection (a)(2) prior to 60 days after the plaintiff has given notice of such action to the Administrator,

except that such action may be brought immediately after such notification in the case of an action under this section respecting a violation of section 112(c)(1)(B) or an order issued by the Administrator pursuant to section 113(a). Notice under this subsection shall be given in such manner as the Administrator shall prescribe by regulation.

(c)(1) Any action respecting a violation by a stationary source of an emission standard or limitation or an order respecting such standard or limitation may be brought only in the judicial district in which such source is located.

(2) In such action under this section, the Administrator, if not a party, may intervene as a matter of right.

(d) The court, in issuing any final order in any action brought pursuant to subsection (a) of this section, may award costs of litigation (including reasonable attorney and expert witness fees) to any party, whenever the court determines such award is appropriate. The court may, if a temporary restraining order or preliminary injunction is sought, require the filing of a bond or equivalent security in accordance with the Federal Rules of Civil Procedure.

(e) Nothing in this section shall restrict any right which any person (or class of persons) may have under any statute or common law to seek enforcement of any emission standard or limitation or to seek any other relief (including relief against the Administrator or a State agency). Nothing in this section or in any other law of the United States shall be construed to prohibit, exclude, or restrict any State, local, or interstate authority from—

(1) bringing any enforcement action or obtaining any judicial remedy or sanction in any State or or local court, or

(2) bringing any administrative enforcement action or obtaining any administrative remedy or sanction in any State or local administrative agency, department or instrumentality,

against the United States, any department, agency, or instrumentality thereof, or any officer, agent, or employee thereof under State or local law respecting control and abatement of air pollution. For provisions requiring compliance by the United States, departments, agencies, instrumentalities, officers, agents, and employees in the same manner as nongovernmental entities, see section 118.

(f) For purposes of this section, the term "emission standard or limitation under this Act" means—

(1) a schedule or timetable of compliance, emission limitation, standard of performance or emission standard,

(2) a control or prohibition respecting a motor vehicle fuel or fuel additive, which is in effect under this Act (including a requirement applicable by reason of section 118) or under an applicable implementation plan, or

(3) any condition or requirement of a permit under part C of title I (relating to significant deterioration of air quality) or part D of title I (relating to nonattainment), any condition or requirement of section 113(d) (relating to certain enforcement orders), section 119 (relating to primary nonferrous smelter orders), any condition or requirement under an applicable implementation plan relating to transportation control measures, air quality maintenance plans, vehicle inspection and maintenance programs or vapor recovery requirements, section 211 (e) and (f) (relating to fuels and fuel additives), section 169A (relating to visibility protection), any condition or requirement under part B of title I (relating to ozone protection), or any requirement under section 111 or 112 (without regard to whether such requirement is expressed as an emission standard or otherwise).

REPRESENTATION IN LITIGATION

SEC. 305. (a) The Administrator shall request the Attorney General to appear and represent him in any civil action instituted under this Act to which the Administrator is a party. Unless the Attorney General notifies the Administrator that he will appear in such action, within a reasonable time, attorneys appointed by the Administrator shall appear and represent him.

(b) In the event the Attorney General agrees to appear and represent the Administrator in any such action, such representation shall be conducted in accordance with, and shall include participation by, attorneys appointed by the Administrator to the extent authorized by, the memorandum of understanding between the Department of Justice and the Environmental Protection Agency, dated June 13, 1977, respecting representation of the agency by the department in civil litigation.

FEDERAL PROCUREMENT

SEC. 306. (a) No Federal agency may enter into any contract with any person who is convicted of any offense under section 113(c)(1) for the procurement of goods, materials, and services to perform such contract at any facility at which the violation which gave rise to such conviction occurred if such facility is owned, leased, or supervised by such person. The prohibition in the preceding sentence shall continue until the Administrator certifies that the condition giving rise to such a conviction has been corrected.

(b) The Administrator shall establish procedures to provide all Federal agencies with the notification necessary for the purposes of subsection (a).

(c) In order to implement the purposes and policy of this Act to protect and enhance the quality of the Nation's air, the President shall, not more than 180 days after enactment of the Clean Air Amendments of 1970 cause to be issued an order (1) requiring each Federal agency authorized to enter into contracts and each Federal agency which is empowered to extend Federal assistance by way of grant, loan, or contract to effectuate the purpose and policy of this Act in such contracting or assistance activities, and (2) setting forth procedures, sanctions, penalties, and such other provisions, as the President determines necessary to carry out such requirement.

(d) The President may exempt any contract, loan, or grant from all or part of the provisions of this section where he determines such exemption is necessary in the paramount interest of the United States and he shall notify the Congress of such exemption.

(e) The President shall annually report to the Congress on measures taken toward implementing the purpose and intent of this section, including but not limited to the progress and problems associated with implementation of this section.

GENERAL PROVISIONS RELATING TO ADMINISTRATIVE PROCEEDINGS AND JUDICIAL REVIEW

SEC. 307. (a)(1) In connection with any determination under section 110(f) or section 202(b)(5), or for purposes of obtaining information under section 202(b)(4) or 211(c)(3), the Administrator may issue subpenas for the attendance and testimony of witnesses and the production of relevant papers, books, and documents, and he may administer oaths. Except for emission data, upon a showing satisfactory to the Administrator by such owner or operator that such papers, books, documents, or information or particular part thereof, if made public, would divulge trade secrets or secret processes of such owner or operator, the Administrator shall consider such record, report, or information or particular portion thereof confidential in accordance with the purposes of section 1905 of title 18 of the United States Code, except that such paper, book, document, or information may be discussed to other officers, employees, or authorized representatives of the United States concerned with carrying out this Act, to persons carrying out the National Academy of Sciences' study and investigation provided for in section 202(c), or when relevant in any proceeding under this Act. Witnesses summoned shall be paid the same fees and mileage that are paid witnesses in the courts of the United States. In cases of contumacy or refusal to obey a subpena served upon any person under this subparagraph, the district court of the United States for any district in which such person is found or resides or transacts business, upon application by the United States and after notice to such person, shall have jurisdiction to issue an order requiring such person to appear and give testimony before the Administrator to appear and produce papers, books, and documents before the Administrator, or both, and any failure to obey such order of the court may be punished by such court as a contempt thereof.

(b) (1) A petition for review of action of the Administrator in promulgating any national primary or secondary ambient air quality standard, any emission standard or requirement under section 112, any standard of performance or requirement under section 111,[7] any standard under section 202 (other than a standard required to be prescribed under section 202(b) (1)), any determination under section 202(b) (5), any control or prohibition under section 211, any standard under section 231, any rule issued under section 113, 119, or under section 120, or any other nationally applicable regulations promulgated, or final action taken, by the Administrator under this Act may be filed only in the United States Court of Appeals for the District of Columbia. A petition for review of the Administrator's action in approving or promulgating any implementation plan under section 110 or section 111(d), any order under section 111(j), under section 112(c), under section 113(d), under section 119, or under section 120, or his action under section 119 (c)(2) (A), (B), or (C) (as in effect before the date of enactment of the Clean Air Act Amendments of 1977) or under regulations thereunder, or any other final action of the Administrator under this Act (including any denial or disapproval by the Administrator under title I) which is local or regionally applicable may be filed only in the United States Court of Appeals for the appropriate circuit. Notwithstanding the preceding sentence a peti-

---

[7] Public Law 95–95 inserted the additional "," after the words "under section 111".

tion for review of any action referred to in such sentence may be filed only in the United States Court of Appeals for the District of Columbia if such action is based on a determination of nationwide scope or effect and if in taking such action the Administrator finds and publishes that such action is based on such a determination. Any petition for review under this subsection shall be filed within sixty days from the date notice of such promulgation, approval, or action appears in the Federal Register, except that if such petition is based solely on grounds arising after such sixtieth day, then any petition for review under this subsection shall be filed within sixty days after such grounds arise.

(2) Action of the Administrator with respect to which review could have been obtained under paragraph (1) shall not be subject to judicial review in civil or criminal proceedings for enforcement.

(c) In any judicial proceeding in which review is sought of a determination under this Act required to be made on the record after notice and opportunity for hearing, if any party applies to the court for leave to adduce additional evidence, and shows to the satisfaction of the court that such additional evidence is material and that there were reasonable grounds for the failure to adduce such evidence in the proceeding before the Administrator, the court may order such additional evidence (and evidence in rebuttal thereof) to be taken before the Administrator, in such manner and upon such terms and conditions as the court may deem proper. The Administrator may modify his findings as to the facts, or make new findings, by reason of the additional evidence so taken and he shall file such modified or new findings, and his recommendation, if any, for the modification or setting aside of his original determination, with the return of such additional evidence.

(d) (1) This subsection applies to—

(A) the promulgation or revision of any national ambient air quality standard under section 109,

(B) the promulgation or revision of an implementation plan by the Administrator under section 110 (c),

(C) the promulgation or revision of any standard of performance under section 111 or emission standard under section 112,

(D) the promulgation or revision of any regulation pertaining to any fuel or fuel additive under section 211,

(E) the promulgation or revision of any aircraft emission standard under section 231,

(F) promulgation or revision of regulations pertaining to orders for coal conversion under section 113(d)(5) (but not including orders granting or denying any such orders),

(G) promulgation or revision of regulations pertaining to primary nonferrous smelter orders under section 119 (but not including the granting or denying of any such order),

(H) promulgation or revision of regulations under subtitle B of title I (relating to stratosphere and ozone protection),

(I) promulgation or revision of regulations under subtitle C of title I (relating to prevention of significant deterioration of air quality and protection of visibility),

(J) promulgation or revision of regulations under section 202 and test procedures for new motor vehicles or engines under sectoin 206, and the revision of a standard under section 202(a)(3),

(K) promulgation or revision of regulations for noncompliance penalties under section 120,

(L) promulgation or revision of any regulations promulgated under section 207 (relating to warranties and compliance by vehicles in actual use),

(M) action of the Administrator under section 126 (relating to interstate pollution abatement), and

"(N) such other actions as the Administrator may determine. The provisions of section 553 through 557 and section 706 of title 5 of the United States Code shall not, except as expressly provided in this subsection, apply to action to which this subsection applies. This subsection shall not apply in the case of any rule or circumstance referred to in subparagraphs (A) or (B) of subsection 553(b) of title 5 of the United States Code.

(2) Not later than the date of proposal of any action to which this subsection applies, the Administrator shall establish a rulemaking docket for such action (hereinafter in this subsection referred to as a "rule"). Whenever a rule applies only within a particular State, a second (identical) docket shall be established in the appropriate regional office of the Environmental Protection Agency.

(3) In the case of any rule to which this subsection applies, notice of proposed rulemaking shall be published in the Federal Register, as provided under section 553(b) of title 5, United States Code, shall be accompanied by a statement of its basis and purpose and shall specify the period available for public comment (hereinafter referred to as the "comment period"). The notice of proposed rulemaking shall also state the docket number, the location or locations of the docket, and the times it will be open to public inspection. The statement of basis and purpose shall include a summary of—

(A) the factual data on which the proposed rule is based;

(B) the methodology used in obtaining the data and in analyzing the data; and

(C) the major legal interpretations and policy considerations underlying the proposed rule.

The statement shall also set forth or summarize and provide a reference to any pertinent findings, recommendations, and comments by the Scientific Review Committee established under section 109(d) and the National Academy of Sciences, and, if the proposal differs in any important respect from any of these recommendations, an explanation of the reasons for such differences. All data, information, and documents referred to in this paragraph on which the proposed rule relies shall be included in the docket on the date of publication of the proposed rule.

(4) (A) The rulemaking docket required under paragraph (2) shall be open for inspection by the public at reasonable times specified in the notice of proposed rulemaking. Any person may copy documents contained in the docket. The Administrator shall provide copying facilities which may be used at the expense of the person seeking copies, but the Administrator may waive or reduce such expenses in such instances as the public interest requires. Any person may request copies by mail if the person pays the expenses, including personnel costs to do the copying.

(B) (i) Promptly upon receipt by the agency, all written comments and documentary information on the proposed rule received from any person for inclusion in the docket during the comment period shall be placed in the docket. The transcript of public hearings, if any, on the proposed rule shall also be included in the docket promptly upon receipt from the person who transcribed such hearings. All documents which become available after the proposed rule has been published and which the Administrator determines are of central relevance to the rulemaking shall be placed in the docket as soon as possible after their availability.

(ii) The drafts of proposed rules submitted by the Administrator to the Office of Management and Budget for any interagency review process prior to proposal of any such rule, all documents accompanying such drafts, and all written comments thereon by other agencies and all written responses to such written comments by the Administrator shall be placed in the docket no later than the date of proposal of the rule. The drafts of the final rule submitted for such review process prior to promulgation and all such written comments thereon, all documents accompanying such drafts, and written responses thereto shall be placed in the docket no later than the date of promulgation.

(5) In promulgating a rule to which this subsection applies (i) the Administrator shall allow any person to submit written comments, data, or documentary information; (ii) the Administrator shall give interested persons an opportunity for the oral presentation of data, views, or arguments, in addition to an opportunity to make written submissions; (iii) a transcript shall be kept of any oral presentation; and (iv) the Administrator shall keep the record of such proceeding open for thirty days after completion of the proceeding to provide an opportunity for submission of rubuttal and supplementary information.

(6) (A) The promulgated rule shall be accompanied by (i) a statement of basis and purpose like that referred to in paragraph (3) with respect to a proposed rule and (ii) an explanation of the reasons for any major changes in the promulgated rule from the proposed rule.

(B) The promulgated rule shall also be accompanied by a response to each of the significant comments, criticisms, and new data submitted in written or oral presentations during the comment period.

(C) The promulgated rule may not be based (in part or whole) on any information or data which has not been placed in the docket as of the date of such promulgation.

(7) (A) The record for judicial review shall consist exclusively of the material referred to in paragraph (3), clause (i) of paragraph (4) (B), and subparagraphs (A) and (B) of paragraph (6).

(B) Only an objection to a rule or procedure which was raised with reasonable specificity during the period for public comment (including any public hearing) may be raised during judicial review. If the person raising an objection can demonstrate to the Administrator that it was impracticable to raise such objection within such time or if the grounds for such objection arose after the period for public comment (but within the time specified for judicial review) and if such objection is of central relevance to the outcome of the rule, the Administrator shall convene a proceeding for reconsideration of the rule and provide the same procedural rights as would have been afforded had the information been available at the time the rule was proposed. If the Administrator refuses to convene such a proceeding, such person may seek review of such refusal in the United States court of appeals for the appropriate circuit (as provided in subsection (b)). Such reconsideration shall not postpone the effectiveness of the rule. The effectiveness of the rule may be stayed during such reconsideration, however, by the Administrator or the court for a period not to exceed three months.

(8) The sole forum for challenging procedural determinations made by the Administrator under this subsection shall be in the United States court of appeals for

the appropriate circuit (as provided in subsection (b)) at the time of the substantive review of the rule. No interlocutory appeals shall be permitted with respect to such procedural determinations. In reviewing alleged procedural errors, the court may invalidate the rule only if the errors were so serious and related to matters of such central relevance to the rule that there is a substantial likelihood that the rule would have been significantly changed if such errors had not been made.

(9) In the case of review of any action of the Administrator to which this subsection applies, the court may reverse any such action found to be—

(A) arbitrary, capricious, an abuse of discretion, or otherwise not in accordance with law;

(B) contrary to constitutional right, power, privilege, or immunity;

(C) in excess of statutory jurisdiction, authority, or limitations, or short of statutory right; or

(D) without observance of procedure required by law, if (i) such failure to observe such procedure is arbitrary or capricious, (ii) the requirement of paragraph (7)(B) has been met, and (iii) the condition of the last sentence of paragraph (8) is met.

(10) Each statutory deadline for promulgation of rules to which this subsection applies which requires promulgation less than six months after date of proposal may be extended to not more than six months after date of proposal by the Administrator upon a determination that such extension is necessary to afford the public, and the agency, adequate opportunity to carry out the purposes of this subsection.

(11) The requirements of this subsection shall take effect with respect to any rule the proposal of which occurs after ninety days after the date of enactment of the Clean Air Act Amendments of 1977.

(e) Nothing in this Act shall be construed to authorize judicial review of regulations or orders of the Administrator under this Act, except as provided in this section.

(f) In any judicial proceeding under this section, the court may award costs of litigation (including reasonable attorney and expert witness fees) whenever it determines that such award is appropriate.

(g) In any action respecting the promulgation of regulations under section 120 or the administration or enforcement of section 120 no court shall grant any stay, injunctive, or similar relief before final judgment by such court in such action.

MANDATORY LICENSING

Sec. 308. Whenever the Attorney General determines upon application of the Administrator—

(1) that—

(A) in the implementation of the requirements of section 111, 112, or 202 of this Act, a right under any United States letters patent, which is being used or intended for public or commercial use and not otherwise reasonably available, is necessary to enable any person required to comply with such limitation to so comply, and

(B) there are no reasonable alternative methods to accomplish such purpose, and

(2) that the unavailability of such right may result in a substantial lessening of competition or tendency to create a monopoly in any line of commerce in any section of the country,

the Attorney General may so certify to a district court of the United States, which may issue an order requiring the person who owns such patent to license it on such reasonable terms and conditions as the court, after hearing, may determine. Such certification may be made to the district court for the district in which the person owning the patent resides, does business, or is found.

POLICY REVIEW

SEC. 309. (a) The Administrator shall review and comment in writing on the environmental impact of any matter relating to duties and responsibilities granted pursuant to this Act or other provisions of the authority of the Administrator, contained in any (1) legislation proposed by any Federal department or agency, (2) newly authorized Federal projects for construction and any major Federal agency action (other than a project for construction) to which section 102(2)(C) of Public Law 91–190 applies, and (3) proposed regulations published by any department or agency of the Federal Government. Such written comment shall be made public at the conclusion of any such review.

(b) In the event the Administrator determines that any such legislation, action, or regulation is unsatisfactory from the standpoint of public health or welfare or environmental quality, he shall publish his determination and the matter shall be referred to the Council on Environmental Quality.

OTHER AUTHORITY NOT AFFECTED

SEC. 310. (a) Except as provided in subsection (b) of this section, this Act shall not be construed as superseding or limiting the authorities and responsibilities, under any other provision of law, of the Administrator or any other Federal officer, department, or agency.

(b) No appropriation shall be authorized or made under section 301, 311, or 314 of the Public Health Service Act for any fiscal year after the fiscal year ending

June 30, 1964, for any purpose for which appropriations may be made under authority of this Act.

RECORDS AND AUDIT

SEC. 311. (a) Each recipient of assistance under this Act shall keep such records as the Administrator shall prescribe, including records which fully disclose the amount and disposition by such recipient of the proceeds of such assistance, the total cost of the project or undertaking in connection with which such assistance is given or used, and the amount of that portion of the cost of the project or undertaking supplied by other sources, and such other records as will facilitate an effective audit.

(b) The Administrator and the Comptroller General of the United States, or any of their duly authorized representatives, shall have access for the purpose of audit and examinations to any books, documents, papers, and records of the recipients that are pertinent to the grants received under this Act.

COMPREHENSIVE ECONOMIC COST STUDIES AND STUDIES OF COST-EFFECTIVENESS ANALYSIS

SEC. 312. (a) In order to provide the basis for evaluating programs authorized by this act and the development of new programs and to furnish the Congress with the information necessary for authorization of appropriations by fiscal years beginning after June 30, 1969, the Administrator, in cooperation with State, interstate, and local air pollution control agencies, shall make a detailed estimate of the cost of carrying out the provisions of this Act; a comprehensive study of the cost of program implementation by affected units of government; and a comprehensive study of the economic impact of air quality standards on the Nation's industries, communities, and other contributing sources of pollution, including an analysis of the national requirements for and the cost of controlling emissions to attain such standards of air quality as may be established pursuant to this Act or applicable State law. The Administrator shall submit such detailed estimate and the results of such comprehensive study of cost for the five-year period beginning July 1, 1969, and the results of such other studies, to the Congress not later than January 10, 1969, and shall submit a reevaluation of such estimate and studies annually thereafter.

(b) The Administrator shall also make a complete investigation and study to determine (1) the need for additional trained State and local personnel to carry out programs assisted pursuant to this Act and other programs for the same purpose as this Act; (2) means of using existing Federal training programs to train such personnel; and (3) the need for additional trained personnel to develop, operate and maintain those pollution control facilities designed and installed to implement air quality standards. He shall report the results of such investigation and study to the President and the Congress not later than July 1, 1969.

(c) Not later than January 1, 1979, the Administrator shall study the possibility of increased use of cost-effectiveness analyses in devising strategies for the control of air pollution and shall report its recommendations to the Congress, including any recommendations for revisions in any provision of this Act. Such study shall also include an analysis and report to Congress concerning whether or not existing air pollution control strategies are adequate to achieve the purposes of this Act.

ADDITIONAL REPORTS TO CONGRESS

SEC. 313. Not later than six months after the effective date of this section and not later than January 10 of each calendar year beginning after such date, the Administrator shall report to the Congress on measures taken toward implementing the purpose and intent of this Act including, but not limited to, (1) the progress and problems associated with control of automotive exhaust emissions and the research efforts related thereto; (2) the development of air quality criteria and recommended emission control requirements; (3) the status of enforcement actions taken pursuant to this Act; (4) the status of State ambient air standards setting, including such plans for implementation and enforcement as have been developed; (5) the extent of development and expansion of air pollution monitoring systems: (6) progress and problems related to development of new and improved control techniques; (7) the development of quantitative and qualitative instrumentation to monitor emissions and air quality; (8) standards set or under consideration pursuant to title II of this Act; (9) the status of State, interstate, and local pollution control programs established pursuant to and assisted by this Act; (10) the reports and recommendations made by the President's Air Quality Advisory Board; and (11)(A) the status of plan provisions developed by States as required under section 110(a)(2)(F)(v), and an accounting of States failing to develop suitable plans; (B) the number of annual incidents of air pollution reaching or exceeding levels determined to present an imminent and substantial endangerment to health (within the meaning of section 303) by location, date, pollution source, and the duration of the emergency; (C) measures taken pursuant to section 110(a)(2)(F)(v), and an evaluation of their effectiveness in reducing pollution; and (D) an accounting of those instances in which an air pollution alert, warning, or emergency is declared as required under regulations of the Administrator and in which no action is taken by either the Administrator, State, or local officials, together with an explanation for the failure to take action.

LABOR STANDARDS

SEC. 314. The Administrator shall take such action as may be necessary to insure that all laborers and mechanics employed by contractors or subcontractors on projects assisted under this Act shall be paid wages at rates not less than those prevailing for the same type of work on similar construction in the locality as determined by the Secretary of Labor, in accordance with the Act of March 3, 1931, as amended, known as the Davis-Bacon Act (46 Stat. 1494; 40 U.S.C. 276a–276a–5). The Secretary of Labor shall have, with respect to the labor standards specified in this subsection, the authority and functions set forth in Reorganization Plan Numbered 14 of 1950 (15 F.R. 3176; 64 Stat. 1267) and section 2 of the Act of June 13, 1934, as amended (48 Stat. 948; 40 U.S.C. 276c).

SEPARABILITY

SEC. 315. If any provision of this Act, or the application of any provision of this Act to any person or circumstance, is held invalid, the application of such provision to other persons or circumstances, and the remainder of this Act, shall not be affected thereby.

SEWAGE TREATMENT GRANTS

SEC. 316. (a) No grant which the Administrator is authorized to make to any applicant for construction of sewage treatment works in any area in any State may be withheld, conditioned, or restricted by the Administrator on the basis of any requirement of this Act except as provided in subsection (b).

(b) The Administrator may withhold, condition, or restrict the making of any grant for construction referred to in subsection (a) only if he determines that—

(1) such treatment works will not comply with applicable standards under section 111 or 112,

(2) the State does not have in effect, or is not carrying out, a State implementation plan approved by the Administrator which expressly quantifies and provides for the increase in emissions of each air pollutant (from stationary and mobile sources in any area to which either part C or part D of title I applies for such pollutant) which increase may reasonably be anticipated to result directly or indirectly from the new sewage treatment capacity which would be created by such construction.

(3) the construction of such treatment works would create new sewage treatment capacity which—

(A) may reasonably be anticipated to cause or contribute to, directly or indirectly, an increase in emissions of any air pollutant in excess of the increase provided for under the provisions referred to in paragraph (2) for any such area, or

(B) would otherwise not be in conformity with the applicable implementation plan, or

(4) such increase in emissions would interfere with, or be inconsistent with, the applicable implementation plan for any other State.

In the case of construction of a treatment works which would result, directly or indirectly, in an increase in emissions of any air pollutant from stationary and mobile sources in an area to which part D of title I applies, the quantification of emissions referred to in paragraph (2) shall include the emissions of any such pollutant resulting directly or indirectly from areawide and nonmajor stationary source growth (mobile and stationary) for each such area.

(c) Nothing in this section shall be construed to amend or alter any provision of the National Environmental Policy Act or to affect any determination as to whether or not the requirements of such Act have been met in the case of the construction of any sewage treatment works.

ECONOMIC IMPACT ASSESSMENT

SEC. 317. (a) This section applies to action of the Administrator is promulgating or revising—

(1) any new source standard of performance under section 111(b),

(2) any regulation under section 111(d),

(3) any regulation under part B of title I (relating to ozone and stratosphere protection),

(4) any regulation under part C of title I (relating to prevention of significant deterioration of air quality),

(5) any regulation establishing emission standards under section 202 and any other regulation promulgated under that section,

(6) any regulation controlling or prohibiting any fuel or fuel additive under section 211(c), and

(7) any aircraft emission standard under section 231.

Nothing in this section shall apply to any standard or regulation described in paragraphs (1) through (7) of this subseciton unless the notice of proposed rulemaking in connection with such standard or regulation is published in the Federal Register after the date ninety days after the date of enactment of this section. In the case of revisions of such standards or regulations, this section shall apply only to revisions which the Administrator determines to be substantial revisions.

(b) Before publication of notice of proposed rulemaking with respect to any standard or regulation to which this section applies, the Administrator shall prepare an economic impact assessment respecting such standard or regulation. Such assessment shall be included in the docket required under section 307(d)(2) and shall be available to the public as provided in section 307(d)(4). Notice of proposed rulemaking shall include notice of such availability together with an explanation of the extent and manner in which the Administrator has considered the analysis contained in such economic impact assessment in proposing the action. The Administrator shall also provide such an explanation in his notice of promulgation of any regulation or standard referred to in subsection (a). Each such explanation shall be part of the statements of basis and purpose required under sections 307(d)(3) and 307(d)(6).

(c) Subject to subsection (d), the assessment required under this section with respect to any standard or regulation shall contain an analysis of—

(1) the costs of compliance with any such standard or regulation, including extent to which the costs of compliance will vary depending on (A) the effective date of the standard or regulation, and (B) the development of less expensive, more efficient means or methods of compliance with the standard or regulation;

(2) the potential inflationary or recessionary effects of the standard or regulation;

(3) the effects on competition of the standard or regulation with respect to small business;

(4) the effects of the standard or regulation on consumer costs; and

(5) the effects of the standard or regulation on energy use.

Nothing in this section shall be construed to provide that the analysis of the factors specified in this subsection affects or alters the factors which the Administrator is required to consider in taking any action referred to in subsection (a).

(d) The assessment required under this section shall be as extensive as practicable, in the judgment of the Administrator taking into account the time and resources available to the Environmental Protection Agency and other duties and authorities which the Administrator is required to carry out under this Act.

(e) Nothing in this section shall be construed—

(1) to alter the basis on which a standard or regulation is promulgated under this Act;

(2) to preclude the Administrator from carrying out his responsibility under this Act to protect public health and welfare; or

(3) to authorize or require any judicial review of any such standard or regulation, or any stay or injunction of the proposal, promulgation, or effectiveness of such standard or regulation on the basis of failure to comply with this section.

(f) The requirements imposed on the Administrator under this section shall be treated as nondiscretionary duties for purposes of section 304(a)(2), relating to citizen suits. The sole method for enforcement of the Administrator's duty under this section shall be by bringing a citizen suit under such section 304(a)(2) for a court order to compel the Administrator to perform such duty. Violation of any such order shall subject the Administrator to penalties for contempt of court.

(g) In the case of any provision of this Act in which costs are expressly required to be taken into account, the adequacy or inadequacy of any assessment required under this section may be taken into consideration, but shall not be treated for purposes of judicial review of any such provision as conclusive with respect to compliance or noncompliance with the requirement of such provision to take cost into account.

FINANCIAL DISCLOSURE; CONFLICTS OF INTEREST

SEC. 318. (a) Each person who—

(1) has any known financial interest in (A) any person subject to this Act, or (B) any person who applies for or receives any grant, contract, or other form of financial assistance pursuant to this Act, and

(2) is (A) an officer or employee of the Environmental Protection Agency who performs any function of duty under this Act, (B) a member of the National Commission on Air Quality appointed as a member of the public, or (C) a member of the scientific review committee under section 109(d)

shall, beginning six months after the date of enactment of this section, annually file with the Administrator, a written statement concerning all such interests held by such officer, employee, or member during the preceding calendar year. Such statement shall be available to the public.

(b) The Administrator shall—

(1) act within ninety days after the date of enactment of the Clean Air Act Amendments of 1977—

(A) to define the term "known financial interest" for purposes of subsection (a) of this section;

(B) to establish the methods by which the requirement to file written statements specified in subsection (a) of this section will be monitored and enforced, including appropriate provisions for the filing by such officers, employees and members of such statements and the review by the Administrator (or the Commission in the case of members of the Commission) of such statements; and

(2) report to the Congress on June 1 of each calendar year with respect to such statements to the Administrator and the actions taken in regard thereto during the preceding calendar year.

(c) After the date one year after the date of the enactment of this section, no person who—

(1) is employed by, serves as attorney for, acts as a consultant for, or holds any other official or contractual relationship to—

(A) the owner or operator of any major stationary source or any stationary source which is subject to a standard of performance or emission standard under section 111 or 112,

(B) any manufacturer of any class or category of mobile sources if such mobile sources are subject to regulation under this Act,

(C) any trade or business association of which such owner or operator referred to in subparagraph (A) or such manufacturer referred to in subparagraph (B) is a member or

(D) any organization (whether or not nonprofit) which is a party to litigation, or engaged in political, educational, or informational activities, relating to air quality, or

(2) owns, or has any financial interest in, any stock, bonds, or other financial interest which ownership or interest may be inconsistent with a position as an officer or employee of the Environmental Protection Agency, as determined under regulations of the Administrator,

may concurrently serve as such an officer or employee of the Environmental Protection Agency.

(d) The Administrator shall promulgate rules for purposes of subsections (b) and (c) which—

(1) identify specific offices or positions within such agency which are of a nonregulatory or nonpolicymaking nature and provide that officers or employees occupying such positions shall be exempt from the requirements of this section, and

(2) identify the ownership or financial interests which may be inconsistent with particular regulatory or policymaking offices or positions within the Environmental Protection Agency.

(e) Any officer or employee of the Environmental Protection Agency or member of the National Commission on Air Quality or of the scientific review committee under section 109(d) who is subject to, and knowingly violates, this section or any regulation issued thereunder, shall be fined not more than $2,500 or imprisoned not more than one year, or both.

(f) Nothing in this section shall be construed to affect or impair any other Federal statutory requirements respecting disclosure or conflict of interest applicable to the Environmental Protection Agency. Subsections (c) and (d) of this section shall not apply after the effective date of any such requirements respecting conflicts of interest which are generally applicable to departments, agencies, and instrumentalities of the United States.

AIR QUALITY MONITORING

SEC. 319. Not later than one year after the date of enactment of the Clean Air Act Amendments of 1977 and after notice and opportunity for public hearing, the Administrator shall promulgate regulations establishing an air quality monitoring system throughout the United States which—

(1) utilizes uniform air quality monitoring criteria and methodology and measures such air quality according to a uniform air quality index,

(2) provides for air quality monitoring stations in major urban areas and other appropriate areas throughout the United States to provide monitoring such as will supplement (but not duplicate) air quality monitoring carried out by the States required under any applicable implementation plan,

(3) provides for daily analysis and reporting of air quality based upon such uniform air quality index, and

(4) provides for recordkeeping with respect to such monitoring data and for periodic analysis and reporting to the general public by the Administrator with respect to air quality based upon such data.

The operation of such air quality monitoring system may be carried out by the Administrator or by such other departments, agencies, or entities of the Federal Government (including the National Weather Service) as the President may deem appropriate. Any air quality monitoring system required under any applicable implementation plan under section 110 shall, as soon as practicable following promulgation of regulations under this section, utilize the standard criteria and methodology, and measure air quality according to the standard index, established under such regulations.

STANDARDIZED AIR QUALITY MODELING

SEC. 320. (a) Not later than six months after the date of the enactment of the Clean Air Act Amendments of

1977, and at least every three years thereafter, the Administrator shall conduct a conference on air quality modeling. In conducting such conference, special attention shall be given to appropriate modeling necessary for carrying out part C of title I (relating to prevention of significant deterioration of air quality).

(b) The conference conducted under this section shall provide for participation by the National Academy of Sciences, representatives of State and local air pollution control agencies, and appropriate Federal agencies, including the National Science Foundation; the National Oceanic and Atmospheric Administration, and the National Bureau of Standards.

(c) Interested persons shall be permitted to submit written comments and a verbatim transcript of the conference proceedings shall be maintained.

(d) The comments submitted and the transcript maintained pursuant to subsection (c) shall be included in the docket required to be established for purposes of promulgating or revising any regulation relating to air quality modeling under part C of title I.

EMPLOYMENT EFFECTS

SEC. 321. (a) The Administrator shall conduct continuing evaluations of potential loss or shifts of employment which may result from the administration or enforcement of the provision of this Act and applicable implementation plans, including where appropriate, investigating threatened plant closures or reductions in employment allegedly resulting from such administration or enforcement.

(b) Any employee, or any representative of such employee, who is discharged or laid off, threatened with discharge or layoff, or whose employment is otherwise adversely affected or threatened to be adversely affected because of the alleged results of any requirement imposed or proposed to be imposed under this Act, including any requirement applicable to Federal facilities and any requirement imposed by a State or political subdivision thereof, may request the Administrator to conduct a full investigation of the matter. Any such request shall be reduced to writing, shall set forth with reasonable particularity the grounds for the request, and shall be signed by the employee, or representative of such employee, making the request. The Administrator shall thereupon investigate the matter and, at the request of any party, shall hold public hearings on not less than five days' notice. At such hearings, the Administrator shall require the parties, including the employer involved, to present information relating to the actual or potential effect of such requirements on employment and the detailed reasons or justification therefor. If the Administrator determines that there are no reasonable grounds for conducting a public hearing he shall notify (in writing) the party requesting such hearing of such a determination and the reasons therefor. If the Administrator does convene such a hearing, the hearing shall be on the record. Upon receiving the report of such investigation, the Administrator shall make findings of fact as to the effect of such requirements on employment and on the alleged actual or potential discharge, layoff, or other adverse effect on employment, and shall make such recommendations as he deems appropriate. Such report, findings, and recommendations shall be available to the public.

(c) In connection with any investigation or public hearing conducted under subsection (b) of this section or as authorized in section 119 (relating to primary nonferrous smelter orders), the Administrator may issue subpenas for the attendance and testimony of witnesses and the production of revelant papers, books and documents, and he may administer oaths. Except for emission data, upon a showing satisfactory to the Administrator by such owner or operator that such papers, books, documents, or information or particular part thereof, if made public, would divulge trade secrets or secret processes of such owner, or operator, the Administrator shall consider such record, report, or information or particular portion thereof confidential in accordance with the purposes of section 1905 of title 18 of the United States Code, except that such paper, book, document, or information may be disclosed to other officers, employees, or authorized representatives of the United States concerned with carrying out this Act, or when relevant in any proceeding under this Act. Witnesses summoned shall be paid the same fees and mileage that are paid witnesses in the courts of the United States. In cases of contumacy or refusal to obey a subpena served upon any person under this subparagraph, the district court of the United States for any district in which such person is found or resides or transacts business, upon application by the United States and after notice to such person, shall have jurisdiction to issue an order requiring such person to appear and give testimony before the Administrator, to appear and produce papers, books, and documents before the Administrator, or both, and any failure to obey such order of the court may be punished by such court as a contempt thereof.

(d) Nothing in this section shall be construed to require or authorize the Administrator, the States, or political subdivisions thereof, to modify or withdraw any requirement imposed or proposed to be imposed under this Act.

EMPLOYEE PROTECTION

SEC. 322. (a) No employer may discharge any employee or otherwise discriminate against any employee with respect to his compensation, terms, conditions, or privileges of employment because the employee (or any person acting pursuant to a request of the employee)—

(1) commenced, caused to be commenced, or is about to commence or cause to be commenced a proceeding under this Act or a proceeding for the administration or enforcement of any requirement imposed under this Act or under any applicable implementation plan.

(2) testified or is about to testify in any such proceeding, or

(3) assisted or participated or is about to assist or participate in any manner in such a proceeding or in any other action to carry out the purposes of this Act.

(b)(1) Any employee who believes that he has been discharged or otherwise discriminated against by any person in violation of subsection (a) may, within thirty days after such violation occurs, file (or have any person file on his behalf) a complaint with the Secretary of Labor (hereinafter in this subsection referred to as the "Secretary") alleging such discharge or discrimination. Upon receipt of such a complaint, the Secretary shall notify the person named in the complaint of the filing of the complaint.

(2)(A) Upon receipt of a complaint filed under paragraph (1), the Secretary shall conduct an investigation of the violation alleged in the complaint. Within thirty days of the receipt of such complaint, the Secretary shall complete such investigation and shall notify in writing the complainant (and any person acting in his behalf) and the person alleged to have committed such violation of the results of the investigation conducted pursuant to this subparagraph. Within ninety days of the receipt of such complaint the Secretary shall, unless the proceeding on the complaint is terminated by the Secretary on the basis of a settlement entered into by the Secretary and the person alleged to have committed such violation, issue an order either providing the relief prescribed by subparagraph (B) or denying the complaint. An order of the Secretary shall be made on the record after notice and opportunity for public hearing. The Secretary may not enter into a settlement terminating a proceeding on a complaint without the participation and consent of the complainant.

(B) If, in response to a complaint filed under paragraph (1), the Secretary determines that a violation of subsection (a) has occurred, the Secretary shall order the person who committed such violation to (i) take affirmative action to abate the violation, and (ii) reinstate the complainant to his former position together with the compensation (including back pay), terms, conditions, and privileges of his employment, and the Secretary may order such person to provide compensatory damages to the complainant. If an order is issued under this paragraph, the Secretary, at the request of the complainant, shall assess against the person against whom the order is issued a sum equal to the aggregate amount of all costs and expenses (including attorneys' and expert witness fees) reasonably incurred, as determined by the Secretary, by the complainant for, or in connection with, the bringing of the complaint upon which the order was issued.

(c)(1) Any person adversely affected or aggrieved by an order issued under subsection (b) may obtain review of the order in the United States court of appeals for the circuit in which the violation, with respect to which the order was issued, allegedly occurred. The petition for review must be filed within sixty days from the issuance of the Secretary's order. Review shall conform to chapter 7 of title 5 of the United States Code. The commencement of proceedings under this subparagraph shall not, unless ordered by the court, operate as a stay of the Secretary's order.

(2) An order of the Secretary with respect to which review could have been obtained under paragraph (1) shall not be subject to judicial review in any criminal or other civil proceeding.

(d) Whenever a person has failed to comply with an order issued under subsection (b)(2), the Secretary may file a civil action in the United States district court for the district in which the violation was found to occur to enforce such order. In actions brought under this subsection, the district courts shall have jurisdiction to grant all appropriate relief including, but not limited to, injunctive relief, compensatory, and exemplary damages.

(e)(1) Any person on whose behalf an order was issued under paragraph (2) of subsection (b) may commence a civil action against the person to whom such order was issued to require compliance with such order. The appropriate United States district court shall have jurisdiction, without regard to the amount in controversy or the citizenship of the parties, to enforce such order.

(2) The court, in issuing any final order under this subsection, may award costs of litigation (including reasonable attorney and expert witness fees) to any party whenever the court determines such award is appropriate.

(f) Any nondiscretionary duty imposed by this section shall be enforceable in a mandamus proceeding brought under section 1361 of title 28 of the United States Code.

(g) Subsection (a) shall not apply with respect to any employee who, acting without direction from his employer (or the employer's agent), deliberately causes a violation of any requirement of this Act.

[The renumbering of the following sections is in accordance with Public Law 96–300].

COST OF EMISSION CONTROL FOR CERTAIN VAPOR RECOVERY TO BE BORNE BY OWNER OF RETAIL OUTLET

SEC. ~~324.~~ *323* (a) The regulations under this Act applicable to vapor recovery with respect to mobile source fuels at retail outlets of such fuels shall provide that the cost of procurement and installation of such vapor recovery shall be borne by the owner of such outlet (as determined under such regulations). Except as provided in subsection (b), such regulations shall provide that no lease of a retail outlet by the owner thereof which is entered into or renewed after the date of enactment of the Clean Air Act Amendments of 1977 may provide for a payment by the lessee of the cost of procurement and installation of vapor recovery equipment. Such regulations shall also provide that the cost of procurement and installation of vapor recovery equipment may be recovered by the owner of such outlet by means of price increases in the cost of any product sold by such owner, notwithstanding any provision of law.

(b) The regulations of the Administrator referred to in subsection (a) shall permit a lease of a retail outlet to provide for payment by the lessee of the cost of procurement and installation of vapor recovery requirement over a reasonable period (as determined in accordance with such regulations), if the owner of such outlet does not sell, trade in, or otherwise dispense any product at wholesale or retail at such outlet.

VAPOR RECOVERY FOR SMALL BUSINESS MARKETERS OF PETROLEUM PRODUCTS

SEC. ~~325.~~ *324* (a) The regulations under this Act applicable to vapor recovery from fueling of motor vehicles at retail outlets of gasoline shall not apply to any outlet owned by an independent small business marketer of gasoline having monthly sales of less than 50,000 gallons. In the case of any other outlet owned by an independent small business marketer, such regulations shall provide, with respect to independent small business marketers of gasoline, for a three-year phase-in period for the installation of such vapor recovery equipment at such outlets under which such marketers shall have—

(1) 33 percent of such outlets in compliance at the end of the first year during which such regulations apply to such marketers,

(2) 66 percent at the end of such second year, and

(3) 100 percent at the end of the third year.

(b) Nothing in subsection (a) shall be construed to prohibit any State from adopting or enforcing, with respect to independent small business marketers of gasoline

having monthly sales of less than 50,000 gallons, any vapor recovery requirements for mobile source fuels at retail outlets. Any vapor recovery requirement which is adopted by a State and submitted to the Administrator as part of its implementation plan may be approved and enforced by the Administrator as part of the applicable implementation plan for that State.

(c) For purposes of this section, an independent small business marketer of gasoline is a person engaged in the marketing of gasoline who would be required to pay for procurement and installation of vapor recovery equipment under section 324 of this Act or under regulations of the Administrator, unless such person—

(1) (A) is a refiner, or

(B) controls, is controlled by, or is under common control with, a refiner.

(C) is otherwise directly or indirectly affiliated (as determined under the regulations of the Administrator) with a refiner or with a person who controls, is controlled by, or is under a common control with a refiner (unless the sole affiliation referred to herein is by means of a supply contract or an agreement or contract to use a trademark, trade name, service mark, or other identifying symbol or name owned by such refiner or any such person), or

(2) receives less than 50 percent of his annual income from refining or marketing of gasoline.

For the purpose of this section, the term "refiner" shall not include any refiner whose total refinery capacity (including the refinery capacity of any person who controls, is controlled by, or is under common control with, such refiner) does not exceed 65,000 barrels per day. For purposes of this section, "control" of a corporation means ownership of more than 50 percent of its stock.

CONSTRUCTION OF CERTAIN CLAUSES

SEC. ~~326.~~ *325* The parenthetical cross references in any provision of this Act to other provisions of the Act, or other provisions of law, where the words "relating to" or "pertaining to" are used, are made only for convenience, and shall be given no legal effect.

APPROPRIATIONS

SEC. ~~327.~~ *326* (a) There are authorized to be appropriated to carry out this Act (other than provisions for which amounts are authorized under subsection (b)), $200,000,000 for the fiscal year 1978 and for each of the three fiscal years beginning thereafter.

(b) (1) There are authorized to be appropriated to carry out section 175 beginning in fiscal year 1978, $75,000,000 to be available until expended.

(2) There are authorized to be appropriated for use in carrying out section 323 (relating to National Commission on Air Quality), not to exceed $10,000,000 beginning in fiscal year 1978. For the study authorized under section 323 there shall be made available by contract to the National Commission on Air Quality from the appropriation to the Environmental Protection Agency for fiscal year 1977 the sum of $1,000,000.

(3) There are authorized to be appropriated to carry out section 127 (relating to grants for public notification) $4,000,000 for the fiscal year 1978 and each of the three succeeding fiscal years.

(4) For purposes of section 103(a)(5), there are authorized to be appropriated $7,500,000 for the fiscal year 1978 and each of the three fiscal years beginning after the date of enactment of the Clean Air Act Amendments of 1977.

(5) For the purpose of carrying out the provisions of part B of title I relating to studies and reports, there are authorized to be appropriated—

(A) to the National Aeronautics and Space Administration, the National Science Foundation, and the Department of State, such sums as may be necessary for the fiscal year ending September 30, 1977, and the fiscal year ending September 30, 1978;

(B) to the Environmental Protection Agency, $157,000,000 for fiscal year 1978; and

(C) to all other agencies such sums as may be necessary.

(6) There are authorized to be appropriated for carrying out research, development and demonstration under sections 103 and 104 of this Act $120,000,000 for fiscal year 1978.

PROVISIONS OF PUBLIC LAW 95-95 WHICH DO NOT AMEND THE CLEAN AIR ACT

* * * * *

TRAINING

SEC. 101. (a) * * *

* * * * *

(c) The Administrator of the Environmental Protection Agency shall consult with the House Committee on Science and Technology on the environmental and atmospheric research, development, and demonstration aspects of this Act. In addition, the reports and studies required by this Act that relate to research, development, and demonstration issues shall be transmitted to the Committee on Science and Technology at the same time they are made available to other committees of the Congress.

* * * * *

COMPLIANCE ORDERS (INCLUDING COAL CONVERSION)

SEC. 112. (a) * * *

* * * * *

(b)(1) Section 119 of such Act is hereby repealed. All references to such section 119 or subsections thereof in section 2 of the Energy Supply and Environmental Coordination Act of 1974 (Public Law 93-319) or any amendment thereto, or any subsequent enactment which supersedes such Act, shall be construed to refer to section 113(d) of the Clean Air Act and to paragraph (5) thereof in particular. Any certification or notification required to be given by the Administrator of the Environmental Protection Agency under section 2 of the Energy Supply and Environmental Coordination Act of 1974 or any amendment thereto, or any subsequent enactment which supersedes such Act, shall be given only when the Governor of the State in which is located the source to which the proposed order under section 113(d)(5) of the Clean Air Act is to be issued gives his prior written concurrence.

(2) In the case of any major stationary source to which any requirement is applicable under section 113(d)(5)(B) of the Clean Air Act and for which certification is required under section 2 of the Energy Supply and Environmental Coordination Act of 1974 or any amendment thereto, or any subsequent enactment which

supersedes such Act, the Administrator of the Environmental Protection Agency shall certify the date which he determines is the earliest date that such source will be able to comply with all such requirements. In the case of any plant or installation which the Administrator of the Environmental Protection Agency determines (after consultation with the State) will not be subject to an order under section 113(d) of the Clean Air Act and for which certification is required under section 2 of the Energy Supply and Environmental Coordination Act of 1974 or any amendment thereto, or any subsequent enactment which supersedes such Act, the Administrator of the Environmental Protection Agency shall certify the date which he determines is the earliest date that such plant or installation will be able to burn coal in compliance with all applicable emission limitations under the implementation plan.

(3) Any certification required under section 2 of the Energy Supply and Environmental Coordination Act of 1974 or any amendment thereto, or any subsequent enactment which supersedes such Act, or under this subsection may be provided in an order under section 113(d) of the Clean Air Act.

* * * * *

UNREGULATED POLLUTANTS

SEC. 120. (a) * * *

* * * * *

(b) The Administrator of the Environmental Protection Agency shall conduct a study, in conjunction with other appropriate agencies, concerning the effect on the public health and welfare of sulfates, radioactive pollutants, cadmium, arsenic, and polycyclic organic matter which are present or may reasonably be anticipated to occur in the ambient air. Such study shall include a thorough investigation of how sulfates are formed and how to protect public health and welfare from the injurious effects, if any, of sulfates, cadmium, arsenic, and polycyclic organic matter.

* * * * *

PREVENTION OF SIGNIFICANT DETERIORATION

SEC. 127. (a) * * *

* * * * *

(b) Within one year from the date of enactment of this Act the Administrator shall report to the Congress on the consequences of that portion of the definition of "major emitting facility" under the amendment made by subsection (a) which applies to facilities with the potential to emit two hundred and fifty tons per year or more. Such study shall examine the type of facilities covered, the air quality benefits of including such facilities, and the administrative aspect of regulating such facilities.

(c) Not later than one year after the date of enactment of this Act, the Administrator shall publish a guidance document to assist the States in carrying out their functions under part C of title I of the Clean Air Act (relating to prevention of significant deterioration of air quality) with respect to pollutants, other than sulfur oxides and particulates, for which national ambient air quality standards are promulgated. Such guidance document shall include recommended strategies for controlling photochemical oxidants on a regional or multistate basis for the purpose of implementing part C and section 110 of such Act.

(d) Not later than two years after the date of enactment of this Act, the Administrator shall complete a study and report to the Congress on the progress made in carrying out part C of title I of the Clean Air Act (relating to significant deterioration of air quality) and the problems associated with carrying out such section, including recommendations for legislative changes necessary to implement strategies for controlling photochemical oxidants on a regional or multistate basis.

* * * * *

NONATTAINMENT AREAS

SEC. 129. (a)(1) Before July 1, 1979, the interpretative regulation of the Administrator of the Environmental Protection Agency published in 41 Federal Register 55524–30, December 21, 1976, as may be modified by rule of the Administrator, shall apply except that the baseline to be used for determination of appropriate emission offsets under such regulation shall be the applicable implementation plan of the State in effect at the time of application for a permit by a proposed major stationary source (within the meaning of section 302 of the Clean Air Act).

(2) Before July 1, 1979, the requirements of the regulation referred to in paragraph (1) shall be waived by the Administrator with respect to any pollutant if he determines that the State has—

(A) an inventory of emissions of the applicable pollutant for each nonattainment area (as defined in section 171 of the Clean Air Act) that identifies the type, quantity, and source of such pollutant so as to provide information sufficient to demonstrate that the requirements of subparagraph (C) are being met;

(B) an enforceable permit program which—

(i) requires new or modified major stationary sources to meet emission limitations at least as stringent as required under the permit requirements referred to in paragraphs (2) and (3) of section 173 of the Clean Air Act (relating to lowest achievable emission rate and compliance by other sources) and which assures compliance with the annual reduction requirements of subparagraph (C); and

(ii) requires existing sources to achieve such reduction in emissions in the area as may be obtained through the adoption, at a minimum of reasonably available control technology, and

(C) a program which requires reductions in total allowable emissions in the area prior to July 1, 1979, so as to provide for the same level of emission reduction as would result from the application of the regulation referred to in paragraph (1).

The Administrator shall terminate such waiver if in his judgment the reduction in emissions actually being attained is less than the reduction on which the waiver was conditioned pursuant to subparagraph (C), or if the Administrator determines that the State is no longer in compliance with any requirement of this paragraph. Upon application by the State, the Administrator may reinstate a waiver terminated under the preceding sentence if he is satisfied that such State is in compliance with all requirements of this subsection.

(3) Operating permits may be issued to those applicants who were properly granted construction permits, in accordance with the law and applicable regulations in effect at the time granted, for construction of a new or modified source in areas exceeding national primary air quality standards on or before the date of the enactment of this Act if such construction permits were granted prior to the date of the enactment of this Act and the person issued any such permit is able to demonstrate that the emissions from the source will be within the limitations set forth in such construction permit.

* * * * *

(c) Notwithstanding the requirements of section 406(d)(2) (relating to date required for submission of certain implementation plan revisions), for purposes of section 110(a)(2) of the Clean Air Act each State in which there is any nonattainment area (as defined in part D of title I of the Clean Air Act) shall adopt and submit an implementation plan revision which meets the requirements of section 110(a)(2)(I) and part D of title I of the Clean Air Act not later than January 1, 1979. In the case of any State for which a plan revision adopted and submitted before such date has made the demonstration required under section 172(a)(2) of the Clean Air Act (respecting impossibility of attainment before 1983), such State shall adopt and submit to the Administrator a plan revision before July 1, 1982, which meets the requirements of section 172 (b) and (c) of such Act.

* * * * *

STUDIES AND RESEARCH OBJECTIVES FOR OXIDES OF NITROGEN

SEC. 202. (a) The Administrator of the Environmental Protection Agency shall conduct a study of the public health implications of attaining an emission standard on oxides of nitrogen from light duty vehicles of 0.4 gram per vehicle mile, the cost and technological capability of attaining such standard, and the need for such a standard to protect public health or welfare. The Administrator shall submit a report of such study to the Congress, together with recommendations not later than July 1, 1980.

* * * * *

STUDY AND REPORT OF FUEL CONSUMPTION

SEC. 203. (a) Following each motor vehicle model year, the Administrator of the Environmental Protection Agency shall report to the Congress respecting the motor vehicle fuel consumption associated with the standards applicable for the immediately preceding model year.

(b) The Secretary of Transportation and the Secretary of Energy shall each submit to Congress, as promptly as practicable following submission by the Administrator of the fuel consumption report referred to in subsection (a), separate reports respecting such fuel consumption.

* * * * *

CARBON MONOXIDE INTRUSION INTO SUSTAINED USE VEHICLES

SEC. 226. (a) The Administrator, in conjunction with the Secretary of Transportation, shall study the problem of carbon monoxide intrusion into the passenger area of sustained-use motor vehicles. Such study shall include an analysis of the sources and levels of carbon monoxide in the passenger area of such vehicles and a determination of the effects of carbon monoxide upon the passengers. The study shall also review available methods of monitoring and testing for the presence of carbon monoxide and shall analyze the cost and effectiveness of alternative methods of monitoring and testing. The study shall analyze the cost and effectiveness of alternative strategies for attaining and maintaining acceptable levels of carbon monoxide in the passenger area of such vehicles. Within one year the Administrator shall report to the Congress respecting the results of such study.

(b) For the purpose of this section, the term "sustained-use motor vehicle" means any diesel or gasoline fueled motor vehicle (whether light or heavy duty) which, as determined by the Administrator (in conjunction with the Secretary), is normally used and occupied for a sustained, continuous, or extensive period of time, including buses, taxicabs, and police vehicles.

* * * * *

INTERAGENCY COOPERATION ON PREVENTION OF ENVIRONMENTAL CANCER AND HEART AND LUNG DISEASE

SEC. 402. (a) Not later than three months after the date of enactment of this section, there shall be established a Task Force on Environmental Cancer and Heart and Lung Disease (hereinafter referred to as the 'Task Force'). The Task Force shall include representatives of the Environmental Protection Agency, the National Cancer Institute, the National Heart, Lung, and Blood Institute, the National Institute of Occupational Safety and Health, and the National Institute on Environmental Health Sciences, and shall be chaired by the Administrator (or his delegate).

(b) The Task Force shall—

(1) recommend a comprehensive research program to determine and quantify the relationship between environmental pollution and human cancer and heart and lung disease;

(2) recommend comprehensive strategies to reduce or eliminate the risks of cancer or such other diseases associated with environmental pollution;

(3) recommend research and such other measures as may be appropriate to prevent or reduce the incidence of environmentally related cancer and heart and lung diseases;

(4) coordinate research by, and stimulate cooperation between, the Environmental Protection Agency, the Department of Health, Education, and Welfare, and such other agencies as may be appropriate to prevent environmentally related cancer and heart and lung diseases: and

(5) report to Congress, not later than one year after the date of enactment of this section and annually thereafter, on the problems and progress in carrying out this section.

STUDIES

SEC. 403. (a) Not later than eighteen months after the date of the enactment of this Act, the Administrator of the Environmental Protection Agency, in cooperation with the National Academy of Sciences, shall study and report to Congress on (1) the relationship between the size, weight, and chemical composition of suspended particulate matter and the nature and degree of the endangerment to public health or welfare presented by such particulate matter (especially with respect to fine particulate matter) and (2) the availability of technology for controlling such particulate matter.

(b) The Administrator of the Environmental Protection Agency shall conduct a study and report to the Congress not later than January 1, 1979, on the effects on public health and welfare of odors or odorous emissions, the sources of such emissions, the technology or other measures available for control of such emissions and the costs of such technology or measures, and the costs and benefits of alternative measures or strategies to abate such emissions. Such report shall include an evaluation of whether air quality criteria or national ambient air quality standards should be published under the Clean Air Act for odors, and what other strategies or authorities under the Clean Air Act are available or appropriate for abating such emissions.

(c) (1) Not later than twelve months after the date of enactment of this Act the Administrator of the Environmental Protection Agency shall publish throughout the United States a list of all known chemical contaminants resulting from environmental pollution which have been found in human tissue including blood, urine, breast milk, and all other human tissue. Such list shall be prepared for the United States and shall indicate the approximate number of cases, the range of levels found, and the mean levels found.

(2) Not later than eighteen months after the date of enactment of this Act the Administrator shall publish in the same manner an explanation of what is known about the manner in which the chemicals described in paragraph (1) entered the environment and thereafter human tissue.

(3) The Administrator, in consultation with National Institutes of Health, the National Center for Health Statistics, and the National Center for Health Services Research and Development, shall, if feasible, conduct an epidemiological study to demonstrate the relationship between levels of chemicals in the environment and in human tissue. Such study shall be made in appropriate regions or areas of the United States in order to determine any different results in such regions or areas. The results of such study shall, as soon as practicable, be reported to the appropriate committee of the Congress.

(d) The Administrator of the Environmental Protection Agency shall conduct a study of air quality in various areas throughout the country including the gulf coast region. Such study shall include analysis of liquid and solid aerosols and other fine particulate matter and the contribution of such substances to visibility and public health problems in such areas. For the purposes of this study, the Administrator shall use environmental health experts from the National Institutes of Health and other outside agencies and organizations.

(e) (1) The Secretary of Labor, in consultation with the Administrator, shall conduct a study of potential dislocation of employees due to implementation of laws administered by the Administrator. Such study shall estimate the number of employees so affected, identify existing sources of assistance available to such employees, assess the adequacy of such assistance, and recommend additional adjustment measures, if justified.

(2) The Secretary shall submit to Congress the results of the study conducted under paragraph (1) not more than one year after the date of enactment of this section.

(f) The Administrator of the Environmental Protection Agency shall undertake to enter into appropriate arrangements with the National Academy of Sciences to conduct continuing comprehensive studies and investigations of the effects on public health and welfare of emissions subject to section 202(a) of the Clean Air Act (including sulfur compounds) and the technological feasibility of meeting emission standards required to be prescribed by the Administrator by section 202(b) of such Act. The Administrator shall report to the Congress within six months of the date of enactment of this section and each year thereafter regarding the status of the contractual arrangements and conditions necessary to implement this paragraph.

(g) The Administrator of the Environmental Protection Agency shall conduct a study and report to Congress by the date one year after the date of the enactment of this section, on the emission of sulfur-bearing compounds from motor vehicles and motor vehicle engines and aircraft engines. Such study and report shall include but not be limited to a review of the effects of such emissions on public health and welfare and an analysis of the costs and benefits of alternatives to reduce or eliminate such emissions (including desulfurization of fuel, short-term allocation of low sulfur crude oil, technological devices used in conjunction with current engine technologies, alternative engine technologies, and other methods) as may be required to achieve any proposed or promulgated emission standards for sulfur compounds.

RAILROAD EMISSION STUDY

SEC. 404. (a) The Administrator of the Environmental Protection Agency shall conduct a study and investigation of emissions of air pollutants from railroad locomotives, locomotive engines, and secondary power sources on railroad rolling stock, in order to determine—

(1) the extent to which such emissions affect air quality in air quality control regions throughout the United States,

(2) the technological feasibility and the current state of technology for controlling such emissions, and

(3) the status and effect of current and proposed State and local regulations affecting such emissions.

(b) Within one hundred and eighty days after commencing such study and investigation, the Administrator shall submit a report of such study and investigation, together with recommendations for appropriate legislation, to the Senate Committee on Environment and Public Works and the House Committee on Interstate and Foreign Commerce.

STUDY AND REPORT CONCERNING ECONOMIC APPROACHES TO CONTROLLING AIR POLLUTION

SEC. 405. (a) The Administrator, in conjunction with the Council of Economic Advisors (hereinafter in this section referred to as 'the Council'), shall undertake a study and assessment of economic measures for the control of air pollution which could—

(1) strengthen the effectiveness of existing methods of controlling air pollution,

(2) provide incentives to abate air pollution to a greater degree than is required by existing provisions of the Clean Air Act (and regulations thereunder), and

(3) serve as the primary incentive for controlling air pollution problems not addressed by any provision of the Clean Air Act (or any regulation thereunder).

(b) The study of measures referred to in paragraph (1) of subsection (a) shall concentrate on (1) identification of air pollution problems for which existing methods of control are not effective because of economic incentives to delay compliance and (2) formulation of economic measures which could be taken with respect to each such air pollution problem which would provide an incentive to comply without interfering with such existing methods of control.

(c) The study of measures referred to in paragraph (2) of subsection (a) shall concentrate on (1) identification of air pollution problems for which existing methods of control may not be sufficiently extensive to achieve all desired environmental goals and (2) formulation of economic measures for each such air pollution problem which would provide additional incentives to reduce air pollution without—

(A) interfering with the effectiveness of existing methods of control, or

(B) creating problems similar to those which prevent alternative regulatory methods from being used to reach such environmental goals.

(d) The study of the measures referred to in paragraph (3) of subsection (a) shall concentrate on (1) identification of air pollution problems for which no existing methods of control exist, (2) formulation of economic measures to reduce such pollution, and (3) comparison of the environmental and economic impacts of the economic measures with those of any alternative regulatory methods which can be identified.

(e) In conducting the study under this section, a preliminary screening should be made of the problems referred to in subsections (b)(1), (c)(1), and (d)(1) and economic measures should be formulated under subsections (b)(2), (c)(2), and (d)(2) in the most promising cases, giving special attention to structural and administrative problems. In formulating any such measure which provides for a charge, the appropriate level of the charge should be determined, if possible, and the environmental and economic impacts should be identified.

(f) Within one year after the date of enactment of this Act, the Administrator shall complete a study and report to the Congress on the advantages and disadvantages (including an analysis of the feasibility) of establishing a system of penalties for stationary sources on emissions of oxides of nitrogen and make recommendations regarding the establishment of such a system. Such study shall determine if such a system will effectively encourage the development of more effective systems and technologies for control of emissions of oxides of nitrogen for new major emitting facilities, or existing major emitting facilities, or both. In any case in which a proposed penalty system is recommended by the Administrator, the report should include—

(1) a recommendation respecting the appropriate period during which such system of penalties should apply, and the appropriate termination date or dates for such system, if any, taking into account—

(A) the time at which adequate technology may reasonably be anticipated to be available to control oxides of nitrogen for that category of facilities,

(B) the degree to which such technology can be expected to be used on such facilities, and

(C) the Administrator's authorities to require the use of such technology, and

(2) recommendations respecting the compilation of records by facilities subject to such penalties for purposes of determining the applicability and amount of such penalty.

(g) Not later than two years after the date of the enactment of this section, the Administrator and the Council shall conclude the study and assessment under this section and submit a report containing the results thereof to the President and to the Congress. Interim reports on specific pollution problems and solutions recommended shall be made available to the President and the Congress by the Administrator whenever available.

SAVING PROVISION; EFFECTIVE DATES

SEC. 406. (a) No suit, action, or other proceeding lawfully commenced by or against the Administrator or any other officer or employee of the United States in his official capacity or in relation to the discharge of his official duties under the Clean Air Act, as in effect immediately prior to the date of enactment of this Act shall abate by reason of the taking effect of the amendments made by this Act. The court may, on its own motion or that of any party made at any time within twelve months after such taking effect, allow the same to be maintained by or against the Administrator or such officer or employee.

(b) All rules, regulations, orders, determinations, contracts, certifications, authorizations, delegations, or other actions duly issued, made, or taken by or pursuant to the Clean Air Act as in effect immediately prior to the date of enactment of this Act, and pertaining to any functions, powers, requirements, and duties under the Clean Air Act, as in effect immediately prior to the date of enactment of this Act, and not suspended by the Administrator or the courts, shall continue in full force and effect after the date of enactment of this Act until modified or rescinded in accordance with the Clean Air Act as amended by this Act.

(c) Nothing in this Act nor any action taken pursuant to this Act shall in any way affect any requirement of an approved implementation plan in effect under section 110 of the Clean Air Act or any other provision of the Act in effect under the Clean Air Act before the date of enactment of this section until modified or rescinded in accordance with the Clean Air Act as amended by this Act.

(d)(1) Except as otherwise expressly provided, the amendments made by this Act shall be effective on date of enactment.

(2) Except as otherwise expressly provided, each State required to revise its applicable implementation plan by reason of any amendment made by this Act shall adopt and submit to the Administrator of the Environmental Protection Administration such plan revision before the later of the date—

(A) one year after the date of enactment of this Act, or

(B) nine months after the date of promulgation by the Administrator of the Environmental Protection Administration of any regulations under an amendment made by this Act which are necessary for the approval of such plan revision.

NOTE

Public Law 96–300 amended the following section and also provided for its repeal effective on the date the National Commission on Air Quality ceased to exist. It is shown here for information purposes only and is no longer a part of the Clean Air Act.

NATIONAL COMMISSION ON AIR QUALITY

SEC. 323. (a) There is established a National Commission on Air Quality which shall study and report to the Congress on—

(1) available alternatives, including enforcement mechanisms to protect and enhance the quality of the Nation's air resources so as to promote the public health and welfare and to achieve the other purposes of the Act, including achievement and maintenance of national ambient air quality standards and in accordance with subsection (b)(2) of this section the prevention of significant deterioration of air quality;

(2) the economic, technology, and environmental consequences of achieving or not achieving the purposes of this Act and programs authorized by it;

(3) the technological capability of achieving and the economic, energy, and environmental and health effects of achieving or not achieving required emission control levels for mobile sources of oxides of nitrogen in relation to and independent of regulation of emissions of oxides of nitrogen from stationary sources;

(4) air pollutants not presently regulated, which pose or may in the future pose a threat to public health or public welfare and options available to regulate emissions of such pollutants;

(5) the adequacy of research, development, and demonstrations being carried out by Federal, State, local, and nongovernmental entities to protect and enhance air quality;

(6) the ability of (including financial resources, manpower, and statutory authority) Federal, State, and local institutions to implement the purposes of the Act;

(7) the extent to which the reduction of hydrocarbon emissions is an adequate or appropriate method to achieve primary standards for photochemical oxidants. Such study shall include—

(A) a description and analysis of the various pollutants which are commonly referred to as "photochemical oxidants" or chemical precursers to photochemical oxidants;

(B) an analysis of any pollutants or combination of pollutants which need to be reduced to achieve any photochemical oxidant standard, and the amount of such reduction;

(C) the relationship between the reductions of hydrocarbons, oxides of nitrogen, and any other pollutants and the achievement of applicable standards for photochemical oxidants;

(D) the degree to which background or natural sources and long-range transportation of pollutants contribute to measured ambient levels of photochemical oxidants;

(E) any other oxidant-related issues which the Commission determines to be appropriate; and

(8) (A) the special problems of small businesses and government agencies in obtaining reductions of emissions from existing sources in order to offset increases in emissions from new sources for the purposes of this Act; and

(B) alternative strategies for permitting, without impeding the achievement of national ambient air quality standards as expeditiously as possible, the construction of new facilities and the modification of existing facilities in air quality control regions exceeding the national ambient air quality standard for any pollutant regulated under the Act.

The Commission's study and report under paragraph (4) shall include analysis of the health effects of pollutants which are derivates of oxides of nitrogen.

(b) (1) Studies and investigations conducted pursuant to subsection (a) shall include the effects of existing or proposed national ambient air quality standards on employment, energy, and the economy (including State and local), their relationship to objective scientific and medical data collected to determine their validity at existing levels, as well as their other social and environmental effects.

(2) The Commission shall, in carrying out the study authorized under this section, give priority to a study of the implementation of the provisions of part C of this Act (relating to prevention of significant deterioration of air quality) and its effects on the States and the Federal Government. In carrying out such study, the Commission shall study, among other questions, the following:

(A) whether the provisions relating to the designation of, and protection of air quality in class I areas under part C are appropriate to protect the air quality over lands of special national significance, including recommendations for, and methods to (i) add to or delete lands from such designation, and (ii) provide appropriate protection of the air quality over such lands;

(B) whether the provisions of part C, including the three-hour and twenty-four-hour increments, (i) affect the location and size of major emitting facilities, and (ii) whether such effects are in conflict or consonance with other national policies regarding the development of such facilities;

(C) whether the technology is available to control emissions from the major emitting facilities which are subject to regulation under part C, including an analysis of the costs associated with that technology;

(D) whether the exclusion of nonmajor emitting sources from the regulatory framework under this Act will affect the protection of air quality in class I and class II regions designated under this Act;

(E) whether the increments of change of air quality under this Act are appropriate to prevent significant deterioration of air quality in class I and class II regions designated under part C of title I;

(F) whether the choice of predictive air quality models and the assumptions of those models are appropriate to protect air quality in the class I and class II regions designated under part C of title I for the pollutants subject to regulation under part C; and

(G) the effects of such provisions on employment, energy, the economy (including State and local), the relationship of such policy to the protection of the public health and welfare as well as other national priorities such as economic growth and national defense, and its other social and environmental effects.

(c) The Commission shall, as a part of any study conducted under subsection (b)(2) of this section, specifically identify any loss or irretrievable commitment of resources (taking into account feasibility), including mineral, agricultural and water resources, as well as land surface-use resources.

(d) Such Commission shall be composed of thirteen members, including the chairman and the ranking minority member of the Senate Committee on Public Works and the House Committee on Interstate and Foreign Commence (or delegates of such chairmen or member appointed by them from among representatives of such committees) and nine members of the public appointed by the President. The chairman of the Commission shall be elected from among the members thereof. Not more than one-third of the members of the Commission may have any interest in any business or activity regulated under this Act.

(e) The heads of the departments, agencies, and instrumentalities of the executive branch of the Federal Government shall cooperate with the Commission in carrying out the requirements of this section, and shall furnish to the Commission such information as the Commission deems necessary to carry out this section.

(f) A report, together with any appropriate recommendations, shall be submitted to the Congress on the results of the investigation and study concerning subsection (a)(3) of this section no later than March 1, 1978, and the results of the investigation and study concerning subsection (b)(2) of this section no later than two years after the date of enactment of the Clean Air Act Amendments of 1977. A report, together with any appropriate recommendations, shall be submitted to the Congress on the results of the investigation and study concerning paragraphs (3) and (8) of subsection (a) of this section no later than March 1, 1978, in order that Congress may have this information in a timely fashion if it deems further changes are needed in the requirements for control of emissions of oxides of nitrogen under this Act, and for other purposes. The Administrator shall undertake to enter into appropriate arrangements with the National Academy of Sciences to conduct a study of the same matters required to be studied by the Commission under subsection (b)(2) and to submit such study to the Congress. at the same time as required for the report of the Commission concerning such subsection. Funds shall be available in the same manner, and the Administrator shall have the same authorities and duties respecting such study, as provided in the case of the study authorized pursuant to section 202(c).

(g) A report shall be submitted with regard to all Commission studies and investigations other than those referred to in subsection (f), together with any appropriate recommendations, not later than three years after the date of enactment of this section. Upon submission of such report or upon expiration of such three-year period, which is sooner, the Commission shall cease to exist. *Not later than March 1, 1981, a report shall be submitted containing the results of all Commission studies and investigations under this section, together with any appropriate recommendations. The Commission shall cease to exist—*

(1) on March 1, 1981, if the report is not submitted in accordance with the preceding sentence on the date specified in the preceding sentence; or

(2) on such date (but not later than May 1, 1981) as may be determined by the Commission, by order if the report is submitted in accordance with the preceding sentence on the date specified in such preceding sentence.

The members of the Commission who are not officers or employees of the United States, while attending conferences or meetings of the Commission or while otherwise serving at the request of the Chairman shall be entitled to receive compensation at a rate not in excess of the maximum rate of pay for grade GS–18, as provided in the General Schedule under section 5332 of title V of the United States Code, including traveltime and while away from their homes or regular places of business they may be allowed travel expenses, including per diem in lieu of subsistence as authorized by law (5 U.S.C. 73b–2) for persons in the Government service employed intermittently.

~~(j)~~ *(h)* In the conduct of the study, the Commission is authorized to contract with nongovernmental entities that are competent to perform research or investigations in areas within the Commission's mandate, and to hold public hearings, forums, and workshops to enable full public participation. The Commission may contract with nonprofit technical and scientific organizations, including the National Academy of Sciences, for the purpose of developing necessary technical information for the study authorized by subsection (a)(7) of this section.[8]
(i) The Commission may appoint and fix the pay of such staff as it deems necessary.

THE FEDERAL INSECTICIDE, FUNGICIDE, AND RODENTICIDE ACT
as amended[1]

An Act

86 STAT. 973-999

To amend the Federal Insecticide, Fungicide, and Rodenticide Act, and for other purposes.

Be it enacted by the Senate and House Representatives of the United States of America in Congress assembled, That this Act may be cited as the "Federal Environmental Pesticide Control Act of 1972."

Amendments to Federal Insecticide, Fungicide, and Rodenticide Act

Sec. 2. The Federal Insecticide, Fungicide, and Rodenticide Act (7 U.S.C. 136 et seq.) is amended to read as follows:

---

[1] Public Law 92-516, October 21, 1982; Public Law 94-51, July 2, 1975; Public Law 94-109, October 10, 1975; Public Law 94-140, November 28, 1975; Public Law 95-251, March 27, 1978; Public Law 95-396, September 30, 1978; Public Law 96-539, December 17, 1980.

"SECTION 1. SHORT TITLE AND TABLE OF CONTENTS.

(a) *Short Title* — This Act may be cited as the 'Federal Insecticide, Fungicide, and Rodenticide Act'.
(b) *Table of Contents* —

"SEC. 2. DEFINITIONS.

"For purposes of this Act—

"(a) *Active Ingredient.*—The term 'active ingredient' means—

"(1) in the case of a pesticide other than a plant regulator, defoliant, or desiccant, an ingredient which will prevent, destroy, repel, or mitigate any pest;

"(2) in the case of a plant regulator, an ingredient which, through physiological action, will accelerate or retard the rate of growth or rate of maturation or otherwise alter the behavior of ornamental or crop plants or the product thereof;

"(3) in the case of a defoliant, an ingredient which will cause the leaves or foliage to drop from a plant; and

"(4) in the case of a desiccant, an ingredient which will artificially accelerate the drying of plant tissue.

"(b) *Administrator.*—The term 'Administrator' means the Administrator of the Environmental Protection Agency.

"(c) *Adulterated.*—The term 'adulterated' applies to any pesticide if:

"(1) its strength or purity falls below the professed standard of quality as expressed on its labeling under which it is sold;

"(2) any substance has been substituted wholly or in part for the pesticide; or

"(3) any valuable constituent of the pesticide has been wholly or in part abstracted.

"(d) *Animal.*—The term 'animal' means all vertebrate and invertebrate species, including but not limited to man and other mammals, birds, fish, and the shellfish.

"(e) *Certified Applicator, Etc.*—

"(1) *Certified applicator.*—The term 'certified applicator' means any individual who is certified under section 4 as authorized to use or supervise the use of any pesticide which is classified for restricted use. Any applicator who holds or applies registered pesticides, or use dilutions of registered pesticides consistent with section 2(ee) of this Act, only to provide a service of controlling pests without delivering any unapplied pesticide to any person so served is not deemed to be a seller or distributor of pesticides under this Act.

"(2) *Private applicator.*—The term 'private applicator' means a certified applicator who uses or supervises the use of any pesticide which is classified for restricted use for purposes of producing any agricultural commodity on property owned or rented by him or his employer or (if applied without compensation other than trading of personal services between producers of agricultural commodities) on the property of another person.

"(3) *Commercial applicator.*—The term 'commercial applicator' means an applicator (whether or not he is private applicator with respect to some uses) who uses or supervises the use of any pesticide which is classified for restricted use for any purpose or on any property other than as provided by paragraph (2).

"(4) *Under the direct supervision of a certified applicator.*—Unless otherwise prescribed by its labeling, a pesticide shall be considered to be applied under the direct supervision of a certified applicator if it is applied by a competent person acting under the instructions and control of a certified applicator who is available if and when needed, even though such certified applicator is not physically present at the time and place the pesticide is applied.

"(f) *Defoliant.*—The term 'defoliant' means any substance or mixture of substances intended for causing the leaves or foliage to drop from a plant, with or without causing abscission.

"(g) *Desiccant.*—The term 'desiccant' means any substance or mixture of substances intended for artificially accelerating the drying of plant tissue.

"(h) *Device.*—The term 'device' means any instrument or contrivance (other than a firearm) which is intended for trapping, destroying, repelling, or mitigating any pest or any other form of plant or animal life (other than man and other than bacteria, virus, or other microorganism on or in living man or other living animals); but not including equipment used for the application of pesticides when sold separately therefrom.

"(i) *District Court.*—The term 'district court' means a United States district court, the District Court of Guam, the District Court of the Virgin Islands, and the highest court of American Samoa.

"(j) *Environment.*—The term 'environment' includes water, air, land, and all plants and man and other animals living therein, and the interrelationships which exist among these.

"(k) *Fungus.*—The term 'fungus' means any non-chlorophyll-bearing thallophyte (that is, any non-chlorophyll-bearing plant of a lower order than mosses and liverworts), as for example, rust, smut, mildew, mold, yeast, and bacteria, except those on or in living man or other animals and those on or in processed food, beverages, or pharmaceuticals.

"l) *Imminent Hazard.*—The term 'imminent hazard' means a situation which exists when the continued use of a pesticide during the time required for cancellation proceeding would be likely to result in unreasonable adverse effects on the environment or will involve unreasonable hazard to the survival of a species declared endangered by the Secretary of the Interior under Public Law 91-135.

"(m) *Inert Ingredient.*—The term "inert ingredient' means an ingredient which is not active.

"(n) *Ingredient Statement.*—The term 'ingredient statement' means a statement which contains—

"(1) the name and percentage of each active ingredient, and the total percentage of all inert ingredients, in the pesticide; and

"(2) if the pesticide contains arsenic in any form, a statement of the percentages of total and water soluble arsenic, calculated as elementary arsenic.

"(o) *Insect.*—The term 'insect' means any of the numerous small invertebrate animals generally having the body more or less obviously segmented, for the most part belonging to the class insecta, comprising six-legged, usually winged forms, as for example, beetles, bugs, bees, flies, and to other allied classes of arthropods whose members are wingless and usually have more than six legs, as for example, spiders, mites, ticks, centipedes, and wood lice.

"(p) *Label and Labeling.*—

"(1) *Label.*—The term 'label' means the written, printed, or graphic matter on, or attached to, the pesticide or device or any of its containers or wrappers.

"(2) *Labeling.*—The term "labeling' means all labels and all other written, printed, or graphic matter—

"(A) accompanying the pesticide or device at any time; or

"(B) to which reference is made on the label or in literature accompanying the pesticide or device, except to current official publications of the Environmental Protection Agency, the United States Departments of Agriculture and Interior, the Department of Health, Education, and Welfare, State experiment stations, State agricultural colleges, and other similiar Federal or State institutions or agencies authorized by law to conduct research in the field of pesticides.

"(q) *Misbranded.*—

"(1) A pesticide is misbranded if—

"(A) its labeling bears any statement, design, or graphic representation relative thereto or to its ingredients which is false or misleading in any particular;

"(B) it is contained in a package or other container or wrapping which does not conform to the standards established by the Administrator pursuant to section 25(c)(3);

"(C) it is an imitation of, or is offered for sale under the name of, another pesticide;

"(D) its label does not bear the registration number assigned under section 7 to each establishment in which it was produced;

"(E) any word, statement, or other information required by or under authority of this Act to appear on the label or labeling is not prominently placed thereon with such conspicuousness (as compared with other words, statements, designs, or graphic matter in the labeling) and in such terms as to render it likely to be read and understood by the ordinary individual under customary conditions of purchase and use;

"(F) the labeling accompanying it does not contain directions for use which are necessary for effecting the purpose for which the product is intended and if complied with, together with any requirements imposed under section 3(d) of this Act, are adequate to protect health and the environment;

"(G) the label does not contain a warning or caution statement which may be necessary and if compiled with, together with any requirements imposed under section 3(d) of this Act, is adequate to protect health and the environment; or

"(H) in the case of a pesticide not registered in accordance with section 3 of this Act and intended for export, the label does not contain, in words prominently placed thereon with such conspicuousness (as compared with other words, statements, designs, or graphic matter in the labeling) as to render it likely to be noted by the ordinary individual under customary conditions of purchase and use, the following: 'Not Registered for Use in the United States of America'.

"(2) A pesticide is misbranded if—

"(A) the label does not bear an ingredient statement on that part of the immediate container (and on the outside container or wrapper of the retail package, if there be one, through which the ingredient statement on the immediate container cannot be clearly read) which is presented or displayed under customary conditions of purchase, except that a pesticide is not misbranded under this subparagraph if:

"(i) the size of form of the immediate container, or the outside container or wrapper of the retail package, makes it impracticable to place the ingredient statement on the part which is presented or displayed under customary conditions of purchase: and

"(ii) the ingredient statement appears prominently on another part of the immediate container, or outside container or wrapper, permitted by the Administrator;

"(B) the labeling does not contain a statement of the use classification under which the product is registered;

"(C) there is not affixed to its container, and to the outside container or wrapper of the retail package, if there be one, through which the required information on the immediate container cannot be clearly read, a label bearing—

"(i) the name and address of the producer, registrant, or person for whom produced;

"(ii) the name, brand, or trademark under which the pesticide is sold;

"(iii) the net weight or measure of the content; *Provided,* That the Administrator may permit reasonable variations; and

"(iv) when required by regulation of the Administrator to effectuate the purposes of this Act, the registration number assigned to the pesticide under this Act, and the use classification; and

"(D) the pesticide contains any substance or substances in quantities highly toxic to man, unless the label shall bear, in addition to any other matter required by this Act—

"(i) the skull and crossbones;

"(ii) the word 'poison' prominently in red on a background of distinctly contrasting color; and

"(iii) a statement of a practical treatment (first aid or otherwise) in case of poisoning by the pesticide.

"(r) *Nematode.*—The term 'nematode' means invertebrate animals of the phylum nemathelminthes and class nematoda, that is, unsegmented round worms with elongated, fusiform, or saclike bodies covered with cuticle, and inhabiting soil, water, plants, or plant parts; may also be called nemas or eelworms.

"(s) *Person.*—The term 'person' means any individual, partnership, association, corporation, or any organized group of persons whether incorporated or not.

"(t) *Pest.*—The term 'pest' means (1) any insect, rodent, nematode, fungus, weed, or (2) any other form of terrestrial or aquatic plant or animal life or virus, bacteria, or other micro-organism (except viruses, bacteria, or other micro-organisms on or in living man or other living animals) which the Administrator declares to be a pest under section 25(c)(1).

"(u) *Pesticide.*—The term 'pesticide' means (1) any substance or mixture of substances intended for preventing, destroying, repelling, or mitigating any pest, and (2) any substance or mixture of substances intended for use as a plant regulator, defoliant, or desiccant: *Provided,* That the term 'pesticide' shall not include any article (1)(a) that is a 'new animal drug' within the meaning of section 201(w) of the Federal Food, Drug, and Cosmetic Act (21 U.S.C. 321(w)), or (b) that has been determined by the Secretary of Health, Education, and Welfare not to be a new animal drug by a regulation establishing conditions of use for the article, or (2) that is an animal feed within the meaning of section 201(x) of such Act (21 U.S.C.321(x)) bearing or containing an article covered by clause (1) of this proviso."

"(v) *Plant Regulator.*—The term 'plant regulator' means any substance or mixture of substances intended, through physiological action, for accelerating or retarding the rate of growth or rate of maturation, or for otherwise altering the behavior of plants or the produce thereof, but shall not include substances to the extent that they are intended as plant nutrients, trace elements, nutritional chemicals, plant inoculants, and soil amendments. Also, the term 'plant regulator' shall not be required to include any of such of those nutrient mixtures or soil amendments as are commonly known as vitamin-hormone horticultural products, intended for improvement, maintenance, survival, health, and propagation of plants, and as are not for pest destruction and are nontoxic, nonpoisonous in the undiluted packaged concentration.

"(w) *Producer and Produce.*—The term 'producer' means the person who manufactures, prepares, compounds, propagates, or processes any pesticide or device or active ingredient used in producing a pesticide. The term 'produce' means to manufacture, prepare, compound, propagate, or process any pesticide or device, or active ingredient used in producing a pesticide. The dilution by individuals of formulated pesticides for their own use and according to the directions on registered labels shall not of itself result in such individuals being included in the definition of 'producer' for the purposes of this Act."

"(x) *Protect Health and the Environment.*—The terms 'protect health and the environment' and 'protection of health and the environment' mean protection against any unreasonable adverse effects on the environment.

"(y) *Registrant.*—The term 'registrant' means a person who has registered any pesticide pursuant to the provisions of this Act.

"(z) *Registration.*—The term 'registration' includes reregistration.

"(aa) *State.*—The term 'State' means a State, the District of Columbia, the Commonwealth of Puerto Rico, the Virgin Islands, Guam, the Trust Territory of the Pacific Islands, and American Samoa.

"(bb) *Unreasonable Adverse Effects on the Environment.*—The term 'unreasonable adverse effects on the environment' means any unreasonable risk to man or the environment, taking into account the economic, social, and environmental costs and benefits of the use of any pesticide.

"(cc) *Weed.*—The term 'weed' means any plant which grows where not wanted.

"(dd) *Establishment.*--The term 'establishment' means any place where a pesticide or device or active ingredient used in producing a pesticide is produced, or held, for distribution or sale.

"(ee) *To Use Any Registered Pesticide in a Manner Inconsistent With Its Labeling.*—The term 'to use any registered pestiscide in a manner inconsistent with its labeling' means to use any registered pesticide in a manner not permitted by the labeling: Provided, That the term shall not include (1) applying a pesticide at any dosage, concentration, or frequency less than that specified on the labeling, (2) applying a pesticide against any target pest not specified on the labeling if the application is to the crop, animal, or site specified on the labeling, unless the Administrator has required that the labeling specifically state that the pesticide may be used only for the pests specified on the labeling after the Administrator has determined that the use of the pesticide against other pests would cause an unreasonable adverse effect on the environment, (3) employing any method of application not prohibited by the labeling, or (4) mixing a pesticide or pesticides with a fertilizer when such mixture is not prohibited by the labeling: Provided further, That the term also shall not include any use of a pesticide inconformance with section 5, 18, or 24 of this Act, or any use of a pesticide in a manner that the Administrator determines to be consistent with the purposes of this Act: And provided further, That after March 31, 1979, the term shall not include the use of a pesticide for agricultural or forestry purposes at a dilution less than label dosage unless before or after that date the Administrator issues a regulation or advisory opinion consistent with the study provided for in section 27(b) of the Federal Pesticide Act of 1978, which regulation or advisory opinion specifically requires the use of definite amounts of dilution.

"SEC. 3. REGISTRATION OF PESTICIDES.

"(a) *Requirement.*—Except as otherwise provided by this Act, no person in any State may distribute, sell, offer for sale, hold for sale, ship, deliver for shipment, or receive and (having so received) delivery or offer to deliver, to any person any pesticide which is not registered with the Administrator.

"(b) *Exemptions.*—A pesticide which is not registered with the Administrator may be transferred if—

"(1) the transfer is from one registered establishment to another registered establishment operated by the same producer solely for packaging at the second establishment or for use as a constituent part of another pesticide produced at the second establishment; or

"(2) the transfer is pursuant to and in accordance with the requirements of an experimental use permit.

"(c) *Procedure for Registration.*—

(1) *Statement required.*—Each applicant for registration of a pesticide shall file with the Administrator a statement which includes—

"(A) the name and address of the applicant and of any other person whose name will appear on the labeling;

"(B) the name of the pesticide;

"(C) a complete copy of the labeling of the pesticide, a statement of all claims to be made for it, and any directions for its use;

"(D) except as otherwise provided in subsection (c)(2)(D) of this section, if requested by the Administrator, a full description of the tests made and the results thereof upon which the claims are based, or alternatively a citation to data that appears in the public literature or that previously had been submitted to the Administrator and that

---

Note:
Section 2(b) of the Federal Pesticide Act of 1978 provides, The amendment to section 3(c)(1)(D) of the Federal Insecticide, Fungicide, and Rodenticide Act made by this section shall apply with respect to all applications for registration approved after September 30, 1978.

the Administrator may consider in accordance with the following provisions:

"(i) with respect to pesticides containing active ingredients that are initially registered under this Act after September 30, 1978, data submitted to support the application for the original registration of the pesticide, or an application for an amendment adding any new use to the registration and that pertains solely to such new use, shall not, without the written permission of the original data submitter, be considered by the Administrator to support an application by another person during a period of ten years following the date the Administrator first registers the pesticides: Provided, That such permission shall not be required in the case of defensive data;

"(ii) except as otherwise provided in subparagraph (D)(i) of this paragraph, with respect to data submitted after December 31, 1969, by an applicant or registrant to support an application for registration, experimental use permit, or amendment adding a new use to an existing registration, to support or maintain in effect an existing registration, or for reregistration, the Administrator may, without the permission of the original data submitter, consider any such item of data in support of an application by any other person (hereinafter in this subparagraph referred to as the 'applicant') within the fifteen-year period following the date the data were originally submitted only if the applicant has made an offer to compensate the original data submitter and submitted such offer to the Administrator accompanied by evidence of delivery to the original data submitter of the offer. The terms and amount of compensation may be fixed by agreement between the original data submitter and the applicant, or, failing such agreement, binding arbitration under this subparagraph. If, at the end of ninety days after the date of delivery to the original data submitter of the offer to compensate, the original data submitter and the applicant have neither agreed on the amount and terms of compensation nor on a procedure for reaching an agreement on the amount and terms of compensation, either person may initiate binding arbitration proceedings by requesting the Federal Mediation and Conciliation Service to appoint an arbitrator from the roster of arbitrators maintained by such Service. The procedure and rules of the Service shall be applicable to the selection of such arbitrator and to such arbitration proceedings, and the findings and determination of the arbitrator shall be final and conclusive, and no official or court of the United States shall have power or jurisdiction to review any such findings and determination, except for fraud, misrepresentation, or other misconduct by one of the parties to the arbitration or the arbitrator where there is a verified complaint with supporting affidavits attesting to specific instances of such fraud, misrepresentation, or other misconduct. The parties to the arbitration shall share equally in the payment of the fee and expenses of the arbitrator. If the Administrator determines that an original data submitter has failed to participate in a procedure for reaching an agreement or in an arbitration proceeding as required by this subparagraph, or failed to comply with the terms of an agreement or arbitration decision concerning compensation under this subparagraph, the original data submitter shall forfeit the right to compensation for the use of the data in support of the application. Notwithstanding any other provision of this Act, if the Administrator determines that an applicant has failed to participate in a procedure for reaching an agreement or in an arbitration proceeding as required by this subparagraph, or failed to comply with the terms of an agreement or arbitration decision concerning compensation under this subparagraph, the

Administrator shall deny the application or cancel the registration of the pesticide in support of which the data were used without further hearing. Before the Administrator takes action under either of the preceding two sentences, the Administrator shall furnish to the affected person, by certified mail, notice of intent to take actions and allow fifteen days from the date of delivery of the notice for the affected person to respond. If a registration is denied or canceled under this subparagraph, the Administrator may make such order as the Administrator deems appropriate concerning the continued sale and use of existing stocks of such pesticide. Registration action by the Administrator shall not be delayed pending the fixing of compensation;

"(iii) after expiration of any period of exclusive use and any period for which compensation is required for the use of an item of data under subparagraphs (D)(i) and (D)(ii) of this paragraph, the Administrator may consider such item of data in support of an application by any other applicant without the permission of the original data submitter and without an offer having been received to compensate the original data submitter for the use of such item of data;

"(E) the complete formula of the pesticide; and

"(F) a request that the pesticide be classified for general use, for restricted use, or for both.

"(2) (A) *Data in support of registration.*—The Administrator shall publish guidelines specifying the kinds of information which will be required to support the registration of a pesticide and shall revise such guidelines from time to time. If thereafter he requires any additional kind of information under subparagraph (B) of this paragraph, he shall permit sufficient time for applicants to obtain such additional information. The Administrator, in establishing standards for data requirements for the registration of pesticides with respect to minor uses, shall make such standards commensurate with the anticipated extent of use, pattern of use, and the level and degree of potential exposure of man and the environment to the pesticide. In the development of these standards, the Administrator shall consider the economic factors of potential national volume of use, extent of distribution, and the impact of the cost of meeting the requirements on the incentives for any potential registrant to undertake the development of the required data. Except as provided by section 10, within 30 days after the Administrator registers a pesticide under this Act he shall make available to the public the data called for in the registration statement together with such other scientific information as he deems relevant to his decision.

"(B) *Additional data to support existing registrations.*—

"(i) If the Administrator determines that additional data are required to maintain in effect an existing registration of a pesticide, the Administrator shall notify all existing registrants of the pesticide to which the determination relates and provide a list of such registrants to any interested person.

"(ii) Each registrant of such pesticide shall provide evidence within ninety days after receipt of notification that it is taking appropriate steps to secure the additional data that are required . Two or more registrants may agree to develop jointly, or to share in the cost of developing, such data if they agree and advise the Administrator of their intent within ninety days after notification. Any registrant who agrees to share in the cost of producing the data shall be entitled to examine and rely upon such data in support of maintenance of such registration.

"(iii) If, at the end of sixty days after advising the Administrator of their agreement to develop jointly, or share in the cost of developing, data, the registrants have not further agreed on the terms of the data development arrangement or on a procedure for reaching such agreement, any of such registrants may initiate binding arbitration proceedings by requesting the Federal Mediation and Conciliation Service to appoint an arbitrator from the roster of arbitrators maintained by such Service. The procedure and rules of the Service shall be applicable to the selection of such arbitrator and to such arbitration proceedings, and the findings and determination of the arbitrator shall be final and conclusive, and no official or court of the United States shall have power or jurisdiction to review any such findings and determination, except for fraud, misrepresentation, or other misconduct by one of the parties to the arbitration or the arbitrator where there is a verified complaint with supporting affidavits attesting to specific instances of such fraud, misrepresentation, or other misconduct. All parties to the arbitration shall share equally in the payment of the fee and expenses of the arbitrator.

"(iv) Notwithstanding any other provision of this Act, if the Administrator determines that a registrant, within the time required by the Administrator, has failed to take appropriate steps to secure the data required under this subparagraph, to participate in a procedure for reaching agreement concerning a joint data development arrangement under this subparagraph or in an arbitration proceeding as required by this subparagraph, or to comply with the terms of an agreement or arbitration decision concerning a joint data development arrangement under this subparagraph, the Administrator may issue a notice of intent to suspend such registrant's registration of the pesticide for which additional data is required. The Administrator may include in the notice of intent to suspend such provisions as the Administrator deems appropriate concerning the continued sale and use of existing stocks of such pesticide. Any suspension proposed under this subparagraph shall become final and effective at the end of thirty days from receipt by the registrant of the notice of intent to suspend, unless during that time a request for hearing is made by a person adversely affected by the notice or the registrant has satisfied the Administrator that the registrant has complied fully with the requirements that served as a basis for the notice of intent to suspend. If a hearing is requested, a hearing shall be conducted under section 6(d) of this Act: Provided, That the only matters for resolution at that hearing shall be whether the registrant has failed to take the action that served as the basis for the notice of intent to suspend the registration of the pesticide for which additional data is required, and whether the Administrator's determination with respect to the disposition of existing stocks is consistent with this Act. If a hearing is held, a decision after completion of such hearing shall be final. Notwithstanding any other provision of this Act, a hearing shall be held and a determination made within seventy-five days after receipt of a request for such hearing. Any registration suspended under this subparagraph shall be reinstated by the Administrator if the Administrator determines that the registrant has compiled fully with the requirements that served as a basis for the suspension of the registration.

"(v) Any data submitted under this subparagraph shall be subject to the provisions of subsection (c)(1)(D) of this section. Whenever such data are submitted jointly by two or more registrants, an agent shall be agreed on at the time of the joint submission to handle any subsequent data compensation matters for the joint submitters of such data.".

"(C) *Simplified procedures.*—Within nine months after date of enactment of this subparagraph, the Administrator shall by regulation, prescribe simplified procedures for the registration of pesticides, which shall include the provisions of subparagraph (D) of this paragraph.

"(D) *Exemption.*—No applicant for registration of a pesticide who proposes to purchase a registered pesticide from another producer in order to formulate such purchased pesticide into an end-use product shall be required to—

"(i) submit or cite data pertaining to the safety of such purchased product; or

"(ii) offer to pay reasonable compensation otherwise required by paragraph (1)(D) of this subsection for the use of any such data.".

"(3) *Time for acting with respect to application.*—The Administrator shall review the data after receipt of the application and shall, as expeditiously as possible, either register the pesticide in accordance with paragraph (5), or notify the applicant of his determination that it does not comply with the provisions of the Act in accordance with paragraph (6).

"(4) *Notice of application.*—The Administrator shall publish in the Federal Register, promptly after receipt of the statement and other data required pursuant to paragraphs (1) and (2), a notice of each application for registration of any pesticide if it contains any new active ingredient or if it would entail a changed use pattern. The notice shall provide for a period of 30 days in which any Federal agency or any other interested person may comment.

"(5) *Approval of registration.*—The Administrator shall register a pesticide if he determines that, when considered with any restrictions imposed under subsection (d)—

"(A) its composition is such as to warrant the proposed claims for it;

"(B) its labeling and other material required to be submitted comply with the requirements of this Act;

"(C) it will perform its intended function without unreasonable adverse effects on the environment; and

"(D) when used in accordance with widespread and commonly recognized practice it will not generally cause unreasonable adverse effects on the environment.

The Administrator shall not make any lack of essentiality a criterion for denying registration of any pesticide. Where two pesticides meet the requirements of this paragraph, one should not be registered in preference to the other. In considering an application for the registration of a pesticide, the Administrator may waive data requirements pertaining to efficacy, in which event the Administrator may register the pesticide without determining that the pesticide's composition is such as to warrant proposed claims of efficacy. If a pesticide is found to be efficacious by any State under section 24(c) of this Act, a presumption is established that the Administrator shall waive data requirements pertaining to efficacy for use of the pesticide in such State.

"(6) *Denial of registration.*—If the Administrator determines that the requirements of paragraph (5) for registration are not satisfied, he shall notify the applicant for registration of his determination and of his reasons (including the factual basis) therefor, and that, unless the applicant corrects the conditions and notifies the Administrator thereof during the 30-day period beginning with the day after the date on which the applicant receives the notice, the Administrator may refuse to register the pesticide. Whenever the Administrator refuses to register a pesticide, he shall notify the applicant of his decision and of his reasons (including the factual basis) therefor. The Administrator shall promptly publish in the Federal Register notice of such denial of registration and the reasons therefor. Upon such notification, the applicant for registration or other interested person with the concurrence of the applicant shall have the same remedies as provided for in section 6.

"(7) *Registration under special circumstances.*—Notwithstanding the provisions of subsection (c)(5) of this section—

"(A) The Administrator may conditionally register or amend the registration of a pesticide if the Administrator determines that (i) the pesticide and proposed use are identical or substantially similar to any currently registered pesticide and use thereof, or differ only in ways that would not significantly increase the risk of unreasonable adverse effects on the environment, and (ii) approving the registration or amendment in the manner proposed by the applicant would not significantly increase the risk of any unreasonable adverse effect on the environment. An applicant seeking conditional registration or amended registration under this subparagraph shall submit such data as would be required to obtain registration of a similar pesticide under subsection (c)(5) of this section: Provided, That, if the applicant is unable to submit an item of data because it has not yet been generated, the Administrator may register or amend the registration of the pesticide under such conditions as will require the submission of such data not later than the time such data are required to be submitted with respect to similar pesticides already registered under this Act.

"(B) The Administrator may conditionally amend the registration of a pesticide to permit additional uses of such pesticide notwithstanding that data concerning the pesticide may be insufficient to support an unconditional amendment, if the Administrator determines that (i) the applicant has submitted satisfactory data pertaining to the proposed additional use, and (ii) amending the registration in the manner proposed by the applicant would not significantly increase the risk of any unreasonable adverse effect on the environment. Notwithstanding the foregoing provisions of this subparagraph, no registration of a pesticide may be amended to permit an additional use of such pesticide if the Administrator has issued a notice stating that such pesticide, or any ingredient thereof, meets or exceeds risk criteria associated in whole or in part with human dietary exposure enumerated in regulations isued under this Act, and during the pendency of any risk-benefit evaluation initiated by such notice, if (i) the additional use of such pesticide involves a major food or feed crop, or (ii) the additional use of such pesticide involves a minor food or feed crop and the Administrator determines, with the concurrence of the Secretary of Agriculture, there is available an effective alternative pesticide that does not meet or exceed such risk criteria. An applicant seeking amended registration under this subparagraph shall submit such data as would be required to obtain registration of a similar pesticide under subsection (c)(5) of this section: Provided, That, if the applicant is unable to submit an item of data (other than data pertaining to the proposed additional use) because it has not yet been generated, the Administrator may amend the registration under such conditions as will require the submission of such data not later than the time such data are required to be submitted with respect to similar pesticides already registered under this Act.

"(C) The Administrator may conditionally register a pesticide containing an active ingredient not contained in any currently registered pesticide for a period reasonably sufficient for the generation and submission of required data (which are lacking because a period reasonably sufficient for generation of the data has not elapsed since the Administrator first imposed the data requirement) on the condition that by the end of such period the Administrator receives such data and the data do not meet or exceed risk criteria enumerated in regulations issued under this Act, and on such other conditions as the Administrator may prescribe: Provided, That a conditional registration under this subparagraph shall be granted only if the Administrator determines that use of the pesticide during such period will not cause any unreasonable adverse effect on the environment, and that use of the pesticide is, in the public interest.

"(8) *Interim administrative review.*—Notwithstanding any other provision of this Act, the Administrator may not initiate a public interim administrative review process to develop a risk-benefit evaluation of the ingredients of a pesticide or any of its uses prior to initiating a formal action to cancel, suspend, or deny registration of such pesticide, required under this Act, unless such interim administrative process is based on a validated test or other significant evidence raising prudent concerns of unreasonable adverse risk to man or to the environment. Notice of the definition of the terms 'validated test' and 'other significant evidence' as used herein shall be published by the Administrator in the Federal Register."

"(d) *Classification of Pesticides.*—

"(1) *Classification for general use, restricted use, or both.*—

"(A) As a part of the registration of a pesticide the Administrator shall classify it as being for general use or for restricted use, provided that if the Administrator determines that some of the uses for which the pesticide is registered should be for general use and that other uses for which it is registered should be for restricted use, he shall classify it for both general use and restricted use. Pesticide uses may be classified by regulation on the initial classification, and registered pesticides may be classified prior to reregistration. If some of the uses of the pesticide are classified for general use and other uses are classified for restricted use, the directions relating to its general uses shall be clearly separated and distinguished from those directions relating to its restricted uses: *Provided, however,* That the Administrator may require that its packaging and labeling for restricted uses shall be clearly distinguishable from its packaging and labeling for general uses.

"(B) If the Administrator determines that the pesticide, when applied in accordance with its directions for use, warnings and cautions and for the uses for which it is registered, or for one or more of such uses, or in accordance with a widespread and commonly recognized practice, will not generally cause unreasonable adverse effects on the environment, he will classify the pesticide, or the particular use or uses of the pesticide to which the determination applies, for general use.

"(C) If the Administrator determines that the pesticide, when applied in accordance with its directions for use, warnings and cautions and for the uses for which it is registered, or for one or more of such uses, or in accordance with a widespread and commonly recognized practice, may generally cause, without additional regulatory restrictions, unreasonable adverse effects on the environment, including injury to the applicator, he shall classify the pesticide, or the particular use or uses to which the determination applies, for restricted use:

"(i) If the Administrator classifies a pesticide, or one or more uses of such pesticide, for restricted use because of a determination that the acute dermal or inhalation toxicity of the pesticide presents a hazard to the applicator or other persons, the pesticide shall be applied for any use to which the restricted classification applies only by or under the direct supervision of a certified applicator.

"(ii) If the Administrator classifies a pesticide, or one or more uses of such pesticide, for restricted use because of a determination that its use without additional regulatory restriction may cause unreasonable adverse effects on the environment, the pesticide shall be applied for any use to which the determination applies only by or under the direct supervision of a certified applicator, or subject to such other restrictions as the Administrator may provide by regulation. Any such regulation shall be reviewable in the appropriate court of appeals upon petition of a person adversely affected filed within 60 days of the publication of the regulation in final form.

"(2) *Change in classification.*—If the Administrator determines that a change in the classification of any use of a pesticide from general use to restricted use is necessary to prevent unreasonable adverse effects on the environment, he shall notify the registrant of such pesticide of such determination at least forty-five days before making the change and shall publish the proposed change in the Federal Register. The registrant, or other interested person with the concurrence of the registrant, may seek relief from such determination under section 6(b).

"(3) *Change in classification from restricted use to general use.*—The registrant of any pesticide with one or more uses classified for restricted use may petition the Administrator to change any such classification from restricted to general use. Such petition shall set out the basis for the registrant's position that restricted use classification is unnecessary because classification of the pesticide for general use would not cause unreasonable adverse effects on the environment. The Administrator, within sixty days after receiving such petition, shall notify the registrant whether the petition has been granted or denied. Any denial shall contain an explanation therefor and any such denial shall be subject to judicial review under section 16 of this Act.

"(e) *Products With Same Formulation and Claims.*—Products which have the same formulation, are manufactured by the same person, the labeling of which contains the same claims, and the labels of which bear a designation identifying the product as the same pesticide may be registered as a single pesticide; and additional names and labels shall be added to the registration by supplemental statements.

"(f) *Miscellaneous.*—

"(1) *Effect of change of labeling or formulation.*—If the labeling or formulation for a pesticide is changed, the registration shall be amended to reflect such change if the Administrator determines that the change will not violate any provision of this Act.

"(2) *Registration not a defense.*—In no event shall registration of an article be construed as a defense for the commission of any offense under this Act: *Provided,* That as long as no cancellation proceedings are in effect registration of a pesticide shall be prima facie evidence that the pesticide, its labeling and packaging comply with the registration provisions of the Act.

"(3) *Authority to consult other Federal agencies.*—In connection with consideration of any registration or application for registration under this section, the Administrator may consult with any other Federal agency.

"(g) *Reregistration of Pesticides.*—The Administrator shall accomplish the reregistration of all pesticides in the most expeditious manner practicable: *Provided,* That, to the extent appropriate, any pesticide that results in a postharvest residue in or on food or feed crops shall be given priority in the reregistration process.

"SEC. 4. USE OF RESTRICTED USE PESTICIDES; CERTIFIED APPLICATORS.

"(a) *Certification Procedure.*—

"(1) *Federal certification.*—In any State for which a State plan for applicator certification has not been approved by the Administrator, the Administrator, in consultation with the Governor of such State, shall conduct a program for the certification of applicators of pesticides: *Provided,* That such program shall conform to the requirements imposed upon the States under the provisions of subsection (a)(2) of this section and shall not require private applicators to take any examination to establish competency in the use of pesticides. Prior to the implementation of the program, the Administrator shall publish in the Federal Register for review and comment a summary of the Federal plan for applicator certification and shall make generally available within the State copies of the plan. The Administrator shall hold public hearings at one or more locations within the State if so requested by the Governor of such State during the thirty days following publication of the Federal Register notice inviting comment on the Federal plan. The hearings shall be held within thirty days following receipt of the request from the Governor. In any State in which the Administrator conducts a certification program, the Administrator may require any person engaging in the commercial application, sale, offering for sale, holding for sale, or distribution of any pesticide one or more uses of which have been classified for restricted use to maintain such records and submit such reports concerning the commercial application, sale, or distribution of such pesticide as the Administrator may by regulation prescribe. Subject to paragraph (2), the Administrator shall prescribe standards for the certification of applicators of pesticides. Such standards shall provide that to be certified, an individual must be determined to be competent with respect to the use and handling of pesticides, or to the use and handling of the pesticide or class of pesticides covered by such individual's certification: *Provided, however,* That the certification standard for a private applicator shall, under a State plan submitted for approval, be deemed fulfilled by his completing a certification form. The Administrator shall further assure that such form contains adequate information and affirmations to carry out the intent of this Act, and may include in the form an affirmation that the private applicator has completed a training program approved by the Administrator so long as the program does not require the private applicator to take, pursuant to requirement prescribed by the Administrator, any examination to establish competency in the use of the pestiscide. The Administrator may require any pesticide dealer participating in a certification program to be licensed under a State licensing program approved by him.

"(2) *State certification.*—If any State, at any time, desires to certify applicators of pesticides, the Governor of such State shall submit a State plan for such purpose. The Administrator shall approve the plan submitted by any State, or any modification thereof, if such plan in his judgment—

"(A) designates a State agency as the agency responsible for administering the plan throughout the State;

"(B) contains satisfactory assurances that such agency has or will have the legal authority and qualified personnel necessary to carry out the plan;

"(C) gives satisfactory assurances that the State will devote adequate funds to the administration of the plan;

"(D) provides that the State agency will make such reports to the Administrator in such form and containing such information as the Administrator may from time to time require; and

"(E) contains satisfactory assurances that State standards for the certification of applicators of pesticides conform with those standards prescribed by the Administrator under paragraph (1).

Any State certification program under this section shall be maintained in accordance with the State plan approved under this section.

"(b) *State Plans.*—If the Administrator rejects a plan submitted under this paragraph, he shall afford the State submitting the plan due notice and opportunity for hearing before so doing. If the Administrator approves a plan submitted under this paragraph, then such State shall certify applicators of pesticides with respect to such State. Whenever the Administrator determines that a State is not administering the certification program in accordance with the plan approved under this section, he shall so notify the State and provide for a hearing at the request of the State, and, if appropriate corrective action is not taken within a reasonable time, not to exceed ninety days, the Administrator shall withdraw approval of such plan.

"(c) *Instruction in Integrated Pest Management Techniques.*—Standards prescribed by the Administrator for the certification of applicators of pesticides under subsection (a), and the State plans submitted to the Administrator under subsection (a) and (b), shall include provisions for making instructional materials concerning integrated pest management techniques available to individuals at their request in accordance with the provisions of section 23(c) of this Act, but such plans may not require that any individual receive instruction concerning such techniques or be shown to be competent with respect to the use of such techniques. The Administrator and States implementing such plans shall provide that all interested individuals are notified of the availability of such instructional materials."

"SEC. 5. EXPERIMENTAL USE PERMITS.

"(a) *Issuance.*—Any person may apply to the Administrator for an experimental use permit for a pesticide. The Administrator shall review the application. After completion of the review, but not later than one hundred and twenty days after receipt of the application and all required supporting data, the Administrator shall either issue the permit or notify the applicant of the Administrator's determination not to issue the permit and the reasons therefor. The applicant may correct the application or request a waiver of the conditions for such permit within thirty days of receipt by the applicant of such notification. The Administrator may issue an experimental use permit only if the Administrator determines that the applicant needs such permit in order to accumulate information necessary to register a pesticide under section 3 of this Act. An application for an experimental use permit may be filed at any time.

"(b) *Temporary Tolerance Level.*—If the Administrator determines that the use of a pesticide may reasonably be expected to result in any residue on or in food or feed, he may establish a temporary tolerance level for the residue of the pesticide before issuing the experimental use permit.

"(c) *Use Under Permit.*—Use of a pesticide under an experimental use permit shall be under the supervision of the Adminstrator, and shall be subject to such terms and conditions and be for such period of time as the Administrator may prescribe in the permit.

"(d) *Studies.*—When any experimental use permit is issued for a pesticide containing any chemical or combination of chemicals which has not been included in any previously registered pesticide, the Administrator may specify that studies be conducted to detect whether the use of the pesticide under the permit may cause unreasonable adverse effects on the environment. All results of such studies shall be reported to the Administrator before such pesticide may be registered under section 3.

"(e) *Revocation.*—The Administrator may revoke any experimental use permit, at any time, if he finds that its terms or conditions are being violated, or that its terms and conditions are inadequate to avoid unreasonable adverse effects on the environment.

"(f) *State Issuance of Permits.*—Notwithstanding the foregoing provisions of this section, the Adminsitrator shall,under such terms and conditions as he may by regulations prescribe, authorize any State to issue an experimental use permit for a pesticide. All provisions of section 4 relating to State plans shall apply with equal force to a State plan for the issuance of experimental use permits under this section.

"(g) *Exemption for Agricultural Research Agencies.*—Notwithstanding the foregoing provisions of this section, the Administrator may issue an experimental use permit for a pesticide to any public or private agricultural research agency or educational institution which applies for such permit. Each permit shall not exceed more than a one-year period or such other specific time as the Administrator may prescribe. Such permit shall be issued under such terms and conditions restricting the use of the pesticide as the Administrator may require: *Provided,* That such pesticide may be used only by such research agency or educational institution for purposes of experimentation."

"SEC. 6. ADMINISTRATIVE REVIEW; SUSPENSION.

"(a) *Cancellation After Five Years.*—

"(1) *Procedure.*—The Administrator shall cancel the registration of any pesticide at the end of the five-year period which begins on the date of its registration (or at the end of any five-year period thereafter) unless the registrant, or other interested person with the concurrence of the registra before the end of such period, requests in accordance with regulations prescribed by the Administrator that the registration be continued in effect: *Provided,* That the Administrator may permit the continued sale and use of existing stocks of a pesticide whose registration is canceled under this subsection or subsection (b) to such extent, under such conditions, and for such uses as he may specify if he determines that such sale or use is not inconsistent with the purposes of this Act and will not have unreasonable adverse effects on the environment. The Administrator shall publish in the Federal Register, at least 30 days prior to the expiration of such five-year period, notice that the registration will be canceled if the registrant or other interested person with the concurrence of the registrant does not request that the registration be continued in effect.

"(2) *Information.*—If at any time after the registration of a pesticide the registrant has additional factual information regarding unreasonable adverse effects on the environment of the pesticide, he shall submit such information to the Administrator.

"(b) *Cancellation and Chance in Classification.*—If it appears to the Administrator that a pesticide or its labeling or other material required to be submitted does not comply with the provisions of this Act or when used in accordance with widespread and commonly recognized practice, generally causes unreasonable adverse effects on the environment, the Administrator may issue a notice of his intent either—

"(1) to cancel its registration or to change its classification together with the reasons (including the factual basis) for his action, or

"(2) to hold a hearing to determine whether or not its registration should be canceled or its classification changed.

Such notice shall be sent to the registrant and made public. In determining whether to issue any such notice, the Administrator shall include among those factors to be taken into account the impact of the action proposed in such notice on production and prices of agricultural commodities, retail food prices, and otherwise on the agricultural economy. At least 60 days prior to sending such notice to the registrant or making public such notice, whichever occurs first, the Administrator shall provide the Secretary of Agriculture with a copy of such notice and an analysis of such impact on the agricultural economy. If the Secretary comments in writing to the Administrator regarding the notice and analysis within 30 days after receiving them, the Administrator shall publish in the Federal Register (with the notice) the comments of the Secretary and the response of the Administrator with regard to the Secretary's comments. If the Secretary does not comment in writing to the Administrator regarding the notice and analysis within 30 days after receiving them, the Administrator may notify the registrant and make public the notice at any time after such 30-day period notwithstanding the foregoing 60-day time requirement. The time requirements imposed by the preceding 3 sentences may be waived or modified to the extent agreed upon by the Administrator and the Secretary. Notwithstanding any other provision of this subsection (b) and section 25(d), in the event that the Administrator determines that suspension of a pesticide registration is necessary to prevent an imminent hazard to human health, then upon such a finding the Administrator may waive the requirement of notice to and consultation with the Secretary of Agriculture pursuant to subsection (b) and of submission to the Scientific Advisory Panel pursuant to section 25(d) and proceed in accordance with subsection (c). The proposed action shall become final and effective at the end of 30 days from receipt by the registrant, or publication, of a notice issued under paragraph (1), whichever occurs later, unless within that time either (i) the registrant makes the necessary corrections, if possible, or (ii) a request for a hearing is made by a person adversely affected by the notice. In the event a hearing is held pursuant to such a request or to the Administrator's determination under paragraph (2), a decision pertaining to registration or classification issued after completion of such hearing shall be final.

In taking any final action under this subsection, the Administrator shall consider restricting a pesticide's use or uses as an alternative to cancellation and shall fully explain the reasons for these restrictions, and shall include among those factors to be taken into account the impact of such final action on production and prices of agricultural commodities, retail food prices, and otherwise on the agricultural economy, and he shall publish in the Federal Register an analysis of such impact.

"(c) *Suspension.*—

"(1) *Order.*—If the Administrator determines that action is necessary to prevent an imminent hazard during the time required for cancellation or change in classification proceedings he may, by order, suspend the registration of the pesticide immediately. No order of suspension may be issued unless the Administrator has issued or at the same time issues notice of his intention to cancel the registration or change the classification of the pesticide.

Except as provided in paragraph (3), the Administration shall notify the registrant prior to issuing any suspension order. Such notice shall include findings pertaining to the question of 'imminent hazard'. The registrant shall then have an opportunity, in accordance with the provisions of paragraph (2), for an expedited hearing before the Agency on the question of whether an imminent hazard exists.

"(2) *Expedite hearing.*—If no request for a hearing is submitted to the Agency within five days of the registrant's receipt of the notification provided for by paragraph (1), the suspension order may be issued and shall take effect and shall not be reviewable by a court. If a hearing is requested, it shall commence within five days of the receipt of the request for such hearing unless the registrant and the Agency agree that it shall commence at a later time. The hearing shall be held in accordance with the provisions of subchapter II of title 5 of the United States Code, except that the presiding officer need not be a certified hearing examiner. The presiding officer shall have ten days from the conclusion of the presentation of evidence to submit recommended findings and conclusions to the Administrator, who shall then have seven days to render a final order on the issue of suspension.

"(3) *Emergency order.*—Whenever the Administrator determines that an emergency exists that does not permit him to hold a hearing before suspending, he may issue a suspension order in advance of notification to the registrant. In that case, paragraph (2) shall apply except that (i) the order of suspension shall be in effect pending the expeditious completion of the remedies provided by that paragraph and the issuance of a final order on suspension, and (ii) no party other than the registrant and the Agency shall participate except that any person adversely affected may file briefs within the time allotted by the Agency's rules. Any person so filing briefs shall be considered a party to such proceeding for the purpose of section 16(b).

"(4) *Judicial review.*—A final order on the question of suspension following a hearing shall be reviewable in accordance with Section 16 of this Act, notwithstanding the fact that any related cancellation proceedings have not been completed. Petitions to review orders on the issue of suspension shall be advanced on the docket of the courts of appeals. Any order of suspension entered prior to a hearing before the Administrator shall be subject to immediate review in an action by the registrant or other interested person with the concurrence of the registrant in an appropriate district court, solely to determine whether the order of suspension was arbitrary, capricious or an abuse of discretion, or whether the order was issued in accordance with the procedures established by law. The effect of any order of the court will be only to stay the effectiveness of the suspension order, pending the Administrator's final decision with respect to cancellation or change in classification. This action may be maintained simultaneously with any administrative review proceeding under this section. The commencement of proceedings under this paragraph shall not operate as a stay of order, unless ordered by the court.

"(d) *Public Hearings and Scientific Review.*—In the event a hearing is requested pursuant to subsection (b) or determined upon by the Administrator pursuant to subsection (b), such hearing shall be held after due notice for the purpose of receiving evidence relevant and material to the issues raised by the objections filed by the applicant or other interested parties, or to the issues stated by the Administrator, if the hearing is called by the Administrator rather than by the filing of objections. Upon a showing of relevance and reasonable scope of evidence sought by any party to a public hearing, the Hearing Examiner shall issue a subpoena to compel testimony or production of documents from any person. The Hearing Examiner shall be guided by the principles of the Federal Rules of Civil Procedure in making any order for the protection of the witness or the content of documents produced and shall order the payment of reasonable fees and expenses as a condition to requiring testimony of the witness. On contest, the subpoena may be enforced by an appropriate United States district court in accordance with the principles stated herein. Upon the request of any party to a public hearing and when in the Hearing Examiner's judgment it is necessary or desirable, the Hearing Examiner shall at any time before the hearing record is closed refer to a Committee of the National Academy of Sciences the relevant questions of scientific fact involved in the public hearing. No member of any committee of the National Academy of Sciences established to carry out the functions of this section shall have a financial or other conflict of interest with respect to any matter considered by such committee. The Committee of the National Academy of Sciences shall report in writing to the Hearing Examiner within 60 days after such referral on these questions of scientific fact. The report shall be made public and shall be considered as part of the hearing record. The Administrator shall enter into appropriate arrangements with the National Academy of Sciences to assure an objective and competent scientific review of the questions presented to Committees of the Academy and to provide such other scientific advisory services as may be required by the Administrator for carrying out the purposes of this Act. As soon as practicable after completion of the hearing (including the report of the Academy) but not later than 90 days thereafter, the Administrator shall evaluate the data and reports before him and issue an order either revoking his notice of intention issued pursuant to this section, or shall issue an order either canceling the registration, changing the classification, denying the registration, or requiring modification of the labeling or packaging of the article. Such order shall be based only on substantial evidence of record of such hearing and shall set forth detailed findings of fact upon which the order is based.

"(e) *Conditional Registration.*—

"(1) The Administrator shall issue a notice of intent to cancel a registration issued under section 3(c)(7) of this Act if (A) the Administrator, at any time during the period provided for satisfaction of any condition imposed, determines that the registrant has failed to initiate and pursue appropriate action toward fulfilling any condition imposed, or (B) at the end of the period provided for satisfaction of any condition imposed, that condition has not been met: *Provided,* That the Administrator may permit the continued sale and use of existing stocks of a pesticide whose conditional registration has been canceled under this subsection to such extent, under such conditions, and for such uses as the Administrator may specify if the Administrator determines that such sale or use is not inconsistent with the purposes of this Act and will not have unreasonable adverse effects on the environment.

"(2) A cancellation proposed under this subsection shall become final and effective at the end of thirty days from receipt by the registrant of the notice of intent to cancel unless during that time a request for hearing is made by a person adversely affected by the notice. If a hearing is requested, a hearing shall be conducted under subsection (d) of this section: *Provided,* That the only matters for resolution at that hearing shall be whether the registrant has initiated and pursued appropriate action to comply with the condition or conditions within the time provided or whether the condition or conditions have been satisfied within the time provided, and whether the Administrator's determination with respect to the disposition of existing stocks is consistent with this Act. A decision after completion of such hearing shall be final. Notwithstanding any other provision of this section, a hearing shall be held and a determination made within seventy-five days after receipt of a request for such hearing.

"(f) *Judicial Review.*—Final orders of the Administrator under this section shall be subject to judicial review pursuant to section 16.

"SEC. 7. REGISTRATION OF ESTABLISHMENTS.

"(a) *Requirement.*—No person shall produce any pesticide subject to this Act or active ingredient used in producing a pesticide subject to this Act in any State unless the establishment in which it is produced is registered with the Administrator. The application for registration of any establishment shall include the name and address of the establishment and of the producer who operates such establishment.

"(b) *Registration.*—Whenever the Administrator receives an application under subsection (a), he shall register the establishment and assign it an establishment number.

"(c) *Information Required.*—

"(1) Any producer operating an establishment registered under this section shall inform the Administrator within 30 days after it is registered of the types and amounts of pesticides and, if applicable, active ingredients used in producing pesticides—

"(A) which he is currently producing;

"(B) which he has produced during the past year; and

"(C) which he has sold or distributed during the past year.

The information required by this paragraph shall be kept current and submitted to the Administrator annually as required under such regulations as the Administrator may prescribe.

"(2) Any such producer shall, upon the request of the Administrator for the purpose of issuing a stop sale order pursuant to section 13, inform him of the name and address of any recipient of any pesticide produced in any registered establishment which he operates.

"(d) *Confidential Records and Information.*—Any information submitted to the Administrator pursuant to subsection (c) other than the names of the pesticides or active ingredients used in producing pesticides produced, sold, or distributed at an establishment shall be considered confidential and shall be subject to the provisions of section 10.

"SEC. 8. BOOKS AND RECORDS.

"(a) *Requirements.*—The Administrator may prescribe regulations requiring producers to maintain such records with respect to their operations and the pesticides and devices produced as he determines are necessary for the effective enforcement of this Act. No records required under this subsection shall extend to financial data, sales data other than shipment data, pricing data, personnel data, and research data (other than data relating to registered pesticides or to a pesticide for which an application for registration has been filed).

"(b) *Inspection.*—For the purposes of enforcing the provisions of this Act, any producer, distributor, carrier, dealer, or any other person who sells or offers for sale, delivers or offers for delivery any pesticide or device subject to this Act, shall, upon request of any officer or employee of the Environmental Protection Agency or of any State or political subdivision, duly designated by the Administrator, furnish or permit such person at all reasonable times to have access to, and to copy: (1) all records showing the delivery, movement, or holding of such pesticide or device, including the quantity, the date of shipment and receipt, and the name of the consignor and consignee; or (2) in the event of the inability of any person to produce records containing such information, all other records and information relating to such delivery, movement, or holding of the pesticide or device. Any inspection with respect to any records and information referred to in this subsection shall not extend to financial data, sales data other than shipment data, pricing data, personnel data, and research data (other than data relating to registered pesticides or to a pesticide for which an application for registration has been filed).

Before undertaking an inspection under this subsection, the officer or employee must present to the owner, operator, or agent in charge of the establishment or other place where pesticides or devices are held for distribution or sale, appropriate credentials and a written statement as to the reason for the inspection, including a statement as to whether a violation of the law is suspected. If no violation is suspected, an alternate and sufficient reason shall be given in writing. Each such inspection shall be commenced and completed with reasonable promptness.

"SEC. 9. INSPECTION OF ESTABLISHMENTS, ETC.

"(a) *In General.*—For purposes of enforcing the provisions of this Act, officers or employees duly designated by the Administrator are authorized to enter at reasonable times, any establishment or other place where pesticides or devices are held for distribution or sale for the purpose of inspecting and obtaining samples of any pesticides or devices, packaged, labeled , and released for shipment, and samples of any containers or labeling for such pesticides or devices.

Before undertaking such inspection, the officers or employees must present to the owner, operator, or agent in charge of the establishment or other place where pesticides or devices are held for distribution or sale, appropriate credentials and a written statement as to the reason for the inspection, including a statement as to whether a violation of the law is suspected. If no violation is suspected, an alternate and sufficient reason shall be given in writing. Each such inspection shall be commenced and completed with reasonable promptness. If the officer or employee obtains any samples, prior to leaving the premises, he shall give to the owner, operator, or agent in charge a receipt describing the samples obtained and, if requested, a portion of each such sample equal in volume or weight to the portion retained. If an analysis is made of such samples, a copy of the results of such analysis shall be furnished promptly to the owner, operator, or agent in charge.

"(b) *Warrants.*—For purposes of enforcing the provisions of this Act and upon a showing to an officer or court of competent jurisdiction that there is reason to believe that the provisions of this Act have been violated, officers or employees duly designated by the Administrator are empowered to obtain and to execute warrants authorizing—

"(1) entry for the purpose of this section;

"(2) inspection and reproduction of all records showing the quantity, date of shipment, and the name of consignor and consignee of any pesticide or device found in the establishment which is adulterated, misbranded, not registered (in the case of a pesticide) or otherwise in violation of this Act and in the event of the inability of any person to produce records containing such information, all other records and information relating to such delivery, movement, or holding of the pesticide or device; and

"(3) the seizure of any pesticide or device which is in violation of this Act.

"(c) *Enforcement.*—

"(1) *Certification of facts to attorney general.*—The examination of pesticides or devices shall be made in the Environmental Protection Agency or elsewhere as the Administrator may designate for the purpose of determining from such examinations whether they comply with the requirements of this Act. If it shall appear from any such examination that they fail to comply with the requirements of this Act, the Administrator shall cause notice to be given to the person against whom criminal or civil proceedings are contemplated. Any person so notified shall be given an opportunity to present his views, either orally or in writing, with regard to such contemplated proceedings, and if in the opinion of the Administrator it appears that the provisions of this Act have been violated by such person, then the Administrator shall certify the facts to the Attorney General, with a copy of the results of the analysis or the examination of such pesticide for the institution of a criminal proceeding pursuant to section 14(b) or a civil proceeding under section 14(a), when the Administrator determines that such action will be sufficient to effectuate the purposes of this Act.

"(2) *Notice not required.*—The notice of contemplated proceedings and opportunity to present views set forth in this subsection are not prerequisites to the institution of any proceeding by the Attorney General.

"(3) *Warning notices.*—Nothing in this Act shall be construed as requiring the Administrator to institute proceedings for prosecution of minor violations of this Act whenever he believes that the public interest will be adequately served by a suitable written notice of warning.

"SEC. 10. PROTECTION OF TRADE SECRETS AND OTHER INFORMATION.

"(a) *In General.*—In submitting data required by this Act, the applicant may (1) clearly mark any portions thereof which in his opinion are trade secrets or commercial or financial information and (2) submit such marked materials separately from other material required to be submitted under this Act.

"(b) *Disclosure.*—Nothwithstanding any other provision of this Act, and subject to the limitations in subsections (d) and (e) of this section the Administrator shall not make public information which in his judgment contains or relates to trade secrets or commercial or financial information obtained from a person and privileged or confidential, except that, when necessary to carry out the provisions of this Act, information relating to formulas of products acquired by authorization of this Act may be revealed to any Federal agency consulted and may be revealed at a public hearing or in findings of fact issued by the Administrator.

"(c) *Disputes.*—If the Administrator proposes to release for inspection information which the applicant or registrant believes to be protected from disclosure under subsection (b), he shall notify the applicant or registrant, in writing, by certified mail. The Administrator shall not thereafter make available for inspection such data until thirty days after receipt of the notice by the applicant or registrant. During this period, the applicant or registrant may institute an action in an appropriate district court for a declaratory judgment as to whether such information is subject to protection under subsection (b).

"(d) *Limitations.*—

"(1) All information concerning the objectives, methodology, results, or significance of any test or experiment performed on or with a registered or previously registered pesticide or its separate ingredients, impurities, or degradation products, and any information concerning the effects of such pesticide on any organism or the behavior of such pesticide in the environment, including, but not limited to, data on safety to fish and wildlife, humans and other mammals, plants, animals, and soil, and studies on persistence, translocation and fate in the environment, and metabolism, shall be available for disclosure to the public: *Provided,* That the use of such data for any registration purpose shall be governed by section 3 of this Act: *Provided further,* That this paragraph does not authorize the disclosure of any information that—

"(A) discloses maufacturing or quality control processes,

"(B) discloses the details of any methods for testing, detecting, or measuring the quantity of any delibrately added inert ingredient of a pesticide, or

"(C) discloses the identity or percentage quantity of any deliberately added inert ingredient of a pesticide, unless the Administrator has first determined that disclosure is necessary to protect against an unreasonable risk of injury to health or the environment.

"(2) Information concerning production, distribution, sale, or inventories of a pesticide that is otherwise entitled to confidential treatment under subsection (b) of this section may be publicly disclosed in connection with a public proceeding to determine whether a pesticide, or any ingredient of a pesticide, causes unreasonable adverse effects on health or the environment, if the Administrator determines that such disclosure is necessary in the public interest.

"(3) If the Administrator proposes to disclose information described in clause (A), (B), or (C) of paragraph (1) or in paragraph (2) of this subsection, the Administrator shall notify by certified mail the submitter of such information of the intent to release such information. The Administrator may not release such information, without the submitter's consent, until thirty days after the submitter has been furnished such notice: *Provided,* That where the Administrator finds that disclosure of information described in clause (A), (B), (C) of paragraph (1) of this subsection is necessary to avoid or lessen an imminent and substantial risk of injury to the public health, the Administrator may set such shorter period of notice (but not less than ten days) and such method of notice as the Administrator finds appropriate. During such period the data submitter may institute an action in an appropriate district court to enjoin or limit the proposed disclosure. The court shall give expedited consideration to any such action. The court may enjoin disclosure, or limit the disclosure or the parties to whom disclosure shall be made, to the extent that—

"(A) in the case of information described in clause (A), (B), or (C) of paragraph (1) of this subsection, the proposed disclosure is not required to protect against an unreasonable risk of injury to health or the environment; or

"(B) in the case of information described in paragraph (2) of this subsection, the public interest in availability of the information in the public proceeding does not outweigh the interests in preserving the confidentiality of the information.

"(e) *Disclosure to Contractors.*—Information otherwise protected from disclosure to the public subsection (b) of this section may be disclosed to contractors with the United States and employees of such contractors if, in the opinion of the Administrator, such disclosure is necessary for the satisfactory performance by the contractor of a contract with the United States for the performance of work in connection with this Act and under such conditions as the Administrator may specify. The Administrator shall require as a condition to the disclosure of information under this subsection that the person receiving it take such security precautions respecting the information as the Administrator shall by regulation prescribe.

"(f) *Penalty for disclosure by Federal Employees.*—

"(1) Any officer or employee of the United States or former officer or employee of the United States who, by virtue of such employment or official position, has obtained possession of, or has access to, material the disclosure of which is prohibited by subsection (b) of this section, and who, knowing that disclosure of such material is prohibited by such subsection, willfully discloses the material in any manner to any person not entitled to receive it, shall be fined not more than $10,000 or imprisoned for not more than one year, or both. Section 1905 of title 18 of the United States Code shall not apply with respect to the publishing, divulging, disclosure, or making known of, or making available, information reported or otherwise obtained under this Act. Nothing in this Act shall preempt any civil remedy under State or Federal law for wrongful disclosure of trade secrets.

"(2) For the purposes of this section, any contractor with the United States who is furnished information as authorized by subsection (e) of this section, or any employee of any such contractor, shall be considered to be an employee of the United States.

"(g) *Disclosure to Foreign and Multinational Pesticide Producers.*—

"(1) The Administrator shall not knowingly disclose information submitted by an applicant or registrant under this Act to any employee or agent of any business or other entity engaged in the production, sale, or distribution of pesticides in countries other than the United States or in addition to the United States or to any other person who intends to deliver such data to such foreign or multinational business or entity unless the applicant or registrant has consented to such disclosure. The Administrator shall require an affirmation from any person who intends to inspect data that such person does not seek access to the data for purposes of delivering it or offering it for sale to any such business or entity or its agents or employees and will not purposefully deliver or negligently cause the data to be delivered to such business or entity or its agents or employees. Notwithstanding any other provision of this subsection, the Administrator may disclose information to any person in connection with a public proceeding under law or regulation, subject to restrictions on the availability of information contained elsewhere in this Act, which information is relevant to the determination by the Administrator with respect to whether a pesticide, or any ingredient of a pesticide, causes unreasonable adverse effects on health or the environment.

"(2) The Administrator shall maintain records of the names of persons to whom data are disclosed under this subsection and the persons or organizations they represent and shall inform the applicant or registrant of the names and affiliation of such persons.

"(3) Section 1001 of title 18 of the United States Code shall apply to any affirmation made under paragraph (1) of this subsection.

"SEC. 11. STANDARDS APPLICABLE TO PESTICIDE APPLICATORS.

"(a) *In General.*—No regulations prescribed by the Administrator for carrying out the provisions of this Act shall require any private applicator to maintain any records or file any reports or other documents.

"(b) *Separate Standards.*—When establishing or approving standards for licensing or certification, the Administrator shall establish separate standards for commercial and private applicators.

"SEC. 12. UNLAWFUL ACTS.

"(a) *In General.*—

"(1) Except as provided by subsection (b), it shall be unlawful for any person in any State to distribute, sell, offer for sale, hold for sale, ship, deliver for shipment, or receive and (having so received) deliver or offer to deliver, to any person—

"(A) any pesticide which is not registered under section 3, except as provided by section 6(a)(1);

"(B) any registered pesticide if any claims made for it as a part of its distribution or sale substantially differ from any claims made for it as a part of the statement required in connection with its registration under section 3;

"(C) any registered pesticide the composition of which differs at the time of its distribution or sale from its composition as described in the statement required in connection with its registration under section 3;

"(D) any pesticide which has not been colored or discolored pursuant to the provisions of section 25(c)(5);

"(E) any pesticide which is adulterated or misbranded; or

"(F) any device which is misbranded.

"(2) It shall be unlawful for any person—

"(A) to detach, alter, deface, or destroy, in whole or in part, any labeling required under this Act;

"(B) to refuse to keep any records required pursuant to section 8, or to refuse to allow the inspection of any records or establishment pursuant to section 8 or 9, or to refuse to allow an officer or employee of the Environmental Protection Agency to take a sample of any pesticide pursuant to section 9;

"(C) to give a guaranty or undertaking provided for in subsection (b) which is false in any particular, except that a person who receives and relies upon a guaranty authorized under subsection (b) may give a guaranty to the same effect. which guaranty shall contain, in addition to his own name and address, the name and address of the person residing in the United States from whom he received the guaranty or undertaking;

"(D) to use for his own advantage or to reveal, other than to the Administrator, or officials or employees of the Environmental Protection Agency or other Federal executive agencies, or to the courts, or to physicians, pharmacists, and other qualified persons, needing such information for the performance of their duties, in accordance with such directions as the Administrator may prescribe, any information acquired by authority of this Act which is confidential under this Act;

"(E) who is a registrant, wholesaler, dealer, retailer, or other distributor to advertise a produce registered under this Act for restricted use without giving the classification of the product assigned to it under section 3;

"(F) to make available for use, or to use, any registered pesticide classified for restricted use for some or all purposes other than in accordance with section 3(d) and any regulations thereunder; *Provided,* That it shall not be unlawful to sell, under regulations issued by the Administrator, a restricted use pesticide to a person who is not a certified applicator for application by a certified applicator;

"(G) to use any registered pesticide in a manner inconsistent with its labeling;

"(H) to use any pesticide which is under an experimental use permit contrary to the provisions of such permit;

"(I) to violate any order issued under section 13;

"(J) to violate any suspension order issued under section 6;

"(K) to violate any cancellation of registration of a pesticide under section 6, except as provided by section 6(a)(1);

"(L) who is a producer to violate any of the provisions of section 7;

"(M) to knowingly falsify all or part of any application for registration, application for experimental use permit, any information submitted to the Administrator pursuant to section 7, any records required to be maintained pursuant to section 8, any report filed under this Act, or any information marked as confidential and submitted to the Administrator under any provision of this act;

"(N) who is a registrant, wholesaler, dealer, retailer, or other distributor to fail to file reports required by this Act;

"(O) to add any substance to, or take any substance from, any pesticide in a manner that may defeat the purpose of this Act; or

"(P) to use any pesticide in tests on human beings unless such human beings (i) are fully informed of the nature and purposes of the test and of any physical and mental health consequences which are reasonably foreseeable therefrom, and (ii) freely volunteer to participate in the test.

"(b) *Exemptions.*—The penalties provided for a violation of paragraph (1) of subsection (a) shall not apply to—

"(1) any person who establishes a guaranty signed by, and containing the name and address of, the registrant or person residing in the United States from whom he purchased or received in good faith the pesticide in the same unbroken package, to the effect that the pesticide was lawfully registered at the time of sale and delivery to him, and that it complies with the other requirements of this Act, and in such case the guarantor shall be subject to the penalties which would otherwise attach to the person holding the guaranty under the provisions of this Act;

"(2) any carrier while lawfully shipping, transporting, or delivering for shipment any pesticide or device, if such carrier upon request of any officer or employee duly designated by the Administrator shall permit such officer or employee to copy all of its records concerning such pesticide or device;

"(3) any public official while engaged in the performance of his official duties;

"(4) any person using or possessing any pesticide as provided by an experimental use permit in effect with respect to such pesticide and such use or possession; or

"(5) any person who ships a substance or mixture of substances being put through tests in which the purpose is only to determine its value for pesticide purposes or to determine its toxicity or other properties and from which the user does not expect to receive any benefit in pest control from its use.

"SEC. 13. STOP SALE, USE, REMOVAL, AND SEIZURE.

"(a) *Stop Sale, Etc., Orders.*—Whenever any pesticide or device is found by the Administrator in any State and there is reason to believe on the basis of inspection or tests that such pesticide or device is in violation of any of the provisions of this Act, or that such pesticide or device has been or is intended to be distributed or sold in violation of any such provisions, or when the registration of the pesticide has been canceled by a final order or has been suspended, the Administrator may issue a written or printed 'stop sale, use, or removal' order to any person who owns, controls, or has custody of such pesticide or device, and after receipt of such order no person shall sell, use, or remove the pesticide or device described in the order except in accordance with the provisions of the order.

"(b) *Seizure.*—Any pesticide or device that is being transported or, having been transported, remains unsold or in original unbroken packages, or that is sold or offered for sale in any State, or that is imported from a foreign country, shall be liable to be proceeded against in any district court in the district where it is found and seized for confiscation by a process in rem for condemnation if—

"(1) in the case of a pesticide—

"(A) it is adulterated or misbranded;

"(B) it is not registered pursuant to the provisions of section 3;

"(C) its labeling fails to bear the information required by this Act;

"(D) it is not colored or discolored and such coloring or discoloring is required under this Act; or

"(E) any of the claims made for it or any of the directions for its use differ in substance from the representations made in connection with its registration;

"(2) in the case of a device, it is misbranded; or

"(3) in the case of a pesticide or device, when used in accordance with the requirements imposed under this Act and as directed by the labeling, it nevertheless causes unreasonable adverse effects on the environment. In the case of a plant regulator, defoliant, or desiccant, used in accordance with the label claims and recommendations, physical or physiological effects on plants or parts thereof shall not be deemed to be injury when such effects are the purpose for which the plant regulator, defoliant, or desiccant was applied.

"(c) *Disposition After Condemnation.*—If the pesticide or device is condemned it shall, after entry of the decree, be disposed of by destruction or sale as the court may direct and the proceeds, if sold, less the court costs, shall be paid into the Treasury of the United States, but the pesticide or device shall not be sold contrary to the provisions of this Act or the laws of the jurisdiction in which it is sold; *Provided,* That upon payment of the costs of the condemnation proceedings and the execution and delivery of a good and sufficient bond conditioned that the pesticide or device shall not be sold or otherwise disposed of contrary to the provisions of the Act or the laws of any jurisdiction in which sold, the court may direct that such pesticide or device be delivered to the owner thereof. The proceedings of such condemnation cases shall conform, as near as may be to the proceedings in admiralty, except that either party may demand trial by jury of any issue of fact joined in any case, and all such proceedings shall be at the suit of and in the name of the United States.

"(d) *Court Costs, Etc.*—When a decree of condemnation is entered against the pesticide or device, court costs and fees, storage, and other proper expenses shall be awarded against the person, if any, intervening as claimant of the pesticide or device.

"SEC. 14. PENALTIES.

"(a) *Civil Penalties.*—

"(1) *In General.*—Any registrant, commercial applicator, wholesaler, dealer, retailer, or other distributor who violates any provision of this Act may be assessed a civil penalty by the Administrator of not more than $5,000 for each offense.

"(2) *Private Applicator.*—Any private applicator or other person not included in paragraph (1) who violates any provision of this Act subsequent to receiving a written warning from the Administrator or following a citation for a prior violation, may be assessed a civil penalty by the Administrator of not more than $1,000 for each offense: *Provided,* That any applicator not included under paragraph (1) of this subsection who holds or applies registered pesticides, or use dilutions of registered pesticides, only to provide a service of controlling pests without delivering any unapplied pesticide to any person so served, and who violates any provision of this Act may be assessed a civil penalty by the Administrator of not more than $500 for the first offense nor more than $1,000 for each subsequent offense.

"(3) *Hearing.*—No civil penalty shall be assessed unless the person charged shall have been given notice and opportunity for a hearing on such charge in the county, parish, or incorporated city of the residence of the person charged.

"(4) *Determination of Penalty.*—In determining the amount of the penalty, the Administrator shall consider the appropriateness of such penalty to the size of the business of the person charged, the effect on the person's ability to continue in business, and the gravity of the violation. Whenever the Administrator finds that the violation occurred despite the exercise of due care or did not cause significant harm to health or the environment, the Administrator may issue a warning in lieu of assessing a penalty.".

"(5) *References to Attorney General.—In case of inability to collect such civil penalty or failure of any person to pay all, or such portion of such civil penalty as the Administrator may determine, the Administrator shall refer the matter to the Attorney General, who shall recover such amount by action in the appropriate United States district court.*

"(b) Criminal Penalties.—

"(1) In General.—Any registrant, commercial applicator, wholesaler, dealer, retailer, or other distributor who knowingly violates any provision of this Act shall be guilty of a misdemeanor and shall on conviction be fined not more than $25,000, or imprisoned for not more than one year, or both.

"(2) *Private applicator.*—Any private applicator or other person not included in paragraph (1) who knowingly violates any provision of this Act shall be guilty of a misdemeanor and shall on conviction be fined not more than $1,000, or imprisoned for not more than 30 days, or both.

"(3) *Disclosure of information.*—Any person, who, with intent to defraud, uses or reveals information relative to formulas of products acquired under the authority of section 3, shall be fined not more than $10,000, or imprisoned for not more than three years, or both.

"(4) *Acts of officers, agents, etc.*—When construing and enforcing the provisions of this Act, the act, omission, or failure of any officer, agent, or other person acting for or employed by any person shall in every case be also deemed to be the act, omission, or failure of such person as well as that of the person employed.

"SEC. 15. INDEMNITIES.

"(a) *Requirement.*—If—

"(1) the Administrator notifies a registrant that he has suspended the registration of a pesticide because such action is necessary to prevent an imminent hazard;

"(2) the registration of the pesticide is canceled as a result of a final determination that the use of such pesticide will create an imminent hazard; and

"(3) any person who owned any quantity of such pesticide immediately before the notice to the registrant under paragraph (1) suffered losses by reason of suspension or cancellation of the registration. The Administrator shall make an indemnity payment to such person, unless the Administrator finds that such person (i) had knowledge of facts which, in themselves, would have shown that such pesticide did not meet the requirements of section 3(c)(5) for registration, and (ii) continued thereafter to produce such pesticide without giving timely notice of such facts to the Administrator.

"(b) *Amount of Payment.*—

"(1) *In General.*—The amount of the indemnity payment under subsection (a) to any person shall be determined on the basis of the cost of the pesticide owned by such person immediately before the notice to the registrant referred to in subsection (a)(1); except that in no event shall an indemnity payment to any person exceed the fair market value of the pesticide owned by such person immediately before the notice referred to in subsection (a)(1).

"(2) *Special rule.*—Notwithstanding any other provision of his Act, the Administrator may provide a reasonable time for use or other disposal of such pesticide. In determining the quantity of any pesticide for which indemnity shall be paid under this subsection, proper adjustment s' ·ll be made for any pesticide used or otherwise disposed of by such o\.,ıer.

"SEC. 16. ADMINISTRATIVE PROCEDURE; JUDICIAL REVIEW.

"(a) *District Court Review.*—Except as is otherwise provided in this Act, Agency refusals to cancel or suspend registrations or change classifications not following a hearing and other final Agency actions not committed to Agency discretion by law are judicially reviewable in the district courts.

"(b) *Review by Court of Appeals.*—In the case of actual controversy as to the validity of any order issued by the Administrator following a public hearing, any person who will be adversely affected by such order and who had been a party to the proceedings may obtain judicial review by filing in the United States court of appeals for the circuit wherein such person resides or has a place of business, within 60 days after the entry of such order, a petition praying that the order be set aside in whole or in part. A copy of the petition shall be forthwith transmitted by the clerk of the court to the Administrator or any officer designated by him for that purpose, and thereupon the Administrator shall file in the court the record of the proceedings on which he based his order, as provided in section 2112 of title 28, United States Code. Upon the filing of such petition the court shall have exclusive jurisdiction to affirm or set aside the order complained of in whole or in part. The court shall consider all evidence of record. The order ot the Administrator shall be sustained if it is supported by substantial evidence when considered on the record as a whole. The judgment of the court affirming or setting aside, in whole or in part, any order under this section shall be final, subject to review by the Supreme Court of the United States upon certiorari or certification as provided in section 1254 of title 28 of the United States Code. The commencement of proceedings under this section shall not, unless specifically ordered by the court to the contrary, operate as a stay of an order. The court shall advance on the docket and expedite the disposition of all cases filed therein pursuant to this section.

"(c) *Jurisdiction of District Courts.*—The district courts of the United States are vested with jurisdiction specifically to enforce, and to prevent and restrain violations of this Act.

"(d) *Notice of Judgments.*—The Administrator shall, by publication in such manner as he may prescribe, give notice of all judgments entered in actions instituted under the authority of this Act.

"SEC. 17. IMPORTS AND EXPORTS.

"(a) *Pesticides and Devices Intended for Export.*—Notwithstanding any other provision of this Act, no pesticide or device or active ingredient used in

---

Section 18 (b) of the Federal Pesticide Act of 1978 provides, The amendment [to Section 17(a)] made by subsection (a)(1) of this section shall become effective March 29, 1979.

producing a pesticide intended solely for export to any foreign country shall be deemed in violation of this Act—

"(1) when prepared or packed according to the specifications or directions of the foreign purchaser, except that producers of such pesticides and devices and active ingredients used in producing pesticides shall be subject to sections 2(p), 2(q)(1) (A), (C), (D), (E), (G), and (H), 2(q)(2) (A), (B), (C) (i) and (iii), and (D), 7, and 8 of this Act; and

"(2) in the case of any pesticide other than a pesticide registered under section 3 or sold under section 6(a)(1) of this Act, if, prior to export, the foreign purchaser has signed a statement acknowledging that the purchaser understands that such pesticide is not registered for use in the United States and cannot be sold in the United States under this Act. A copy of that statement shall be transmitted to an appropriate official of the government of the importing country.

"(b) *Cancellation Notices Furnished to Foreign Governments.*—Whenever a registration, or a cancellation or suspension of the registration of a pesticide becomes effective, or ceases to be effective, the Administrator shall transmit through the State Department notification thereof to the governments of other countries and to appropriate international agencies. Such notification shall, upon request, include all information related to the cancellation or suspension of the registration of the pesticide and information concerning other pesticides that are registered under section 3 of this Act and that could be used in lieu of such pesticide.

"(c) *Importation of Pesticides and Devices.*—The Secretary of the Treasury shall notify the Administrator of the arrival of pesticides and devices and shall deliver to the Administrator, upon his request, samples of pesticides or devices which are being imported into the United States, giving notice to the owner or consignee, who may appear before the Administrator and have the right to introduce testimony. If it appears from the examination of a sample that it is adulterated, or misbranded or otherwise violates the provisions set forth in this Act, or is otherwise injurious to health or the environment, the pesticide or device may be refused admission, and the Secretary of the Treasury shall refuse delivery to the consignee and shall cause the destruction of any pesticide or device refused delivery which shall not be exported by the consignee within 90 days from the date of notice of such refusal under such regulations as the Secretary of Treasury may prescribe: *Provided,* That the Secretary of the Treasury may deliver to the consignee such pesticide or device pending examination and decision in the matter on execution of bond for the amount of the full invoice value of such pesticide or device, together with the duty thereon, and on refusal to return such pesticide or device for any cause to the custody of the Secretary of the Treasury, when demanded, for the purpose of excluding them from the country, or for any other purpose, said consignee shall forfeit the full amount of said bond: *And provided further,* That all charges for storage, cartage, and labor on pesticides or devices which are refused admission or delivery shall be paid by the owner or consignee, and in default of such payment shall constitute a lien against any future importation made by such owner or consignee.

"(d) *Cooperation in International Efforts.*—The Administrator shall in cooperation with the Department of State and any other appropriate Federal agency, participate and cooperate in any international efforts to develop improved pesticide research and regulations.

"(e) *Regulations.*—The Secretary of the Treasury, in consultation with the Administrator, shall prescribe regulations for the enforcement of subsection (c) of this section.

"SEC. 18. EXEMPTION OF FEDERAL AGENCIES.

"The Administrator may, at his discretion, exempt any Federal or State agency from any provision of this Act if he determines that emergency conditions exist which require such exemption.

"The Administrator, in determining whether or not such emergency conditions exist, shall consult with the Secretary of Agriculture and the Governor of any State concerned if they request such determination."

"SEC. 19. DISPOSAL AND TRANSPORTATION.

"(a) *Procedures.*—The Administrator shall, after consultation with other interested Federal agencies, establish procedures and regulations for the disposal or storage of packages and containers of pesticides and for disposal or storage of excess amounts of such pesticides, and accept at convenient locations for safe disposal a pesticide the registration of which is canceled under section 6(c) if requested by the owner of the pesticide.

"(b) *Advice to Secretary of Transportation.*—The Administrator shall provide advice and assistance to the Secretary of Transportation with respect to his functions relating to the transportation of hazardous materials under the Department of Transportation Act (49 U.S.C. 1657), the Transportation of Explosives Act (18 U.S.C. 831-835), the Federal Aviation Act of 1958 (49 U.S.C. 1421-1430, 1472 II), and the Hazardous Cargo Act (46 U.S.C. 170, 375, 416).

"(c) *Provisions for unused quantities.*—Notification of cancellation of any pesticide shall include specific provisions for the disposal of the unused quantities of such pesticide.

"SEC. 20. RESEARCH AND MONITORING.

"(a) *Research.*—The Administrator shall undertake research, including research by grant or contract with other Federal agencies, universities, or others as may be necessary to carry out the purposes of this Act, and he shall conduct research into integrated pest management in coordination with the Secretary of Agriculture. The Administrator shall also take care to insure that such research does not duplicate research being undertaken by any other Federal agency.

"(b) *National Monitoring Plan.*—The Administrator shall formulate and periodically revise, in cooperation with other Federal, State, or local agencies, a national plan for monitoring pesticides.

"(c) *Monitoring.*—The Administrator shall undertake such monitoring activities, including, but not limited to, monitoring in air, soil, water, man, plants, and animals, as may be necessary for the implementation of this Act and of the national pesticide monitoring plan. The Administrator shall establish procedures for the monitoring of man and animals and their environment for incidental pesticide exposure, including, but not limited to, the quantification of incidental human and environmental pesticide pollution and the secular trends thereof, and identification of the sources of contamination and their relationship to human and environmental effects. Such activities shall be carried out in cooperation with other Federal, State, and local agencies.

"SEC. 21. SOLICITATION OF COMMENTS; NOTICE OF PUBLIC HEARINGS.

"(a) The Administrator, before publishing regulations under this Act, shall solicit the views of the Secretary of Agriculture in accordance with the procedure described in section 25(a).

"(b) In addition to any other authority relating to public hearings and solicitation of views, in connection with the suspension or cancellation of a pesticide registration or any other actions authorized under this Act, the Administrator may, at his discretion, solicit the views of all interested persons, either orally or in writing, and seek such advice from scientists, farmers, farm organizations, and other qualified persons as he deems proper.

"(c) In connection with all public hearings under this Act the Administrator shall publish timely notice of such hearings in the Federal Register.

"SEC. 22. DELEGATION AND COOPERATION.

"(a) *Delegation.*—All authority vested in the Administrator by virtue of the provisions of this Act may with like force and effect be executed by such employees of the Environmental Protection Agency as the Administrator may designate for the purpose.

"(b) *Cooperation.*—The Administrator shall cooperate with the Department of Agriculture, any other Federal agency, and any appropriate agency of any State or any political subdivision thereof, in carrying out the provisions of this Act, and in securing uniformity of regulations.

"SEC. 23. STATE COOPERATION, AID, AND TRAINING.

"(a) *Cooperative Agreements.*—The Administrator may enter into cooperative agreements with States and Indian tribes—

"(1) to delegate to any State or Indian tribe the authority to cooperate in the enforcement of this Act through the use of its personnel or facilities, to train personnel of the State or Indian tribe to cooperate in the enforcement of this Act, and to assist States and Indian tribes in implementing cooperative enforcement programs through grants-in-aid; and

"(2) to assist States in developing and administering State programs, and Indian tribes that enter into cooperative agreements, to train and certify applicators consistent with the standards the Administrator prescribes.

Effective with the fiscal year beginning October 1, 1978, there are authorized to be appropriated annually such funds as may be necessary for the Administrator to provide through cooperative agreements an amount equal to 50 percent of the anticipated cost to each State or Indian tribe, as agreed to under such cooperative agreements, of conducting training and certification programs during such fiscal year. If funds sufficient to pay 50 percent of the costs for any year are not appropriated, the share of each State and Indian tribe shall be reduced in a like proportion in allocating available funds.

"(b) *Contracts for Training.*—In addition, the Administrator may enter into contracts with Federal, State, or Indian tribal agencies for the purpose of encouraging the training of certified applicators.

"(c) *Information and Education.*—The Administrator shall, in cooperation with the Secretary of Agriculture, use the services of the cooperative State extension services to inform and educate pesticide users about accepted uses and other regulations made under this Act.

"SEC. 24. AUTHORITY OF STATES.

"(a) A State may regulate the sale or use of any federally registered pesticide or device in the State, but only if and to the extent the regulation does not permit any sale or use prohibited by this Act.

"(b) Such State shall not impose or continue in effect any requirements for labeling or packaging in addition to or different from those required under this Act.

"(c)(1) A State may provide registration for additional uses of federally registered pesticides formulated for distribution and use within that State to meet special local needs in accord with the purposes of this Act and if registration for such use has not previously been denied, disapproved, or cancelled by the Administrator. Such registration shall be deemed registration under section 3 for all purposes of this Act, but shall authorize distribution and use only within such State.

"(2) A registration issued by a State under this subsection shall not be effective for more than ninety days if disapproved by the Administrator within that period. Prior to disapproval, the Administrator shall, except as provided in paragraph (3) of this subsection, advise the State of the Administrator's intention to disapprove and the reasons therefor, and provide the State time to respond. The Administrator shall not prohibit or disapprove a registration issued by a State under this subsection (A) on the basis of lack of essentiality of a pesticide or (B) except as provided in paragraph (3) of this subsection, if its composition and use patterns are similar to those of a federally registered pesticide.

"(3) In no instance may a State issue a registration for a food or feed use unless there exists a tolerance or exemption under the Federal Food, Drug, and Cosmetic Act that permits the residues of the pesticide on the food or feed. If the Administrator determines that a registration issued by a State is inconsistent with the Federal Food, Drug, and Cosmetic Act, or the use of a pesticide under a registration issued by a State constitutes an imminent hazard, the Administrator may immediately disapprove the registration.

"(4) If the Administrator finds, in accordance with standards set forth in regulations issued under section 25 of this Act, that a State is not capable of exercising adequate controls to assure that State registration under this station will be in accord with the purposes of this act or has failed to exercise adequate controls, the Administrator may suspend the authority of the State to register pesticides until such time as the Administrator is satisfied that the State can and will exercise adequate controls. Prior to any such suspension, the Administrator shall advise the State of the Administrator's intention to suspend and the reasons therefor and provide the State time to respond.".

"SEC. 25. AUTHORITY OF ADMINISTRATOR.

"(a)(1) *Regulations.*—The Administrator is authorized in accordance with the procedure described in paragraph (2), to prescribe regulations to carry out the provisions of this Act. Such regulations shall take into account the difference in concept and usage between various classes of pesticides and differences in environmental risk and the appropriate data for evaluating such risk between agricultural and nonagricultural pesticides.

(2) *Procedure.*—

"(A) *Proposed regulations.*—At least 60 days prior to signing any proposed regulation for publication in the Federal Register, the Administrator shall provide the Secretary of Agriculture with a copy of such regulation. If the Secretary comments in writing to the Administrator regarding any such regulation within 30 days after receiving it, the Administrator shall publish in the Federal Register (with the proposed regulation) the comments of the Secretary and the response of the Administrator with regard to the Secretary's comments. If the Secretary does not comment in writing to the Administrator regarding the regulation within 30 days after receiving it, the Administrator may sign such regulation for publication in the Federal Register any time after such 30-day period notwithstanding the foregoing 60-day time requirement.

"(B)" Final regulations. — At least 30 days prior to signing any regulation in final form for publication in the Federal Register, the Administrator shall provide the Secretary of Agriculture with a copy of such regulation. If the Secretary comments in writing to the Administrator regarding any such final regulation within 15 days after receiving it, the Administrator shall publish in the Federal Register (with the final regulation) the comments of the Secretary, if requested by the Secretary, and the response of the Administrator concerning the Secretary's comments. If the Secretary does not comment in writing to the Administrator regarding the regulation within 15 days after receiving it, the Administrator may sign such regulation for publication in the Federal Register at any time after such 15-day period notwithstanding the foregoing 30-day time requirement.

In taking any final action under this subsection, the Administrator shall include among those factors to be taken into account the effect of the regulation on production and prices of agricultural commodities, retail food prices, and otherwise on the agricultural economy, and the Administrator shall publish in the Federal Register an analysis of such effect.

"(C) Time requirements. — The time requirements imposed by subparagraphs (A) and (B) may be waived or modified to the extent agreed upon by the Administrator and the Secretary.

"(D) Publications in the federal register. — The Administrator shall, simultaneously with any notifiction to the Secretary of Agriculture under this paragraph prior to the issuance of any proposed or final regulation, publish such notification in the Federal Register.".

"(3) Congressional Committees. — At such time as the Administrator is required under paragraph (2) of tihs subsection to provide the Secretary of Agriculture with a copy of proposed regulations and a copy of the final form of regulations, he shall also furnish a copy of such regulations to the Committee on Agriculture of the House of Representatives and the Committee on Agriculture and Forestry of the Senate.

"(4) Rule and Regulation Review. —

"(A) Congressional review. — Notwithstanding any other provision of this Act, simultaneously with promulgation of any rule or regulation under this Act, the Administrator shall transmit a copy thereof to the Secretary of the Senate and the Clerk of the House of Representatives. Except as provided in subparagraph (B), the rule or regulation shall not become effective, if within 90 calendar days of continuous session of Congress after the date of promulgation, both Houses of Congress adopt a concurrent resolution, the matter after the resolving clause of which is as follows: "That Congress disapproves the rule or regulation promulgated by the Administrator of the Environmental Protection Agency dealing with the matter of __________, which rule or regulation was transmitted to Congress on __________', the blank spaces therein being appropriately filled.

"(B) Effective date. — If at the end of 60 calendar days of continuous session of Congress after the date of promulgation of a rule or regulation, no committee of either House of Congress has reported or been discharged from further consideration of a concurrent resolution, disapproving the rule or regulation, and neither House has adopted such a resolution, the rule or regulation may go into effect immediately. If, within such 60 calendar days, such a committee has reported or been discharged from further consideration of such a resolution, or either House has adopted such a resolution, the rule or regulation may go into effect not sooner than 90 calendar days of continuous session of Congress after its promulgation unless disapproved as provided in subparagraph (A).

"(C) For the purposes of subparagraphs (A) and (B) of this paragraph —

(i) continuity of session is broken only by an adjournment of Congress sine die; and

(ii) the days on which either House is not is session because of an adjournment of more than 3 days to a day certain are excluded in the computation of 60 and 90 calendar days of continuous session of Congress.

"(D) Effect of congressional inaction. — Congressional inaction on or rejection of a resolution of disapproval shall not be deemed an expression of approval of such rule.

"(E) Judicial review. —

(i) Any interested party, including any person who participated in the rulemaking involved, may institute such actions in the appropriate district court of the United States, including actions for declaratory judgment, as may be appropriate to construe the constitutionality of any provision of this paragraph. The district court immediately shall certify all questions of the constitutionality of this paragraph to the United States court of appeals for the circuit involved, which shall hear the matter sitting en banc.

(ii) Notwithstanding any other provision of law, any decision on a matter certified under clause (i) of this subparagraph shall be reviewable by appeal directly to the Supreme Court of the United States. Such appeal shall be brought not later than 20 days after the decision of the court of appeals.

"(iii) It shall be the duty of the Court of appeals and of the Supreme Court of the United States to advance on the docket and to expedite to the greatest possible extent the disposition of any matter certified under clause (i) of this subparagraph.".

"(b) Exemption of Pesticides. — The Administrator may exempt from the requirements of this Act by regulation any pesticide which he determines either (1) to be adequately regulated by another Federal agency, or (2) to be of a character which is unnecessary to be subject to this Act in order to carry out the purposes of this Act.

"(c) Other Authority. — The Administrator, after notice and opportunity for hearing, is authorized —

"(1) to declare a pest any form of plant or animal life (other than man and other than bacteria, virus, and other micro-organisms on or in living man or other living animals) which is injurious to health or the environment;

"(2) to determine any pesticide which contains any substance or substances in quantities highly toxic to man;

"(3) to establish standards (which shall be consistent with those established under the authority of the Poison Prevention Packaging Act (Public Law 91-601)) with respect to the package, container, or wrapping in which a pesticide or device is enclosed for use or consumption, in order to protect children and adults from serious injury or illness resulting from accidential ingestion or contact with pesticides or devices regulated by this Act as well as to accomplish the other purposes of thie Act;

"(4) to specify those classes of devices which shall be subject to any provision of paragraph 2(q)(1) or section 7 of this Act upon his determination that application of such provision is necessary to effectuate the purposes of this Act;

"(5) to prescribe regulations requiring any pesticide to be colored or discolored if he determines that such requirement is feasible and is necessary for the protection of health and the environment; and

"(6) to determine and establish suitable names to be used in the ingredient statement

"(d) Scientific Advisory Panel. — The Administrator shall submit to an advisory panel for comment as to the impact on health and the environment of the action proposed in notices of intent issued under Section 6(b) and of the proposed and final form of regulations issued under section 25(a) within the same time periods as provided for the comments of the Secretary of Agriculture under such sections. The time requirements for notices of intent and proposed and final forms of regulation may not be modified or waived and unless in addition to meeting the requirements of section 6(b) or 25(a), as applicable, the advisory panel has failed to comment on the proposed action within the prescribed time period or has agreed to the modification or waiver. The Administrator shall also solicit from the advisory panel comments, evaluations, and recommendations for operating guidelines to improve the effectiveness and quality of scientific analyses made by personnel of the Environmental Protection Agency that lead to decisions by the Administrator in carrying out the provisions of this Act. The comments, evaluations, and recommendations of the advisory panel and the response of the Administrator shall be published in the Federal Register in the same manner as provided for publication of the comments of the Secretary of Agriculture under such sections. The Chairman of the advisory panel, after consultation with the Administrator, may create temporary subpanels on specific projects to assist the full advisory panel in expediting and preparing its evaluations, comments, and recommendations. The subpanels may be composed of scientists other than members of the advisory panel, as deemed necessary for the purpose of evaluating scientific studies relied upon by the Administrator with respect to proposed action. Such additional scientists shall be selected by the advisory panel. The panel referred to in this subsection shall consist of seven members appointed by the Administrator from a list of 12 nominees, six nominated by the National Institutes of Health, and six by the National Science Foundation. The Administrator may require such information from the nominees to the advisory panel as he deems necessary, and he shall publish in the Federal Register the name, address, and professional affiliations of each nominee. Each member of the panel shall receive per diem compensation at a rate not in excess of that fixed for GS-18 of the General Schedule as may be determined by the Administrator, except that any such member who holds another office or position under the Federal Government the compensation for which exceeds such rate may elect to receive compensation at the rate provided for such other office or position in lieu of the compensation provided by this subsection. In order to assure the objectivity of the advisory panel, the Administrator shall promulgate regulations regarding conflicts of interest with respect to the members of the panel. The advisory panel established under this subsection shall terminate September 30, 1981. In performing the functions assigned by this Act, the panel shall consult and coordinate its activities with the Science Advisory Board established under the Environmental Research, Development, and Demonstration Authorization Act of 1978. Whenever the Administrator exercises authority under section 6(c) of this Act to immediately suspend the registration of any pesticide to prevent an imminent hazard, the Administrator shall promptly submit to the advisory panel for comment, as to the impact on health and the environment, the action taken to suspend the registration of such pesticide.

"(e) Peer Review. — The Administrator shall, by written procedures, provide for peer review with respect to the design, protocols, and conduct of major scientific studies conducted under this Act by the Environmental Protection Agency or by any other Federal agency, any State or political subdivision thereof, or any institution or individual under grant, contract, or cooperative agreement from or with the Environmental Protection Agency. In such procedures, the

Administrator may take relating to the change in classification, suspension, or cancellation of a pesticide. Provided, That whenever the Administrator determines that circumstances do not permit the peer review of the results of any such scientific study prior to the Administrator's exercising authority under section 6(c) of this Act to immediately suspend the registration of any pesticide to prevent an imminent hazard, the Administrator shall promptly thereafter provide for the conduct of peer review as provided in this sentence. The evaluations and relevant documentation constituting the peer review that relate to the proposed scientific studies and the results of the completed scientific studies shall be included in the submission for comment forwarded by the Administrator to the advisory panel as provided in subsection (d). As used in this subsection, the term 'peer review' shall mean an independent evaluation by scientific experts, either within or outside the Environmental Protection Agency, in the appropriate disciplines.

[*Editor's note:* Section 2(b) of PL 96-539 provides:

"(b) The provisions of this section shall become effective upon publication in the Federal Register of final procedures for peer review as provided in this section, but in no event shall such provisions become effective later than one year after the date of enactment of this Act."]

"SEC. 26. STATE PRIMARY ENFORCEMENT RESPONSIBILITY.

"(a) For the purposes of this Act, a State shall have primary enforcement responsibility for pesticide use violations during any period for which the Administrator determines that such State—

"(1) has adopted adequate pesticide use laws and regulations; *Provided,* That the Administrator may not require a State to have pesticide use laws that are more stringent than this Act;

"(2) has adopted and is implementing adequate procedures for the enforcement of such State laws and regulations; and

"(3) will keep such records and make such reports showing compliance with paragraphs (1) and (2) of this subsection as the Administrator may require by regulation.

"(b) Notwithstanding the provisions of subsection (a) of this section, any State that enters into a cooperative agreement with the Administrator under section 23 of this Act for the enforcement of pesticide use restrictions shall have the primary enforcement responsibility for pesticide use violations. Any State that has a plan approved by the Administrator in accordance with the requirements of section 4 of this Act that the Administrator determines meets the criteria set out in subsection (a) of this section shall have the primary enforcement responsibility for pesticide use violations. The Administrator shall make such determinations with respect to State plans under Section 4 of this Act in effect on September 30, 1978 not later than March 31, 1979.

"(c) the Administrator shall have primary enforcement responsibility for those States that do not have primary enforcement responsibility under this Act. Notwithstanding the provisions of section 2(e) (1) of this Act, during any period when the Administrator has such enforcement responsibility, section 8(b) of this Act shall apply to the books and records of commercial applicators and to any applicator who holds or applies pesticides, or use dilutions of pesticides, only to provide a service of controlling pests without delivering any unapplied pesticide to any person so served, and section 9(a) of this Act shall apply to the establishment or other place where pesticides or devices are held for application by such persons with respect to pesticides or devices held for such application.

"SEC. 27. FAILURE BY THE STATE TO ASSURE ENFORCEMENT OF STATE PESTICIDE USE REGULATIONS.

"(a) Upon receipt of any complaint or other information alleging or indicating a significant violation of the pesticide use provisions of this Act, the Administrator shall refer the matter to the appropriate State officials for their investigation of the matter consistent with the requirements of this Act. If, within thirty days, the State has not commenced appropriate enforcement action, the Administrator may act upon the complaint or information to the extent authorized under this Act.

"(b) Whenever the Administrator determines that a State having primary enforcement responsibility for pesticide use violations is not carrying out (or cannot carry out due to the lack of adequate legal authority) such responsibility, the Administrator shall notify the State. Such notice shall specify those aspects of the administration of the State program that are determined to be inadequate. The State shall have ninety days after receipt of the notice to correct any deficiencies. If after that time the Administrator determines that the State program remains inadequate, the Administrator may rescind, in whole or in part, the State's primary enforcement responsibility for pesticide use violations.

"(c) Neither section 26 of this Act nor this section shall limit the authority of the Administrator to enforce this Act, where the Adminstrator determines that emergency conditions exist that require immediate action on the part of the Administrator and the State authority is unwilling or unable adequately to respond to the emergency.

"SEC. 28. IDENTIFICATION OF PESTS; COOPERATION WITH DEPARTMENT OF AGRICULTURE'S PROGRAM.

"The Administrator, in coordination with the Secretary of Agriculture, shall identify those pests that must be brought under control. The Administrator shall also coordinate and cooperate with the Secretary of Agriculture's research and implementation programs to develop and improve the safe use and effectiveness of chemical, biological, and alternative methods to combat and control pests that reduce the quality and economical production and distribution of agricultural products to domestic and foreign consumers.

"SEC. 29. ANNUAL REPORT.

"The Administrator shall submit an annual report to Congress before February 16 of each year and the first report shall be due February 15, 1979. The report shall include the total number of applications for conditional registration under section 3(c)(7)(B) and 3(c)(7)(C) of this Act that were filed during the immediately preceding fiscal year, and, with respect to those applications approved, the Administrator shall report the Administrator's findings in each case, the conditions imposed and any modification of such conditions in each case, and the quantities produced of such pesticides.

"SEC. 30. SEVERABILITY.

"If any provision of this Act or the application thereof to any person or circumstance is held invalid, the invalidity shall not affect other provisions or applications of this Act which can be given effect without regard to the invalid provision or application, and to this end the provisions of this Act are severable.

"SEC. 31. AUTHORIZATION FOR APPROPRIATIONS.

"There is authorized to be appropriated such sums as may be necessary to carry out the provisions of this Act for each of the fiscal years ending June 30, 1973, June 30, 1974, and June 30, 1975. The amounts authorized to be appropriated for any fiscal year ending after June 30, 1975, shall be the sums hereafter provided by law."

There is hereby authorized to be appropriated to carry out the provisions of this Act for the period beginning July 1, 1975, and ending September 30, 1975, the sum of $11,967,000.

There is hereby authorized to be appropriated to carry out the provisions of this Act for the period beginning October 1, 1975, and ending November 15, 1975, the sum of $5,983,500.

"There are hereby authorized to be appropriated to carry out the provisions of this Act for the period beginning October 1, 1975, and ending September 30, 1976, the sum of $47,868,000 and for the period beginning October 1, 1976, and ending September 30, 1977, the sum of $46,636,000, and for the period beginning October 1, 1977, and ending September 30, 1978, the sum of $54,500,000, and for the period beginning October 1, 1978, and ending September 30, 1979, such sums as may be necessary, but not in excess of $70,000,000. There are hereby authorized to be appropriated to carry out the provisions of this Act for the period beginning October 1, 1979, and ending September 30, 1980, such sums as may be necessary, but not in excess of $72,160,000, and for the period beginning October 1, 1980, and ending September 30, 1981, such sums as may be necessary, but not in excess of $77,500,000.

AMENDMENTS TO OTHER ACTS

SEC. 3. The following Acts are amended by striking out the terms "economic poisons" and "an economic poison" wherever they appear and inserting in lieu thereof "pesticides" and "a pesticide" respectively:

(1) The Federal Hazardous Substances Act, as amended (15 U.S.C. 1261 et seq.);

(2) The Poison Prevention Packaging Act, as amended (15 U.S.C. 1471 et seq.); and

(3) The Federal Food, Drug, and Cosmetic Act, as amended (21 U.S.C. 301 et seq.).

EFFECTIVE DATES OF PROVISIONS OF ACT

SEC. 4. (a) Except as otherwise provided in the Federal Insecticide, Fungicide, and Rodenticide Act, as amended by this Act, and as otherwise provided by this section, the amendments made by this Act shall take effect at the close of the date of the enactment of this Act, provided if regulations are necessary for the implementation of any provision that becomes effective on the date of enactment, such regulations shall be promulgated and shall become effective within 90 days from the date of enactment of this Act.

(b) The provisions of the Federal Insecticide, Fungicide, and Rodenticide Act and the regulations thereunder as such existed prior to the enactment of this Act shall remain in effect until superseded by the amendments made by this Act and regulations thereunder.

(c) (1) Two years after the enactment of this Act the Administrator shall have promulgated regulations providing for the registration and classification of pesticides under the provisions of this Act and thereafter shall register all new applications under such provisions.

(2) Any requirements that a pesticide be registered for use only by a certified applicator shall not be effective until five years from the date of enactment of this Act.

(3) A period of five years from date of enactment shall be provided for certification of applicators.

(A) One year after the enactment of this Act the Administrator shall have prescribed the standards for the certification of applicators.

(B) Each State desiring to certify applicators shall submit a State plan to the Administrator for the purpose provided by section 4(b).

(C) As promptly as possible but in no event more than one year after submission of a State plan, the Administrator shall approve the State plan or disapprove it and indicate the reasons for disapproval. Consideration of plans resubmitted by States shall be expedited.

(4) One year after the enactment of this Act the Administrator shall have promulgated and shall make effective regulations relating to the registration of establishments, permits for experimental use, and the keeping of books and records under the provisions of this Act.

(d) No person shall be subject to any criminal or civil penalty imposed by the Federal Insecticide, Fungicide, and Rodenticide Act, as amended by this Act, for any act (or failure to act) occurring before the expiration of 60 days after the Administrator has published effective regulations in the Federal Register and taken such other action as may be necessary to permit compliance with the provisions under which the penalty is to be imposed.

(e) For purposes of determining any criminal or civil penalty or liability to any third person in respect of any act or omission occurring before the expiration of the periods referred to in this section, the Federal Insecticide, Fungicide, and Rodenticide Act shall be treated as continuing in effect as if this Act had not been enacted.

STUDIES

(a) The Administrator of the Environmental Protection Agency shall perform a study examining the feasibility of assessing and collecting fees from persons applying to register, or amend the registration of, pesticides to cover the costs incurred by the Environmental Protection Agency in processing such applications under the provisions of the Federal Insecticide, Fungicide, and Rodenticide Act. The Administrator shall complete this study and submit a report setting forth the findings of the study and recommendations for the implementation of these findings to the Senate Committee on Agriculture, Nutrition, and Forestry and the House Committee on Agriculture, not later than nine months after the date of enactment of this Act.

(b) The Administrator, in cooperation with the Secretary of Agriculture, and after consultation with appropriate State officials, shall review available scientific information dealing with issues involved in the methods of pesticide application, including, but not limited to, the advisability of ultra-low-volume methods of application, and shall recommend to the Senate Committee on Agriculture, Nutrition, and Forestry and the House Committee on Agriculture such changes as the Administrator may deem necessary in existing law relative to provisions of the Act pertaining to the use of a registered pesticide in a manner inconsistent with its labeling. The report shall be submitted as soon as practicable, but not later than six months after the date of enactment of this Act.

(c) The Administrator shall submit an updated study examining the problems of minor uses of pesticides not specifically permitted by labeling. The Administrator shall complete this study and submit a report setting forth the findings of the study and recommendations for the implementation of these findings to the Senate Committee on Agriculture, Nutrition, and Forestry and the House Committee on Agriculture, not later than nine months after the date of enactment of this Act.

FEDERAL WATER POLLUTION CONTROL ACT (CLEAN WATER ACT)

as amended[1]

(33 U.S.C. 466 et seq.)

AN ACT To provide for water pollution control activities in the Public Health Service of the Federal Security Agency and in the Federal Works Agency, and for other purposes.

Be it enacted by the Senate and House of Representatives of the United States of America in Congress assembled,

TITLE I—RESEARCH AND RELATED PROGRAMS

DECLARATION OF GOALS AND POLICY

SEC. 101. (a) The objective of this Act is to restore and maintain the chemical, physical, and biological integrity of the Nation's waters. In order to achieve this objective it is hereby declared that, consistent with the provisions of this Act—

(1) it is the national goal that the discharge of pollutants into the navigable waters be eliminated by 1985;

(2) it is the national goal that wherever attainable, an interim goal of water quality which provides for the protection and propagation of fish, shellfish, and wildlife and provides for recreation in and on the water be achieved by July 1, 1983;

(3) it is the national policy that the discharge of toxic pollutants in toxic amounts be prohibited;

(4) it is the national policy that Federal financial assistance be provided to construct publicly owned waste treatment works;

(5) it is the national policy that areawide waste treatment management planning processes be developed and implemented to assure adequate control of sources of pollutants in each State; and

(6) it is the national policy that a major research and demonstration effort be made to develop technology necessary to eliminate the discharge of pollutants into the navigable waters, waters of the contiguous zone, and the oceans.

(b) It is the policy of the Congress to recognize, preserve, and protect the primary responsibilities and rights of States to prevent, reduce, and eliminate pollution, to plan the development and use (including restoration, preservation, and enhancement) of land and water resources, and to consult with the Administrator in the exercise of his authority under this Act. It is the policy of Congress that the

---

[1] The Federal Water Pollution Control Act was amended by the Clean Water Act of 1977 and is commonly known as the Clean Water Act. The Federal Water Pollution Control Act was enacted by PL 92-500, October 18, 1972, and amended by PL 93-207, December 28, 1973; 93-243, January 2, 1974; PL 93-592, January 2, 1975; PL 94-238, March 23, 1976; PL 94-273, April 21, 1976; 94-558, October 19, 1976; PL 95-217, December 28, 1977; PL 95-576, November 2, 1978; PL 96-148, December 16, 1979; PL 96-478 and PL 96-483, October 21, 1980; PL 96-561, December 22, 1980; PL 97-35, August 13, 1981; PL 96-510, December 11, 1981; PL 97-117; December 29, 1981; PL 97-164, April 2, 1982; PL 97-216, July 18, 1982; PL 97-272, September 30, 1982; PL 97-440, January 8, 1983.

States manage the construction grant program under this Act and implement the permit programs under sections 402 and 404 of this Act. It is further the policy of the Congress to support and aid research relating to the prevention, reduction, and elimination of pollution, and to provide Federal technical services and financial aid to State and interstate agencies and municipalities in connection with the prevention, reduction, and elimination of pollution.

(c) It is further the policy of Congress that the President, acting through the Secretary of State and such national and international organizations as he determines appropriate, shall take such action as may be necessary to insure that to the fullest extent possible all foreign countries shall take meaningful action for the prevention, reduction, and elimination of pollution in their waters and in international waters and for the achievement of goals regarding the elimination of discharge of pollutants and the improvement of water quality to at least the same extent as the United States does under its laws.

(d) Except as otherwise expressly provided in this Act, the Administrator of the Environmental Protection Agency (hereinafter in this Act called "Administrator") shall administer this Act.

(e) Public participation in the development, revision, and enforcement of any regulation, standard, effluent limitation, plan, or program established by the Administrator or any State under this Act shall be provided for, encouraged, and assisted by the Administrator and the States. The Administrator, in cooperation with the States, shall develop and publish regulations specifying minimum guidelines for public participation in such processes.

(f) It is the national policy that to the maximum extent possible the procedures utilized for implementing this Act shall encourage the drastic minimization of paperwork and interagency decision procedures, and the best use of available manpower and funds, so as to prevent needless duplication and unnecessary delays at all levels of government.

(g) It is the policy of Congress that the authority of each State to allocate quantities of water within its jurisdiction shall not be superseded, abrogated or otherwise impaired by this Act. It is the further policy of Congress that nothing in this Act shall be construed to supersede or abrogate rights to quantities of water which have been established by any State. Federal agencies shall cooperate with State and local agencies to develop comprehensive solutions to prevent, reduce, and eliminate pollution in concert with programs for managing water resources.

COMPREHENSIVE PROGRAMS FOR WATER POLLUTION CONTROL

SEC. 102. (a) The Administrator shall, after careful investigation, and in cooperation with other Federal agencies, State water pollution control agencies, interstate agencies, and the municipalities and industries involved, prepare or develop comprehensive programs for preventing, reducing, or eliminating the pollution of the navigable waters and ground waters and improving the sanitary condition of surface and underground water. In the development of such comprehensive programs due regard shall be given to the improvements which are necessary to conserve such waters for the protection and propagation of fish and aquatic life and wildlife, recreational purposes, and the withdrawal of such waters for public water supply, agricultural, industrial, and other purposes. For the purpose of this section, the Administrator is authorized to make joint investigations with any such agencies of the condition of any waters in any State or States, and of the discharges of any sewage, industrial wastes, or substance which may adversely affect such waters.

(b)(1) In the survey of planning of any reservoir by the Corps of Engineers, Bureau of Reclamation, or other Federal agency, consideration shall be given to inclusion of storage for regulation of streamflow, except that any such storage and water releases shall not be provided as a substitute for adequate treatment or other methods of controlling waste at the source.

(2) The need for and the value of storage for regulation of streamflow (other than for water quality) including but not limited to navigation, salt water intrusion, recreation, esthetics, and fish and wildlife, shall be determined by the Corps of Engineers, Bureau of Reclamation, or other Federal agencies.

(3) The need for, the value of, and the impact of, storage for water quality control shall be determined by the Administrator, and his views on these matters shall be set forth in any report or presentation to Congress proposing authorization or construction of any reservoir including such storage.

(4) The value of such storage shall be taken into account in determining the economic value of the entire project of which it is a part, and costs shall be allocated to the purpose of regulation of streamflow in a manner which will insure that all project purposes, share equitably in the benefits of multiple-purpose construction.

(5) Costs of regulation of streamflow features incorporated in any Federal reservoir or other impoundment under the provisions of this Act shall be determined and the beneficiaries identified and if the benefits are widespread or national in scope, the cost of such features shall be nonreimbursable.

(6) No license granted by the Federal Power Commission for a hydroelectric power project shall include storage for regulation of streamflow for the purpose of water quality control unless the Administrator shall recommend its inclusion and such reservoir storage capacity shall not exceed such proportion of the total storage required for the water quality control plan as the drainage area of such reservoir bears to the drainage area of the river basin or basins involved in such water quality control plan.

(c)(1) The Administrator shall, at the request of the Governor of a State, or a majority of the Governors when more than one State is involved, make a grant to pay not to exceed 50 per centum of the administrative expenses of a planning agency for a period not to exceed three years, which period shall begin after the date of enactment of the Federal Water Pollution Control Act Amendments of 1972, if such agency provides for adequate representation of appropriate State, interstate, local or (when appropriate) international interests in the basin or portion thereof involved and is capable of developing an effective, comprehensive water quality control plan for a basin or portion thereof.

(2) Each planning agency receiving a grant under this subsection shall develop a comprehensive pollution control plan for the basin or portion thereof which—

(A) is consistent with any applicable water quality standards, effluent and other limitations, and thermal discharge regulations established pursuant to current law within the basin;

(B) recommends such treatment works as will provide the most effective and economical means of collection, storage, treatment, and elimination of pollutants and recommends means to encourage both municipal and industrial use of such works;

(C) recommends maintenance and improvement of water quality within the basin or portion thereof and recommends methods of adequately financing those facilities as may be necessary to implement the plan; and

(D) as appropriate, is developed in cooperation with, and is consistent with any comprehensive plan prepared by the Water Resources Council, any areawide waste management plans developed pursuant to section 208 of this Act, and any State plan developed pursuant to section 303(e) of this Act.

(3) For the purposes of this subsection the term "basin" includes, but is not limited to, rivers and their tributaries, streams, coastal waters, sounds, estuaries, bays, lakes, and portions thereof, as well as the lands drained thereby.

(d) The Administrator, after consultation with the States, and River Basin Commissions established under the Water Resources Planning Act, shall submit a report to Congress on or before July 1, 1978, which analyzes the relationship between programs under this Act, and the programs by which States and Federal agencies allocate quantities of water. Such report shall include recommendations concerning the policy in section 101(g) of the Act to improve coordination of efforts to reduce and eliminate pollution in concert with programs fo managing water resources.

INTERSTATE COOPERATION AND UNIFORM LAWS

SEC. 103. (a) The Administrator shall encourage cooperative activities by the States for the prevention, reduction, and elimination of pollution, encourage the enactment of improved and, so far as practicable, uniform State laws relating to the prevention, reduction, and elimination of pollution; and encourage compacts between States for the prevention and control of pollution.

(b) The consent of the Congress is hereby given to two or more States to negotiate and enter into agreements or compacts, not in conflict with any law or treaty of the United States, for (1) cooperative effort and mutual assistance for the prevention and control of pollution and the enforcement of their respective laws relating thereto, and (2) the establishment of such agencies, joint or otherwise, as they may deem desirable for making effective such agreements and compacts. No such agreement or compact shall be binding or obligatory upon any State a party thereto unless and until it has been approved by the Congress.

RESEARCH, INVESTIGATIONS, TRAINING, AND INFORMATION

SEC. 104. (a) The Administrator shall establish national programs for the prevention, reduction, and elimination of pollution and as part of such programs shall—

(1) in cooperation with other Federal, State, and local agencies, conduct and promote the coordination and acceleration of,

research, investigations, experiments, training, demonstrations, surveys, and studies relating to the causes, effects, extent, prevention, reduction, and elimination of pollution;

(2) encourage, cooperate with, and render technical services to pollution control agencies and other appropriate public or private agencies, institutions, and organizations, and individuals, including the general public, in the conduct of activities referred to in paragraph (1) of this subsection;

(3) conduct, in cooperation with State water pollution control agencies and other interested agencies, organizations and persons, public investigations concerning the pollution of any navigable waters, and report on the results of such investigations;

(4) establish advisory committees composed of recognized experts in various aspects of pollution and representatives of the public to assist in the examination and evaluation of research progress and proposals and to avoid duplication of research;

(5) in cooperation with the States, and their political subdivisions, and other Federal agencies establish, equip, and maintain a water quality surveillance system for the purpose of monitoring the quality of the navigable waters and ground waters and the contiguous zone and the oceans and the Administrator shall, to the extent practicable, conduct such surveillance by utilizing the resources of the National Aeronautics and Space Administration, the National Oceanic and Atmospheric Administration, the Geological Survey, and the Coast Guard, and shall report on such quality in the report required under subsection (a) of section 516; and

(6) initiate and to promote the coordination and acceleration of research designed to develop the most effective practicable tools and techniques for measuring the social and economic costs and benefits of activities which are subject to regulation under this Act; and shall transmit a report on the results of such research to the Congress not later than January 1, 1974.

(b) In carrying out the provisions of subsection (a) of this section the Administrator is authorized to—

(1) collect and make available, through publications and other appropriate means, the results of and other information, including appropriate recommendations by him in connection therewith, pertaining to such research and other activities referred to in paragraph (1) of subsection (a);

(2) cooperate with other Federal departments and agencies, State water pollution control agencies, interstate agencies, other public and private agencies, institutions, organizations, industries involved, and individuals, in the preparation and conduct of such research and other activities referred to in paragraph (1) of subsection (a);

(3) make grants to State water pollution control agencies, interstate agencies, other public or nonprofit private agencies, institutions, organizations, and individuals, for purposes stated in paragraph (1) of subsection (a) of this section;

(4) contract with public or private agencies, institutions, organizations, and individuals, without regard to sections 3648 and 3709 of the Revised Statutes (31 U.S.C. 529; 41 U.S.C. 5), referred to in paragraph (1) of subsection (a);

(5) establish and maintain research fellowships at public or

nonprofit private educational institutions or research organizations;

(6) collect and disseminate, in cooperation with other Federal departments and agencies, and with other public or private agencies, institutions, and organizations having related responsibilities, basic data on chemical, physical, and biological effects of varying water quality and other information pertaining to pollution and the prevention, reduction, and elimination thereof; and

(7) develop effective and practical processes, methods, and prototype devices for the prevention, reduction, and elimination of pollution.

(c) In carrying out the provisions of subsection (a) of this section the Administrator shall conduct research on, and survey the results of other scientific studies on, the harmful effects on the health or welfare of persons caused by pollutants. In order to avoid duplication of effort, the Administrator shall, to the extent practicable, conduct such research in cooperation with and through the facilities of the Secretary of Health, Education, and Welfare.

(d) In carrying out the provisions of this section the Administrator shall develop and demonstrate under varied conditions (including conducting such basic and applied research, studies, and experiments as may be necessary):

(1) Practicable means of treating municipal sewage, and other waterborne wastes to implement the requirements of section 201 of this act;

(2) Improved methods and procedures to identify and measure the effects of pollutants, including those pollutants created by new technological developments; and

(3) Methods and procedures for evaluating the effects on water quality of augmented streamflows to control pollution not susceptible to other means of prevention, reduction, or elimination.

(e) The Administrator shall establish, equip, and maintain field laboratory and research facilities, including, but not limited to, one to be located in the northeastern area of the United States, one in the Middle Atlantic area, one in the southeastern area, one in the midwestern area, one in the southwestern area, one in the Pacific Northwest, and one in the State of Alaska, for the conduct of research, investigations, experiments, field demonstrations and studies, and training relating to the prevention, reduction and elimination of pollution. Insofar as practicable, each such facility shall be located near institutions of higher learning in which graduate training in such research might be carried out. In conjunction with the development of criteria under section 403 of this Act, the Administrator shall construct the facilities authorized for the National Marine Water Quality Laboratory established under this subsection.

(f) The Administrator shall conduct research and technical development work, and make studies, with respect to the quality of the waters of the Great Lakes, including an analysis of the present and projected future water quality of the Great Lakes under varying conditions of waste treatment and disposal, an evaluation of the water quality needs of those to be served by such waters, an evaluation of municipal, industrial, and vessel waste treatment and disposal practices with respect to such waters, and a study of alternate means of solving pollution problems (including additional waste treatment measures) with respect to such waters.

(g)(1) For the purpose of providing an adequate supply of trained personnel to operate and maintain existing and future treatment works and related activities, and for the purpose of enhancing substantially the proficiency of those engaged in such activities, the Administrator shall finance pilot programs, in cooperation with State and interstate agencies, municipalities, educational institutions, and other organizations and individuals, of manpower development and training and retraining of persons in, on entering into, the field of operation and maintenance of treatment works and related activities. Such program and any funds expended for such a program shall supplement, not supplant, other manpower and training programs and funds available for the purposes of this paragraph. The Administrator is authorized, under such terms and conditions as he deems appropriate, to enter into agreements with one or more States, acting jointly or severally, or with other public or private agencies or institutions for the development and implementation of such a program.

(2) The Administrator is authorized to enter into agreements with public and private agencies and institutions, and individuals to develop and maintain an effective system for forecasting the supply of, and demand for, various professional and other occupational categories needed for the prevention, reduction, and elimination of pollution in each region, State, or area of the United States and, from time to time, publish the results of such forecasts.

(3) In furtherance of the purposes of this Act, the Administrator is authorized to—

(A) make grants to public or private agencies and institutions and to individuals for training projects, and provide for the conduct of training by contract with public or private agencies and institutions and with individuals without regard to sections 3648 and 3709 of the Revised Statutes;

(B) establish and maintain research fellowships in the Environmental Protection Agency with such stipends and allowances, including traveling and subsistence expenses, as he may deem necessary to procure the assistance of the most promising research fellows; and

(C) provide, in addition to the program established under paragraph (1) of this subsection, training in technical matters relating to the causes, prevention, reduction, and elimination of pollution for personnel of public agencies and other persons with suitable qualifications.

(4) The Administrator shall submit, through the President, a report to the Congress not later than December 31, 1973, summarizing the actions taken under this subsection and the effectiveness of such actions, and setting forth the number of persons trained, the occupational categories for which training was provided, the effectiveness of other Federal, State, and local training programs in this field, together with estimates of future needs, recommendations on improving training programs, and such other information and recommendations, including legislative recommendations, as he deems appropriate.

(h) The Administrator is authorized to enter into contracts with, or make grants to, public or private agencies and organizations and individuals for (A) the purpose of developing and demonstrating new or improved methods for the prevention, removal, reduction, and elimination of pollution in lakes, including the undesirable effects of nutrients and vegetation, and (B) the construction of publicly owned research facilities for such purpose.

(i) The Administrator, in cooperation with the Secretary of the department in which the Coast Guard is operating, shall—

(1) engage in such research, studies, experiments, and demonstrations as he deems appropriate, relative to the removal of oil from any waters and to the prevention, control, and elimination of oil and hazardous substances pollution;

(2) publish from time to time the results of such activities; and

(3) from time to time, develop and publish in the Federal Register specifications and other technical information on the various chemical compounds used in the control of oil and hazardous substances spills.

In carrying out this subsection, the Administrator may enter into contracts with, or make grants to, public or private agencies and organizations and individuals.

(j) The Secretary of the department in which the Coast Guard is operating shall engage in such research, studies, experiments, and demonstrations as he deems appropriate relative to equipment which is to be installed on board a vessel and is designed to receive, retain, treat, or discharge human body wastes and the wastes from toilets and other receptacles intended to receive or retain body wastes with particular emphasis on equipment to be installed on small recreational vessels. The Secretary of the department in which the Coast Guard is operating shall report to Congress the results of such research, studies, experiments, and demonstrations prior to the effective date of any regulations established under section 312 of this Act. In carrying out this subsection the Secretary of the department in which the Coast Guard is operating may enter into contracts with, or make grants to, public or private organizations and individuals.

(k) In carrying out the provisions of this section relating to the conduct by the Administrator of demonstration projects and the development of field laboratories and research facilities, the Administrator may acquire land and interests therein by purchase, with appropriated or donated funds, by donation, or by exchange for acquired or public lands under his jurisdiction which he classifies as suitable for disposition. The values of the properties so exchanged either shall be approximately equal, or if they are not approximately equal, the values shall be equalized by the payment of cash to the grantor or to the Administrator as the circumstances require.

(l)(1) The Administrator shall, after consultation with appropriate local, State, and Federal agencies, public and private organizations, and interested individuals, as soon as practicable but not later than January 1, 1973, develop and issue to the States for the purpose of carrying out this Act the latest scientific knowledge available in indicating the kind and extent of effects on health and welfare which may be expected from the presence of pesticides in the water in varying quantities. He shall revise and add to such information whenever necessary to reflect developing scientific knowledge.

(2) The President shall, in consultation with appropriate local, State, and Federal agencies, public and private organizations, and interested individuals, conduct studies and investigations of methods to control the release of pesticides into the environment which study shall include examination of the persistency of pesticides in the water

environment and alternatives thereto. The President shall submit reports, from time to time, on such investigations to Congress together with his recommendations for any necesssary legislation.

(m)(1) The Administrator shall, in an effort to prevent degradation of the environment from the disposal of waste oil, conduct a study of (A) the generation of used engine, machine, cooling, and similar waste oil, including quantities generated, the nature and quality of such oil, present collecting methods and disposal practices, and alternate uses of such oil; (B) the long-term, chronic biological effects of the disposal of such waste oil; and (C) the potential market for such oils, including the economic and legal factors relating to the sale of products made from such oils, the level of subsidy, if any, needed to encourage the purchase by public and private nonprofit agencies of products from such oil, and the practicability of Federal procurement, on a priority basis, of products made from such oil. In conducting such study, the Administrator shall consult with affected industries and other persons.

(2) The Administrator shall report the preliminary results of such study to Congress within six months after the date of enactment of the Federal Water Pollution Control Act Amendments of 1972, and shall submit a final report to Congress within 18 months after such date of enactment.

(n)(1) The Administrator shall, in cooperation with the Secretary of the Army, the Secretary of Agriculture, the Water Resources Council, and with other appropriate Federal, State, interstate, or local public bodies and private organizations, institutions, and individuals, conduct and promote, encourage contributions to, continuing comprehensive studies of the effects of pollution, including sedimentation, in the estuaries and estuarine zones of the United States on fish and wildlife, on sport and commercial fishing, on recreation, on water supply and water power, and on other beneficial purposes. Such studies shall also consider the effect of demographic trends, the exploitation of mineral resources and fossil fuels, land and industrial development, navigation, flood and erosion control, and other uses of estuaries and estuarine zones upon the pollution of the waters therein.

(2) In conducting such studies, the Administrator shall assemble, coordinate, and organize all existing pertinent information on the Nation's estuaries and estuarine zones; carry out a program of investigations and surveys to supplement existing information in representative estuaries and estuarine zones; and identify the problems and areas where further research and study are required.

(3) The Administrator shall submit to Congress, from time to time, reports of the studies authorized by this subsection but at least one such report during any six-year period. Copies of each such report shall be made available to all interested parties, public and private.

(4) For the purpose of this subsection, the term "estuarine zones" means an environmental system consisting of an estuary and those transitional areas which are consistently influenced or affected by water from an estuary such as, but not limited to, salt marshes, coastal and intertidal areas, bays, harbors, lagoons, inshore waters, and channels, and the term "estuary" means all or part of the mouth of a river or stream or other body of water having unimpaired natural connection with open sea and within which the sea water is measurably diluted with fresh water derived from land drainage.

(o)(1) The Administrator shall conduct research and investigations on devices, systems, incentives, pricing policy, and other methods of reducing the total flow of sewage, including, but not limited to, unnecessary water consumption in order to reduce the requirements for, and the costs of, sewage and waste treatment services. Such research and investigations shall be directed to develop devices, systems, policies, and methods capable of achieving the maximum reduction of unnecessary water consumption.

(2) The Administrator shall report the preliminary results of such studies and investigations to the Congress within one year after the date of enactment of the Federal Water Pollution Control Act Amendments of 1972, and annually thereafter in the report required under subsection (a) of section 516. Such report shall include recommendations for any legislation that may be required to provide for the adoption and use of devices, systems, policies, or other methods of reducing water consumption and reducing the total flow of sewage. Such report shall include an estimate of the benefits to be derived from adoption and use of such devices, systems, policies, or other methods and also shall reflect estimates of any increase in private, public, or other cost that would be occasioned thereby.

(p) In carrying out the provisions of subsection (a) of this section the Administrator shall, in cooperation with the Secretary of Agriculture, other Federal agencies, and the States, carry out a comprehensive study and research program to determine new and improved methods and the better application of existing methods of preventing, reducing, and eliminating pollution from agriculture, including the legal, economic, and other implications of the use of such methods.

(q)(1) The Administrator shall conduct a comprehensive program of research and investigation and pilot project implementation into new and improved methods of preventing, reducing, storing, collecting, treating, or otherwise eliminating pollution from sewage in rural and other areas where collection of sewage in conventional, communitywide sewage collection systems is impractical, uneconomical, or otherwise infeasible, or where soil conditions or other factors preclude the use of septic tank and drainage field systems.

(2) The Administrator shall conduct a comprehensive program of research and investigation and pilot project implementation into new and improved methods for the collection and treatment of sewage and other liquid wastes combined with the treatment and disposal of solid wastes.

(3) The Administrator shall establish, either within the Environmental Protection Agency, or through contract with an appropriate public or private non-profit organization, a national clearinghouse which shall (A) receive reports and information resulting from research, demonstrations, and other projects funded under this Act related to paragraph (1) of this subsection and to subsection (e)(2) of section 105; (B) coordinate and disseminate such reports and information for use by Federal and State agencies, municipalities, institutions, and persons in developing new and improved methods pursuant to this subsection; and (C) provide for the collection and dissemination of reports and information relevant to this subsection from other Federal and State agencies, institutions, universities, and persons.

(r) The Administrator is authorized to make grants to colleges and universities to conduct basic research into the structure and function of fresh water aquatic ecosystems, and to improve understanding of the ecological characteristics necessary to the maintenance of the chemical, physical, and biological integrity of fresh water aquatic ecosystems.

(s) The Administrator is authorized to make grants to one or more institutions of higher education (regionally located and to be designated as "River Study Centers") for the purpose of conducting and reporting on interdisciplinary studies on the nature of river systems, including hydrology, biology, ecology, economics, the relationship between river uses and land uses, and the effects of development within river basins on river systems and on the value of water resources and water related activities. No such grant in any fiscal year shall exceed $1,000,000.

(t) The Administrator shall, in cooperation with State and Federal agencies and public and private organizations, conduct continuing comprehensive studies of the effects and methods of control of thermal discharges. In evaluating alternative methods of control the studies shall consider (1) such data as are available on the latest available technology, economic feasibility including cost-effectiveness analysis, and (2) the total impact on the environment, considering not only water quality but also air quality, land use, and effective utilization and conservation of fresh water and other natural resources. Such studies shall consider methods of minimizing adverse effects and maximizing beneficial effects of thermal discharges. The results of these studies shall be reported by the Administrator as soon as practicable, but not later than 270 days after enactment of this subsection, and shall be made available to the public and the States, and considered as they become available by the Administrator in carrying out section 316 of this Act and by the States in proposing thermal water quality standards.

(u) There is authorized to be appropriated (1) not to exceed $100,000,000 per fiscal year for the fiscal year ending June 30, 1973, the fiscal year ending June 30, 1974, and the fiscal year ending June 30, 1975, and not to exceed $14,039,000 for the fiscal year ending September 30, 1980, and not to exceed $20,697,000 for the fiscal year ending September 30, 1981, and not to exceed $22,770,000 for the fiscal year ending September 30, 1982 for carrying out the provisions of this section, other than subsections (g) (1) and (2), (p), (r), and (t), except that such authorizations are not for any research, development, or demonstration activity pursuant to such provisions; (2) not to exceed $7,500,000 for fiscal years 1973, 1974, and 1975, $2,000,000 for fiscal year 1977, $3,000,000 for fiscal year 1978, $3,000,000 for fiscal year 1979, $3,000,000 for fiscal year 1980, $3,000,000 for fiscal year 1981, and $3,000,000 for fiscal year 1982 for carrying out the provisions of subsection (g)(1); (3) not to exceed $2,500,000 for fiscal year 1973, 1974, and 1975, $1,000,000 for fiscal year 1977, $1,500,000 for fiscal year 1978, $1,500,000 for fiscal year 1979, $1,500,000 for fiscal year 1980, $1,500,000 for fiscal year 1981, and $1,500,000 for fiscal year 1982 for carrying out the provisions of subsection (g)(2); (4) not to exceed $10,000,000 for each of the fiscal years ending June 30, 1973, June 30, 1974, and June 30, 1975, for carrying out the provisions of subsection (p); (5) not to exceed $15,000,000 per fiscal year for the fiscal years ending June 30, 1973, June 30, 1974, and June 30, 1975, for carrying out the provisions of subsection (r); and (6) not to exceed $10,000,000 per fiscal year for the fiscal years ending June 30, 1973, June 30, 1974, and June 30, 1975, for carrying out the provisions of subsection (t).

GRANTS FOR RESEARCH AND DEVELOPMENT

SEC. 105. (a) The Administrator is authorized to conduct in the Environmental Protection Agency, and to make grants to any State, municipality, or intermunicipal or interstate agency for the purpose of assisting in the development of—

(1) any project which will demonstrate a new or improved method of preventing, reducing, and eliminating the discharge into any waters of pollutants from sewers which carry storm water or both storm water and pollutants; or

(2) any project which will demonstrate advanced waste treatment and water purification methods (including the temporary use of new or improved chemical additives which provide substantial immediate improvement to existing treatment processes), or new or improved methods of joint treatment systems for municipal and industrial wastes;

and to include in such grants such amounts as are necessary for the purpose of reports, plans and specifications in connection therewith.

(b) The Administrator is authorized to make grants to any State or States or interstate agency to demonstrate, in river basins or portions thereof, advanced treatment and environmental enhancement techniques to control pollution from all sources, within such basins or portions thereof, including nonpoint sources, together with in stream water quality improvement techniques.

(c) In order to carry out the purposes of section 301 of this Act, the Administrator is authorized to (1) conduct in the Environmental Protection Agency, (2) make grants to persons, and (3) enter into contracts with persons, for research and demonstration projects for prevention of pollution of any waters by industry including, but not limited to, the prevention, reduction, and elimination of the discharge of pollutants. No grant shall be made for any project under this subsection unless the Administrator determines that such project will develop or demonstrate a new or improved method of treating industrial wastes or otherwise prevent pollution by industry, which method shall have industry wide application.

(d) In carrying out the provisions of this section, the Administrator shall conduct, on a priority basis, an accelerated effort to develop, refine, and achieve practical application of:

(1) waste management methods applicable to point and nonpoint sources of pollutants to eliminate the discharge of pollutants, including, but not limited to, elimination of runoff of pollutants and the effects of pollutants from inplace or accumulated sources;

(2) advanced waste treatment methods applicable to point and nonpoint sources, including inplace or accumulated sources of pollutants, and methods for reclaiming and recycling water and confining pollutants so they will not migrate to cause water or other environmental pollution; and

(3) improved methods and procedures to identify and measure the effects of pollutants on the chemical, physical, and biological integrity of water, including those pollutants created by new technological developments.

(e)(1) The Administrator is authorized to (A) make, in consultation with the Secretary of Agriculture, grants to persons for research and demonstration projects with respect to new and improved methods of preventing, reducing, and eliminating pollution from agriculture, and (B) disseminate, in cooperation with the Secretary of Agriculture, such information obtained under this subsection, section 104(p), and section 304 as will encourage and enable the adoption of such methods in the agricultural industry.

(2) The Administrator is authorized, (A) in consultation with other interested Federal agencies, to make grants for demonstration projects with respect to new and improved methods of preventing, reducing, storing, collecting, treating, or otherwise eliminating pollution from sewage in rural and other areas where collection of sewage in conventional, community-wide sewage collection systems is impractical, uneconomical, or otherwise infeasible, or where soil conditions or other factors preclude the use of septic tank and drainage field systems, and (B) in cooperation with other interested Federal and State agencies, to disseminate such information obtained under this subsection as will encourage and enable the adoption of new and improved methods developed pursuant to this subsection.

(f) Federal grants under subsection (a) of this section shall be subject to the following limitations:

(1) No grant shall be made for any project unless such project shall have been approved by the appropriate State water pollution control agency or agencies and by the Administrator;

(2) No grant shall be made for any project in an amount exceeding 75 per centum of cost thereof as determined by the Administrator; and

(3) No grant shall be made for any project unless the Administrator determines that such project will serve as a useful demonstration for the purpose set forth in clause (1) or (2) of subsection (a).

(g) Federal grants under subsections (c) and (d) of this section shall not exceed 75 per centum of the cost of the project.

(h) For the purpose of this section there is authorized to be appropriated $75,000,000 per fiscal year for the fiscal year ending June 30, 1973, the fiscal year ending June 30, 1974, and the fiscal year ending June 30, 1975, and from such appropriations at least 10 per centum of the funds actually appropriated in each fiscal year shall be available only for the purposes of subsection (e).

(i) The Administrator is authorized to make grants to a municipality to assist in the costs of operating and maintaining a project which received a grant under this section, section 104, or section 113 of this Act prior to the date of enactment of this subsection so as to reduce the operation and maintenance costs borne by the recipients of services from such project to costs comparable to those for projects assisted under title II of this Act.

(j) The Administrator is authorized to make a grant to any grantee who received an increased grant pursuant to section 202(a)(2) of this Act. Such grant may pay up to 100 per centum of the costs of technical evaluation of the operation of the treatment works, cost of training of persons (other than employees of the grantee), and costs of disseminating technical information on the operation of the treatment works.

GRANTS FOR POLLUTION CONTROL PROGRAMS

SEC. 106. (a) There are hereby authorized to be appropriated the following sums, to remain available until expended, to carry out the purposes of this section—

(1) $60,000,000 for the fiscal year ending June 30, 1973; and

(2) $75,000,000 for the fiscal year ending June 30, 1974 and the fiscal year ending June 30, 1975, $100,000,000 per fiscal year for the fiscal years 1977, 1978, 1979, and 1980 $75,000,000 per fiscal year for the fiscal years 1981 and 1982

for grants to States and to interstate agencies to assist them in administering programs for the prevention, reduction, and elimination of pollution, including enforcement directly or through appropriate State law enforcement officers or agencies.

(b) From the sums appropriated in any fiscal year, the Administrator shall make allotments to the several States and interstate agencies in accordance with regulations promulgated by him on the basis of the extent of the pollution problem in the respective States.

(c) The Administrator is authorized to pay to each State and interstate agency each fiscal year either—

(1) the allotment of such State or agency for such fiscal year under subsection (b), or

(2) the reasonable costs as determined by the Administrator of developing and carrying out a pollution program by such State or agency during such fiscal year,

whichever amount is the lesser.

(d) No grant shall be made under this section to any State or interstate agency for any fiscal year when the expenditure of non-Federal funds by such State or interstate agency during such fiscal year for the recurrent expenses of carrying out its pollution control program are less than the expenditure by such State or interstate agency of non-Federal funds for such recurrent program expenses during the fiscal year ending June 30, 1971.

(e) Beginning in fiscal year 1974 the Administrator shall not make any grant under this section to any State which has not provided or is not carrying out as a part of its program—

(1) the establishment and operation of appropriate devices, methods, systems, and procedures necessary to monitor, and to compile and analyze data on (including classification according to eutrophic condition), the quality of navigable waters and to the extent practicable, ground waters including biological monitoring; and provision for annually updating such data and including it in the report required under section 305 of this Act;

(2) authority comparable to that in section 504 of this Act and adequate contingency plans to implement such authority.

(f) Grants shall be made under this section on condition that—

(1) Such State (or interstate agency) filed with the Administrator within one hundred and twenty days after the date of enactment of this section:

(A) a summary report of the current status of the State pollution control program, including the criteria used by the State in determining priority of treatment works; and

(B) such additional information, data, and reports as the Administrator may require.

(2) No federally assumed enforcement as defined in section 309 (a)(2) is in effect with respect to such State or interstate agency.

(3) Such State (or interstate agency) submits within one hundred and twenty days after the date of enactment of this section and

before October 1 of each year thereafter for the Administrator's approval of its program for the prevention, reduction, and elimination of pollution in accordance with purposes and provisions of this Act in such form and content as the Administrator may prescribe.

(g) Any sums allotted under subsection (b) in any fiscal year which are not paid shall be reallotted by the Administrator in accordance with regulations promulgated by him.

MINE WATER POLLUTION CONTROL DEMONSTRATIONS

SEC. 107. (a) The Administrator in cooperation with the Appalachian Regional Commission and other Federal agencies is authorized to conduct, to make grants for, or to contract for, projects to demonstrate comprehensive approaches to the elimination or control of acid or other mine water pollution resulting from active or abandoned mining operations and other environmental pollution affecting water quality within all or part of a watershed or river basin, including siltation from surface mining. Such projects shall demonstrate the engineering and economic feasibility and practicality of various abatement techniques which will contribute substantially to effective and practical methods of acid or other mine water pollution elimination or control, and other pollution affecting water quality, including techniques that demonstrate the engineering and economic feasibility and practicality of using sewage sludge materials and other municipal wastes to diminish or prevent pollution affecting water quality from acid, sedimentation, or other pollutants and in such projects to restore affected lands to usefulness for forestry, agriculture, recreation, or other beneficial purposes.

(b) Prior to undertaking any demonstration project under this section in the Appalachian region (as defined in section 403 of the Appalachian Regional Development Act of 1965, as amended), the Appalachian Regional Commission shall determine that such demonstration project is consistent with the objectives of the Appalachian Regional Development Act of 1965, as amended.

(c) The Administrator, in selecting watersheds for the purposes of this section, shall be satisfied that the project area will not be affected adversely by the influx of acid or other mine water pollution from nearby sources.

(d) Federal participation in such projects shall be subject to the conditions—

(1) that the State shall acquire any land or interests therein necessary for such project; and

(2) that the State shall provide legal and practical protection to the project area to insure against any activities which will cause future acid or other mine water pollution.

(e) There is authorized to be appropriated $30,000,000 to carry out the provisions of this section, which sum shall be available until expended.

POLLUTION CONTROL IN GREAT LAKES

SEC. 108. (a) The Administrator, in cooperation with other Federal departments, agencies, and instrumentalities is authorized to enter into agreements with any State, political subdivision, interstate agency, or other public agency, or combination thereof, to carry out one or more projects to demonstrate new methods and techniques and tod evelop preliminary plans for the elimination or control of pollution, within all or any part of the watersheds of the Great Lakes. Such projects shall demonstrate the engineering and economic feasibility and practicality of removal of pollutants and prevention of any polluting matter from entering into the Great Lakes in the future and other reduction and remedial techniques which will contribute substantially to effective and practical methods of pollution prevention, reduction, or elimination.

(b) Federal participation in such projects shall be subject to the condition that the State, political subdivision, interstate agency, or other public agency, or combination thereof, shall pay not less than 25 per centum of the actual project costs, which payment may be in any form, including, but not limited to, land or interests therein that is needed for the project, and personal property or services the value of which shall be determined by the Administrator.

(c) There is authorized to be appropriated $20,000,000 to carry out the provisions of subsections (a) and (b) of this section, which sum shall be available until expended.

(d) (1) In recognition of the serious conditions which exist in Lake Erie, the Secretary of the Army, acting through the Chief of Engineers, is directed to design and develop a demonstration waste water management program for the rehabilitation and environmental repair of Lake Erie. Prior to the initiation of detailed engineering and design, the program, along with the specific recommendations of the Chief of Engineers and recommendations for its financing, shall be submitted to the Congress for statutory approval. This authority is in addition to, and not in lieu of, other waste water studies aimed at eliminating pollution emanating from select sources around Lake Erie.

(2) This program is to be developed in cooperation with the Environmental Protection Agency, other interested departments, agencies, and instrumentalities of the Federal Government, and the States and their political subdivisions. This program shall set forth alternative systems for managing waste water on a regional basis and shall provide local and State governments with a range of choice as to the type of system to be used for the treatment of waste water. These alternative systems shall include both advanced waste treatment technology and land disposal systems including aerated treatment-spray irrigation technology and will also include provisions for the disposal of solid wastes, including sludge. Such program should include measures to control point sources of pollution, area sources of pollution, including acid-mine drainage, urban runoff and rural runoff, and in place sources of pollution, including bottom loads, sludge banks, and polluted harbor dredgings.

(e) There is authorized to be appropriated $5,000,000 to carry out the provisions of subsection (d) of this section, which sum shall be available until expended.

TRAINING GRANTS AND CONTRACTS

SEC. 109. (a) The Administrator is authorized to make grants to or contracts with institutions of higher education, or combinations of such institutions, to assist them in planning, developing strengthening, improving, or carrying out programs or projects for the preparation of undergraduate students to enter an occupation which involves the design, operation, and maintenance of treatment works, and other facilities whose purpose is water quality control. Such grants or contracts may include payment of all or part of the cost of programs or projects such as—

(A) planning for the development or expansion of programs or projects for training persons in the operation and maintenance of treatment works;

(B) training and retraining of faculty members;

(C) conduct of short-term or regular session institutes for study by persons engaged in, or preparing to engage in, the preparation of students preparing to enter an occupation involving the operation and maintenance of treatment works;

(D) carrying out innovative and experimental programs of cooperative education involving alternate periods of full-time or part-time academic study at the institution and periods of full-time or part-time employment involving the operation and maintenance of treatment works; and

(E) research into, and development of, methods of training students or faculty, including the preparation of teaching materials and the planning of curriculum.

(b) (1) The Administrator may pay 100 per centum of any additional cost of construction of treatment works required for a facility to train and upgrade waste treatment works operation and maintenance personnel and for the costs of other State treatment works operator training programs, including mobile training units, classroom rental, specialized instructors, and instructional material.

(2) The Administrator shall make no more than one grant for such additional construction in any State (to serve a group of States, where, in his judgment, efficient training programs require multi-State programs), and shall make such grant after consultation with and approval by the State or States on the basis of (A) the suitability of such facility for training operation and maintenance personnel for treatment works throughout such State or States; and (B) a commitment by the State agency or agencies to carry out at such facility a program of training approved by the Administrator. In any case where a grant is made to serve two or more States, the Administrator is authorized to make an additional grant for a supplemental facility in each such State.

(3) The Administrator may make such grant out of the sums allocated to a State under section 205 of this Act, except that in no event shall the Federal cost of any such training facilities exceed $500,000.

(4) The Administrator may exempt a grant under this section from any requirement under section 204(a)(3) of this Act. Any grantee who received a grant under this section prior to enactment of the Clean Water Act of 1977 shall be eligible to have its grant increased by funds made available under such Act.

APPLICATION FOR TRAINING GRANT OR CONTRACT; ALLOCATION OF GRANTS OR CONTRACTS

SEC. 110. (1) A grant or contract authorized by section 109 may be made only upon application to the Administrator at such time or times and containing such information as he may prescribe, except that no such application shall be approved unless it—

(A) sets forth programs, activities, research, or development for which a grant is authorized under section 109 and describes the relation to any program set forth by the applicant in an application, if any, submitted pursuant to section 111;

(B) provides such fiscal control and fund accounting procedures as may be necessary to assure proper disbursement of and accounting for Federal funds paid to the applicant under this section; and

(C) provides for making such reports, in such form and containing such information, as the Administrator may require to carry out his functions under this section, and for keeping such records and for affording such access thereto as the Administrator may find necessary to assure the correctness and vertification of such reports.

(2) The Administrator shall allocate grants or contracts under section 109 in such manner as will most nearly provide an equitable distribution of the grants or contracts throughout the United States among institutions of higher education which show promise of being able to use funds effectively for the purpose of this section.

(3)(A) Payments under this section may be used in accordance with regulations of the Administrator, and subject to the terms and conditions set forth in an application approved under paragraph (1), to pay part of the compensation of students employed in connection with the operation and maintenance of treatment works, other than as an employee in connection with the operation and maintenance of treatment works or as an employee in any branch of the Government of the United States, as part of a program for which a grant has been approved pursuant to this section.

(B) Departments and agencies of the United States are encouraged, to the extent consistent with efficient administration, to enter into arrangements with institutions of higher education for the full-time, part-time, or temporary employment, whether in the competitive or excepted service, of students enrolled in programs set forth in applications approved under paragraph (1).

AWARD OF SCHOLARSHIPS

SEC. 111. (1) The Administrator is authorized to award scholarships in accordance with the provisions of this section for undergraduate study by persons who plan to enter an occupation involving the operation and maintenance of treatment works. Such scholarships shall be awarded for such periods as the Administrator may determine but not to exceed four academic years.

(2) The Administrator shall allocate scholarships under this section among institutions of higher education with programs approved under the provisions of this section for the use of individuals accepted into such programs, in such manner and accordance to such plan as will insofar as practicable—

(A) provide an equitable distribution of such scholarships throughout the United States; and

(B) attract recent graduates of secondary schools to enter an occupation involving the operation and maintenance of treatment works.

(3) The Administrator shall approve a program of any institution

of higher education for the purposes of this section only upon application by the institution and only upon his finding—

(A) that such program has a principal objective the education and training of persons in the operation and maintenance of treatment works;

(B) that such program is in effect and of high quality, or can be readily put into effect and may reasonably be expected to be of high quality;

(C) that the application, describes the relation of such program to any program, activity, research, or development set forth by the applicant in an application, if any, submitted pursuant to section 110 of this Act; and

(D) that the application contains satisfactory assurances that (i) the institution will recommend to the Administrator for the award of scholarships under this section, for study in such program, only persons who have demonstrated to the satisfaction of the institution a serious intent, upon completing the program, to enter an occupation involving the operation and maintenance of treatment works, and (ii) the institution will make reasonable continuing efforts to encourage recipients of scholarships under this section, enrolled in such program, to enter occupations involving the operation and maintenance of treatment works upon completing the program.

(4)(A) The Administrator shall pay to persons awarded scholarships under this section such stipends (including such allowances for subsistence and other expenses for such persons and their dependents) as he may determine to be consistent with prevailing practices under comparable federally supported programs.

(B) The Administrator shall (in addition to the stipends paid to persons under paragraph (1) pay to the institution of higher education at which such person is pursuing his course of study such amount as he may determine to be consistent with prevailing practices under comparable federally supported programs.

(5) A person awarded a scholarship under the provisions of this section shall continue to receive the payments provided in this section only during such periods as the Administrator finds that he is maintaining satisfactory proficiency and devoting full time to study or research in the field in which such scholarship was awarded in an institution of higher education, and is not engaging in gainful employment other than employment approved by the Administrator by or pursuant to regulation.

(6) The Administrator shall by regulation provide that any person awarded a scholarship under this section shall agree in writing to enter and remain in an occupation involving the design, operation, or maintenance of treatment works for such period after completion of his course of studies as the Administrator determines appropriate.

DEFINITIONS AND AUTHORIZATIONS

SEC. 112. (a) As used in sections 109 through 112 of this Act—

(1) The term "institution of higher education" means an educational institution described in the first sentence of section 1201 of the Higher Education Act of 1965 (other than an institution of any agency of the United States) which is accredited by a nationally recognized accrediting agency or association

approved by the Administrator for this purpose. For purposes of this subsection, the Administrator shall publish a list of nationally recognized accrediting agencies or associations which he determines to be reliable authority as to the quality of training offered.

(2) The term "academic year" means an academic year or its equivalent, as determined by the Administrator.

(b) The Administrator shall annually report his activities under sections 109 through 112 of this Act, including recommendations for needed revisions in the provisions thereof.

(c) There are authorized to be appropriated $25,000,000 per fiscal year for the fiscal years ending June 30, 1973, June 30, 1974, and June 30, 1975, $6,000,000 for the fiscal year ending September 30, 1977, $7,000,000 for the fiscal year ending September 30, 1978, $7,000,000 for the fiscal year ending September 30, 1979, $7,000,000 for the fiscal year ending September 30, 1980, $7,000,000 for the fiscal year ending September 30, 1981, and $7,000,000 for the fiscal year ending September 30, 1982 to carry out sections 109 through 112 of this Act.

ALASKA VILLAGE DEMONSTRATION PROJECTS

SEC. 113. (a) The Administrator is authorized to enter into agreements with the State of Alaska to carry out one or more projects to demonstrate methods to provide for central community facilities for safe water and elimination or control of pollution in those native villages of Alaska without such facilities. Such projects shall include provisions for community safe water supply systems, toilets, bathing and laundry facilities, sewage disposal facilities, and other similar facilities, and educational and informational facilities and programs relating to health and hygiene. Such demonstration projects shall be for the further purpose of developing preliminary plans for providing such safe water and such elimination or control of pollution for all native villages in such State.

(b) In carrying out this section the Administrator shall cooperate with the Secretary of Health, Education, and Welfare for the purpose of utilizing such of the personnel and facilities of that Department as may be appropriate.

(c) The Administrator shall report to Congress not later than July 1, 1973, the results of the demonstration projects authorized by this section together with his recommendations, including any necessary legislation, relating to the establishment of a statewide program.

(d) There is authorized to be appropriated not to exceed $2,000,000 to carry out this section. In addition, there is authorized to be appropriated to carry out this section not to exceed $200,000 for the fiscal year ending September 30, 1978, and $220,000 for the fiscal year ending September 30, 1979.

(e) The Administrator is authorized to coordinate with the Secretary of the Department of Health, Education, and Welfare, the Secretary of the Department of Housing and Urban Development, the Secretary of the Department of the Interior, the Secretary of the Department of Agriculture, and the heads of any other departments or agencies he may deem appropriate to conduct a joint study with representatives of the State of Alaska and the appropriate Native organizations (as defined in Public Law 92–203) to develop a comprehensive program for achieving adequate sanitation services in Alaska villages. This study shall be coordinated with the programs and projects authorized by sections 104(q) and 105(e)(2) of this Act. The Administrator shall submit a report of the results of the study, together with appropriate supporting data and such recommendations as he deems desirable, to the Committee on Environment and Public Works of the Senate and to the Committee on Public Works and Transportation of the House of Representatives not later than December 31, 1979. The Administrator shall also submit recommended administrative actions, procedures, and any proposed legislation necessary to implement the recommendations of the study no later than June 30, 1980.

(f) The Administrator is authorized to provide technical, financial and management assistance for operation and maintenance of the demonstration projects constructed under this section, until such time as the recommendations of subsection (e) are implemented.

(g) For the purpose of this section, the term "village" shall mean an incorporated or unincorporated community with a population of ten to six hundred people living within a two-mile radius. The term "sanitation services" shall mean water supply, sewage disposal, solid waste disposal and other services necessary to maintain generally accepted standards of personal hygiene and public health.

LAKE TAHOE STUDY

SEC. 114. (a) The Administrator, in consultation with the Tahoe Regional Planning Agency, the Secretary of Agriculture, other Federal agencies, representatives of State and local governments, and members of the public, shall conduct a thorough and complete study on the adequacy of and need for extending Federal oversight and control in order to preserve the fragile ecology of Lake Tahoe.

(b) Such study shall include an examination of the interrelationships and responsibilities of the various agencies of the Federal Government and State and local governments with a view to establishing the necessity for redefinition of legal and other arrangements between these various governments, and making specific legislative recommendations to Congress. Such study shall consider the effect of various actions in terms of their environmental impact on the Tahoe Basin, treated as an ecosystem.

(c) The Administrator shall report on such study to Congress not later than one year after the date of enactment of this subsection.

(d) There is authorized to be appropriated to carry out this section not to exceed $500,000.

IN-PLACE TOXIC POLLUTANTS

SEC. 115. The Administrator is directed to identify the location of in-place pollutants with emphasis on toxic pollutants in harbors and navigable waterways and is authorized, acting through the Secretary of the Army, to make contracts for the removal and appropriate disposal of such materials from critical port and harbor areas. There is authorized to be appropriated $15,000,000 to carry out the provisions of this section, which sum shall be available until expended.

HUDSON RIVER PCB RECLAMATION DEMONSTRATION PROJECT

SEC. 116. (a) The Administrator is authorized to enter into contracts and other agreements with the State of New York to carry out a project to demonstrate methods for the selective removal of polychlorinated biphenyls contaminating bottom sediments of the Hudson River, treating such sediments as required, burying such sediments in secure landfills, and installing monitoring systems for such landfills. Such demonstration project shall be for the purpose of determining the feasibility of indefinite storage in secure landfills of toxic substances and of ascertaining the improvement of the rate of recovery of a toxic contaminated national waterway. No pollutants removed pursuant to this paragraph shall be placed in any landfill unless the Administrator first determines that disposal of the pollutants in such landfill would provide a higher standard of protection of the public health, safety, and welfare than disposal of such pollutants by any other method including, but not limited to, incineration or a chemical destruction process.

(b) The Administrator is authorized to make grants to the State of New York to carry out this section from funds allotted to such State under section 205(a) of this Act, except that the amount of any such grant shall be equal to 75 per centum of the cost of the project and such grant shall be made on condition that non-Federal sources provide the remainder of the cost of such project. The authority of this section shall be available until September 30, 1983. Funds allotted to the State of New York under section 205(a) shall be available under this subsection only to the extent that funds are not available, as determined by the Administrator, to the State of New York for the work authorized by this section under section 115 or 311 of this Act or a comprehensive hazardous substance response and clean up fund. Any funds used under the authority of this subsection shall be deducted from any estimate of the needs of the State of New York prepared under section 616(b) of this Act. The Administrator may not obligate or expend more than $20,000,000 to carry out this section.

TITLE II—GRANTS FOR CONSTRUCTION OF TREATMENT WORKS

PURPOSE

SEC. 201. (a) It is the purpose of this title to require and to assist the development and implementation of waste treatment management plans and practices which will achieve the goals of this Act.

(b) Waste treatment management plans and practices shall provide for the application of the best practicable waste treatment technology before any discharge into receiving waters, including reclaiming and recycling of water, and confined disposal of pollutants so they will not migrate to cause water or other environmental pollution and shall provide for consideration of advanced waste treatment techniques.

(c) To the extent practicable, waste treatment management shall be on an areawide basis and provide control or treatment of all point and nonpoint sources of pollution, including in place or accumulated pollution sources.

(d) The Administrator shall encourage waste treatment management which results in the construction of revenue producing facilities providing for—

(1) the recycling of potential sewage pollutants through the production of agriculture, silviculture, or aquaculture products, or any combination thereof;

(2) the confined and contained disposal of pollutants not recycled;

(3) the reclamation of wastewater; and

(4) the ultimate disposal of sludge in a manner that will not result in environmental hazards.

(e) The Administrator shall encourage waste treatment management which results in integrating facilities for sewage treatment and recycling with facilities to treat, dispose of, or utilize other industrial and municipal wastes, including but not limited to solid waste and waste heat and thermal discharges. Such integrated facilities shall be designed and operated to produce revenues in excess of capital and operation and maintenance costs and such revenues shall be used by the designated regional management agency to aid in financing other environmental improvement programs.

(f) The Administrator shall encourage waste treatment management which combines "open space" and recreational considerations with such management.

(g)(1) The Administrator is authorized to make grants to any State, municipality, or intermunicipal or interstate agency for the construction of publicly owned treatment works. *On and after October 1, 1984, grants under this title shall be made only for projects for secondary treatment or more stringent treatment, or any cost effective alternative thereto, new interceptors and appurtenances, and infiltration-in-flow correction. Notwithstanding the preceding sentence, the Administrator may make grants on and after October 1, 1984, for any project within the definition set forth in section 212(2) of this Act, other than for a project referred to in the preceding sentence, except that not more than 20 per centum (as determined by the Governor of the State) of the amount allotted to a State under section 205 of this Act for any fiscal year shall be obligated in such State under authority of this sentence.*

(2) The Administrator shall not make grants from funds authorized for any fiscal year beginning after June 30, 1974, to any State, municipality, or intermunicipal or interstate agency for the erection, building, acquisition, alteration, remodeling, improvement, or extension of treatment works unless the grant applicant has satisfactorily demonstrated to the Administrator that—

(A) alternative waste management techniques have been studied and evaluated and the works proposed for grant assistance will provide for the application of the best practicable waste treatment technology over the life of the works consistent with the purposes of this title; and

(B) as appropriate, the works proposed for grant assistance will take into account and allow to the extent practicable the application of technology at a later date which will provide for the reclaiming or recycling of water or otherwise eliminate the discharge of pollutants.

(3) The Administrator shall not approve any grant after July 1, 1973, for treatment works under this section unless the applicant shows

to the satisfaction of the Administrator that each sewer collection system discharging into such treatment works is not subject to excessive infiltration.

(4) The Administrator is authorized to make grants to applicants for treatment works grants under this section for such sewer system evaluation studies as may be necessary to carry out the requirements of paragraph (3) of this subsection. Such grants shall be made in accordance with rules and regulations promulgated by the Administrator. Initial rules and regulations shall be promulgated under this paragraph not later than 120 days after the date of enactment of the Federal Water Pollution Control Act Amendments of 1972.

(5) The Administrator shall not make grants from funds authorized for any fiscal year beginning after September 30, 1978, to any State, municipality, or intermunicipal or interstate agency for the erection, building, acquisition, alteration, remodeling, improvement, or extension of treatment works unless the grant applicant has satisfactorily demonstrated to the Administrator that innovative and alternative wastewater treatment processes and techniques which provide for the reclaiming and reuse of water, otherwise eliminate the discharge of pollutants, and utilize recycling techniques, land treatment, new or improved methods of waste treatment management for municipal and industrial waste (discharged into municipal systems) and the confined disposal of pollutants, so that pollutants will not migrate to cause water or other environmental pollution, have been fully studied and evaluated by the applicant taking into account section 201(d) of this Act and taking into account and allowing to the extent practicable the more efficient use of energy and resources.

(6) The Administrator shall not make grants from funds authorized for any fiscal year beginning after September 30, 1978, to any State, municipality, or intermunicipal or interstate agency for the erection, building, acquisition, alteration, remodeling, improvement, or extension of treatment works unless the grant applicant has satisfactorily demonstrated to the Administrator that the applicant has analyzed the potential recreation and open space opportunities in the planning of the proposed treatment works.

(h) A grant may be made under this section to construct a privately owned treatment works serving one or more principal residences or small commercial establishments constructed prior to, and inhabited on the date of enactment of this subsection where the Administrator finds that—

(1) a public body otherwise eligible for a grant under subsection (g) of this section has applied on behalf of a number of such units and certified that public ownership of such works is not feasible;

(2) such public body has entered into an agreement with the Administrator which guarantees that such treatment works will be properly operated and maintained and will comply with all other requirements of section 204 of this Act and includes a system of charges to assure that each recipient of waste treatment services under such a grant will pay its proportionate share of the cost of operation and maintenance (including replacement); and

(3) the total cost and environmental impact of providing waste treatment services to such residences or commercial

establishments will be less than the cost of providing a system of collection and central treatment of such wastes.

(i) The Administrator shall encourage waste treatment management methods, processes, and techniques which will reduce total energy requirements.

(j) The Administrator is authorized to make a grant for any treatment works utilizing processes and techniques meeting the guidelines promulgated under section 304(d)(3) of this Act, if the Administrator determines it is in the public interest and if in the cost effectiveness study made of the construction grant application for the purpose of evaluating alternative treatment works, the life cycle cost of the treatment works for which the grant is to be made does not exceed the life cycle cost of the most effective alternative by more than 15 per centum.

(k) No grant made after November 15, 1981, for a publicly owned treatment works, other than for facility planning and the preparation of construction plans and specifications, shall be used to treat, store, or convey the flow of any industrial user into such treatment works in excess of a flow per day equivalent to fifty thousand gallons per day of sanitary waste. This subsection shall not apply to any project proposed by a grantee which is carrying out an approved project to prepare construction plans and specifications for a facility to treat wastewater, which received its grant approval before May 15, 1980. *This subsection shall not be in effect after November 15, 1981.*

(l) (1) After the date of enactment of this subsection, Federal grants shall not be made for the purpose of providing assistance solely for facility plans, or plans, specifications, and estimates for any proposed project for the construction of treatment works. In the event that the proposed project receives a grant under this section for construction, the Administrator shall make an allowance in such grant for non-Federal funds expended during the facility planning and advanced engineering and design phase at the prevailing Federal share under section 202(a) of this Act, based on the percentage of total project costs which the Administrator determines is the general experience for such projects.

(2) (A) Each State shall use a portion of the funds allotted to such State each fiscal year, but not to exceed 10 per centum of such funds, to advance to potential grant applicants under this title the costs of facility planning or the preparation of plans, specifications, and estimates.

(B) Such an advance shall be limited to the allowance for such costs which the Administrator establishes under paragraph (1) of this subsection, and shall be provided only to a potential grant applicant which is a small community and which in the judgment of the State would otherwise be unable to prepare a request for a grant for construction costs under this section.

(C) In the event a grant for construction costs is made under this section for a project for which an advance has been made under this paragraph, the Administrator shall reduce the amount of such grant by the allowance established under paragraph (1) of this subsection. In the event no such grant is made, the State is authorized to seek repayment of such advance on such terms and conditions as it may determine.

(m)(1) Notwithstanding any other provisions of this title, the Administrator is authorized to make a grant from any funds otherwise allotted to the State of California under section 205 of this Act to the project (and in the amount) specified in Order WQG 81–1 of the California State Water Resources Control Board.

(2) Notwithstanding any other provision of this Act, the Administrator shall make a grant from any funds otherwise allotted to the State of California to the city of Eureka, California, in connection with project numbered C–06–2772, for the purchase of one hundred and thirty-nine acres of property as environmental mitigation for siting of the proposed treatment plant.

(3) Notwithstanding any other provision of this Act, the Administrator shall make a grant from any funds otherwise allotted to the State of California to the city of San Diego, California, in connection with that city's aquaculture sewage process (total resources recovery system) as an innovative and alternative waste treatment process.

(n)(1) On and after October 1, 1984, upon the request of the Governor of an affected State, the Administrator is authorized to use funds available to such State under section 205 to address water quality problems due to the impacts of discharges from combined storm water and sanitary sewer overflows, which are not otherwise eligible under this subsection, where correction of such discharges is a major priority for such State.

(2) Beginning fiscal year 1983, the Administrator shall have available $200,000,000 per fiscal year in addition to those funds authorized in section 207 of this Act to be utilized to address water quality problems of marine bays and estuaries subject to lower levels of water quality due to the impacts of discharges from combined storm water and sanitary sewer overflows from adjacent urban complexes, not otherwise eligible under this subsection. Such sums may be used as deemed appropriate by the Administrator as provided in paragraphs (1) and (2) of this subsection, upon the request of and demonstration of water quality benefits by the Governor of an affected State.

(o) The Administrator shall encourage and assist applicants for grant assistance under this title to develop and file with the Administrator a capital financing plan which, at a minimum—

(1) projects the future requirements for waste treatment services within the applicant's jurisdiction for a period of no less than ten years;

(2) projects the nature, extent, timing, and costs of future expansion and reconstruction of treatment works which will be necessary to satisfy the applicant's projected future requirements for waste treatment services; and

(3) sets forth with specificity the manner in which the applicant intends to finance such future expansion and reconstruction.

FEDERAL SHARE

SEC. 202. (a)(1) The amount of any grant for treatment works made under this Act from funds authorized for any fiscal year beginning after June 30, 1971 *and ending before October 1, 1984*, shall be 75 per centum of the cost of construction thereof (as approved by the Administrator), *and for any fiscal year beginning on or after October 1, 1984, shall be 55 per centum of the cost of construction thereof (as approved by the Administrator)* unless modified to a lower percentage rate uniform throughout a State by the Governor of that State with the concurrence of the Administrator. Within ninety days after the enactment of this sentence the Administrator shall issue guidelines for concurrence in any such modification, which shall provide for the consideration of the unobligated balance of sums allocated to the State under section 205 of this Act, the need for assistance under this title in such State, and the availability of State grant assistance to replace the Federal share reduced by such modification. The payment of any such reduced Federal share shall not constitute an obligation on the part of the United States or a claim on the part of any State or grantee to reimbursement for the portion of the Federal share reduced in any such State. Any grant (other than for reimbursement) made prior to the date of enactment of the Federal Water Pollution Control Act Amendments of 1972 from any funds authorized for any fiscal year beginning after June 30, 1971, shall, upon the request of the applicant, be increased to the applicable percentage under this section. *Notwithstanding the first sentence of this paragraph, in any case where a primary, secondary, or advanced waste treatment facility or its related interceptors or a project for infiltration-in-flow correction has received a grant for erection, building, acquisition, alteration, remodeling, improvement, extension, or correction before October 1, 1984, all segments and phases of such facility, interceptors and project for infiltration-in-flow correction shall be eligible for grants at 75 per centum of the cost of construction thereof.*

(2) The amount of any grant made after September 30, 1978, and before October 1, 1981, for any eligible treatment works or significant portion thereof utilizing innovative or alternative wastewater treatment processes and techniques referred to in section 201(g)(5) shall be 85 per centum of the cost of construction thereof, unless modified by the Governor of the State with the concurrence of the Administrator to a percentage rate no less than 15 per centum greater than the modified uniform percentage rate in which the Administrator has concurred pursuant to paragraph (1) of this subsection. *The amount of any grant made after September 30, 1981, for any eligible treatment works or unit processes and techniques thereof utilizing innovative or alternative wastewater treatment processes and techniques referred to in section 201(g)(5) shall be a percentage of the cost of construction thereof equal to 20 per centum greater than the percentage in effect under paragraph (1) of this subsection for such works or unit processes and techniques, but in no event greater than 85 per centum of the cost of construction thereof.* No grant shall be made under this paragraph for construction of a treatment works in any State unless the proportion of the State contribution to the non-Federal share of construction costs for all treatment works in such State receiving a grant under this paragraph is the same as or greater than the proportion of the State contribution (if any) to the non-Federal share of construction costs for all treatment works receiving grants in such State under paragraph (1) of this subsection.

(3) In addition to any grant made pursuant to paragraph (2) of **this subsection, the Administrator is authorized to make a grant to fund all of the costs of the modification or replacement of any facilities**

constructed with a grant made pursuant to paragraph (2) if the Administrator finds that such facilities have not met design performance specifications unless such failure is attributable to negligence on the part of any person and if such failure has significantly increased capital or operating and maintenance expenditures.

(4) For the purposes of this section, the term "eligible treatment works" means those treatment works in each State which meet the requirements of section 201(g)(5) of this Act and which can be fully funded from funds available for such purpose in such State. ~~in the fiscal years ending September 30, 1979, September 30, 1980, and September 30, 1981. Such term does not include collector sewers, interceptors, storm or sanitary sewers or the separation thereof, or major sewer rehabilitation~~.

(b) The amount of the grant for any project approved by the Administrator after January 1, 1971, and before July 1, 1971, for the construction of treatment works, the actual erection, building or acquisition of which was not commenced prior to July 1, 1971, shall, upon the request of the applicant, be increased to the applicable percentage under subsection (a) of this section for grants for treatment works from funds for fiscal years beginning after June 30, 1971, with respect to the cost of such actual erection, building, or acquisition. Such increased amount shall be paid from any funds allocated to the State in which the treatment works is located without regard to the fiscal year for which such funds were authorized. Such increased amount shall be paid for such project only if—

(1) a sewage collection system that is a part of the same total waste treatment system as the treatment works for which such grant was approved is under construction or is to be constructed for use in conjunction with such treatment works, and if the cost of such sewage collection system exceeds the cost of such treatment works, and

(2) the State water pollution control agency or other appropriate State authority certifies that the quantity of available ground water will be insufficient, inadequate, or unsuitable for public use, including the ecological preservation and recreational use of surface water bodies, unless effluents from publicly owned treatment works after adequate treatment are returned to the ground water consistent with acceptable technological standards.

PLANS, SPECIFICATIONS, ESTIMATES, AND PAYMENTS

SEC. 203. (a) Each applicant for a grant shall submit to the Administrator for his approval, plans, specifications, and estimates for each proposed project for the construction of treatment works for which a grant is applied for under section 201(g)(1) from funds allotted to the State under section 205 and which otherwise meets the requirements of this Act. The Administrator shall act upon such plans, specifications, and estimates as soon as practicable after the same have been submitted, and his approval of any such plans, specifications, and estimates shall be deemed a contractual obligation of the United States for the payment of its proportional contribution to such project. In the case of a treatment works that has an estimated total cost of ~~$4,000,000~~ *$8,000,000* or less (as determined by the Administrator, and the population of the applicant municipality is twenty-five thousand or less (according to the most recent United States census), upon completion of an approved facility plan, a single grant may be awarded for the combined Federal share of the cost of preparing construction plans and specifications, and the building and erection of the treatment works. ~~If any State is found by the Administrator to have unusually high costs of construction, the Administrator may authorize a single grant under the preceding sentence where the estimated total cost of the treatment works does not exceed $5,000,000.~~

(b) The Administrator shall, from time to time as the work progresses, make payments to the recipient of a grant for costs of construction incurred on a project. These payments shall at no time exceed the Federal share of the cost of construction incurred to the date of the voucher covering such payment plus the Federal share of the value of the materials which have been stockpiled in the vicinity of such construction in conformity to plans and specifications for the project.

(c) After completion of a project and approval of the final voucher by the Administrator, he shall pay out of the appropriate sums the unpaid balance of the Federal share payable on account of such project.

(d) Nothing in this Act shall be construed to require, or to authorize the Administrator to require, that grants under this Act for construction of treatment works be made only for projects which are operable units usable for sewage collection, transportation, storage, waste treatment, or for similar purposes without additional construction.

(e) At the request of a grantee under this title, the Administrator is authorized to provide technical and legal assistance in the administration and enforcement of any contract in connection with treatment works assisted under this title, and to intervene any civil action involving the enforcement of such a contract.

LIMITATIONS AND CONDITIONS

SEC. 204. (a) Before approving grants for any project for any treatment works under section 201(g)(1) the Administrator shall determine—

(1) that such works are included in any applicable areawide waste treatment management plan developed under section 208 of this Act;

(2) that such works are in conformity with any applicable State plan under section 303(e) of this Act;

(3) that such works have been certified by the appropriate State water pollution control agency as entitled to priority over such other works in the State in accordance with any applicable State plan under section 303(e) of this Act, except that any priority list developed pursuant to section 303(e)(3)(H) may be modified by such State in accordance with regulations promulgated by the Administrator to give higher priority for grants for the Federal share of the cost of preparing construction drawings and specifications for any treatment works utilizing processes and techniques meeting the guidelines promulgated under section 304(d)(3) of this Act and for grants for the combined Federal share of the cost of preparing construction drawings and specifications and the building and erection of any treatment works meeting the requirements of the next to the last sentence of section 203(a) of this Act which utilizes processes and techniques meeting the guidelines promulgated under section 304(d)(3) of this Act;

(4) that the applicant proposing to construct such works agrees to pay the non-Federal costs of such works and has made ade-

quate provisions satisfactory to the Administrator for assuring proper and efficient operation, including the employment of trained management and operations personnel, and the maintenance of such works in accordance with a plan of operation approved by the State water pollution control agency or, as appropriate, the interstate agency, after construction therof;

(5) that the size and capacity of such works relate directly to the needs to be served by such works, including sufficient reserve capacity. The amount of reserve capacity provided shall be approved by the Administrator on the basis of a comparison of the cost of constructing such reserves as a part of the works to be funded and the anticipated cost of providing expanded capacity at a date when such capacity will be required after taking into account, in accordance with regulations promulgated by the Administrator, efforts to reduce total flow of sewage and unnecessary water consumption. The amount of reserve capacity eligible for a grant under this title shall be determined by the Administrator taking into account the projected population and associated commercial and industrial establishments within the jurisdiction of the applicant to be served by such treatment works as identified in an approved facilities plan, an areawide plan under section 208, or an applicable municipal master plan of development. For the purpose of this paragraph, section 208, and any such plan, projected population shall be determined on the basis of the latest information available from the United States Department of Commerce or from the States as the Administrator, by regulation, determines appropriate. *Beginning October 1, 1984, no grant shall be made under this title to construct that portion of any treatment works providing reserve capacity in excess of existing needs (including existing needs of residential, commercial, industrial, and other users) on the date of approval of a grant for the erection, building, acquisition, alteration, remodeling, improvement, or extension of a project for secondary treatment or more stringent treatment or new interceptors and appurtenances, except that in no event shall reserve capacity of a facility and its related interceptors to which this subsection applies be in excess of existing needs on October 1, 1990. In any case in which an applicant proposes to provide reserve capacity greater than that eligible for Federal financial assistance under this title, the incremental costs of the additional reserve capacity shall be paid by the applicant;*

(6) that no specification for bids in connection with such works shall be written in such a manner as to contain proprietary, exclusionary, or discriminatory requirements other than those based upon performance, unless such requirements are necessary to test or demonstrate a specific thing or to provide for necessary interchangeability of parts and equipment.

When in the judgment of the grantee, it is impractical or uneconomical to make a clear and accurate description of the technical requirements, a "brand name or equal" description may be used as a means to define the performance or other salient requirements of a procurement, and in doing so the grantee need not establish the existence of any source other than the brand or source so named.

(b)(1) Notwithstanding any other provision of this title, the Administrator shall not approve any grant for any treatment works under section 201(g)(1) after March 1, 1973, unless he shall first have determined that the applicant (A) has adopted or will adopt a system of charges to assure that each recipient of waste treatment services within the applicant's jurisdiction, as determined by the Administrator, will pay its proportionate share (except as otherwise provided in this paragraph) of the costs of operation and maintenance (including replacement) of any waste treatment services provided by the applicant; and (B) has legal, instiutional, managerial, and financial capability to insure adequate construction, operation, and maintenance of treatment works throughout the applicant's jurisdiction, as determined by the Administrator. In any case where an applicant which, as of the date of enactment of this sentence, uses a system of dedicated ad valorem taxes and the Administrator determines that the applicant has a system of charges which results in the distribution of operation and maintenance costs for treatment works within the applicant's jurisdiction, to each user class, in proportion to the contribution to the total cost of operation and maintenance of such works by each user class (taking into account total waste water loading of such works, the constituent elements of the waste, and other appropriate factors), and such applicant is otherwise in compliance with clause (A) of this paragraph with respect to each industrial user, then such dedicated ad valorem tax system shall be deemed to be the user charge system meeting the requirements of clause (A) of this paragraph for the residential user class and such small non-residential user classes as defined by the Administrator. In defining small non-residential users, the Administrator shall consider the volume of wastes discharged into the treatment works by such users and the constituent elements of such wastes as well as such other factors as he deems appropriate.

(2) The Administrator shall, within one hundred and eighty days after the date of enactment of the Federal Water Pollution Control Act Amendments of 1972, and after consultation with appropriate State, interstate, municipal, and intermunicipal agencies, issue guidelines applicable to payment of waste treatment costs by industrial and nonindustrial recipients of waste treatment services which shall establish (A) classes of users of such services, including categories of industrial users; (B) criteria against which to determine the adequacy of charges imposed on classes and categories of users reflecting all factors that influence the cost of waste treatment, including strength, volume, and delivery flow rate characteristics of waste; and (C) model systems and rates of user charges typical of various treatment works serving municipal-industrial communities.

(3) Approval by the Administrator of a grant to an interstate agency established by interstate compact for any treatment works shall satisfy any other requirement that such works be authorized by Act of Congress.

(4) A system of charges which meets the requirement of clause (A) of paragraph (1) of this subsection may be based on something other than metering the sewage or water supply flow of residential recipients of waste treatment services, including ad valorem taxes. If the system of charges is based on something other than metering, the Administrator shall require (A) the applicant to establish a system by which the necessary funds will be available for the proper operation and maintenance of the treatment works; and (B) the applicant to establish a procedure under which the residential user will be notified

as to that portion of his total payment which will be allocated to the costs of the waste treatment services.

(c) The next to the last sentence of paragraph (5) of subsection (a) of this section shall not apply in any case where a primary, secondary, or advanced waste treatment facility or its related interceptors has received a grant for erection, building, acquisition, alteration, remodeling, improvement, or extension before October 1, 1984, and all segments and phases of such facility and interceptors shall be funded based on a 20-year reserve capacity in the case of such facility and a 20-year reserve capacity in the case of such interceptors, except that, if a grant for such interceptors has been approved prior to the date of enactment of the Municipal Wastewater Treatment Construction Grant Amendments of 1981, such interceptors shall be funded based on the approved reserve capacity not to exceed 40 years.

(d)(1) A grant for the construction of treatment works under this title shall provide that the engineer or engineering firm supervising construction or providing architect engineering services during construction shall continue its relationship to the grant applicant for a period of one year after the completion of construction and initial operation of such treatment works. During such period such engineer or engineering firm shall supervise operation of the treatment works, train operating personnel, and prepare curricula and training material for operating personnel. Costs associated with the implementation of this paragraph shall be eligible for Federal assistance in accordance with this title.

(2) On the date one year after the completion of construction and initial operation of such treatment works, the owner and operator of such treatment works shall certify to the Administrator whether or not such treatment works meet the design specifications and effluent limitations contained in the grant agreement and permit pursuant to section 402 of the Act for such works. If the owner and operator of such treatment works cannot certify that such treatment works meet such design specifications and effluent limitations, any failure to meet such design specifications and effluent limitations shall be corrected in a timely manner, to allow such affirmative certification, at other than Federal expense.

(3) Nothing in this section shall be construed to prohibit a grantee under this title from requiring more assurances, guarantees, or indemnity or other contractual requirements from any party to a contract pertaining to a project assisted under this title, than in those provided under this subsection.

ALLOTMENT

SEC. 205. (a) Sums authorized to be appropriated pursuant to section 207 for each fiscal year beginning after June 30, 1972, and before September 30, 1977, shall be allotted by the Administrator not later than the January 1st immediately preceding the beginning of the fiscal year for which authorized, except that the allotment for fiscal year 1973 shall be made not later than 30 days after the date of enactment of the Federal Water Pollution Control Act Amendments of 1972. Such sums shall be allotted among the States by the Administrator in accordance with regulations promulgated by him, in the ratio that the estimated cost of constructing all needed publicly owned treatment works in each State bears to the estimated cost of construction of all needed publicly owned treatment works in all of the States. For the fiscal years ending June 30, 1973, and June 30, 1974, such ratio shall be determined on the basis of table III of House Public Works Committee Print No. 92–50. For the fiscal year ending June 30, 1975, such ratio shall be determined one-half on the basis of table I of House Public Works Committee Print Numbered 93–28 and one-half on the basis of table II of such print, except that no State shall recieve an allotment less than that which it received for the fiscal year ending June 30, 1972, as set forth in table III of such print. Allotments for fiscal years which begin after the fiscal year ending June 30, 1975 shall be made only in accordance with a revised cost estimate made and submitted to Congress in accordance with section 516(b) of this Act and only after such revised cost estimate shall have been approved by law specifically enacted hereafter.

(b)(1) Any sums allotted to a State under subsection (a) shall be available for obligation under section 203 on and after the date of such allotment. Such sums shall continue available for obligation in such State for a period of one year after the close ot the fiscal year for which such sums are authorized. Any amounts so allotted which are not obligated by the end of such one-year period shall be immediately reallotted by the Administrator, in accordance with regulations promulgated by him, generally on the basis of the ratio used in making the last allotment of sums under this section. Such reallotted sums shall be added to the last allotments made to the States. Any sum made available to a State by reallotment under this subsection shall be in addition to any funds otherwise allotted to such State for grants under this title during any fiscal year.

(2) Any sums which have been obligated under section 203 and which are released by the payment of the final voucher for the project shall be immediately credited to the State to which such sums were last allotted. Such released sums shall be added to the amounts last allotted to such State and shall be immediately available for obligation in the same manner and to the same extent as such last allotment.

(c) *(1)* Sums authorized to be appropriated pursuant to section 207 for the fiscal years during the period beginning October 1, 1977, and ending September 30, 1981, shall be allotted for each such year by the Administrator not later than the tenth day which begins after the date of enactment of the Clean Water Act of 1977. Notwithstanding any other provisions of law, sums authorized for the fiscal years ending September 30, 1978, September 30, 1979, September 30, 1980, and September 30, 1981, shall be allotted in accordance with table 3 of Committee Print Numbered 95–30 of the Committee on Public Works and Transportation of the House of Representatives.

(2) Sums authorized to be appropriated pursuant to section 207 for the fiscal years 1982, 1983, 1984, and 1985 shall be allotted for each such year by the Administrator not later than the tenth day which begins after the date of enactment of the Municipal Wastewater Treatment Construction Grant Amendments of 1981. Notwithstanding any other provision of law, sums authorized for the fiscal year ending September 30, 1982, shall be allotted in accordance with table 3 of Committee Print Numbered 95–30 of the Committee on Public

Works and Transportation of the House of Representatives. Sums authorized for the fiscal years ending September 30, 1983, September 30, 1984, and September 30, 1985, shall be allotted in accordance with the following table:

States:	Fiscal years 1983 through 1985
Alabama	.011398
Alaska	.006101
Arizona	.006885
Arkansas	.006668
California	.072901
Colorado	.008154
Connecticut	.012487
Delaware	.004965
District of Columbia	.004965
Florida	.034407
Georgia	.017234
Hawaii	.007895
Idaho	.004965
Illinois	.046101
Indiana	.024566
Iowa	.013796
Kansas	.009201
Kentucky	.012973
Louisiana	.011205
Maine	.007788
Maryland	.024653
Massachusetts	.034608
Michigan	.043829
Minnesota	.018735
Mississippi	.009184
Missouri	.028257
Montana	.004965
Nebraska	.005214
Nevada	.004965
New Hampshire	.010186
New Jersey	.041654
New Mexico	.004965
New York	.113097
North Carolina	.018396
North Dakota	.004965
Ohio	.057383
Oklahoma	.008235
Oregon	.011515
Pennsylvania	.040377
Rhode Island	.006750
South Carolina	.010442
South Dakota	.004965
Tennessee	.014807
Texas	.038726
Utah	.005371
Vermont	.004965
Virginia	.020861
Washington	.017726
West Virginia	.015890
Wisconsin	.027557
Wyoming	.004965
Samoa	.000915
Guam	.000662
Northern Marianas	.000425
Puerto Rico	.013295
Pacific Trust Territories	.001305
Virgin Islands	.000531
United States totals	.999996

(d) Sums allotted to the States for a fiscal year shall remain available for obligation for the fiscal year for which authorized and for the period of the next succeeding twelve months. The amount of any allotment not obligated by the end of such twenty-four-month period shall be immediately reallotted by the Administrator on the basis of the same ratio as applicable to sums allotted for the then current fiscal year, except that none of the funds reallotted by the Administrator for fiscal year 1978 and for fiscal years thereafter shall be allotted to any State which failed to obligate any of the funds being reallotted. Any sum made available to a State by reallotment under this subsection shall be in addition to any funds otherwise allotted to such State for grants under this title during any fiscal year.

(e) For the fiscal years 1978, 1979, 1980, ~~and 1981,~~ *1981, 1982, 1983, 1984, and 1985*, no State shall receive less than one-half of 1 per centum of the total allotment under subsection (c) of this section, except that in the case of Guam, Virgin Islands, American Samoa, and the Trust Territories not more than thirty-three one-hundredths of 1 per centum in the aggregate shall be allotted to all four of these jurisdictions. For the purpose of carrying out this subsection there are authorized to be appropriated, subject to such amounts as are provided in appropriation Acts, not to exceed $75,000,000 for each of fiscal years 1978, 1979, 1980, ~~and 1981~~ *1981, 1982, 1983, 1984, and 1985*. If for any fiscal year the amount appropriated under authority of this subsection is less than the amount necessary to carry out this subsection the amount each State receives under this subsection for such year shall bear the same ratio to the amount such State would have received under this subsection in such year if the amount necessary to carry it out had been appropriated as the amount appropriated for such year bears to the amount necessary to carry out this subsection for such year.

(f) Notwithstanding any other provision of this section, sums made available between January 1, 1975, and March 1, 1975, by the Administrator for obligation shall be available for obligation until September 30, 1978.

(g)(1) The Administrator is authorized to reserve each fiscal year not to exceed 2 per centum of the amount authorized under section 207 of this title for purposes of the allotment made to each State under this section on or after October 1, 1977, *except in the case of any fiscal year beginning on or after October 1, 1981, and ending before October 1, 1985, in which case the percentage authorized to be reserved shall not exceed 4 per centum*, or $400,000, whichever amount is the greater. Sums so reserved shall be available for making grants to such State under paragraph (2) of this subsection for the same period as sums are available from such allotment under subsection (d) of this section, and any such grant shall be available for obligation only during such period. Any grant made from sums reserved under this subsection which has not been obligated by the end of the period for which available shall be added to the amount last allotted to such State under this section and shall be immediately available for obligation in the same manner and to the same extent as such last allotment. *Sums authorized to be reserved by this paragraph shall be in addition to and not in lieu of any other funds which may be authorized to carry out this subsection.*

(2) The Administrator is authorized to grant to any State from amounts reserved to such State under this subsection, the reasonable costs of administering any aspects of sections 201, 203, 204, and 212 of this Act the responsibility for administration of which the Administrator has delegated to such State. The Administrator may increase such grant to take into account the reasonable costs of administering an approved program under section 402 or 404, administering a statewide waste treatment management planning program under section 208(b)(4), and managing waste treatment construction grants for small communities.

(h) The Administrator shall set aside from funds authorized for each fiscal year beginning on or after October 1, 1978, four per centum of the sums allotted to any State with a rural population of 25 per centum or more of the total population of such State, as determined by the Bureau of the Census. The Administrator may set aside no more than four per centum of the sums allotted to any other State for which the Governor requests such action. Such sums shall be available only for alternatives to conventional sewage treatment works for municipalities having a population of three thousand five hundred or less, or for the highly dispersed sections of larger municipalities, as defined by the Administrator.

(i) Not less than one-half of one per centum of funds allotted to a State for each of the fiscal years ending September 30, 1979, September 30, 1980, ~~and September 30, 1981~~, *September 30, 1981, September 30, 1982, September 30, 1983, September 30, 1984, and September 30, 1985*, under subsection (a) of this section shall be expended only for increasing the Federal share of grants for construction of treatment works utilizing innovative processes and techniques from 75 per centum to 85 per centum pursuant to section 202(a)(2) of this Act. Including the expenditures authorized by the preceding sentence, a total of 2 per centum of the funds allotted to a State for each of the fiscal years ending September 30, 1979, and September 30, 1980, and 3 per centum of the funds allotted to a State for the fiscal year ending September 30, 1981, under subsection (a) of this section shall be expended only for increasing grants for construction of treatment works ~~from 75 per centum to 85 per centum~~ pursuant to section 202(a)(2) of this Act. *Including the expenditures authorized by the first sentence of this subsection, a total (as determined by the Governor of the State) of not less than 4 per centum nor more than 7½ per centum of the funds allotted to such State for any fiscal year beginning after September 30, 1981, under subsection (c) of this section shall be expended only for increasing the Federal share of grants for construction of treatment works pursuant to section 202(a)(2) of this Act.*

(j)(1) The Administrator shall reserve each fiscal year not to exceed 1 per centum of the sums allotted and available for obligation to each State under this section for each fiscal year beginning on or after October 1, 1981, or $100,000, whichever amount is the greater.

(2) Such sums shall be used by the Administrator to make grants to the States to carry out water quality management planning, including, but not limited to—

(A) identifying most cost effective and locally acceptable facility and non-point measures to meet and maintain water quality standards;

(B) developing an implementation plan to obtain State and

local financial and regulatory commitments to implement measures developed under subparagraph (A);

(C) determining the nature, extent, and causes of water quality problems in various areas of the State and interstate region, and reporting on these annually; and

(D) determining those publicly owned treatment works which should be constructed with assistance under this title, in which areas and in what sequence, taking into account the relative degree of effluent reduction attained, the relative contributions to water quality of other point or nonpoint sources, and the consideration of alternatives to such construction, and implementing section 303(e) of this Act.

(3) In carrying out planning with grants made under paragraph (2) of this subsection, a State shall develop jointly with local, regional, and interstate entities, a plan for carrying out the program and give funding priority to such entities and designated or undesignated public comprehensive planning organizations to carry out the purposes of this subsection.

(4) All activities undertaken under this subsection shall be in coordination with other related provisions of this Act.

(k) The Administrator shall allot to the State of New York from sums authorized to be appropriated for the fiscal year ending September 30, 1982, an amount necessary to pay the entire cost of conveying sewage from the Convention Center of the city of New York to the Newtown sewage treatment plant, Brooklyn-Queens area, New York. The amount allotted under this subsection shall be in addition to and not in lieu of any other amounts authorized to be allotted to such State under this Act.

REIMBURSEMENT AND ADVANCED CONSTRUCTION

SEC. 206. (a) Any publicly owned treatment works in a State on which construction was initiated after June 30, 1966, but before July 1, 1973, which was approved by the appropriate State water pollution control agency and which the Administrator finds meet the requirements of section 8 of this Act in effect at the time of the initiation of construction shall be reimbursed a total amount equal to the difference between the amount of Federal financial assistance, if any, received under such section 8 for such project and 50 per centum of the cost of such project, or 55 per centum of the project cost where the Administrator also determines that such treatment works was constructed in conformity with a comprehensive metropolitan treatment plan as described in section 8(f) of the Federal Water Pollution Control Act as in effect immediately prior to the date of enactment of the Federal Water Pollution Control Act Amendments of 1972. Nothing in this subsection shall result in any such works receiving Federal grants from all sources in excess of 80 per centum of the cost of such project.

(b) Any publicly owned treatment works constructed with or eligible for Federal financial assistance under this Act in a State between June 30, 1956, and June 30, 1966, which was approved by the State water pollution control agency and which the Administrator finds meets the requirements of section 8 of this Act prior to the date of enactment of the Federal Water Pollution Control Act Amendments of 1972 but which was constructed without assistance under such section 8 or which received such assistance in an amount less than 30 per centum of the cost of such project shall qualify for payments and reimbursement of State or local funds used for such project from sums allocated to such State under this section in an amount which shall not exceed the difference between the amount of such assistance, if any, received for such project and 30 per centum of the cost of such project.

(c) No publicly owned treatment works shall receive any payment or reimbursement under subsection (a) or (b) of this section unless an application for such assistance is filed with the Administrator within the one year period which begins on the date of enactment of the Federal Water Pollution Control Act Amendments of 1972. Any application filed within such one year period may be revised from time to time as may be necessary.

[Section 206(c) was amended by Public Law 93-207 as follows:

"Sec. 29. Nothwithstanding section 206(c) of the Federal Water Pollution Control Act and section 2 of Public Law 93-207, in the case of publicly owned treatment works for which a grant was made under the Federal Water Pollution Control Act, as amended by the Water Pollution Control Act Amendments of 1956 (Public Law 660, 84th Congress) before July 1, 1972, and on which construction was initiated before July 1, 1973, applications for assistance under such section 206 shall be filed not later than the ninetieth day after the date of enactment of the Clean Water Act of 1977."]

(d) The Administrator shall allocate to each qualified project under subsection (a) of this section each fiscal year for which funds are appropriated under subsection (e) of this section an amount which bears the same ratio to the unpaid balance of the reimbursement due such project as the total of such funds for such year bears to the total unpaid balance of reimbursement due all such approved projects on the date of enactment of such appropriation. The Administrator shall allocate to each qualified project under subsection (b) of this section each fiscal year for which funds are appropriated under subsection (e) of this section an amount which bears the same ratio to the unpaid balance of the reimbursement due such project as the total of such funds for such year bears to the total unpaid balance of reimbursement due all such approved projects on the date of enactment of such appropriation.

[Section 206(d) was amended by Public Law 93-207 as follows:

"Sec. 3. Funds available for reimbursement under Public Law 92-399 shall be allocated in accordance with subsection (d) of section 206 of the Federal Water Pollution Control Act (86 Stat. 838), pro rata among all projects eligible under subsection (a) of such section 206 for which applications have been submitted and approved by the Administrator pursuant to such Act. Nothwithstanding the provisions of subsection (d) of such section 206, (1) the Administrator is authorized to make interim payments to each such project for which an application has been approved on the basis of estimates of maximum pro rata entitlement of all applicants under section 206(a) and (2) for the purpose of determining allocation of sums available under Public Law 92-399, the unpaid balance of reimbursement due such projects shall be computed as of January 31, 1974. Upon completion by the Administrator of his audit and approval of all projects for which an application has been filed under subsection (a) of such section 206, the Administrator shall, within the limits of appropriated funds, allocate to each such qualified project the amount remaining, if any, of its total entitlement. Amounts allocated to projects which are later determined to be in excess of entitlement shall be available for reallocation, until expended, to other qualified projects under subsection (a) of such section 206. In no event, however, shall any payments exceed the Federal share of the cost of construction incurred to the date of the voucher covering such payments plus the Federal Share of the value of the materials which have been stockpiled in the vicinity of such construction in conformity to plans and specifications for the project."]

(e) There is authorized to be appropriated to carry out subection (a) of this section not to exceed $2,600,000,000 and, to carry out subsection (b) of this section, not to exceed $750,000,000. The authorizations contained in this subsection shall be the sole source of funds for reimbursements authorized by this section.

(f)(1) In any case where a substantial portion of the funds allotted to a State for the current fiscal year under this title have been obligated under section 201(g), or will be so obligated in a timely manner (as determined by the Administrator), and there is construction of any treatment work project without the aid of Federal funds and in accordance with all procedures and all requirements applicable to treatment works projects, except those procedures and requirements which limit construction of projects to those constructed with the aid of previously allotted Federal funds, the Administrator, upon his approval of an application made under this subsection therefor, is authorized to pay the Federal share of the cost of construction of such project when additional funds are allotted to the State under this title if prior to the construction of the project the Administrator approves plans, specifications, and estimates therefor in the same manner as other treatment works projects. The Administrator may not approve an application under this subsection unless an authorization is in effect for the first fiscal year in the period for

which the application requests payment and such requested payment for that fiscal year does not exceed the State's expected allotment from such authorization. The Administrator shall not be required to make such requested payment for any fiscal year—

(A) to the extent that such payment would exceed such State's allotment of the amount appropriated for such fiscal year; and

(B) unless such payment is for a project which, on the basis of an approved funding priority list of such State, is eligible to receive such payment based on the allotment appropriation for such fiscal year.

To the extent that sufficient funds are not appropriated to pay the full Federal share with respect to a project for which obligations under the provisions of this subsection have been made, the Administrator shall reduce the Federal share to such amount less than 75 per centum as such appropriations do provide.

(2) In determining the allotment for any fiscal year under this title, any treatment works project constructed in accordance with this section and without the aid of Federal funds shall not be considered completed until an application under the provisions of this subsection with respect to such project has been approved by the Administrator, or the availability of funds from which this project is eligible for reimbursement has expired, whichever first occurs.

AUTHORIZATION

[SEC. 207. There is authorized to be appropriated to carry out this title, other than sections 206(e), 208 and 209, for the fiscal year ending June 30, 1973, not to exceed $5,000,000,000, for the fiscal year ending June 30, 1974, not to exceed $6,000,000,000, and for the fiscal year ending June 30, 1975, not to exceed $7,000,000,000, and, subject to such amounts as are provided in appropriation Acts for the fiscal year ending September 30, 1977, $1,000,000,000 for the fiscal year ending September 30, 1978, $4,500,000,000 and for the fiscal years ending September 30, 1979, September 30, 1980, ~~September 30, 1981, and September 30, 1982, not to exceed $5,000,000,000 per fiscal year.~~ *not to exceed $5,000,000,000 for the fiscal year ending September 30 1981, not to exceed $2,548,837,000; and for the fiscal year ending September 30, 1982, not to exceed $0, unless there is enacted legislation establishing an allotment formula for fiscal year 1982 construction grant funds and otherwise reforming the municipal sewage treatment construction grant program under this title, in which case the authorization for fiscal year 1982 shall be an amount not to exceed $2,400,000,000.*] [1]

SEC. 207. There is authorized to be appropriated to carry out this time, other than section 206(e), 208 and 209, for the fiscal year ending June 30, 1973, not to exceed $5,000,000,000, for the fiscal year ending June 30, 1974, not to exceed $6,000,000,000, and for the fiscal year ending June 30, 1975, not to exceed $7,000,000,000, and, subject to such amounts as are provided in appropriation Acts for the fiscal year ending September 30, 1977, $1,000,000,000 for the fiscal year ending September 30, 1978, $4,500,000,000 and for the fiscal years ending September 30, 1979, September 30, 1980, not to exceed $5,000,000,000; for the fiscal year ending September 30, 1981, not to exceed $2,548,-837,000; and for the fiscal years ending September 30, 1982, September 30, 1983, September 30, 1984, and September 30, 1985, not to exceed $2,400,000,000 per fiscal year.[2]

---

[1] This version of section 207 (enclosed in brackets) shows amendments made by Public Law 97-35, the Omnibus Budget Reconciliation Act of 1981, Aug. 13, 1981.

[2] This version shows amendments made by Public Law 97-117, the Municipal Wastewater Treatment Construction Grant Amendments of 1981, Dec. 29, 1981.

AREAWIDE WASTE TREATMENT MANAGEMENT

SEC. 208. (a) For the purpose of encouraging and facilitating the development and implementation of areawide waste treatment management plans—

(1) The Administrator, within ninety days after the date of enactment of this Act and after consultation with appropriate Federal, State, and local authorities, shall by regulation publish guidelines for the identification of those areas, which as a result of urban-industrial concentrations or other factors, have substantial water quality control problems.

(2) The Governor of each State, within sixty days after publication of the guidelines issued pursuant to paragraph (1) of this subsection, shall identify each area within the State which, as a result of urban-industrial concentrations or other factors, has substantial water quality control problems. Not later than one hundred and twenty days following such identification and after consultation with appropriate elected and other officials of local governments having jurisdiction in such areas, the Governor shall designate (A) the boundaries of each such area, and (B) a single representative organization, including elected officials from local governments or their designees, capable of developing effective areawide waste treatment management plans for such area. The Governor may in the same manner at any later time identify any additional area (or modify an existing area) for which he determines areawide waste treatment management to be appropriate, designate the boundaries of such area, and designate an organization capable of developing effective areawide waste treatment management plans for such area.

(3) With respect to any area which, pursuant to the guidelines published under paragraph (1) of this subsection, is located in two or more States, the Governors of the respective States shall consult and cooperate in carrying out the provisions of paragraph (2), with a view toward designating the boundaries of the interstate area having common water quality control problems and for which areawide waste treatment management plans would be most effective, and toward designating, within one hundred and eighty days after publication of guidelines issued pursuant to paragraph (1) of this subsection, of a single representative organization capable of developing effective areawide waste treatment management plans for such area.

(4) If a Governor does not act, either by designating or determining not to make a designation under paragraph (2) of this subsection, within the time required by such paragraph, or if, in the case of an interstate area, the Governors of the States involved do not designate a planning organization within the time required by paragraph (3) of this subsection, the chief elected officials of local governments within an area may be agreement designate (A) the boundaries for such an area, and (B) a single

representative organization including elected officials from such local governments, or their designees, capable of developing an areawide waste treatment management plan for such area.

(5) Existing regional agencies may be designated under paragraphs (2), (3), and (4) of this subsection.

(6) The State shall act as a planning agency for all portions of such State which are not designated under paragraph (2), (3), or (4) of this subsection.

(7) Designations under this subsection shall be subject to the approval of the Administrator.

(b)(1)(A) Not later than one year after the date of designation of any organization under subsection (a) of this section such organization shall have in operation a continuing areawide waste treatment management planning process consistent with section 201 of this Act. Plans prepared in accordance with this process shall contain alternatives for waste treatment management, and be applicable to all wastes generated within the area involved. The initial plan prepared in accordance with such process shall be certified by the Governor and submitted to the Administrator not later than two years after the planning process is in operation.

(B) For any agency designated after 1975 under subsection (a) of this section and for all portions of a State for which the State is required to act as the planning agency in accordance with subsection (a)(6), the initial plan prepared in accordance with such process shall be certified by the Governor and submitted to the Administrator not later than three years after the receipt of the initial grant award authorized under subsection (f) of this section.

(2) Any plan prepared under such process shall include, but not be limited to—

(A) the identification of treatment works necessary to meet the anticipated municipal and industrial waste treatment needs of the area over a twenty-year period, annually updated (including an analysis of alternative waste treatment systems), including any requirements for the acquisition of land for treatment purposes; the necessary waste water collection and urban storm water runoff systems; and a program to provide the necessary financial arrangements for the development of such treatment works, and an identification of open space and recreation opportunities that can be expected to result from improved water quality, including consideration of potential use of lands associated with treatment works and increased access to water-based recreation;

(B) the establishment of construction priorities for such treatment works and time schedules for the initiation and completion of all treatment works;

(C) the establishment of a regulatory program to—

(i) implement the waste treatment management requirements of section 201(c),

(ii) regulate the location, modification, and construction of any facilities within such area which may result in any discharge in such area, and

(iii) assure that any industrial or commercial waste discharged into any treatment works in such area meet applicable pretreatment requirements;

(D) the identification of those agencies necessary to construct, operate, and maintain all facilities required by the plan and otherwise to carry out the plan;

(E) the identification of the measures necessary to carry out the plan (including financing), the period of time necessary to carry out the plan, the costs of carrying out the plan within such time, and the economic, social, and environmental impact of carrying out the plan within such time;

(F) a process to (i) identify, if appropriate, agriculturally and silviculturally related nonpoint sources of pollution, including return flows from irrigated agriculture, and their cumulative effects, runoff from manure disposal areas, and from land used for livestock and crop production, and (ii) set forth procedures and methods (including land use requirements) to control to the extent feasible such sources;

(G) a process of (i) identify, if appropriate, mine-related sources of pollution including new, current, and abandoned surface and underground mine runoff, and (ii) set forth procedures and methods (including land use requirements) to control to the extent feasible such sources;

(H) a. process to (i) identify construction activity related sources of pollution, and (ii) set forth procedures and methods (including land use requirements) to control to the extent feasible such sources;

(I) a process to (i) identify, if appropriate, salt water intrusion into rivers, lakes, and estuaries resulting from reduction of fresh water flow from any cause, including irrigation, obstruction, ground water extraction, and diversion, and (ii) set forth procedures and methods to control such intrusion to the extent feasible where such procedures and methods are otherwise a part of the waste treatment management plan;

(J) a process to control the disposition of all residual waste generated in such area which could affect water quality; and

(K) a process to control the disposal of pollutants on land or in subsurface excavations within such area to protect ground and surface water quality.

(3) Areawide waste treatment management plans shall be certified annually by the Governor or his designee (or Governors or their designees, where more than one State is involved) as being consistent with applicable basin plans and such areawide waste treatment management plans shall be submitted to the Administrator for his approval.

(4)(A) Whenever the Governor of any State determines (and notifies the Administrator) that consistency with a statewide regulatory program under section 303 so requires, the requirements of clauses (F) through (K) of paragraph (2) of this subsection shall be developed and submitted by the Governor to the Administrator for approval for application to a class or category of activity throughout such State.

(B) Any program submitted under subparagraph (A) of this paragraph which, in whole or in part, is to control the discharge or other placement of dredged or fill material into the navigable waters shall include the following:

(i) A consultation process which includes the State agency with primary jurisdiction over fish and wildlife resources.

(ii) A process to identify and manage the discharge or other placement of dredged or fill material which adversely affects navigable waters, which shall complement and be coordinated with a State program under section 404 conducted pursuant to this Act.

(iii) A process to assure that any activity conducted pursuant to a best management practice will comply with the guidelines established under section 404(b)(1), and sections 307 and 403 of this Act.

(iv) A process to assure that any activity conducted pursuant to a best management practice can be terminated or modified for cause including, but not limited to, the following:

(I) violation of any condition of the best management practice;

(II) change in any activity that requires either a temporary or permanent reduction or elimination of the discharge pursuant to the best management practice.

(v) A process to assure continued coordination with Federal and Federal-State water-related planning and receiving processes, including the National Wetlands Inventory.

(C) If the Governor of a State obtains approval from the Administrator of a statewide regulatory program which meets the requirements of subparagraph (B) of this paragraph and if such State is administering a permit program under section 404 of this Act, no person shall be required to obtain an individual permit pursuant to such section, or to comply with a general permit issued pursuant to such section, with respect to any appropriate activity within such State for which a best management practice has been approved by the Administrator under the program approved by the Administrator pursuant to this paragraph.

(D)(i) Whenever the Administrator determines after public hearing that a State is not administering a program approved under this section in accordance with the requirements of this section, the Administrator shall so notify the State, and if appropriate corrective action is not taken within a reasonable time, not to exceed ninety days, the Administrator shall withdraw approval of such program. The Administrator shall not withdraw approval of any such program unless he shall first have notified the State, and made public, in writing, the reasons for such withdrawal.

(ii) In the case of a State with a program submitted and approved under this paragraph, the Administrator shall withdraw approval of such program under this subparagraph only for a substantial failure of the State to administer its program in accordance with the requirements of this paragraph.

(c)(1) The Governor of each State, in consultation with the planning agency designated under subsection (a) of this section, at the time a plan is submitted to the Administrator, shall designate one or more waste treatment management agencies (which may be an existing or newly created local, regional or State agency or potential subdivision) for each area designated under subsection (a) of this section and submit such designations to the Administrator.

(2) The Administrator shall accept any such designation, unless, within 120 days of such designation, he finds that the designated management agency (or agencies) does not have adequate authority—

(A) to carry out appropriate portions of an areawide waste treatment management plan developed under subsection (b) of this section;

(B) to manage effectively waste treatment works and related facilities serving such area in conformance with any plan required by subsection (b) of this section;

(C) directly or by contract, to design and construct new works, and to operate and maintain new and existing works as required by any plan developed pursuant to subsection (b) of this section;

(D) to accept and utilize grants, or other funds from any source, for waste treatment management purposes;

(E) to raise revenues, including the assessment of waste treatment charges;

(F) to incur short- and long-term indebtedness;

(G) to assure in implementation of an areawide waste treatment management plan that each participating community pays its proportionate share of treatment costs;

(H) to refuse to receive any wastes from any municipality or subdivision thereof, which does not comply with any provisions of an approved plan under this section applicable to such area; and

(I) to accept for treatment industrial wastes.

(d) After a waste treatment management agency having the authority required by subsection (c) has been designated under such subsection for an area and a plan for such area has been approved under subsection (b) of this section, the Administrator shall not make any grant for construction of a publicly owned treatment works under section 201(g)(1) within such area except to such designated agency and for works in conformity with such plan.

(e) No permit under section 402 of this Act shall be issued for any point source which is in conflict with a plan approved pursuant to subsection (b) of this section.

(f)(1) The Administrator shall make grants to any agency designated under subsection (a) of this section for payment of the reasonable costs of developing and operating a continuing areawide waste treatment management planning process under subsection (b) of this section.

(2) For the two-year period beginning on the date the first grant is made under paragraph (1) of this subsection to an agency, if such first grant is made before October 1, 1977, the amount of each such grant to such agency shall be 100 per centum of the costs of developing and operating a continuing areawide waste treatment management planning process under subsection (b) of this section, and thereafter the amount granted to such agency shall not exceed 75 per centum of such costs in each succeeding one-year period. In the case of any other grant made to an agency under such paragraph (1) of this subsection, the amount of such grant shall not exceed 75 per centum of the costs of developing and operating a continuing areawide waste treatment management planning process in any year.

(3) Each applicant for a grant under this subsection shall submit to the Administrator for his approval each proposal for which a grant is applied for under this subsection. The Administrator shall act upon such proposal as soon as practicable after it has been submitted, and his approval of that proposal shall be deemed a contractual obligation of the United States for the payment of its contribution to such proposal, subject to such amounts as are provided in appropriation Acts. There is authorized to be appropriated to carry out this subsection

not to exceed $50,000,000 for the fiscal year ending June 30, 1973, not to exceed $100,000,000 for the fiscal year ending June 30, 1974, and not to exceed $150,000,000 per fiscal year for the fiscal years ending June 30, 1975, September 30, 1977, September 30, 1978, September 30, 1979, and September 30, 1980, and not to exceed $100,000,000 per fiscal year for the fiscal years ending September 30, 1981, and September 30, 1982.

(g) The Administrator is authorized, upon request of the Governor or the designated planning agency, and without reimbursement, to consult with, and provide technical assistance to, any agency designated under subsection (a) of this section in the development of areawide waste treatment management plans under subsection (b) of this section.

(h)(1) The Secretary of the Army, acting through the Chief of Engineers, in cooperation with the Administrator is authorized and directed, upon request of the Governor or the designated planning organization, to consult with, and provide technical assistance to, any agency designed under subsection (a) of this section in developing and operating a continuing areawide waste treatment management planning process under subsection (b) of this section.

(2) There is authorized to be appropriated to the Secretary of the Army, to carry out this subsection, not to exceed $50,000,000 per fiscal year for the fiscal years ending June 30, 1973, and June 30, 1974.

(i)(1) The Secretary of the Interior, acting through the Director of the United States Fish and Wildlife Service, shall, upon request of the Governor of a State, and without reimbursement, provide technical assistance to such State in developing a statewide program for submission to the Administrator under subsection (b)(4)(B) of this section and in implementing such program after its approval.

(2) There is authorized to be appropriated to the Secretary of the Interior $6,000,000 to complete the National Wetlands Inventory of the United States, by December 31, 1981, and to provide information from such Inventory to States as it becomes available to assist such States in the development and operation of programs under this Act.

(j)(1) The Secretary of Agriculture, with the concurrence of the Administrator, and acting through the Soil Conservation Service and such other agencies of the Department of Agriculture as the Secretary may designate, is authorized and directed to establish and administer a program to enter into contracts, subject to such amounts as are provided in advance by appropriation acts, of not less than five years nor more than ten years with owners and operators having control of rural land for the purpose of installing and maintaining measures incorporating best management practices to control nonpoint source pollution for improved water quality in those States or areas for which the Administrator has approved a plan under subsection (b) of this section where the practices to which the contracts apply are certified by the management agency designated under subsection (c)(1) of this section to be consistent with such plans and will result in improved water quality. Such contracts may be entered into during the period ending not later than September 31, 1988. Under such contracts the land owner or operator shall agree—

(i) to effectuate a plan approved by a soil conservation district, where one exists, under this section for his farm, ranch, or other land substantially in accordance with the schedule outlined therein unless any requirement thereof is waived or modified by the Secretary;

(ii) to forfeit all rights to further payments or grants under the contract and refund to the United States all payments and grants received thereunder, with interest, upon his violation of the contract at any stage during the time he has control of the land if the Secretary, after considering the recommendations of the soil conservation district, where one exists, and the Administrator, determines that such violation is of such a nature as to warrant termination of the contract, or to make refunds or accept such payment adjustments as the Secretary may deem appropriate if he determines that the violation by the owner or operator does not warrant termination of the contract;

(iii) upon transfer of his right and interest in the farm, ranch, or other land during the contract period to forfeit all rights to further payments or grants under the contract and refund to the United States all payments or grants received thereunder, with interest, unless the transferee of any such land agrees with the Secretary to assume all obligations of the contract;

(iv) not to adopt any practice specified by the Secretary on the advice of the Administrator in the contract as a practice which would tend to defeat the purposes of the contract;

(v) to such additional provisions as the Secretary determines are desirable and includes in the contract to effectuate the purposes of the program or to facilitate the practical administration of the program.

(2) In return for such agreement by the landowner or operator the Secretary shall agree to provide technical assistance and share the cost of carrying out those conservation practices and measures set forth in the contract for which he determines that cost sharing is appropriate and in the public interest and which are approved for cost sharing by the agency designated to implement the plan developed under subsection (b) of this section. The portion of such cost (including labor) to be shared shall be that part which the Secretary determines is necessary and appropriate to effectuate the installation of the water quality management practices and measures under the contract, but not to exceed 50 per centum of the total cost of the measures set forth in the contract; except the Secretary may increase the matching cost share where he determines that (1) the main benefits to be derived from the measures are related to improving offsite water quality, and (2) the matching share requirement would place a burden on the landowner which would probably prevent him from participating in the program.

(3) The Secretary may terminate any contract with a landowner or operator by mutual agreement with the owner or operator if the Secretary determines that such termination would be in the public interest, and may agree to such modification of contracts previously entered into as he may determine to be desirable to carry out the purposes of the program or facilitate the practical administration thereof or to accomplish equitable treatment with respect to other conservation, land use, or water quality programs.

(4) In providing assistance under this subsection the Secretary will give priority to those areas and sources that have the most significant effect upon water quality. Additional investigations or plans

may be made, where necessary, to supplement approved water quality management plans, in order to determine priorities.

(5) The Secretary shall, where practicable, enter into agreements with soil conservation districts, State soil and water conservation agencies, or State water quality agencies to administer all or part of the program established in this subsection under regulations developed by the Secretary. Such agreements shall provide for the submission of such reports as the Secretary deems necessary, and for payment by the United States of such portion of the costs incurred in the administration of the program as the Secretary may deem appropriate.

(6) The contracts under this subsection shall be entered into only in areas where the management agency designated under subsection (c)(1) of this section assures an adequate level of participation by owners and operators having control of rural land in such areas. Within such areas the local soil conservation district, where one exists, together with the Secretary of Agriculture, will determine the priority of assistance among individual land owners and operators to assure that the most critical water quality problems are addressed.

(7) The Secretary, in consultation with the Administrator and subject to section 304(k) of this Act, shall, not later than September 30, 1978, promulgate regulations for carrying out this subsection and for support and cooperation with other Federal and non-Federal agencies for implementation of this subsection.

(8) This program shall not be used to authorize or finance projects that would otherwise be eligible for assistance under the terms of Public Law 83-566.

(9) There are hereby authorized to be appropriated to the Secretary of Agriculture $200,000,000 for fiscal year 1979, $400,000,000 for fiscal year 1980, $100,000,000 for fiscal year 1981, and $100,000,000 for fiscal year 1982 to carry out this subsection. The program authorized under this subsection shall be in addition to, and not in substitution of, other programs in such area authorized by this or any other public law.

BASIN PLANNING

SEC. 209. (a) The President, acting through the Water Resources Council, shall, as soon as practicable, prepare a Level B plan under the Water Resources Planning Act for all basins in the United States. All such plans shall be completed not later than January 1, 1980, except that priority in the preparation of such plans shall be given to those basins and portions thereof which are within those areas designated under paragraphs (2), (3), and (4) of subsection (a) of section 208 of this Act.

(b) The President, acting through the Water Resources Council, shall report annually to Congress on progress being made in carrying out this section. The first such report shall be submitted not later than January 31, 1973.

(c) There is authorized to be appropriated to carry out this section not to exceed $200,000,000.

ANNUAL SURVEY

SEC. 210. The Administrator shall annually make a survey to determine the efficiency of the operation and maintenance of treatment works constructed with grants made under this Act, as compared to the efficiency planned at the time the grant was made. The results of such annual survey shall be included in the report required under section 516(a) of this Act.

SEWAGE COLLECTION SYSTEMS

SEC. 211. (a) No grant shall be made for a sewage collection system under this title unless such grant (1) is for replacement or major rehabilitation of an existing collection system and is necessary to the total integrity and performance of the waste treatment works servicing such community, or (2) is for a new collection system in an existing community with sufficient existing or planned capacity adequately to treat such collected sewage and is consistent with section 201 of this Act.

(b) If the Administrator uses population density as a test for determining the eligibility of a collector sewer for assistance it shall be only for the purpose of evaluating alternatives and determining the needs for such system in relation to ground or surface water quality impact.

(c) No grant shall be made under this title from funds authorized for any fiscal year during the period beginning October 1, 1977, and ending ~~September 30, 1982~~, *September 30, 1985*, for treatment works for control of pollutant discharges from separate storm sewer systems.

DEFINITIONS

SEC. 212. As used in this title—

(1) The term "construction" means any one or more of the following: preliminary planning to determine the feasibility of treatment works, engineering, architectural, legal, fiscal, or economic investigations or studies, surveys, designs, plans, working drawings, specifications, procedures, *field testing of innovative or alternative waste water treatment processes and techniques meeting guidelines promulgated under section 304(d)(3) of this Act*, or other necessary actions, erection, building, acquisition, alteration, remodeling, improvement, or extension of treatment works, or the inspection or supervision of any of the foregoing items.

(2) (A) The term "treatment works" means any devices and systems used in the storage, treatment, recycling, and reclamation of municipal sewage or industrial wastes of a liquid nature to implement section 201 of this act, or necessary to recycle or reuse water at the most economical cost over the estimated life of the works, including intercepting sewers, outfall sewers, sewage collection systems, pumping power, and other equipment, and their appurtenances; extensions, improvements, remodeling, additions, and alterations thereof; elements essential to provide a reliable recycled supply such as standby treatment units and clear well facilities; and any works, including site acquisition of the land that will be an integral part of the treatment process (including land use for the storage of treated wastewater in land treatment systems prior to land application) or is used for ultimate disposal of residues resulting from such treatment.

(B) In addition to the definition contained in subparagraph (A) of this paragraph, "treatment works" means any other method or system for preventing, abating, reducing, storing, treating, separating, or disposing of municipal waste, including storm water runoff, or industrial waste, including waste in combined storm water and sanitary sewer systems. Any application for construction grants which includes wholly or in part such methods or systems shall, in accordance with guidelines published by the Administrator pursuant to subparagraph (C) of this paragraph, contain adequate data and analysis demonstrating such proposal to be, over the life of such works, the most cost efficient alternative to comply with section 301 or 302 of this act, or the requirements of section 201 of this act.

(C) For the purposes of subparagraph (B) of this paragraph, the Administrator shall, within one hundred and eighty days after the date of enactment of this title, publish and thereafter revise no less often than annually, guidelines for the evaluation of methods, including cost-effective analysis, described in subparagraph (B) of this paragraph.

(3) The term "replacement" as used in this title means those expenditures for obtaining and installing equipment, accessories, or appurtenances during the useful life of the treatment works necessary to maintain the capacity and performance for which such works are designed and constructed.

LOAN GUARANTEES FOR CONSTRUCTION OF TREATMENT WORKS

SEC. 213. (a) Subject to the conditions of this section and to such terms and conditions as the Administrator determines to be necessary to carry out the purposes of this title, the Administrator is authorized to guarantee, and to make commitments to guarantee, the principal and interest (including interest accruing between the date of default and the date of the payment in full of the guarantee) of any loan, obligation, or participation therein of any State, municipality, or intermunicipal or interstate agency issued directly and exclusively to the Federal Financing Bank to finance that part of the cost of any grant-eligible project for the construction of publicly owned treatment works not paid for with Federal financial assistance under this title (other than this section), which project the Administrator has determined to be eligible for such financial assistance under this title, including, but not limited to, projects eligible for reimbursement under section 206 of this title.

(b) No guarantee, or commitment to make a guarantee, may be made pursuant to this section—

(1) unless the Administrator certifies that the issuing body is unable to obtain on reasonable terms sufficient credit to finance its actual needs without such guarantee; and

(2) unless the Administrator determines that there is a reasonable assurance of repayment of the loan, obligation, or participation therein.

A determination of whether financing is available at reasonable rates shall be made by the Secretary of the Treasury with relationship to the current average yield on outstanding marketable obligations of municipalities of comparable maturity.

(c) The Administrator is authorized to charge reasonable fees for the investigation of an application for a guarantee and for the issuance of a commitment to make a guarantee.

(d) The Administrator, in determining whether there is a reasonable assurance of repayment, may require a commitment which would apply to such repayment. Such commitment may include, but not be limited to, any funds received by such grantee from the amounts appropriated under section 206 of this act.

PUBLIC INFORMATION

SEC. 214. The Administrator shall develop and operate within one year of the date of enactment of this section, a continuing program of public information and education on recycling and reuse of wastewater (including sludge), the use of land treatment, and methods for the reduction of wastewater volume.

REQUIREMENTS FOR AMERICAN MATERIALS

SEC. 215. Notwithstanding any other provision of law, no grant for which application is made after February 1, 1978, shall be made under this title for any treatment works unless only such unmanufactured articles, materials, and supplies as have been mined or produced in the United States, and only such manufactured articles, materials, and supplies as have been manufactured in the United States, substantially all from articles, materials, or supplies mined, produced, or manufactured, as the case may be, in the United States will be used in such treatment works. This section shall not apply in any case where the Administrator determines, based upon those factors the Administrator deems relevant, including the available resources of the agency, it to be inconsistent with the public interest (including multilateral government procurement agreements) or the cost to be unreasonable, or if articles, materials, or supplies of the class or kind to be used or the articles, materials, or supplies from which they are manufactured are not mined, produced, or manufactured, as the case may be, in the United States in sufficient and reasonably available commercial quantities and of a satisfactory quality.

DETERMINATION OF PRIORITY

SEC. 216. Notwithstanding any other provision of this Act, the determination of the priority to be given each category of projects for construction of publicly owned treatment works within each State shall be made solely by that State, except that if the Administrator, after a public hearing, determines that a specific project will not result in compliance with the enforceable requirements of this Act, such project shall be removed from the State's priority list and such State shall submit a revised priority list. These categories shall include, but not be limited to (A) secondary treatment, (B) more stringent treatment, (C) infiltration-in-flow correction, (D) major sewer system rehabilitation, (E) new collector sewers and appurtenances, (F) new interceptors and appurtenances, and (G) correction of combined sewer overflows. Not less than 25 per centum of funds allocated to a State in any fiscal year under this title for construction of publicly owned treatment works in such State shall be obligated for those types of projects referred to in clauses (D), (E), (F), and (G) of this section, if such projects are on such State's priority list for that year and are otherwise eligible for funding in that fiscal year. *It is the policy of Congress that projects for wastewater treatment and management undertaken with Federal financial assistance under this Act by any State, municipality, or intermunicipal or interstate agency shall be projects which, in the estimation of the State, are designed to achieve optimum water quality management, consistent with the public health and water quality goals and requirements of the Act.*

COST-EFFECTIVENESS GUIDELINES

SEC. 217. Any guidelines for cost-effectiveness analysis published **by the Administrator under this title shall provide for the identification and selection of cost effective alternatives to comply with the objective and goals of this Act and sections 201(b), 201(d), 201(g)(2)(A), and 301(b)(2)(B) of this Act.**

COST EFFECTIVENESS

SEC. 218. (a) It is the policy of Congress that a project for waste treatment and management undertaken with Federal financial assistance under this Act by any State, municipality, or intermunicipal or interstate agency shall be considered as an overall waste treatment system for waste treatment and management, and shall be that system which constitutes the most economical and cost-effective combination of devices and systems used in the storage, treatment, recycling, and reclamation of municipal sewage or industrial wastes of a liquid nature to implement section 201 of this Act, or necessary to recycle or reuse water at the most economical cost over the estimated life of the works, including intercepting sewers, outfall sewers, sewage collection systems, pumping power, and other equipment, and their appurtenances; extension, improvements, remodeling, additions, and alterations thereof; elements essential to provide a reliable recycled supply such as standby treatment units and clear well facilities; and any works, including site acquisition of the land that will be an integral part of the treatment process (including land use for the storage of treated wastewater in land treatment systems prior to land application) or which is used for ultimate disposal of residues resulting from such treatment; water efficiency measures and devices; and any other method or system for preventing, abating, reducing, storing, treating, separating, or disposing of municipal waste, including storm water runoff, or industrial waste, including waste in combined storm water and sanitary sewer systems; to meet the requirements of this Act.

(b) In accordance with the policy set forth in subsection (a) of this section, before the Administrator approves any grant to any State, municipality, or intermunicipal or interstate agency for the erection, building, acquisition, alteration, remodeling, improvement, or extension of any treatment works the Administrator shall determine that the facilities plan of which such treatment works are a part constitutes the most economical and cost-effective combination of treatment works over the life of the project to meet the requirements of this Act, including, but not limited to, consideration of construction costs, operation, maintenance, and replacement costs.

(c) In furtherance of the policy set forth in subsection (a) of this section, the Administrator shall require value engineering review in connection with any treatment works, prior to approval of any grant for the erection, building, acquisition, alteration, remodeling, improvement, or extension of such treatment works, in any case in which the cost of such erection, building, acquisition, alteration, remodeling, improvement, or extension is projected to be in excess of $10,000,000. For purposes of this subsection, the term "value engineering review" means a specialized cost control technique which uses a systematic and creative approach to identify and to focus on unnecessarily high cost in

a project in order to arrive at a cost saving without sacrificing the reliability or efficiency of the project.

(d) This section applies to projects for waste treatment and management for which no treatment works including a facilities plan for such project have received Federal financial assistance for the preparation of construction plans and specifications under this Act before the date of enactment of this section.

STATE CERTIFICATION OF PROJECTS

Sec. 219. Whenever the Governor of a State which has been delegated sufficient authority to administer the construction grant program under this title in that State certifies to the Administrator that a grant application meets applicable requirements of Federal and State law for assistance under this title, the Administrator shall approve or disapprove such application within 45 days of the date of receipt of such application. If the Administrator does not approve or disapprove such application within 45 days of receipt, the application shall be deemed approved. If the Administrator disapproves such application the Administrator shall state in writing the reasons for such disapproval. Any grant approved or deemed approved under this section shall be subject to amounts provided in appropriation Acts.

TITLE III—STANDARDS AND ENFORCEMENT

EFFLUENT LIMITATIONS

Sec. 301. (a) Except as in compliance with this section and sections 302, 306, 307, 318, 402, and 404 of this Act, the discharge of any pollutant by any person shall be unlawful.

(b) In order to carry out the objective of this Act there shall be achieved—

(1)(A) not later than July 1, 1977, effluent limitations for point sources, other than publicly owned treatment works, (i) which shall require the application of the best practicable control technology currently available as defined by the Administrator pursuant to section 304(b) of this Act, or (ii) in the case of a discharge into a publicly owned treatment works which meets the requirements of subparagraph (B) of this paragraph, which shall require compliance with any applicable pretreatment requirements and any requirements under section 307 of this Act; and

(B) for publicly owned treatment works in existence on July 1, 1977, or approved pursuant to section 203 of this Act prior to June 30, 1974 (for which construction must be completed within four years of approval), effluent limitations based upon secondary treatment as defined by the Administrator pursuant to section 304(d)(1) of this Act; or,

(C) not later than July 1, 1977, any more stringent limitation, including those necessary to meet water quality standards, treatment standards, or schedule of compliance, established pursuant to any State law or regulations (under authority preserved by section 510), or any other Federal law or regulation, or required to implement any applicable water quality standard established pursuant to this Act.

(2)(A) for pollutants identified in subparagraphs (C), (D), and (F) of this paragraph effluent limitations for categories and classes of point sources, other than publicly owned treatment works, which (i) shall require application of the best available technology economically achievable for such category or class, which will result in reasonable further progress toward the national goal of eliminating the discharge of all pollutants, as determined in accordance with regulations issued by the Administrator pursuant to section 304(b)(2) of this Act, which such effluent limitations shall require the elimination of discharges of all pollutants if the Administrator finds, on the basis of information available to him (including information developed pursuant to section 315), that such elimination is technologically and economically achievable for category or class of point sources as determined in accordance with regulations issued by the Administrator pursuant to section 304(b)(2) of this Act or (ii) in the case of the introduction of a pollutant into a publicly owned treatment works which meets the requirements of subparagraph (B) of this paragraph, shall require compliance with any applicable pretreatment requirements and any other requirement under section 307 of this Act;

~~(B) not later than July 1, 1983, compliance by all publicly owned treatment works with the requirements set forth in section 201(g)(2)(A) of this Act;~~

(C) not later than July 1, 1984, with respect to all toxic pollutants referred to in table 1 of Committee Print Numbered 95–30 of the Committee on Public Works and Transportation of the House of Representatives compliance with effluent limitations in accordance with subparagraph (A) of this paragraph;

(D) for all toxic pollutants listed under paragraph (1) of subsection (a) of section 307 of this Act which are not referred to in subparagraph (C) of this paragraph compliance with effluent limitation in accordance with subparagraph (A) of this paragraph not later than three years after the date such limitations are established;

(E) not later than July 1, 1984, effluent limitations for categories and classes of point sources, other than publicly owned treatment works, which in the case of pollutants identified pursuant to section 304(a)(4) of this Act shall require application of the best conventional pollutant control technology as determined in accordance with regulations issued by the Administrator pursuant to section 304(b)(4) of this Act; and

(F) for all pollutants (other than those subject to subparagraphs (C), (D), or (E) of this paragraph) compliance with effluent limitations in accordance with subparagraph (A) of this paragraph not later than 3 years after the date such limitations are established, or not later than July 1, 1984, whichever is later, but in no case later than July 1, 1987.

(c) The Administrator may modify the requirements of subsection (b)(2)(A) of this section with respect to any point source for which a permit application is filed after July 1, 1977, upon a showing by the owner or operator of such point source satisfactory to the Administrator that such modified requirements (1) will represent the maximum use of technology within the economic capability of the owner or operator; and (2) will result in reasonable further progress toward the elimination of the discharge of pollutants.

(d) Any effluent limitation required by paragraph (2) of subsection (b) of this section shall be reviewed at least every five years and, if appropriate, revised pursuant to the procedure established under such paragraph.

(e) Effluent limitations established pursuant to this section or section 302 of this Act shall be applied to all point sources of discharge of pollutants in accordance with the provisions of this Act.

(f) Notwithstanding any other provisions of this Act it shall be unlawful to discharge any radiological, chemical, or biological warfare agent or high-level radioactive waste into the navigable waters.

(g) (1) The Administrator, with the concurrence of the State, shall modify the requirements of subsection (b)(2)(A) of this section with respect to the discharge of any pollutant (other than pollutants identified pursuant to section 304(a)(4) of this Act, toxic pollutants subject to section 307(a) of this Act, and the thermal component of discharges) from any point source upon a showing by the owner or operator of such point source satisfactory to the Administator that—

(A) Such modified requirements will result at a minimum in compliance with the requirements of subsection (b)(1)(A) or (C) of this section, whichever is applicable;

(B) such modified requirements will not result in any additional requirements on any other point or nonpoint source; and

(C) such modification will not interfere with the attainment or maintenance of that water quality which shall assure protection of public water supplies, and the protection and propagation of a balanced population of shellfish, fish, and wildlife, and allow recreational activities, in and on the water and such modification will not result in the discharge of pollutants in quantities which may reasonably be anticipated to pose an unacceptable risk to human health or the environment because of bioaccumulation, persistency in the environment, acute toxicity, chronic toxicity (including carcinogenicity, mutagenicity or teratogenicity), or synergistic propensities.

(2) If an owner or operator of a point source applies for a modification under this subsection with respect to the discharge of any pollutant, such owner or operator shall be eligible to apply for modification under subsection (c) of this section with respect to such pollutant only during the same time-period as he is eligible to apply for a modification under this subsection.

(h) The Administrator, with the concurrence of the State, may issue a permit under section 402 which modifies the requirements of subsection (b)(1)(B) of this section with respect to the discharge of any pollutant ~~in an existing discharge~~ from a publicly owned treatment works into marine waters, if the applicant demonstrates to the satisfaction of the Administrator that—

(1) there is an applicable water quality standard specific to the pollutant for which the modification is requested, which has been identified under section 304(a)(6) of this Act;

(2) such modified requirements will not interfere with the attainment or maintenance of that ater quality which assures protection of public water supplies and the protection and propagation of a balanced, indigenous population of shellfish, fish and wildlife, and allows recreational activities, in and on the water;

(3) the applicant has established a system for monitoring the impact of such discharge on a representative sample of aquatic biota, to the extent practicable;

(4) such modified requirements will not result in any additional requirements on any other point or nonpoint source;

(5) all applicable pretreatment requirements for sources introducing waste into such treatment works will be enforced;

(6) to the extent practicable, the applicant has established a schedule of activities designed to eliminate the entrance of toxic pollutants from nonindustrial sources into such treatment works;

(7) there will be no new or substantially increased discharges from the point source of the pollutant to which the modification applies above that volume of discharge specified in the permit.

~~(8) any funds available to the owner of such treatment works under title II of this Act will be used to achieve the degree of effluent reduction required by section 201 (b) and (g) (2) (A) or to carry out the requirements of this subsection.~~

For the purposes of this subsection the phrase "the discharge of any pollutant into marine waters" refers to a discharge into deep waters of the territorial sea or the waters of the contiguous zone, or into saline estuarine waters where there is strong tidal movement and other hydrological and geological characteristics which the Administrator determines necessary to allow compliance with paragraph (2) of this subsection, and section 101(a)(2) of this Act. *A municipality which applies secondary treatment shall be eligible to receive a permit pursuant to this subsection which modifies the requirements of subsection (b)(1)(B) of this section with respect to the discharge of any pollutant from any treatment works owned by such municipality into marine waters. No permit issued under this subsection shall authorize the discharge of sewage sludge into marine waters.*

(i)(1) Where construction is required in order for a planned or existing publicly owned treatment works to achieve limitations under subsection (b)(1)(B) or (b)(1)(C) of this section, but (A) construction cannot be completed within the time required in such subsection, or (B) the United States has failed to make financial assistance under this Act available in time to achieve such limitations by the time specified in such subsection, the owner or operator of such treatment works may request the Administrator (or if appropriate the State) to issue a permit pursuant to section 402 of this Act or to modify a permit issued pursuant to that section to extend such time for compliance. Any such request shall be filed with the Administrator (or if appropriate the State) within 180 days after the date of enactment of this subsection. The Administrator (or if appropriate the State) may grant such request and issue or modify such a permit, which shall contain a schedule of compliance for the publicly owned treatment works based on the earliest date by which such financial assistance will be available from the United States and construction can be completed, but in no event later than ~~July 1, 1983,~~ *July 1, 1988,*[3] and shall contain such other terms and conditions, including those necessary to carry out subsection (b) through (g) of section 201 of this Act, section 307 of this

[3] Section 21(a), Public Law 97–117. . . . The amendment made by this subsection shall not be interpreted or applied to extend the date for compliance with section 301(b)(1)(B) or (C) of the Federal Water Pollution Control Act beyond schedules for compliance in effect as of the date of enactment of this Act, except in cases where reductions in the amount of financial assistance under this Act or changed conditions affecting the rate of construction beyond the control of the owner or operator will make it impossible to complete construction by July 1, 1983.

Act, and such interim effluent limitations applicable to that treatment works as the Administrator determines are necessary to carry out the provisions of this Act.

(2) (A) Where a point source (other than a publicly owned treatment works) will not achieve the requirements of subsections (b)(1) (A) and (b)(1)(C) of this section and—

(i) if a permit issued prior to July 1, 1977, to such point source is based upon a discharge into a publicly owned treatment works; or

(ii) if such point source (other than a publicly owned treatment works) had before July 1, 1977, a contract (enforceable against such point source) to discharge into a publicly owned treatment works; or

(ii) if either an application made before July 1, 1977, for a construction grant under this Act for a publicly owned treatment works, or engineering or architectural plans or working drawings made before July 1, 1977, for a publicly owned treatment works, show that such point source was to discharge into such publicly owned treatment works,

and such publicly owned treatment works is presently unable to accept such discharge without construction, and in the case of a discharge to an existing publicly owned treatment works, such treatment works has an extension pursuant to paragraph (1) of this subsection, the owner or operator of such point source may request the Administrator (or if appropriate the State) to issue or modify such a permit pursuant to such section 402 to extend such time for compliance. Any such request shall be filed with the Administrator (or if appropriate the State) within 180 days after the date of enactment of this subsection or the filing of a request by the appropriate publicly owned treatment works under paragraph (1) of this subsection, whichever is later. If the Administrator (or if appropriate the State) finds that the owner or operator of such point source has acted in good faith, he may grant such request and issue or modify such a permit, which shall contain a schedule of compliance for the point source to achieve the requirements of subsections (b)(1) (A) and (C) of this section and shall contain such other terms and conditions, including pretreatment and interim effluent limitations and water conservation requirements applicable to that point source, as the Administrator determines are necessary to carry out the provisions of this Act.

(B) No time modification granted by the Administrator (or if appropriate the State) pursuant to paragraph (2)(A) of this subsection shall extend beyond the earliest date practicable for compliance or beyond the date of any extension granted to the appropriate publicly owned treatment works pursuant to paragraph (1) of this subsection, but in no event shall it extend beyond ~~July 1, 1983,~~ *July 1, 1988;* [4] and no such time modification shall be granted unless (i) the publicly owned treatment works will be in operation and available to the point source before ~~July 1, 1983,~~ *July 1, 1988;* [4] and will meet the requirements to subsections (b) (1) (B) and (C) of this section after receiving

[4] Section 21(a), Public Law 97–117. . . . The amendment made by this subsection shall not be interpreted or applied to extend the date for compliance with section 301(b) (1) (B) or (C) of the Federal Water Pollution Control Act beyond schedules for compliance in effect as of the date of enactment of this Act, except in cases where reductions in the amount of financial assistance under this Act or changed conditions affecting the rate of construction beyond the control of the owner or operator will make it impossible to complete construction by July 1, 1983.

the discharge from that point source; and (ii) the point source and the publicly owned treatment works have entered into an enforceable contract requiring the point source to discharge into the publicly owned treatment works the owner or operator of such point source to pay the costs required under section 204 of this Act, and the publicly owned treatment works to accept the discharge from the point source; and (iii) the permit for such point source requires point source to meet all requirements under section 307 (a) and (b) during the period of such time modification.

(j)(1) Any application filed under this section for a modification of the provisions of—

~~(A) subsection (b)(1)(B) under subsection (h) of this section shall be filed not later than 270 days after the date of enactment of the Clean Water Act of 1977;~~

(A) subsection (b)(1)(B) under subsection (h) of this section shall be filed not later that the 365th day which begins after the date of enactment of the Municipal Wastewater Treatment Construction Grant Amendments of 1981; [5]

(B) subsection (b)(2)(A) as it applies to pollutants identified in subsection(b)(2)(F) shall be filed not later than 270 days after the date of promulgation of an applicable effluent guideline under section 304 or not later than 270 days after the date of enactment of the Clean Water Act of 1977, whichever is later.

(2) Any application for a modification filed under subsection (g) of this section shall not operate to stay any requirement under this Act, unless in the judgment of the Administrator such a stay or the modification sought will not result in the discharge of pollutants in quantities which may reasonably be anticipated to pose an unacceptable risk to human health or the environment because of bioaccumulation, persistency in the environment, acute toxicity, chronic toxicity (including carcinogenicity, mutagenicity or teratogenicity), or synergistic propensities, and that there is a substantial likelihood that the applicant will succeed on the merits of such application. In the case of an application filed under subsection (g) of this section, the Administrator may condition any stay granted under this paragraph on requiring the filing of a bond or other appropriate security to assure timely compliance with the requirements from which a modification is sought.

(k) In the case of any facility subject to a permit under section 402 which proposes to comply with the requirements of subsection (b)(2)(A) of this section by replacing existing production capacity with an innovative production process which will result in an effluent reduction significantly greater than that required by the limitation otherwise applicable to such facility and moves toward the national goal of eliminating the discharge of all pollutants, or with the installation of an innovative control technique that has a substantial likelihood for enabling the facility to comply with the applicable effluent limitation by

---

[5] Public Law 97–117.
SEC. 22(a) * * *

* * * * * * *

(e) The amendments made by this section shall take effect on the date of enactment of this Act, except that no applicant, other than the city of Avalon, California, who applies after the date of enactment of this Act for a permit pursuant to subsection (h) of section 301 of the Federal Water Pollution Control Act which modifies the requirements of subsection (b)(1)(B) of section 301 of such Act shall receive such permit during the one-year period which begins on the date of enactment of this Act.

achieving a significantly greater effluent reduction than that required by the applicable effluent limitation and moves toward the national goal of eliminating the discharge of all pollutants, or by achieving the required reduction with an innovative system that has the potential for significantly lower costs than the systems which have been determined by the Administrator to be economically achievable, the Administrator (or the State with an approved program under section 402, in consultation with the Administrator) may establish a date for compliance under subsection (b)(2)(A) of this section no later than July 1, 1987, if it is also determined that such innovative system has the potential for industrywide application.

(l) The Administrator may not modify any requirement of this section as it applies to any specific pollutant which is on the toxic pollutant list under section 307(a)(1) of this Act.

"(m)(1) The Administrator, with the concurrence of the State, may issue a permit under section 402 which modifies the requirements of subsections (b)(1)(A) and (b)(2)(E) of this section, and of section 403, with respect to effluent limitations to the extent such limitations relate to biochemical oxygen demand and pH from discharges by an industrial discharger in such State into deep waters of the territorial seas, if the applicant demonstrates and the Administrator finds that—

"(A) the facility for which modification is sought is covered at the time of the enactment of this subsection by National Pollutant Discharge Elimination System permit number CA0005894 or CA0005282;

"(B) the energy and environmental costs of meeting such requirements of subsections (b)(1)(A) and (b)(2)(E) and section 403 exceed by an unreasonable amount the benefits to be obtained, including the objectives of this Act;

"(C) the applicant has established a system for monitoring the impact of such discharges on a representative sample of aquatic biota;

"(D) such modified requirements will not result in any additional requirements on any other point or nonpoint source;

"(E) there will be no new or substantially increased discharges from the point source of the pollutant to which the modification applies above that volume of discharge specified in the permit;

"(F) the discharge is into waters where there is strong tidal movement and other hydrological and geological characteristics which are necessary to allow compliance with this subsection and section 101(a)(2) of this Act;

"(G) the applicant accepts as a condition to the permit a contractural obligation to use funds in the amount required (but not less than $250,000 per year for ten years) for research and development of water pollution control technology, including but not limited to closed cycle technology;

"(H) the facts and circumstances present a unique situation which, if relief is granted, will not establish a precedent or the relaxation of the requirements of this Act applicable to similarly situated discharges; and

"(I) no owner or operator of a facility comparable to that of the applicant situated in the United States has demonstrated that it would be put at a competitive disadvantage to the applicant (or the parent company or any subsidiary thereof) as a result of the issuance of a permit under this subsection.

"(2) The effluent limitations established under a permit issued under paragraph (1) shall be sufficient to implement the applicable State water quality standards, to assure the protection of public water supplies and protection and propagation of a balanced, indigenous population of shellfish, fish, fauna, wildlife, and other aquatic organisms, and to allow recreational activities in and on the water. In setting such limitations, the Administrator shall take into account any seasonal variations and the need for an adequate margin of safety, considering the lack of essential knowledge concerning the relationship between effluent limitations and water quality and the lack of essential knowledge of the effects of discharges on beneficial uses of the receiving waters.

"(3) A permit under this subsection may be issued for a period not to exceed five years, and such a permit may be renewed for one additional period not to exceed five years upon a demonstration by the applicant and a finding by the Administrator at the time of application for any such renewal that the provisions of this subsection are met.

"(4) The Administrator may terminate a permit issued under this subsection if the Administrator determines that there has been a decline in ambient water quality of the receiving waters during the period of the permit even if a direct cause and effect relationship cannot be shown: *Provided*, That if the effluent from a source with a permit issued under this subsection is contributing to a decline in ambient water quality of the receiving waters, the Administrator shall terminate such permit.".

WATER QUALITY RELATED EFFLUENT LIMITATIONS

SEC. 302. (a) Whenever, in the judgment of the Administrator, discharges of pollutants from a point source or group of point sources, with the application of effluent limitations required under section 301 (b)(2) of this Act, would interfere with the attainment or maintenance of that water quality in a specific portion of the navigable waters which shall assure protection of public water supplies, agricultural and industrial uses, and the protection and propagation of a balanced population of shellfish, fish and wildlife, and allow recreational activities in and on the water, effluent limitations (including alternative effluent control strategies) for such point source or sources shall be established which can reasonably be expected to contribute to the attainment or maintenance of such water quality.

(b) (1) Prior to establishment of any effluent limitation pursuant to subsection (a) of this section,. the Administrator shall issue notice of intent to establish such limitation and within ninety days of such notice hold a public hearing to determine the relationship of the economic and social costs of achieving any such limitation or limitations, including any economic or social dislocation in the affected community or communities, to the social and economic benefits to be obtained (including the attainment of the objective of this Act) and to determine whether or not such effluent limitations can be implemented with available technology or other alternative control strategies.

(2) If a person affected by such limitation demonstrates at such hearing that (whether or not such technology or other alternative control strategies are available) there is no reasonable relationship between the economic and social costs and the benefits to be obtained (including attainment of the objective of this Act), such limitation shall not become effective and the Administrator shall adjust such limitation as it applies to such person.

(c) The establishment of effluent limitations under this section shall not operate to delay the application of any effluent limitation established under section 301 of this Act.

WATER QUALITY STANDARDS AND IMPLEMENTATION PLANS

SEC. 303. (a)(1) In order to carry out the purpose of this Act, any water quality standard applicable to interstate waters which was adopted by any State and submitted to, and approved by, or is awaiting approval by, the Administrator pursuant to this Act as in effect immediately prior to the date of enactment of the Federal Water Pollution Control Act Amendments of 1972, shall remain in effect unless the Administrator determined that such standard is not consistent with the applicable requirements of this Act as in effect immediately prior to the date of enactment of the Federal Water Pollution Control Act Amendments of 1972. If the Administrator makes such a determination he shall, within three months after the date of enactment of the Federal Water Pollution Control Act Amendments of 1972, notify the State and specify the changes needed to meet such requirements. If such changes are not adopted by the State within ninety days after the date of such notification, the Administrator shall promulgate such changes in accordance with subsection (b) of this section.

(2) Any State which, before the date of enactment of the Federal Water Pollution Control Act Amendments of 1972, has adopted, pursuant to its own law, water quality standards applicable to intrastate waters shall submit such standards to the Administrator ithin thirty days after the date of enactment of the Federal Water Pollution Control Act Amendments of 1972. Each such standard shall remain in effect, in the same manner and to the same extent as any other water quality standard established under this Act unless the Administrator determines that such standard is inconsistent with the applicable requirements of this Act as in effect immediately prior to the date of enactment of the Federal Water Pollution Control Act Amendments of 1972. If the Administrator makes such a determination he shall not later than the one hundred and twentieth day after the date of submission of such standards, notify the State and specify the changes needed to meet such requirements. If such changes are not adopted by the State within ninety days after such notification, the Administrator shall promulgate such changes in accordance with subsection (b) of this section.

(3)(A) Any State which prior to the date of enactment of the Federal Water Pollution Control Act Amendments of 1972 has not adopted pursuant to its own laws water quality standards applicable to intrastate waters shall, not later than one hundred and eighty days after the date of enactment of the Federal Water Pollution Control Act Amendments of 1972, adopt and submit such standards to the Administrator.

(B) If the Administrator determines that any such standards are consistent with the applicable requirements of this Act as in effect immediately prior to the date of enactment of the Federal Water Pollution Control Act Amendments of 1972, he shall approve such standards.

(C) If the Administrator determines that any such standards are not consistent with the applicable requirements of this Act as in effect immediately prior to the date of enactment of the Federal Water Pollution Control Act Amendments of 1972, he shall, not later than the ninetieth day after the date of submission of such standards, notify the State and specify the changes to meet such requirements. If such changes are not adopted by the State within ninety days after the date of notification, the Administrator shall promulgate such standards pursuant to subsection (b) of this section.

(b)(1) The Administrator shall promptly prepare and publish proposed regulations setting forth water quality standards for a State in accordance with the applicable requirements of this Act as in effect immediately prior to the date of enactment of the Federal Water Pollution Control Act Amendments of 1972, if—

(A) the State fails to submit water quality standards within the times prescribed in subsection (a) of this section,

(B) a water quality standard submitted by such State under subsection (a) of this section is determined by the Administrator not to be consistent with the applicable requirements of subsection (a) of this section.

(2) The Administrator shall promulgate any water quality standard published in a proposed regulation not later than one hundred and ninety days after the date he publishes any such proposed standard, unless prior to such promulgation, such State has adopted a water quality standard which the Administrator determines to be in accordance with subsection (a) of this section.

(c)(1) The Governor of a State or the State water pollution control agency of such State shall from time to time (but at least once each three year period beginning with the date of enactment of the Federal Water Pollution Control Act Amendments of 1972) hold public hearings for the purpose of reviewing applicable water quality standards and, as appropriate, modifying and adopting standards. Results of such review shall be made available to the Administrator.

(2) Whenever the State revises or adopts a new standard, such revised or new standard shall be submitted to the Administrator. Such revised or new water quality standard shall consist of the designated uses of the navigable waters involved and the water quality criteria for such waters based upon such uses. Such standards shall be such as to protect the public health or welfare, enhance the quality of water and serve the purposes of this Act. Such standards shall be established taking into consideration their use and value for public water supplies, propagation of fish and wildlife, recreational purposes, and agricultural, industrial, and other purposes, and also taking into consideration their use and value for navigation.

(3) If the Administrator, within sixty days after the date of submission of the revised or new standard, determines that such standard meets the requirements of this Act, such standard shall thereafter be the water quality standard for the applicable waters of that State. If the Administrator determines that any such revised or new standard is not consistent with the applicable requirements of this Act, he shall not later than the ninetieth day after the date of submission of such standard notify the State and specify the changes to meet such requirements. If such changes are not adopted by the State within ninety days after the date of notification, the Administrator shall promulgate such standard pursuant to paragraph (4) of this subsection.

(4) The Administrator shall promptly prepare and publish proposed regulations setting forth a revised or new water quality standard for the navigable waters involved—

(A) if a revised or new water quality standard submitted by such State under paragraph (3) of this subsection for such waters is determined by the Administrator not to be consistent with the applicable requirements of this Act, or

(B) in any case where the Administrator determines that a revised or new standard is necessary to meet the requirements of this Act.

The Administrator shall promulgate any revised or new standard under this paragraph not later than ninety days after he publishes such proposed standards, unless prior to such promulgation, such State has adopted a revised or new water quality standard which the Administrator determines to be in accordance with this Act.

(d)(1)(A) Each State shall identify those waters within its boundaries for which the effluent limitations required by section 301(b)(1)(A) and section 301(b)(1)(B) are not stringent enough to implement any water quality standard applicable to such waters. The State shall establish a priority ranking for such waters, taking into account the severity of the pollution and the uses to be made of such waters.

(B) Each State shall identify those waters or parts thereof within its boundaries for which controls on thermal discharges under section 301 are not stringent enough to assure protection and propagation of a balanced indigenous population of shellfish, fish, and wildlife

(C) Each State shall establish for the waters identified in paragraph (1)(A) of this subsection, and in accordance with the priority ranking, the total maximum daily load, for those pollutants which the Administrator identifies under section 304(a)(2) as suitable for such calculation. Such load shall be established at a level necessary to implement the applicable water quality standards with seasonal variations and a margin of safety which takes into account any lack of knowledge concerning the relationship between effluent limitations and water quality.

(D) Each State shall estimate for the waters identified in paragraph (1)(D) of this subsection the total maximum daily thermal load required to assure protection and propagation of a balanced, indigenous population of shellfish, fish and wildlife. Such estimates shall take into account the normal water temperatures, flow rates, seasonal variations, existing sources of heat input, and the dissipative capacity of the identified waters or parts thereof. Such estimates shall include a calculation of the maximum heat input that can be made into each such part and shall include a margin of safety which takes into account any lack of knowledge concerning the development of thermal water quality criteria for such protection and propagation in the identified waters or parts thereof.

(2) Each State shall submit to the Administrator from time to time, with the first such submission not later than one hundred and eighty days after the date of publication of the first identification of pollutants under section 304(a)(2)(D), for his approval the waters identified and the loads established under paragraphs (1)(A), (1)(B), (1)(C), and (1)(D) of this subsection. The Administrator shall either approve or disapprove such identification and load not later than thirty days after the date of submission. If the Administrator approves such identification and load, such State shall incorporate them into its current plan under subsection (e) of this section. If the Administrator disapproves such identification and load, he shall not later than thirty days after the date of such disapproval identify such waters in such State and establish such loads for such waters as he determines necessary to implement the water quality standards applicable to such waters and upon such identification and establishment the State shall incorporate them into its current plan under subsection (e) of this section.

(3) For the specific purpose of developing information, each State shall identify all waters within its boundaries which it has not identified under paragraph (1)(A) and (1)(B) of this subsection

and estimate for such waters the total maximum daily load with seasonal variations and margins of safety, for those pollutants which the Administrator identifies under section 304(a)(2) as suitable for such calculation and for thermal discharges, at a level that would assure protection and propagation of a balanced indigenous population of fish, shellfish and wildlife.

(e)(1) Each State shall have a continuing planning process approved under paragraph (2) of this subsection which is consistent with this Act.

(2) Each State shall submit not later than 120 days after the date of the enactment of the Water Pollution Control Admendments of 1972 to the Administrator for his approval a proposed continuing planning process which is consistent with this Act. Not later than thirty days after the date of submission of such a process the Administrator shall either approve or disapprove such process. The Administrator shall from time to time review each State's approved planning process for the purpose of insuring that such planning process is at all times consistent with this Act. The Administrator shall not approve any State permit program under title IV of this Act for any State which does not have an approved continuing planning process under this section.

(3) The Administrator shall approve any continuing planning process submitted to him under this section which will result in plans for all navigable waters within such State, which include, but are not limited to, the following:

(A) effluent limitations and schedules of compliance at least as stringent as those required by section 301(b)(1), section 301 (b)(2), section 306, and section 307, and at least as stringent as any requirements contained in any applicable water quality standard in effect under authority of this section;

(B) the incorporation of all elements of any applicable areawide waste management plans under section 208, and applicable basin plans under section 209 of this Act;

(C) total maximum daily load for pollutants in accordance with subsection (d) of this section;

(D) procedures for revision;

(E) adequate authority for intergovernmental cooperation;

(F) adequate implementation, including schedules of compliance, for revised or new water quality standards, under subsection (c) of this section;

(G) controls over the disposition of all residual waste from any water treatment processing;

(H) an inventory and ranking, in order of priority, of needs for construction of waste treatment works required to meet the applicable requirements of sections 301 and 302.

(f) Nothing in this section shall be construed to affect any effluent limitation, or schedule of compliance required by any State to be implemented prior to the dates set forth in sections 301(b)(1) and 301(b)(2) nor to preclude any State from requiring compliance with any effluent limitation or schedule of compliance at dates earlier than such dates.

(g) Water quality standards relating to heat shall be consistent with the requirements of section 316 of this Act.

(h) For the purposes of this Act the term "water quality standards" includes thermal water quality standards.

INFORMATION AND GUIDELINES

SEC. 304. (a)(1) The Administrator, after consultation with appropriate Federal and State agencies and other interested persons, shall develop and publish, within one year after the date of enactment of this title (and from time to time thereafter revise) criteria for water quality accurately reflecting the latest scientific knowledge (A) on the kind and extent of all identifiable effects on health and welfare including, but not limited to, plankton, fish, shellfish, wildlife, plant life, shorelines, beaches, esthetics, and recreation which may be expected from the presence of pollutants in any body of water, including ground water; (B) on the concentration and dispersal of pollutants, or their byproducts, through biological, physical, and chemical processes; and (C) on the effects of pollutants on biological community diversity, productivity, and stability, including information on the factors affecting rates of eutrophication and rates of organic and inorganic sedimentation for varying types of receiving waters.

(2) The Administrator, after consulation with appropriate Federal and State agencies and other interested persons, shall develop and publish, within one year after the date of enactment of this title (and from time to time thereafter revise) information (A) on the factors necessary to restore and maintain the chemical, physical, and biological integrity of all navigable waters, ground waters, waters of the contiguous zone, and the oceans; (B) on the factors necessary for the protection and propagation of shellfish, fish, and wildlife for classes and categories of receiving waters and to allow recreational activities in and on the water; and (C) on the measurement and classification of water quality; and (D) for the purpose of section 303, on and the identification of pollutants suitable for maximum daily load measurement correlated with the achievement of water quality objectives.

(3) Such criteria and information and revisions thereof shall be issued to the States and shall be published in the Federal Register and otherwise made available to the public.

(4) The Administrator shall, within 90 days after the date of enactment of the Clean Water Act of 1977 and from time to time thereafter, publish and revise as appropriate information identifying conventional pollutants, including but not limited to, pollutants classified as biological oxygen demanding, suspended solids, fecal coliform, and pH. The thermal component of any discharge shall not be identified as a conventional pollutant under this paragraph.

(5)(A) The Administrator, to the extent practicable before consideration of any request under section 301(g) of this Act and within six months after the date of enactment of the Clean Water Act of 1977, shall develop and publish information on the factors necessary for the protection of public water supplies, and the protection and propagation of a balanced population of shellfish, fish and wildlife, and to allow recreational activities. in and on the water.

(B) The Administrator, to the extent practicable before consideration of any application under section 301(h) of this Act and within six months after the date of enactment of the Clean Water Act of 1977, shall develop and publish information on the factors necessary for the protection of public water supplies, and the protection and propagation of a balanced indigenous population of shellfish, fish and wildlife, and to allow recreational activities, in and on the water.

(6) The Administrator shall, within three months after enactment of the Clean Water Act of 1977 and annually thereafter, for purposes of section 301(h) of this Act publish and revise as appropriate information identifying each water quality standard in effect under this Act of State law, the specific pollutants associated with such water quality standard, and the particular waters to which such water quality standard applies.

(b) For the purpose of adopting or revising effluent limitations under this Act the Adminitrator shall, after consultaton with appropriate Federal and State agencies and other interested person, publish within one year of enactment of this title, regulations, providing guidelines for effluent limitations, and, at east annually thereafter, revise, if appropriate, such regulations. Such regulations shall—

(1)(A) identify, in terms of amounts of constituents and chemical, physical, and biological characteristics of pollutants, the degree of effluent reduction attainable through the application of the best practicable control technology currently available for classes and categories of point sources (other than publicly owned treatment works); and

(B) specify factors to be taken into account in determining the control measures and practices to be applicable to point sources (other than publicly owned treatment works) within such categories or classes. Factors relating to the assessment of best practicable control technology currently available to comply with subsection (b)(1) of section 301 of this Act shall include consideration of the total cost of application of technology in relation to the effluent reduction benefits to be achieved from such application, and shall also take into account the age of equipment and facilities involved, the process employed, the engineering aspects of the application of various types of control techniques, process changes, non-water quality environmental impact (including energy requirements), and such other factors as the Administrator deems appropriate;

(2)(A) identify, in terms of amounts of constituents and chemical, physical, and biological characteristics of pollutants, the degree of effluent reduction attainable through the application of the best control measures and practices achievable including treatment techniques, process and procedure innovations, operating methods, and other alternatives for classes and categories of point sources (other than publicly owned treatment works); and

(B) specify factors to be taken into account in determining the best measures and practices available to comply with subsection (b)(2) of section 301 of this Act to be applicable to any point source (other than publicly owned treatment works) within such categories of classes. Factors relating to the assessment of best available technology shall take into account the age of equipment and facilities involved, the process employed, the engineering aspects of the application of various types of control techniques, process changes, the cost of achieving such effluent reduction, non-water quality environmental impact (including energy requirements), and such other factors as the Administrator deems appropriate;

(3) identify control measures and practices available to eliminate the discharge of pollutants from categories and classes of

point sources, taking into account the cost of achieving such elimination of the discharge of pollutants; and

(4) (A) identify, in terms of amounts of constituents and chemical, physical, and biological characteristics of pollutants, the degree of effluent reduction attainable through the application of the best conventional pollutant control technology (including measures and practices) for classes and categories of point sources (other than publicly owned treatment works); and

(B) specify factors to be taken into account in determining the best conventional pollutant control technology measures and practices to comply with section 301(b)(2)(E) of this Act to be applicable to any point source (other than publicly owned treatment works) within such categories or classes. Factors relating to the assessment of best conventional pollutant control technology (including measures and practices) shall include consideration of the reasonableness of the relationship between the costs of attaining a reduction in effluents and the effluent reduction benefits derived and the comparison of the cost and level of reduction of such pollutants from the discharge from publicly owned treatment works to the cost and level of reduction of such pollutants from a class or category of industrial sources, and shall take into account the age of equipment and facilities involved, the process employed, the engineering aspects of the application of various types of control techniques, process changes, non-water quality environmental impact (including energy requirements), and such other factors as the Administrator deems appropriate.

(c) The Administrator, after consultation, with appropriate Federal and State agencies and other interested persons, shall issue to the States and appropriate water pollution control agencies within 270 days after enactment of this title (and from time to time thereafter) information on the processes, procedures, or operating methods which result in the elimination or reduction of the discharge of pollutants to implement standards of performance under section 306 of this Act. Such information shall include technical and other data, including costs, as are available on alternative methods of elimination or reduction of the discharge of pollutants. Such information, and revisions thereof, shall be published in the Federal Register and otherwise shall be made available to the public.

(d)(1) The Administrator, after consultation with appropriate Federal and State agencies and other interested persons, shall publish within sixty days after enactment of this title (and from time to time thereafter) information, in terms of amounts of constituents and chemical, physical, and biological characteristics of pollutants, on the degree of effluent reduction attainable through the application of secondary treatment.

(2) The Administrator, after consultation with appropriate Federal and State agencies and other interested persons, shall publish within nine months after the date of enactment of this title (and from time to time thereafter) information on alternative waste treatment management techniques and systems available to implement section 201 of this Act.

(3) The Administrator, after consultation with appropriate Federal and State agencies and other interested persons, shall promulgate

within one hundred and eighty days after the date of enactment of this subsection guidelines for identifying and evaluating innovative and alternative wastewater treatment processes and techniques referred to in section 201(g)(5) of this Act.

(4) For the purposes of this subsection, such biological treatment facilities as oxidation ponds, lagoons, and ditches and trickling filters shall be deemed the equivalent of secondary treatment. The Administrator shall provide guidance under paragraph (1) of this subsection on design criteria for such facilities, taking into account pollutant removal efficiencies and, consistent with the objective of the Act, assuring that water quality will not be adversely affected by deeming such facilities as the equivalent of secondary treatment.

(e) The Administrator, after consultation with appropriate Federal and State agencies and other interested persons, may publish regulations, supplemental to any effluent limitations specified under subsections (b) and (c) of this section for a class or category of point sources, for any specific pollutant which the Administrator is charged with a duty to regulate as a toxic or hazardous pollutant under section 307 (a)(1) or 311 of this Act, to control plant site runoff, spillage or leaks, sludge or waste disposal, and drainage from raw material storage which the Administrator determines are associated with or ancillary to the industrial manufacturing or treatment process within such class or category of point sources and may contribute significant amounts of such pollutants to navigable waters. Any applicable controls established under this subsection shall be included as a requirement for the purposes of section 301, 302, 306, 307, or 403, as the case may be, in any permit issued to a point source pursuant to section 402 of this Act.

(f) The Administrator, after consultation with appropriate Federal and State agencies and other interested persons, shall issue to appropriate Federal agencies, the States, water pollution control agencies, and agencies designated under section 208 of this Act, within one year after the effective date of this subsection (and from time to time thereafter) information including (1) guidelines for identifying and evaluating the nature and extent of nonpoint sources of pollutants, and (2) processes, procedures, and methods to control pollution resulting from—

(A) agricultural and silvicultural activities, including runoff from fields and crop and forest lands;

(B) mining activities, including runoff and siltation from new, currently operating, and abandoned surface and underground mines;

(C) all construction activity, including runoff from the facilities resulting from such construction;

(D) the disposal of pollutants in wells or in subsurface excavations;

(E) salt water intrusion resulting from reductions of fresh water flow from any cause, including extraction of ground water, irrigation, obstruction, and diversion; and

(F) changes in the movement, flow, or circulation of any navigable waters or ground waters, including changes caused by the construction of dams, levees, channels, causeways, or flow diversion facilities.

Such information and revisions thereof shall be published in the Federal Register and otherwise made available to the public.

(g)(1) For the purpose of assisting States in carrying out programs under section 402 of this Act, the Administrator shall publish, within one hundred and twenty days after the date of enactment of this title, and review at least annually thereafter and, if appropriate, revise guidelines for pretreatment of pollutants which he determines are not susceptible to treatment by publicly owned treatment works. **Guidelines under this subsection shall be established to control and prevent the discharge into the navigable waters, the contiguous zone, or the ocean (either directly or through publicly owned treatment works) of any pollutant which interferes with, passes through or otherwise is incompatible with such works.**

(2) When publishing guidelines under this subsection, the Administrator shall designate the category or categories of treatment works to which the guidelines shall apply.

(h) The Administrator shall, within one hundred and eighty days from the date of enactment of this title, promulgate guidelines establishing test procedures for the analysis of pollutants that shall include the factors which must be provided in any certification pursuant to section 401 of the Act or permit application pursuant to section 402 of this Act.

(i) The Administrator shall (1) within sixty days after the enactment of this title promulgate guidelines for the purpose of establishing uniform application forms and other minimum requirements for the acquisition of information from owners and operators or point-sources of discharge subject to any State program under section 402 of this Act, and (2) within sixty days from the date of enactment of this title promulgate guidelines establishing the minimum procedural and other elements of any State program under section 402 of this Act which shall include:

(A) monitoring requirements;

(B) reporting requirements (including procedures to make information available to the public);

(C) enforcement provisions; and.

(D) funding, personnel qualifications, and manpower requirements (including a requirement that no board or body which approves permit applications or portions thereof shall include, as a member, any person who receives, or has during the previous two years received, a significant portion of his income directly or indirectly from permit holders or applicants for a permit).

(j) The Administrator shall issue information biennually on methods, procedures, and processes as may be appropriate to restore and enhance the quality of the Nation's publicly owned freshwater lakes.

(k)(1) The Administrator shall enter into agreements with the **Secretary of Agriculture, the Secretary of the Army, and the Secretary of the Interior, and the heads of such other departments, agencies, and instrumentalities of the United States as the Administrator determines, to provide for the maximum utilization of other Federal laws and programs for the purpose of achieving and maintaining water quality through appropriate implementation of plans approved under section 208 of this Act.**

(2) The Administrator is authorized to transfer to the Secretary **of Agriculture, the Secretary of the Army, and the Secretary of the Interior and the heads of such other departments, agencies, and in-**

strumentalities of the United States as the Administrator determines, any funds appropriated under paragraph (3) of this subsection to supplement funds otherwise appropriated to programs authorized pursuant to any agreement under paragraph (1).

(3) There is authorized to be appropriated to carry out the provisions of this subsection $100,000,000 per fiscal year for the fiscal years 1979 through 1983.

WATER QUALITY INVENTORY

SEC. 305. (a) The Administrator, in cooperation with the States and with the assistance of appropriate Federal agencies, shall prepare a report to be submitted to the Congress on or before January 1, 1974, which shall—

(1) describe the specific quality, during 1973, with appropriate supplemental descriptions as shall be required to take into account seasonal, tidal, and other variations, of all navigable waters and the waters of the contiguous zone;

(2) include an inventory of all point sources of discharge (based on a qualitative and quantitative analysis of discharges) of pollutants, into all navigable waters and the waters of the contiguous zone; and

(3) identify specifically those navigable waters, the quality of which—

(A) is adequate to provide for the protection and propagation of a balanced population of shellfish, fish, and wildlife and allow recreational activities in and on the water;

(B) can reasonably be expected to attain such level by 1977 or 1983; and

(C) can reasonably be expected to attain such level by any later date.

(b)(1) Each State shall prepare and submit to the Administratro by April 1, 1975, and shall bring up to date by April 1, 1976, and biennially thereafter, a report which shall include—

(A) a description of the water quality of all navigable waters in such State during the preceding year, with appropriate supplemental descriptions as shall be required to take into account seasonal, tidal, and other variations, correlated with the quality of water required by the objective of this Act (as identified by the Administrator pursuant to criteria published under section 304(a) of this Act) and the water quality described in subparagraph (B) of this paragraph;

(B) an analysis of the extent to which all navigable waters of such State provide for the protection and propagation of a balanced population of shellfish, fish, and wildlife, and allow recreational activities in and on the water;

(C) an analysis of the extent to which the elimination of the discharge of pollutants and a level of water quality which provides for the protection and propagation of a balanced population of shellfish, fish, and wildlife and allows recreational activities in and on the water, have been or will be achieved by the requirements of this Act, together with recommendations as to additional action necessary to achieve such objectives and for what waters such additional action is necessary;

(D) an estimate of (i) the environmental impact, (ii) the economic and social costs necessary to achieve the objective of this Act in such State, (iii) the economic and social benefits of such achievement, and (iv) an estimate of the date of such achievement; and

(E) a description of the nature and extent of nonpoint sources of pollutants, and recommendations as to the programs which must be undertaken to control each category of such sources, including an estimate of the costs of implementing such programs.

(2) The Administrator shall transmit such State reports, together with an analysis thereof, to Congress on or before October 1, 1975, and October 1, 1976, and biennially thereafter.

NATIONAL STANDARDS OF PERFORMANCE

SEC. 306. (a) For purposes of this section:

(1) The term "standard of performance" means a standard for the control of the discharge of pollutants which reflects the greatest degree of effluent reduction which the Administrator determines to be achievable through application of the best available demonstrated control technology, processes, operating methods, or other alternatives, including, where practicable, a standard permitting no discharge of pollutants.

(2) The term "new source" means any source, the construction of which is commenced after the publication of proposed regulations prescribing a standard of performance under this section which will be applicable to such source, if such standard is thereafter promulgated in accordance with this section.

(3) The term "source" means any building, structure, facility, or installation from which there is or may be the discharge of pollutants.

(4) The term "owner or operator" means any person who owns, leases, operates, controls, or supervises a source.

(5) The term "construction" means any placement, assembly, or installation of facilities or equipment (including contractual obligations to purchase such facilities or equipment) at the premises where such equipment will be used, including preparation work at such premises.

(b)(1)(A) The Administrator shall, within ninety days after the date of enactment of this title publish (and from time to time thereafter shall revise) a list of categories of sources, which shall at the minimum, include:

pulp and paper mills;
paperboard, builders paper and board mills;
meat product and rendering processing;
dairy product processing;
grain mills;
canned and preserved fruits and vegetables processing;
canned and preserved seafood processing;
sugar processing;
textile mills;
cement manufacturing;
feedlots;
electroplating;
organic chemicals manufacturing;
inorganic chemicals manufacturing;
plastic and synthetic materials manufacturing;
soap and detergent manufacturing;

fertilizer manufacturing;
petroleum refining;
iron and steel manufacturing;
nonferrous metals manufacturing;
phosphate manufacturing;
steam electric powerplants;
ferroalloy manufacturing;
leather tanning and finishing;
glass and asbestos manufacturing;
rubber processing; and
timber products processing.

(B) As soon as practicable, but in no case more than one year, after a category of sources is included in a list under subparagraph (A) of this paragraph, the Administrator shall propose and publish regulations establishing Federal standards of performance for new sources within such category. The Administrator shall afford interested persons an opportunity for written comment on such proposed regulations. After considering such comments, he shall promulgate, within one hundred and twenty days after publication of such proposed regulations, such standards with such adjustments as he deems appropriate. The Administrator shall, from time to time, as technology and alternatives change, revise such standards following the procedure required by this subsection for promulgation of such standards. Standards of performance, or revisions thereof, shall become effective upon promulgation. In establishing or revising Federal standards of performance for new sources under this section, the Administrator shall take into consideration the cost of achieving such effluent reduction, and any non-water quality environmental impact and energy requirements.

(2) The Administrator may distinguish among classes, types, and sizes within categories of new sources for the purpose of establishing such standards and shall consider the type of process employed (including whether batch or continuous).

(3) The provisions of this section shall apply to any new source owned or operated by the United States.

(c) Each State may develop and submit to the Administrator a procedure under State law for applying and enforcing standards of performance for new sources located in such State. If the Administrator finds that the procedure and the law of any State require the application and enforcement of standards of performance to at least the same extent as required by this section, such State is authorized to apply and enforce such standards of performance (except with respect to new sources owned or operated by the United States).

(d) Notwithstanding any other provision of this Act, any point source the construction of which is commended after the date of enactment of the Federal Water Pollution Control Act Amendments of 1972 and which is so constructed as to meet all applicable standards of performance shall not be subject to any more stringent standard of performance during a ten-year period beginning on the date of completion of such construction or during the period of depreciation or amortization of such facility for the purposes of section 167 or 169 (or both) of the Internal Revenue Code of 1954, whichever period ends first.

(e) After the effective date of standards of performance promulgated under this section, it shall be unlawful for any owner or operator of any new source to operate such source in violation of any standard of performance applicable to such source.

TOXIC AND PRETREATMENT EFFLUENT STANDARDS

SEC. 307. (a)(1) On and after the date of enactment of the Clean Water Act of 1977, the list of toxic pollutants or combination of pollutants subject to this Act shall consist of those toxic pollutants listed in table 1 of Committee Print Numbered 95–30 of the Committee on Public Works and Transportation of the House of Representatives, and the Administrator shall publish, not later than the thirtieth day after the date of enactment of the Clean Water Act of 1977, that list. From time to time thereafter, the Administrator may revise such list and the Administrator is authorized to add to or remove from such list any pollutant. The Administrator in publishing any revised list, including the addition or removal of any pollutant from such list, shall take into account the toxicity of the pollutant, its persistence, degradability, the usual or potential presence of the affected organisms in any waters, the importance of the affected organisms, and the nature and extent of the effect of the toxic pollutant on such organisms. A determination of the Administrator under this paragraph shall be final except that if, on judicial review, such determination was based on arbitrary and capricious action of the Administrator, the Administrator shall make a redetermination.

(2) Each toxic pollutant listed in accordance with paragraph (1) of the subsection shall be subject to effluent limitations resulting from the application of the best available technology economically achieveable for the applicable category or class of point sources established in accordance with section 301(b)(2)(A) and 304(b)(2) of this Act. The Administrator, in his discretion, may publish in the Federal Register a proposed effluent standard (which may include a prohibition) establishing requirements for a toxic pollutant which, if an effluent limitation is applicable to a class or category of point sources, shall be applicable to such category or class only if such standard imposes more stringent requirements. Such published effluent standard (or prohibition) shall take into account the toxicity of the pollutant, its persistence, degradability, the usual or potential presence of the affected organisms in any waters, the importance of the affected organisms and the nature and extent of the effect of the toxic pollutant on such organisms, and the extent to which effective control is being or may be achieved under other regulatory authority. The Administrator shall allow a period of not less than sixty days following publication of any such proposed effluent standard (or prohibition) for written comment by interested persons on such proposed standard. In addition, if within thirty days of publication of any such proposed effluent standard (or prohibition) any interested person so requests, the Administrator shall hold a public hearing in connection therewith. Such a public hearing shall provide an opportunity for oral and written presentations, such cross-examination as the Administrator determines is appropriate on disputed issues of material fact, and the transcription of a verbatim record which shall be available to the

public. After consideration of such comments and any information and material presented at any public hearing held on such proposed standard or prohibition, the Administrator shall promulgate such standards (or prohibition) with such modifications as the Administrator finds are justified. Such promulgation by the Administrator shall be made within two hundred and seventy days after publication of proposed standard (or prohibition). Such standard (or prohibition) shall be final except that if, on judicial review, such standard was not based on substantial evidence, the Administrator shall promulgate a revised standard. Effluent limitations shall be established in accordance with sections 301(b)(2)(A) and 304(b)(2) for every toxic pollutant referred to in table 1 of Committee Print Numbered 95–30 of the Committee on Public Works and Transportation of the House of Representatives as soon as practicable after the date of enactment of the Clean Water Act of 1977, but no later than July 1, 1980. Such effluent limitations or effluent standards (or prohibitions) shall be established for every other toxic pollutant listed under paragraph (1) of this subsection as soon as practicable after it is so listed.

(3) Each such effluent standard (or prohibition) shall be reviewed and, if appropriate, revised at least every three years.

(4) Any effluent standard promulgated under this section shall be at that level which the Administrator determines provides an ample margin of safety.

(5) When proposing or promulgating any effluent standard (or prohibition) under this section, the Administrator shall designate the category or categories of sources to which the effluent standard (or prohibition) shall apply. Any disposal of dredged material may be included in such a category of sources after consultation with the Secretary of the Army.

(6) Any effluent standard (or prohibition) established pursuant to this section shall take effect on such date or dates as specified in the order promulgating such standard, but in no case, more than one year from the date of such promulgation. If the Administrator determines that compliance within one year from the date of promulgation is technologically infeasible for a category of sources, the Administrator may establish the effective date of the effluent standard (or prohibition) for such category at the earliest date upon which compliance can be feasibly attained by sources within such category, but in no event more than three years after the date of such promulgation.

(7) Prior to publishing any regulations pursuant to this section the Administrator shall, to the maximum extent practicable within the time provided, consult with appropriate advisory committees, States, independent experts, and Federal departments and agencies.

(b)(1) The Administrator shall, within one hundred and eighty days after the date of enactment of this title and from time to time thereafter, publish proposed regulations establishing pretreatment standards for introduction of pollutants into treatment works (as defined in section 212 of this Act) which are publicly owned for those pollutants which are determined not to be susceptible to treatment by such treatment works or which would interfere with the operation of such treatment works. Not later than ninety days after such publication, and after opportunity for public hearing, the Administrator shall promulgate such pretreatment standards. Pretreatment standards under this subsection shall specify a time for compliance not to exceed three years from the date of promulgation and shall be established to prevent the discharge of any pollutant through treatment works (as defined in section 212 of this Act) which are publicly owned, which pollutant interferes with, passes through, or otherwise is incompatible with such works. If, in the case of any toxic pollutant under subsection (a) of this section introduced by a source into a publicly owned treatment works, the treatment by such works removes all or any part of such toxic pollutant and the discharge from such works does not violate that effluent limitation or standard which would be applicable to such toxic pollutant if it were discharged by such source other than through a publicly owned treatment works, and does not prevent sludge use or disposal by such works in accordance with section 405 of this Act, then the pretreatment requirements for the sources actually discharging such toxic pollutant into such publicly owned treatment works may be revised by the owner or operator of such works to reflect the removal of such toxic pollutant by such works.

(2) The Administrator shall, from time to time, as control technology, processes, operating methods, or other alternative change, revise such standards following the procedure established by this subsection for promulgation of such standards.

(3) When proposing or promulgating any pretreatment standard under this section, the Administrator shall designate the category or categories of sources to which such standard shall apply.

(4) Nothing in this subsection shall affect any pretreatment requirement established by any State or local law not in conflict with any pretreatment standard established under this subsection.

(c) In order to insure that any source introducing pollutants into a publicly owned treatment works, which source would be a new source subject to section 306 if it were to discharge pollutants, will not cause a violation of the effluent limitations established for any such treatment works, the Administrator shall promulgate pretreatment standards for the category of such sources simultaneously with the promulgation of standards of performance under section 306 for the equivalent category of new sources. Such pretreatment standards shall prevent the discharge of any pollutant into such treatment works, which pollutant may interfere with, pass through, or otherwise be incompatible with such works.

(d) After the effective date of any effluent standard or prohibition or pretreatment standard promulgated under this section, it shall be unlawful for any owner or operator of any source to operate any source in violation of any such effluent standard or prohibition or pretreatment standard.

INSPECTIONS, MONITORING, AND ENTRY

SEC. 308. (a) Whenever required to carry out the objective of this Act, including but not limited to (1) developing or assisting in the development of any effluent limitation, or other limitation, prohibition, or effluent standard, pretreatment standard, or standard of performance under this Act; (2) determining whether any person is in violation of any such effluent limitation, or other limitation, prohibition or effluent standard, pretreatment standard, or standard of performance; (3) any requirement established under this section; or (4) carrying out section 305, 311, 402, 404 (relating to State permit programs), and 504 of this Act—

(A) the Administrator shall require the owner or operator of any point source to (i) establish and maintain such records, (ii) make such reports, (iii) install, use, and maintain such monitoring equipment or methods (including where appropriate, biological monitoring methods), (iv) sample such effluents (in accordance with such methods, at such locations, at such intervals, and in such manner as the Administrator shall prescribe), and (v) provide such other information as he may reasonably require; and

(B) the Administrator or his authorized representative, upon presentation of his credentials—

(i) shall have a right of entry to, upon, or through any premises in which an effluent source is located in or which any records required to be maintained under clause (A) of this subsection are located, and

(ii) may at reasonable times have access to any copy any records, inspect any monitoring equipment or method required under clause (A), and sample any effluents which the owner or operator of such sources is required to sample under such clause.

(b) Any records, reports, or information obtained under this section (1) shall, in the case of effluent data, be related to any applicable effluent limitations, toxic pretreatment, or new source performance standards, and (2) shall be available to the public, except that upon a showing satisfactory to the Administrator by any person that records, reports, or information, or particular part thereof (other than effluent data), to which the Administrator has access under this section, if made public would divulge methods or processes entitled to protection as trade secrets of such person, the Administrator shall consider such record, report, or information, or particular portion thereof confidential in accordance with the purposes of section 1905 of title 18 of the United States Code, except that such record, report, or information may be disclosed to other officers, employees, or authorized representatives of the United States concerned with carrying out this Act or when relevant in any proceeding under this Act.

(c) Each State may develop and submit to the Administrator procedures under State law for inspection, monitoring, and entry with respect to point sources located in such State. If the Administrator finds that the procedures and the law of any State relating to inspection, monitoring, and entry are applicable to at least the same extent as those required by this section, such State is authorized to apply and enforce its procedures for inspection, monitoring, and entry with respect to point sources located in such State (except with respect to point sources owned or operated by the United States).

FEDERAL ENFORCEMENT

SEC. 309. (a)(1) Whenever, on the basis of any information available to him, the Administrator finds that any person is in violation of any condition or limitation which implements section 301, 302, 306,

307, 308, 318, or 405 of this Act in a permit issued by a State under an approved permit program under section 402 or 404 of this Act, he shall proceed under his authority in paragraph (3) of this subsection or he shall notify the person in alleged violation and such State or such finding. If beyond the thirtieth day after the Administrator's notification the State has not commenced appropriate enforcement action, the Administrator shall issue an order requiring such person to comply with such condition or limitation or shall bring a civil action in accordance with subsection (b) of this section.

(2) Whenever, on the the basis of information available to him, the Administrator finds that violations of permit conditions or limitations as set forth in paragraph (1) of this subsection are so widespread that such violations appear to result from a failure of the State to enforce such permit conditions or limitations effectively, he shall so notify the State. If the Administrator finds such failure extends beyond the thirtieth day after such notice, he shall give public notice of such finding. During the period beginning with such public notice and lending when such State satisfies the Administrator that it will enforce such conditions and limitations (hereafter referred to in this section as the period of "federally assumed enforcement"), except where an extension has been granted under paragraph (5)(B) of this subsection, the Administrator shall enforce any permit condition or limitation with respect to any person—

(A) by issuing an order to comply with such condition or limitation, or

(B) by bringing a civil action under subsection (b) of this section.

(3) Whenever on the basis of any information available to him the Administrator finds that any person is in violation of section 301, 302, 306, 307, 308, 318, or 405 of this Act, or is in violation of any permit condition or limitation implementing any of such sections in a permit issued under section 402 of this Act by him or by a State or in a permit issued under section 404 of this Act by a State, he shall issue an order requiring such person to comply with such section or requirement, or he shall bring a civil action in accordance with subsection (b) of this section.

(4) A copy of any order issued under this subsection shall be sent immediately by the Administrator to the State in which the violation occurs and other affected States. In any case in which an order under this subsection (or notice to a violator under paragraph (1) of this subsection) is issued to a corporation, a copy of such order (or notice) shall be served on any appropriate corporate officers. An order issued under this subsection relating to a violation of section 308 of this Act shall not take effect until the person to whom it is issued has had an opportunity to confer with the Administrator concerning the alleged violation.

(5)(A) Any order issued under this subsection shall be by personal service, shall state with reasonable specificity the nature of the violation, and shall specify a time for compliance not to exceed thirty days in the case of a violation of an interim compliance schedule or operation and maintenance requirement and not to exceed a time the Administrator determines to be reasonable in the case of a violation of a final deadline, taking into account the seriousness of the violation and any good faith efforts to comply with applicable requirements.

(B) The Administrator may, if he determines (i) that any person who is a violator of, or any person who is otherwise not in compliance with, the time requirements under this Act or in any permit issued under this Act, has acted in good faith, and has made a commitment (in the form of contracts or other securities) of necessary resources to achieve compliance by the earliest possible date after July 1, 1977, but not later than April 1, 1979; (ii) that any extension under this provision will not result in the imposition of any additional controls on any other point or nonpoint source; (iii) that an application for a permit under section 402 of this Act was filed for such person prior to December 31, 1974; and (iv) that the facilities necessary for compliance with such requirements are under construction, grant an extension of the date referred to in section 301(b)(1)(A) to a date which will achieve compliance at the earliest time possible but not later than April 1, 1979.

(6) Whenever, on the basis of information available to him, the Administrator finds (A) that any person is in violation of section 301(b)(1) (A) or (C) of this Act, (B) that such person cannot meet the requirements for a time extension under section 301(i)(2) of this Act, and (C) that the most expeditious and appropriate means of compliance with this Act by such person is to discharge into a publicly owned treatment works, then, upon request of such person, the Administrator may issue an order requiring such person to comply with this Act at the earliest date practicable, but not later than July 1, 1983, by discharging into a publicly owned treatment works if such works concur with such order. Such order shall include a schedule of compliance.

(b) The Administrator is authorized to commence a civil action for appropriate relief, including a permanent or temporary injunction, for any violation for which he is authorized to issue a compliance order under subsection(a) of this section. Any action under this subsection may be brought in the district court of the United States for the district in which the defendant is located or resides or is doing business, and such court shall have jurisdiction to restrain such violation and to require compliance. Notice of the commencement of such action shall be given immediately to the appropriate State.

(c)(1) Any person who willfully or negligently violates section 301, 302, 306, 307, or 308 of this Act, or any permit condition or limitation implementing any of such actions in a permit issued under section 402 of this Act by the Administrator or by a State, or in a permit issued under section 404 of this Act by a State shall be published by a fine of not less than $2,500 nor more than $25,000 per day of violation, or by imprisonment for not more than one year, or by both. If the conviction is for a violation committed after a first conviction of such person under this paragraph, punishment shall be by a fine of not more than $50,000 per day of violation, or by imprisonment for not more than two years, or by both.

(2) Any person who knowingly makes any false statement, representation, or certification in any application, record, report, plan, or other document filed or required to be maintained under this Act or who falsifies, tampers with, or knowingly renders inaccurate any monitoring device or method required to be maintained under this Act, shall upon conviction, be punished by a fine of not more than $10,000, or by imprisonment for not more than six months, or by both.

(3) For the purposes of this subsection, the term "person" shall mean, in addition to the definition contained in section 502(5) of this Act, any responsbile corporate officer.

(d) Any person who violates section 301, 302, 306, 307, 308, 318 or 405 of this Act, or any permit condition or limitation implementing any of such sections in a permit issued under section 402 of this Act by the Administrator, or by a State, or in a permit issued under section 404 of this Act by a State and any person who violates any order issued by the Administrator under subsection (a) of this section, shall be subject to a civil penalty, not to exceed $10,000 per day of such violation.

(e) Whenever a municipality is a party to a civil action brought by the United States under this section, the State in which such municipality is located shall be joined as a party. Such State shall be liable for payment of any judgment, or any expenses incurred as a result of complying with any judgment, entered against the municipality in such action to the extent that the laws of that State prevent the municipality from raising revenues needed to comply with such judgment.

(f) Whenever, on the basis of any information available to him, the Administrator finds that an owner or operator of any source is introducing a pollutant into a treatment works in violation of subsection (d) of section 307, the Administrator may notify the owner or operator of such treatment works and the State of such violation. If the owner or operator of the treatment works does not commence appropriate enforcement action within 30 days of the date of such notification, the Administrator may commence a civil action for appropriate relief, including but not limited to, a permanent or temporary injunction, against the owner or operator of such treatment works. In any such civil action the Administrator shall join the owner or operator of such source as a party to the action. Such action shall be brought in the district court of the United States in the district in which the treatment works is located. Such court shall have jurisdiction to restrain such violation and to require the owner or operator of the treatment works and the owner or operator of the source to take such action as may be necessary to come into compliance with this Act. Notice of commencement of any such action shall be given the State. Nothing in this subsection shall be construed to limit or prohibit any other authority the Administrator may have under this Act.

INTERNATIONAL POLLUTION ABATEMENT

SEC. 310. (a) Whenever the Administrator, upon receipts of reports, surveys, or studies from any duly constituted international agency, has reason to believe that pollution is occurring which endangers the health or welfare of persons in a foreign country, and the Secretary of State requests him to abate such pollution, he shall give formal notification thereof to the State water pollution control agency of the State or States in which such discharge or discharges originate and to the appropriate interstate agency, if any. He shall also promptly call such a hearing, if he believes that such pollution is occurring in sufficient quantity to warrant such action, and if such foreign country has given the United States essentially the same rights with respect to the prevention and control of pollution occurring in that country as is given that country by this subsection. The Administrator, through the Secretary of State, shall invite the foreign country which may be adversely affected by the pollution to attend and participate in the hearing, and the representative of such country shall, for the purpose of the hearing and any further proceeding resulting from such hearing, have all the rights of a State water pollution control agency. Nothing in this subsection shall be construed to modify, amend, repeal, or otherwise affect the provisions of the 1909 Boundary Waters Treaty between Canada and the United States or the Water Utilization Treaty of 1944 between Mexico and the United States (59 Stat. 1219), relative to the control and abatement of pollution in waters covered by those treaties.

(b) The calling of a hearing under this section shall not be construed by the courts, the Administrator, or any person as limiting, modifying, or otherwise affecting the functions and responsibilities of the Administrator under this section to establish and enforce water quality requirements under this Act.

(c) The Administrator shall publish in the Federal Register a notice of a public hearing before a hearing board of five or more persons appointed by the Administrator. A majority of the members of the board and the chairman who shall be designated by the Administrator shall not be officers or employees of Federal, State, or local governments. On the basis of the evidence presented at such hearing, the board shall within sixty days after completion of the hearing make findings of fact as to whether or not such pollution is occurring and shall thereupon by decision, incorporating its findings therein, make such recommendations to abate the pollution as may be appropriate and shall transmit such decision and the record of the hearings to the Administrator. All such decisions shall be public. Upon receipt of such decision. the Administrator shall promptly implement the board's decision in accordance with the provisions of this Act.

(d) In connection with any hearing called under this subsection, the board is authorized to require any person whose alleged activities result in discharges causing or contributing to pollution to file with it in such forms as it may prescribe, a report based on existing data, furnishing such information as may reasonably be required as to the character, kind, and quantity of such discharges and the use of facilities or other means to prevent or reduce such discharges by the person filing such a report. Such report shall be made under oath or otherwise, as the board may prescribe, and shall be filed with the board within such reasonable period as it may prescribe, unless additional time is granted by it. Upon a showing satisfactory to the board by the person filing such report that such report or portion thereof (other than effluent data), to which the Administrator has access under this section, if made public would divulge trade secrets or secret processes of such person, the board shall consider such report or portion thereof confidential for the purposes of section 1905 of title 18 of the United States Code. If any person required to file any report under this paragraph shall fail to do so within the time fixed by the board for filing the same, and such failure shall continue for thirty days after notice of such default, such person shall forfeit to the United States the sum of $1,000 for each and every day of the continuance of such failure, which forfeiture shall be payable into the Treasury of the United

States, and shall be recoverable in a civil suit in the name of the United States in the district court of the United States where such person has his principal office or in any district in which he does business. The Administrator may upon application therefor remit or mitigate any forfeiture provided for under this subsection.

(e) Board members, other than officers or employees of Federal, State, or local governments, shall be for each day (including traveltime) during which they are performing board business, entitled to receive compensation at a rate fixed by the Administrator but not in excess of the maximum rate of pay for grade GS–18, as provided in the General Schedule under section 5332 of title 5 of the United States Code, and shall, notwithstanding the limitations of sections 5703 and 5704 of title 5 of the United States Code, be fully reimbursed for travel, subsistence, and related expenses.

(f) When any such recommendation adopted by the Administrator involves the institution of enforcement proceedings against any person to obtain the abatement of pollution subject to such recommendation, the Administrator shall institute such proceedings if he believes that the evidence warrants such proceedings. The district court of the United States shall consider and determine de novo all relevant issues, but shall receive in evidence the record of the proceedings before the conference or hearing board. The court shall have jurisdiction to enter such judgment and orders enforcing such judgment as it deems appropriate or to remand such proceedings to the Administrator for such further action as it may direct.

OIL AND HAZARDOUS SUBSTANCE LIABILITY

SEC. 311. (a) For the purpose of this section, the term—

(1) "oil" means oil of any kind or in any form, including, but not limited to, petroleum, fuel oil, sludge, oil refuse, and oil mixed with wastes other than dredged spoil;

(2) "discharge" includes, but is not limited to, any spilling, leaking, pumping, pouring, emitting, emptying or dumping, but excludes (A) discharges in compliance with a permit under section 402 of this Act, (B) discharges resulting from circumstances identified and reviewed and made a part of the public record with respect to a permit issued or modified under section 402 of this Act, and subject to a condition in such permit, and (C) continuous or anticipated intermittent discharges from a point source, identified in a permit or permit application under section 402 of this Act, which are caused by events occurring within the scope or revelant operating or treatment systems.

(3) "vessel" means every description of watercraft or other artificial contrivance used, or capable of being used, as a means of transportation on water other than a public vessel;

(4) "public vessel" means a vessel owned or bareboat-chartered and operated by the United States, or by a State or political subdivision thereof, or by a foreign nation, except when such vessel is engaged in commerce;

(5) "United States" means the States, the District of Columbia, the Commonwealth of Puerto Rico, the Canal Zone, Guam, American Samoa, the Virgin Islands, and the Trust Territory of the Pacific Islands;

(6) "owner or operator" means (A) in the case of a vessel, any person owning, operating, or chartering by demise, such vessel, and (B) in the case of an onshore facility, and an offshore facility, any person owning or operating such onshore facility or offshore facility, and (C) in the case of any abandoned offshore facility, the person who owned or operated such facility immediately prior to such abandonment:

(7) "person" includes an individual, firm, corporation, association, and a partnership;

(8) "remove" or "removal" refers to removal of the oil or hazardous substances from the water and shorelines or the taking of such other actions as may be necessary to minimize or mitigate damage to the public health or welfare, including, but not limited to, fish, shellfish, wildlife, and public and private property, shorelines, and beaches;

(9) "contiguous zone" means the entire zone established or to be established by the United States under article 24 of the Convention on the Territorial Sea and the Contiguous Zone;

(10) "onshore facility" means any facility (including, but not limited to, motor vehicles and rolling stock) of any kind located in, on, or under, any land within the United States other than submerged land;

(11) "offshore facility" means any facility of any kind located in, on, or under, any of the navigable waters of the United States, and any facility of any kind which is subject to the jurisdiction of the United States and is located in, on, or under any other waters, other than a vessel or a public vessel;

(12) "act of God" means an act occasioned by an unanticipated grave natural disaster;

(13) "barrel" means 42 United States gallons at 60 degrees Fahrenheit;

(14) "hazardous substance" means any substance designated pursuant to subsection (b)(2) of this section;

(15) "inland oil barge" means a non-self-propelled vessel carrying oil in bulk as cargo and certificated to operate only in the inland waters of the United States, while operating in such waters;

(16) "inland waters of the United States" means those waters of the United States lying inside the baseline from which the territorial sea is measured and those waters outside such baseline which are a part of the Gulf Intracoastal Waterway;

(17) "Otherwise subject to the jurisdiction of the United States" means subject to the jurisdiction of the United States by virtue of United States citizenship, United States vessel documentation or numbering, or as provided for by international agreement to which the United States is a party.

(b)(1) The Congress hereby declares that it is the policy of the United States that there should be no discharges of oil or hazardous substances into or upon the navigable waters of the United States, adjoining shorelines, or into or upon the waters of the contiguous zone; or in connection with activities under the Outer Continental Shelf Lands Act or the Deepwater Port Act of 1977, or which may affect natural resources belonging to, appertaining to, or under the exclusive management authority of the United States (including resources under the Fishery Conservation and Management Act of 1976.

(2)(A) The Administrator shall develop, promulgate, and revises a may be appropriate, regulations designating as hazardous substances, other than oil as defined in this section, such elements and compounds which, when discharged in any quantity into or upon the navigable waters of the United States or adjoining shorelines or the waters of the contiguous zone or in connection with activities under the Outer Continental Shelf Lands Act or the Deepwater Port Act of 1974, or which may affect natural resources belonging to, appertaining to, or under the exclusive management authority of the United States (including resources under the Fishery Conservation and Management Act of 1976), present an imminent and substantial danger to the public health or welfare, including, but not limited to, fish, shellfish, wildlife, shorelines, and beaches.

(B) The Administrator shall within 18 months after the date of enactment of this paragraph, conduct a study and report to the Congress on methods, mechanisms, and procedures to create incentives to achieve a higher standard of care in all aspects of the management and movement of hazardous substances on the part of owners, operators, or persons in charge of onshore facilities, offshore facilities, or vessels. The Administrator shall include in such study (1) limits of liability, (2) liability for third party damages, (3) penalties and fees, (4) spill prevention plans, (5) current practices in the insurance and banking industries, and (6) whether the penalty enacted in subclause (bb) of clause (iii) of subparagraph (B) of subsection (b)(2) of section 311 of Public Law 92–500 should be enacted.

[311 (b)(2)(B) was revised by PL 95-576. Subclause (bb) (PL 92-500) reads as follows:

"(bb) a penalty determined by the number of units discharged multiplied by the amount established for such unit under clause (iv) of this subparagraph, but such penalty shall not be more than $5,000,000 in the case of a discharge from a vessel and $500,000 in the case of a discharge from an onshore or offshore facility."]

(3) The discharge of oil or hazardous substances (i) into or upon the navigable waters of the United States, adjoining shorelines, or into or upon the waters of the contiguous zone, or (ii) in connection with activities under the Outer Continental Shelf Lands Act or the Deepwater Port Act of 1974, or which may affect natural resources belonging to, appertaining to, or under the exclusive management authority of the United States (including resources under the Fishery Conservation and Management Act of 1976), in such quantities as may be harmful as determined by the President under paragraph (4) of this subsection, is prohibited, except (A) in the case of such discharges of oil into the waters of the contiguous zone or which may affect natural resources belonging to, appertaining to, or under the exclusive management authority of the United States (including resources under the Fishery Conservation and Management Act of 1976), where permitted under the Protocol of 1978 Relating to the International Convention for the Pre-

vention of Pollution from Ships, 1973 and (B) where permitted in quantities and at times and locations or under such circumstances or conditions as the President may, by regulation, determine not to be harmful. Any regulations issued under this subsection shall be consistent with maritime safety and with marine and navigation laws and regulations and applicable water quality standards.

(4) The President shall by regulation determine for the purposes of this section those quantities of oil and any hazardous substances the discharge of which may be harmful to the public health or welfare of the United States, including but not limited to fish, shellfish, wildlife, and public and private property, shorelines, and beaches.

(5) Any person in charge of a vessel or of an onshore facility or an offshore facility shall, as soon as he has knowledge of any discharge of oil or a hazardous substance from such vessel or facility in violation of paragraph (3) of this subsection, immediately notify the appropriate agency of the United States Government of such discharge. Any such person (A) in charge of a vessel from which oil or a hazardous substance is discharged in violation of paragraph (3)(i) of this subsection, or (B) in charge of a vessel from which oil or a hazardous substance is discharged in violation of paragraph (3)(ii) of this subsection and who is otherwise subject to the jurisdiction of the United States at the time of the discharge, or (C) in charge of an onshore facility or an offshore facility, who fails to notify immediately such agency of such discharge shall, upon conviction, be fined not more than $10,000, or imprisoned for not more than one year, or both. Notification received pursuant to this paragraph or information obtained by the exploitation of such notification shall not be used against any such person in any criminal case, except a prosecution for perjury or for giving a false statement.

(6)(A) Any owner, operator, or person in charge of any onshore facility or offshore facility from which oil or a hazardous substance is discharged in violation of paragraph (3) of this subsection shall be assessed a civil penalty by the Secretary of the department in which the Coast Guard is operating of not more than $5,000 for each offense. Any owner, operator, or person in charge of any vessel from which oil or a hazardous substance is discharged in violation of paragraph (3)(i) of this subsection, and any owner, operator, or person in charge of a vessel from which oil or a hazardous substance is discharged in violation of paragraph (3)(ii) who is otherwise subject to the jurisdiction of the United States at the time of discharge, shall be assessed a civil penalty by the Secretary of the department in which the Coast Guard is operating of not more than $5,000 for each offense. No penalty shall be assessed unless the owner or operator charged shall have been given notice and opportunity for a hearing on such charge. Each violation is a separate offense. Any such civil penalty may be compromised by such Secretary. In determining the amount of the penalty, or the amount agreed upon in compromise, the appropriateness of such penalty to the size of the business of the owner or operator charged, the effect on the owner or operator's ability to continue in business, and the gravity of the violation, shall be considered by such Secretary. The Secretary of the Treasury shall withhold at the request of such Secretary the clearance required by section 4197 of the Revised Statutes of the United States, as amended (46 U.S.C. 91), of any vessel the owner or operator of which is subject to the foregoing penalty. Clearance may be granted in such cases upon the filing of a bond or other surety satisfactory to such Secretary.

(B) The Administrator, taking into account the gravity of the offense, and the standard of care manifested by the owner, operator, or person in charge, may commence a civil action against any such person subject to the penalty under subparagraph (A) of this paragraph to impose a penalty based on consideration of the size of the business of the owner or operator, the effect on the ability of the owner or operator to continue in business, the gravity of the violation, and the nature, extent, and degree of success of any efforts made by the owner, operator, or person in charge to minimize or mitigate the effects of such discharge. The amount of such penalty shall not exceed $50,000, except that where the United States can show that such discharge was the result of willful negligence or willful misconduct within the privity and knowledge of the owner, operator, or person in charge, such penalty shall not exceed $250,000. Each violation is a separate offense. Any action under this subparagraph may be brought in the district court of the United States for the district in which the defendant is located or resides or is doing business, and such court shall have jurisdiction to assess such penalty. No action may be commenced under this clause where a penalty has been assessed under clause (A) of this paragraph.

(C) In addition to establishing a penalty for the discharge of a hazardous substance, the Administrator may act to mitigate the damage to the public health or welfare caused by such discharge. The cost of such mitigation shall be deemed a cost incurred under subsection (c) of this section for the removal of such substance by the United States Government.

(D) Any costs of removal incurred in connection with a discharge excluded by subsection (a)(2)(C) of this section shall be recoverable from the owner or operator of the source of the discharge in an action brought under section 309(b) of this Act.

(E) Civil penalties shall not be assessed under both this section and section 309 for the same discharge.

(c)(1) Whenever any oil or a hazardous substance is discharged, or there is a substantial threat of such discharge, into or upon the navigable waters of the United States, adjoining shorelines, or into or upon the waters of the contiguous zone, or in connection with activities under the Outer Continental Shelf Lands Act or the Deepwater Port Act of 1974, or which may affect natural resources belonging to, appertaining to, or under the exclusive management authority of the United States (including resources under the Fishery Conservation and Management Act of 1976) the President is authorized to act to remove or arrange for the removal of such oil or substance at any time, unless he determines such removal will be done properly by the owner or operator of the vessel, onshore facility, or offshore facility, from which the discharge occurs.

(2) Within sixty days after the effective date of this section, the President shall prepare and publish a National Contingency Plan for removal of oil and hazardous substances, pursuant to this subsection. Such National Contingency Plan shall provide for efficient, coordinated, and effective action to minimize damage from oil and hazardous substance discharges, including containment, dispersal, and removal of oil and hazardous substances, and shall include, but not be limited to—

(A) assignment of duties and responsibilities among Federal departments and agencies in coordination with State and local agencies, including, but not limited to, water pollution control, conservation, and port authorities;

(B) identification, procurement, maintenance, and storage of equipment and supplies;

(C) establishment or designation of a strike force consisting of personnel who shall be trained, prepared, and available to provide necessary services to carry out the Plan, including the establishment at major ports, to be determined by the President, of emergency task forces of trained personnel, adequate oil and hazardous substance pollution control equipment and material, and a detailed oil and hazardous substance pollution prevention and removal plan;

(D) a system of surveillance and notice designed to insure earliest possible notice of discharges of oil and hazardous substances and imminent threats of such discharges to the appropriate State and Federal agencies;

(E) establishment of a national center to provide coordination and direction for operations in carrying out the Plan;

(F) procedures and techniques to be employed in identifying, containing, dispersing, and removing oil and hazardous substances;

(G) a schedule, prepared in cooperation with the States, identifying (i) dispersants and other chemicals, if any, that may be used in carrying out the Plan, (ii) the waters in which such dispersants and chemicals may be used, and (iii) the quantities of such dispersant or chemical which can be used safely in such waters, which schedule shall provide in the case of any dispersant, chemical, or waters not specifically identified in such schedule that the President, or his delegate, may, on a case-by-case basis, identify the dispersants and other chemicals which may be used, the waters in which they may be used, and the quantities which can be used safely in such waters; and

(H) a system whereby the State or States affected by a discharge of oil or hazardous substance may act where necessary to remove such discharge and such State or States may be reimbursed from the fund established under subsection (k) of this section for the reasonable costs incurred in such removal.

The President may, from time to time, as he deems advisable revise or otherwise amend the National Contingency Plan. After publication of the National Contingency Plan, the removal of oil and hazardous substances and actions to minimize damage from oil and hazardous substance discharges shall, to the greatest extent possible, be in accordance with the National Contingency Plan.

(d) Whenever a marine disaster in or upon the navigable waters of the United States has created a substantial threat of a pollution hazard to the public health or welfare of the United States, including, but not limited to, fish, shellfish, wildlife and the public and private shorelines and beaches of the United States, because of a discharge, or an imminent discharge, of large quantities of oil, or of a hazardous substance from a vessel the United States may (A) coordinate and direct all public and private efforts directed at the removal or elimination of such threat; and (B) summarily remove, and, if necessary, destroy such vessel by whatever means are available without regard to any provisions of law governing the employment of personnel or the expenditure of appropriated funds. Any expense incurred under this subsection or under the Intervention on the High Seas Act (or the convention defined in section 2(3) thereof) shall be a cost incurred by the United States Government for the purposes of subsection (f) in the removal of oil or hazardous substance.

(e) In addition to any other action taken by a State or local government, when the President determines there is an imminent and substantial threat to the public health or welfare of the United States, including, but not limited to, fish, shellfish, and wildlife and public and, private property shorelines, and beaches within the United States, because of an actual or threatened discharge of oil or hazardous substance into or upon the navigable waters of the United States from an onshore or offshore facility, the President may require the United States attorney of the district in which the threat occurs to secure such relief as may be necessary to abate such threat, and the district courts of the United States shall have jurisdiction to grant such relief as the public interest and the equities of the case may require.

(f)(1) Except where an owner or operator can prove that a discharge was caused solely by (A) an act of God, (B) an act of war, (C) negligence on the part of the United States Government, or (D) an act or omission of a third party without regard to whether any such act or omission was or was not negligent, or any combination of the foregoing clauses, such owner or operator of any vessel from which oil or a hazardous substance is discharged in violation of subsection (b)(3) of this section shall, notwithstanding any other provision of law, be liable to the United States Government for the actual costs incurred under subsection (c) for the removal of such oil or substance by the United States Government in an amount not to exceed in the case of an inland oil barge $125 per gross ton of such barge, or $125,000, whichever is greater, and in the case of any other vessel, $150 per gross ton of such vessel (or, for a vessel carrying oil or hazardous substances as cargo, $250,000), whichever is greater, except that where the United States can show that such discharge was the result of willful negligence or willful misconduct within the privity and knowledge of the owner, such owner or operator shall be liable to the United States Government for the full amount of such cost. Such costs shall constitute a maritime lien on such vessel which may be recovered in an action in rem in the district court of the United

States for any district within which any vessel may be found. The United States may also bring an action against the owner or operator of such vessel in any court of competent jurisdiction to recover such costs.

[Sec. 58(d)(2) of the Clean Water Act of 1977 increased liability under Subsection 311(f)(1) of the Act. Sec. 58(j) of the 1977 Act provides:

"(j) No vessel subject to the increased amounts which result from the amendments made by subsections (d)(2), (d)(3), and (d)(4) of this section shall be required to establish any evidence of financial responsibility under section 311(p) of the Federal Water Pollution Control Act for such increased amounts before October 1, 1978."]

(2) Except where an owner or operator of an onshore facility can prove that a discharge was caused solely by (A) an act of God, (B) an act of war, (C) negligence on the part of the United States Government, or (D) an act or omission of a third party without regard to whether any such act or omission was or was not negligent, or any combination of the foregoing clauses, such owner or operator of any such facility from which oil or a hazardous substance is discharged in violation of subsection (b)(3) of this section shall be liable to the United States Government for the actual costs incurred under subsection (c) for the removal of such oil or substance by the United States Government in an amount not to exceed $50,000,000 except that where the United States can show that such discharge was the result of willful negligence or willful misconduct within the privity and knowledge of the owner, such owner or operator shall be liable to the United States Government for the full amount of such costs. The United States may bring an action against the owner or operator of such facility in any court of competent jurisdiction to recover such costs. The Administrator is authorized, by regulation, after consultation with the Secretary of Commerce and the Small Business Administration, to establish reasonable and equitable classifications of those onshore facilities having a total fixed storage capacity of 1,000 barrels or less which he determines because of size, type, and location do not present a substantial risk of the discharge of oil or a hazardous substance in violation of subsection (b)(3) of this section, and apply with respect to such classifications differing limits of liability which may be less than the amount contained in this paragraph.

(3) Except where an owner or operator of an offshore facility can prove that a discharge was caused solely by (A) an act of God, (B) an act of war, (C) negligence on the part of the United States Government, or (D) an act or omission of a third party without regard to whether any such act or omission was or was not negligent, or any combination of the foregoing clauses, such owner or operator of any such facility from which oil or a hazardous substance is discharged in violation of subsection (b)(3) of this section shall, notwithstanding any other provision of law, be liable to the United States Government for the actual costs incurred under subsection (c) for the removal of such oil or substance by the United States Government in an amount not to exceed $50,000,000, except that where the United States can show that such discharge was the result of willful negligence or willful misconduct within the privity and knowledge of the owner, such owner or operator shall be liable to the United States Government for the full amount of such costs. The United States may bring an action against the owner or operator of such a facility in any court of competent jurisdiction to recover such costs.

[Liability of $50,000 in Section 311(f)(2) and Section 311(f)(3) was established by the Clean Water Act of 1977. Under Sec. 58(h) of the 1977 Act, liability is to be $8,000,000 until June 1978.]

(4) The costs of removal of oil or a hazardous substance for which the owner or operator of a vessel or onshore or offshore facility is liable under subsection (f) of this section shall include any costs or expenses incurred by the Federal Government or any State government in the restoration or replacement of natural resources damaged or destroyed as a result of a discharge of oil or a hazardous substance in violation of subsection (b) of this section.

(5) The President, or the authorized representative of any State, shall act on behalf of the public as trustee of the natural resources to recover for the costs of replacing or restoring such resources. Sums recovered shall be used to restore, rehabilitate, or acquire the equivalent of such natural resources by the appropriate agencies of the Federal Government, or the State government.

(g) Where the owner or operator of a vessel (other than an inland oil barge) carrying oil or hazardous substances as cargo or an onshore or offshore facility which handles or stores oil or hazardous substances in bulk, from which oil or a hazardous substance is discharged in violation of subsection (b) of this section, alleges that such discharge was caused solely by an act or omission of a third party, such owner or operator shall pay to the United States Government the actual costs incurred under subsection (c) for removal of such oil or substance and shall be entitled by subrogation to all rights of the United States Government to recover such costs from such third party under this subsection. In any case where an owner or operator of a vessel, of an onshore facility, or of an offshore facility, from which oil or a hazardous substance is discharged in violation of subsection (b)(3) of this section, proves that such discharge of oil or hazardous substance was caused solely by an act or omission of a third party, or was caused solely by such an act or omission in combination with an act of God, an act of war, or negligence on the part of the United States Government, such third party shall, notwithstanding any other provision of law, be liable to the United States Government for the actual costs incurred under subsection (c) for removal of such oil or substance by the United States Government, except where such third party can prove that such discharge was caused solely by (A) an act of God, (B) an act of war, (C) negligence on the part of the United States Government, or (D) an act or omission of another party without regard to whether such act or omission was or was not negligent, or any combination of the foregoing clauses. If such third party was the owner or operator of a vessel which caused the discharge of oil or a hazardous substance in violation of subsection (b)(3) of this section, the liability of such third party under this subsection shall not exceed, in the case of an inland oil barge $125 per gross ton of such barge, $125,000, whichever is greater, and in the case of any other vessel, $150 per gross ton of such vessel (or, for a vessel carrying oil or hazardous substances as cargo, $250,000), whichever is greater. In any other case the liability of such third party shall not exceed the limitation which would have been applicable to the owner or operator of the vessel or the onshore or offshore facility from which the discharge actually occurred if such owner or operator were liable. If the United States can show that the discharge of oil or a hazardous substance in violation of subsection (b)(3) of this section was the result of willful negligence or willful misconduct within the privity and knowledge of such third party, such third party shall be liable to the United States Government for the full amount of such removal costs. The United States may bring an action against the third party in any court of competent jurisdiction to recover such removal costs.

(h) The liabilities established by this section shall in no way affect any rights which (1) the owner or operator of a vessel or of an onshore facility or an offshore facility may have against any third party whose acts may in any way have caused or contributed to such discharge, or (2) the United States Government may have against any third party whose actions may in any way have caused or contributed to the discharge of oil or hazardous substance.

(i)(1) In any case where an owner or operator of a vessel or an onshore facility or an offshore facility from which oil or a hazardous substance is discharged in violation of subsection (b)(3) of this section acts to remove such oil or substance in accordance with regulations promulgated pursuant to this section, such owner or operator shall be entitled to recover the reasonable costs incurred in such removal upon establishing, in a suit which may be brought against the United States Government in the United States Claims Court,* that such discharge was caused solely by (A) an act of God, (B) an act of war, (C) negligence on the part of the United States Government, or (D) an act or omission of a third party without regard to whether such act or omission was or was not negligent, or of any combination of the foregoing clauses.

(2) The provisions of this subsection shall not apply in any case where liability is established pursuant to the Outer Continental Shelf Lands Act, or the Deepwater Port Act of 1974.

(3) Any amount paid in accordance with a judgment of the United States Claims Court* pursuant to this section shall be paid from the funds established pursuant to subsection (k).

(j)(1) Consistent with the National Contingency Plan required by subsection (c)(2) of this section, as soon as practicable after the effective date of this section, and from time to time thereafter, the President shall issue regulations consistent with maritime safety and with marine and navigation laws (A) establishing methods and procedures for removal of discharged oil and hazardous substances, (B) establishing criteria for the development and implementation of local and regional oil and hazardous substance removal contingency plans, (C) establishing procedures, methods, and equipment and other requirements for equipment to prevent discharges of oil and hazardous substances from vessels and from onshore facilities and offshore facilities, and to contain such discharges, and (D) governing the inspection of vessels carrying cargoes of oil and hazardous substances and the inspection of such cargoes in order to reduce the likelihood of discharges of oil from vessels in violation of this section.

(2) Any owner or operator of a vessel or an onshore facility or an offshore facility and any other person subject to any regulation issued under paragraph (1) of this subsection who fails or refuses to comply with the provisions of any such regulations, shall be liable to a civil penalty of not more than $5,000 for each such violation. This para-

---

*Amended by PL 97-164, April 2, 1982.

graph shall not apply to any owner or operator of any vessel from which oil or a hazardous substance is discharged in violation of paragraph (3)(ii) of subsection (b) unless such owner, operator, or person in charge is otherwise subject to the jurisdiction of the United States. Each violation shall be a separate offense. The President may assess and compromise such penalty. No penalty shall be assessed until the owner, operator, or other person charged shall have been given notice and an opportunity for a hearing on such charge. In determining the amount of the penalty, or the amount agreed upon in compromise, the gravity of the violation, and the demonstrated good faith of the owner, operator, or other person charged in attempting to achieve rapid compliance after notification of a violation, shall be considered by the President.

(k) (1) There is hereby authorized to be appropriated to a revolving fund to be established in the Treasury such sums as may be necessary to maintain such fund at a level of $35,000,000 to carry out the provisions of subsections (c), (d), (i), and (l) of this section. Any other funds received by the United States under this section shall also be deposited in said fund for such purposes. All sums appropriated to or deposited in, said fund shall remain available until expended.

(2) The Secretary of Transportation shall notify the Congress whenever the unobligated balance of the fund is less than $12,000,000, and shall include in such notification a recommendation for a supplemental appropriation relating to the sums that are needed to maintain the fund at the level provided in paragraph (1).

[Section 304(b) and (c) of the Comprehensive Environmental Response, Compensation and Liability Act of 1980 (PL 96-510) provides:

"(b) One-half of the unobligated balance remaining before the date of the enactment of this Act under subsection (k) of section 311 of the Federal Water Pollution Control Act and all sums appropriated under section 504(b) of the Federal Water Pollution Control Act shall be transferred to the Fund established under title II of this Act.

(c) In any case in which any provision of section 311 of the Federal Water Pollution Control Act is determined to be in conflict with any provisions of this Act, the provisions of this Act shall apply."]

(l) The President is authorized to delegate the administration of this section to the heads of those Federal departments, agencies, and instrumentalities which he determines to be appropriate. Any moneys in the fund established by subsection (k) of this section shall be available to such Federal departments, agencies, and instrumentalities to carry out the provisions of subsections (c) and (i) of this section. Each such department, agency, and instrumentality, in order to avoid duplication of effort, shall, whenever appropriate, utilize the personnel, services, and facilities of other Federal departments, agencies, and instrumentalities.

(m) Anyone authorized by the President to enforce the provisions of this section may, except as to public vessels, (A) board and inspect any vessel upon the navigable waters of the United States or the waters of the contiguous zone, (B) with or without a warrant arrest any person who violates the provisions of this section or any regulation issued thereunder in his presence or view, and (C) execute any warrant or other process issued by an officer or court of competent jurisdiction.

(n) The several district courts of the United States are invested with jurisdiction for any actions, other than actions pursuant to subsection (i)(1), arising under this section. In the case of Guam and the Trust Territory of the Pacific Islands, such actions may be brought

in the district court of Guam, and in the case of the Virgin Islands such actions may be brought in the district court of the Virgin Islands. In the case of American Samoa and the Trust Territory of the Pacific Islands, such actions may be brought in the District Court of the United States for the District of Hawaii and such court shall have jurisdiction of such actions. In the case of the Canal Zone, such actions may be brought in the United States District Court for the District of the Canal Zone.

(o)(1) Nothing in this section shall affect or modify in any way the obligations of any owner or operator of any vessel, or of any owner or operator of any onshore facility or offshore facility to any person or agency under any provision of law for damages to any publicly owned or privately owned property resulting from a discharge of any oil or hazardous substance or from the removal of any such oil or hazardous substance.

(2) Nothing in this section shall be construed as preempting any State or political subdivision thereof from imposing any requirement or liability with respect to the discharge of oil or hazardous substance into any waters within such State.

(3) Nothing in this section shall be construed as affecting or modifying any other existing authority of any Federal department, agency, or instrumentality, relative to onshore or offshore facilities under this Act or any other provision of law, or to affect any State or local law not in conflict with this section.

(p)(1) Any vessel over three hundred gross tons, including any barge of equivalent size, but not including any barge that is not self-propelled and that does not carry oil or hazardous substances as cargo or fuel, using any port or place in the United States or the navigable waters of the United States for any purpose shall establish and maintain under regulations to be prescribed from time to time by the President, evidence of financial responsibility of, in the case of an inland oil barge $125 per gross ton of such barge, or $125,000 whichever is greater, and in the case of any other vessel, $150 per gross ton of such vessel (or, for a vessel carrying oil or hazardous substances as cargo, $250,000), whichever is greater, to meet the liability to the United States which such vessel could be subjected under this section. In cases where an owner or operator owns, operates, or charters more than one such vessel, financial responsibility need only be established to meet the maximum liability to which the largest of such vessels could be subjected. Financial responsibility may be established by any one of, or a combination of, the following methods acceptable to the President: (A) evidence of insurance, (B) surety bonds, (C) qualification as a self-insurer, or (D) other evidence of financial responsibility. Any bond filed shall be issued by a bonding company authorized to do business in the United States.

(2) The provisions of paragraph (1) of this subsection shall be effective April 3, 1971, with respect to oil and one year after the date of enactment of this section with respect to hazardous substances. The President shall delegate the responsibility to carry out the provisions of this subsection to the appropriate agency within sixty days after the date of enactment of this section. Regulations necessary to implement this subsection shall be issued within six months after the date of enactment of this section.

(3) Any claim for costs incurred by such vessel may be brought directly against the insurer or any other person providing evidence of

financial responsibility as required under this subsection. In the case of any action pursuant to this subsection such insurer or other person shall be entitled to invoke all rights and defenses which would have been available to the owner or operator if an action had been brought against him by the claimant, and which would have been available to him if an action had been brought against him by the owner or operator.

(4) Any owner or operator of a vessel subject to this subsection, who fails to comply with the provisions of this subsection or any regulation issued thereunder, shall be subject to a fine or not more than $10,000.

(5) The Secretary of the Treasury may refuse the clearance required by section 4197 of the Revised Statutes of the United States, as amended (4 U.S.C. 91), to any vessel subject to this subsection, which does not have evidence furnished by the President that the financial responsibility provisions of paragraph (1) of this subsection have been complied with.

(6) The Secretary of the Department in which the Coast Guard is operated may (A) deny entry to any port or place in the United States or the navigable waters of the United States, to, and (B) detain at the port or place in the United States from which it is about to depart for any other port or place in the United States, any vessel subject to this subsection, which upon request, does not produce evidence furnished by the President that the financial responsibility provisions of paragraph (1) of this subsection have been complied with.

(q) The President is authorized to establish, with respect to any class or category of onshore or offshore facilities, a maximum limit of liability under subsections (f) (2) and (3) of this section of less than $50,000,000, but not less than $8,000,000.

(r) Nothing in this section shall be construed to impose, or authorize the imposition of any limitation on liability under the Outer Continental Shelf Lands Act or the Deepwater Port Act of 1974.

MARINE SANITATION DEVICES

SEC. 312. (a) For the purpose of this section, the term—

(1) "new vessel" includes every description of watercraft or other artificial contrivance used, or capable of being used, as a means of transportation on the navigable waters, the construction of which is initiated after promulgation of standards and regulations under this section;

(2) "existing vessel" includes every description of watercraft or other artificial contrivance used, or capable of being used, as a means of transportation on the navigable waters, the construction of which is initiated before promulgation of standards and regulations under this section;

(3) "public vessel" means a vessel owned or bareboat chartered and operated by the United States, by a State or political subdivision thereof, or by a foreign nation, except when such vessel is engaged in commerce;

(4) "United States" includes the States, the District of Columbia, the Commonwealth of Puerto Rico, the Virgin Islands, Guam,

American Samoa, the Canal Zone, and the Trust Territory of the Pacific Islands;

(5) "marine sanitation device" includes any equipment for installation on board a vessel which is designed to receive, retain, treat, or discharge sewage, and any process to treat such sewage;

(6) "sewage" means human body wastes and the waste from toilets and other receptacles intended to receive or retain body wastes except that, with respect to commercial vessels on the Great Lakes such term shall include graywater;

(7) "manufacture" means any person engaged in the manufacturing, assembling, or importation or marine sanitation devices or of vessels subject to standards and regulations promulgated under this section;

(8) "person" means an individual, partnership, firm, corporation, or association, but does not include an individual on board a public vessel;

(9) "discharge" includes, but is not limited to, any spilling, leaking, pumping, pouring, emitting, emptying or dumping;

(10) "commercial vessels" means those vessels used in the business of transporting property for compensation or hire, or in transporting property in the business of the owner, lessees, or operator of the vessel;

(11) "graywater" means galley, bath, and shower water.

(b)(1) As soon as possible, after the enactment of this section and subject to the provisions of section 104(j) of this Act, the Administrator, after consultation with the Secretary of the department in which the Coast Guard is operating, after giving appropriate consideration to the economic costs involved, and within the limits of available technology, shall promulgate Federal standards of performance for marine sanitation devices (hereafter in this section referred to as "standards") which shall be designed to prevent the discharge of untreated or inadequately treated sewage into or upon the navigable waters from new vessels and existing vessels, except vessel not equipped with installed toilet facilities. Such standards and standards established under subsection (c)(1)(B) of this section shall be consistent with maritime safety and the marine and navigation laws and regulations and shall be coordinated with the regulations issued under this subsection by the Secretary of the department in which the Coast Guard is operating. The Secretary of the department in which the Coast Guard is operating shall promulgate regulations, which are consistent with standards promulgated under this subsection and subsection (c) of this section and with maritime safety and the marine and navigation laws and regulations governing the design, construction, installation, and operation of any marine sanitation device on board such vessels.

(2) Any existing vessel equipped with a marine sanitation device on the date of promulgation of initial standards and regulations under this section, which device is in compliance with such initial standards and regulations, shall be deemed in compliance with this section until such time as the device is replaced or is found not to be in compliance with such initial standards and regulations.

(c)(1)(A) Initial standards and regulations under this section shall become effective for new vessels two years after promulgation; and for existing vessels five years after promulgation. Revisions of standards and regulations shall be effective upon promulgation, unless another effective date is specified, except that no revision shall take effect before the effective date of the standard or regulation being revised.

(B) The Administrator shall, with respect to commercial vessels on the Great Lakes, establish standards which require at a minimum the equivalent of secondary treatment as defined under section 304(d) of this Act. Such standards and regulations shall take effect for existing vessels after such time as the Administrator determines to be reasonable for the upgrading of marine sanitation devices to attain such standard.

(2) The Secretary of the department in which the Coast Guard is operating with regard to his regulatory authority established by this section, after consultation with the Administrator, may distinguish among classes, types, and sizes of vessels as well as between new and existing vessels, and may waive applicability of standards and regulations as necessary or appropriate for such classes, types, and sizes of vessels (including existing vessels equipped with marine sanitation devices on the date of promulgation of the initial standards required by this section), and, upon application, for individual vessels.

(d) The provisions of this section and the standards and regulations promulgated hereunder apply to vessels owned and operated by the United States unless the Secretary of Defense finds that compliance would not be in the interest of national security. With respect to vessels owned and operated by the Department of Defense, regulations under the last sentence of subsection (b)(1) of this section and certifications under subsection (g)(2) of this section shall be promulgated and issued by the Secretary of Defense.

(e) Before the standards and regulations under this section are promulgated, the Administrator and the Secretary of the department in which the Coast Guard is operating shall consult with the Secretary of State; the Secretary of Health, Education, and Welfare; the Secretary of Defense; the Secretary of the Treasury; the Secretary of Commerce; other interested Federal agencies; and the States and industries interested; and otherwise comply with the requirements of section 553 of title 5 of the United States Code.

(f)(1) After the effective date of the initial standards and regulations promulgated under this section, no State or political subdivision thereof shall adopt or enforce any statute or regulation of such State or political subdivision with respect to the design, manufacture, or installation or use of any marine sanitation device on any vessel subject to the provisions of this section.

(2) If after promulgation of the initial standards and regulations and prior to their effective date, a vessel is equipped with a marine sanitation device in compliance with such standards and regulations and the installation and operation of such device is in accordance with such standards and regulations, such standards and regulations shall, for the purposes of paragraph (1) of this subsection, become effective with respect to such vessel on the date of such compliance.

(3) After the effective date of the initial standards and regulations promulgated under this section, if any State determines that the protection and enhancement of the quality of some or all of the

waters within such States require greater environmental protection, such State may completely prohibit the discharge from all vessels of any sewage, whether treated or not, into such waters, except that no such prohibition shall apply until the Administrator determines that adequate facilities for the safe and sanitary removal and treatment of sewage from all vessels are reasonably available for such water to which such prohibition would apply. Upon application of the State, the Administrator shall make such determination within 90 days of the date of such application.

(4)(A) If the Administrator determines upon application by a State that the protection and enhancement of the quality of specified waters within such State requires such a prohibition, he shall by regulation completely prohibit the discharge from a vessel of any sewage (whether treated or not) into such waters.

(B) Upon application by a State, the Administrator shall, by regulation, establish a drinking water intake zone in any waters within such State and prohibit the discharge of sewage from vessels within that zone.

(g)(1) No manufacturer of a marine sanitation device shall sell, offer for sale, or introduce or deliver for introduction in interstate commerce, or import into the United States for sale or resale any marine sanitation device manufactured after the effective date of the standards and regulations promulgated under this section unless such device is in all material respects substantially the same as a test device certified under this subsection.

(2) Upon application of the manufacturer, the Secretary of the department in which the Coast Guard is operating shall so certify a marine sanitation device, if he determines, in accordance with the provisions of this paragraph, that it meets the appropriate standards and regulations promulgated under this section. The Secretary of the department in which the Coast Guard is operating shall test or require such testing of the device in accordance with procedures set forth by the Administrator as to standards of performance and for such other purposes as may be appropriate. If the Secretary of the department in which the Coast Guard is operating determines that the device is satisfactory from the standpoint of safety and any other requirements of maritime law or regulation, and after consideration of the design, installation, operation, material, or other appropriate factors, he shall certify the device. Any device manufactured by such manufacturer which is in all material respects substantially the same as the certified test device shall be deemed to be in conformity with the appropriate standards and regulations established under this section.

(3) Every manufacturer shall establish and maintain such records, make such reports, and provide such information as the Administrator or the Secretary of the department in which the Coast Guard is operating may reasonably require to enable him to determine whether such manufacturer has acted or is acting in compliance with this section and regulations issued thereunder and shall, upon request of an officer or employee duly designated by the Administrator or the Secretary of the department in which the Coast Guard is operating, permit such officer or employee at reasonable times to have access to and copy such records. All information reported to or otherwise obtained by the Administrator or the Secretary of the department

in which the Coast Guard is operating or their representatives pursuant to this subsection which contains or relates to a trade secret or other matter referred to in section 1905 of title 18 of the United States Code shall be considered confidential for the purpose of that section, except that such information may be disclosed to other officers or employees concerned with carrying out this section. This paragraph shall not apply in the case of the construction of a vessel by an individual for his own use.

(h) After the effective date of standards and regulations promulgated under this section, it shall be unlawful—

(1) for the manufacturer of any vessel subject to such standards and regulations to manufacture for sale, to sell or offer for sale, or to distribute for sale or resale any such vessel unless it is equipped with a marine sanitation device which is in all material respects substantially the same as the appropriate test device certified pursuant to this section;

(2) for any person, prior to the sale or delivery of a vessel subject to such standards and regulations to the ultimate purchaser, wrongfully to remove or render inoperative any certified marine sanitation device or element of design of such device installed in such vessel;

(3) for any person to fail or refuse to permit access to or copying of records or to fail to make reports or provide information required under this section; and

(4) for a vessel subject to such standards and regulations to operate on the navigable waters of the United States, if such vessel is not equipped with an operable marine sanitation device certified pursuant to this section.

(i) The district courts of the United States shall have jurisdictions to restrain violations of subsection (g)(1) of this section and subsections (h) (1) through (3) of this section. Actions to restrain such violations shall be brought by, and in, the name of the United States. In case of contumacy or refusal to obey a subpena served upon any person under this subsection, the district court of the United States for any district in which such person is found or resides or transacts business, upon application by the United States and after notice to such person, shall have jurisdiction to issue an order requiring such person to appear and give testimony or to appear and produce documents, and any failure to obey such order of the court may be punished by such court as a contempt thereof.

(j) Any person who violates subsection (g)(1) of this section or clause (1) or (2) of subsection (h) of this section shall be liable to a civil penalty of not more than $5,000 for each violation Any person who violates clause (4) of subsection (h) of this section or any regulation issued pursuant to this section shall be liable to a civil penalty of not more than $2,000 for each violation Each violation shall be a separate offense. The Secretary of the department in which the Coast Guard is operating may assess and compromise any such penalty. No penalty shall be assessed until the person charged shall have been given notice and an opportunity for a hearing on such charge. In determining the amount of the penalty, or the amount agreed upon in compromise, the gravity of the violation, and the demonstrated good faith of the person charged in attempting to achieve rapid compliance, after notification of a violation, shall be considered by said Secretary.

(k) The provisions of this section shall be enforced by the Secretary of the department in which the Coast Guard is operating and he may utilize by agreement, with or without reimbursement, law enforcement officers or other personnel and facilities of the Administrator, other Federal agencies, or the States to carrry out the provisions of this section.

(l) Anyone authorized by the Secretary of the department in which the Coast Guard is operating to enforce the provisions of this section may, except as to public vessels, (1) board and inspect any vessel upon the navigable waters of the United States and (2) execute any warrant or other process issued by an officer or court of competent jurisdiction.

(m) In the case of Guam and the Trust Territory of the Pacific Islands, actions arising under this section may be brought in the district court of Guam, and in the case of the Virgin Islands such actions may be brought in the district court of the Virgin Islands. In the case of American Samoa and the Trust Territory of the Pacific Islands, such actions may be brought in the District Court of the United States for the District of Hawaii and such court shall have jurisdiction of such actions. In the case of the Canal Zone, such actions may be brought in the District Court for the District of the Canal Zone.

FEDERAL FACILITIES POLLUTION CONTROL

SEC. 313. (a) Each department, agency, or instrumentality of the executive, legislative, and judicial branches of the Federal Government (1) having jurisdiction over any property or facility, or (2) engaged in any activity resulting, or which may result, in the discharge or runoff of pollutants, and each officer, agent, or employee thereof in the performance of his official duties, shall be subject to, and comply with, all Federal, State, interstate, and local requirements, administrative authority, and process and sanctions respecting the control and abatement of water pollution in the same manner, and to the same extent as any nongovernmental entity including the payment of reasonable service charges. The preceding sentence shall apply (A) to any requirement whether substantive or procedural (including any recordkeeping or reporting requirement, any requirement respecting permits and any other requirement, whatsoever), (B) to the exercise of any Federal, State, or local administrative authority, and (C) to any process and sanction, whether enforced in Federal, State, or local courts or in any other manner. This subsection shall apply notwithstanding any immunity of such agencies, officers, agents, or employees under any law or rule of law. Nothing in this section shall be construed to prevent any department, agency, or instrumentality of the Federal Government, or any officer, agent, or employee thereof in the performance of his official duties, from removing to the appropriate Federal district court any proceeding to which the department, agency, or instrumentality or officer, agent, or employee thereof is subject pursuant to this section, and any such proceeding may be removed in accordance with 28 U.S.C. 1441 et seq. No officer, agent, or employee of the United States shall be personally liable for any civil penalty arising from the performance of his official duties, for which he is not otherwise liable, and the United States shall be liable only for those civil penalties arising under Federal law or imposed by a State or local court to enforce an order or the process of such court. The President may exempt any effluent source of any department, agency, or instrumentality in the executive branch from compliance with any such a requirement if he determines it to be in the paramount interest of the United States to do so; except that no exemption may be granted from the requirements of section 306 or 307 of this Act. No such exemptions shall be granted due to lack of appropriation unless the President shall have specifically requested such appropriation as a part of the budgetary process and the Congress shall have failed to make available such requested appropriation. Any exemption shall be for a period not in excess of one year, but additional exemptions may be granted for periods of not to exceed one year upon the President's making a new determination. The President shall report each January to the Congress all exemptions from the requirements of this section granted during the preceding calendar year, together with his reason for granting such exemption. In addition to any such exemption of a particular effluent source, the President may, if he determines it to be in the paramount interest of the United States to do so, issue regulations exempting from compliance with the requirements of this section any weaponry, equipment, aircraft, vessels, vehicles, or other classes or categories of property, and access to such property, which are owned or operated by the Armed Forces of the United States (including the Coast Guard) or by the National Guard of any State and which are uniquely military in nature. The President shall reconsider the need for such regulations at three-year intervals.

(b)(1) The Administrator shall coordinate with the head of each department, agency, or instrumentality of the Federal Government having jurisdiction over any property or facility utilizing federally owned wastewater facilities to develop a program of cooperation for utilizing wastewater control systems utilizing those innovative treatment processes and techniques for which guidelines have been promulgated under section 304(d)(3). Such program shall include an inventory of property and facilities which could utilize such processes and techniques.

(2) Construction shall not be initiated for facilities for treatment of wastewater at any Federal property or facility after September 30, 1979, if alternative methods for wastewater treatment at such property or facility utilizing innovative treatment processes and techniques, including but not limited to methods utilizing recycle and reuse techniques and land treatment are not utilized, unless the life cycle cost of the alternative treatment works exceeds the life cycle cost of the most cost effective alternative by more than 15 per centum. The Administrator may waive the application of this paragraph in any case where the Administrator determines it to be in the public interest, or that compliance with this paragraph would interfere with the orderly compliance with conditions of a permit issued pursuant to section 402 of this Act.

CLEAN LAKES

SEC. 314. (a) Each State shall prepare or establish, and submit to the Administrator for his approval—

(1) an identification and classification according to eutrophic condition of all publicly owned fresh water lakes in such State;

(2) procedures, processes, and methods (including land use requirements), to control sources of pollution of such lakes; and

(3) methods and procedures, in conjunction with appropriate Federal agencies, to restore the quality of such lakes.

(b) The Administrator shall provide financial assistance to States in order to carry out methods and procedures approved by him under this section. The Administrator shall provide financial assistance, to States to prepare the identification and classification surveys required in subsection (a) (1) of this section.

(c)(1) The amount granted to any State for any fiscal year under this section shall not exceed 70 per centum of the funds expended by such State in such year for carrying out approved methods and procedures under this section.

(2) There is authorized to be appropriated $50,000,000 for the fiscal year ending June 30, 1973; $100,000,000 for the fiscal year 1974; $150,000,000 for the fiscal year 1975, $50,000,000 for fiscal year 1977, $60,000,000 for fiscal year 1978, $60,000,000 for fiscal year 1979, $60,000,000 for fiscal year 1980, $30,000,000 for fiscal year 1981, and $30,000,000 for fiscal year 1982 for grants to States under this section which such sums shall remain available until expended. The Administrator shall provide for an equitable distribution of such sums to the States with approved methods and procedures under this section.

NATIONAL STUDY COMMISSION

SEC. 315. (a) There is established a National Study Commission, which shall make a full and complete investigation and study of all of the technological aspects of achieving, and all aspects of the total economic, social, and environmental effects of achieving or not achieving, the effluent limitations and goals set fort hfor 1983 in section 301(b)(2) of this Act.

(b) Such Commission shall be composed of fifteen members, including five members of the Senate, who are members of the Public Works Committee, appointed by the President of the Senate, five members of the House, who are members of the Public Works Committee, appointed by the Speaker of the House, and five members of the public appointed by the President. The Chairman of such Commission shall be elected from among its members.

(c) In the conduct of such study, the Commission is authorized to contract with the National Academy of Sciences and the National Academy of Engineering (acting through the National Research Council), the National Institute of Ecology, Brookings Institution, and other nongovernmental entities, for the investigation of matters within their competence.

(d) The heads of the departments, agencies and instrumentalities of the executive branch of the Federal Government shall cooperate with the Commission in carrying out the requirements of this section, and shall furnish to the Commission such information as the Commission deems necessary to carry out this section.

(e) A report shall be submitted to the Congress of the results of such investigation and study, together with recommendations, not later than three years after the date of enactment of this title.

(f) The members of the Commission who are not officers or employees of the United States, while attending conferences or meetings of the Commission or while otherwise serving at the request of the Chairman shall be entitled to receive compensation at a rate not in excess of the maximum rate of pay for grade GS–18, as provided in the General Schedule under section 5332 of title V of the United States Code, including traveltime and while away from their homes or regular places of business they may be allowed travel expenses, including per diem in lieu of subsistence as authorized by law (5 U.S.C. 73b–2) for persons in the Government service employed intermittently.

(g) In addition to authority to appoint personnel subject to the provisions of title 5, United States Code, governing appointments in the competitive service, and to pay such personnel in accordance with the provisions of chapter 51 and subchapter III of chapter 53 of such title relating to classification and General Schedule pay rates, the Commission shall have authority to enter into contracts with private or public organizations who shall furnish the Commission with such administrative and technical personnel as may be necessary to carry out the purpose of this section. Personnel furnished by such organizations under this subsection are not, and shall not be considered to be, Federal employees for any purposes, but in the performance of their duties shall be guided by the standards which apply to employees of the legislative branches under rules 41 and 43 of the Senate and House of Representatives, respectively.

(h) There is authorized to be appropriated, for use in carrying out this section, not to exceed $17,250,000.

THERMAL DISCHARGES

SEC. 316. (a) With respect to any point source otherwise subject to the provisions of section 301 or section 306 of this Act, whenever the owner or operator of any such source, after opportunity for public hearing, can demonstrate to the satisfaction of the Administrator (or if appropriate, the State) that any effluent limitation proposed for the control of the thermal component of any discharge from such source will require effluent limitations more stringent than necessary to assure the projection and propagation of a balanced, indigenous population of shellfish, fish, and wildlife in and on the body of water into which the discharge is to be made, the Administrator (or, if appropriate, the State) may impose an effluent limitation under such sections for such plant, with respect to the thermal component of such discharge (taking into account the interaction of such thermal component with other pollutants), that will assure the protection and propagation of a balanced, indigenous population of shellfish, fish, and wildlife in and on that body of water.

(b) Any standard established pursuant to section 301 or section 306 of this Act and applicable to a point source shall require that the location, design, construction, and capacity of cooling water intake structures reflect the best technology available for minimizing adverse environmental impact.

(c) Notwithstanding any other provision of this Act, any point source of a discharge having a thermal component, the modification of which point source is commenced after the date of enactment of the Federal Water Pollution Control Act Amendments of 1972 and which, as modified, meets effluent limitations established under section 301 or, if more stringent, effluent limitations established under section 303 and which effluent limitations will assure protection and propagation of a balanced, indigenous population of shellfish, fish, and wildlife in or on the water into which the discharge is made, shall not be subject to any more stringent effluent limitation with respect to the thermal component of its discharge during a ten year period beginning on the date of completion of such modification or during the period of depreciation or amortization of such facility for the purpose of section 167 or 169 (or both) of the Internal Revenue Code of 1954, whichever period ends first.

FINANCING STUDY

SEC. 317. (a) The Administrator shall continue to investigate and study the feasibility of alternate methods of financing the cost of preventing, controlling and abating pollution as directed in the Water Quality Improvement Act of 1970 (Public Law 91–224), including, but not limited to, the feasibility of establishing a pollution abatement trust fund. The results of such investigation and study shall be reported to the Congress not later than two years after enactment of this title, together with recommendations of the Administrator for financing the programs for preventing, controlling and abating pollution for the fiscal years beginning after fiscal year 1976, including any necessary legislation.

(b) There is authorized to be appropriated for use in carrying out this section, not to exceed $1,000,000.

AQUACULTURE

SEC. 318. (a) The Administrator is authorized, after public hearings, to permit the discharge of a specific pollutant or pollutants under controlled conditions associated with an approved aquaculture project under Federal or State supervision pursuant to section 402 of this Act.

(b) The Administrator shall by regulation establish any procedures and guidelines which the Administrator deems necessary to carry out this section. Such regulations shall require the application to such discharge of each criterion, factor, procedure, and requirement applicable to a permit issued under section 402 of this title, as the Administrator determines necessary to carry out the objective of this Act.

(c) Each State desiring to administer its own permit program within its jurisdiction for discharge of a specific pollutant or pollutants under controlled conditions associated with an approved aquaculture project may do so if upon submission of such program the Administrator determines such program is adequate to carry out the objective of this Act.

TITLE IV—PERMITS AND LICENSES

CERTIFICATION

SEC. 401. (a)(1) Any applicant for a Federal license or permit to conduct any activity including, but not limited to, the construction or operation of facilities, which may result in any discharge into the navigable waters, shall provide the licensing or permitting agency a certification from the State in which the discharge originates or will originate, or, if appropriate, from the interstate water pollution control agency having jurisdiction over the navigable waters at the point where the discharge originates or will originate, that any such discharge will comply with the applicable provisions of sections 301, 302, 303, 306, and 307 of this Act. In the case of any such activity for which there is not an applicable effluent limitation or other limitation under sections 301(b) and 302, and there is not an applicable standard under sections 306 and 307, the State shall so certify, except that any such certification shall not be deemed to satisfy section 511(c) of this Act. Such State or interstate agency shall establish procedures for public notice in the case of all applications for certification by it and, to the extent it deems appropriate, procedures for public hearings in connection with specific applications. In any case where a State or interstate agency has no authority to give such a certification, such certification shall be from the Administrator. If the State, interstate agency, or Administrator, as the case may be, fails or refuses to act on a request for certification, within a reasonable period of time (which shall not exceed one year) after receipt of such request, the certification requirements of this subsection shall be waived with respect to such Federal application. No license or permit shall be granted until the certification required by this section has been obtained or has been waived as provided in the preceding sentence. No license or permit shall be granted if certification has been denied by the State, interstate agency, or the Administrator, as the case may be.

(2) Upon receipt of such application and certification the licensing or permitting agency shall immediately notify the Administrator of such application and certification. Whenever such a discharge may affect, as determined by the Administrator, the quality of the waters of any other State, the Administrator within thirty days of the date of notice of application for such Federal license or permit shall so notify such other State, the licensing or permitting agency, and the applicant. If, within sixty days after receipt of such notification, such other State determines that such discharge will affect the quality of its waters so as to violate any water quality requirement in such State, and within such sixty-day period notifies the Administrator and the licensing or permitting agency in writing of its objection to the issuance of such license or permit and requests a public hearing on such objection, the licensing or permitting agency shall hold such a hearing. The Administrator shall at such hearing submit his evaluation and recommendations with respect to any such objection to the licensing or permitting agency. Such agency, based upon the recommendations of such State, the Administrator, and upon any additional evidence, if any, presented to the agency at the hearing, shall condition such license or permit in such manner as may be necessary to insure compliance with applicable water quality requirements. If the imposition of conditions cannot insure such compliance such agency shall not issue such license or permit.

(3) The certification obtained pursuant to paragraph (1) of this subsection with respect to the construction of any facility shall fulfill the requirements of this subsection with respect to certification in connection with any other Federal license or permit required for the operation of such facility unless, after notice to the certifying State,

agency, or Administrator, as the case may be, which shall be given by the Federal agency to whom application is made for such operating license or permit, the State, or if appropriate, the interstate agency or the Administrator, notifies such agency within sixty days after receipt of such notice that there is no longer reasonable assurance that there will be compliance with the applicable provisions of section 301, 302, 303, 306, and 307 of this Act because of changes since the construction license or permit certification was issued in (A) the construction or operation of the facility, (B) the characteristics of the waters into which such discharge is made, (C) the water quality criteria applicable to such waters or (D) applicable effluent limitations or other requirements. This paragraph shall be inapplicable in any case where the applicant for such operating license or permit has failed to provide the certifying State, or, if appropriate, the interstate agency or the Administrator, with notice of any proposed changes in the construction or operation of the facility with respect to which a construction license or permit has been granted, which changes may result in violation of section 301, 302, 303, 306, or 307 of this Act.

(4) Prior to the initial operation of any federally licensed or permitted facility or activity which may result in any discharge into the navigable waters and with respect to which a certification has been obtained pursuant to paragraph (1) of this subsection, which facility or activity is not subject to a Federal operating license or permit, the licensee or permittee shall provide an opportunity for such certifying State, or, if appropriate, the interstate agency or the Administrator to review the manner in which the facility or activity shall be operated or conducted for the purposes of assuring that applicable effluent limitations or other limitations or other applicable water quality requirements will not be violated. Upon notification by the certifying State, or if appropriate, the interstate agency or the Administrator that the operation of any such federally licensed or permitted facility or activity will violate applicable effluent limitations or other limitations or other water quality requirements such Federal agency may, after public hearing, suspend such license or permit. If such license or permit is suspended, it shall remain suspended until notification is received from the certifying State, agency, or Administrator, as the case may be, that there is reasonable assurance that such facility or activity will not violate the applicable provisions of section 301, 302, 303, 306, or 307 of this Act.

(5) Any Federal license or permit with respect to which a certification has been obtained under paragraph (1) of this subsection may be suspended or revoked by the Federal agency issuing such license or permit upon the entering of a judgment under this Act that such facility or activity has been operated in violation of the applicable provisions of section 301, 302, 303, 306, or 307 of this Act.

(6) Except with respect to a permit issued under section 402 of this Act, in any case where actual construction of a facility has been lawfully commenced prior to April 3, 1970, no certification shall be required under this subsection for a license or permit issued after April 3, 1970, to operate such facility, except that any such license or permit issued without certification shall terminate April 3, 1973,

unless prior to such term nation date the person having such license or permit submits to the Federal agency which issued such license or permit a certification and otherwise meets the requirements of this section.

(b) Nothing in this section shall be construed to limit the authority of any department or agency pursuant to any other provision of law to require compliance with any applicable water quality requirements. The Administrator shall, upon the request of any Federal department or agency, or State or interstate agency, or applicant, provide, for the purpose of this section, any relevant information on applicable effluent limitations, or other limitations, standards, regulations, or requirements, or water quality criteria, and shall; when requested by any such department or agency or State or interstate agency, or applicant, comment on any methods to comply with such limitations, standards, regulations, requirements, or criteria.

(c) In order to implement the provisions of this section, the Secretary of the Army, acting through the Chief of Engineers, is authorized, if he deems it to be in the public interest, to permit the use of spoil disposal areas under his jurisdiction by Federal licensees or permittees, and to make an appropriate charge for such use. Moneys received from such licensees or permittees shall be deposited in the Treasury as miscellaneous receipts.

(d) Any certification provided under this section shall set forth any effluent limitations and other limitations, and monitoring requirements necessary to assure that any applicant for a Federal license or permit will comply with any applicable effluent limitations and other limitations, under section 301 or 302 of this Act, standard of performance under section 306 of this Act, or prohibition, effluent standard, or pretreatment standard under section 307 of this Act, and with any other appropriate requirement of State law set forth in such certification, and shall become a condition on any Federal license or permit subject to the provisions of this section.

NATIONAL POLLUTANT DISCHARGE ELIMINATION SYSTEM

SEC. 402. (a)(1) Except as provided in sections 318 and 404 of this Act, the Administrator may, after opportunity for public hearing, issue a permit for the discharge of any pollutant, or combination of pollutants, notwithstanding section 301(a), upon condition that such discharge will meet either all applicable requirements under sections 301, 302, 306, 307, 308, and 403 of this Act, or prior to the taking of necessary implementing actions relating to all such requirements, such conditions as the Administrator determines are necessary to carry out the provisions of this Act.

(2) The Administrator shall prescribe conditions for such permits to assure compliance with the requirements of paragraph (1) of this subsection, including conditions on data and information collection, reporting, and such other requirements as he deems appropriate.

(3) The permit program of the Administrator under paragraph (1) of this subsection, and permits issued thereunder, shall be subject to the same terms, conditions, and requirements as apply to a State permit program and permits issued thereunder under subsection (b) of this section.

(4) All permits for discharges into the navigable waters issued pursuant to section 13 of the Act of March 3, 1899, shall be deemed to be permits issued under this title, and permits issued under this title shall be deemed to be permits issued under section 13 of the Act of March 3, 1899, and shall continue in force and effect for their term unless revoked, modified, or suspended in accordance with the provisions of this Act.

(5) No permit for a discharge into the navigable waters shall be issued under section 13 of the Act of March 3, 1899, after the date of enactment of this title. Each application for a permit under section 13 of the Act of March 3, 1899, pending on the date of enactment of this Act shall be deemed to be an application for a permit under this section. The Administrator shall authorize a State, which he determines has the capability of administering a permit program which will carry out the objective of this Act, to issue permits for discharges into the navigable waters within the jurisdiction of such State. The Administrator may exercise the authority granted him by the preceding sentence only during the period which begins on the date of enactment of this Act and ends either on the ninetieth day after the date of the first promulgation of guidelines required by section 304 (h)(2) of this Act, or the date approval by the Administrator of a permit program for such State under subsection (b) of this section, whichever date first occurs, and no such authorization to a State shall extend beyond the last day of such period. Each such permit shall be subject to such conditions as the Administrator determines are necessary to carry out the provisions of this Act. No such permit shall issue if the Administrator objects to such issuance.

(b) At any time after the promulgation of the guidelines required by subsection (h)(2) of section 304 of this Act, the Governor of each State desiring to administer its own permit program for discharges into navigable waters within its jurisdiction may submit to the Administrator a full and complete description of the program it proposes to establish and administer under State law or under an interstate compact. In addition, such State shall submit a statement from the attorney general (or the attorney for those State water pollution control agencies which have independent legal counsel), or from the chief legal officer in the case of an interstate agency, that the laws of such State, or the interstate compact, as the case may be, provide adequate authority to carry out the described program. The Administrator shall approve each such submitted program unless he determines that adequate authority does not exist:

(1) To issue permits which—

(A) apply, and insure compliance with, any applicable requirements of sections 301, 302, 306, 307, and 403;

(B) are for fixed terms not exceeding five years; and

(C) can be terminated or modified for cause including, but not limited to, the following:

(i) violation of any condition of the permit;

(ii) obtaining a permit by misrepresentation, or failure to disclose fully all relevant facts;

(iii) change in any condition that requires either a temporary or permanent reduction or elimination of the permitted discharge;

(D) control the disposal of pollutants into wells;

(2)(A) To issue permits which apply, and insure compliance with, all applicable requirements of section 308 of this Act, or

(B) To inspect, monitor, enter, and require reports to at least the same extent as required in section 308 of this Act;

(3) To insure that the public, and any other State the waters of which may be affected, receive notice of each application for a permit and to provide an opportunity for public hearing before a ruling on each such application;

(4) To insure that the Administrator receives notice of each application (including a copy thereof) for a permit;

(5) To insure that any State (other than the permitting State), whose waters may be affected by the issuance of a permit may submit written recommendations to the permitting State (and the Administrator) with respect to any permit application and, if any part of such written recommendations are not accepted by the permitting State, that the permitting State will notify such affected State (and the Administrator) in writing of its failure to so accept such recommendations together with its reasons for so doing;

(6) To insure that no permit will be issued if, in the judgment of the Secretary of the Army acting through the Chief of Engineers, after consultation with the Secretary of the department in which the Coast Guard is operating, anchorage and navigation of any of the navigable waters would be substantially impaired thereby;

(7) To abate violations of the permit or the permit program, including civil and criminal penalties and other ways and means of enforcement;

(8) To insure that any permit for a discharge from a publicly owned treatment works includes conditions to require the identification in terms of character and volume of pollutants of any significant source introducing pollutants subject to pretreatment standards under section 307(b) of this Act into such works and a program to assure compliance with such pretreatment standards by each such source, in addition to adequate notice to the permitting agency of (A) new introductions into such works of pollutants from any source which would be a new source as defined in section 306 if such source were discharging pollutants, (B) new introductions of pollutants into such works from a source which would be subject to section 301 if it were discharging such pollutants, or (C) a substantial change in volume or character of pollutants being introduced into such works by a source introducing pollutants into such works at the time of issuance of the permit. Such notice shall include information on the quality and quantity of effluent to be introduced into such treatment works and any anticipated impact of such change in the quantity or quality of effluent to be discharged from such publicly owned treatment works; and

(9) To insure that any industrial user of any publicly owned treatment works will comply with sections 204(b), 307, and 308.

(c)(1) Not later than ninety days after the date on which a State has submitted a program (or revision thereof) pursuant to subsection (b) of this section, the Administrator shall suspend the issuance of permits under subsection (a) of this section as to those navigable waters subject to such program unless he determines that the State permit program does not meet the requirements of subsection (b) of this section or does not conform to the guidelines issued under section 304(i)(2) of this Act. If the Administrator so determines, he shall notify the State of any revisions or modifications necessary to conform to such requirements or guidelines.

(2) Any State permit program under this section shall at all times be in accordance with this section and guidelines promulgated pursuant to section 304(h)(2) of this Act.

(3) Whenever the Administrator determines after public hearing that a State is not administering a program approved under this section in accordance with requirements of this section, he shall so notify the State and, if appropriate corrective action is not taken within a reasonable time, not to exceed ninety days, the Administrator shall withdraw approval of such program. The Administrator shall not withdraw approval of any such program unless he shall first have notified the State, and made public, in writing, the reasons for such withdrawal.

(d)(1) Each State shall transmit to the Administrator a copy of each permit application received by such State and provide notice to the Administrator of every action related to the consideration of such permit application, including each permit proposed to be issued by such State.

(2) No permit shall issue (A) if the Administrator within ninety days of the date of his notification under subsection (b)(5) of this section objects in writing to the issuance of such permit, or (B) if the Administrator within ninety days of the date of transmittal of the proposed permit by the State objects in writing to the issuance of such permit as being outside the guidelines and requirements of this Act. Whenever the Administrator objects to the issuance of a permit under this paragraph such written objection shall contain a statement of the reasons for such objection and the effuent limitations and conditions which such permit would include if it were issued by the Administrator.

(3) The Administrator may, as to any permit application, waive paragraph (2) of this subsection.

(4) In any case where, after the date of enactment of this paragraph, the Administrator, pursuant to paragraph (2) of this subsection, objects to the issuance of a permit, on request of the State, a public hearing shall be held by the Administrator on such objection. If the State does not resubmit such permit revised to meet such objection within 30 days after completion of the hearing, or, if no hearing is requested within 90 days after the date of such objection, the Administrator may issue the permit pursuant to subsection (a) of this section for such source in accordance with the guidelines and requirements of this Act.

(e) In accordance with guidelines promulgated pursuant to subsection (h)(2) of section 304 of this Act, the Administrator is authorized to waive the requirements of subsection (d) of this section at the time he approves a program pursuant to subsection (b) of this section for any category (including any class, type, or size within such category) of point sources within the State submitting such program.

(f) The Administrator shall promulgate regulations establishing categories of point sources which he determines shall not be subject to the requirements of subsection (d) of this section in any State with a program approved pursuant to subsection (b) of this section. The Administrator may distinguish among classes, types, and sizes within any category of point sources.

(g) Any permit issued under this section for the discharge of pollutants into the navigable waters from a vessel or other floating craft shall be subject to any applicable regulations promulgated by the Secretary of the Department in which the Coast Guard is operating, establishing specifications for safe transportation, handling, carriage, storage, and stowage of pollutants.

(h) In the event any condition of a permit for discharges from a treatment works (as defined in section 212 of this Act) which is publicly owned is violated, a State with a program approved under subsection (b) of this section or the Administrator, where no State program is approved or where the Administrator determines pursuant to section 309(a) of this Act that a State with an approved program has not commenced appropriate enforcement action with respect to such permit, may proceed in a court of competent jurisdiction to restrict or prohibit the introduction of any pollutant into such treatment works by a source not utilizing such treatment works prior to the finding that such condition was violated.

(i) Nothing in this section shall be contrued to limit the authority of the Administrator to take action pursuant to section 309 of this Act.

(j) A copy of each permit application and each permit issued under this section shall be available to the public. Such permit application or permit, or portion thereof, shall further be available on request for the purpose of reproduction.

(k) Compliance with a permit issued pursuant to this section shall be deemed compliance, for purposes of sections 309 and 505, with sections 301, 302, 306, 307, and 403, except any standard imposed under section 307 for a toxic pollutant injurious to human health. Until December 31, 1974, in any case where a permit for discharge has been applied for pursuant to this section, but final administrative disposition of such application has not been made, such discharge shall not be a violation of (1) section 301, 306, or 402 of this Act, or (2) section 13 of the Act, of March 3, 1899, unless the Administrator or other plaintiff proves that final administrative disposition of such application has not been made because of the failure of the applicant to furnish information reasonably required or requested in order to process the application. For the 180-day period beginning on the date of enactment of the Federal Water Pollution Control Act Amendments of 1972, in the case of any point source discharging any pollutant or combination of pollutants immediately prior to such date of enactment which source is not subject to section 13 of the Act of March 3, 1899, the discharge by such source shall not be a violation of this Act if such a source applies for a permit for discharge pursuant to this section within such 180-day period.

(l) The Administrator shall not require a permit under this section for discharges composed entirely of return flows from irrigated agriculture, nor shall the Administrator directly or indirectly, require any State to require such a permit.

[Sec. 54(c)(2) of the Clean Water Act of 1977 says:

"Any State Permit program approved under section 402 of the Federal Water Pollution Control Act before the date of enactment of the Clean Water Act of 1977, which required modification to conform to the amendment made by paragraph (1) of this subsection, shall not be required to be modified before the end of the one year period which begins on the date of enactment of the Clean Water Act of 1977 unless in order to make the required modification a State must amend or enact a law in which case such modification shall not be required for such State before the end of the two year period which begins on such date of enactment."]

OCEAN DISCHARGE CRITERIA

SEC. 403. (a) No permit under section 402 of this Act for a discharge into the territorial sea, the waters of the contiguous zone, or the oceans shall be issued, after promulgation of guidelines established under subsection (c) of this section, except in compliance with such guidelines. Prior to the promulgation of such guidelines, a permit may be issued under such section 402 if the Administrator determines it to be in the public interest.

(b) The requirements of subsection (d) of section 402 of this Act may not be waived in the case of permits for discharges into the territorial sea.

(c)(1) The Administrator shall, within one hundred and eighty days after enactment of this Act (and from time to time thereafter), promulgate guidelines for determining the degradation of the waters of the territorial seas, the contiguous zone, and the oceans, which shall include:

(A) the effect of disposal of pollutants on human health or welfare, including but not limited to plankton, fish, shellfish, wildlife, shorelines, and beaches;

(B) the effect of disposal of pollutants on marine life including the transfer, concentration, and dispersal of pollutants or their byproducts through biological, physical, and chemical processes; changes in marine ecosystem diversity, productivity, and stability; and species and community population changes;

(C) the effect of disposal, of pollutants on esthetic, recreation, and economic values;

(D) the persistence and permanence of the effects of disposal of pollutants;

(E) the effect of the disposal at varying rates, of particular volumes and concentrations of pollutants;

(F) other possible locations and methods of disposal or recycling of pollutants including land-based alternatives; and

(G) the effect on alternate uses of the oceans, such as mineral exploitation and scientific study.

(2) In any event where insufficient information exists on any proposed discharge to make a reasonable judgment on any of the guidelines established pursuant to this subsection no permit shall be issued under section 402 of this Act.

PERMITS FOR DREDGED OR FILL MATERIAL

SEC. 404. (a) The Secretary may issue permits, after notice and opportunity for public hearings for the discharge of dredged or fill material into the navigable waters at specified disposal sites. Not later than the fifteenth day after the date an applicant submits all the information required to complete an application for a permit under this subsection, the Secretary shall publish the notice required by this subsection.

(b) Subject to subsection (c) of this section, each such disposal site shall be specified for each such permit by the Secretary (1) through the application of guidelines developed by the Administrator, in conjunction with the Secretary, which guidelines shall be based upon criteria comparable to the criteria applicable to the territorial seas, the contiguous zone, and the ocean under section 403(c), and (2) in any case where such guidelines under clause (1) alone would prohibit the specification of a site, through the application additionally of the economic impact of the site on navigation and anchorage.

(c) The Administrator is authorized to prohibit the specification (including the withdrawal of specification) of any defined area as a disposal site, and he is authorized to deny or restrict the use of any defined area for specification (including the withdrawal of specification) as a disposal site, whenever he determines, after notice and opportunity for public hearings, that the discharge of such materials into such area will have an unacceptable adverse effect on municipal water supplies, shellfish beds and fishery areas (including spawning and breeding areas), wildlife, or recreational areas. Before making such determination, the Administrator shall consult with the Secretary. The Administrator shall set forth in writing and make public his findings and his reasons for making any determination under this subsection.

(d) The term "Secretary" as used in this section means the Secretary of the Army, acting through the Chief of Engineers.

(e)(1) In carrying out his functions relating to the discharge of dredged or fill material under this section, the Secretary may, after notice and opportunity for public hearing, issue general permits on a State, regional, or nationwide basis for any category of activities involving discharges of dredged or fill material if the Secretary determines that the activities in such category are similar in nature, will cause only minimal adverse environmental effects when performed separately, and will have only minimal cumulative adverse effect on the environment. Any general permit issued under this subsection shall (A) be based on the guidelines described in subsection (b)(1) of this section, and (B) set forth the requirements and standards which shall apply to any activity authorized by such general permit.

(2) No general permit issued under this subsection shall be for a period of more than five years after the date of its issuance and such general permit may be revoked or modified by the Secretary if, after opportunity for public hearing, the Secretary determines that the activities authorized by such general permit have an adverse impact on the environment or such activities are more appropriately authorized by individual permits.

(f)(1) Except as provided in paragraph (2) of this subsection, the discharge of dredge or fill material—

(A) from normal farming, silviculture, and ranching activities such as plowing, seeding, cultivating, minor drainage, harvesting for the production of food, fiber, and forest products, or upland soil and water conservation practices;

(B) for the purpose of maintenance, including emergency reconstruction of recently damaged parts, of currently serviceable structures such as dikes, dams, levees, groins, riprap, breakwaters, causeways, and bridge abutments or approaches, and transportation structures;

(C) for the purpose of construction or maintenance of farm or stock ponds or irrigation ditches, or the maintenance of drainage ditches;

(D) for the purpose of construction of temporary sedimentation basins on a construction site which does not include placement of fill material into the navigable waters;

(E) for the purpose of construction or maintenance or farm roads or forest roads, or temporary roads for moving mining equipment, where such roads are constructed and maintained, in accordance with best management practices, to assure that flow and circulation patterns and chemical and biological characteristics of the navigable waters are not impaired, that the reach of the navigable waters is not reduced, and that any adverse effect on the aquatic environment will be otherwise minimized;

(F) resulting from any activity with respect to which a State has an approved program, under section 208(b)(4) which meets the requirements of subparagraphs (B) and (C) of such section,

is not prohibited by or otherwise subject to regulation under this section or section 301(a) or 402 of this Act (except for effluent standards or prohibitions under section 307).

(2) Any discharge of dredged or fill material into the navigable waters incidental to any activity having as its purpose bringing an area of the navigable waters into a use to which it was not previously subject, where the flow or circulation of navigable waters may be impaired or the reach of such waters be reduced, shall be required to have a permit under this section.

(g)(1) The Governor of any State desiring to administer its own individual and general permit program for the discharge of dredged or fill material into the navigable waters (other than those waters which are presently used, or are susceptible to use in their natural condition or by reasonable improvement as a means to transport interstate or foreign commerce shoreward to their ordinary high water mark, including all waters which are subject to the ebb and flow of the tide shoreward to their mean high water mark, or mean higher high water mark on the west coast, including wetlands adjacent thereto), within its jurisdiction may submit to the Administrator a full and complete description of the program it proposes to establish and administer under State law or under an interstate compact. In addition, such State shall submit a statement from the attorney general (or the attorney for those State agencies which have independent legal counsel), or from the chief legal officer in the case of an interstate agency, that the laws of such State, or the interstate compact, as the case may be, provide adequate authority to carry out the described program.

(2) Not later than the tenth day after the date of the receipt of the program and statement submitted by any State under paragraph (1) of this subsection, the Administrator shall provide copies of such program and statement to the Secretary and the Secretary of the Interior, acting through the Director of the United States Fish and Wildlife Service.

(3) No later than the ninetieth day after the date of the receipt by the Administrator of the program and statement submitted by any State, under paragraph (1) of this subsection, the Secretary and the Secretary of the Interior, acting through the Director of the United States Fish and Wildlife Service, shall submit any comments with respect to such program and statement to the Administrator in writing.

(h)(1) Not later than the one-hundred-twentieth day after the date of the receipt by the Administrator of a program and statement submitted by any State under paragraph (1) of this subsection, the Administrator shall determine, taking into account any comments submitted by the Secretary and the Secretary of the Interior, acting through the Director of the United States Fish and Wildlife Service, pursuant to subsection (g) of this section, whether such State has the following authority with respect to the issuance of permits pursuant to such program:

(A) To issue permits which—

(i) apply, and assure compliance with, any applicable requirements of this section, including, but not limited to, the guidelines established under subsection (b)(1) of this section, and sections 307 and 403 of this Act;

(ii) are for fixed terms not exceeding five years; and

(iii) can be terminated or modified for cause including, but not limited to, the following:

(I) violation of any condition of the permit;

(II) obtaining a permit by misrepresentation, or failure to disclose fully all relevant facts;

(III) change in any condition that requires either a temporary or permanent reduction or elimination of the permitted discharge.

(B) To issue permits which apply, and assure compliance with, all applicable requirements of section 308 of this Act, or to inspect, monitor, enter, and require reports to at least the same extent as required in section 308 of this Act.

(C) To assure that the public, and any other State the waters of which may be affected, receive notice of each application for a permit and to provide an opportunity for public hearing before a ruling on each such application.

(D) To assure that the Administrator receives notice of each application (including a copy thereof) for a permit.

(E) To assure that any State (other than the permitting State), whose waters may be affected by the issuance of a permit may submit written recommendation to the permitting State (and the Administrator) with respect to any permit application and, if any part of such written recommendations are not accepted by the permitting State, that the permitting State will notify such affected State (and the Administrator) in writing of its failure to so accept such recommendations together with its reasons for so doing.

(F) To assure that no permit will be issued if, in the judgment of the Secretary, after consultation with the Secretary of the department in which the Coast Guard is operating, anchorage and navigation of any of the navigable waters would be substantially impaired thereby.

(G) To abate violations of the permit or the permit program, including civil and criminal penalties and other ways and means of enforcement.

(H) To assure continued coordination with Federal and Federal-State water-related planning and review processes.

(2) If, with respect to a State program submitted under subsection (g)(1) of this section, the Administrator determines that such State—

(A) has the authority set forth in paragraph (1) of this subsection, the Administrator shall approve the program and so notify (i) such State, and (ii) the Secretary, who upon subsequent notification from such State that it is administering such program, shall suspend the issuance of permits under subsections (a) and (e) of this section for activities with respect to which a permit may be issued pursuant to such State program; or

(B) does not have the authority set forth in paragraph (1) of this subsection, the Administrator shall so notify such State, which notification shall also describe the revisions or modifications necessary so that such State may resubmit such program for a determination by the Administrator under this subsection.

(3) If the Administrator fails to make a determination with respect to any program submitted by a State under subsection (g)(1) of this section within one-hundred-twenty days after the date of the receipt of such program, such program shall be deemed approved pursuant to paragraph (2)(A) of this subsection and the Administrator shall so notify such State and the Secretary who, upon subsequent notification from such State that it is administering such program, shall suspend the issuance of permits under subsection (a) and (e) of this section for activities with respect to which a permit may be issued by such State.

(4) After the Secretary receives notification from the Administrator under paragraph (2) or (3) of this subsection that a State permit program has been approved, the Secretary shall transfer any applications for permits pending before the Secretary for activities with respect to which a permit may be issued pursuant to such State program to such State for appropriate action.

(5) Upon notification from a State with a permit program approved under this subsection that such State intends to administer and enforce the terms and conditions of a general permit issued by the Secretary under subsection (e) of this section with respect to activities in such State to which such general permit applies, the Secretary shall suspend the administration and enforcement of such general permit with respect to such activities.

(i) Whenever the Administrator determines after public hearing that a State is not administering a program approved under section (h)(2)(A) of this section, in accordance with this section, including, but not limited to, the guidelines established under subsection (b)(1) of this section, the Administrator shall so notify the State, and, if appropriate corrective action is not taken within a reasonable time, not to exceed ninety days after the date of the receipt of such notification, the Administrator shall (1) withdraw approval of such program until the Administrator determines such corrective action has been taken, and (2) notify the Secretary that the Secretary shall resume the programs for the issuance of permits under subsections (a) and (e) of this section for activities with respect to which the State was issuing permits and that such authority of the Secretary shall continue in effect until such time as the Administrator makes the determination described in clause (1) of this subsection and such State again has an approved program.

(j) Each State which is administering a permit program pursuant to this section shall transmit to the Administrator (1) a copy of each permit application received by such State and provide notice to the Administrator of every action related to the consideration of such permit application, including each permit proposed to be issued by such State, and (2) a copy of each proposed general permit which such State intends to issue. Not later than the tenth day after the date of the receipt of such permit application or such proposed general permit, the Administrator shall provide copies of such permit application or such proposed general permit to the Secretary and the Secretary of the Interior, acting through the Director of the United States Fish and Wildlife Service. If the Administrator intends to provide written comments to such State with respect to such permit application or such proposed general permit, he shall so notify such State not later than the thirtieth day after the date of the receipt of such application or such proposed general permit and provide such written comments to such State, after consideration of any comments made in writing with respect to such application or such proposed general permit by the Secretary and the Secretary of the Interior, acting through the Director of the United States Fish and Wildlife Service, not later than the ninetieth day after the date of such receipt. If such State is so notified by the Administrator, it shall not issue the proposed permit until after the receipt of such comments from the Administrator, or after such ninetieth day, whichever first occurs. Such State shall not issue such proposed permit after such ninetieth day if it has received such written comments in which the Administrator objects (A) to the issuance of such proposed permit and such proposed permit is one that has been submitted to the Administrator pursuant to subsection (h)(1)(E), or (B) to the issuance of such proposed permit as being outside the requirements of this section, including, but not limited to, the guidelines developed under subsection (b)(1) of this section unless it modifies such proposed permit in accordance with such comments. Whenever the Administrator objects to the issuance of a permit under the preceding sentence such written objection shall contain a statement of the reasons for such objection and the conditions which such permit would include if it were issued by the Administrator. In any case where the Administrator objects to the issuance of a permit, on request of the State, a public hearing shall be held by the Administrator on such objection. If the State does not resubmit such permit revised to meet such objection within 30 days after completion of the hearing or, if no hearing is requested within 90 days after the date of such objection, the Secretary may issue the permit pursuant to subsection (a) or (e) of this section, as the case may be, for such source in accordance with the guidelines and requirements of this Act.

(k) In accordance with guidelines promulgated pursuant to subsection (i)(2) of section 304 of this Act, the Administrator is authorized to waive the requirements of subsection (j) of this section at the time of the approval of a program pursuant to subsection (h)(2)(A) of this section for any category (including any class, type, or size within such category) of discharge within the State submitting such program.

(l) The Administrator shall promulgate regulations establishing categories of discharges which he determines shall not be subject to the requirements of subsection (j) of this section in any State with a program approved pursuant to subsection (h)(2)(A) of this section. The Administrator may distinguish among classes, types, and sizes within any category of discharges.

(m) Not later than the ninetieth day after the date on which the Secretary notifies the Secretary of the Interior, acting through the Director of the United States Fish and Wildlife Service that (1) an application for a permit under subsection (a) of this section has been received by the Secretary, or (2) the Secretary proposes to issue a general permit under subsection (e) of this section, the Secretary of the Interior, acting through the Director of the United States Fish and Wildlife Service, shall submit any comments with respect to such application or such proposed general permit in writing to the Secretary.

(n) Nothing in this section shall be construed to limit the authority of the Administrator to take action pursuant to section 309 of this Act.

(o) A copy of each permit application and each permit issued under this section shall be available to the public. Such permit application or portion thereof, shall further be available on request for the purpose of reproduction.

(p) Compliance with a permit issued pursuant to this section, including any activity carried out pursuant to a general permit issued under this section, shall be deemed compliance, for purposes of sections 309 and 505, with sections 301, 307, and 403.

(q) Not later than the one-hundred-eightieth day after the date of enactment of this subsection, the Secretary shall enter into agreements with the Administrator, the Secretaries of the Departments of Agriculture, Commerce, Interior, and Transportation, and the heads of other appropriate Federal agencies to minimize, to the maximum extent practicable, duplication, needless paperwork, and delays in the issuance of permits under this section. Such agreements shall be developed to assure that, to the maximum extent practicable, a decision with respect to an application for a permit under subsection (a) of this section will be made not later than the ninetieth day after the date the notice of such application is published under subsection (a) of this section.

(r) The discharge of dredged or fill material as part of the construction of a Federal project specifically authorized by Congress, whether prior to or on or after the date of enactment of this subsection, is not prohibited by or otherwise subject to regulation under this section, or a State program approved under this section, or section 301(a) or 402 of the Act (except for effluent standards or prohibitions under section 307), if information on the effects of such discharge, including consideration of the guidelines developed under subsection (b)(1) of this section, is included in an environmental impact statement for such project pursuant to the National Environmental Policy Act of 1969 and such environmental impact statement has been submitted to Congress before the actual discharge of dredged or fill material in connection with the construction of such project and prior to either authorization of such project or an appropriation of funds for each construction.

(s)(1) Whenever on the basis of any information available to him the Secretary finds that any person is in violation of any condition or limitation set forth in a permit issued by the Secretary under this section, the Secretary shall issue an order requiring such persons to comply with such condition or limitation, or the Secretary shall bring a civil action in accordance with paragraph (3) of this subsection.

(2) A copy of any order issued under this subsection shall be sent immediately by the Secretary to the State in which the violation occurs and other affected States. Any order issued under this subsection shall be by personal service and shall state with reasonable specificity the nature of the violation, specify a time for compliance, not to exceed thirty days, which the Secretary determines is reasonable, taking into account the seriousness of the violation and any good faith efforts to comply with applicable requirements. In any case in which an order under this subsection is issued to a corporation, a copy of such order shall be served on any appropriate corporate officers.

(3) The Secretary is authorized to commence a civil action for appropriate relief, including a permanent or temporary injunction for any violation for which he is authorized to issue a compliance order under paragraph (1) of this subsection. Any action under this paragraph may be brought in the district court of the United States for the district in which the defendant is located or resides or is doing business, and such court shall have jurisdiction to restrain such violation and to require compliance. Notice of the commencement of sucb action shall be given immediately to the appropriate State.

(4)(A) Any person who willfully or negligently violates any condition or limitation in a permit issued by the Secretary under this section shall be punished by a fine of not less than $2,500 nor more than $25,000 per day of violation, or by imprisonment for not more than one year, or by both. If the conviction is for a violation committed after a first conviction of such person under this paragraph, punishment shall be by a fine of not more than $50,000 per day of violation, or by imprisonment for not more than two years, or by both.

(B) For the purposes of this paragraph, the term "person" shall mean, in addition to the definition contained in section 502(5) of this Act, any responsible corporate officer.

(5) Any person who violates any condition or limitation in a permit issued by the Secretary under this section, and any person who violates any order issued by the Secretary under paragraph (1) of this subsection, shall be subject to a civil penalty not to exceed $10,000 per day of such violation.

(t) Nothing in this section shall preclude or deny the right of any State or interstate agency to control the discharge of dredged or fill material in any portion of the navigable waters within the jurisdiction of such State, including any activity of any Federal agency, and each such agency shall comply with such State or interstate requirements both substantive and procedural to control the discharge of dredged or fill material to the same extent that any person is subject to such requirements. This section shall not be construed as affecting or impairing the authority of the Secretary to maintain navigation.

DISPOSAL OF SEWAGE SLUDGE

SEC. 405. (a) Notwithstanding any other provision of this Act, or of any other law, in the case where the disposal of sewage sludge resulting from the operation of a treatment works as defined in section 212 of this Act (including the removal of in-place sewage sludge from one location and its deposit at another location) would result in any pollutant from such sewage sludge entering the navigable waters, such disposal is prohibited except in accordance with a permit issued by the Administrator under section 402 of this Act.

(b) The Administrator shall issue regulations governing the issuance of permits for the disposal of sewage sludge subject to subsection (a) of this section and section 402 of this Act. Such regulations shall require the application to such disposal of each criterion, factor, procedure, and requirement applicable to a permit issued under section 402 of this title.

(c) Each State desiring to administer its own permit program for disposal of sewage sludge subject to subsection (a) of this section within its jurisdiction may do so, in accordance with section 402 of this Act.

(d) The Administrator, after consultation with appropriate Federal and State agencies and other interested persons, shall develop and publish, within one year after the date of enactment of this subsection and from time to time thereafter, regulations providing guidelines for the disposal of sludge and the utilization of sludge for various purposes. Such regulations shall—

(1) identify uses for sludge, including disposal;

(2) specify factors to be taken into account in determining the measures and practices applicable to each such use or disposal (including publication of information on costs);

(3) identify concentrations of pollutants which interfere with each such use or disposal.

The Administrator is authorized to revise any regulation issued under this subsection.

(e) The determination of the manner of disposal or use of sludge is a local determination except that it shall be unlawful for the owner or operator of any publicly owned treatment works to dispose of sludge from such works for any use for which guidelines have been established pursuant to subsection (d) of this section, except in accordance with such guidelines.

TITLE V—GENERAL PROVISIONS

ADMINISTRATION

SEC. 501. (a) The Administrator is authorized to prescribe such regulations as are necessary to carry out his functions under this Act.

(b) The Administrator, with the consent of the head of any other agency of the United States, may utilize such officers and employees of such agency as may be found necessary to assist in carrying out the purposes of this Act.

(c) Each recipient of financial assistance under this Act shall keep such records as the Administrator shall prescribe, including records which fully disclose the amount and disposition by such recipient of the proceeds of such assistance, the total cost of the project or undertaking in connection with which such assistance is given or used, and the amount of that portion of the cost of the project or undertaking supplied by other sources, and such other records as will facilitate an effective audit.

(d) The Administrator and the Comptroller General of the United States, or any of their duly authorized representatives, shall have access, for the purpose of audit and examination, to any books, documents, papers, and records of the recipients that are pertinent to the grants received under this Act.

(e)(1) It is the purpose of this subsection to authorize a program which will provide official recognition by the United States Government to those industrial organizations and political subdivisions of States which during the preceding year demonstrated an outstanding technological achievement or an innovative process, method, or device in their waste treatment and pollution abatement programs. The Administrator shall, in consultation with the appropriate State water pollution control agencies, establish regulations under which such recognition may be applied for and granted, except that no applicant shall be eligible for an award under this subsection if such applicant is not in total compliance with all applicable water quality requirements under this Act, or otherwise does not have a satisfactory record with respect to environmental quality.

(2) The Administrator shall award a certificate or plaque of suitable design to each industrial organization or political subdivision which qualifies for such recognition under regulations established under this subsection.

(3) The President of the United States, the Governor of the appropriate State, the Speaker of the House of Representatives, and the President pro tempore of the Senate shall be notified of the award by the Administrator and the awarding of such recognition shall be published in the Federal Register.

(f) Upon the request of a State water pollution control agency, personnel of the Environmental Protection Agency may be detailed to such agency for the purpose of carrying out the provisions of this Act.

GENERAL DEFINITIONS

SEC. 502. Except as otherwise specifically provided, when used in this Act:

(1) The term "State water pollution control agency" means the State agency designated by the Governor having responsibility for enforcing State laws relating to the abatement of pollution.

(2) The term "interstate agency" means an agency of two or more States established by or pursuant to an agreement or compact approved by the Congress, or any other agency of two or more States, having substantial powers or duties pertaining to the control of pollution as determined and approved by the Administrator.

(3) The term "State" means a State, the District of Columbia, the Commonwealth of Puerto Rico, the Virgin Islands, Guam, American Samoa, and the Trust Territory of the Pacific Islands.

(4) The term "municipality" means a city, town, borough, county, parish, district, association, or other public body created by or pursuant to State law and having jurisdiction over disposal of sewage, industrial wastes, or other wastes, or an Indian tribe or an authorized Indian tribal organization, or a designated and approved management agency under section 208 of this Act.

(5) The term "person" means an individual, corporation, partnership, association, State, municipality, commission, or political subdivision of a State, or any interstate body.

(6) The term "pollutant" means dredged spoil, solid waste, incinerator residue, sewage, garbage, sewage sludge, munitions, chemical wastes, biological materials, radioactive materials, heat, wrecked or discarded equipment, rock, sand, celler dirt and industrial, municipal, and agricultural waste discharged into water. This term does not mean (A) "sewage from vessels" within the meaning of section 312 of this Act; or (B) water, gas, or other material which is injected into a well to facilitate production of oil or gas, or water derived in association with oil or gas production and disposed of in a well, if the well used either to facilitate production or for disposal purposes is approved by authority of the State in which the well is located, and if such State determines that such injection or disposal will not result in the degradation of ground or surface water resources.

(7) The term "navigable waters" means the waters of the United States, including the territorial seas.

(8) The term "territorial seas" means the belt of the seas measured from the line of ordinary low water along that portion of the coast which is in direct contact with the open sea and the line marking the seaward limit of inland waters, and extending seaward a distance of three miles.

(9) The term "contiguous zone" means the entire zone established or to be established by the United States under article 24 of the Convention of the Territorial Sea and the Contiguous Zone.

(10) The term "ocean" means any portion of the high seas beyond the contiguous zone.

(11) The term "effluent limitation" means any restriction established by a State or the Administrator on quantities, rates, and concentrations of chemical, physical, biological, and other constituents which are discharged from point sources into navigable waters, the waters of the contiguous zone, or the ocean, including schedules of compliance.

(12) The term "discharge of a pollutant" and the term "discharge of pollutants" each means (A) any addition of any pollutant to navigable waters from any point source, (B) any addition of any pollutant to the waters of the contiguous zone or the ocean from any point source other than a vessel or other floating craft.

(13) The term "toxic pollutant" means those pollutants, or combinations of pollutants, including disease-causing agents, which after discharge and upon exposure, ingestion, inhalation or assimilation into any organism, either directly from the environment or indirectly by ingestion through food chains, will, on the basis of information available to the Administrator, cause death, disease, behavioral abnormalities, cancer, genetic mutations, physiological malfunctions (including malfunctions in reproduction) or physical deformations, in such organisms or their offspring.

(14) The term "point source" means any discernible, confined and discrete conveyance, including but not limited to any pipe, ditch, channel, tunnel, conduit, well, discrete fissure, container, rolling stock, concentrated animal feeding operation, or vessel or other floating craft, from which pollutants are or may be discharged. This term does not include return flows from irrigated agriculture.

(15) The term "biological monitoring" shall mean the determination of the effects on aquatic life, including accumulation of pollutants in tissue, in receiving waters due to the discharge of pollutants (A) by techniques and procedures, including sampling of organisms representative of appropriate levels of the food chain appropriate to the volume and the physical, chemical, and biological characteristics of the effluent and (B) at appropriate frequencies and locations.

(16) The term "discharge" when used without qualification includes a discharge of a pollutant, and a discharge of pollutants.

(17) The term "schedule of compliance" means a schedule of remedial measures including an enforceable sequence of actions or operations leading to compliance with an effluent limitation, other limitation prohibition, or standard.

(18) The term "industrial user" means those industries identified in the Standard Industrial Classification Manual, Bureau of the Budget, 1967, as amended and supplemented, under the category "Division D—Manufacturing" and such other classes of significant waste producers as, by regulation, the Administrator deems appropriate.

(19) The term "pollution" means the man-made or man-induced alteration of the chemical, physical, biological, and radiological integrity of water.

WATER POLLUTION CONTROL ADVISORY BOARD

SEC. 503. (a)(1) There is hereby established in the Environmental Protection Agency a Water Pollution Control Advisory Board, composed of the Administrator or his designee, who shall be Chairman, and nine members appointed by the President, none of whom shall be Federal officers or employees. The appointed members, having due regard for the purposes of this Act, shall be selected from among representatives of various State, interstate, and local governmental agencies, of public or private interests contributing to, affected by, or concerned with pollution, and of other public and private agencies, organizations, or groups demonstrating an active interest in the field of pollution prevention and control, as well as other individuals who are expert in this field.

(2)(A) Each member appointed by the President shall hold office for a term of three years, except that (i) any member appointed to fill a vacancy occurring prior to the expiration of the term for which his predecessor was appointed shall be appointed for the remainder of such term, and (ii) the terms of office of the members first taking office after June 30, 1956, shall expire as follows: three at the end of one year after such date, three at the end of two years after such date, and three at the end of three years after such date, as designated by the President at the time of appointment, and (iii) the term of any member under the preceding provisions shall be extended until the date on which his successor's appointment is effective. None of the members appointed by the President shall be eligible for reappointment within one year after the end of his preceding term.

(B) The members of the Board who are not officers or employees of the United States, while attending conferences or meetings of the Board or while otherwise serving at the request of the Administrator, shall be entitled to receive compensation at a rate to be fixed by the Administrator, but not exceeding $100 per diem, including traveltime, and while away from their homes or regular places of business they may be allowed travel expenses, including per diem in lieu of subsistence, as authorized by law (5 U.S.C. 73b–2) for persons in the Government service employed intermittently.

(b) The Board shall advise, consult with, and make recommendations to the Administrator on matters of policy relating to the activities and functions of the Administrator under this Act.

(c) Such clerical and technical assistance as may be necessary to discharge the duties of the Board shall be provided from the personnel of the Environmental Protection Agency.

EMERGENCY POWERS

SEC. 504. Notwithstanding any other provision of this Act, the Administrator upon receipt of evidence that a pollution source or combination of sources is presenting an imminent and substantial endangerment to the health of persons or to the welfare of persons where such endangerment is to the livelihood of such persons, such as inability to market shellfish, may bring suit on behalf of the United States in the appropriate district court to immediately restrain any person causing or contributing to the alleged pollution to stop the discharge of pollutants causing or contributing to such pollution or to take such other action as may be necessary.

CITIZEN SUITS

SEC. 505. (a) Except as provided in subsection (b) of this section, any citizen may commence a civil action on his own behalf—

(1) against any person (including (i) the United States, and (ii) any other governmental instrumentality or agency to the extent permitted by the eleventh amendment to the Constitution) who is alleged to be in violation of (A) an effluent standard or limitation under this Act or (B) an order issued by the Administrator or a State with respect to such a standard or limitation, or

(2) against the Administrator where there is alleged a failure of the Administrator to perform any act or duty under this Act which is not discretionary with the Administrator.

The district courts shall have jurisdiction, without regard to the amount in controversy or the citizenship of the parties, to enforce such an effluent standard or limitation, or such an order, or to order the Administrator to perform such act or duty, as the case may be, and to apply any appropriate civil penalties under section 309(d) of this Act.

(b) No action may be commenced—

(1) under subsection (a)(1) of this section—

(A) prior to sixty days after the plaintiff has given notice of the alleged violation (i) to the Administrator, (ii) to the State in which the alleged violation occurs, and (iii) to any alleged violator of the standard, limitation, or order, or

(B) if the Administrator or State has commenced and is diligently prosecuting a civil or criminal action in a court of the United States, or a State to require compliance with the standard, limitation, or order, but in any such action in a court of the United States any citizen may intervene as a matter of right,

(2) under subsection (a)(2) of this section prior to sixty days after the plaintiff has given notice of such action to the Administrator,

except that such action may be brought immediately after such notification in the case of an action under this section respecting a violation of sections 306 and 307(a) of this Act. Notice under this subsection shall be given in such manner as the Administrator shall prescribe by regulation.

(c)(1) Any action respecting a violation by a discharge source of an effluent standard or limitation or an order respecting such standard or limitation may be brought under this section only in the judicial district in which such source is located.

(2) In such action under this section, the Administrator, if not a party, may intervene as a matter of right.

(d) The court, in issuing any final order in any action brought pursuant to this section, may award costs of litigation (including reasonable attorney and expert witness fees) to any party, whenever the court determines such award is appropriate. The court may, if a temporary restraining order or preliminary injunction is sought, require the filing of a bond or equivalent security in accordance with the Federal Rules of Civil Procedure.

(e) Nothing in this section shall restrict any right which any person (or class of persons) may have under any statute or common law to seek enforcement of any effluent standard or limitation or to seek any other relief (including relief against the Administrator or a State agency).

(f) For purposes of this section, the term "effluent standard or limitation under this Act" means (1) effective July 1, 1973, an unlawful act under subsection (a) of section 301 of this Act; (2) an effluent limitation or other limitation under section 301 or 302 of this Act; (3) standard or performance under section 306 of this Act; (3) prohibition, effluent standard or pretreatment standards under section 307 of this Act; (5) certification under section 401 of this Act; or (6) a permit or condition thereof issued under section 402 of this Act, which is in effect under this Act (including a requirement applicable by reason of section 313 of this Act).

(g) For the purposes of this section the term "citizen" means a person or persons having an interest which is or may be adversely affected.

(h) A Governor of a State may commence a civil action under subsection (a), without regard to the limitations of subsection (b) of this section, against the Administrator where there is alleged a failure of the Administrator to enforce an effluent standard or limitation under this Act the violation of which is occurring in another State and is causing an adverse effect on the public health or welfare in his State or is causing a violation of any water quality requirement in his State.

APPEARANCE

SEC. 506. The Administrator shall request the Attorney General to appear and represent the United States in any civil or criminal action instituted under this Act to which the Administrator is a party. Unless the Attorney General notifies the Administrator within a reasonable time, that he will appear in a civil action, attorneys who are officers or employees of the Environmental Protection Agency shall appear and represent the United States in such action.

EMPLOYEE PROTECTION

SEC. 507. (a) No person shall fire, or in any other way discriminate against, or cause to be fired or discriminated against, any employee or any authorized representative of employees by reason of the fact that such employee or representative has filed, instituted, or caused to be filed or instituted any proceeding under this Act, or has testified or is about to testify in any proceeding resulting from the administration or enforcement of the provisions of this Act.

(b) Any employee or a representative of employees who believes that he has been fired or otherwise discriminated against by any person in violation of subsection (a) of this section may, within thirty days after such alleged violation occurs, apply to the Secretary of Labor for a review of such firing or alleged discrimination. A copy of the application shall be sent to such person who shall be the respondent. Upon receipt of such application, the Secretary of Labor shall cause such investigation to be made as he deems appropriate. Such investigation shall provide an opportunity for a public hearing at the request of any party to such review to enable the parties to present information relating to such alleged violation. The parties shall be given written notice of the time and place of the hearing at least five days prior to the hearing. Any such hearing shall be of record and shall be subject to section 554 of title 5 of the United States Code. Upon receiving the report of such investigation, the Secretary of Labor shall make findings of fact. If he finds that such violation did occur, he shall issue a decision, incorporating an order therein and his findings, requiring the party committing such violation to take such affirmative action to abate the violation as the Secretary of Labor deems appropriate, including, but not limited to, the rehiring or reinstatement of the employee or representative of employees to his former position with compensation. If he finds that there was no such violation, he shall issue an order denying the application. Such order issued by the Secretary of Labor under this subparagraph shall be subject to judicial review in the same manner as orders and decisions of the Administrator are subject to judicial review under this Act.

(c) Whenever an order is issued under this section to abate such violation, at the request of the applicant, a sum equal to the aggregate amount of all costs and expenses (including the attorney's fees), as determined by the Secretary of Labor, to have been reasonably incurred by the applicant for, or in connection with, the institution and prosecution of such proceedings, shall be assessed against the person committing such violation.

(d) This section shall have no application to any employee who, acting without direction from his employer (or his agent) deliberately violates any prohibition of effluent limitation or other limitation under section 301 or 302 of this Act, standards of performance under section 306 of this Act, effluent standard, prohibition or pretreatment standard under section 307 of this Act, or any other prohibition or limitation established under this Act.

(e) The Administrator shall conduct continuing evaluations of potential loss or shifts of employment which may result from the issuance of any effluent limitation or order under this Act, including, where appropriate, investigating threatened plant closures or reductions in employment allegedly resulting from such limitation or order. Any employee who is discharged or laid off, threatened with discharge or lay-off, or otherwise discriminated against by any person because of the alleged results of any effluent limitation or order issued under this Act, or any representative of such employee, may request the Administrator to conduct a full investigation of the matter. The Administrator shall thereupon investigate the matter and, at the request of any party, shall hold public hearings on not less than five days notice, and shall at such hearings require the parties, including the employer involved, to present information relating to the actual or potential effect of such limitation or order on employment and on any alleged discharge, lay-off, or other discrimination and the detailed reasons or justification therefor. Any such hearing shall be of record and shall be subject to section 554 of title 5 of the United States Code. Upon receiving the report of such investigation, the Administrator shall make findings of fact as to the effect of such effluent limitation or order on employment and on the alleged discharge, lay-off, or discrimination and shall make such recommendations as he deems appropriate. Such report, findings, and recommendations shall be available to the public. Nothing in this subsection shall be construed to require or authorize the Administrator to modify or withdraw any effluent limitation or order issued under this Act.

FEDERAL PROCUREMENT

SEC. 508. (a) No Federal agency may enter into any contract with any person, who has been convicted of any offense under section 309 (c) of this Act, for the procurement of goods, materials, and services if such contract is to be performed at any facility at which the violation which gave rise to such conviction occurred, and if such facility is owned, leased, or supervised by such person. The prohibition in the preceding sentence shall continue until the Administrator certifies that the condition giving rise to such conviction has been corrected.

(b) The Administrator shall establish procedures to provide all Federal agencies with the notification necessary for the purposes of subsection (a) of this section.

(c) In order to implement the purposes and policy of this Act to protect and enhance the quality of the Nation's water, the President shall, not more than one hundred and eighty days after enactment of this Act, cause to be issued an order (1) requiring each Federal agency authorized to enter into contracts and each Federal agency which is empowered to extend Federal assistance by way of grant, loan, or contract to effectuate the purpose and policy of this Act in such contracting or assistance activities, and (2) setting forth procedures, sanctions, penalties, and such other provisions, as the President determines necessary to carry out such requirement.

(d) The President may exempt any contract, loan, or grant from all or part of the provisions of this section where he determines such exemption is necessary in the paramount interest of the United States and he shall notify the Congress of such exemption.

(e) The President shall annually report to the Congress on measures taken in compliance with the purpose and intent of this section, including, but not limited to, the progress and problems associated with such compliance.

ADMINISTRATIVE PROCEDURE AND JUDICIAL REVIEW

SEC. 509. (a)(1) For purposes of obtaining information under section 305 of this Act, or carrying out section 507(e) of this Act, the Administrator may issue subpenas for the attendance and testimony of witnesses and the production of relevant papers, books, and documents, and he may administer oaths. Except for effluent data, upon a showing satisfactory to the Administrator that such papers, books, documents, or information or particular part thereof, if made public, would divulge trade secrets or secret processes, the Administrator shall consider such record, report, or information or particular portion thereof confidential in accordance with the purposes of section 1905 of title 18 of the United States Code, except that such paper, book, document, or information may be disclosed to other officers, employees, or authorized representatives of the United States concerned with carrying out this Act, or when relevant in any proceeding under this Act. Witnesses summoned shall be paid the same fees and mileage that are paid witnesses in the courts of the United States. In case of contumacy or refusal to obey a subpena served upon any person under this subsection, the district court of the United States for any district in which such person is found or resides or transacts business, upon application by the United States and after notice to such person, shall have jurisdiction to issue an order requiring such person to appear and give testimony before the Administrator, to appear and produce papers, books, and documents before the Administrator, or both, and any failure to obey such order of the court may be punished by such court as a contempt thereof.

(2) The district courts of the United States are authorized, upon application by the Administrator, to issue subpenas for attendance and testimony of witnesses and the production of relevant papers, books, and documents, for purposes of obtaining information under section 304 (b) and (c) of this Act. Any papers, books, documents, or other information or part thereof, obtained by reason of such a subpena shall be subject to the same requirements as are provided in paragraph (1) of this subsection.

(b)(1) Review of the Administrator's action (A) in promulgating any standard of performance under section 306, (B) in making any determination pursuant to section 306(b)(1)(C), (C) in promulgating any effluent standard, prohibition, or pretreatment standard under section 307, (D) in making any determination as to a State permit program submitted under section 402(b), (E) in approving or promulgating any effluent limitation or other limitation under section 301, 302, or 306, and (F) in issuing or denying any permit under section 402, may be had by any interested person in the Circuit Court of Appeals of the United States for the Federal judicial district in which such person resides or transacts such business upon application by such person. Any such application shall be made within ninety days from the date of such determination, approval, promulgation, issuance or denial, or after such date only if such application is based solely on grounds which arose after such ninetieth day.

(2) Action of the Administrator with respect to which review could have been obtained under paragraph (1) of this subsection shall not be subject to judicial review in any civil or criminal proceeding for enforcement.

(c) In any judicial proceeding brought under subsection (b) of this section in which review is sought of a determination under this Act required to be made on the record after notice and opportunity for hearing, if any party applies to the court for leave to adduce additional evidence, and shows to the satisfaction of the court that such additional evidence is material and that there were reasonable grounds for the failure to adduce such evidence in the proceeding before the Administrator, the court may order such additional evidence (and evidence in rebuttal thereof) to be taken before the Administrator, in such manner and upon such terms and conditions as the court may deem proper. The Administrator may modify his findings as to the facts, or make new findings, by reason of the additional evidence so taken and he shall file such modified or new findings, and his recommendation, if any, for the modification or setting aside of his original determination, with the return of such additional evidence.

STATE AUTHORITY

SEC. 510. Except as expressly provided in this Act, nothing in this Act shall (1) preclude or deny the right of any State or political subdivision thereof or interstate agency to adopt or enforce (A) any standard of limitation respecting discharges of pollutants, or (B) any requirement respecting control or abatement of pollution; except that if an effluent limitation, or other limitation, effluent standard, prohibition, pretreatment standard, or standard of performacne is in effect under this Act, such State or political subdivision or interstate agency may not adopt or enforce any effluent limitation, or other limitation, effluent standard, prohibition, pretreatment standard, or standard of performance which is less stringent than the effluent limitation, or other limitation, effluent standard, prohibition, pretreatment standard, or standard of performance under this Act; or (2) be construed as impairing or in any manner affecting any right or jurisdiction of the States with respect to the waters (including boundary waters) of such States.

OTHER AFFECTED AUTHORITY

SEC. 511. (a) This Act shall not be construed as (1) limiting the authority or functions of any officer or agency of the United States under any other law or regulation not inconsistent with this Act; (2) affecting or impairing the authority of the Secretary of the Army

(A) to maintain navigation or (B) under the Act of March 3, 1899 (30 Stat. 1112), except that any permit issued under section 404 of this Act shall be conclusive as to the effect on water quality of any discharge resulting from any activity subject to section 10 of the Act of March 3, 1899, or (3) affecting or impairing the provisions of any treaty of the United States.

(b) Discharges of pollutants into the navigable waters subject to the Rivers and Harbors Act of 1910 (36 Stat. 593; 33 U.S.C. 421) and the Supervisory Harbors Act of 1888 (25 Stat. 209; 33 U.S.C. 441–451b) shall be regulated pursuant to this Act, and not subject to such Act of 1910 and the Act of 1888 except as to effect on navigation and anchorage.

(c)(1) Except for the provision of Federal financial assistance for the purpose of assisting the construction of publicly owned treatment works as authorized by section 201 of this Act, and the issuance of a permit under section 402 of this Act for the discharge of any pollutant by a new source as defined in section 306 of this Act, no action of the Administrator taken pursuant to this Act shall be deemed a major Federal action significantly affecting the quality of the human environment within the meaning of the National Environmental Policy Act of 1969 (83 Stat. 852); and

(2) Nothing in the National Environmental Policy Act of 1969 (83 Stat. 852) shall be deemed to—

(A) authorize any Federal agency authorized to license or permit the conduct of any activity which may result in the discharge of a pollutant into the navigable waters to review any effluent limitation or other requirement established pursuant to this Act or the adequacy of any certification under section 401 of this Act; or

(B) authorize any such agency to impose, as a condition precedent to the issuance of any license or permit, any effluent limitation other than any such limitation established pursuant to this Act.

(d) Notwithstanding this Act or any other provision of law, the Administrator (1) shall not require any State to consider in the development of the ranking in order of priority of needs for the construction of treatment works (as defined in title II of this Act), any water pollution control agreement which may have been entered into between the United States and any other nation, and (2) shall not consider any such agreement in the approval of any such priority ranking.

SEPARABILITY

SEC. 512. If any provision of this Act, or the application of any provision of this Act to any person or circumstance, is held invalid, the application of such provision to other persons or circumstances, and the remainder of this Act, shall not be affected thereby.

LABOR STANDARDS

SEC. 513. The Administrator shall take such action as may be necessary to insure that all laborers and mechanics employed by contractors or subcontractors on treatment works for which grants are made under this Act shall be paid wages at rates not less than those prevailing for the same type of work on similar construction in the immediate locality, as determined by the Secretary of Labor, in accordance with the Act of March 3, 1931, as amended, known as the Davis-Bacon Act (46 Stat. 1494; 40 U.S.C., sec. 276a through 276a–5). The Secretary of Labor shall have, with respect to the labor standards specified in this subsection, the authority and functions set forth in Reorganization Plan Numbered 14 of 1950 (15 F.R. 3176) and section 2 of the Act of June 13, 1934, as amended (48 Stat. 948; 40 U.S.C. 276c).

PUBLIC HEALTH AGENCY COORDINATION

SEC. 514. The permitting agency under section 402 shall assist the applicant for a permit under such section in coordinating the requirements of this Act with those of the appropriate public health agencies.

EFFLUENT STANDARDS AND WATER QUALITY INFORMATION ADVISORY COMMITTEE

SEC. 515. (a)(1) There is established on Effluent Standards and Water Quality Information Advisory Committee, which shall be composed of a Chairman and eight members who shall be appointed by the administrator within sixty days after the date of enactment of this Act.

(2) All members of the Committee shall be selected from the scientific community, qualified by education, training, and experience to provide, assess, and evaluate scientific and technical information on effluent standards and limitations.

(3) Members of the Committee shall serve for a term of four years, and may be reappointed.

(b)(1) No later than one hundred and eighty days prior to the date on which the Administrator is required to publish any proposed regulations required by section 304(b) of this Act, any proposed standard of performance for new sources required by section 306 of this Act, or any proposed toxic effluent standard required by section 307 of this Act, he shall transmit to the Committee a notice of intent to propose such regulations. The Chairman of the Committee within ten days after receipt of such notice may publish a notice of a public hearing by the Committee, to be held within thirty days.

(2) No later than one hundred and twenty days after receipt of such notice, the Committee shall transmit to the Administrator such scientific and technical information as is in its possession, including that presented at any public hearing, related to the subject matter contained in such notice.

(3) Information so transmitted to the Administrator shall constitute a part of the administrative record and comments on any proposed regulations or standards as information to be considered with other comments and information in making any final determinations.

(4) In preparing information for transmittal, the Committee shall avail itself of the technical and scientific services of any Federal agency, including the United States Geological Survey and any national environmental laboratories which may be established.

(c)(1) The Committee shall appoint and prescribe the duties of a Secretary, and such legal counsel as it deems necessary. The Committee shall appoint such other employees as it deems necessary to exercise and fulfills its powers and responsibilities. The compensation of all employees appointed by the Committee shall be fixed in accordance with chapter 51 and subchapter III of chapter 53 of title V of the United States Code.

(2) Members of the Committee shall be entitled to receive compensation at a rate to be fixed by the President but not in excess of the maximum rate of pay grade for GS-18, as provided in the General Schedule under section 5332 of title V of the United States Code.

(d) Five members of the Committee shall constitute a quorum, and official actions of the Committee shall be taken only on the affirmative vote of at least five members. A special panel composed of one or more members upon order of the Committee shall conduct any hearing authorized by this section and submit the transcript of such hearing to the entire Committee for its action thereon.

(e) The Committee is authorized to make such rules as are necessary for the orderly transaction of its business.

REPORTS TO CONGRESS

SEC. 516. (a) Within ninety days following the convening of each session of Congress, the Administrator shall submit to the Congress a report, in addition to any other report required by this Act, on measures taken toward implementing the objective of this Act, including, but not limited to, (1) the progress and problems associated with developing comprehensive plans under section 102 of this Act, areawide plans under section 208 of this Act, basin plans under section 209 of this Act, and plans under section 303(e) of this Act; (2) a summary of actions taken and results achieved in the field of water pollution control research, experiments, studies, and related matters by the Administrator and other Federal agencies and by other persons and agencies under Federal grants or contracts; (3) the progress and problems associated with the development of effluent limitations and recommended control techniques; (4) the status of State programs, including a detailed summary of the progress obtained as compared to that planned under State program plans for development and enforcement of water quality requirements; (5) the identification and status of enforcement actions pending or completed under such Act during the preceding year; (6) the status of State, interstate, and local pollution control programs established pursuant to, and assisted by, this Act; (7) a summary of the results of the survey required to be taken under section 210 of this Act; (8) his activities including recommendations under sections 109 through 111 of this Act; and (9) all reports and recommendations made by the Water Pollution Control Advisory Board.

(b)(1) The Administrator, in cooperation with the States, including water pollution control agencies and other water pollution control planning agencies, shall make (A) a detailed estimate of the cost of carrying out the provisions of this Act; (B) a detailed estimate, biennially revised, of the cost of construction of all needed publicly owned treatment works in all of the States and of the cost of construction of all needed publicly owned treatment works in each of the States; (C) a comprehensive study of the economic impact on affected units of government of the cost of installation of treatment facilities; and (D) a comprehensive analysis of the national requirements for and the cost of treating municipal, industrial, and other effluent to attain the water quality objectives as established by this Act or applicable State law. The Administrator shall submit such detailed estimate and such comprehensive study of such cost to the Congress no later than February 10 of each odd-numbered year. Whenever the Administrator, pursuant to this subsection, requests and receives an estimate of cost from a State, he shall furnish copies of such estimate together with such detailed estimate to Congress.

(2) Notwithstanding the second sentence of paragraph (1) of this subsection, the Administrator shall make a preliminary detailed estimate called for by subparagraph (B) of such paragraph and shall submit such preliminary detailed estimate to the Congress no later than September 3, 1974. The Administrator shall require each State to prepare an estimate of cost for such State, and shall utilize the survey form EPA-1, O.M.B. No. 158-R0017, prepared for the 1973 detailed estimate, except that such estimate shall include all costs of compliance with section 201(g)(2)(A) of this Act and water quality standards established pursuant to section 303 of this Act, and all costs of treatment works as defined in section 212(2), including all eligible costs of constructing sewage collection systems and correcting excessive infiltration or inflow and all eligible costs of correcting combined storm and sanitary sewer problems and treating storm water flows. The survey form shall be distributed by the Administrator to each State no later than January 31, 1974.

(c) The Administrator shall submit to the Congress by October 1, 1978, a report on the status of combined sewer overflows in municipal treatment works operations. The report shall include (1) the status of any projects funded under this Act to address combined sewer overflows, (2) a listing by State of combined sewer overflow needs identified in the 1977 State priority listings, (3) an estimate for each applicable municipality of the number of years necessary, assuming an annual authorization and appropriation for the construction grants program of $5,000,000,000 to correct combined sewer overflow problems, (4) an analysis using representative municipalities faced with major combined sewer overflow needs, of the annual discharges of pollutants from overflows in comparison to treated effluent discharges, (5) an analysis of the technological alternatives available to municipalities to correct major combined sewer overflow problems, and (6) any recommendations of the Administrator for legislation to address the problem of combined sewer overflows, including whether a separate authorization and grant program should be established by the Congress to address combined sewer overflows.

(d) The Administrator shall submit to the Congress by October 1, 1978, a report on the status of the use of municipal secondary effluent and sludge for agricultural and other purposes that utilize the nutrient value of treated wastewater effluent. The report shall include (1) a summary of results of research and development programs, grants, and contracts carried out by the Environmental Protection Agency pursuant to sections 104 and 105 of this Act, regarding alternatives to disposal, landfill, or incineration of secondary effluent of sludge, (2) an estimate of the amount of sludge generated by public treatment works and its disposition, including an estimate of annual energy costs to incinerate sludge, (3) an analysis of current technologies for the utilization, reprocessing, and other uses of sludge to utilize the nutrient value of sludge, (4) legal, institutional, public health, economic, and other impediments to the greater utilization of treated sludge, and (5) any recommendations of the Administrator for legislation to encourage or require the expanded utilization of sludge for agricultural and other purposes. In carrying out this subsection, the Administrator shall consult with, and use the services of the Tennessee Valley Authority and other departments, agencies, and instrumentalities of the United States, to the extent it is appropriate to do so.

(e) The Administrator, in cooperation with the States, including water pollution control agencies, and other water pollution control planning agencies, and water supply and water resources agencies of the States and the United States shall submit to Congress, within two years of the date of enactment of this section, a report with recommendations for legislation on a program to require coordination between water supply and wastewater control plans as a condition to grants for construction of treatment works under this Act. No such report shall be submitted except after opportunity for public hearings on such proposed report.

GENERAL AUTHORIZATION

SEC. 517. There are authorized to be appropriated to carry out this Act, other than sections 104, 105, 106(a), 107, 108, 112, 113, 114, 115, 206, 207, 208 (f) and (h), 209, 304, 311 (c), (d), (i), (l), and (k), 314, 315, and 317, $250,000,000 for the fiscal year ending June 30, 1973, $300,000,000 for the fiscal year ending June 30, 1974, $350,000,000 for the fiscal year ending June 30, 1975, $100,000,000 for the fiscal year ending September 30, 1977, $150,000,000 for the fiscal year ending September 30, 1978, $150,000,000 for the fiscal year ending September 30, 1979, $150,000,000 for the fiscal year ending September 30, 1980, $150,000,000 for the fiscal year ending September 30, 1981, and $160,000,000 for the fiscal year ending September 30, 1982.

SHORT TITLE

SEC. 518. This Act may be cited as the "Federal Water Pollution Control Act" (commonly referred to as the Clean Water Act).

NOTE

The following provisions of Public Law 96-483 do not amend the Clean Water Act.

SEC. 2(a) * * *

* * * * * * *

(c) The Administrator of the Environmental Protection Agency shall take such action as may be necessary to remove from any grant made under section 201(g)(1) of the Federal Water Pollution Control Act after March 1, 1973, and prior to the date of enactment of this Act, any condition or requirement no longer applicable as a result of the repeals made by subsections (a) and (b) of this section or release any grant recipient of the obligations established by such conditions of other requirement.

* * * * * * *

(f)(1) Section 75(b) of the Federal Water Pollution Control Act of 1977 (91 Stat. 1610) is hereby repealed.

(2) Section 75(d) of the Clean Water Act of 1977 (91 Stat. 1610) is hereby repealed.

(g) The amendments made by this section shall take effect on December 27, 1977.

* * * * * * *

SEC. 4. The Administrator of the Environmental Protection Agency shall study and report to the Congress not later than March 15, 1981, on the effect of the amendment made by section 3 on the construction of publicly owned treatment works, industrial participation in publicly owned treatments works, treatment of industrial discharges, and the appropriate degree of Federal and non-Federal participation in the funding of publicly owned treatment works.

* * * * * * *

SEC. 7. Notwithstanding section 205(d) of the Federal Water Pollution Control Act (33 U.S.C. 1285), sums allotted to the States for the fiscal year 1979 shall remain available for obligation for the fiscal year for which authorized and for the period of the next succeeding twenty-four months. The amount of any allotment not obligated by the end of such thirty-six month period shall be immediately reallotted by the Administrator on the basis of the same ratio as applicable to sums allotted for the then current fiscal year, except that none of the funds reallotted by the Administrator for fiscal year 1979 shall be allotted to any State which failed to obligate any of the funds being reallotted. Any sum made available to a State by reallotment under this section shall be in addition to any funds otherwise allotted to such State for grants under title II of the Federal Water Pollution Control Act during any fiscal year. This section shall take effect on September 30, 1980.

* * * * * * *

SEC. 12. The Administrator of the Environmental Protection Agency is authorized to make grants to States to undertake a demonstration program for the cleanup of State-owned abandoned mines which can be used as hazardous waste disposal sites. The State shall pay 10 per centum of project costs. At a minimum, the Administrator shall undertake projects under such program in the States of Ohio, Illinois, and West Virginia. There are authorized to be appropriated $10,000,000 per fiscal year for each of the fiscal years ending September 30, 1982, September 30, 1983, and September 30, 1984, to carry out this section. Such projects shall be undertaken in accordance with all applicable laws and regulations.

The following provisions of Public Law 97-117 do not amend the Clean Water Act.

REVISED WATER QUALITY STANDARDS

SEC. 24. The review, revision, and adoption or promulgation of revised or new water quality standards pursuant to section 303(c) of the Federal Water Pollution Control Act shall be completed by th date three years after the enactment of the Municipal Wastewater Treatment Construction Grant Amendments of 1981. No grant shall be made under title II of the Federal Water Pollution Control Act after such date until water quality standards are reviewed and revised pursuant to section 303(c), except where the State has in good faith submitted such revised water quality standards and the Administrator has not acted to approve or disapprove such submission within one hundred and twenty days of receipt.

NEEDS SURVEY

SEC. 25. The Administrator of the Environmental Protection Agency shall submit to the Congress, not later than December 31, 1982, a report containing the detailed estimates, comprehensive study, and comprehensive analysis required by section 516(b) of the Federal Water Pollution Control Act, including an estimate of the total cost and the amount of Federal funds necessary for the construction of needed publicly owned treatment facilities. Such report shall be prepared in the same manner as is required by such section and shall reflect the changes made in the Federal water pollution control program by this Act and the amendments made by this Act. In preparing this report, the Administrator shall give emphasis to the effects of the amendment made by section 2(a) of this Act in addressing water quality needs adequately and appropriately.

JUDICIAL NOTICE

SEC. 26. It is the sense of Congress that judicial notice should be taken of this Act and of the amendments to the Federal Water Pollution Control Act made by this Act, including reduced authorization levels under section 207 of such Act, and that the parties to Federal consent decrees establishing a deadline, schedule, or timetable for the construction of publicly owned treatment works are encouraged to reexamine the provisions of such consent decrees and, where required by equity, to make appropriate adjustments in such provisions.

BATH TOWNSHIP

SEC. 27. For purposes of the Federal Water Pollution Control Act, the project for publicly owned treatment works for Bath Township, Michigan, shall be eligible for payments from sums allocated to the State of Michigan under such Act in an amount equal to the amount such works would be eligible for under section 202 of such Act if such works were to be constructed after the date of enactment of this Act, at the original construction cost.

NOTE

The following provision of Public Law 97-216 does not amend the Clean Water Act.

CONSTRUCTION GRANTS

For necessary expenses to carry out title II of the Federal Water Pollution Control Act, as amended, other than sections 201(m), 205(k), except that for the project authorized by said section the Administrator shall allocate to the State of New York an amount equal to one-third of the total cost from the amount made available under this paragraph to the State of New York, one-third from the amount made available to the State of New Jersey, and one-third from the amounts made available to the remaining States, 206, 208, and 209, $2,400,000,000, including grants for biological treatment facilities to repair or replace small community systems but not to exceed three systems suffering operational problems outside the warranty period where the existing Environmental Protection Agency planned systems have proven to be inoperable by the local municipalities, where determined to be necessary, to remain available until expended: *Provided*, That of such amount, $3,965,426 in additional funds (the amount which was withheld from the State of Kansas by reason of an accounting error by the Federal Government) shall be made available to the State of Kansas: *Provided further*, That nothing herein shall prohibit any project specified in section 201(m) from receiving a grant under section 201(g), in compliance with all relevant procedures under title II of the Federal Water Pollution Control Act, as amended, and paid from funds allotted to the State by section 205 and appropriated by this Act: *Provided further*, That the Administrator, upon application by the Governor of the State of Ohio, with the approval of the Committees on Appropriations, shall before October 1, 1982, commit existing unobligated funds from the State's Wastewater Construction Grant allotments to fund the Solid Waste Energy facility in Akron, Ohio.

NOTE

The following provision was provided by Public Law 97-272.

CONSTRUCTION GRANTS

For necessary expenses to carry out title II of the Federal Water Pollution Control Act, as amended, including sections 201(n)(2) and 201(m)(3), other than sections 206, 208, and 209, $2,430,000,000, to remain available until expended.

Section 307(a)(1) refers to the following Table.

TABLE I.—SECTION 307—TOXIC POLLUTANTS

Acenaphthene
Acrolein
Acrylonitrile
Aldrin/Dieldrin
Antimony and compounds*
Arsenic and compounds
Asbestos
Benzene
Benzidine
Beryllium and compounds
Cadmium and compounds
Carbon tetrachloride
Chlordane (technical mixture and metabolites)
Chlorinated benzenes (other than dichlorobenzenes)
Chlorinated ethanes (including 1,2-dichloroethane, 1,1,1-trichloroethane, and hexachloroethane)
Chloroalkyl ethers (chloromethyl, chloroethyl, and mixed ethers)
Chlorinated naphthalene
Chlorinated phenols (other than those listed elsewhere; includes trichlorophenols and chlorinated cresols)
Chloroform
2-chlorophenol
Chromium and compounds
Copper and compounds
Cyanides
DDT and metabolites
Dichlorobenzenes (1,2-, 1,3-, and 1,4-dichlorobenzenes)
Dichlorobenzidine
Dichloroethylenes (1,1- and 1,2-dichloroethylene)
2,4-dichlorophenol
Dichloropropane and dichloropropene
2,4-dimethylphenol
Dinitrotoluene
Diphenylhydrazine
Endosulfan and metabolites
Endrin and metabolites
Ethylbenzene
Fluoranthene
Haloethers (other than those listed elsewhere; includes chlorophenylphenyl ethers, bromophenylphenyl ether, bis(dischloroisopropyl) ether, bis-(chloroethoxy) methane and polychlorinated diphenyl ethers)
Halomethanes (other than those listed elsewhere; includes methylene chlorid methylchloride, methylbromide, bromoform, dichlorobromomethane, trichlorofluoromethane, dichlorodifluoromethane)
Heptachlor and metabolites
Hexachlorobutadiene
Hexachlorocyclohexane (all isomers)
Hexachlorocyclopentadiene
Isophorone
Lead and compounds
Mercury and compounds
Naphthalene
Nickel and compounds
Nitrobenzene
Nitrophenols (Including 2,4-dinitrophenol) dinitrocresol)
Nitrosamines
Pentachlorophenol
Phenol
Phthalate esters
Polychlorinated biphenyls (PCSs)
Polynuclear aromatic hydrocarbons (including benzanthracenes, benzopyrenes, benzofluoranthene, chrysenes, dibenzanthracenes, and indenopyrenes)
Selenium and compounds
Silver and compounds
2,3,7,8- Tetrachlorodibenzo-p-dioxin (TCDD)
Tetrachloroethylene
Thallium and compounds
Toluene
Toxaphene
Trichloroethylene
Vinyl chloride
Zinc and compounds

* The term "compounds" shall include organic and inorganic compounds.

MARINE PROTECTION, RESEARCH, AND SANCTUARIES ACT OF 1972

as amended[1]

An Act to regulate the transportation for dumping, and the dumping of material into ocean waters, and for other purposes.

This Act may be cited as the "Marine Protection, Research, and Sanctuaries Act of 1972."

Finding, Policy, and Purpose

"Sec. 2 (a) Unregulated dumping of material into ocean waters endangers human health, welfare, and amenities, and the marine environment, ecological systems, and economic potentialities.

"(b) The Congress declares that it is the policy of the United States to regulate the dumping of all types of materials into ocean waters and to prevent or strictly limit the dumping into ocean waters of any material which would adversely affect human health, welfare, or amenities, or the marine environment, ecological systems, or economic potentialities.

"(c) It is the purpose of this Act to regulate

"(1) the transportation by any person of material from the United States and, in the case of United States vessels, aircraft, or agencies, the transportation of material from a location outside the United States, when in either case the transportation is for the purpose of dumping the material into ocean waters, and

"(2) the dumping of material transported by any person from a location outside the United States if the dumping occurs in the territorial sea or the contiguous zone of the United States.

"Sec. 3. For the purposes of this Act the term —

"(a) "Administrator" means the Administrator of the Environmental Protection Agency.

"(b) "Ocean waters" means those waters of the open seas lying seaward of the base line from which the territorial sea is measured, as provided for in the Convention on the Territorial Sea and the Contiguous Zone (15 UST 1606; TIAS 5639).

"(c) "Material" means matter of any kind or description, including, but not limited to, dredged material, solid waste, incinerator residue, garbage, sewage, sewage sludge, munitions, radiological, chemical, and biological warfare agents, radioactive materials, chemicals, biological and laboratory waste, wreck or discarded equipment, rock, sand, excavation debris, and industrial, municipal, agricultural, and other waste, but such term does not mean sewage from vessels within the meaning of sections 312 of the Federal Water Pollution Control Act, as amended (33 USC 1322). Oil within the meaning of section 311 of the Federal Water Pollution Control Act, as amended (33 USC 1321), shall be included only to the extent that such oil is taken on board a vessel or aircraft for the purpose of dumping.

---

[1] Enacted by PL 92-532, October 23, 1972, 86 Stat. 1052; 33 U.S.C. 1401 et seq.; As amended by PL 93-254, March 22, 1974; PL 93-472, October 26, 1974; PL 94-62, July 25, 1975; PL 94-326, June 30, 1976; PL 95-153, November 4, 1977; PL 96-332, August 29, 1980; PL 96-381, October 6, 1980; PL 96-470, October 19, 1980; PL 96-572, December 22, 1980; PL 97-16, June 23, 1981; PL 97-109, December 26, 1981; PL 97-424, January 6, 1983.

"(d) "United States" includes the several States, the District of Columbia, the Commonwealth of Puerto Rico, the Canal Zone, the territories and possessions of the United States, and the Trust Territory of the Pacific Islands.

"(e) "Person" means any private person or entity, or any officer, employee, agent, department, agency, or instrumentality of the Federal Government, of any State or local unit of government, or of any foreign government.

"(f) "Dumping" means a disposition of material: Provided, That it does not mean a disposition of any effluent from any outfall structure to the extent that such disposition is regulated under the provisions of the Federal Water Pollution Control Act, as amended (33 USC 1251-1376) under the provisions of section 13 of the Rivers and Harbors Act of 1899, as amended (33 USC 407), or under the provisions of the Atomic Energy Act of 1954, as amended (42 USC 2011, et seq.), nor does it mean a routine discharge of effluent incidental to the propulsion of, or operation of motor-driven equipment on, vessels. Provided further, That it does not mean the construction of any fixed structure or artificial island nor the intentional placement of any device in ocean waters or on or in the submerged land beneath such waters, for a purpose other than disposal, when such construction or such placement is otherwise regulated by Federal or State law or occurs pursuant to an authorized Federal or State program. And provided further, That it does not include the deposit of oyster shells or other materials when such deposit is made for the purpose of developing, maintaining, or harvesting fisheries resources and is otherwise regulated by Federal or State law or occurs pursuant to an authorized Federal or State program.

"(g) "District Court of the United States" includes the District Court of Guam, the District Court of the Virgin Islands, the District Court of Puerto Rico, the District Court of the Canal Zone, and in the case of American Samoa and the Trust Territory of the Pacific Islands, the District Court of the United States for the District of Hawaii, which court shall have jursidiction over actions arising therein.

"(h) "Secretary" means the Secretary of the Army.

"(i) "Dredged material" means any material excavated or dredged from the navigable waters of the United States.

"(j) "High-level radioactive waste" means the aqueous waste resulting from the operation of the first cycle solvent extraction system, or equivalent, and the concentrated waste from subsequent extraction cycles, or equivalent, in a facility for reprocessing irradiated reactor fuels, or irradiated fuel from nuclear power reactors.

"(k) "Transport" or "transportation" refers to the carriage and related handling of any material by a vessel, or by any other vehicle, including aircraft.

"(l) "Convention" means the Convention on the Prevention of Marine Pollution by Dumping of Wastes and Other Matter.

TITLE I — OCEAN DUMPING
Prohibited Acts

"Sec. 101 (a) Except as may be authorized by a permit issued pursuant to section 102 or section 103 of this title, and subject to regulations issued pursuant to section 108 of this title,

"(1) no person shall transport from the United States, and

"(2) in the case of a vessel or aircraft registered in the United States or flying the United States flag or in the case of a United States department, agency, or instrumentality, no person shall transport from any location any material for the purpose of dumping it into ocean waters.

"(b) Except as may be authorized by a permit issued pursuant to section 102 of this title, and subject to regulations issued pursuant to section 108 of this title, no person shall dump any material transported from a location outside the United States (1) into the territorial sea of the United States, or (2) into a zone contiguous to the territorial sea of the United States, extending to a line twelve nautical miles seaward from the base line from which the breadth of the territorial sea is measured, to the extent that it may affect the territorial sea or the territory of the United States.

"Sec. 4 (a) The Administrator of the Environmental Protection Agency (hereinafter referred to in this section as the "Administrator") shall end the dumping of sewage sludge and industrial waste into ocean waters, or into waters described in section 101(b) of the Marine Protection, Research and Sanctuaries Act of 1972, as soon as possible after the date of enactment of this section, but except as provided in subsections (b) and (c) in no case may the Administrator issue any permit, or any renewal thereof (under title I of such Act of 1972) which authorizes any such dumping after December 31, 1981.

"(b) After December 31, 1981, the Administrator may issue permits under such title I for the dumping of industrial waste into ocean waters, or into waters described in such section 101(b), if the Administrator determines --

"(1) that the proposed dumping is necessary to conduct research --

"(A) on new technology related to ocean dumping, or

"(B) to determine whether the dumping of such substance will unreasonably degrade or endanger human health, welfare, or amenities, or the marine environment, ecological systems, or economic potentialities;

"(2) that the scale of the proposed dumping is such that the dumping will have minimal adverse impact upon the human health, welfare, and amenities, and the marine environment, ecological systems, and economic potentialities; and

"(3) after consultation with the Secretary of Commerce, that the potential benefits of such research will outweigh any such adverse impact.

Each permit issued pursuant to this subsection shall be subject to such conditions and restrictions as the Administrator determines to be necessary to minimize possible adverse impacts of such dumping. No permit issued by the Administrator pursuant to this subsection may have an effective period of more than six consecutive months.

"(c) After December 31, 1981, the Administrator may issue emergency permits under such title I for the dumping of industrial waste into ocean waters, or into waters described in such section 101(b), if the Administrator determines that there has been demonstrated to exist an emergency, requiring the dumping of such waste, which poses an unacceptable risk relating to human health and admits of no other feasible solution. As used herein, "emergency" refers to situations requiring action with a marked degree of urgency.

"(d) For purposes of this section --

"(1) the term "sewage sludge" means any solid, semisolid, or liquid waste generated by a municipal wastewater treatment plant the ocean dumping of which may unreasonably degrade or endanger human health, welfare, or amenities, or the marine environment, ecological systems, and economic potentialities; and

"(2) the term "industrial waste" means any solid, semisolid, or liquid waste generated by a manufacturing or processing plant the ocean dumping of which may unreasonably degrade or endanger human health, welfare, or amenities, or the marine environment, ecological systems, and economic potentialities.

Environmental Protection Agency Permits

"Sec. 102 (a) Except in relation to dredged material as provided for in section 103 of this title, and in relation to radiological, chemical, and biological warfare agents and high-level radioactive waste, for which no permit may be issued, the Administrator may issue permits, after notice and opportunity for public hearings, for the transportation from the United States or, in the case of an agency or instrumentality of the United States, for the transportation from a location outside the United States, of material for the purpose of dumping it into ocean waters, or for the dumping of material into the waters described in section 101(b), where the Administrator determines that such dumping will not unreasonably degrade or endanger human health, welfare, or amenities, or the marine environment, ecological systems, or economic potentialities. The Administrator shall establish and apply criteria for reviewing and evaluating such permit applications, and, in establishing or revising such criteria, shall consider, but not by limited in his consideration to, the following:

"(A) The need for the proposed dumping.

"(B) The effect of such dumping on human health and welfare, including economic, esthetic, and recreational values.

"(C) The effect of such dumping on fisheries resources, plankton, fish, shellfish, wildlife, shore lines and beaches.

"(D) The effect of such dumping on marine ecosystems, particularly with respect to —

"(i) the transfer, concentration, and dispersion of such material and its byproducts through biological, physical, and chemical processes,

"(ii) potential changes in marine ecosystem diversity, productivity, and stability, and

"(iii) species and community population dynamics.

"(E) The persistence and permanence of the effects of the dumping.

"(F) The effect of dumping particular volumes and concentrations of such materials.

"(G) Appropraite locations and methods of disposal or recycling, including land-based alternatives and the probable impact of requiring use of such alternate locations or methods upon considerations affecting the public interest.

"(H) The effect on alternate uses of oceans, such as scientific study, fishing, and other living resource exploitatation, and nonliving resource exploitation.

"(I) In designating recommended sites, the Administrator shall utilize wherever feasible locations beyond the edge of the Continental Shelf.

In establishing or revising such criteria, the Administrator shall consult with Federal, State and local officials, and interested members of the general public, as may appear appropriate to the Administrator with respect to such criteria as may affect the civil works program of the Department of the Army, the Administrator shall also consult with the Secretary. In reviewing applications for permits, the Administrator shall make such provision for consultation with interested Federal and State agencies as he deems useful or necessary. No permit shall be issued for a dumping of material which will violate applicable water quality standards.

To the extent that he may do so without relaxing the requirements of this title, the Administrator, in establishing or revising such criteria, shall apply the standards and criteria binding upon the United States under the Convention, including its Annexes.

"(b) The Administrator may establish and issue various categories of permits, including the general permits described in section 104(c).

"(c) The Administrator may, considering the criteria established pursuant to subsection (a) of this section, designate recommended sites or times for dumping and, when he finds it necessary to protect critical areas, shall, after consultation with the Secretary, also designate sites or times within which certain materials may not be dumped.

"(d) No permit is required under this title for the transportation for dumping or the dumping of fish wastes, except when deposited in harbors or other protected or enclosed coastal waters, or where the Administrator finds that such deposits could endanger health, the environment, or ecological systems in a specific location. Where the Administrator makes such a finding, such material may be deposited only as authorized by a permit issued by the Administrator under this section.

"(e) In the case of transportation of material, by an agency or instrumentality of the United States or by a vessel or aircraft registered in the United States or flying the United States flag, from a location in a foreign State Party to the Convention, a permit issued pursuant to the authority of that foreign State Party, in accordance with Convention requirements, and which otherwise could have been issued pursuant to subsection (a) hereof, shall be accepted for the purposes of this title, as if it were issued by the Administrator under the authority of this section: Provided, That in the case of an agency or instrumentality of the United States, no application shall be made for a permit to be issued pursuant to the authority of a foreign State Party to the Convention unless the Administrator concurs in the filing of such application.

Corps of Engineers Permits

"Sec. 103 (a) Subject to the provisions of subsections (b), (c), and (d) of this section, the Secretary may issue permits, after notice and opportunity for public hearings, for the transportation of dredged material for the purpose of dumping it into ocean waters, where the Secretary determines that the dumping will not unreasonably degrade or endanger human health, welfare, or amenities, or the marine environment, ecological systems, or economic potentialities.

"(b) In making the determination required by subsection (a), the Secretary shall apply those criteria, established pursuant to section 102(a), relating to the effects of the dumping. Based upon an evaluation of the potential effect of a permit denial on navigation, economic and industrial development, and foreign and domestic commerce of the United States, the Secretary shall make an independent determination as to the need for the dumping. The Secretary shall also make an independent determination as to other possible methods of disposal and as to appropriate locations for the dumping. In considering appropriate locations, he shall, to the extent feasible, utilize the recomended sites designated by the Administrator pursuant to section 102(c).

"(c) Prior to issuing any permit under this section, the Secretary shall first notify the Administrator of his intention to do so. In any case in which the Administrator disagrees with the determination of the Secretary as to compliance with the criteria established pursuant to section 102(a) relating to the effects of the dumping or with the restrictions established pursuant to section 102(c), relating to critical areas, the determination of the Administrator shall prevail. Unless the Administrator grants a waiver pursuant to subsection (d), the Secretary shall not issue a permit which does not comply with such criteria and with such restrictions.

"(d) If, in any case, the Secretary finds that, in the disposition of dredged material, there is no economically feasible method or site available other than a dumping site the utilization of which would result in noncompliance with the criteria established pursuant to section 102(a) relating to the effects of dumping or with the restrictions established pursuant to section 102(c) relating to critical areas, he shall so certify and request a waiver from the Administrator of the specific requirements involved. Within thirty days of the receipt of the waiver request, unless the Administrator finds that the dumping of the material will result in an unacceptably adverse impact on municipal water supplies, shellfish beds, wildlife, fisheries (including spawning and breeding areas), or recreational areas, he shall grant the waiver.

"(e) In connection with Federal projects involving dredged material, the Secretary may, in lieu of the permit procedure, issue regulations which will require the application to such projects of the same criteria, other factors to be evaluated, the same procedures and the same requirements which apply to the issuance of permits under subsections (a), (b), (c), and (d) of this section.

Permit Conditions

"Sec. 104 (a) Permits issued under this title shall designate and include

"(1) the type of material authorized to be transported for dumping or to be dumped;

"(2) the amount of material authorized to be transported for dumping or to be dumped;

"(3) the location where such transport for dumping will be terminated or where such dumping will occur;

"(4) the length of time for which the permits are valid and their expiration date;

"(5) any special provisions deemed necessary by the Administrator or the Secretary, as the case may be, after consultation with the Secretary of the Department in which the Coast Guard is operating, for the monitoring and surveillance of the transportation or dumping; and

"(6) such other matters and the Administrator or the Secretary, as the case may be, deems appropriate.

"(b) The Administrator or the Secretary, as the case may be, may prescribe such processing fees for permits and such reporting requirements for actions taken pursuant to permits issued by him under this title as he deems appropriate.

"(c) Consistent with the requirements of sections 102 and 103, but in lieu of a requirement for specific permits in such case, the Administrator or the Secretary, as the case may be, may issue general permits for the transportation for dumping, or dumping, or both, of specified materials or classes of materials for which he may issue permits, which he determines will have a minimal adverse environmental impact.

"(d) Any permit issued under this title shall be reviewed periodically and, if appropriate, revised. The Administrator or the Secretary, as the case may be, may limit or deny the issuance of permits, or he may alter or revoke partially or entirely the terms of permits issued by him under this title, for the transportation for dumping, or for the dumping, or both, of specified materials or classes of materials, where he finds that such materials cannot be dumped consistently with the criteria and other factors required to be applied in evaluating the permit application. No action shall be taken under this subsection unless the affected person or permittee shall have been given notice and opportunity for a hearing on such action as proposed.

"(e) The Administrator or the Secretary, as the case may be, shall require an applicant for a permit under this title to provide such information as he may consider necessary to review and evaluate such application.

"(f) Information received by the Administrator or the Secretary, as the case may be, as a part of any application or in connection with any permit granted under this title shall be available to the public as a matter of public record, at every stage of the proceeding. The final determination of the Administrator or the Secretary, as the case may be, shall be likewise available.

"(g) A copy of any permit issued under this title shall be placed in a conspicuous place in the vessel which will be used for the transportation or dumping authorized by such permit, and an additional copy shall be furnished by the issuing official to the Secretary of the department in which the Coast Guard is operating, or its designee.

"(h) Notwithstanding any provision of title I of the Marine Protection, Research, and Sanctuaries Act of 1972 to the contrary, during the two-year period beginning on the date of enactment of this subsection, no permit may be issued under such title I that authorizes the dumping of any low-level radioactive waste unless the Administrator of the Environmental Protection Agency determines --

"(1) that the proposed dumping is necessary to conduct research --

"(A) on new technology related to ocean dumping, or

"(B) to determine the degree to which the dumping of such substance will degrade the marine environment;

"(2) that the scale of the proposed dumping is limited to the smallest amount of such material and the shortest duration of time that is necessary to fulfill the purposes of the research, such that the dumping will have minimal adverse impact upon human health, welfare, and amenities, and the marine environment, ecological systems, economic potentialities, and other legitimate uses;

"(3) after consultation with the Secretary of Commerce, that the potential benefits of such research will outweigh any such adverse impact; and

"(4) that the proposed dumping will be preceded by appropriate baseline monitoring studies of the proposed dump site and its surrounding environment.

Each permit issued pursuant to this subsection shall be subject to such conditions and restrictions as the Administrator determines to be necessary to minimize possible adverse impacts of such dumping.

"(i) (1) Two years after the date of enactment of this subsection, the Administrator may not issue a permit under this title for the disposal of radioactive waste material until the applicant, in addition to complying with all other requirements of this title, prepares, with respect to the site at which the disposal is proposed, a Radioactive Material Disposal Impact Assessment which shall include --

"(A) a listing of all radioactive materials in each container to be disposed, the number of containers to be dumped, the structural diagrams of each container, the number of curies of each material in each container, and the exposure levels in rems at the inside and outside of each container;

"(B) an analysis of the environmental impact of the proposed action, at the site at which the applicant desires to dispose of the material, upon human health and welfare and marine life;

"(C) any adverse environmental effects at the site which

cannot be avoided should the proposal be implemented;

"(D) an analysis of the resulting environmental and economic conditions if the containers fail to contain the radioactive waste material when initially deposited at the specific site;

"(E) a plan for the removal or containment of the disposed nuclear material if the container leaks or decomposes;

"(F) a determination by each affected State whether the proposed action is consistent with its approved Coastal Zone Management Program;

"(G) an analysis of the economic impact upon other users of marine resources;

"(H) alternatives to the proposed action;

"(I) comments and results of consultation with State officials and public hearings held in the coastal States that are nearest to the affected areas;

"(J) a comprehensive monitoring plan to be carried out by the applicant to determine the full effect of the disposal on the marine environment, living resources, or human health, which plan shall include, but not be limited to, the monitoring of exterior container radiation samples, the taking of water and sediment samples, and fish and benthic animal samples, adjacent to the containers, and the acquisition of such other information as the Administrator may require; and

"(K) such other information which the Administrator may require in order to determine the full effects of such disposal.

"(2) The Administrator shall include, in any permit to which paragraph (1) applies, such terms and conditions as may be necessary to ensure that the monitoring plan required under paragraph (1)(J) is fully implemented, including the analysis by the Administrator of the samples required to be taken under the plan.

"(3) The Administrator shall submit a copy of the assessment prepared under paragraph (1) with respect to any permit to the Committee on Merchant Marine and Fisheries of the House of Representatives and the Committee on Environment and Public Works of the Senate.

"(4) (A) Upon a determination by the Administrator that a permit to which this subsection applies should be issued, the Administrator shall transmit such a recommendation to the House of Representatives and the Senate.

"(B) No permit may be issued by the Administrator under this Act for the disposal of radioactive materials in the ocean unless the Congress, by approval of a resolution described in paragraph (D) within 90 days of continuous session of the Congress beginning on the date after the date of receipt by the Senate and the House of Representatives of such recommendation, authorizes the Administrator to grant a permit to dispose of radioactive material under this Act.

"(C) For purposes of this subsection —

"(i) continuity of session of the Congress is broken only by an adjournment sine die;

"(ii) the days on which either House is not in session because of an adjournment of more than three days to a day certain are excluded in the computation of the 90 day calendar period.

"(D) For the purposes of this subsection, the term 'resolution' means a joint resolution, the resolving clause of which is as follows: "That the House of Representatives and the Senate approve and authorize the Administrator of the Environmental Protection Agency to grant a permit under the Marine Protection, Research, and Sanctuaries Act of 1972 to dispose of radioactive materials in the ocean as recommended by the Administrator to the Congress on ___________, 19___'; the first blank space therein to be filled with the appropriate applicant to dispose of nuclear material and the second blank therein to be filled with the date on which the Administrator submits the recommendation to the House of Representatives and the Senate.

Penalties

"Sec. 105 (a) Any person who violates any provision of this title, or of the regulations promulgated under this title, or a permit issued under this title shall be liable to a civil penalty of not more than $50,000 for each violation to be assessed by the Administrator. No penalty shall be assessed until the person charged shall have been given notice and an opportunity for a hearing of such violation. In determining the amount of the penalty, the gravity of the violation, prior violations, and the demonstrated good faith of the person charged in attempting to achieve rapid compliance after notification of a violation shall be considered by said Administrator. For good cause shown, the Administrator may remit or mitigate such penalty. Upon failure of the offending party to pay the penalty the Administrator may request the Attorney General to commence an action, in the appropriate district court of the United States for such relief as may be appropriate.

"(b) In addition to any action which may be brought under subsection (a) of this section, a person who knowingly violates this title, regulations promulgated under this title or a permit issued under this title shall be fined not more than $50,000 or imprisoned for not more than one year, or both.

"(c) For the purpose of imposing civil penalties and criminal fines under this section each day of a continuing violation shall constitute a separate offense as shall the dumping from each of several vessels, or other sources.

"(d) The Attorney General or his delegate may bring actions for equitable relief to enjoin an imminent or continuing violation of this title, or regulations promulgated under this title, or of permits issued under this title, and the district courts of the United States shall have jurisdiction to grant such relief as the equities of the case may require.

"(e) A vessel, except a public vessel within the meaning of section 13 of the Federal Water Pollution Control Act, as amended (33 USC 1163), used in a violation, shall be liable in rem for any civil penalty assessed or criminal fine imposed and may be proceeded against in any district court of the United States having jurisdiction thereof; but no vessel shall be liable unless it shall appear that one or more of the owners, or bareboat charterers, was at the time of the violation a consenting party or privy to such violation.

"(f) If the provisions of any permit issued under section 102 or 103 are violated, the Administrator or the Secretary, as the case may be, may revoke the permit or may suspend the permit for a specified period of time. No permit shall be revoked or suspended unless the permittee shall have been given notice and opportunity for a hearing on such violation and proposed suspension or revocation.

"(g) (1) Except as provided in paragraph (2) of this subsection any person may commence a civil suit on his own behalf to enjoin any person, including the United States and any other governmental instrumentality or agency (to the extent permitted by the eleventh amendment to the Constitution), who is alleged to be in violation of any prohibition, limitation, criterion, or permit established or issued by or under this title. The district courts shall have jurisdiction, without regard to the amount in controversy or the citizenship of the parties, to enforce such prohibition, limitation, criterion, or permit, as the case may be.

"(2) No action may be commenced --

"(A) prior to sixty days after notice of the violation has been given to the Administrator or the Secretary, and to any alleged violator of the prohibition, limitation, criterion, or permit, or

"(B) if the Attorney General has commenced, and is diligently prosecuting a civil action in a court of the United States to require compliance with the prohibition, limitation, criterion, or permit; or

"(C) if the Administrator has commenced action to impose a penalty pursuant to subsection (a) of this section, or if the Administrator, or the Secretary, has initiated permit revocation or suspension proceedings under subsection (f) of this section; or

"(D) if the United States has commenced and is diligently pursuing a criminal action in a court of the United States or a State to redress a violation of this title;

"(3) (A) Any suit under this subsection may be brought in the judicial district in which the violation occurs.

"(B) In any such suit under this subsection in which the United States is not a party, the Attorney General, at the request of the Administrator or Secretary, may intervene on behalf of the United States as a matter of right.

"(4) The court, in issuing any final order in any suit brought pursuant to paragraph (1) of this subsection may award costs of litigation (including reasonable attorney and expert witness fees) to any party, whenever the court determines such award is appropriate.

"(5) The injunctive relief provided by this subsection shall not restrict any right which any person (or class of persons) may have under any statute or common law to seek enforcement of any standard or limitation or to seek any other relief (including relief against the Administrator, the Secretary, or a State agency).

"(h) No person shall be subject to a civil penalty or to a criminal fine or imprisonment for dumping materials from a vessel if such materials are dumped in an emergency to safeguard life at sea. Any such emergency dumping shall be reported to the Administrator under such conditions as he may prescribe.

Relationship to Other Laws

"Sec. 106 (a) After the effective date of this title, all licenses, permits, and authorizations other than those issued pursuant to this title shall be void and of no legal effect, to the extent that they purport to authorize any activity regulated by this title, and whether issued before or after the effective date of this title.

"(b) The provisions of subsection (a) shall not apply to actions taken before the effective date of this title under the authority of the Rivers and Harbors Act of 1899 (30 Stat. 1151), as amended (33 U.S.C. 401 et seq.).

"(c) Prior to issuing any permit under this title, if it appears to the Administrator that the disposition of material, other than dredged material, may adversely affect navigation in the territorial sea of the United States, or in the approaches to any harbor of the United States, or may create an artificial island on the Outer Continental Shelf, the Administrator shall consult with the Secretary and no permit shall be issued if the Secretary determines that navigation will be unreasonably impaired.

"(d) After the effective date of this title, no State shall adopt or enforce any rule or regulation relating to any activity regulated by this title. Any State may, however, propose to the Administrator criteria relating to the dumping of materials into ocean waters within its jurisdiction, or into other ocean waters to the extent that such dumping may affect waters within the jurisdiction of such State, and if the Administrator determines, after notice and opportunity for hearing, that the proposed criteria are not inconsistent with the purposes of this title, may adopt those criteria and may issue regulations to implement such criteria. Such determination shall be made by the Administrator within one hundred and twenty days of receipt of the proposed criteria. For the purposes of this subsection, the term "state" means any State, interstate or regional authority, Federal territory or Commonwealth or the District of Columbia.

"(e) Nothing in this title shall be deemed to affect in any manner or to any extent any provision of the Fish and Wildlife Coordination Act as amended (16 U.S.C. 661-666c).

"(f) In addition to other provisions of law and notwithstanding the specific exclusion relating to dredged material in the first sentence in section 102(a) of this Act, the dumping of dredged material in Long Island Sound from any Federal project (or pursuant to Federal authorization) or from a dredging project by a non-Federal applicant exceeding 25,000 cubic yards shall comply with the criteria established pursuant to the second sentence of section 102(a) of the Act relating to the effects of dumping. Subsection (d) of this section shall not apply to this subsection.

Enforcement

"Sec. 107 (a) The Administrator or the Secretary, as the case may be, may, whenever appropriate, utilize by agreement, the personnel, services and facilities of other Federal departments, agencies, and instrumentalities, or State agencies or instrumentalities, whether on a reimbursable or a nonreimbursable basis, in carrying out his responsibilities under this title.

"(b) The Administrator or the Secretary may delegate responsibility and authority for reviewing and evaluating permit applications, including the decision as to whether a permit will be issued, to an officer of his agency, or he may delegate, by agreement, such responsibility and authority to the heads of other Federal departments or agencies, whether on a reimbursable or nonreimbursable basis.

"(c) The Secretary of the department in which the Coast Guard is operating shall conduct surveillance and other appropriate enforcement activity to prevent unlawful transportation of material for dumping, or unlawful dumping. Such enforcement activity shall include, but not be limited to, enforcement of regulations issued by him pursuant to section 108, relating to safe transportation, handling, carriage, storage, and stowage. The Secretary of the department in which the Coast Guard is operating shall supply to the Administrator and to the Attorney General, as appropriate, such information of enforcement activities and such evidentiary material assembled as they may require in carrying out their duties relative to penalty assessments, criminal prosecutions, or other actions involving litigation pursuant to the provisions of this title.

Regulations

"Sec. 108 In carrying out the responsibilities and authority conferred by this title, the Administrator, the Secretary, and the Secretary of the department in which the Coast Guard is operating are authorized to issue such regulations as they may deem appropriate.

International Cooperation

"Sec. 109 The Secretary of State, in consultation with the Administrator, shall seek effective international action and cooperation to insure protection of the marine environment, and may, for this purpose, formulate, present or support specific proposals in the United Nations and other competent international organizations for the development of appropriate international rules and regulations in support of the policy of this Act.

Effective Date and Savings Provisions

"Sec. 110 (a) This title shall take effect six months after the date of the enactment of this Act.

"(b) No legal action begun, or right of action accrued, prior to the effective date of this title shall be affected by any provision of this title.

"Sec. 111 There are hereby authorized to be appropriated not to exceed $3,600,000 for fiscal year 1973, not to exceed $5,500,000 for each of the fiscal years 1974 and 1975, not to exceed $5,300,000 for fiscal year 1976, not to exceed $1,325,000 for the transition period (July 1 through September 30, 1976), not to exceed $4,800,000 for fiscal year 1977, and not to exceed $4,800,000 for fiscal year 1978, not to exceed $2,000,000 for each of fiscal year 1980, fiscal year 1981, and not to exceed $4,213,000 for fiscal year 1982 for the purposes and administration of this title, and for succeeding fiscal years only such sums as the Congress may authorize by law.

"Sec. 112 The Administrator, the Secretary, and the Secretary of the department in which the Coast Guard is operating shall each individually report annually, on or before March 1 of each year, with the first report to be made on or before June 30, 1973 to the Congress, on his administration of this title, including recommendations for additional legislation if deemed necessary.

TITLE II — COMPREHENSIVE RESEARCH ON OCEAN DUMPING

"Sec. 201 The Secretary of Commerce, in coordination with the Secretary of the Department in which the Coast Guard is operating and with the Administrator shall, within six months of the enactment of this Act, initiate a comprehensive and continuing program of monitoring and research regarding the effects of the dumping of material into ocean waters or other coastal waters where the tide ebbs and flows or into the Great Lakes or their connecting waters and shall report from time to time, not less frequently than annually, his findings (including an evaluation of the short-term ecological effects and the social and economic factors involved) to the Congress.

"Sec. 202 (a) The Secretary of Commerce, in consultation with other appropriate Federal departments, agencies, and instrumentalities shall, within six months of the enactment of this Act, initiate a comprehensive and continuing program of research with respect to the possible long-range effects of pollution, overfishing, and man-induced changes of ocean ecosystems. These responsibilities shall include the scientific assessment of damages to the natural resources from spills of petroleum or petroleum products. In carrying out such research, the Secretary of Commerce shall take into account such factors as existing and proposed international policies affecting oceanic problems, economic considerations involved in both the protection and the use of the oceans, possible alternatives to existing programs, and ways in which the health of the oceans may best be preserved for the benefit of succeeding generations of mankind.

"(b) In carrying out his responsibilities under this section, the Secretary of Commerce, under the foreign policy guidance of the President and pursuant to international agreements and treaties made by the President with the advice and consent of the Senate, may act alone or in conjunction with any other nation or group of nations, and shall make known the reults of his activities by such channels of communication as may appear appropriate.

"(c) In March of each year, the Secretary of Commerce shall report to the Congress on the results of activities undertaken by him pursuant to this section during the previous fiscal year. The Secretary shall include in this report the report to Congress of activities of the Department of Commerce under section 5 of the Act of March 10, 1934 (48 Stat. 401; 16 U.S.C. 665) required by that section.

"(d) Each department, agency, and independent instrumentality of the Federal Government is authorized and directed to cooperate with the Secretary of Commerce in carrying out the purposes of this section and, to the extent permitted by law, to furnish such information as may be requested.

"(e) The Secretary of Commerce, in carrying out his responsibilities under this section, shall, to the extent feasible, utilize the personnel, services, and facilities of other Federal departments, agencies, and instrumentalities (including those of the Coast Guard for monitoring purposes), and is authorized to enter into appropriate interagency agreements to accomplish this action.

"Sec. 203 (a) The Administrator of the Environmental Protection Agency shall --

"(1) conduct research, investigations, experiments, training, demonstrations, surveys, and studies for the purpose of --

"(A) determining means of minimizing or ending, as soon as possible after the date of the enactment of this section, the dumping into ocean waters, or waters described in section 101(b), of material which may unreasonably degrade or endanger human health, welfare, or amenities, or the marine environment, ecological systems, or economic potentialities, and

"(B) developing disposal methods as alternatives to the dumping described in subparagraph (A); and

"(2) encourage, cooperate with, promote the coordination of, and render financial and other assistance to appropriate public authorities, agencies, and institutions, (whether Federal, State, interstate, or local) and appropriate private agencies, institutions, and individuals in the conduct of research and other activities described in paragraph (1).

"(b) Nothing in this section shall be construed to affect in any way the

December 31, 1981, termination date, established in section 4 of the Act of November 4, 1977 (Public Law 95-153; 33 U.S.C. 1412a) for the dumping of sewage sludge.

"Sec. 204 There are authorized to be appropriated for the first fiscal year after this Act is enacted and for the next two fiscal years thereafter such sums as may be necessary to carry out this title, but the sums appropriated for any such fiscal year may not exceed $6,000,000. There are authorized to be appropriated not to exceed $1,500,000 for the transition period (July 1 through September 30, 1976), not to exceed $5,600,000 for fiscal year 1977, not to exceed $6,500,000 for fiscal year 1978, not to exceed $11,396,000 for fiscal year 1981, and not to exceed $12,000,000 for fiscal year 1982.

"Sec. 205 The Administrator of the Environmental Protection Agency is authorized to conduct a study to assist the city of New York in evaluating the technological options available for the removal of heavy metals and other toxic organic materials from the sewage sludge of the city of New York. The study shall also examine options available to reduce the amount of such pollutants entering the sewage system. The study is to be completed by July 1, 1981.

TITLE III — MARINE SANCTUARIES

"Sec. 301 Notwithstanding the provisions of subsection (h) of section 3 of this Act, the term "Secretary", when used in this title, means Secretary of Commerce. The term "State," when used in this title, means any of the several States or any territory or possession of the United States which has a popularly elected Governor.

"Sec. 302 (a) The Secretary, after consultation with the Secretaries of State, Defense, the Interior, and Transportation, the Administrator, and the heads of other interested Federal agencies, and with the approval of the President, may designate as marine sanctuaries those areas of the ocean waters, as far seaward as the outer edge of the Continental Shelf (15 U.S.T. 74; TIAS 5578), of other coastal waters where the tide ebbs and flows, or of the Great Lakes and their connecting waters, which he determines necessary for the purpose of preserving or restoring such areas for their conservation, recreational, ecological, or esthetic values. The consultation shall include an opportunity to review and comment on a specific proposed designation.

"(b)(1) Prior to designating a marine sanctuary which includes waters lying within the territorial limits of any State or superjacent to the subsoil and seabed within the seaward boundary of a coastal State, as that boundary is defined in section 2 of title 1 of the Act of May 22, 1953 (67 Stat. 29), the Secretary shall consult with, and give due consideration to the views of, the responsible officials of the State involved.

"(2) A designation under this section shall become effective unless--
(A) the Governor of any State described in paragraph (1) certifies to the Secretary, before the end of the sixty-day period beginning on the date of the publication of the designation, that the designation or any of its terms described in subsection (f)(1), are unacceptable to his State, in which case those terms certified as unacceptable will not be effective in the waters described in paragraph (1) in such State until the Governor withdraws his certification of unacceptability; or (B) both Houses of Congress adopt a concurrent resolution in accordance with subsection (h) which disapproves the designation or any of its terms described in subsection (f)(1).

"The Secretary may withdraw the designation after any such certification or resolution of disapproval. If the Secretary does not withdraw the designation, only those portions of the designation not certified as unacceptable under subparagraph (A) or not disapproved under subparagraph (B) shall take effect.

"(c) When a marine sanctuary is designated, pursuant to this section, which includes an area of ocean waters outside the territorial jurisdiction of the United States, the Secretary of State shall take such actions as may be appropriate to enter into negotiations with other Governments for the purpose of arriving at necessary agreements with those governments, in order to protect such sanctuary and to promote the purposes for which it was established.

"(d) The Secretary shall submit an annual report to the Congress, on or before November 1 of each year, setting forth a comprehensive review of his actions during the previous fiscal year undertaken pursuant to the authority of this section, together with appropriate recommendations for legislation considered necessary for the designation and protection of marine sanctuaries.

"(e) Before a marine sanctuary is designated under this section, the Secretary shall hold public hearings in the coastal areas which would be most directly affected by such designation, for the purpose of receiving and giving proper consideration to the views of any interested party. Such hearings shall be held no earlier than thirty days after the publication of a public notice thereof.

"(f) (1) The terms of the designation shall include the geographic area included within the sanctuary; the characteristics of the area that give it conservation, recreational, ecological or esthetic value; and the types of activities that will be subject to regulation by the Secretary in order to protect those characteristics. The terms of the designation may be modified only by the same procedures through which an original designation is made.

"(2) The Secretary, after consultation with other interested Federal and State agencies, shall issue necessary and reasonable regulations to implement the terms of the designation and control the activities described in it, except that all permits, licenses, and other authorizations issued pursuant to any other authority shall be valid unless such regulations otherwise provide.

"(3) The Secretary shall conduct such research as is necessary and reasonable to carry out the purposes of this title.

"(4) The Secretary and the Secretary of the department in which the Coast Guard is operating shall conduct such enforcement activities as are necessary and reasonable to carry out the purposes of this title. The Secretary shall, whenever appropriate and in consultation with the Secretary of the department in which the Coast Guard is operating, utilize by agreement the personnel, services, and facilities of other Federal departments, agencies, and instrumentalities, or State agencies or instrumentalities, whether on a reimbursable or a nonreimbursable basis in carrying out his responsibilities under this title.

"(g) The regulations issued pursuant to subsection (f) shall be applied in accordance with recognized principles of international law, including treaties, conventions, and other agreements to which the United States is signatory. Unless the application of the regulations is in accordance with such principles or is otherwise authorized by an agreement between the United States and the foreign State of which the affected person is a citizen or, in the case of the crew of a foreign vessel, between the United States and flag State of the vessel, no regulation applicable to ocean waters outside the territorial jurisdiction of the United States shall be applied to a person not a citizen of the United States.

"(h) (1) For purposes of subsection (b)(2)(B), the Secretary shall transmit to the Congress a designation of a marine sanctuary at the time of its publication. The concurrent resolution described in subsection (b)(2)(B) is a concurrent resolution which is adopted by both Houses of Congress before the end of the first period of sixty calendar days of continuous session of Congress after the date on which the designation is transmitted, the matter after the resolving clause of which is as follows: 'That the Congress does not favor the taking of effect of the following terms of the marine sanctuary designation numbered ________ transmitted to Congress by the Secretary of Commerce on ________ : ______' the blank space being filled with the number of the designation, the second blank space being filled with the date of the transmittal, and the third blank space being filled with the terms of the designation which are disapproved (or the phrase 'the entire designation' if the entire designation is disapproved).

"(2) For the purpose of paragraph (1) of this subsection —

"(A) continuity of session is broken only by an adjournment of Congress sine die; and

"(B) the days on which either House is not in session because of an adjournment of more than three days to a day certain are excluded in the computation of the sixty-day period.

"(3) A designation which becomes effective, or that portion of a designation which takes effect under subsection (b), shall be printed in the Federal Register.

"Sec. 303 (a) Any person subject to the jurisdiction of the United States who violates any regulation issued pursuant to this title shall be liable to a civil penalty of not more than $50,000 for each such violation, to be assessed by the Secretary. Each day of a continuing violation shall constitute a separate violation.

"(b) No penalty shall be assessed under this section until the person charged has been given notice and an opportunity to be heard. Upon failure of the offending party to pay an assessed penalty, the Attorney General, at the request of the Secretary, shall commence action in the appropriate district court of the United States to collect the penalty and to seek such other relief as may be appropriate.

"(c) A vessel used in the violation of a regulation issued pursuant to this title shall be liable in rem for any civil penalty assessed for such violation and may be proceeded against in any district court of the United States having jurisdiction thereof.

"(d) The district courts of the United States shall have jurisdiction to restrain a violation of the regulations issued pursuant to this title, and to grant such other relief as may be appropriate. Actions shall be brought by the Attorney General in the name of the United States, either on his own initiative or at the request of the Secretary.

"Sec. 304 There are authorized to be appropriated not to exceed $10,000,000 for each of the fiscal years 1973, 1974, and 1975, not to exceed $6,200,000 for fiscal year 1976, not to exceed $1,550,000 for the transition period (July 1 through September 30, 1976), not to exceed $500,000 for fiscal year 1977, not to exceed $500,000 for fiscal year 1978, not to exceed $2,250,000 for fiscal year 1981, not to exceed $2,235,000 for fiscal year 1982, and not to exceed $2,235,000 for fiscal year 1983, to carry out the provisions of this title, including the acquisition, development, and operation of marine sanctuaries designated under this title.

NATIONAL ENVIRONMENTAL POLICY ACT OF 1969

as amended[1]

Be it enacted by the Senate and House of Representatives of the United States of America in Congress assembled, That this Act may be cited as the "National Environmental Policy Act of 1969".

PURPOSE

SEC. 2. The purposes of this Act are: To declare a national policy which will encourage productive and enjoyable harmony between man and his environment; to promote efforts which will prevent or eliminate damage to the environment and biosphere and stimulate the health and welfare of man; to enrich the understanding of the ecological systems and natural resources important to the Nation; and to establish a Council on Environmental Quality.

TITLE I

DECLARATION OF NATIONAL ENVIRONMENTAL POLICY

SEC. 101. (a) The Congress, recognizing the profound impact of man's activity on the interrelations of all components of the natural environment, particularly the profound influences of population growth, high-density urbanization, industrial expansion, resource exploitation, and new and expanding technological advances and recognizing further the critical importance of restoring and maintaining environmental quality to the overall welfare and development of man, declares that it is the continuing policy of the Federal Government, in cooperation with State and local governments, and other concerned public and private organizations, to use all practicable means and measures, including financial and technical assistance, in a manner calculated to foster and promote the general welfare, to create and maintain conditions under which man and nature can exist in productive harmony, and fulfill the social, economic, and other requirements of present and future generations of Americans.

(b) In order to carry out the policy set forth in this Act, it is the continuing responsibility of the Federal Government to use all practicable means, consistent with other essential considerations of national policy, to improve and coordinate Federal plans, functions, programs, and resources to the end that the Nation may—

---

1 PL 91-190, USC 4321-4347, January 1, 1970, as amended by PL 94-83, August 9, 1975.

(1) fulfill the responsibilities of each generation as trustee of the environment for succeeding generations;

(2) assure for all Americans safe, healthful, productive and esthetically and culturally pleasing surroundings;

(3) attain the widest range of beneficial uses of the environment without degradation, risk to health or safety, or other undesirable and unintended consequences;

(4) preserve important historic, cultural, and natural aspects of our national heritage, and maintain, wherever possible, an environment which supports diversity and variety of individual choice;

(5) achieve a balance between population and resource use which will permit high standards of living and a wide sharing of life's amenities; and

(6) enhance the quality of renewable resources and approach the maximum attainable recycling of depletable resources.

(c) The Congress recognizes that each person should enjoy a healthful environment and that each person has a responsibility to contribute to the preservation and enhancement of the environment.

SEC. 102. The Congress authorizes and directs that, to the fullest extent possible: (1) the policies, regulations, and public laws of the United States shall be interpreted and administered in accordance with the policies set forth in this Act, and (2) all agencies of the Federal Government shall—

(A) utilize a systematic, interdisciplinary approach which will insure the integrated use of the natural and social sciences and the environmental design arts in planning and in decisionmaking which may have an impact on man's environment;

(B) identify and develop methods and procedures, in consultation with the Council on Environmental Quality established by title II of this Act, which will insure that presently unquantified environmental amenities and values may be given appropriate consideration in decisionmaking along with economic and technical considerations;

(C) include in every recommendation or report on proposals for legislation and other major Federal actions significantly affecting the quality of the human environment, a detailed statement by the responsible official on—

(i) the environmental impact of the proposed action,

(ii) any adverse environmental effects which cannot be avoided should the proposal be implemented,

(iii) alternatives to the proposed action,

(iv) the relationship between local short-term uses of man's environment and the maintenance and enhancement of long-term productivity, and

(v) any irreversible and irretrievable commitments of resources which would be involved in the proposed action should it be implemented.

Prior to making any detailed statement, the responsible Federal official shall consult with and obtain the comments of any Federal agency which has jurisdiction by law or special expertise with respect to any environmental impact involved. Copies of such statement and the comments and views of the appropriate Federal, State, and local agencies, which are authorized to develop and enforce environmental standards, shall be made available to the President, the Council on Environmental Quality and to the public as provided by section 552 of title 5, United States Code, and shall accompany the proposal through the existing agency review processes;

(D) Any detailed statement required under subparagraph (C) after January 1, 1970, for any major Federal action funded under a program of grants to States shall not be deemed to be legally insufficient solely by reason of having been prepared by a State agency or official, if:

(i) the State agency or official has statewide jurisdiction and has the responsibility for such action,

(ii) the responsible Federal official furnishes guidance and participates in such preparation,

(iii) the responsible Federal official independently evaluates such statement prior to its approval and adoption, and

(iv) after January 1, 1976 the responsible Federal official provides early notification to, and solicits the views of, any other State or any Federal land management entity of any action or any alternative thereto which may have significant impacts upon such State or affected Federal land management entity and, if there is any disagreement on such impacts, prepares a written assessment of such impacts and views for incorporation into such detailed statement.

The procedures in this subparagraph shall not relieve the Federal official of his responsibilities for the scope, objectivity, and content of the entire statement or of any other responsibility under this Act: and further, this subparagraph does not affect the legal sufficiency of statements prepared by State agencies with less than statewide jurisdiction.

(E) study, develop, and describe appropriate alternatives to recommended courses of action in any proposal which involves unresolved conflicts concerning alternative uses of available resources;

(F) recognize the worldwide and long-range character of environmental problems and, where consistent with the foreign policy of the United States, lend appropriate support to initiatives, resolutions, and programs designed to maximize international cooperation in anticipating and preventing a decline in the quality of mankind's world environment;

(G) make available to States, counties, municipalities, institutions, and individuals, advice and information useful in restoring, maintaining, and enhancing the quality of the environment;

(H) initiate and utilize ecological information in the planning and development of resource-oriented projects; and

(I) assist the Council on Environmental Quality established by title II of this Act.

Sec. 103. All agencies of the Federal Government shall review their present statutory authority, administrative regulations, and current policies and procedures for the purpose of determining whether there are any deficiencies or inconsistencies therein which prohibit full compliance with the purposes and provisions of this Act and shall propose to the President not later than July 1, 1971, such measures as may be necessary to bring their authority and policies into conformity with the intent, purposes, and procedures set forth in this Act.

Sec. 104. Nothing in Section 102 or 103 shall in any way affect the specific statutory obligations of any Federal agency (1) to comply with criteria or standards of environmental quality, (2) to coordinate or consult with any other Federal or State agency, or (3) to act, or refrain from acting contingent upon the recommendations or certification of any other Federal or State agency.

Sec. 105. The policies and goals set forth in this Act are supplementary to those set forth in existing authorizations of Federal agencies.

TITLE II

COUNCIL ON ENVIRONMENTAL QUALITY

SEC. 201. The President shall transmit to the Congress annually beginning July 1, 1970, an Environmental Quality Report (hereinafter referred to as the "report") which shall set forth (1) the status and condition of the major natural, manmade, or altered environmental classes of the Nation, including, but not limited to, the air, the aquatic, including marine, estuarine, and fresh water, and the terrestrial environment, including, but not limited to, the forest, dryland, wetland, range, urban, suburban, and rural environment; (2) current and foreseeable trends in the quality, management and utilization of such environments and the effects of those trends on the social, economic, and other requirements of the Nation; (3) the adequacy of available natural resources for fulfilling human and economic requirements of the Nation in the light of expected population pressures; (4) a review of the programs and activities (including regulatory activities) of the Federal Government, the State and local governments, and nongovernmental entities or individuals, with particular reference to their effect on the environment and on the conservation, development and utilization of natural resources; and (5) a program for remedying the deficiencies of existing programs and activities, together with recommendations for legislation.

SEC. 202. There is created in the Executive Office of the President a Council on Environmental Quality (hereinafter referred to as the "Council"). The Council shall be composed of three members who shall be appointed by the President to serve at his pleasure, by and with the advice and consent of the Senate. The President shall designate one of the members of the Council to serve as Chairman. Each member shall be a person who, as a result of his training, experience, and attainments, is exceptionally well qualified to analyze and interpret environmental trends and information of all kinds; to appraise programs and activities of the Federal Government in the light of the policy set forth in title I of this Act; to be conscious of and responsive to the scientific, economic, social, esthetic, and cultural needs and interests of the Nation; and to formulate and recommend national policies to promote the improvement of the quality of the environment.

SEC. 203. The Council may employ such officers and employees as may be necessary to carry out its functions under this Act. In addition, the Council may employ and fix the compensation of such experts and consultants as may be necessary for the carrying out of its functions under this Act, in accordance with section 3109 of title 5, United States Code (but without regard to the last sentence thereof).

SEC. 204. It shall be the duty and function of the Council—

(1) to assist and advise the President in the preparation of the Environmental Quality Report required by section 201;

(2) to gather timely and authoritative information concerning the conditions and trends in the quality of the environment both current and prospective, to analyze and interpret such information for the purpose of determining whether such conditions and trends are interfering, or are likely to interfere, with the achievement of the policy set forth in title I of this Act, and to compile and submit to the President studies relating to such conditions and trends;

(3) to review and appraise the various programs and activities of the Federal Government in the light of the policy set forth in title I of this Act for the purpose of determining the extent to which such programs and activities are contributing to the achievement of such policy, and to make recommendations to the President with respect thereto;

(4) to develop and recommend to the President national policies to foster and promote the improvement of environmental quality to meet the conservation, social, economic, health, and other requirements and goals of the Nation;

(5) to conduct investigations, studies, surveys, research, and analyses relating to ecological systems and environmental quality;

(6) to document and define changes in the natural environment, including the plant and animal systems, and to accumulate necessary data and other information for a continuing analysis of these changes or trends and an interpretation of their underlying causes;

(7) to report at least once each year to the President on the state and condition of the environment; and

(8) to make and furnish such studies, reports thereon, and recommendations with respect to matters of policy and legislation as the President may request.

SEC. 205. In exercising its powers, functions, and duties under this Act, the Council shall—

(1) consult with the Citizens' Advisory Committee on Environmental Quality established by Executive Order numbered 11472, dated May 29, 1969, and with such representatives of science, industry, agriculture, labor, conservation, organizations, State and local governments and other groups, as it deems advisable; and

(2) utilize, to the fullest extent possible, the services, facilities, and information (including statistical information) of public and private agencies and organizations, and individuals, in order that duplication of effort and expense may be avoided, thus assuring that the Council's activities will not unnecessarily overlap or conflict with similar activities authorized by law and performed by established agencies.

SEC. 206. Members of the Council shall serve full time and the Chairman of the Council shall be compensated at the rate provided for Level II of the Executive Schedule Pay Rates (5 U.S.C. 5313). The other members of the Council shall be compensated at the rate provided for Level IV or the Executive Schedule Pay Rates (5 U.S.C. 5315).

SEC. 207. There are authorized to be appropriated to carry out the provisions of this Act not to exceed $300,000 for fiscal year 1970, $700,000 for fiscal year 1971, and $1,000,000 for each fiscal year thereafter.

NOISE CONTROL ACT OF 1972*

SHORT TITLE

SECTION 1. This Act may be cited as the "Noise Control Act of 1972".

FINDINGS AND POLICY

SEC. 2(a) The Congress finds—

(1) that inadequately controlled noise presents a growing danger to the health and welfare of the Nation's population, particularly in urban areas;

(2) that the major sources of noise include transportation vehicles and equipment, machinery, appliances, and other products in commerce; and

(3) that, while primary responsibility for control of noise rests with State and local governments, Federal action is essential to deal with major noise sources in commerce control of which require national uniformity of treatment.

(b) The Congress declares that it is the policy of the United States to promote an environment for all Americans free from noise that jeopardizes their health or welfare. To that end, it is the purpose of this Act to establish a means for effective coordination of Federal research and activities in noise control, to authorize the establishment of Federal noise emission standards for products distributed in commerce, and to provide information to the public respecting the noise emission and noise reduction characteristics of such products.

DEFINITIONS

SEC. 3. For purposes of this Act:

(1) The term "Administrator" means the Administrator of the Environmental Protection Agency.

(2) The term "person" means an individual, corporation, partnership, or association, and (except as provided in sections 11(e) and 12(a)) includes any officer, employee, department, agency, or instrumentality of the United States, a State, or any political subdivision of a State.

(3) The term "product" means any manufactured article or goods or component thereof; except that such term does not include—

---

* Public Law 91-596, December 29, 1970; Public Law 95-609, November 8, 1978.

(A) any aircraft, aircraft engine, propeller, or appliance, as such terms are defined in section 101 of the Federal Aviation Act of 1958; or

(B) (i) any military weapons or equipment which are designed for combat use; (ii) any rockets or equipment which are designed for research, experimental, or developmental work to be performed by the National Aeronautics and Space Administration; or (iii) to the extent provided by regulations of the Administrator, any other machinery or equipment designed for use in experimental work done by or for the Federal Government.

(4) The term "ultimate purchaser" means the first person who in good faith purchases a product for purposes other than resale.

(5) The term "new product" means (A) a product the equitable or legal title of which has never been transferred to an ultimate purchaser, or (B) a product which is imported or offered for importation into the United States and which is manufactured after the effective date of a regulation under section 6 or section 8 which would have been applicable to such product had it been manufactured in the United States.

(6) The term "manufacturer" means any person engaged in the manufacturing or assembling of new products, or the importing of new products for resale, or who acts for, and is controlled by, any such person in connection with the distribution of such products.

(7) The term "commerce" means trade, traffic, commerce, or transportation—

(A) between a place in a State and any place outside thereof, or

(B) which affects trade, traffic, commerce, or transportation described in subparagraph (A).

(8) The term "distribute in commerce" means sell in, offer for sale in, or introduce or deliver for introduction into, commerce.

(9) The term "State" includes the District of Columbia, the Commonwealth of Puerto Rico, the Virgin Islands, American Samoa, Guam, and the Trust Territory of the Pacific Islands.

(10) The term "Federal agency" means an executive agency (as defined in section 105 of title 5, United States Code) and includes the United States Postal Service.

(11) The term "environmental noise" means the intensity, duration, and the character of sounds from all sources.

FEDERAL PROGRAMS

SEC. 4. (a) The Congress authorizes and directs that Federal agencies shall, to the fullest extent consistent with their authority under Federal laws administered by them, carry out the programs within their control in such a manner as to further the policy declared in section 2(b).

(b) Each department, agency, or instrumentality of the executive, legislative, and judicial branches of the Federal Government—

(1) having jurisdiction over any property or facility, or

(2) engaged in any activity resulting, or which may result, in the emission of noise,

shall comply with Federal, State, interstate, and local requirements respecting control and abatement of environmental noise to the same extent that any person is subject to such requirements. The President may exempt any single activity or facility, including noise emission sources or classes thereof, of any department, agency, or instrumentality in the executive branch from compliance with any such requirement if he determines it to be in the paramount interest of the United States to do so; except that no exemption, other than for those products referred to in section 3(3)(B) of this Act, may be granted from the requirements of sections 6, 17, and 18 of this Act. No such exemption shall be granted due to lack of appropriation unless the President shall have specifically requested such appropriation as a part of the budgetary process and the Congress shall have failed to make available such requested appropriation. Any exemption shall be for a period not in excess of one year, but additional exemptions may be granted for periods of not to exceed one year upon the President's making a new determination. The President shall report each January to the Congress all exemptions from the requirements of this section granted during the preceding calendar year, together with his reason for granting such exemption.

(c)(1) The Administrator shall coordinate the programs of all Federal agencies relating to noise research and noise control. Each Federal agency shall, upon request, furnish to the Administrator such information as he may reasonably require to determine the nature, scope, and results of the noise-research and noise-control programs of the agency.

(2) Each Federal agency shall consult with the Administrator in prescribing standards or regulations respecting noise. If at any time the Administrator has reason to believe that a standard or regulation, or any proposed standard or regulation, of any Federal agency respecting noise does not protect the public health and

welfare to the extent he believes to be required and feasible, he may request such agency to review and report to him on the advisability of revising such standard or regulation to provide such protection. Any such request may be published in the Federal Register and shall be accompanied by a detailed statement of the information on which it is based. Such agency shall complete the requested review and report to the Administrator within such time as the Administrator specifies in the request, but such time specified may not be less than ninety days from the date the request was made. The report shall be published in the Federal Register and shall be accompanied by a detailed statement of the findings and conclusions of the agency respecting the revision of its standard or regulation. With respect to the Federal Aviation Administration, section 611 of the Federal Aviation Act of 1958 (as amended by section 7 of this Act) shall apply in lieu of this paragraph.

(3) On the basis of regular consultation with appropriate Federal agencies, the Administrator shall compile and publish, from time to time, a report on the status and progress of Federal activities relating to noise research and noise control. This report shall describe the noise-control programs of each Federal agency and assess the contributions of those programs to the Federal Government's overall efforts to control noise.

IDENTIFICATION OF MAJOR NOISE SOURCES; NOISE CRITERIA AND CONTROL TECHNOLOGY

SEC. 5. (a)(1) The Administrator shall, after consultation with appropriate Federal agencies and within nine months of the date of the enactment of this Act, develop and publish criteria with respect to noise. Such criteria shall reflect the scientific knowledge most useful in indicating the kind and extent of all identifiable effects on the public health or welfare which may be expected from differing quantities and qualities of noise.

(2) The Administrator shall, after consultation with appropriate Federal agencies and within twelve months of the date of the enactment of this Act, publish information on the levels of environmental noise the attainment and maintenance of which in defined areas under various conditions are requisite to protect the public health and welfare with an adequate margin of safety.

(b) The Administrator shall, after consultation with appropriate Federal agencies, compile and publish a report or series of reports (1) identifying products (or classes of products) which in his judgment are major sources of noise, and (2) giving information on techniques for control of noise from such products, including available data on the technology, costs, and alternative methods of noise control. The first such report shall be published not later than eighteen months after the date of enactment of this Act.

(c) The Administrator shall from time to time review and, as appropriate, revise or supplement any criteria or reports published under this section.

(d) Any report (or revision thereof) under subsection (b)(1) identifying major noise sources shall be published in the Federal Register. The publication or revision under this section of any criteria or information on control techniques shall be announced in the Federal Register, and copies shall be made available to the general public.

NOISE EMISSION STANDARDS FOR PRODUCTS DISTRIBUTED IN COMMERCE

SEC. 6. (a)(1) The Administrator shall publish proposed regulations, meeting the requirements of subsection (c), for each product—

(A) which is identified (or is part of a class identified) in any report published under section 5(b)(1) as a major source of noise,

(B) for which, in his judgment, noise emission standards are feasible, and

(C) which falls in one of the following categories:

(i) Construction equipment.

(ii) Transportation equipment (including recreational vehicles and related equipment).

(iii) Any motor or engine (including any equipment of which an engine or motor is an integral part).

(iv) Electrical or electronic equipment.

(2)(A) Initial proposed regulations under paragraph (1) shall be published not later than eighteen months after the date of enactment of this Act, and shall apply to any product described in paragraph (1) which is identified (or is a part of a class identified) as a major source of noise in any report published under section 5(b)(1) on or before the date of publication of such initial proposed regulations.

(B) In the case of any product described in paragraph (1) which is identified (or is part of a class identified) as a major source of noise in a report published under section 5(b)(1) after publication of the initial proposed regulations under subparagraph (A) of this paragraph, regulations under paragraph (1) for such product shall be proposed and published by the Administrator not later than eighteen months after such report is published.

(3) After proposed regulations respecting a product have been published under paragraph (2), the Adminis-

trator shall, unless in his judgment noise emission standards are not feasible for such product, prescribe regulations, meeting the requirements of subsection (c), for such product—

(A) not earlier than six months after publication of such proposed regulations, and

(B) not later than—

(i) twenty-four months after the date of enactment of this Act, in the case of a product subject to proposed regulations published under paragraph (2)(A), or

(ii) in the case of any other product, twenty-four months after the publication of the report under section 5(b)(1) identifying it (or a class of products of which it is a part) as a major source of noise.

(b) The Administrator may publish proposed regulations, meeting the requirements of subsection (c), for any product for which he is not required by subsection (a) to prescribe regulations but for which, in his judgment, noise emission standards are feasible and are requisite to protect the public health and welfare. Not earlier than six months after the date of publication of such proposed regulations respecting such product, he may prescribe regulations, meeting the requirements of subsection (c), for such product.

(c)(1) Any regulation prescribed under subsection (a) or (b) of this section (and any revision thereof) respecting a product shall include a noise emission standard which shall set limits on noise emissions from such product and shall be a standard which in the Administrator's judgment, based on criteria published under section 5, is requisite to protect the public health and welfare, taking into account the magnitude and conditions of use of such product (alone or in combination with other noise sources), the degree of noise reduction achievable through the application of the best available technology and the cost of compliance. In establishing such a standard for any product, the Administrator shall give appropriate consideration to standards under other laws designed to safeguard the health and welfare of persons, including any standards under the National Traffic and Motor Vehicle Safety Act of 1966, the Clean Air Act, and the Federal Water Pollution Control Act. Any such noise emission standards shall be a performance standard. In addition, any regulation under subsection (a) or (b) (and any revision thereof) may contain testing procedures necessary to assure compliance with the emission standard in such regulation, and may contain provisions respecting instructions of the manufacturer for the maintenance, use, or repair of the product.

(2) After publication of any proposed regulations under this section, the Administrator shall allow interested persons an opportunity to participate in rulemaking in accordance with the first sentence of section 553(c) of title 5, United States Code.

(3) The Administrator may revise any regulation prescribed by him under this section by (A) publication of proposed revised regulations, and (B) the promulgation, not earlier than six months after the date of such publication, of regulations making the revision; except that a revision which makes only technical or clerical corrections in a regulation under this section may be promulgated earlier than six months after such date if the Administrator finds that such earlier promulgation is in the public interest.

(d)(1) On and after the effective date of any regulation prescribed under subsection (a) or (b) of this section, the manufacturer of each new product to which such regulation applies shall warrant to the ultimate purchaser and each subsequent purchaser that such product is designed, built, and equipped so as to conform at the time of sale with such regulation.

(2) Any cost obligation of any dealer incurred as a result of any requirement imposed by paragraph (1) of this subsection shall be borne by the manufacturer. The transfer of any such cost obligation from a manufacturer to any dealer through franchise or other agreement is prohibited.

(3) If a manufacturer includes in any advertisement a statement respecting the cost or value of noise emission control devices or systems, such manufacturer shall set forth in such statement the cost or value attributed to such devices or systems by the Secretary of Labor (through the Bureau of Labor Statistics). The Secretary of Labor and his representatives, shall have the same access for this purpose to the books, documents, papers, and records of a manufacturer as the Comptroller General has to those of a recipient of assistance for purposes of section 311 of the Clean Air Act.

(e)(1) No State or political subdivision thereof may adopt or enforce—

(A) with respect to any new product for which a regulation has been prescribed by the Administrator under this section, any law or regulation which sets a limit on noise emissions from such new product and which is not identical to such regulation of the Administrator; or

(B) with respect to any component incorporated into such new product by the manufacturer of such product, any law or regulation setting a limit on noise emissions from such component when so incorporated.

(2) Subject to sections 17 and 18, nothing in this section precludes or denies the right of any State or political subdivision thereof to establish and enforce controls on environmental noise (or one or more sources thereof) through the licensing, regulation, or restriction of the use, operation, or movement of any product or combination of products.

AIRCRAFT NOISE STANDARDS

SEC. 7. (a) The Administrator, after consultation with appropriate Federal, State, and local agencies and interested persons, shall conduct a study of the (1) adequacy of Federal Aviation Administration flight and operational noise controls; (2) adequacy of noise emission standards on new and existing aircraft, together with recommendations on the retrofitting and phaseout of existing aircraft; (3) implications of identifying and achieving levels of cumulative noise exposure around airports; and (4) additional measures available to airport operators and local governments to control aircraft noise. He shall report on such study to the Committee on Interstate and Foreign Commerce of the House of Representatives and the Committees on Commerce and Public Works of the Senate within nine months after the date of the enactment of this Act.

(b) Section 611 of the Federal Aviation Act of 1958 (49 U.S.C. 1431) is amended to read as follows:

"CONTROL AND ABATEMENT OF AIRCRAFT NOISE AND SONIC BOOM

"SEC. 611. (a) For purposes of this section:

"(1) The term 'FAA' means Administrator of the Federal Aviation Administration.

"(2) The term 'EPA' means the Administrator of the Environmental Protection Agency.

"(b)(1) In order to afford present and future relief and protection to the public health and welfare from aircraft noise and sonic boom, the FAA, after consultation with the Secretary of Transportation and with EPA, shall prescribe and amend standards for the measurement of aircraft noise and sonic boom and shall prescribe and amend such regulations as the FAA may find necessary to provide for the control and abatement of aircraft noise and sonic boom, including the application of such standards and regulations in the issuance, amendment, modification, suspension, or revocation of any certificate authorized by this title. No exemption with respect to any standard or regulation under this section may be granted under any provision of this Act unless the FAA shall have consulted with EPA before such exemption is granted, except that if the FAA determines that safety in air commerce or air transportation requires that such an exemption be granted before EPA can be consulted, the FAA shall consult with EPA as soon as practicable after the exemption is granted.

"(2) The FAA shall not issue an original type certificate under section 603(a) of this Act for any aircraft for which substantial noise abatement can be achieved by prescribing standards and regulations in accordance with this section, unless he shall have prescribed standards and regulations in accordance with this section which apply to such aircraft and which protect the public from aircraft noise and sonic boom, consistent with the considerations listed in subsection (d).

"(c)(1) Not earlier than the date of submission of the report required by section 7(a) of the Noise Control Act of 1972, EPA shall submit to the FAA proposed regulations to provide such control and abatement of aircraft noise and sonic boom (including control and abatement through the exercise of any of the FAA's regulatory authority over air commerce or transportation or over aircraft or airport operations) as EPA determines is necessary to protect the public health and welfare. The FAA shall consider such proposed regulations submitted by EPA under this paragraph and shall, within thirty days of the date of its submission to the FAA, publish the proposed regulations in a notice of proposed rulemaking. Within sixty days after such publication, the FAA shall commence a hearing at which interested persons shall be afforded an opportunity for oral (as well as written) presentations of data, views, and arguments. Within a reasonable time after the conclusion of such hearing and after consultation with EPA, the FAA shall—

"(A) in accordance with subsection (b), prescribe regulations (i) substantially as they were submitted by EPA, or (ii) which are a modification of the proposed regulations submitted by EPA, or

"(B) publish in the Federal Register a notice that it is not prescribing any regulation in response to EPA's submission of proposed regulations, together with a detailed explanation providing reasons for the decision not to prescribe such regulations.

"(2) If EPA has reason to believe that the FAA's action with respect to a regulation proposed by EPA under paragraph (1)(A)(ii) or (1)(B) of this subsection does not protect the public health and welfare from aircraft noise or sonic boom, consistent with the considerations listed in subsection (d) of this section, EPA shall consult with the FAA and may request the FAA to review, and report to EPA on, the advisability of prescribing the regulation originally proposed by EPA. Any such request shall be published in the Federal Register and shall include a detailed statement of the information on which it is based. The FAA shall complete the review requested and shall report to EPA within such time as EPA specifies in the request, but such time specified may not be less than ninety days from the date the request was made. The FAA's report shall be accompanied by a detailed statement of the FAA's findings and the reasons for the FAA's conclusions; shall identify any statement filed pursuant to section 102(2)(C) of the National Environmental Policy Act of 1969 with respect to such action of the FAA under paragraph (1) of this subsection; and shall specify whether (and where) such statements are available for public inspection. The FAA's report shall be published in the Federal Register, except in a case in which EPA's request proposed specific action to be taken by the FAA, and FAA's report indicates such action will be taken.

"(3) If, in the case of a matter described in paragraph (2) of this subsection with respect to which no statement is required to be filed under such section 102(2)(C), the report of the FAA indicates that the proposed regulation originally submitted by EPA should not be made, then EPA may request the FAA to file a supplemental report, which shall be published in the Federal Register within such a period as EPA may specify (but such time specified shall not be less than ninety days from the date the request was made), and which shall contain a comparison of (A) the environmental effects (including those which cannot be avoided) of the action actually taken by the FAA in response to EPA's proposed regulations, and (B) EPA's proposed regulations.

"(d) In prescribing and amending standards and regulations under this section, the FAA shall—

"(1) consider relevant available data relating to aircraft noise and sonic boom, including the results of research, development, testing, and evaluation activities conducted pursuant to this Act and the Department of Transportation Act;

"(2) consult with such Federal, State, and interstate agencies as he deems appropriate;

"(3) consider whether any proposed standard or regulation is consistent with the highest degree of safety in air commerce or air transportation in the public interest;

"(4) consider whether any proposed standard or regulation is economically reasonable, technologically practicable, and appropriate for the particular type of aircraft, aircraft engine, appliance, or certificate to which it will apply; and

"(5) consider the extent to which such standard or regulation will contribute to carrying out the purposes of this section.

"(e) In any action to amend, modify, suspend, or revoke a certificate in which violation of aircraft noise or sonic boom standards or regulations is at issue, the certificate holder shall have the same notice and appeal rights as are contained in section 609, and in any appeal to the National Transportation Safety Board, the Board may amend, modify, or reverse the order of the FAA if it finds that control or abatement of aircraft noise or sonic boom and the public health and welfare do not require the affirmation of such order, or that such order is not consistent with safety in air commerce or air transportation."

(c) All—

(1) standards, rules, and regulations prescribed under section 611 of the Federal Aviation Act of 1958, and

(2) exemptions, granted under any provision of the Federal Aviation Act of 1958, with respect to such standards, rules, and regulations,

which are in effect on the date of the enactment of this Act, shall continue in effect according to their terms until modified, terminated, superseded, set aside, or repealed by the Administrator of the Federal Aviation Administration in the exercise of any authority vested in him, by a court of competent jurisdiction, or by operation of law.

LABELING

SEC. 8. (a) The Administrator shall by regulation designate any product (or class thereof)—

(1) which emits noise capable of adversely affecting the public health or welfare; or

(2) which is sold wholly or in part on the basis of its effectiveness in reducing noise.

(b) For each product (or class thereof) designated under subsection (a) the Administrator shall by regulation require that notice be given to the prospective user of the level of the noise the product emits, or of its effectiveness in reducing noise, as the case may be. Such regulations shall specify (1) whether such notice shall be affixed to the product or to the outside of its container, or to both, at the time of its sale to the ultimate purchaser or whether such notice shall be given to the prospective user in some other manner, (2) the form of the notice, and (3) the methods and units of measurement to be used. Sections 6(c)(2) shall apply to the prescribing of any regulation under this section.

(c) This section does not prevent any State or political subdivision thereof from regulating product labeling or information respecting products in any way not in conflict with regulations prescribed by the Administrator under this section.

IMPORTS

SEC. 9. The Secretary of the Treasury shall, in consultation with the Administrator, issue regulations to carry out the provisions of this Act with respect to new products imported or offered for importation.

PROHIBITED ACTS

SEC. 10. (a) Except as otherwise provided in subsection (b), the following acts or the causing thereof are prohibited:

(1) In the case of a manufacturer, to distribute in commerce any new product manufactured after the effective date of a regulation prescribed under section 6 which is applicable to such product, except in conformity with such regulation.

(2) (A) The removal or rendering inoperative by any person, other than for purposes of maintenance, repair, or replacement, of any device or element of design incorporated into any product in compliance with regulations under section 6, prior to its sale or delivery to the ultimate purchaser or while it is in use, or (B) the use of a product after such device or element of design has been removed or rendered inoperative by any person.

(3) In the case of a manufacturer, to distribute in commerce any new product manufactured after the effective date of a regulation prescribed under section 8(b) (requiring information respecting noise) which is applicable to such product, except in conformity with such regulation.

(4) The removal by any person of any notice affixed to a product or container pursuant to regulations prescribed under section 8(b), prior to sale of the product to the ultimate purchaser.

(5) The importation into the United States by any person of any new product in violation of a regulation prescribed under section 9 which is applicable to such product.

(6) The failure or refusal by any person to comply with any requirement of section 11(d) or 13(a) or regulations prescribed under section 13(a), 17, or 18.

(b)(1) For the purpose of research, investigations, studies, demonstrations, or training, or for reasons of national security, the Administrator may exempt for a specified period of time any product, or class thereof, from paragraphs (1), (2), (3), and (5) of subsection (a), upon such terms and conditions as he may find necessary to protect the public health or welfare.

(2) Paragraphs (1), (2), (3), and (4) of subsection (a) shall not apply with respect to any product which

is manufactured solely for use outside any State and which (and the container of which) is labeled or otherwise marked to show that it is manufactured solely for use outside any State; except that such paragraphs shall apply to such product if it is in fact distributed in commerce for use in any State.

ENFORCEMENT

SEC. 11. (a) Any person who willfully or knowingly violates paragraph (1), (3), (5), or (6) of subsection (a) of section 10 of this Act shall be punished by a fine of not more than $25,000 per day of violation, or by imprisonment for not more than one year, or by both. If the conviction is for a violation committed after a first conviction of such person under this subsection, punishment shall be by a fine of not more than $50,000 per day of violation, or by imprisonment for not more than two years, or by both.

(b) For the purpose of this section, each day of violation of any paragraph of section 10(a) shall constitute a separate violation of that section.

(c) The district courts of the United States shall have jurisdiction of actions brought by and in the name of the United States to restrain any violations of section 10(a) of this Act.

(d)(1) Whenever any person is in violation of section 10(a) of this Act, the Administrator may issue an order specifying such relief as he determines is necessary to protect the public health and welfare.

(2) Any order under this subsection shall be issued only after notice and opportunity for a hearing in accordance with section 554 of title 5 of the United States Code.

(e) The term "person," as used in this section, does not include a department, agency, or instrumentality of the United States.

CITIZEN SUITS

SEC. 12. (a) Except as provided in subsection (b), any person (other than the United States) may commence a civil action on his own behalf—

(1) against any person (including (A) the United States, and (B) any other governmental instrumentality or agency to the extent permitted by the eleventh amendment to the Constitution) who is alleged to be in violation of any noise control requirement (as defined in subsection (e)), or

(2) against—

(A) the Administrator of the Environmental Protection Agency where there is alleged a failure of such Administrator to perform any act or duty under this Act which is not discretionary with such Administrator, or

(B) the Administrator of the Federal Aviation Administration where there is alleged a failure of such Administrator to perform any act or duty under section 611 of the Federal Aviation Act of 1958 which is not discretionary with such Administrator.

The district courts of the United States shall have jurisdiction, without regard to the amount in controversy, to restrain such person from violating such noise control requirement or to order such Administrator to perform such act or duty, as the case may be.

(b) No action may be commenced—

(1) under subsection (a)(1)—

(A) prior to sixty days after the plaintiff has given notice of the violation (i) to the Administrator of the Environmental Protection Agency (and to the Federal Aviation Administrator in the case of a violation of a noise control requirement under such section 611) and (ii) to any alleged violator of such requirement, or

(B) if an Administrator has commenced and is diligently prosecuting a civil action to require compliance with the noise control requirement, but in any such action in a court of the United States any person may intervene as a matter of right, or

(2) under subsection (a)(2) prior to sixty days after the plaintiff has given notice to the defendant that he will commence such action.

Notice under this subsection shall be given in such manner as the Administrator of the Environmental Protection Agency shall prescribe by regulation.

(c) In an action under this section, the Administrator of the Environmental Protection Agency, if not a party, may intervene as a matter of right. In an action under this section respecting a noise control requirement under section 611 of the Federal Aviation Act of 1958, the Administrator of the Federal Aviation Administration, if not a party, may also intervene as a matter of right.

(d) The court, in issuing any final order in any action brought pursuant to subsection (a) of this section, may award costs of litigation (including reasonable attorney and expert witness fees) to any party, whenever the court determines such an award is appropriate.

(e) Nothing in this section shall restrict any right which any person (or class of persons) may have under any statute or common law to seek enforcement of any noise control requirement or to seek any other relief (inincluding relief against an Administrator).

(f) For purposes of this section, the term "noise control requirement" means paragraph (1), (2), (3), (4), or

(5) of section 10(a), or a standard, rule, or regulation issued under section 17 or 18 of this Act or under section 611 of the Federal Aviation Act of 1958.

RECORDS, REPORTS, AND INFORMATION

SEC. 13. (a) Each manufacturer of a product to which regulations under section 6 or section 8 apply shall—

(1) establish and maintain such records, make such reports, provide such information, and make such tests, as the Administrator may reasonably require to enable him to determine whether such manufacturer has acted or is acting in compliance with this Act.

(2) upon request of an officer or employee duly designated by the Administrator, permit such officer or employee at reasonable times to have access to such information and the results of such tests and to copy such records, and

(3) to the extent required by regulations of the Administrator, make products coming off the assembly line or otherwise in the hands of the manufacturer available for testing by the Administrator.

(b) (1) All information obtained by the Administrator or his representatives pursuant to subsection (a) of this section, which information contains or relates to a trade secret or other matter referred to in section 1905 of title 18 of the United States Code, shall be considered confidential for the purpose of that section, except that such information may be disclosed to other Federal officers or employees, in whose possession it shall remain confidential, or when relevant to the matter in controversy in any proceeding under this Act.

(2) Nothing in this subsection shall authorize the withholding of information by the Administrator, or by any officers or employees under his control, from the duly authorized committees of the Congress.

(c) Any person who knowingly makes any false statement, representation, or certification in any application, record, report, plan, or other document filed or required to be maintained under this Act or who falsifies, tampers with, or knowingly renders inaccurate any monitoring device or method required to be maintained under this Act, shall upon conviction be punished by a fine of not more than $10,000, or by imprisonment for not more than six months, or by both.

RESEARCH, TECHNICAL ASSISTANCE, AND PUBLIC INFORMATION

SEC. 14. In furtherance of his responsibilities under this Act and to complement, as necessary, the noise-research programs of other Federal agencies, the Administrator is authorized to:

(1) Conduct research, and finance research by contract with any person, on the effects, measurement, and control of noise, including but not limited to—

(A) investigation of the psychological and physiological effects of noise on humans and the effects of noise on domestic animals, wildlife, and property, and determination of acceptable levels of noise on the basis of such effects;

(B) development of improved methods and standards for measurement and monitoring of noise, in cooperation with the National Bureau of Standards, Department of Commerce; and

(C) determination of the most effective and practicable means of controlling noise emission.

(2) Provide technical assistance to State and local governments to facilitate their development and enforcement of ambient noise standards, including but not limited to—

(A) advice on training of noise-control personnel and on selection and operation of noise-abatement equipment; and

(B) preparation of model State or local legislation for noise control.

(3) Disseminate to the public information on the effects of noise, acceptable noise levels, and techniques for noise measurement and control.

DEVELOPMENT OF LOW-NOISE-EMISSION PRODUCTS

SEC. 15. (a) For the purpose of this section:

(1) The term "Committee" means the Low-Noise-Emission Product Advisory Committee.

(2) The term "Federal Government" includes the legislative, executive, and judicial branches of the Government of the United States, and the government of the District of Columbia.

(3) The term "low-noise-emission product" means any product which emits noise in amounts significantly below the levels specified in noise emission standards under regulations applicable under section 6 at the time of procurement to that type of product.

(4) The term "retail price" means (A) the maximum statutory price applicable to any type of product; or (B) in any case where there is no applicable maximum statutory price, the most recent procurement price paid for any type of product.

(b)(1) The Administrator shall determine which products qualify as low-noise-emission products in accordance with the provisions of this section.

(2) The Administrator shall certify any product—

(A) for which a certification application has been filed in accordance with paragraph (5)(A) of this subsection;

(B) which is a low-noise-emission product as determined by the Administrator; and

(C) which he determines is suitable for use as a substitute for a type of product at that time in use by agencies of the Federal Government.

(3) The Administrator may establish a Low-Noise-Emission Product Advisory Committee to assist him in determining which products qualify as low-noise-emission products for purposes of this section. The Committee shall include the Administrator or his designee, a representative of the National Bureau of Standards, and representatives of such other Federal agencies and private individuals as the Administrator may deem necessary from time to time. Any member of the Committee not employed on a full-time basis by the United States may receive the daily equivalent of the annual rate of basic pay in effect for grade GS–18 of the General Schedule for each day such member is engaged upon work of the Committee. Each member of the Committee shall be reimbursed for travel expenses, including per diem in lieu of subsistence as authorized by section 5703 of title 5, United States Code, for persons in the Government service employed intermittently.

(4) Certification under this section shall be effective for a period of one year from the date of issuance.

(5)(A) Any person seeking to have a class or model of product certified under this section shall file a certification application in accordance with regulations prescribed by the Administrator.

(B) The Administrator shall publish in the Federal Register a notice of each application received.

(C) The Administrator shall make determinations for the purposes of this section in accordance with procedures prescribed by him by regulation.

(D) The Administrator shall conduct whatever investigation is necessary, including actual inspection of the product at a place designated in regulations prescribed under subparagraph (A).

(E) The Administrator shall receive and evaluate written comments and documents from interested persons in support of, or in opposition to, certification of the class or model of product under consideration.

(F) Within ninety days after the receipt of a properly filed certification application the Administrator shall determine whether such product is a low-noise-emission product for purposes of this section. If the Administrator determines that such product is a low-noise-emission product, then within one hundred and eighty days of such determination the Administrator shall reach a decision as to whether such product is a suitable substitute for any class or classes of products presently being purchased by the Federal Government for use by its agencies.

(G) Immediately upon making any determination or decision under subparagraph (F), the Administrator shall publish in the Federal Register notice of such determination or decision, including reasons therefor.

(c) (1) Certified low-noise-emission products shall be acquired by purchase or lease by the Federal Government for use by the Federal Government in lieu of other products if the Administrator of General Services determines that such certified products have procurement costs which are no more than 125 per centum of the retail price of the least expensive type of product for which they are certified substitutes.

(2) Data relied upon by the Administrator in determining that a product is a certified low-noise-emission product shall be incorporated in any contract for the procurement of such product.

(d) The procuring agency shall be required to purchase available certified low-noise-emission products which are eligible for purchase to the extent they are available before purchasing any other products for which any low-noise-emission product is a certified substitute. In making purchasing selections between competing eligible certified low-noise-emission products, the procuring agency shall give priority to any class or model which does not require extensive periodic maintenance to retain its low-noise emission qualities or which does not involve operating costs significantly in excess of those products for which it is a certified substitute.

(e) For the purpose of procuring certified low-noise-emission products any statutory price limitations shall be waived.

(f) The Administrator shall, from time to time as he deems appropriate, test the emissions of noise from certified low-noise-emission products purchased by the Federal Government. If at any time he finds that the noise-emission levels exceed the levels on which certification under this section was based, the Administrator shall give the supplier of such product written notice of this finding, issue public notice of it, and give the supplier an opportunity to make necessary repairs, adjustments, or replacements. If no such repairs, adjustments, or replacements are made within a period to be set by the Administrator, he may order the supplier to show cause why the product involved should be eligible for recertification.

(g) There are authorized to be appropriated for paying additional amounts for products pursuant to, and for carrying out the provisions of, this section, $1,000,000 for the fiscal year ending June 30, 1973, and $2,000,000 for each of the two succeeding fiscal years, $2,200,000 for the fiscal year ending June 30, 1976, $550,000 for the transition period of July 1, 1976, through September 30, 1976, and $2,420,000 for the fiscal year ending September 30, 1977.

(h) The Administrator shall promulgate the procedures required to implement this section within one hundred and eighty days after the date of enactment of this Act.

JUDICIAL REVIEW; WITNESSES

Sec. 16. (a) A petition for review of action of the Administrator of the Environmental Protection Agency in promulgating any standard or regulation under section 6, 17, or 18 of this Act or any labeling regulation under section 8 of this Act may be filed only in the United States Court of Appeals for the District of Columbia Circuit, and a petition for review of action of the Administrator of the Federal Aviation Administration in promulgating any standard or regulation under section 611 of the Federal Aviation Act of 1958 may be filed only in such court. Any such petition shall be filed within ninety days from the date of such promulgation, or after such date if such petition is based solely on grounds arising after such ninetieth day. Action of either Administrator with respect to which review could have been obtained under this subsection shall not be subject to judicial review in civil or criminal proceedings for enforcement.

(b) If a party seeking review under this Act applies to the court for leave to adduce additional evidence, and shows to the satisfaction of the court that the information is material and was not available at the time of the proceeding before the Administrator of such Agency or Administration (as the case may be), the court may order such additional evidence (and evidence in rebuttal thereof) to be taken before such Administrator, and to be adduced upon the hearing, in such manner and upon such terms and conditions as the court may deem proper. Such Administrator may modify his findings as to the facts, or make new findings, by reason of the additional evidence so taken, and he shall file with the court such modified or new findings, and his recommendation, if any, for the modification or setting aside of his original order, with the return of such additional evidence.

(c) With respect to relief pending review of an action by either Administrator, no stay of an agency action may be granted unless the reviewing court determines that the party seeking such stay is (1) likely to prevail on the merits in the review proceeding and (2) will suffer irreparable harm pending such proceeding.

(d) For the purpose of obtaining information to carry out this Act, the Administrator of the Environmental Protection Agency may issue subpenas for the attendance and testimony of witnesses and the production of relevant papers, books, and documents, and he may administer oaths. Witnesses summoned shall be paid the same fees and mileage that are paid witnesses in the courts of the United States. In cases of contumacy or refusal to obey a subpena served upon any person under this subsection, the district court of the United States for any district in which such person is found or resides or transacts business, upon application by the United States and after notice to such person, shall have jurisdiction to issue an order requiring such person to appear and give testimony before the Administrator, to appear and produce papers, books, and documents before the Administrator, or both, and any failure to obey such order of the court may be punished by such court as a contempt thereof.

RAILROAD NOISE EMISSION STANDARDS

SEC. 17. (a)(1) Within nine months after the date of enactment of this Act, the Administrator shall publish proposed noise emission regulations for surface carriers engaged in interstate commerce by railroad. Such proposed regulations shall include noise emission standards setting such limits on noise emissions resulting from operation of the equipment and facilities of surface carriers engaged in interstate commerce by railroad which reflect the degree of noise reduction achievable through the application of the best available technology, taking into account the cost of compliance. These regulations shall be in addition to any regulations that may be proposed under section 6 of this Act.

(2) Within ninety days after the publication of such regulations as may be proposed under paragraph (1) of this subsection, and subject to the provisions of section 16 of this Act, the Administrator shall promulgate final regulations. Such regulations may be revised, from time to time, in accordance with this subsection.

(3) Any standard or regulation, or revision thereof, proposed under this subsection shall be promulgated only after consultation with the Secretary of Transportation in order to assure appropriate consideration for safety and technological availability.

(4) Any regulation or revision thereof promulgated under this subsection shall take effect after such period as the Administrator finds necessary, after consultation with the Secretary of Transportation, to permit the development and application of the requisite technology, giving appropriate consideration to the cost of compliance within such period.

(b) The Secretary of Transportation, after consultation with the Administrator, shall promulgate regulations to insure compliance with all standards promulgated by the Administrator under this section. The Secretary of Transportation shall carry out such regulations through the use of his powers and duties of enforcement and inspection authorized by the Safety Appliance Acts, the Interstate Commerce Act, and the Department of Transportation Act. Regulations promulgated under this section shall be subject to the provisions of sections 10, 11, 12, and 16 of this Act.

(c) (1) Subject to paragraph (2) but notwithstanding any other provision of this Act, after the effective date of a regulation under this section applicable to noise emissions resulting from the operation of any equipment or facility of a surface carrier engaged in interstate commerce by railroad, no State or political subdivision thereof may adopt or enforce any standard applicable to noise emissions resulting from the operation of the same equipment or facility of such carrier unless such standard is identical to a standard applicable to noise emissions resulting from such operation prescribed by any regulation under this section.

(2) Nothing in this section shall diminish or enhance the rights of any State or political subdivision thereof to establish and enforce standards or controls on levels of environmental noise, or to control, license, regulate, or restrict the use, operation, or movement of any product if the Administrator, after consultation with the Secretary of Transportation, determines that such standard, control, license, regulation, or restriction is necessitated by special local conditions and is not in conflict with regulations promulgated under this section.

(d) The terms "carrier" and "railroad" as used in this section shall have the same meaning and such terms have under the first section of the Act of February 17, 1911 (45 U.S.C. 22).

MOTOR CARRIER NOISE EMISSION STANDARDS

SEC. 18. (a) (1) Within nine months after the date of enactment of this Act, the Administrator shall publish proposed noise emission regulations for motor carriers engaged in interstate commerce. Such proposed regulations shall include noise emission standards setting such limits on noise emissions resulting from operation of motor carriers engaged in interstate commerce which reflect the degree of noise reduction achievable through the application of the best available technology, taking into account the cost of compliance. These regulations shall be in addition to any regulations that may be proposed under section 6 of this Act.

(2) Within ninety days after the publication of such regulations as may be proposed under paragraph (1) of

this subsection, and subject to the provisions of section 16 of this Act, the Administrator shall promulgate final regulations. Such regulations may be revised from time to time, in accordance with this subsection.

(3) Any standard or regulation, or revision thereof, proposed under this subsection shall be promulgated only after consultation with the Secretary of Transportation in order to assure appropriate consideration for safety and technological availability.

(4) Any regulation or revision thereof promulgated under this subsection shall take effect after such period as the Administrator finds necessary, after consultation with the Secretary of Transportation, to permit the development and application of the requisite technology, giving appropriate consideration to the cost of compliance within such period.

(b) The Secretary of Transportation, after consultation with the Administrator shall promulgate regulations to insure compliance with all standards promulgated by the Administrator under this section. The Secretary of Transportation shall carry out such regulations through the use of his powers and duties of enforcement and inspection authorized by the Interstate Commerce Act and the Department of Transportation Act. Regulations promulgated under this section shall be subject to the provisions of sections 10, 11, 12, and 16 of this Act.

(c)(1) Subject to paragraph (2) of this subsection but notwithstanding any other provision of this Act, after the effective date of a regulation under this section applicable to noise emissions resulting from the operation of any motor carrier engaged in interstate commerce, no State or political subdivision thereof may adopt or enforce any standard applicable to the same operation of such motor carrier, unless such standard is identical to a standard applicable to noise emissions resulting from such operation prescribed by any regulation under this section.

(2) Nothing in this section shall diminish or enhance the rights of any State or political subdivision thereof to establish and enforce standards or controls on levels of environmental noise, or to control, license, regulate, or restrict the use, operation, or movement of any product if the Administrator, after consultation with the Secretary of Transportation, determines that such standard, control, license, regulation, or restriction is necessitated by special local conditions and is not in conflict with regulations promulgated under this section.

(d) For purposes of this section, the term "motor carrier" includes a common carrier by motor vehicle, a contract carrier by motor vehicle, and a private carrier of property by motor vehicle as those terms are defined by paragraphs (14), (15), and (17) of section 203(a) of the Interstate Commerce Act (49 U.S.C. 303(a)).

AUTHORIZATION OF APPROPRIATIONS

SEC. 19. There is authorized to be appropriated to carry out this Act (other than section 15) $3,000,000 for the fiscal year ending June 30, 1973; $6,000,000 for the fiscal year ending June 30, 1974; $12,000,000 for the fiscal year ending June 30, 1975; $11,090,000 for the fiscal year ending June 30, 1976; $2,772,500 for the transition period of July 1, 1976, through September 30, 1976; and $12,199,000 for the fiscal year ending September 30, 1977; except that no part of any amount appropriated pursuant to this section or section 15 for any period after the fiscal year ending June 30, 1975, shall be available for research or development.

Public Law 95–609
95th Congress

An Act

To extend provisions of the Noise Control Act of 1972 for one year, and for other purposes.

Be it enacted by the Senate and House of Representatives of the United States of America in Congress assembled, That this Act may be cited as the "Quiet Communities Act of 1978".

SEC. 2. Section 14 of the Noise Control Act of 1972 is amended to read as follows:

"QUIET COMMUNITIES, RESEARCH, PUBLIC INFORMATION

"SEC. 14. To promote the development of effective State and local noise control programs, to provide an adequate Federal noise control research program designed to meet the objectives of this Act, and to otherwise carry out the policy of this Act, the Administrator shall, in cooperation with other Federal agencies and through the use of grants, contracts, and direct Federal actions—

"(a) develop and disseminate information and educational materials to all segments of the public on the public health and other effects of noise and the most effective means for noise control, through the use of materials for school curricula, volunteer organizations, radio and television programs, publication, and other means;

"(b) conduct or finance research directly or with any public or private organization or any person on the effects, measurement, and control of noise, including but not limited to—

"(1) investigation of the psychological and physiological effects of noise on humans and the effects of noise on domestic animals, wildlife, and property, and the determination of dose/response relationships suitable for use in decision-making, with special emphasis on the nonauditory effects of noise;

"(2) investigation, development, and demonstration of noise control technology for products subject to possible regulation under sections 6, 7, and 8 of this Act;

"(3) investigation, development, and demonstration of monitoring equipment and other technology especially suited for use by State and local noise control programs;

"(4) investigation of the economic impact of noise on property and human activities; and

"(5) investigation and demonstration of the use of economic incentives (including emission charges) in the control of noise;

"(c) administer a nationwide Quiet Communities Program which shall include, but not be limited to—

"(1) grants to States, local governments, and authorized regional planning agencies for the purpose of—

"(A) identifying and determining the nature and extent of the noise problem within the subject jurisdiction;

"(B) planning, developing, and establishing a noise control capacity in such jurisdiction, including purchasing initial equipment;

"(C) developing abatement plans for areas around major transportation facilities (including airports, highways, and rail yards) and other major stationary sources of noise, and, where appropriate, for the facility or source itself; and,

"(D) evaluating techniques for controlling noise (including institutional arrangements) and demonstrating the best available techniques in such jurisdiction;

"(2) purchase of monitoring and other equipment for loan to State and local noise control programs to meet special needs or assist in the beginning implementation of a noise control program or project;

"(3) development and implementation of a quality assurance program for equipment and monitoring procedures of State and local noise control programs to help communities assure that their data collection activities are accurate;

"(4) conduct of studies and demonstrations to determine the resource and personnel needs of States and local governments required for the establishment and implementation of effective noise abatement and control programs; and

"(5) development of educational and training materials and programs, including national and regional workshops, to support State and local noise abatement and control programs;

except that no actions, plans or programs hereunder shall be inconsistent with existing Federal authority under this Act to regulate sources of noise in interstate commerce;

"(d) develop and implement a national noise environmental assessment program to identify trends in noise exposure and response, ambient levels, and compliance data and to determine otherwise the effectiveness of noise abatement actions through the collection of physical, social, and human response data;

"(e) establish regional technical assistance centers which use the capabilities of university and private organizations to assist State and local noise control programs;

"(f) provide technical assistance to State and local governments to facilitate their development and enforcement of noise control, including direct onsite assistance of agency or other personnel with technical expertise, and preparation of model State or local legislation for noise control; and

"(g) provide for the maximum use in programs assisted under this section of senior citizens and persons eligible for participation in programs under the Older Americans Act.".

SEC. 3. The fourth sentence of section 611(c)(1) of the Federal Aviation Act, as amended by section 7 of the Noise Control Act of 1972, is amended by striking "a reasonable time" and inserting in lieu thereof "ninety days", and by adding before the period "and a detailed analysis of and response to all documentation or other information submitted by the Environmental Protection Agency with such proposed regulations".

SEC. 4. Section 11(a) of the Noise Control Act of 1972 is amended by inserting "(1)" after "(a)" and by adding the following new paragraph:

"(2) Any person who violates paragraph (1), (3), (5), or (6) of subsection (a) of section 10 of this Act shall be subject to a civil penalty not to exceed $10,000 per day of such violation".

SEC. 5. Section 6 of the Noise Control Act of 1972 is amended by adding the following subsection:

"(f) At any time after the promulgation of regulations respecting a product under this section, a State or political subdivision thereof may petition the Administrator to revise such standard on the grounds that a more stringent standard under subsection (c) of this section is necessary to protect the public health and welfare. The Administration shall publish notice of receipt of such petition in the Federal Register and shall within ninety days of receipt of such petition respond by (1) publication of proposed revised regulations in accordance with subsection (c)(3) of this section, or (2) publication in the Federal Register of a decision not to publish such proposed revised regulations at that time, together with a detailed explanation for such decision.".

SEC. 6. Section 19 of the Noise Control Act of 1972 is amended to read as follows:

"AUTHORIZATION OF APPROPRIATIONS

"SEC. 19. There are authorized to be appropriated to carry out this Act (other than for research and development) $15,000,000 for the fiscal year ending September 30, 1979.".

SEC. 7. (a) Section 1002(a)(4) of the Solid Waste Disposal Act is amended by deleting the hyphen between the words "solid" and "waste" in the last line.

(b) Section 1004 of the Solid Waste Disposal Act is amended by—

(1) revising paragraph (8) by striking out everything after "improvement of land";

(2) revising paragraph (10) by striking out "disposal" and inserting in lieu thereof "management";

(3) by revising paragraph (29) to read as follows:

"(29) The term 'solid waste management facility' includes—

"(A) any resource recovery system or component thereof,

"(B) any system, program, or facility for resource conservation, and

"(C) any facility for the collection, source separation, storage, transportation, transfer, processing, treatment or disposal of solid wastes, including hazardous wastes, whether such facility is associated with facilities generating such wastes or otherwise.".

(c) Section 1008(a)(3) of the Solid Waste Disposal Act is amended by striking out "title IV" and inserting in lieu thereof "subtitle D".

(d) Section 1008(b) of the Solid Waste Disposal Act is amended by striking ", pursuant to this section" and by inserting after "suggested guidelines" each time it appears the phrase "or proposed regulations under this Act".

(e) Section 2003 of the Solid Waste Disposal Act is amended by inserting "Federal agencies," after "to provide".

(f) Section 3002 of the Solid Waste Disposal Act is amended by—

(1) revising paragraph (5) by striking out the semicolon after "subtitle" and substituting a comma, and by striking out "and" and inserting in lieu thereof "or pursuant to title I of the Marine Protection, Research, and Sanctuaries Act (86 Stat. 1052); and"; and

(2) revising paragraph (6) by adding a close parenthesis after "subtitle" the first time it appears.

(g) Section 3003 of the Solid Waste Disposal Act is amended by—

(1) revising subsection (a)(4) by striking out the period after "subtitle" and substituting a comma, and by adding at the end thereof "or pursuant to title I of the Marine Protection, Research, and Sanctuaries Act (86 Stat. 1052)."; and

(2) revising subsection (b) by striking out "subtitle" after "the regulations promulgated by the Administrator under this" and inserting in lieu thereof "section".

(h) Section 3005(a) of the Solid Waste Disposal Act is amended by inserting "treatment, storage, or" after "and upon and after such date the".

(i) Section 3006(c) of the Solid Waste Disposal Act is amended by—

(1) striking out "required for" wherever it appears in the subsection and inserting in lieu thereof "of"; and

(2) inserting the word "may" immediately after "3005," and before "submit".

(j) Section 3007(a)(1) of the Solid Waste Disposal Act is amended by striking out "or disposed of" and inserting in lieu thereof "disposed of, or transported from".

(k) Section 3008 of the Solid Waste Disposal Act is amended by—

(1) revising subsection (d)(1) to read as follows:

"(1) transports any hazardous waste identified or listed under this subtitle to a facility which does not have a permit under section 3005 (or 3006 in the case of a State program), or pursuant to title I of the Marine Protection, Research, and Sanctuaries Act (86 Stat. 1052),"; and

(2) revising subsection (d)(2) to read as follows:

"(2) treats, stores, or disposes of any hazardous waste identified or listed under this subtitle without having obtained a permit under section 3005 (or 3006 in the case of a State program) or pursuant to title I of the Marine Protection, Research, and Sanctuaries Act (86 Stat. 1052)."

(l) Section 4007(C) of the Solid Waste Disposal Act is amended by redesignating subsection "(C)" as "(c)".

(m) Section 6001 of the Solid Waste Disposal Act is amended by inserting "or management" between "disposal" and "of solid waste".

(n) Section 6002 of the Solid Waste Disposal Act is amended by—

(1) deleting "(A)" after "(1)" in subsection (c) and changing "(B)" and "(C)" to "(2)" and "(3)", respectively: and changing "(i)", "(ii)", and "(iii)" to "(A)", "(B)", and "(C)", respectively;

(2) in subsection (c)(3) as redesignated, striking "Contracting" and inserting in lieu thereof "After the date specified in any applicable guidelines prepared pursuant to subsection (e) of this section, contracting"; and

(3) inserting in the second sentence of subsection (e) after "containing such materials" the phrase "and with respect to certification by vendors of the percentage of recovered materials used,".

(o) Section 6004 of the Solid Waste Disposal Act is amended by—

(1) revising subsection (a)(1)(A) by striking out "disposal" and inserting in lieu thereof "management";

(2) revising subsection (a)(1)(B) by striking out "disposal" and inserting in lieu thereof "management"; and

(3) revising subsection (b) by striking out "Secretary" and inserting in lieu thereof "Administrator".

(p) Section 7002 of the Solid Waste Disposal Act is amended by—

(1) revising subsection (c) by striking out "section 212" and inserting in lieu thereof "subtitle C"; and

(2) revising subsection (e) by striking out "requiring" and inserting in lieu thereof "require".

(q) Section 7003 of the Solid Waste Disposal Act is amended by striking out "for" before "contributing to the alleged disposal".

(r) Section 7007 of the Solid Waste Disposal Act is amended by—

(1) revising subsection (b)(1)(A) by striking out "disposal" and inserting "management"; and by striking out "resources" and inserting "resource";

(2) revising subsection (b)(1)(B) by striking out "disposal" and inserting "management"; and

(3) revising subsection (c)(3) by striking out "disposal" and inserting "management" in lieu thereof.

(s) Section 8001(a) of the Solid Waste Disposal Act is amended by—

(1) revising paragraph (2) by striking out "disposal" and inserting "management" in lieu thereof; and

(2) revising paragraph (13) by inserting "treatment," after "for purpose of".

(t) Section 8002 of the Solid Waste Disposal Act is amended by—

(1) revising paragraph (1) of subsection (g) by inserting a comma between "shale" and "liquefaction";

(2) revising paragraph (1) of subsection (j) by inserting "the Secretary of Energy, the Chairman of the Council of Economic Advisors," before "and a representative of the Office of Management and Budget,";

(3) revising paragraph (2) of subsection (j) by striking "(2)(D)" and inserting "(1)(D)" in lieu thereof;

(4) revising paragraph (3) of subsection (j) by striking "(2)(D)" and inserting "(1)" in lieu thereof; and

(5) revising subsection (1) by striking out "required under subsection (a), (h), (i) and (j)" and inserting in lieu thereof "required under subsections (a), (h), and (i)".

(u) Section 8003(a)(3) of the Solid Waste Disposal Act is amended by striking out "discarded materials" and inserting "solid waste" in lieu thereof.

(v) Section 8004(a)(1) of the Solid Waste Disposal Act is amended by striking out "discarded material" and inserting "solid waste" in lieu thereof.

SEC. 8. (a) The Secretary of Transportation and the Administrator of the Environmental Protection Agency shall jointly study the aircraft noise effects from an airport on communities located in a State other than the State in which the airport is located. The criteria to be used in selecting the airport to be studied shall include:

(1) the airport shall be operated by a State, a unit of general purpose local government of a State, or a special purpose entity constituted for the purpose of operating an airport, and

(2) the airport shall have a point on the airport boundary within one nautical mile from a State boundary, and

(3) the airport shall have had in excess of sixty thousand scheduled air carrier departures during the preceding calendar year.

(b) The study shall be conducted in cooperation with the airport operator, appropriate Federal, State, and local officials, and the appropriate Metropolitan Planning Organization.

(c) The Secretary and the Administrator shall prepare and submit to Congress a report within nine months of the conclusion of the study, but no later than twenty-four months after enactment of this section.

Approved November 8, 1978.

OCCUPATIONAL SAFETY AND HEALTH ACT

AN ACT To assure safe and healthful working conditions for working men and women; by authorizing enforcement of the standards developed under the Act; by assisting and encouraging the States in their efforts to assure safe and healthful working conditions; by providing for research, information, education, and training in the field of occupational safety and health; and for other purposes.

Be it enacted by the Senate and House of Representatives of the United States of America in Congress assembled, That this Act may be cited as the "Occupational Safety and Health Act of 1970".

CONGRESSIONAL FINDINGS AND PURPOSE

SEC. (2) The Congress finds that personal injuries and illnesses arising out of work situations impose a substantial burden upon, and are a hindrance to, interstate commerce in terms of lost production, wage loss, medical expenses, and disability compensation payments.

(b) The Congress declares it to be its purpose and policy, through the exercise of its powers to regulate commerce among the several States and with foreign nations and to provide for the general welfare, to assure so far as possible every working man and woman in the Nation safe and healthful working conditions and to preserve our human resources—

(1) by encouraging employers and employees in their efforts to reduce the number of occupational safety and health hazards at their places of employment, and to stimulate employers and employees to institute new and to perfect existing programs for providing safe and healthful working conditions;

(2) by providing that employers and employees have separate but dependent responsibilities and rights with respect to achieving safe and healthful working conditions;

(3) by authorizing the Secretary of Labor to set mandatory occupational safety and health standards applicable to businesses affecting interstate commerce, and by creating an Occupational Safety and Health Review Commission for carrying out adjudicatory functions under the Act;

(4) by building upon advances already made through employer and employee initiative for providing safe and healthful working conditions;

---

* Public Law 91-596, December 29, 1970.

(5) by providing for research in the field of occupational safety and health, including the psychological factors involved, and by developing innovative methods, techniques, and approaches for dealing with occupational safety and health problems;

(6) by exploring ways to discover latent diseases, establishing causal connections between diseases and work in environmental conditions, and conducting other research relating to health problems, in recognition of the fact that occupational health standards present problems often different from those involved in occupational safety;

(7) by providing medical criteria which will assure insofar as practicable that no employee will suffer diminished health, functional capacity, or life expectancy as a result of his work experience;

(8) by providing for training programs to increase the number and competence of personnel engaged in the field of occupational safety and health;

(9) by providing for the development and promulgation of occupational safety and health standards;

(10) by providing an effective enforcement program which shall include a prohibition against giving advance notice of any inspection and sanctions for any individual violating this prohibition;

(11) by encouraging the States to assume the fullest responsibility for the administration and enforcement of their occupational safety and health laws by providing grants to the States to assist in identifying their needs and responsibilities in the area of occupational safety and health, to develop plans in accordance with the provisions of this Act, to improve the administration and enforcement of State occupational safety and health laws, and to conduct experimental and demonstration projects in connection therewith;

(12) by providing for appropriate reporting procedures with respect to occupational safety and health which procedures will help achieve the objectives of this Act and accurately describe the nature of the occupational safety and health problem;

(13) by encouraging joint labor-management efforts to reduce injuries and disease arising out of employment.

DEFINITIONS

SEC. 3. For the purposes of this Act—

(1) The term "Secretary" means the Secretary of Labor.

(2) The term "Commission" means the Occupational Safety and Health Review Commission established under this Act.

(3) The term "commerce" means trade, traffic, commerce, transportation, or communication among the several States, or between a State and any place outside thereof, or within the District of Columbia, or a possession of the United States (other than the Trust Territory of the Pacific Islands), or between points in the same State but through a point outside thereof.

(4) The term "person" means one or more individuals, partnerships, associations, corporations, business trusts, legal representatives, or any organized group of persons.

(5) The term "employer" means a person engaged in a business affecting commerce who has employees, but does not include the United States or any State or political subdivision of a State.

(6) The term "employee" means an employee of an employer who is employed in a business of his employer which affects commerce.

(7) The term "State" includes a State of the United States, the District of Columbia, Puerto Rico, the Virgin Islands, American Samoa, Guam, and the Trust Territory of the Pacific Islands.

(8) The term "occupational safety and health standard" means a standard which requires conditions, or the adoption or use of one or more practices, means, methods, operations, or processes, reasonably necessary or appropriate to provide safe or healthful employment and places of employment.

(9) The term "national consensus standard" means any occupational safety and health standard or modification thereof which (1) has been adopted and promulgated by a nationally recognized standards-producing organization under procedures whereby it can be determined by the Secretary that persons interested and affected by the scope or provisions of the standard have reached substantial agreement on its adoption, (2) was formulated in a manner which afforded an opportunity for diverse views to be considered and (3) has been designated as such a standard by the Secretary, after consultation with other appropriate Federal agencies.

(10) The term "established Federal standard" means any operative occupational safety and health standard established by any agency of the United States and presently in effect, or contained in any Act of Congress in force on the date of enactment of this Act.

(11) The term "Committee" means the National Advisory Committee on Occupational Safety and Health established under this Act.

(12) The term "Director" means the Director of the National Institute for Occupational Safety and Health.

(13) The term "Institute" means the National Institute for Occupational Safety and Health established under this Act.

(14) The term "Workmen's Compensation Commission" means the National Commission on State Workmen's Compensation Laws established under this Act.

APPLICABILITY OF THIS ACT

SEC. 4. (a) This Act shall apply with respect to employment performed in a workplace in a State, the District of Columbia, the Commonwealth of Puerto Rico, the Virgin Islands, American Samoa, Guam, the Trust Territory of the Pacific Islands, Wake Island, Outer Continental Shelf lands defined in the Outer Continental Shelf Lands Act, Johnston Island, and the Canal Zone. The Secretary of the Interior shall, by regulation, provide for judicial enforcement of this Act by the courts established for areas in which there are no United States district courts having jurisdiction.

(b)(1) Nothing in this Act shall apply to working conditions of employees with respect to which other Federal agencies, and State agencies acting under section 274 of the Atomic Energy Act of 1954, as amended (42 U.S.C. 2021), exercise statutory authority to prescribe or enforce standards or regulations affecting occupational safety or health.

(2) The safety and health standards promulgated under the Act of June 30, 1936, commonly known as the Walsh-Healey Act (41 U.S.C. 35 et seq.), the Service Contract Act of 1965 (41 U.S.C. 351 et seq.), Public Law 91–54, Act of August 9, 1969 (40 U.S.C. 333), Public Law 85–742, Act of August 23, 1958 (33 U.S.C. 941), and the National Foundation on Arts and Humanities Act (20 U.S.C. 951 et seq.) are superseded on the effective date of corresponding standards, promulgated under this Act, which are determined by the Secretary to be more effective. Standards issued under the laws listed in this paragraph and in effect on or after the effective date of this Act shall be deemed to be occupational safety and health standards issued under this Act, as well as under such other Acts.

(3) The Secretary shall, within three years after the effective date of this Act, report to the Congress his recommendations for legislation to avoid unnecessary duplication and to achieve coordination between this Act and other Federal laws.

(4) Nothing in this Act shall be construed to supersede or in any manner affect any workmen's compensation law or to enlarge or diminish or affect in any other manner the common law or statutory rights, duties, or liabilities of employers and employees under any law with respect to injuries, diseases, or death of employees arising out of, or in the course of, employment.

DUTIES

SEC. 5. (a) Each employer—

(1) shall furnish to each of his employees employment and a place of employment which are free from recognized hazards that are causing or are likely to cause death or serious physical harm to his employees;

(2) shall comply with occupational safety and health standards promulgated under this Act.

(b) Each employee shall comply with occupational safety and health standards and all rules, regulations, and orders issued pursuant to this Act which are applicable to his own actions and conduct.

OCCUPATIONAL SAFETY AND HEALTH STANDARDS

SEC. 6. (a) Without regard to chapter 5 of title 5, United States Code, or to the other subsections of this section, the Secretary shall, as soon as practicable during the period beginning with the effective date of this Act and ending two years after such date, by rule promulgate as an occupational safety or health standard any national consensus standard, and any established Federal standard, unless he determines that the promulgation of such a standard would not result in improved safety or health for specifically designated employees. In the event of conflict among any such standards, the Secretary shall promulgate the standard which assures the greatest protection of the safety or health of the affected employees.

(b) The Secretary may by rule promulgate, modify, or revoke any occupational safety or health standard in the following manner:

(1) Whenever the Secretary, upon the basis of information submitted to him in writing by an interested person, a representative of any organization of employers or employees, a nationally recognized standards-producing organization, the Secretary of Health, Education, and Welfare, the National Institute for Occupational Safety and Health, or a State or political subdivision, or on the basis of information developed by the Secretary or otherwise available to him, determines that a rule should be

promulgated in order to serve the objectives of this Act, the Secretary may request the recommendations of an advisory committee appointed under section 7 of this Act. The Secretary shall provide such an advisory committee with any proposals of his own or of the Secretary of Health, Education, and Welfare, together with all pertinent factual information developed by the Secretary or the Secretary of Health, Education, and Welfare, or otherwise available, including the results of research, demonstrations, and experiments. An advisory committee shall submit to the Secretary its recommendations regarding the rule to be promulgated within ninety days from the date of its appointment or within such longer or shorter period as may be prescribed by the Secretary, but in no event for a period which is longer than two hundred and seventy days.

(2) The Secretary shall publish a proposed rule promulgating, modifying, or revoking an occupational safety or health standard in the Federal Register and shall afford interested persons a period of thirty days after publication to submit written data or comments. Where an advisory committee is appointed and the Secretary determines that a rule should be issued, he shall publish the proposed rule within sixty days after the submission of the advisory committee's recommendations or the expiration of the period prescribed by the Secretary for such submission.

(3) On or before the last day of the period provided for the submission of written data or comments under paragraph (2), any interested person may file with the Secretary written objections to the proposed rule, stating the grounds therefor and requesting a public hearing on such objections. Within thirty days after the last day for filing such objections, the Secretary shall publish in the Federal Register a notice specifying the occupational safety or health standard to which objections have been filed and a hearing requested, and specifying a time and place for such hearing.

(4) Within sixty days after the expiration of the period provided for the submission of written data or comments under paragraph (2), or within sixty days after the completion of any hearing held under paragraph (3), the Secretary shall issue a rule promulgating, modifying, or revoking an occupational safety or health standard or make a determination that a rule should not be issued. Such a rule may contain a provision delaying its effective date for such period (not in excess of ninety days) as the Secretary determines may be necessary to insure that affected employers and employees will be informed of the existence of the standard and of its terms and that employers affected are given an opportunity to familiarize themselves and their employees with the existence of the requirements of the standard.

(5) The Secretary, in promulgating standards dealing with toxic materials or harmful physical agents under this subsection, shall set the standard which most adequately assures, to the extent feasible, on the basis of the best available evidence, that no employee will suffer material impairment of health or functional capacity even if such employee has regular exposure to the hazard dealt with by such standard for the period of his working life. Development of standards under this subsection shall be based upon research, demonstrations, experiments, and such other information as may be appropriate. In addition to the attainment of the highest degree of health and safety protection for the employee, other considerations shall be the latest available scientific data in the field, the feasibility of the standards, and experience gained under this and other health and safety laws. Whenever practicable, the standard promulgated shall be expressed in terms of objective criteria and of the performance desired.

(6)(A) Any employer may apply to the Secretary for a temporary order granting a variance from a standard or any provision thereof promulgated under this section. Such temporary order shall be granted only if the employer files an application which meets the requirements of clause (B) and establishes that (i) he is unable to comply with a standard by its effective date because of unavailability of professional or technical personnel or of materials and equipment needed to come into compliance with the standard or because necessary construction or alteration of facilities cannot be completed by the effective date, (ii) he is taking all available steps to safeguard his employees against the hazards covered by the standard, and (iii) he has an effective program for coming into compliance with the standard as quickly as practicable. Any temporary order issued under this paragraph shall prescribe the practices, means, methods, operations, and processes which the employer must adopt and use while the order is in effect and state in detail his program for coming into compliance with the standard. Such a temporary order may be granted only after notice to employees and an opportunity for a hearing: *Provided*, That the Secretary may issue one interim order to be effective until a decision is made on the basis of the hearing. No temporary order may be in effect for longer than the period needed by the employer to achieve compliance with the standard or one year, whichever is shorter, except that such an order may be renewed not more than twice (I) so long as the requirements of this paragraph are met and (II) if an application for renewal is filed at least 90 days prior to the expiration date of the order. No interim renewal of an order may remain in effect for longer than 180 days.

(B) An application for a temporary order under this paragraph (6) shall contain:

(i) a specification of the standard or portion thereof from which the employer seeks a variance,

(ii) a representation by the employer, supported by representations from qualified persons having firsthand knowledge of the facts represented, that he is unable to comply with the standard or portion thereof and a detailed statement of the reasons therefor,

(iii) a statement of the steps he has taken and will take (with specific dates) to protect employees against the hazard covered by the standard,

(iv) a statement of when he expects to be able to comply with the standard and what steps he has taken and what steps he will take (with dates specified) to come into compliance with the standard, and

(v) a certification that he has informed his employees of the application by giving a copy thereof to their authorized representative, posting a statement giving a summary of the application and specifying where a copy may be examined at the place or places where notices to employees are normally posted, and by other appropriate means.

A description of how employees have been informed shall be contained in the certification. The information to employees shall also inform them of their right to petition the Secretary for a hearing.

(C) The Secretary is authorized to grant a variance from any standard or portion thereof whenever he determines, or the Secretary of Health, Education, and Welfare certifies, that such variance is necessary to permit an employer to participate in an experiment approved by him or the Secretary of Health, Education, and Welfare designed to demonstrate or validate new and improved techniques to safeguard the health or safety of workers.

(7) Any standard promulgated under this subsection shall prescribe the use of labels or other appropriate forms of warning as are necessary to insure that employees are apprised of all hazards to which they are exposed, relevant symptoms and appropriate emergency treatment, and proper conditions and precautions of safe use or exposure. Where appropriate, such standard shall also prescribe suitable protective equipment and control or technological procedures to be used in connection with such hazards and shall provide for monitoring or measuring employee exposure at such locations and intervals, and in such manner as may be necessary for the protection of employees. In addition, where appropriate, any such standard shall prescribe the type and frequency of medical examinations or other tests which shall be made

available, by the employer or at his cost, to employees exposed to such hazards in order to most effectively determine whether the health of such employees is adversely affected by such exposure. In the event such medical examinations are in the nature of research, as determined by the Secretary of Health, Education, and Welfare, such examinations may be furnished at the expense of the Secretary of Health, Education, and Welfare. The results of such examinations or tests shall be furnished only to the Secretary or the Secretary of Health, Education, and Welfare, and, at the request of the employee, to his physician. The Secretary, in consultation with the Secretary of Health, Education, and Welfare, may by rule promulgated pursuant to section 553 of title 5, United States Code, make appropriate modifications in the foregoing requirements relating to the use of labels or other forms of warning, monitoring or measuring, and medical examinations, as may be warranted by experience, information, or medical or technological developments acquired subsequent to the promulgation of the relevant standard.

(8) Whenever a rule promulgated by the Secretary differs substantially from an existing national consensus standard, the Secretary shall, at the same time, publish in the Federal Register a statement of the reasons why the rule as adopted will better effectuate the purposes of this Act than the national consensus standard.

(c)(1) The Secretary shall provide, without regard to the requirements of chapter 5, title 5, United States Code, for an emergency temporary standard to take immediate effect upon publication in the Federal Register if he determines (A) that employees are exposed to grave danger from exposure to substances or agents determined to be toxic or physically harmful or from new hazards, and (B) that such emergency standard is necessary to protect employees from such danger.

(2) Such standard shall be effective until superseded by standard promulgated in accordance with the procedures prescribed in paragraph (3) of this subsection.

(3) Upon publication of such standard in the Federal Register the Secretary shall commence a proceeding in accordance with section 6(b) of this Act, and the standard as published shall also serve as a proposed rule for the proceeding. The Secretary shall promulgate a standard under this paragraph no later than six months after publication of the emergency standard as provided in paragraph (2) of this subsection.

(d) Any affected employer may apply to the Secretary for a rule or order for a variance from a standard promulgated under this section. Affected employees shall be given notice of each such application and an opportunity to participate in a hearing. The Secretary shall issue such rule or order if he determines on the record, after opportunity for an inspection where appropriate and a hearing, that the proponent of the variance has demonstrated by a preponderance of the evidence that the conditions, practices, means, methods, operations, or processes used or proposed to be used by an employer will provide employment and places of employment to his employees which are as safe and healthful as those which would prevail if he complied with the standard. The rule or order so issued shall prescribe the conditions the employer must maintain, and the practices, means, methods, operations, and processes which he must adopt and utilize to the extent they differ from the standard in question. Such a rule or order may be modified or revoked upon application by an employer, employees, or by the Secretary on his own motion, in the manner prescribed for its issuance under this subsection at any time after six months from its issuance.

(e) Whenever the Secretary promulgates any standard, makes any rule, order, or decision, grants any exemption or extension of time, or compromises, mitigates, or settles any penalty assessed under this Act, he shall include a statement of the reasons for such action, which shall be published in the Federal Register.

(f) Any person who may be adversely affected by a standard issued under this section may at any time prior to the sixtieth day after such standard is promulgated file a petition challenging the validity of such standard with the United States court of appeals for the circuit wherein such person resides or has his principal place of business, for a judicial review of such standard. A copy of the petition shall be forthwith transmitted by the clerk of the court to the Secretary. The filing of such petition shall not, unless otherwise ordered by the court, operate as a stay of the standard. The determinations of the Secretary shall be conclusive if supported by substantial evidence in the record considered as a whole.

(g) In determining the priority for establishing standards under this section, the Secretary shall give due regard to the urgency of the need for mandatory safety and health standards for particular industries, trades, crafts, occupations, businesses, workplaces or work environments. The Secretary shall also give due regard to the recommendations of the Secretary of Health, Education, and Welfare regarding the need for mandatory standards in determining the priority for establishing such standards.

ADVISORY COMMITTEES; ADMINISTRATION

SEC. 7 (a)(1) There is hereby established a National Advisory Committee on Occupational Safety and Health consisting of twelve members appointed by the Secretary, four of whom are to be designated by the Secretary of Health, Education, and Welfare, without regard to the provisions of title 5, United States Code, governing appointments in the competitive service, and composed of representatives of management, labor, occupational safety and occupational health professions, and of the public. The Secretary shall designate one of the public members as Chairman. The members shall be selected upon the basis of their experience and competence in the field of occupational safety and health.

(2) The Committee shall advise, consult with, and make recommendations to the Secretary and the Secretary of Health, Education, and Welfare on matters relating to the administration of the Act. The Committee shall hold no fewer than two meetings during each calendar year. All meetings of the Committee shall be open to the public and a transcript shall be kept and made available for public inspection.

(3) The members of the Committee shall be compensated in accordance with the provisions of section 3109 of title 5, United States Code.

(4) The Secretary shall furnish to the Committee an executive secretary and such secretarial, clerical, and other services as are deemed necessary to the conduct of its business.

(b) An advisory committee may be appointed by the Secretary to assist him in his standard-setting functions under section 6 of this Act. Each such committee shall consist of not more than fifteen members and shall include as a member one or more designees of the Secretary of Health, Education, and Welfare, and shall include among its members an equal number of persons qualified by experience and affiliation to present the viewpoint of the employers involved, and of persons similarly qualified to present the viewpoint of the workers involved, as well as one or more representatives of health and safety agencies of the States. An advisory committee may also include such other persons as the Secretary may appoint who are qualified by knowledge and experience to make a useful contribution to the work of such committee, including one or more representatives of professional organizations of technicians or professionals specializing in occupational safety or health, and one or more representatives of nationally recognized standards-producing organizations, but the number of persons so appointed to any such advisory committee shall not exceed the number appointed to such committee as representatives of Federal and State agencies. Persons appointed to advisory committees from private life shall be compensated in the same manner as consultants or experts under section 3109 of title 5, United States Code.

The Secretary shall pay to any State which is the employer of a member of such a committee who is a representative of the health or safety agency of that State, reimbursement sufficient to cover the actual cost to the State resulting from such representative's membership on such committee. Any meeting of such committee shall be open to the public and an accurate record shall be kept and made available to the public. No member of such committee (other than representatives of employers and employees) shall have an economic interest in any proposed rule.

(c) In carrying out his responsibilities under this Act, the Secretary is authorized to—

(1) use, with the consent of any Federal agency, the services, facilities, and personnel of such agency, with or without reimbursement, and with the consent of any State or political subdivision thereof, accept and use the services, facilities, and personnel of any agency of such State or subdivision with reimbursement; and

(2) employ experts and consultants or organizations thereof as authorized by section 3109 of title 5, United States Code, except that contracts for such employment may be renewed annually; compensate individuals so employed at rates not in excess of the rate specified at the time of service for grade GS–18 under section 5332 of title 5, United States Code, including traveltime, and allow them while away from their homes or regular places of business, travel expenses (including per diem in lieu of subsistence) as authorized by section 5703 of title 5, United States Code, for persons in the Government service employed intermittently, while so employed.

INSPECTIONS, INVESTIGATIONS, AND RECORDKEEPING

SEC. 8. (a) In order to carry out the purposes of this Act, the Secretary, upon presenting appropriate credentials to the owner, operator, or agent in charge, is authorized—

(1) to enter without delay and at reasonable times any factory, plant, establishment, construction site, or other area, workplace or environment where work is performed by an employee of an employer; and

(2) to inspect and investigate during regular working hours and at other reasonable times, and within reasonable limits and in a reasonable manner, any such place of employment and all pertinent conditions, structures, machines, apparatus, devices, equipment, and materials therein, and to question privately any such employer, owner, operator, agent or employee.

(b) In making his inspections and investigations under this Act the Secretary may require the attendance and testimony of witnesses and the production of evidence under oath. Witnesses shall be paid the same fees and mileage that are paid witnesses in the courts of the United States. In case of a contumacy, failure, or refusal of any person to obey such an order, any district court of the United States or the United States courts of any territory or possession, within the jurisdiction of which such person is found, or resides or transacts business, upon the application by the Secretary, shall have jurisdiction to issue to such person an order requiring such person to appear to produce evidence if, as, and when so ordered, and to give testimony relating to the matter under investigation or in question, and any failure to obey such order of the court may be punished by said court as a contempt thereof.

(c)(1) Each employer shall make, keep and preserve, and make available to the Secretary or the Secretary of Health, Education, and Welfare, such records regarding his activities relating to this Act as the Secretary, in cooperation with the Secretary of Health, Education, and Welfare, may prescribe by regulation as necessary or appropriate for the enforcement of this Act or for developing information regarding the causes and prevention of occupational accidents and illnesses. In order to carry out the provisions of this paragraph such regulations may include provisions requiring employers to conduct periodic inspections. The Secretary shall also issue regulations requiring that employers, through posting of notices or other appropriate means, keep their employees informed of their protections and obligations under this Act, including the provisions of applicable standards.

(2) The Secretary, in cooperation with the Secretary of Health, Education, and Welfare, shall prescribe regulations requiring employers to maintain accurate records of, and to make periodic reports on, work-related deaths, injuries and illnesses other than minor injuries requiring only first aid treatment and which do not involve medical treatment, loss of consciousness, restriction of work or motion, or transfer to another job.

(3) The Secretary, in cooperation with the Secretary of Health, Education, and Welfare, shall issue regulations requiring employers to maintain accurate records of employee exposures to potentially toxic materials or harmful physical agents which are required to be monitored or measured under section 6. Such regulations shall provide employees or their representatives with an opportunity to observe such monitoring or measuring, and to have access to the records thereof. Such regulations shall also make appropriate provision for each employee or

former employee to have access to such records as will indicate his own exposure to toxic materials or harmful physical agents. Each employer shall promptly notify any employee who has been or is being exposed to toxic materials or harmful physical agents in concentrations or at levels which exceed those prescribed by an applicable occupational safety and health standard promulgated under section 6, and shall inform any employee who is being thus exposed of the corrective action being taken.

(d) Any information obtained by the Secretary, the Secretary of Health, Education, and Welfare, or a State agency under this Act shall be obtained with a minimum burden upon employers, especially those operating small businesses. Unnecessary duplication of efforts in obtaining information shall be reduced to the maximum extent feasible.

(e) Subject to regulations issued by the Secretary, a representative of the employer and a representative authorized by his employees shall be given an opportunity to accompany the Secretary or his authorized representative during the physical inspection of any workplace under subsection (a) for the purpose of aiding such inspection. Where there is no authorized employee representative, the Secretary or his authorized representative shall consult with a reasonable number of employees concerning matters of health and safety in the workplace.

(f) (1) Any employees or representative of employees who believe that a violation of a safety or health standard exists that threatens physical harm, or that an imminent danger exists, may request an inspection by giving notice to the Secretary or his authorized representative of such violation or danger. Any such notice shall be reduced to writing, shall set forth with reasonable particularity the grounds for the notice, and shall be signed by the employees or representative of employees, and a copy shall be provided the employer or his agent no later than at the time of inspection, except that, upon the request of the person giving such notice, his name and the names of individual employees referred to therein shall not appear in such copy or on any record published, released, or made available pursuant to subsection (g) of this section. If upon receipt of such notification the Secretary determines there are reasonable grounds to believe that such violation or danger exists, he shall make a special inspection in accordance with the provisions of this section as soon as practicable, to determine if such violation or danger exists. If the Secretary determines there are no reasonable grounds to believe that a violation or danger exists he shall notify the employees or representative of the employees in writing of such determination.

(2) Prior to or during any inspection of a workplace, any employees or representative of employees employed

in such workplace may notify the Secretary or any representative of the Secretary responsible for conducting the inspection, in writing, of any violation of this Act which they have reason to believe exists in such workplace. The Secretary shall, by regulation, establish procedures for informal review of any refusal by a representative of the Secretary to issue a citation with respect to any such alleged violation and shall furnish the employees or representative of employees requesting such review a written statement of the reasons for the Secretary's final disposition of the case.

(g) (1) The Secretary and Secretary of Health, Education, and Welfare are authorized to compile, analyze, and publish, either in summary or detailed form, all reports or information obtained under this section.

(2) The Secretary and the Secretary of Health, Education, and Welfare shall each prescribe such rules and regulations as he may deem necessary to carry out their responsibilities under this Act, including rules and regulations dealing with the inspection of an employer's establishment.

CITATIONS

SEC. 9. (a) If, upon inspection or investigation, the Secretary or his authorized representative believes that an employer has violated a requirement of section 5 of this Act, of any standard, rule or order promulgated pursuant to section 6 of this Act, or of any regulations prescribed pursuant to this Act, he shall with reasonable promptness issue a citation to the employer. Each citation shall be in writing and shall describe with particularity the nature of the violation, including a reference to the provision of the Act, standard, rule, regulation, or order alleged to have been violated. In addition, the citation shall fix a reasonable time for the abatement of the violation. The Secretary may prescribe procedures for the issuance of a notice in lieu of a citation with respect to de minimis violations which have no direct or immediate relationship to safety or health.

(b) Each citation issued under this section, or a copy or copies thereof, shall be prominently posted, as prescribed in regulations issued by the Secretary, at or near each place a violation referred to in the citation occurred.

(c) No citation may be issued under this section after the expiration of six months following the occurrence of any violation.

PROCEDURE FOR ENFORCEMENT

SEC. 10. (a) If, after an inspection or investigation, the Secretary issues a citation under section 9(a), he shall, within a reasonable time after the termination of such inspection or investigation, notify the employer by certified mail of the penalty, if any, proposed to be assessed under section 17 and that the employer has fifteen working days within which to notify the Secretary that he wishes to contest the citation or proposed assessment of penalty. If, within fifteen working days from the receipt of the notice issued by the Secretary the employer fails to notify the Secretary that he intends to contest the citation or proposed assessment of penalty, and no notice is filed by any employee or representative of employees under subsection (c) within such time, the citation and the assessment, as proposed, shall be deemed a final order of the Commission and not subject to review by any court or agency.

(b) If the Secretary has reason to believe that an employer has failed to correct a violation for which a citation has been issued within the period permitted for its correction (which period shall not begin to run until the entry of a final order by the Commission in the case of any review proceedings under this section initiated by the employer in good faith and not solely for delay or avoidance of penalties), the Secretary shall notify the employer by certified mail of such failure and of the penalty proposed to be assessed under section 17 by reason of such failure, and that the employer has fifteen working days within which to notify the Secretary that he wishes to contest the Secretary's notification or the proposed assessment of penalty. If, within fifteen working days from the receipt of notification issued by the Secretary, the employer fails to notify the Secretary that he intends to contest the notification or proposed assessment of penalty, the notification and assessment, as proposed, shall be deemed a final order of the Commission and not subject to review by any court or agency.

(c) If an employer notifies the Secretary that he intends to contest a citation issued under section 9(a) or notification issued under subsection (a) or (b) of this section, or if, within fifteen working days of the issuance of a citation under section 9(a), any employee or representative of employees files a notice with the Secretary alleging that the period of time fixed in the citation for the abatement of the violation is unreasonable, the Secretary shall immediately advise the Commission of such notification, and the Commission shall afford an opportunity for a hearing (in accordance with section 554 of title 5, United States Code, but without regard to subsection (a)(3) of such section). The Commission shall thereafter issue an order, based on findings of fact, affirming, modifying, or vacating the Secretary's citation or proposed penalty, or directing other appropriate relief, and such order shall become final thirty days after its issuance. Upon a showing by an employer of a good faith effort to comply with the abatement requirements of a citation, and that abatement has not been completed because of factors beyond his reasonable control, the Secretary, after an opportunity for a hearing as provided in this subsection, shall issue an order affirming or modifying the abatement requirements in such citation. The rules of procedure prescribed by the Commission shall provide affected employees or representatives of affected employees an opportunity to participate as parties to hearings under this subsection.

JUDICIAL REVIEW

Sec. 11. (a) Any person adversely affected or aggrieved by an order of the Commission issued under subsection (c) of section 10 may obtain a review of such order in any United States court of appeals for the circuit in which the violation is alleged to have occurred or where the employer has its principal office, or in the Court of Appeals for the District of Columbia Circuit, by filing in such court within sixty days following the issuance of such order a written petition praying that the order be modified or set aside. A copy of such petition shall be forthwith transmitted by the clerk of the court to the Commission and to the other parties, and thereupon the Commission shall file in the court the record in the proceeding as provided in section 2112 of title 28, United States Code. Upon such filing, the court shall have jurisdiction of the proceeding and of the question determined therein, and shall have power to grant such temporary relief or restraining order as it deems just and proper, and to make and enter upon the pleadings, testimony, and proceedings set forth in such record a decree affirming, modifying, or setting aside in whole or in part, the order of the Commission and enforcing the same to the extent that such order is affirmed or modified. The commencement of proceedings under this subsection shall not, unless ordered by the court, operate as a stay of the order of the Commission. No objection that has not been urged before the Commission shall be considered by the court, unless the failure or neglect to urge such objection shall be excused because of extraordinary circumstances. The findings of the Commission with respect to questions of fact, if supported by substantial evidence on the record considered as a whole, shall be conclusive. If any party shall apply to the court for leave to adduce additional evidence and shall show to the satisfaction of the court that such additional evidence is material and that there were reasonable grounds for the failure to adduce such evidence in the hearing before the Commission, the court may order such additional evidence to be taken before the Commission and to be made a part of the record. The Commission may modify its findings as to the facts, or make new findings, by reason of additional evidence so taken and filed, and it shall file such modified or new findings, which findings with respect to questions of fact, if supported by substantial evidence on the record considered as a whole, shall be conclusive, and its recommendations, if any, for the modification or setting aside of its original order. Upon the filing of the record with it, the jurisdiction of the court shall be exclusive and its judgment and decree shall be final, except that the same shall be subject to review by the Supreme Court of the United States, as provided in section 1254 of title 28, United States Code. Petitions filed under this subsection shall be heard expeditiously.

(b) The Secretary may also obtain review or enforcement of any final order of the Commission by filing a petition for such relief in the United States court of appeals for the circuit in which the alleged violation occurred or in which the employer has its principal office, and the provisions of subsection (a) shall govern such proceedings to the extent applicable. If no petition for review, as provided in subsection (a), is filed within sixty days after service of the Commission's order, the Commission's findings of fact and order shall be conclusive in connection with any petition for enforcement which is filed by the Secretary after the expiration of such sixty-day period. In any such case, as well as in the case of a noncontested citation or notification by the Secretary which has become a final order of the Commission under subsection (a) or (b) of section 10, the clerk of the court, unless otherwise ordered by the court, shall forthwith enter a decree enforcing the order and shall transmit a copy of such decree to the Secretary and the employer named in the petition. In any contempt proceeding brought to enforce a decree of a court of appeals entered pursuant to this subsection or subsection (a), the court of appeals may assess the penalties provided in section 17, in addition to invoking any other available remedies.

(c) (1) No person shall discharge or in any manner discriminate against any employee because such employee has filed any complaint or instituted or caused to be instituted any proceeding under or related to this Act or has testified or is about to testify in any such proceeding or because of the exercise by such employee on behalf of himself or others of any right afforded by this Act.

(2) Any employee who believes that he has been discharged or otherwise discriminated against by any person in violation of this subsection may, within thirty days after such violation occurs, file a complaint with the Secretary alleging such discrimination. Upon receipt of such complaint, the Secretary shall cause such investigation to be made as he deems appropriate. If upon such investigation, the Secretary determines that the pro-

visions of this subsection have been violated, he shall bring an action in any appropriate United States district court against such person. In any such action the United States district courts shall have jurisdiction, for cause shown to restrain violations of paragraph (1) of this subsection and order all appropriate relief including rehiring or reinstatement of the employee to his former position with back pay.

(3) Within 90 days of the receipt of a complaint filed under this subsection the Secretary shall notify the complainant of his determination under paragraph 2 of this subsection.

THE OCCUPATIONAL SAFETY AND HEALTH REVIEW COMMISSION

SEC. 12. (a) The Occupational Safety and Health Review Commission is hereby established. The Commission shall be composed of three members who shall be appointed by the President, by and with the advice and consent of the Senate, from among persons who by reason of training, education, or experience are qualified to carry out the functions of the Commission under this Act. The President shall designate one of the members of the Commission to serve as Chairman.

(b) The terms of members of the Commission shall be six years except that (1) the members of the Commission first taking office shall serve, as designated by the President at the time of appointment, one for a term of two years, one for a term of four years, and one for a term of six years, and (2) a vacancy caused by the death, resignation, or removal of a member prior to the expiration of the term for which he was appointed shall be filled only for the remainder of such unexpired term. A member of the Commission may be removed by the President for inefficiency, neglect of duty, or malfeasance in office.

(c)(1) Section 5314 of title 5, United States Code, is amended by adding at the end thereof the following new paragraph:

"(57) Chairman, Occupational Safety and Health Review Commission."

(2) Section 5315 of title 5, United States Code, is amended by adding at the end thereof the following new paragraph:

"(94) Members, Occupational Safety and Health Review Commission."

(d) The principal office of the Commission shall be in the District of Columbia. Whenever the Commission deems that the convenience of the public or of the parties may be promoted, or delay or expense may be minimized, it may hold hearings or conduct other proceedings at any other place.

(e) The Chairman shall be responsible on behalf of the Commission for the administrative operations of the Commission and shall appoint such hearing examiners and other employees as he deems necessary to assist in the performance of the Commission's functions and to fix their compensation in accordance with the provisions of chapter 51 and subchapter III of chapter 53 of title 5, United States Code, relating to classification and General Schedule pay rates: *Provided*, That assignment, removal and compensation of hearing examiners shall be in accordance with sections 3105, 3344, 5362, and 7521 of title 5, United States Code.

(f) For the purpose of carrying out its functions under this Act, two members of the Commission shall constitute a quorum and official action can be taken only on the affirmative vote of at least two members.

(g) Every official act of the Commission shall be entered of record, and its hearings and records shall be open to the public. The Commission is authorized to make such rules as are necessary for the orderly transaction of its proceedings. Unless the Commission has adopted a different rule, its proceedings shall be in accordance with the Federal Rules of Civil Procedure.

(h) The Commission may order testimony to be taken by deposition in any proceedings pending before it at any state of such proceeding. Any person may be compelled to appear and depose, and to produce books, papers, or documents, in the same manner as witnesses may be compelled to appear and testify and produce like documentary evidence before the Commission. Witnesses whose depositions are taken under this subsection, and the persons taking such depositions, shall be entitled to the same fees as are paid for like services in the courts of the United States.

(i) For the purpose of any proceeding before the Commission, the provisions of section 11 of the National Labor Relations Act (29 U.S.C. 161) are hereby made applicable to the jurisdiction and powers of the Commission.

(j) A hearing examiner appointed by the Commission shall hear, and make a determination upon, any proceeding instituted before the Commission and any motion in connection therewith, assigned to such hearing examiner by the Chairman of the Commission, and shall make a report of any such determination which constitutes his final disposition of the proceedings. The report of the hearing examiner shall become the final order of the Commission within thirty days after such report by the hearing examiner, unless within such period any Commission member has directed that such report shall be reviewed by the Commission.

(k) Except as otherwise provided in this Act, the hearing examiners shall be subject to the laws governing employees in the classified civil service, except that appointments shall be made without regard to section 5108 of title 5, United States Code. Each hearing examiner shall receive compensation at a rate not less than that prescribed for GS-16 under section 5332 of title 5, United States Code.

PROCEDURES TO COUNTERACT IMMINENT DANGERS

SEC. 13. (a) The United States district courts shall have jurisdiction, upon petition of the Secretary, to restrain any conditions or practices in any place of employment which are such that a danger exists which could reasonably be expected to cause death or serious physical harm immediately or before the imminence of such danger can be eliminated through the enforcement procedures otherwise provided by this Act. Any order issued under this section may require such steps to be taken as may be necessary to avoid, correct, or remove such imminent danger and prohibit the employment or presence of any individual in locations or under conditions where such imminent danger exists, except individuals whose presence is necessary to avoid, correct, or remove such imminent danger or to maintain the capacity of a continuous process operation to resume normal operations without a complete cessation of operations, or where a cessation of operations is necessary, to permit such to be accomplished in a safe and orderly manner.

(b) Upon the filing of any such petition the district court shall have jurisdiction to grant such injunctive relief or temporary restraining order pending the outcome of an enforcement proceeding pursuant to this Act. The proceeding shall be as provided by Rule 65 of the Federal Rules, Civil Procedure, except that no temporary restraining order issued without notice shall be effective for a period longer than five days.

(c) Whenever and as soon as an inspector concludes that conditions or practices described in subsection (a) exist in any place of employment, he shall inform the affected employees and employers of the danger and that he is recommending to the Secretary that relief be sought.

(d) If the Secretary arbitrarily or capriciously fails to seek relief under this section, any employee who may be injured by reason of such failure, or the representative of such employees, might bring an action against the Secretary in the United States district court for the district in which the imminent danger is alleged to exist or the employer has its principal office, or for the District of Columbia, for a writ of mandamus to compel the Secretary to seek such an order and for such further relief as may be appropriate.

REPRESENTATION IN CIVIL LITIGATION

SEC. 14. Except as provided in section 518(a) of title 28, United States Code, relating to litigation before the Supreme Court, the Solicitor of Labor may appear for and represent the Secretary in any civil litigation brought under this Act but all such litigation shall be subject to the direction and control of the Attorney General.

CONFIDENTIALITY OF TRADE SECRETS

SEC. 15. All information reported to or otherwise obtained by the Secretary or his representative in connection with any inspection or proceeding under this Act which contains or which might reveal a trade secret referred to in section 1905 of title 18 of the United States Code shall be considered confidential for the purpose of that section, except that such information may be disclosed to other officers or employees concerned with carrying out this Act or when relevant in any proceeding under this Act. In any such proceeding the Secretary, the Commission, or the court shall issue such orders as may be appropriate to protect the confidentiality of trade secrets.

VARIATIONS, TOLERANCES, AND EXEMPTIONS

SEC. 16. The Secretary, on the record, after notice and opportunity for a hearing may provide such reasonable limitations and may make such rules and regulations allowing reasonable variations, tolerances, and exemptions to and from any or all provisions of this Act as he may find necessary and proper to avoid serious impairment of the national defense. Such action shall not be in effect for more than six months without notification to affected employees and an opportunity being afforded for a hearing.

PENALTIES

SEC. 17. (a) Any employer who willfully or repeatedly violates the requirements of section 5 of this Act, any standard, rule, or order promulgated pursuant to section 6 of this Act, or regulations prescribed pursuant to this Act, may be assessed a civil penalty or not more than $10,000 for each violation.

(b) Any employer who has received a citation for a serious violation of the requirements of section 5 of this Act, of any standard, rule, or order promulgated pursuant to section 6 of this Act, or of any regulations prescribed pursuant to this Act, shall be assessed a civil penalty of up to $1,000 for each such violation.

(c) Any employer who has received a citation for a violation of the requirements of section 5 of this Act, of any standard, rule, or order promulgated pursuant to section 6 of this Act, or of regulations prescribed pursuant to this Act, and such violation is specifically determined not to be of a serious nature, may be assessed a civil penalty of up to $1,000 for each such violation.

(d) Any employer who fails to correct a violation for which a citation has been issued under section 9(a) within the period permitted for its correction (which period shall not begin to run until the date of the final order of the Commission in the case of any review proceeding under section 10 initiated by the employer in good faith and not solely for delay or avoidance of penalties), may be assessed a civil penality of not more than $1,000 for each day during which such failure or violation continues.

(e) Any employer who willfully violates any standard, rule, or order promulgated pursuant to section 6 of this Act, or of any regulations prescribed pursuant to this Act, and that violation caused death to any employee, shall, upon conviction, be punished by a fine of not more than $10,000 or by imprisonment for not more than six months, or by both; except that if the conviction is for a violation committed after a first conviction of such person, punishment shall be by a fine of not more than $20,000 or by imprisonment for not more than one year, or by both.

(f) Any person who gives advance notice of any inspection to be conducted under this Act, without authority from the Secretary or his designees, shall upon conviction, be punished by a fine of not more than $1,000 or by imprisonment for not more than six months, or by both.

(g) Whoever knowingly makes any false statement, representation, or certification in any application, record, report, plan, or other document filed or required to be maintained pursuant to this Act shall, upon conviction, be punished by a fine of not more than $10,000, or by imprisonment for not more than six months, or by both.

(h)(1) Section 1114 of title 18, United States Code, is hereby amended by striking out "designated by the Secretary of Health, Education, and Welfare to conduct investigations, or inspections under the Federal Food, Drug, and Cosmetic Act" and inserting in lieu thereof "or of the Department of Labor assigned to perform investigative, inspection, or law enforcement functions".

(2) Notwithstanding the provisions of sections 1111 and 1114 of title 18, United States Code, whoever, in violation of the provisions of section 1114 of such title, kills a person while engaged in or on account of the perform-

ance of investigative, inspection, or law enforcement functions added to such section 1114 by paragraph (1) of this subsection, and who would otherwise be subject to the penalty provisions of such section 1111, shall be punished by imprisonment for any term of years or for life.

(i) Any employer who violates any of the posting requirements, as prescribed under the provisions of this Act, shall be assessed a civil penalty of up to $1,000 for each violation.

(j) The Commission shall have authority to assess all civil penalties provided in this section, giving due consideration to the appropriateness of the penalty with respect to the size of the business of the employer being charged, the gravity of the violation, the good faith of the employer, and the history of previous violations.

(k) For purposes of this section, a serious violation shall be deemed to exist in a place of employment if there is a substantial probability that death or serious physical harm could result from a condition which exists, or from one or more practices, means, methods, operations, or processes which have been adopted or are in use, in such place of employment unless the employer did not, and could not with the exercise of reasonable diligence, know of the presence of the violation.

(l) Civil penalties owed under this Act shall be paid to the Secretary for deposit into the Treasury of the United States and shall accrue to the United States and may be recovered in a civil action in the name of the United States brought in the United States district court for the district where the violation is alleged to have occurred or where the employer has its principal office.

STATE JURISDICTION AND STATE PLANS

SEC. 18. (a) Nothing in this Act shall prevent any State agency or court from asserting jurisdiction under State law over any occupational safety or health issue with respect to which no standard is in effect under section 6.

(b) Any State which, at any time, desires to assume responsibility for development and enforcement therein of occupational safety and health standards relating to any occupational safety or health issue with respect to which a Federal standard has been promulgated under section 6 shall submit a State plan for the development of such standards and their enforcement.

(c) The Secretary shall approve the plan submitted by a State under subsection (b), or any modification thereof, if such plan in his judgment—

(1) designates a State agency or agencies as the agency or agencies responsible for administering the plan throughout the State,

(2) provides for the development and enforcement of safety and health standards relating to one or more safety or health issues, which standards (and the enforcement of which standards) are or will be at least as effective in providing safe and healthful employment and places of employment as the standards promulgated under section 6 which relate to the same issues, and which standards, when applicable to products which are distributed or used in interstate commerce, are required by compelling local conditions and do not unduly burden interstate commerce,

(3) provides for a right of entry and inspection of all workplaces subject to the Act which is at least as effective as that provided in section 8, and includes a prohibition on advance notice of inspections,

(4) contains satisfactory assurances that such agency or agencies have or will have the legal authority and qualified personnel necessary for the enforcement of such standards,

(5) gives satisfactory assurances that such State will devote adequate funds to the administration and enforcement of such standards,

(6) contains satisfactory assurances that such State will, to the extent permitted by its law, establish and maintain an effective and comprehensive occupational safety and health program applicable to all employees of public agencies of the State and its political subdivisions, which program is as effective as the standards contained in an approved plan,

(7) requires employers in the State to make reports to the Secretary in the same manner and to the same extent as if the plan were not in effect, and

(8) provides that the State agency will make such reports to the Secretary in such form and containing such information, as the Secretary shall from time to time require.

(d) If the Secretary rejects a plan submitted under subsection (b), he shall afford the State submitting the plan due notice and opportunity for a hearing before so doing.

(e) After the Secretary approves a State plan submitted under subsection (b), he may, but shall not be required to, exercise his authority under sections 8, 9, 10, 13, and 17 with respect to comparable standards promulgated under section 6, for the period specified in the next sentence. The Secretary may exercise the authority referred to above until he determines, on the basis of actual operations under the State plan, that the criteria set forth in subsection (c) are being applied, but he shall not make such determination for at least three years after the plan's approval under subsection (c). Upon making the determination referred to in the preceding sentence, the provisions of sections 5(a)(2), 8 (except for the purpose of carrying out subsection (f) of this section), 9. 10, 13, and 17, and standards promulgated under section 6 of this Act, shall not apply with respect to any occupational safety or health issues covered under the plan, but the Secretary may retain jurisdiction under the above provisions in any proceeding commenced under section 9 or 10 before the date of determination.

(f) The Secretary shall, on the basis of reports submitted by the State agency and his own inspections make a continuing evaluation of the manner in which each State having a plan approved under this section is carrying out such plan. Whenever the Secretary finds, after affording due notice and opportunity for a hearing, that in the administration of the State plan there is a failure to comply substantially with any provision of the State plan (or any assurance contained therein), he shall notify the State agency of his withdrawal of approval of such plan and upon receipt of such notice such plan shall cease to be in effect, but the State may retain jurisdiction in any case commenced before the withdrawal of the plan in order to enforce standards under the plan whenever the issues involved do not relate to the reasons for the withdrawal of the plan.

(g) The State may obtain a review of a decision of the Secretary withdrawing approval of or rejecting its plan by the United States court of appeals for the circuit in which the State is located by filing in such court within thirty days following receipt of notice of such decision a petition to modify or set aside in whole or in part the action of the Secretary. A copy of such petition shall forthwith be served upon the Secretary, and thereupon the Secretary shall certify and file in the court the record upon which the decision complained of was issued as provided in section 2112 of title 28, United States Code. Unless the court finds that the Secretary's decision in rejecting a proposed State plan or withdrawing his approval of such a plan is not supported by substantial evidence the court shall affirm the Secretary's decision. The judgment of the court shall be subject to review by the Supreme Court of the United States upon certiorari or certification as provided in section 1254 of title 28, United States Code.

(h) The Secretary may enter into an agreement with a State under which the State will be permitted to continue to enforce one or more occupational health and safety standards in effect in such State until final action is taken by the Secretary with respect to a plan submitted by a State under subsection (b) of this section, or two years from the date of enactment of this Act, whichever is earlier.

FEDERAL AGENCY SAFETY PROGRAMS AND RESPONSIBILITIES

SEC. 19. (a) It shall be the responsibility of the head of each Federal agency to establish and maintain an effective and comprehensive occupational safety and health program which is consistent with the standards promulgated under section 6. The head of each agency shall (after consultation with representatives of the employees thereof)—

(1) provide safe and healthful places and conditions of employment, consistent with the standards set under section 6;

(2) acquire, maintain, and require the use of safety equipment, personal protective equipment, and devices reasonably necessary to protect employees;

(3) keep adequate records of all occupational accidents and illnesses for proper evaluation and necessary corrective action;

(4) consult with the Secretary with regard to the adequacy as to form and content of records kept pursuant to subsection (a)(3) of this section; and

(5) make an annual report to the Secretary with respect to occupational accidents and injuries and the agency's program under this section. Such report shall include any report submitted under section 7902 (e)(2) of title 5, United States Code.

(b) The Secretary shall report to the President a summary or digest of reports submitted to him under subsection (a)(5) of this section, together with his evaluations of and recommendations derived from such reports. The President shall transmit annually to the Senate and the House of Representatives a report of the activities of Federal agencies under this section.

(c) Section 7902(c)(1) of title 5, United States Code, is amended by inserting after "agencies" the following: "and of labor organizations representing employees".

(d) The Secretary shall have access to records and reports kept and filed by Federal agencies pursuant to subsections (a) (3) and (5) of this section unless those records and reports are specifically required by Executive order to be kept secret in the interest of the national defense or foreign policy, in which case the Secretary shall have access to such information as will not jeopardize national defense or foreign policy.

RESEARCH AND RELATED ACTIVITIES

SEC. 20. (a)(1) The Secretary of Health, Education, and Welfare, after consultation with the Secretary and with other appropriate Federal departments or agencies, shall conduct (directly or by grants or contracts) research, experiments, and demonstrations relating to occupational safety and health, including studies of psychological factors involved, and relating to innovative methods, techniques, and approaches for dealing with occupational safety and health problems.

(2) The Secretary of Health, Education, and Welfare shall from time to time consult with the Secretary in order to develop specific plans for such research, demonstrations, and experiments as are necessary to produce criteria, including criteria identifying toxic substances, enabling the Secretary to meet his responsibility for the formulation of safety and health standards under this Act; and the Secretary of Health, Education, and Welfare, on the basis of such research, demonstrations, and experiments and any other information available to him, shall develop and publish at least annually such criteria as will effectuate the purposes of this Act.

(3) The Secretary of Health, Education, and Welfare, on the basis of such research, demonstrations, and experiments, and any other information available to him, shall develop criteria dealing with toxic materials and harmful physical agents and substances which will describe exposure levels that are safe for various periods of employment, including but not limited to the exposure levels at which no employee will suffer impaired health or functional capacities or diminished life expectancy as a result of his work experience.

(4) The Secretary of Health, Education, and Welfare shall also conduct special research, experiments, and demonstrations relating to occupational safety and health as are necessary to explore new problems, including those created by new technology in occupational safety and health, which may require ameliorative action beyond that which is otherwise provided for in the operating provisions of this Act. The Secretary of Health, Education, and Welfare shall also conduct research into the motivational and behavioral factors relating to the field of occupational safety and health.

(5) The Secretary of Health, Education, and Welfare, in order to comply with his responsibilities under paragraph (2), and in order to develop needed information regarding potentially toxic substances or harmful physical agents, may prescribe regulations requiring employers to measure, record, and make reports on the exposure of employees to substances or physical agents which the Secretary of Health, Education, and Welfare reasonably believes may endanger the health or safety of employees. The Secretary of Health, Education, and Welfare also is authorized to establish such programs of medical examinations and tests as may be necessary for determining the incidence of occupational illnesses and the suscep-

tibility of employees to such illnesses. Nothing in this or any other provision of this Act shall be deemed to authorize or require medical examination, immunization, or treatment for those who object thereto on religious grounds, except where such is necessary for the protection of the health or safety of others. Upon the request of any employer who is required to measure and record exposure of employees to substances or physical agents as provided under this subsection, the Secretary of Health, Education, and Welfare shall furnish full financial or other assistance to such employer for the purpose of defraying any additional expense incurred by him in carrying out the measuring and recording as provided in this subsection.

(6) The Secretary of Health, Education, and Welfare shall publish within six months of enactment of this Act and thereafter as needed but at least annually a list of all known toxic substances by generic family or other useful grouping, and the concentrations at which such toxicity is known to occur. He shall determine following a written request by any employer or authorized representative of employees, specifying with reasonable particularity the grounds on which the request is made, whether any substance normally found in the place of employment has potentially toxic effects in such concentrations as used or found; and shall submit such determination both to employers and affected employees as soon as possible. If the Secretary of Health, Education, and Welfare determines that any substance is potentially toxic at the concentrations in which it is used or found in a place of employment, and such substance is not covered by an occupational safety or health standard promulgated under section 6, the Secretary of Health, Education, and Welfare shall immediately submit such determination to the Secretary, together with all pertinent criteria.

(7) Within two years of enactment of this Act, and annually thereafter the Secretary of Health, Education, and Welfare shall conduct and publish industrywide studies of the effect of chronic or low-level exposure to industrial materials, processes, and stresses on the potential for illness, disease, or loss of functional capacity in aging adults.

(b) The Secretary of Health, Education, and Welfare is authorized to make inspections and question employers and employees as provided in section 8 of this Act in order to carry out his functions and responsibilities under this section.

(c) The Secretary is authorized to enter into contracts, agreements, or other arrangements with appropriate public agencies or private organizations for the purpose of conducting studies relating to his responsibilities under this Act. In carrying out his responsibilities under this subsection, the Secretary shall cooperate with the Secretary of Health, Education, and Welfare in order to avoid any duplication of efforts under this section.

(d) Information obtained by the Secretary and the Secretary of Health, Education, and Welfare under this section shall be disseminated by the Secretary to employers and employees and organizations thereof.

(e) The functions of the Secretary of Health, Education, and Welfare under this Act shall, to the extent feasible, be delegated to the Director of the National Institute for Occupational Safety and Health established by section 22 of this Act.

TRAINING AND EMPLOYEE EDUCATION

SEC. 21. (a) The Secretary of Health, Education, and Welfare, after consultation with the Secretary and with other appropriate Federal departments and agencies, shall conduct, directly or by grants or contracts (1) education programs to provide an adequate supply of qualified personnel to carry out the purposes of this Act, and (2) informational programs on the importance of and proper use of adequate safety and health equipment.

(b) The Secretary is also authorized to conduct, directly or by grants or contracts, short-term training of personnel engaged in work related to his responsibilities under this Act.

(c) The Secretary, in consultation with the Secretary of Health, Education, and Welfare, shall (1) provide for the establishment and supervision of programs for the education and training of employers and employees in the recognition, avoidance, and prevention of unsafe or unhealthful working conditions in employments covered by this Act, and (2) consult with and advise employers and employees, and organizations representing employers and employees as to effective means of preventing occupational injuries and illnesses.

NATIONAL INSTITUTE FOR OCCUPATIONAL SAFETY AND HEALTH

SEC. 22. (a) It is the purpose of this section to establish a National Institute for Occupational Safety and Health in the Department of Health, Education, and Welfare in order to carry out the policy set forth in section 2 of this Act and to perform the functions of the Secretary of Health, Education, and Welfare under sections 20 and 21 of this Act.

(b) There is hereby established in the Department of Health, Education, and Welfare a National Institute for

Occupational Safety and Health. The Institute shall be headed by a Director who shall be appointed by the Secretary of Health, Education, and Welfare, and who shall serve for a term of six years unless previously removed by the Secretary of Health, Education, and Welfare.

(c) The Institute is authorized to—

(1) develop and establish recommended occupational safety and health standards; and

(2) perform all functions of the Secretary of Health, Education, and Welfare under sections 20 and 21 of this Act.

(d) Upon his own initiative, or upon the request of the Secretary or the Secretary of Health, Education, and Welfare, the Director is authorized (1) to conduct such research and experimental programs as he determines are necessary for the development of criteria for new and improved occupational safety and health standards, and (2) after consideration of the results of such research and experimental programs make recommendations concerning new or improved occupational safety and health standards. Any occupational safety and health standard recommended pursuant to this section shall immediately be forwarded to the Secretary of Labor, and to the Secretary of Health, Education, and Welfare.

(e) In addition to any authority vested in the Institute by the other provisions of this section, the Director, in carrying out the functions of the Institute, is authorized to—

(1) prescribe such regulations as he deems necessary governing the manner in which its functions shall be carried out;

(2) receive money and other property donated, bequeathed, or devised, without condition or restriction other than that it be used for the purposes of the Institute and to use, sell, or otherwise dispose of such property for the purpose of carrying out its functions;

(3) receive (and use, sell, or otherwise dispose of, in accordance with paragraph (2)), money and other property donated, bequeathed, or devised to the Institute with a condition or restriction, including a condition that the Institute use other funds of the Institute for the purposes of the gift;

(4) in accordance with the civil service laws, appoint and fix the compensation of such personnel as may be necessary to carry out the provisions of this section;

(5) obtain the services of experts and consultants in accordance with the provisions of section 3109 of title 5, United States Code;

(6) accept and utilize the services of voluntary and noncompensated personnel and reimburse them for

travel expenses, including per diem, as authorized by section 5703 of title 5, United States Code;

(7) enter into contracts, grants or other arrangements, or modifications thereof to carry out the provisions of this section, and such contracts or modifications thereof may be entered into without performance of other bonds, and without regard to section 3709 of the Revised Statutes, as amended (41 U.S.C. 5), or any other provision of law relating to competitive bidding;

(8) make advance, progress, and other payments which the Director deems necessary under this title without regard to the provisions of section 3648 of the Revised Statutes, as amended (31 U.S.C. 529); and

(9) make other necessary expenditures.

(f) The Director shall submit to the Secretary of Health, Education, and Welfare, to the President, and to the Congress an annual report of the operations of the Institute under this Act, which shall include a detailed statement of all private and public funds received and expended by it, and such recommendations as he deems appropriate.

GRANTS TO THE STATES

SEC. 23. (a) The Secretary is authorized, during the fiscal year ending June 30, 1971, and the two succeeding fiscal years, to make grants to the States which have designated a State agency under section 18 to assist them—

(1) in identifying their needs and responsibilities in the area of occupational safety and health,

(2) in developing State plans under section 18, or

(3) in developing plans for—

(A) establishing systems for the collection of information concerning the nature and frequency of occupational injuries and diseases;

(B) increasing the expertise and enforcement capabilities of their personnel engaged in occupational safety and health programs; or

(C) otherwise improving the administration and enforcement of State occupational safety and health laws, including standards thereunder, consistent with the objectives of this Act.

(b) The Secretary is authorized, during the fiscal year ending June 30, 1971, and the two suceeding fiscal years, to make grants to the States for experimental and demonstration projects consistent with the objectives set forth in subsection (a) of this section.

(c) The Governor of the State shall designate the appropriate State agency for receipt of any grant made by the Secretary under this section.

(d) Any State agency designated by the Governor of the State desiring a grant under this section shall submit an application therefor to the Secretary.

(e) The Secretary shall review the application, and shall, after consultation with the Secretary of Health, Education, and Welfare, approve or reject such application.

(f) The Federal share for each State grant under subsection (a) or (b) of this section may not exceed 90 per centum of the total cost of the application. In the event the Federal share for all States under either such subsection is not the same, the differences among the States shall be established on the basis of objective criteria.

(g) The Secretary is authorized to make grants to the States to assist them in administering and enforcing programs for occupational safety and health contained in State plans approved by the Secretary pursuant to section 18 of this Act. The Federal share for each State grant under this subsection may not exceed 50 per centum of the total cost to the State of such a program. The last sentence of subsection (f) shall be applicable in determining the Federal share under this subsection.

(h) Prior to June 30, 1973, the Secretary shall, after consultation with the Secretary of Health, Education, and Welfare, transmit a report to the President and to the Congress, describing the experience under the grant programs authorized by this section and making any recommendations he may deem appropriate.

STATISTICS

SEC. 24. (a) In order to further the purposes of this Act, the Secretary, in consultation with the Secretary of Health, Education, and Welfare, shall develop and maintain an effective program of collection, compilation, and analysis of occupational safety and health statistics. Such program may cover all employments whether or not subject to any other provisions of this Act but shall not cover employments excluded by section 4 of the Act. The Secretary shall compile accurate statistics on work injuries and illnesses which shall include all disabling, serious, or significant injuries and illnesses, whether or not involving loss of time from work, other than minor injuries requiring only first aid treatment and which do not involve medical treatment, loss of consciousness, restriction of work or motion, or transfer to another job.

(b) To carry out his duties under subsection (a) of this section, the Secretary may—

(1) promote, encourage, or directly engage in programs of studies, information and communication concerning occupational safety and health statistics;

(2) make grants to States or political subdivisions

thereof in order to assist them in developing and administering programs dealing with occupational safety and health statistics; and

(3) arrange, through grants or contracts, for the conduct of such research and investigations as give promise of furthering the objectives of this section.

(c) The Federal share for each grant under subsection (b) of this section may be up to 50 per centum of the State's total cost.

(d) The Secretary may, with the consent of any State or political subdivision thereof, accept and use the services, facilities, and employees of the agencies of such State or political subdivision, with or without reimbursement, in order to assist him in carrying out his functions under this section.

(e) On the basis of the records made and kept pursuant to section 8(c) of this Act, employers shall file such reports with the Secretary as he shall prescribe by regulation, as necessary to carry out his functions under this Act.

(f) Agreements between the Department of Labor and States pertaining to the collection of occupational safety and health statistics already in effect on the effective date of this Act shall remain in effect until superseded by grants or contracts made under this Act.

AUDITS

SEC. 25. (a) Each recipient of a grant under this Act shall keep such records as the Secretary or the Secretary of Health, Education, and Welfare shall prescribe, including records which fully disclose the amount and disposition by such recipient of the proceeds of such grant, the total cost of the project or undertaking in connection with which such grant is made or used, and the amount of that portion of the cost of the project or undertaking supplied by other sources, and such other records as will facilitate an effective audit.

(b) The Secretary or the Secretary of Health, Education, and Welfare, and the Comptroller General of the United States, or any of their duly authorized representatives, shall have access for the purpose of audit and examination to any books, documents, papers, and records of the recipients of any grant under this Act that are pertinent to any such grant.

ANNUAL REPORT

SEC. 26. Within one hundred and twenty days following the convening of each regular session of each Congress, the Secretary and the Secretary of Health, Education, and Welfare shall each prepare and submit to the

President for transmittal to the Congress a report upon the subject matter of this Act, the progress toward achievement of the purpose of this Act, the needs and requirements in the field of occupational safety and health, and any other relevant information. Such reports shall include information regarding occupational safety and health standards, and criteria for such standards, developed during the preceding year; evaluation of standards and criteria previously developed under this Act, defining areas of emphasis for new criteria and standards; an evaluation of the degree of observance of applicable occupational safety and health standards, and a summary of inspection and enforcement activity undertaken; analysis and evaluation of research activities for which results have been obtained under governmental and nongovernmental sponsorship; an analysis of major occupational diseases; evaluation of available control and measurement technology for hazards for which standards or criteria have been developed during the preceding year; description of cooperative efforts undertaken between Government agencies and other interested parties in the implementation of this Act during the preceding year; a progress report on the development of an adequate supply of trained manpower in the field of occupational safety and health, including estimates of future needs and the efforts being made by Government and others to meet those needs; listing of all toxic substances in industrial usage for which labeling requirements, criteria, or standards have not yet been established; and such recommendations for additional legislation as are deemed necessary to protect the safety and health of the worker and improve the administration of this Act.

NATIONAL COMMISSION ON STATE WORKMEN'S COMPENSATION LAWS

SEC. 27. (a) (1) The Congress hereby finds and declares that—

(A) the vast majority of American workers, and their families, are dependent on workmen's compensation for their basic economic security in the event such workers suffer disabling injury or death in the course of their employment; and that the full protection of American workers from job-related injury or death requires an adequate, prompt, and equitable system of workmen's compensation as well as an effective program of occupational health and safety regulation; and

(B) in recent years serious questions have been raised concerning the fairness and adequacy of present workmen's compensation laws in the light of the growth of the economy, the changing nature of the labor force, increases in medical knowledge, changes in the hazards associated with various types of employment, new technology creating new risks to health and safety, and increases in the general level of wages and the cost of living.

(2) The purpose of this section is to authorize an effective study and objective evaluation of State workmen's compensation laws in order to determine if such laws provide an adequate, prompt, and equitable system of compensation for injury or death arising out of or in the course of employment.

(b) There is hereby established a National Commission on State Workmen's Compensation Laws.

(c)(1) The Workmen's Compensation Commission shall be composed of fifteen members to be appointed by the President from among members of State workmen's compensation boards, representatives of insurance carriers, business, labor, members of the medical profession having experience in industrial medicine or in workmen's compensation cases, educators having special expertise in the field of workmen's compensation, and representatives of the general public. The Secretary, the Secretary of Commerce, and the Secretary of Health, Education, and Welfare shall be ex officio members of the Workmen's Compensation Commission:

(2) Any vacancy in the Workmen's Compensation Commission shall not affect its powers.

(3) The President shall designate one of the members to serve as Chairman and one to serve as Vice Chairman of the Workmen's Compensation Commission.

(4) Eight members of the Workmen's Compensation Commission shall constitute a quorum.

(d)(1) The Workmen's Compensation Commission shall undertake a comprehensive study and evaluation of State workmen's compensation laws in order to determine if such laws provide an adequate, prompt, and equitable system of compensation. Such study and evaluation shall include, without being limited to, the following subjects: (A) the amount and duration of permanent and temporary disability benefits and the criteria for determining the maximum limitations thereon, (B) the amount and duration of medical benefits and provisions insuring adequate medical care and free choice of physician, (C) the extent of coverage of workers, including exemptions based on numbers or type of employment, (D) standards for determining which injuries or diseases should be deemed compensable, (E) rehabilitation, (F) coverage under second or subsequent injury funds, (G) time limits on filing claims, (H) waiting periods, (I) compulsory or elective coverage, (J) administration, (K) legal expenses, (L) the feasibility and desirability of a uniform system of reporting information concerning job-related injuries and diseases and the operation of workmen's compensation laws, (M) the resolution of conflict of laws, extraterritoriality and similar problems arising from claims with multistate aspects, (N) the extent to which private insurance carriers are excluded from supplying workmen's compensation coverage and the desirability of such exclusionary practices, to the extent they are found to exist, (O) the relationship between workmen's compensation on the one hand, and old-age, disability, and survivors insurance and other types of insurance, public or private, on the other hand, (P) methods of implementing the recommendations of the Commission.

(2) The Workmen's Compensation Commission shall transmit to the President and to the Congress not later than July 31, 1972, a final report containing a detailed statement of the findings and conclusions of the Commission, together with such recommendations as it deems advisable.

(e) (1) The Workmen's Compensation Commission or, on the authorization of the Workmen's Compensation Commission, any subcommittee or members thereof, may, for the purpose of carrying out the provisions of this title, hold such hearings, take such testimony, and sit and act at such times and places as the Workmen's Compensation Commission deems advisable. Any member authorized by the Workmen's Compensation Commission may administer oaths or affirmations to witnesses appearing before the Workmen's Compensation Commission or any subcommittee or members thereof.

(2) Each department, agency, and instrumentality of the executive branch of the Government, including independent agencies, is authorized and directed to furnish to the Workmen's Compensation Commission, upon request made by the Chairman or Vice Chairman, such information as the Workmen's Compensation Commission deems necessary to carry out its functions under this section.

(f) Subject to such rules and regulations as may be adopted by the Workmen's Compensation Commission, the Chairman shall have the power to—

(1) appoint and fix the compensation of an executive director, and such additional staff personnel as he deems necessary, without regard to the provisions of title 5, United States Code, governing appointments in the competitive service, and without regard to the provisions of chapter 51 and subchapter III of chapter 53 of such title relating to classification and General Schedule pay rates, but at rates not in excess of the maximum rate for GS-18 of the General Schedule under section 5332 of such title, and

(2) procure temporary and intermittent services to the same extent as is authorized by section 3109 of title 5, United States Code.

(g) The Workmen's Compensation Commission is authorized to enter into contracts with Federal or State agencies, private firms, institutions, and individuals for the conduct of research or surveys, the preparation of reports, and other activities necessary to the discharge of its duties.

(h) Members of the Workmen's Compensation Commission shall receive compensation for each day they are engaged in the performance of their duties as members of the Workmen's Compensation Commission at the daily rate prescribed for GS–18 under section 5332 of title 5, United States Code, and shall be entitled to reimbursement for travel, subsistence, and other necessary expenses incurred by them in the performance of their duties as members of the Workmen's Compensation Commission.

(i) There are hereby authorized to be appropriated such sums as may be necessary to carry out the provisions of this section.

(j) On the ninetieth day after the date of submission of its final report to the President, the Workmen's Compensation Commission shall cease to exist.

ECONOMIC ASSISTANCE TO SMALL BUSINESSES

SEC. 28. (a) Section 7(b) of the Small Business Act, as amended, is amended—

(1) by striking out the period at the end of "paragraph (5)" and inserting in lieu thereof "; and"; and

(2) by adding after paragraph (5) a new paragraph as follows:

"(6) to make such loans (either directly or in cooperation with banks or other lending institutions through agreements to participate on an immediate or deferred basis) as the Administration may determine to be necessary or appropriate to assist any small business concern in effecting additions to or alterations in the equipment, facilities, or methods of operation of such business in order to comply with the applicable standards promulgated pursuant to section 6 of the Occupational Safety and Health Act of 1970 or standards adopted by a State pursuant to a plan approved under section 18 of the Occupational Safety and Health Act of 1970, if the Administration determines that such concern is likely to suffer substantial economic injury without assistance under this paragraph."

(b) The third sentence of section 7(b) of the Small Business Act, as amended, is amended by striking out "or (5)" after "paragraph (3)" and inserting a comma followed by "(5) or (6)".

(c) Section 4(c)(1) of the Small Business Act, as amended, is amended by inserting "7(b)(6)," after "7(b)(5),".

(d) Loans may also be made or guaranteed for the purposes set forth in section 7(b)(6) of the Small Business Act, as amended, pursuant to the provisions of section 202 of the Public Works and Economic Development Act of 1965, as amended.

ADDITIONAL ASSISTANT SECRETARY OF LABOR

SEC. 29. (a) Section 2 of the Act of April 17, 1946 (60 Stat. 91) as amended (29 U.S.C. 553) is amended by—

(1) striking out "four" in the first sentence of such section and inserting in lieu thereof "five"; and

(2) adding at the end thereof the following new sentence, "One of such Assistant Secretaries shall be an Assistant Secretary of Labor for Occupational Safety and Health.".

(b) Paragraph (20) of section 5315 of title 5, United States Code, is amended by striking out "(4)" and inserting in lieu thereof "(5)".

ADDITIONAL POSITIONS

SEC. 30. Section 5108(c) of title 5, United States Code, is amended by—

(1) striking out the word "and" at the end of paragraph (8);

(2) striking out the period at the end of paragraph (9) and inserting in lieu thereof a semicolon and the word "and"; and

(3) by adding immediately after paragraph (9) the following new paragraph:

"(10)(A) the Secretary of Labor, subject to the standards and procedures prescribed by this chapter, may place an additional twenty-five positions in the Department of Labor in GS–16, 17, and 18 for the purposes of carrying out his responsibilities under the Occupational Safety and Health Act of 1970;

"(B) the Occupational Safety and Health Review Commission, subject to the standards and procedures prescribed by this chapter, may place ten positions in GS–16, 17, and 18 in carrying out its functions under the Occupational Safety and Health Act of 1970."

EMERGENCY LOCATOR BEACONS

SEC. 31. Section 601 of the Federal Aviation Act of 1958 is amended by inserting at the end thereof a new subsection as follows:

"EMERGENCY LOCATOR BEACONS

"(d)(1) Except with respect to aircraft described in paragraph (2) of this subsection, minimum standards pursuant to this section shall include a requirement that emergency locator beacons shall be installed—

"(A) on any fixed-wing, powered aircraft for use in air commerce the manufacture of which is completed, or which is imported into the United States, after one year following the date of enactment of this subsection; and

"(B) on any fixed-wing, powered aircraft used in air commerce after three years following such date.

"(2) The provisions of this subsection shall not apply to jet-powered aircraft; aircraft used in air transportation (other than air taxis and charter aircraft); military aircraft; aircraft used solely for training purposes not involving flights more than twenty miles from its base; and aircraft used for the aerial application of chemicals."

SEPARABILITY

SEC. 32. If any provision of this Act, or the application of such provision to any person or circumstance, shall be held invalid, the remainder of this Act, or the application of such provision to persons or circumstances other than those as to which it is held invalid, shall not be affected thereby.

APPROPRIATIONS

SEC. 33. There are authorized to be appropriated to carry out this Act for each fiscal year such sums as the Congress shall deem necessary.

EFFECTIVE DATE

SEC. 34. This Act shall take effect one hundred and twenty days after the date of its enactment.

RESOURCE CONSERVATION AND RECOVERY ACT OF 1976

as amended[1]

An Act

Short Title

Section 1. This Act may be cited as the "Resource Conservation and Recovery Act of 1976".

AMENDMENT OF SOLID WASTE DISPOSAL ACT

Section 2. The Solid Waste Disposal Act (42 U.S.C. 3251 and following) is amended to read as follows:

TITLE II - SOLID WASTE DISPOSAL

"Subtitle A—General Provisions

"Short Title and Table of Contents

"Sec. 1001. This title (hereinafter referred to as 'this Act'), together with the following table of contents, may be cited as the 'Solid Waste Disposal Act':

"Subtitle A—General Provisions

---

[1] PL 94-580, October 21, 1976, as amended by the Quiet Communities Act of 1978 (PL 95-609); the Solid Waste Disposal Act of 1980 (PL 96-482); the Used Oil Recycling Act of 1980 (PL 96-463); the Comprehensive Environmental Response, Compensation, and Liability Act of 1980 (PL 96-510); and PL 97-272, September 30, 1982.

"Subtitle H—Research, Development, Demonstration, and Information

"CONGRESSIONAL FINDINGS

"Sec. 1002. (a) SOLID WASTE.—The Congress finds with respect to solid waste—

"(1) that the continuing technological progress and improvement in methods of manufacture, packaging, and marketing of consumer products has resulted in an ever-mounting increase, and in a change in the characteristics, of the mass material discarded by the purchaser of such products;

"(2) that the economic and population growth of our Nation, and the improvements in the standard of living enjoyed by our population, have required increased industrial production to meet our needs, and have made necessary the demolition of old buildings, the construction of new buildings, and the provision of highways and other avenues of transportation, which, together with related industrial, commercial, and agricultural operations, have resulted in a rising tide of scrap, discarded, and waste materials;

"(3) that the continuing concentration of our population in expanding metropolitan and other urban areas has presented these communities with serious financial, management, intergovernmental, and technical problems in the disposal of solid wastes resulting from the industrial, commercial, domestic, and other activities carried on in such areas;

"(4) that while the collection and disposal of solid wastes should continue to be primarily the function of State, regional, and local agencies, the problems of waste disposal as set forth above have become a matter national in scope and in concern and necessitate Federal action through financial and technical assistance and leadership in the development, demonstration, and application of new and improved methods and processes to reduce the amount of waste and unsalvageable materials and to provide for proper and economical solid waste disposal practices.

"(b) ENVIRONMENT AND HEALTH.—The Congress finds with respect to the environment and health, that—

"(1) although land is too valuable a national resource to be needlessly polluted by discarded materials, most solid waste is disposed of on land in open dumps and sanitary landfills;

"(2) disposal of solid waste and hazardous waste in or on the land without careful planning and management can present a danger to human health and the environment;

"(3) as a result of the Clean Air Act, the Water Pollution Control Act, and other Federal and State laws respecting public health and the environment, greater amounts of solid waste (in the form of sludge and other pollution treatment residues) have been created. Similarly, inadequate and environmentally unsound practices for the disposal or use of solid waste have created greater amounts of air and water pollution and other problems for the environment and for health;

"(4) open dumping is particularly harmful to health, contaminates drinking water from underground and surface supplies, and pollutes the air and the land;

"(5) hazardous waste presents, in addition to the problems associated with non-hazardous solid waste, special dangers to health and requires a greater degree of regulation than does non-hazardous solid waste; and

"(6) alternatives to existing methods of land disposal must be developed since many of the cities in the United States will be running out of suitable solid waste disposal sites within five years unless immediate action is taken;

"(c) MATERIALS.—The Congress finds with respect to materials, that—

"(1) millions of tons of recoverable material which could be used are needlessly buried each year;

"(2) methods are available to separate usable materials from solid waste; and

"(3) the recovery and conservation of such materials can reduce the dependence of the United States on foreign resources and reduce the deficit in its balance of payments.

"(d) ENERGY.—The Congress finds with respect to energy, that—

"(1) solid waste represents a potential source of solid fuel, oil, or gas that can be converted into energy;

"(2) the need exists to develop alternative energy sources for public and private consumption in order to reduce our dependence on such sources as petroleum products, natural gas, nuclear and hydroelectric generation; and

"(3) technology exists to produce usable energy from solid waste.

"OBJECTIVES

"Sec. 1003. The objectives of this Act are to promote the protection of health and the environment and to conserve valuable material and energy resources by—

"(1) providing technical and financial assistance to State and local governments and interstate agencies for the development of solid waste management plans (including resource recovery and resource conservation systems) which will promote improved solid waste management techniques (including more effective organizational arrangements), new and improved methods of collection, separation, and recovery of solid waste, and the environmentally safe disposal of nonrecoverable residues;

"(2) providing training grants in occupations involving the design, operation, and maintenance of solid waste disposal systems;

"(3) prohibiting future open dumping on the land and requiring the conversion of existing open dumps to facilities which do not pose a danger to the environment or to health;

"(4) regulating the treatment, storage, transportation, and disposal of hazardous wastes which have adverse effects on health and the environment;

"(5) providing for the promulgation of guidelines for solid waste collection, transport, separation, recovery, and disposal practices and systems;

"(6) promoting a national research and development program for improved solid waste management and resource conservation techniques, more effective organizational arrangements, and new and improved methods of collection, separation, and recovery, and recycling of solid wastes and environmentally safe disposal of nonrecoverable residues;

"(7) promoting the demonstration, construction, and application of solid waste management, resource recovery, and resource conservation systems which preserve and enhance the quality of air, water, and land resources; and

"(8) establishing a cooperative effort among the Federal, State, and local governments and private enterprise in order to recover valuable materials and energy from solid waste.

"DEFINITIONS

"Sec. 1004. As used in this Act:

"(1) The term 'Administrator' means the Administrator of the Environmental Protection Agency.

"(2) The term 'construction,' with respect to any project of construction under this Act, means (A) the erection or building of new structures and acquisition of lands or interests therein, or the acquisition, replacement, expansion, remodeling, alteration, modernization, or extension of existing structures, and (B) the acquisition and installation of initial equipment of, or required in connection with, new or newly acquired structures or the expanded, remodeled, altered, modernized or extended part of existing structures (including trucks and other motor vehicles, and tractors, cranes, and other machinery) necessary for the proper utilization and operation of the facility after completion of the project; and includes preliminary planning to determine the economic and engineering feasibility and the public health and safety aspects of the project, the engineering, architectural, legal, fiscal, and economic investigations and studies, and any surveys, designs, plans, working drawings, specifications, and other action necessary for the carrying out of the project, and (C) the inspection and supervision of the process of carrying out the project to completion.

"(2A) The term 'demonstration' means the initial exhibition of a new technology process or practice or a significantly new combination or use of technologies, processes or practices, subsequent to the development stage, for the purpose of proving technological feasibility and cost effectiveness.

"(3) The term 'disposal' means the discharge, deposit, injection, dumping, spilling, leaking, or placing of any solid waste or hazardous waste into or on any land or water so that such solid waste or hazardous waste or any constituent thereof may enter the environment or be emitted into the air or discharged into any waters, including ground waters.

"(4) The term 'Federal agency' means any department, agency, or other instrumentality of the Federal Government, and any independent agency or establishment of the Federal Government including any Government corporation, and the Government Printing Office.

"(5) The term 'hazardous waste' means a solid waste, or combination of solid wastes, which because of its quantity, concentration, or physical, chemical or infectious characteristics may—

"(A) cause, or significantly contribute to an increase in mortality or an increase in serious irreversible, or incapacitating reversible, illness; or

"(B) pose a substantial present or potential hazard to human health or the environment when improperly treated, stored, transported, or disposed of, or otherwise managed.

"(6) The term 'hazardous waste generation' means the act or process of producing hazardous waste.

"(7) The term 'hazardous waste management' means the systematic control of the collection, source separation, storage, transportation, processing, treatment, recovery, and disposal of hazardous wastes.

"(8) For purposes of Federal financial assistance (other than rural communities assistance), the term 'implementation' does not include the acquisition, leasing, construction, or modification of facilities or equipment or the acquisition, leasing, or improvement of land.

"(9) The term 'intermunicipal agency' means an agency established by two or more municipalities with responsibility for planning or administration of solid waste.

"(10) The term 'interstate agency' means an agency of two or more municipalities in different States, or an agency established by two or more States, with authority to provide for the management of solid wastes and serving two or more municipalities located in different States.

"(11) The term 'long term contract' means, when used in relation to solid waste supply, a contract of sufficient duration to assure the viability of a resource recovery facility (to the extent that such viability depends upon solid waste supply).

"(12) The term 'manifest' means the form used for identifying the quantity, composition, and the origin, routing, and destination of hazardous waste during its transportation from the point of generation to the point of disposal, treatment, or storage.

"(13) The term 'municipality' (A) means a city, town, borough, county, parish, district, or other public body created by or pursuant to State law, with responsibility for the planning or administration of solid waste management, or an Indian tribe or authorized tribal organization or Alaska Native village or organization, and (B) includes any rural community or unincorporated town or village or any other public entity for which an application for assistance is made by a State or political subdivision thereof.

"(14) The term 'open dump' means any facility or site where solid waste is disposed of which is not a sanitary landfill which meets the criteria promulgated under section 4004 and which is not a facility for disposal of hazardous waste.

"(15) The term 'person' means an individual, trust, firm, joint stock company, corporation (including a government corporation), partnership, association, State, municipality, commission, political subdivision of a State, or any interstate body.

"(16) The term 'procurement item' means any device, good, substance, material, product, or other item whether real or personal property which is the subject of any purchase, barter, or other exchange made to procure such an item.

"(17) The term 'procuring agency' means any Federal agency, or any State agency or agency of a political subdivision of a State which is using appropriated Federal funds for such procurement, or any person contracting with any such agency with respect to work performed under such contract.

"(18) The term 'recoverable' refers to the capability and likelihood of being recovered from solid waste for a commercial or industrial use.

"(19) The term 'recovered material' means waste material and byproducts which have been recovered or diverted from solid waste, but such term does not include those materials and byproducts generated from, and commonly reused within, an original manufacturing process.

"(20) The term 'recovered resources' means material or energy recovered from solid waste.

"(21) The term 'resource conservation' means reduction of the amounts of solid waste that are generated, reduction of overall resource consumption, and utilization of recovered resources.

"(22) The term 'resource recovery' means the recovery of material or energy from solid waste.

"(23) The term 'resource recovery system' means a solid waste management system which provides for collection, separation, recycling, and recovery of solid wastes, including disposal of nonrecoverable waste residues.

"(24) The term 'resource recovery facility' means any facility at which solid waste is processed for the purpose of extracting, converting to energy, or otherwise separating and preparing solid waste for reuse.

"(25) The term 'regional authority' means the authority established or designated under section 4006.

"(26) The term 'sanitary landfill' means a facility for the disposal of solid waste which meets the criteria published under section 4004.

"(26A) The term 'sludge' means any solid, semisolid or liquid waste generated from a municipal, commercial, or industrial wastewater treatment plant, water supply treatment plant, or air pollution control facility or any other such waste having similar characteristics and effects.

"(27) The term 'solid waste' means any garbage, refuse, sludge, from a waste treatment plant, water supply treatment plant, or air pollution control facility and other discarded material, including solid, liquid, semisolid, or contained gaseous material resulting from industrial, commercial, mining, and agricultural operations, and from community activities, but does not include solid or dissolved material in domestic sewage, or solid or dissolved materials in irrigation return flows or industrial discharges which are point sources subject to permits under section 402 of the Federal Water Pollution Control Act, as amended (86 Stat. 880), or source, special nuclear, or byproduct material as defined by the Atomic Energy Act of 1954, as amended (68 Stat. 923).

"(28) The term 'solid waste management' means the systematic administration of activities which provide for the collection, source separation, storage, transportation, transfer, processing, treatment, and disposal of solid waste.

"(29) The term 'solid waste management facility' includes—

"(A) any resource recovery system or component thereof,

"(B) any system, program, or facility for resource conservation, and

"(C) any facility for the collection, source separation, storage, transportation, transfer, processing, treatment, or disposal of solid wastes, including hazardous wastes, whether such facility is associated with facilities generating such wastes or otherwise.

"(30) The term 'solid waste planning', 'solid waste management', and 'comprehensive planning' include planning or management respecting resource recovery and resource conservation.

"(31) The term 'State' means any of the several States, the District of Columbia, the Commonwealth of Puerto Rico, the Virgin Islands, Guam, American Samoa, and the Commonwealth of the Northern Mariana Islands.

"(32) The term 'State authority' means the agency established or designated under section 4007.

"(33) The term 'storage', when used in connection with hazardous waste, means the containment of hazardous waste, either on a temporary basis or for a period of years, in such a manner as not to constitute disposal of such hazardous waste.

"(34) The term 'treatment', when used in connection with hazardous waste, means any method, technique, or process, including neutralization, designed to change the physical, chemical, or biological character or composition of any hazardous waste so as to neutralize such waste or so as to render such waste nonhazardous, safer for transport, amenable for recovery, amenable for storage, or reduced in volume. Such term includes any activity or processing designed to change the physical form or chemical composition of hazardous waste so as to render it nonhazardous.

"(35) The term 'virgin material' means a raw material, including previously unused copper, aluminum, lead, zinc, iron, or other metal or metal ore, any undeveloped resource that is, or with new technology will become a source of raw materials.

"(36) The term 'used oil' means any oil which has been—

"(A) refined from crude oil,

"(B) used, and

"(C) as a result of such use, contaminated by physical or chemical impurities.

"(37) The term 'recycled oil' means any used oil which is reused, following its original use, for any purpose (including the purpose for which the oil was originally used). Such term includes oil which is re-refined, reclaimed, burned, or reprocessed.

"(38) The term 'lubricating oil' means the fraction of crude oil which is sold for purposes of reducing friction in any industrial or mechanical device. Such term includes re-refined oil.

"(39) The term 're-refined oil' means used oil from which the physical and chemical contaminants acquired through previous use have been removed through a refining process.

"GOVERNMENTAL COOPERATION

"Sec. 1005. (a) INTERSTATE COOPERATION.—The provisions of this Act to be carried out by States may be carried out by interstate agencies and provisions applicable to States may apply to interstate regions where such agencies and regions have been established by the respective States and approved by the Administrator. In such case, action required to be taken by the Governor of a State, respecting regional designation shall be required to be taken by the Governor of each of the respective States with respect to so much of the interstate region as is within the jurisdiction of that State.

"(b) CONSENT OF CONGRESS TO COMPACTS.—The consent of the Congress is hereby given to two or more states to negotiate and enter into agreements or compacts, not in conflict with any law or treaty of the United States, for—

"(1) cooperative effort and mutual assistance for the management of solid waste or hazardous waste (or both) and the enforcement of their respective laws relating thereto, and

"(2) the establishment of such agencies, joint or otherwise, as they deem desirable for making effective such agreements or compacts.

No such agreement or compact shall be binding or obligatory upon any State a party thereto unless it is agreed upon by all parties to the agreement and until it has been approved by the Administrator and the Congress.

"APPLICATION OF ACT AND INTEGRATION WITH OTHER ACTS

"Sec. 1006. (a) APPLICATION OF ACT.—Nothing in this Act shall be construed to apply to (or to authorize any State, interstate, or local authority to regulate) any activity or substance which is subject to the Federal Water Pollution Control Act (33 U.S.C. 1151 and following), the Safe Drinking Water Act (42 U.S.C. 300f and following), the Marine Protection, Research and Sanctuaries Act of 1972 (33 U.S.C. 1401 and following), or the Atomic Energy Act of 1954 (42 U.S.C. 2011 and following) except to the extent that such application (or regulation) is not inconsistent with the requirements of such Acts.

"(b) INTEGRATION WITH OTHER ACTS.—The Administrator shall integrate all provisions of this Act for purposes of administration and enforcement and shall avoid duplication, to the maximum extent practicable, with the appropriate provisions of the Clean Air Act (42 U.S.C. 1857 and following), the Federal Water Pollution Control Act (33 U.S.C. 1151 and following), the Federal Insecticide, Fungicide, and Rodenticide Act (7 U.S.C. 135 and following), the Safe Drinking Water Act (42 U.S.C. 300f and following), the Marine Protection, Research and Sanctuaries Act of 1972 (33 U.S.C. 1401 and following) and such other Acts of Congress as grant regulatory authority to the Administrator. Such integration shall be effected only to the extent that it can be done in a manner consistent with the goals and policies expressed in this Act and in other acts referred to in this subsection.

"(c) INTEGRATION WITH THE SURFACE MINING CONTROL AND RECLAMATION ACT OF 1977.—(1) No later than 90 days after the date of enactment of the Solid Waste Disposal Act Amendments of 1980, the Administrator shall review any regulations applicable to the treatment, storage, or disposal of any coal mining wastes or overburden promulgated by the Secretary of the Interior under the Surface Mining and Reclamation Act of 1977. If the Administrator determines that any requirement of final regulations promulgated under any section of subtitle C relating to mining wastes or overburden is not adequately addressed in such regulations promulgated by the Secretary, the Administrator shall promptly transmit such determination, together with suggested revisions and supporting documentation, to the Secretary.

"(2) The Secretary of the Interior shall have exclusive responsibility for carrying out any requirement of subtitle C of this Act with respect to coal mining wastes or overburden for which a surface coal mining and reclamation permit is issued or approved under the Surface Mining Control and Reclamation Act of 1977. The Secretary shall, with the concurrence of the Administrator, promulgate such regulations as may be necessary to carry out the purposes of this subsection and shall integrate such regulations with regulations promulgated under the Surface Mining Control and Reclamation Act of 1977.

"FINANCIAL DISCLOSURE

"Sec. 1007. (a) STATEMENT.—Each officer or employee of the Administrator who

"(1) performs any function or duty under this Act; and

"(2) has any known financial interest in any person who applies for or receives financial assistance under this Act

shall, beginning on February 1, 1977, annually file with the Administrator a written statement concerning all such interests held by such officer or employee during the preceding calendar year. Such statement shall be available to the public.

"(b) ACTION BY ADMINISTRATOR.—The Administrator shall—

"(1) act within ninety days after the date of enactment of this Act-

"(A) to define the term 'known financial interest' for purposes of subsection (a) of this section; and

("B) to establish the methods by which the requirement to file written statements specified in subsection (a) of this section will be monitored and enforced, including appropriate provision for the filing by such officers and employees of such statements and the review by the Administrator of such statements; and

"(2) report to the Congress on June 1, 1978, and of each succeeding calendar year with respect to such disclosures and the actions taken in regard thereto during the preceding calendar year.

"(c) EXEMPTION.—In the rules prescribed under subsection (b) of this section, the Administrator may identify specific positions within the Environmental Protection Agency which are of a nonpolicy-making nature and provide that officers or employees occupying such positions shall be exempt from the requirements of this section.

"(d) PENALTY.—Any officer or employee who is subject to, and knowingly violates this section shall be fined not more than $2,500 or imprisoned not more than one year, or both.

"SOLID WASTE MANAGEMENT INFORMATION AND GUIDELINES

"Sec. 1008. (a) GUIDELINES.—Within one year of enactment of this section, and from time to time thereafter, the Administrator shall, in cooperation with appropriate Federal, State, municipal, and inter-municipal agencies, and in consultation with other interested persons, and after public hearings, develop and publish suggested guidelines for solid waste management. Such suggested guidelines shall-

"(1) provide a technical and economic description of the level of performance that can be attained by various available solid waste management practices (including operating practices) which provide for the protection of public health and the environment;

"(2) not later than two years after the enactment of this section, describe levels of performance, including appropriate methods and degrees of control, that provide at a minimum for (A) protection of public health and welfare; (B) protection of the quality of ground waters and surface waters from leachates; (C) protection of the quality of surface waters from runoff through compliance with effluent limitations under the Federal Water Pollution Control Act, as amended; (D) protection of ambient air quality through compliance with new source performance standards or requirements of air quality implementation plans under the Clear Air Act, as amended; (E) disease and vector control; (F) safety; and (G) esthetics; and

"(3) provide minimum criteria to be used by the States to define those solid waste management practices which constitute the open dumping of solid waste or hazardous waste and are to be prohibited under subtitle D of this Act.

Where appropriate, such suggested guidelines also shall include minimum information for use in deciding the adequate location, design, and construction of facilities associated with solid waste management practices, including the consideration of regional, geographic, demographic, and climatic factors.

"(b) NOTICE.—The Administrator shall notify the Committee on Public Works of the Senate and the Committee on Interstate and Foreign Commerce of the House of Representatives a reasonable time before publishing any suggested guidelines or proposed regulations under this Act, of the content of such proposed suggested guidelines or proposed regulations under this Act.

"Subtitle B—Office of Solid Waste; Authorities of the Administrator

"OFFICE OF SOLID WASTE AND INTERAGENCY COORDINATING COMMITTEE

"Sec. 2001. (a) OFFICE OF SOLID WASTE.—The Administrator shall establish within the Environmental Protection Agency an Office of Solid Waste (hereinafter referred to as the 'Office') to be headed by an Assistant Administrator of the Environmental Protection Agency. The duties and responsibilities (other than duties and responsibilities relating to research and development) of the Administrator under this Act (as modified by applicable reorganization plans) shall be carried out through the Office.

"(b) INTERAGENCY COORDINATING COMMITTEE.— (1) There is hereby established an Interagency Coordinating Committee on Federal Resource Conservation and Recovery Activities which shall have the responsibility for coordinating all activities dealing with resource conservation and recovery from solid waste carried out by the Environmental Protection Agency, the Department of Energy, the Department of Commerce, and all other Federal agencies which conduct such activities pursuant to this or any other Act. For purposes of this subsection, the term 'resource conservation and recovery activities' shall include, but not be limited to, all research, development and demonstration projects on resource conservation or energy, or material, recovery from solid waste, and all technical or financial assistance for State or local planning for, or implementation of, projects related to resource conservation or energy or material, recovery from solid waste. The committee shall be chaired by the Administrator of the Environmental Protection Agency or such person as the Administrator may designate. Members of the Committee shall include representatives of the Department of Energy, the Department of Commerce, the Department of the Treasury, and each other Federal agency which the Administrator determines to have programs or responsibilities affecting resource conservation or recovery.

"(2) The Interagency Coordinating Committee shall include oversight of the implementation of

"(A) the May 1979 Memorandum of Understanding on Energy Recovery from Municipal Solid Waste between the Environmental Protection Agency and the Department of Energy;

"(B) the May 30, 1978, Interagency Agency Agreement between the Department of Commerce and the Environmental Protection Agency on the Implementation of the Resource Conservation and Recovery Act; and

"(C) any subsequent agreements between these agencies or other Federal agencies which address Federal resource recovery or conservation activities.

"(3) The Interagency Coordinating Committee shall submit to the Congress by March 1, 1981, and on March 1 each year thereafter, a five-year action plan for Federal resource conservation or recovery activities which shall identify means and propose programs to encourage resource conservation or material and energy recovery and increase private municipal investment in resource conservation or recovery systems, especially those which provide for material conservation or recovery as well as energy conservation or recovery. Such plan shall describe, at a minimum, a coordinated and nonduplicatory plan for resource recovery and conservation activities for the Environmental Protection Agency, the Department of Energy, the Department of Commerce, and all other Federal agencies which conduct such activities.

"AUTHORITIES OF ADMINISTRATOR

"Sec. 2002. (a) AUTHORITIES.--In carrying out this Act, the Administrator is authorized to--

"(1) prescribe, in consultation with Federal, State, and regional authorities, such regulations as are necessary to carry out his functions under this Act;

"(2) consult with or exchange information with other Federal agencies undertaking research, development, demonstration projects, studies, or investigations relating to solid waste;

"(3) provide technical and financial assistance to states or regional agencies in the development and implementation of solid waste plans and hazardous waste management programs;

"(4) consult with representatives of science, industry, agriculture, labor, environmental protection and consumer organizations, and other groups, as he deems advisable;

"(5) utilize the information, facilities, personnel and other resources of Federal agencies, including the National Bureau of Standards and the National Bureau of the Census, on a reimbursable basis, to perform research and analyses and conduct studies and investigations related to resource recovery and conservation and to otherwise carry out the Administrator's functions under this Act, and;

"(6) to delegate to the Secretary of Transportation the performance of any inspection or enforcement function under this Act relating to the transportation of hazardous waste where such delegation would avoid unnecessary duplication of activity and would carry out the objectives of this Act and of the Hazardous Materials Transportation Act.

"(b) REVISION OF REGULATIONS.--Each regulation promulgated under this Act shall be reviewed and, where necessary, revised not less frequently than every three years.

"RESOURCE RECOVERY AND CONSERVATION PANELS

"Sec. 2003. The Administrator shall provide teams of personnel, including Federal, State, and local employees or contractors (hereinafter referred to as 'Resource Conservation and Recovery Panels') to provide Federal agencies, States and local governments upon request with technical assistance on solid waste management, resource recovery, and resource conservation. Such teams shall include technical, marketing, financial, and institutional specialists, and the services of such teams shall be provided without charge to States or local governments.

[Editor's note: Public Law 97-272, an appropriations bill for the Department of Housing and Urban Development and independent agencies, provides the following concerning funds for EPA compliance activities:

ABATEMENT, CONTROL AND COMPLIANCE

"For abatement, control and compliance activities, $369,075,000, to remain available until September 30, 1984: Provided, That none of these funds may be expended for purposes of Resource Conservation and Recovery Panels established under section 2003 of the Resource Conservation and Recovery Act, as amended (42 U.S.C. 6913) or for support to State, regional, local and interstate agencies in accordance with subtitle D of the Solid Waste Disposal Act, as amended, other than section 4008(a)(2) or 4009"...]

"GRANTS FOR DISCARDED TIRE DISPOSAL

"Sec. 2004. (a) GRANTS.--The Administrator shall make available grants equal to 5 percent of the purchase price of tire shredders (including portable shredders attached to tire collection trucks) to those eligible applicants best meeting criteria promulgated under this section. An eligible applicant may be any private purchaser, public body, or public-private joint venture. Criteria for receiving grants shall be promulgated under this section and shall include the policy to offer any private purchaser the first option to receive a grant, the policy to develop widespread geographic distribution of tire shredding facilities, the need for such facilities within a geographic area, and the projected risk and viability of any such venture. In the case of an application under this section from a public body, the Administrator shall first make a determination that there are no private purchasers interested in making an application before approving a grant to a public body.

"(b) AUTHORIZATION.--There is authorized to be appropriated $750,000 for each of the fiscal years 1978 and 1979 to carry out this section.

"LABELING OF CERTAIN OIL

"Sec. 2005. For purposes of any provision of law which requires the labeling of commodities, lubricating oil shall be treated as lawfully labeled only if it bears the following statement, prominently displayed:

"'DON'T POLLUTE—CONSERVE RESOURCES; RETURN USED OIL TO COLLECTION CENTERS'."

"ANNUAL REPORT

"Sec. 2006. The Administrator shall transmit to the Congress and the President, not later than ninety days after the end of each fiscal year, a comprehensive and detailed report on all activities of the Office during the preceding fiscal year. Each such report shall include--

"(1) a statement of specific and detail objectives for the activities and programs conducted and assisted under this Act;

"(2) statements of the Administrator's conclusions as to the effectiveness of such activities and programs in meeting the stated objectives and the purposes of this Act, measured through the end of such fiscal year;

"(3) a summary of outstanding solid waste problems confronting the Administrator, in order of priority;

"(4) recommendations with respect to such legislation which the Administrator deems necessary or desirable to assist in solving problems respecting solid waste;

"(5) all other information required to be submitted to the Congress pursuant to any other provision of this Act; and

"(6) the Administrator's plans for activities and programs respecting solid waste during the next fiscal year.

"GENERAL AUTHORIZATION

"Sec. 2007. (a) GENERAL ADMINISTRATION.—There are authorized to be appropriated to the Administrator for the purpose of carrying out the provision of this Act, $35,000,000 for the fiscal year ending September 30, 1977, $ 38,000,000 for the fiscal year ending September 30, 1978, $42,000,000 for the fiscal year ending September 30, 1979, $70,000,000 for the fiscal year ending September 30, 1980, $80,000,000 for the fiscal year ending September 30, 1981, and $80,000,000 for the fiscal year ending September 30, 1982.

"(b) RESOURCE RECOVERY AND CONSERVATION PANELS.—Not less than 20 percent of the amount appropriated under subsection (a), or $5,000,000 per fiscal year, whichever is less, shall be used only for purposes of Resource Recovery and Conservation Panels established under section 2003 (including travel expenses incurred by such panels in carrying out their functions under this Act).

"(c) HAZARDOUS WASTE.—Not less than 30 percent of the amount appropriated under subsection (a) shall be used only for purposes of carrying out subtitle C of this Act (relating to hazardous waste) other than section 3011.

"(d) STATE AND LOCAL SUPPORT.—Not less than 25 per centum of the total amount appropriated under this title, up to the amount authorized in section 4008(a)(1), shall be used only for purposes of support to State, regional, local, and interstate agencies in accordance with subtitle D of this Act other than section 4008(a)(2) or 4009.

"Subtitle C—Hazardous Waste Management

"IDENTIFICATION AND LISTING OF HAZARDOUS WASTE

"Sec. 3001. (a) CRITERIA FOR IDENTIFICATION OR LISTING.—Not later than eighteen months after the date of the enactment of this Act, the Administrator shall, after notice and opportunity for public hearing, and after consultation with appropriate Federal and State agencies, develop and promulgate criteria for identifying the characteristics of hazardous waste, and for listing hazardous waste, which should be subject to the provisions of this subtitle, taking into account toxicity, persistence, and degradability in nature, potential for accumulation in tissue, and other related factors such as flammability, corrosiveness, and other hazardous characteristics. Such criteria shall be revised from time to time as may be appropriate.

"(b) IDENTIFICATION AND LISTING.—(1) Not later than eighteen months after the date of enactment of this section, and after notice and opportunity or public hearing, the Administrator shall promulgate regulations identifying the characteristics of hazardous waste, and listing particular hazardous wastes (within the meaning of section 1004(5), which shall be subject to the provisions of this subtitle. Such regulations shall be based on the criteria promulgated under subsection (a) and shall be revised from time to time thereafter as may be appropriate.

"(2)(A) Notwithstanding the provisions of paragraph (1) of this subsection, drilling fluids, produced waters, and other wastes associated with the exploration, development, or production of crude oil or natural gas or geothermal energy shall be subject only to existing State or Federal regulatory programs in lieu of subtitle C until at least 24 months after the date of enactment of the Solid Waste Disposal Act Amendments of 1980 and after promulgation of the regulations in accordance with subparagraphs (B) and (C) of this paragraph. It is the sense of the Congress that such State or Federal programs should include, for waste disposal sites which are to be closed, provisions requiring at least the following:

"(i) The identification through surveying, platting, or other measures, together with recordation of such information on the public record, so as to assure that the location where such wastes are disposed of can be located in the future; except however, that no such surveying, platting, or other measure identifying the location of a disposal site for drilling fluids and associated wastes shall be required if the distance from the disposal site to the surveyed or platted location to the associated well is less than two hundred lineal feet; and

(ii) A chemical and physical analysis of a produced water and a composition of a drilling fluid suspected to contain a hazardous material, with such information to be acquired prior to closure and to be placed on the public record.

"(B) Not later than six months after completion and submission of the study required by section 8002(m) of this Act, the Administrator shall, after public hearings and opportunity for comment, determine either to promulgate regulations under this subtitle for drilling fluids, produced waters, and other wastes associated with the exploration, development, or production of crude oil or natural gas or geothermal energy or that such regulations are unwarranted. The Administrator shall publish his decision in the Federal Register accompanied by an explanation and justification of the reasons for it. In making the decision under this paragraph, the Administrator shall utilize the information developed or accumulated pursuant to the study required under section 8002(m).

"(C) The Administrator shall transmit his decision, along with any regulations, if necessary, to both Houses of Congress. Such regulations shall take effect only when authorized by Act of Congress.

"(3)(A) Notwithstanding the provisions of paragraph (1) of this subsection, each waste listed below shall, except as provided in subparagraph (B) of this paragraph, be subject only to regulation under other applicable provisions of Federal or State law in lieu of this subtitle until at least six months after the date of submission of the applicable study required to be conducted under subsection (f), (n), (o), or (p) of section 8002 of this Act and after promulgation of regulations in accordance with subparagraph (C) of this paragraph:

"(i) Fly ash waste, bottom ash waste, slag waste, and flue gas emission control waste generated primarily from the combustion of coal or other fossil fuels.

"(ii) Solid waste from the extraction, beneficiation, and processing of ores and minerals, including phosphate rock and overburden from the mining of uranium ore.

"(iii) Cement kiln dust waste.

"(B)(i) Owners and operators of disposal sites for wastes listed in subparagraph (A) may be required by the Administrator, through regulations prescribed under authority of section 2002 of this Act--

"(I) as to disposal sites for such wastes which are to be closed, to identify the locations of such sites through surveying, platting, or other measures, together with recordation of such information on the public record, to assure that the locations where such wastes are disposed of are known and can be located in the future, and

"(II) to provide chemical and physical analysis and composition of such wastes, based on available information, to be placed on the public record.

"(ii)(I) In conducting any study under subsection (f), (n), (o), or (p), of section 8002 of this Act, any officer, employee, or authorized representative of the Environmental Protection Agency, duly designated by the Administrator, is authorized, at reasonable times and as reasonably necessary for the purposes of such study, to enter any establishment where any waste subject to such study is generated, stored, treated, disposed of, or transported from; to inspect, take samples, and conduct monitoring and testing; and to have access to and copy records relating to such waste. Each such inspection shall be commenced and completed with reasonable promptness. If the officer, employee, or authorized representative obtains any samples prior to leaving the premises, he shall give to the owner, operator, or agent in charge a receipt describing the sample obtained and if requested a portion of each such sample equal in volume or weight to the portion retained. If any analysis is made of such samples, or monitoring and testing performed, a copy of the results shall be furnished promptly to the owner, operator, or agent in charge.

(II) Any records, reports, or information obtained from any person under subclause (I) shall be available to the public, except that upon a showing satisfactory to the Administrator by any person that records, reports, or information, or particular part thereof, to which the Administrator has access under this subparagraph if made public, would divulge information entitled to protection under section 1905 of title 18 of the United States Code, the Administrator shall consider such information or particular portion thereof confidential in accordance with the purposes of that section, except that such record, report, document, or information may be disclosed to other officers, employees, or authorized representatives of the United States concerned with carrying out this Act. Any person not subject to the provisions of section 1905 of title 18 of the United States Code who knowingly and willfully divulges or discloses any information entitled to protection under this subparagraph shall, upon conviction, be subject to a fine of not more than $5,000 or to imprisonment not to exceed one year, or both.

"(iii) The Administrator may prescribe regulations, under the authority of this Act, to prevent radiation exposure which presents an unreasonable risk to human health from the use in construction or land reclamation (with or without revegetation) of (I) solid waste from the extraction, beneficiation, and processing of phosphate rock or (II) overburden from the mining of uranium ore.

"(iv) Whenever on the basis of any information the Administrator determines that any person is in violation of any requirement of this subparagraph, the Administrator shall give notice to the violator of his failure to comply with such requirement. If such violation extends beyond the thirtieth day after the Administrator's notification, the Administrator may issue an order requiring compliance within a specified time period or the Administrator may commence a civil action in the United States district court in the district in which the violation occurred for appropriate relief, including a temporary or permanent injunction.

"(C) not later than six months after the date of submission of the applicable study required to be conducted under subsection (f), (n), (o), or (p), of section 8002 of this Act, the Administrator shall, after public hearings and opportunity for comment, either determine to promulgate regulations under this subtitle for each waste listed in subparagraph (A) of this paragraph or determine that such regulations are unwarranted. The Administrator shall publish his determination, which shall be based on information developed or accumulated pursuant to such study, public hearings, and comment, in the Federal Register accompanied by an explanation and justification of the reasons for it.

"(c) PETITION BY STATE GOVERNOR.--At any time after the date eighteen months after the enactment of this title, the Governor of any State may petition the Administrator to identify or list a material as a hazardous waste. The Administrator shall act upon such petition within ninety days following his receipt thereof and shall notify the Governor of such action. If the Administrator denies such petition because of financial considerations, in providing such notice to the Governor he shall include a statement concerning such considerations.

"STANDARDS APPLICABLE TO GENERATORS OF HAZARDOUS WASTE

"Sec. 3002. Not later than eighteen months after the date of the enactment of this section, and after notice and opportunity for public hearings and after consultation with appropriate Federal and State agencies, the Administrator shall promulgate regulations establishing such standards, applicable to generators of hazardous waste identified or listed under this subtitle, as may be necessary to protect human health and the environment. Such standards shall establish requirements respecting—

"(1) recordkeeping practices that accurately identify the quantities of such hazardous waste generated, the constituents thereof which are significant in quantity or in potential harm to human health or the environment, and the disposition of such wastes;

"(2) labeling practices for any containers used for the storage, transport, or disposal of such hazardous waste such as will identify accurately such waste;

"(3) use of appropriate containers for such hazardous waste;

"(4) furnishing of information on the general chemical composition of such hazardous waste to persons transporting, treating, storing, or disposing of such wastes;

"(5) use of a manifest system and any other reasonable means necessary to assure that all such hazardous waste generated is designated for treatment, storage, or disposal in, and arrives at treatment, storage, or disposal facilities (other than facilities on the premises where the waste is generated) for which a permit has been issued as provided in this subtitle, or pursuant to title I of the Marine Protection, Research, and Sanctuaries Act (86 Stat. 1052); and

"(6) submission of reports to the Administrator (or the State agency in any case in which such agency carries out an authorized permit program pursuant to this subtitle) at such times as the Administrator (or the State agency if appropriate) deems necessary, setting out—

"(A) the quantities of hazardous waste identified or listed under this subtitle that he has generated during a particular time period; and

"(B) the disposition of all hazardous waste reported under subparagraph (A).

"STANDARDS APPLICABLE TO TRANSPORTERS OF HAZARDOUS WASTE

"Sec. 3003. (a) STANDARDS.—Not later than eighteen months after the date of enactment of this section, and after opportunity for public hearings, the Administrator, after consultation with the Secretary of Transportation and the States, shall promulgate regulations establishing such standards, applicable to transporters of hazardous waste identified or listed under this subtitle, as may be necessary to protect human health and the environment. Such standards shall include but need not be limited to requirements respecting—

"(1) recordkeeping concerning such hazardous waste transported, and their source and delivery points;

"(2) transportation of such waste only if properly labeled;

"(3) compliance with the manifest system referred to in section 3002(5); and

"(4) transportation of all such hazardous waste only to the hazardous waste treatment, storage, or disposal facilities which the shipper designates on the manifest form to be a facility holding a permit issued under this subtitle, or pursuant to title I of the Marine Protection, Research, and Sanctuaries Act (86 Stat. 1052).

"(b) COORDINATION WITH REGULATIONS OF SECRETARY OF TRANSPORTATION.—In case of any hazardous waste identified or listed under this subtitle which is subject to the Hazardous Materials Transportation Act (88 Stat. 2156; 49 U.S.C. 1801 and following), the regulations promulgated by the Administrator under this section shall be consistent with the requirements of such Act and the regulations thereunder. The Administrator is authorized to make recommendations to the Secretary of Transportation respecting the regulations of such hazardous waste under the Hazardous Materials Transportation Act and for addition of materials to be covered by such Act.

"STANDARDS APPLICABLE TO OWNERS AND OPERATORS OF HAZARDOUS WASTE TREATMENT, STORAGE, AND DISPOSAL FACILITIES

"Sec. 3004. Not later than eighteen months after the date of enactment of this section, and after opportunity for public hearings and after consultation with appropriate Federal and State agencies, the Administrator shall promulgate regulations establishing such performance standards, applicable to owners and operators of facilities for the treatment, storage, or disposal of hazardous waste identified or listed under this subtitle, as may be necessary to protect human health and the environment. In establishing such standards the Administrator shall, where appropriate, distinguish in such standards between requirements appropriate for new facilities and for facilities in existence on the date of promulgation of such regulations. Such standards shall include, but need not be limited to, requirements respecting—

"(1) maintaining records of all hazardous wastes identified or listed under this title which is treated, stored, or disposed of, as the case may be, and the manner in which such wastes were treated, stored, or disposed of;

"(2) satisfactory reporting, monitoring, and inspection and compliance with the manifest system referred to in section 3002(5);

"(3) treatment, storage, or disposal of all such waste received by the facility pursuant to such operating methods, techniques, and practices as may be satisfactory to the Administrator;

"(4) the location, design, and construction of such hazardous waste treatment, disposal, or storage facilities;

"(5) contingency plans for effective action to minimize unanticipated damage from any treatment, storage, or disposal of any such hazardous waste;

"(6) the maintenance of operation of such facilities and requiring such additional qualifications as to ownership, continuity of operation, training for personnel, and financial responsibility as may be necessary or desirable; and

"(7) compliance with the requirements of section 3005 respecting permits for treatment, storage, or disposal.

No private entity shall be precluded by reason of criteria established under paragraph (6) from the ownership or operation of facilities providing hazardous waste treatment, storage, or disposal services where such entity can provide assurances of financial responsibility and continuity of operation consistent with the degree and duration of risks associated with the treatment, storage, or disposal of specified hazardous waste.

"PERMITS FOR TREATMENT, STORAGE, OR DISPOSAL OF HAZARDOUS WASTE

"Sec. 3005. (a) PERMIT REQUIREMENTS.--Not later than eighteen months after the date of the enactment of this section, the Administrator shall promulgate regulations requiring each person owning or operating a facility for the treatment, storage, or disposal of hazardous waste identified or listed under this subtitle to have a permit issued pursuant to this section. Such regulations shall take effect on the date provided in section 3010 and upon and after such date the treatment, storage, or disposal of any such hazardous waste is prohibited except in accordance with such a permit.

"(b) REQUIREMENTS OF PERMIT APPLICATION.--Each application for a permit under this section shall contain such information as may be required under regulations promulgated by the Administrator, including information respecting--

"(1) estimates with respect to the composition, quantities, and concentrations of any hazardous waste identified or listed under this subtitle, or combinations of any such hazardous waste and any other solid waste, proposed to be disposed of, treated, transported, or stored, and the time, frequency, or rate of which such waste is proposed to be disposed of, treated, transported, or stored; and

"(2) the site at which such hazardous waste or the products of treatment of such hazardous waste will be disposed of, treated, transported to, or stored.

"(c) PERMIT ISSUANCE.--Upon a determination by the Administrator (or a State, if applicable), of compliance by a facility for which a permit is applied for under this section with the requirements of this section and section 3004, the Administrator (or the State) shall issue a permit for such facilities. In the event permit applicants propose modification of their facilities, or in the event the Administrator (or the State) determines that modifications are necessary to conform to the requirements under this section and section 3004, the permit shall specify the time allowed to complete the modifications.

"(d) PERMIT REVOCATION.--Upon a determination by the Administrator (or by a State, in the case of a State having an authorized hazardous waste program under section 3006) of noncompliance by a facility having a permit under this title with the requirements of this section or section 3004, the Administrator (or State, in the case of a State having an authorized hazardous waste program under section 3006) shall revoke such permit.

"(e) INTERIM STATUS.--Any person who--

"(1) owns or operates a facility required to have a permit under this section which facility is in existence on November 19, 1980,

"(2) has complied with the requirements of section 3010(a), and

"(3) has made an application for a permit under this section shall be treated as having been issued such permit until such time as final administrative disposition of such application is made, unless the Administrator or other plaintiff proves that final administrative disposition of such application has not been made bacause of the failure of the applicant to furnish information reasonably required or requested in order to process the application.

"(f) COAL MINING WASTES AND RECLAMATION PERMITS.--Notwithstanding subsection (a) through (e) of this section, any surface coal mining and reclamation permit covering any coal mining wastes or overburden which has been issued or approved under the Surface Mining Control and Reclamation Act of 1977 shall be deemed to be a permit issued pursuant to this section with respect to the treatment, storage, or disposal of such wastes or overburden. Regulations promulgated by the Administrator under this subtitle shall not be applicable to treatment, storage, or disposal of coal mining wastes and overburden which are covered by such a permit.

"AUTHORIZED STATE HAZARDOUS WASTE PROGRAMS

"Sec. 3006. (a) FEDERAL GUIDELINES.--Not later than eighteen months after the date of enactment of this Act, the Administrator, after consultation with State authorities, shall promulgate guidelines to assist States in the development of State hazardous waste programs.

"(b) AUTHORIZATION OF STATE PROGRAM.--Any State which seeks to administer and enforce a hazardous waste program pursuant to this subtitle may develop and, after notice and opportunity for public hearing, submit to the Administrator an application, in such form as he shall require, for authorization of such program. Within ninety days following submission of an application under this subsection, the Administrator shall issued a notice as to whether or not he expects such program to be authorized, and within ninety days following such notice (and after opportunity for public hearing) he shall publish his findings as to whether or not the conditions listed in item (1), (2), and (3) below have been met. Such State is authorized to carry out such program in lieu of the Federal program under this subtitle in such State and to issue and enforce permits for the storage, treatment, or disposal of hazardous waste unless, within ninety days following submission of the application the Administrator notifies such State that such program may not be authorized and, within ninety days following such notice and after opportunity for public hearing, he finds that (1) such State program is not equivalent to the Federal program under this subtitle, (2) such program is not consistent with the Federal or State programs applicable in other States, or (3) such program does not provide adequate enforcement of compliance with the requirements of this subtitle.

"(c) INTERIM AUTHORIZATION.--Any State which has in existence a hazardous waste program pursuant to State law before the date ninety days after the date of promulgation of regulations under sections 3002, 3003, 3004, and 3005, may submit to the Administrator evidence of such existing program and may request a temporary authorization to carry out such program under this subtitle. The Administrator shall, if the evidence submitted shows the existing State program to be substantially equivalent to the Federal program under this subtitle, grant an interim authorization to the State to carry out such program in lieu of the Federal program pursuant to this subtitle for a twenty-four month period beginning on the date six months after the date of promulgation of regulations under sections 3002 through 3005.

"(d) EFFECT OF STATE PERMIT.--Any action taken by a State under a hazardous waste program authorized under this section shall have the same force and effect as action taken by the Administrator under this subtitle.

"(e) WITHDRAWAL OF AUTHORIZATION.--Whenever the Administrator determines after public hearing that a State is not administering and enforcing a program authorized under this section in accordance with requirements of this section, he shall so notify the State and, if appropriate corrective action is not taken within a reasonable time, not to exceed ninety days, the Administrator shall withdraw authorization of such program and establish a Federal program pursuant to this subtitle. The Administrator shall not withdraw authorization of any such program unless he shall first have notified the State, and made public, in writing, the reasons for such withdrawal.

"INSPECTIONS

"Sec. 3007. (a) ACCESS ENTRY.—For purposes of developing or assisting in the development of any regulation or enforcing the provisions of this title, any person who generates, stores, treats, transports, disposes of, or otherwise handles or has handled hazardous wastes shall, upon request of any officer, employee or representative of the Environmental Protection Agency, duly designated by the Administrator, or upon request of any duly designated officer, employee or representative of a State having an authorized hazardous waste program, furnish information relating to such wastes and permit such person at all reasonable times to have access to, and to copy all records relating to such wastes. For the purposes of developing or assisting in the development of any regulation or enforcing the provisions of this title, such officers, employees or representatives are authorized—

"(1) to enter at reasonable times any establishment or other place where hazardous wastes are or have been generated, stored, treated, disposed of, or transported from;

"(2) to inspect and obtain samples from any person of any such wastes and samples of any containers or labeling for such wastes.

Each such inspection shall be commenced and completed with reasonable promptness. If the officer, employee or representative obtains any samples, prior to leaving the premises, he shall give to the owner, operator, or agent in charge a receipt describing the sample obtained and if requested a portion of each such sample equal in volume or weight to the portion retained. If any analysis is made of such samples, a copy of the results of such analysis shall be furnished promptly to the owner, operator, or agent in charge.

"(b) AVAILABILITY TO PUBLIC.—(1) Any records, reports, or information obtained from any person under this section shall be available to the public, except that upon a showing satisfactory to the Administrator (or the State, as the case may be) by any person that records, reports, or information, or particular part thereof, to which the Administrator (or the State, as the case may be) or any officer, employee or representative thereof has access under this section if made public, would divulge information entitled to protection under section 1905 of title 18 of the United States Code, such information or particular portion thereof shall be considered confidential in accordance with the purposes of that section, except that such record, report, document, or information may be disclosed to other officers, employees, or authorized representatives of the United States concerned with carrying out this Act, or when relevant in any proceeding under this Act.

"(2) Any person not subject to the provisions of section 1905 of title 18 of the United States Code who knowingly and willfully divulges or discloses any information entitled to protection under this subsection shall, upon conviction, be subject to a fine of not more than $5,000 or to imprisonment not to exceed one year, or both.

"(3) In submitting data under this Act, a person required to provide such data may—

"(A) designate the data which such person believes is entitled to protection under this subsection, and

"(B) submit such designated data separately from other data submitted under this Act.

A designation under this paragraph shall be made in writing and in such manner as the Administrator may prescribe.

"(4) Notwithstanding any limitation contained in this section or any other provision of law, all information reported to, or otherwise obtained by, the Administrator (or any representative of the Administrator) under this Act shall be made available, upon written request of any duly authorized committee of the Congress, to such committee (including records, reports, or information obtained by representatives of the Environmental Protection Agency).

"FEDERAL ENFORCEMENT

"Sec. 3008. (a) COMPLIANCE ORDERS.—(1) Except as provided in paragraph (2), whenever on the basis of any information the Administrator determines that any person is in violation of any requirement of this subtitle, the Administrator may issue an order requiring compliance immediately or within a specified time period or the Administrator may commence a civil action in the United States district court in the district in which the violation occurred for appropriate relief, including a temporary or permanent injunction.

"(2) In the case of a violation of any requirement of this subtitle where such violation occurs in a State which is authorized to carry out a hazardous waste program under section 3006, the Administrator shall give notice to the State in which such violation has occurred prior to issuing an order or commencing a civil action under this section.

"(3) If such violator fails to take corrective action within the time specified in the order, he shall be liable for a civil penalty of not more than $25,000 for each day of continued noncompliance and the Administrator may suspend or revoke any permit issued to the violator (whether issued by the Administrator or the State).

"(b) PUBLIC HEARING.—Any order shall become final unless, no later than thirty days after the order is served, the person or persons named therein request a public hearing. Upon such request the Administrator shall promptly conduct a public hearing. In connection with any proceeding under this section the Administrator may issue subpoenas for the attendance and testimony of witnesses and the production of relevant papers, books, and documents, and may promulgate rules for discovery procedures.

"(c) REQUIREMENTS OF COMPLIANCE ORDERS.—Any order issued under this section may include a suspension or revocation of a permit issued under this subtitle, and shall state with reasonable specificity the nature of the violation and specify a time for compliance and assess a penalty, if any, which the Administrator determines is reasonable taking into account the seriousness of the violation and any good faith efforts to comply with the applicable requirements.

"(d) CRIMINAL PENALTIES.—Any person who—

"(1) knowingly transports any hazardous waste identified or listed under this subtitle to a facility which does not have a permit under section 3005 (or 3006 in case of a State program), or pursuant to title I of the Marine Protection, Research, and Sanctuaries Act (86 Stat. 1052),

"(2) knowingly treats, stores, or disposes of any hazardous waste identified or listed under this subtitle either—

"(A) without having obtained a permit under section 3005 (or 3006 in the case of a State program) or pursuant to title I of the Marine Protection, Research, and Sanctuaries Act (86 Stat. 1052); or

"(B) in knowing violation of any material condition or requirement of such permit;

"(3) knowingly makes any false material statement or representation in any application, label, manifest, record, report, permit or other document filed, maintained, or used for purposes of compliance with this subtitle; or

"(4) knowingly generates, stores, treats, transports, disposes of, or otherwise handles any hazardous waste (whether such activity took place before or takes place after the date of the enactment of this paragraph) and who knowingly destroys, alters, or conceals any record required to be maintained under regulations promulgated by the Administrator under this subtitle shall, upon conviction, be subject to a fine of not more than $25,000 ($50,000 in the case of a violation of paragraph (1) or (2)) for each day of violation, or to imprisonment not to exceed one year (two years in the case of a violation of paragraph (1) or (2)), or both. If the conviction is for a violation committed after a first conviction of such person under this paragraph, punishment shall be by a fine of not more than $50,000 per day of violation, or by imprisonment for not more than two years, or by both.

"(e) KNOWING ENDANGERMENT.--Any person who knowingly transports, treats, stores, or disposes of any hazardous waste identified or listed under this subtitle--

"(1)(A) in violation of paragraphs (1) or (2) of subsection (d) of this section, or

"(B) having applied for a permit under section 3005 or 3006, and knowingly either--

"(i) has failed to include in his application material information required under regulations promulgated by the Administrator, or

"(ii) fails to comply with the applicable interim status regulations and standards promulgated pursuant to this subtitle,

who knows at that time that he thereby places another person in imminent danger of death or serious bodily injury, and

"(2)(A) if his conduct in the circumstances manifests an unjustified and inexcusable disregard for human life, or

"(B) if his conduct in the circumstances manifests an extreme indifference for human life.

shall, upon conviction, be subject to a fine of not more than $250,000 or imprisonment for not more than 2 years, or both, except that any person who violates subsection (e)(2)(B) shall, upon conviction, be subject to a fine of not more than $250,000 or imprisonment for not more than 5 years, or both. A defendant that is an organization shall, upon conviction of violating this subsection, be subject to a fine of not more than $1,000,000.

"(f) SPECIAL RULES.--For the purposes of subsection (e)--

"(1) A person's state of mind is knowing with respect to--

"(A) his conduct, if he is aware of the nature of his conduct;

"(B) an existing circumstance, if he is aware or believes that the circumstance exists; or

"(C) a result of his conduct, if he is aware or believes that his conduct is substantially certain to cause danger of death or serious bodily injury.

"(2) In determining whether a defendant who is a natural person knew that his conduct placed another person in imminent danger of death or serious bodily injury-

"(A) the person is responsible only for actual awareness or actual belief that he possessed; and

"(B) knowledge possessed by a person other than the defendant but not by the defendant himself may not be attributed to the defendant;

PROVIDED, That in proving the defendant's possession of actual knowledge, circumstantial evidence may be used, including evidence that the defendant took affirmative steps to shield himself from relevant information.

"(3) It is an affirmative defense to prosecution that the conduct charged was consented to by the person endangered and that the danger and conduct charged were reasonably forseeable hazards of —

"(A) an occupation, a business, or a profession; or

"(B) medical treatment or medical or scientific experimentation conducted by professionally approved methods and such other person had been made aware of the risks involved prior to giving consent.

The defendant may establish an affirmative defense under this subsection by a preponderance of the evidence.

"(4) All general defenses, affirmative defenses, and bars to prosecution that may apply with respect to other Federal criminal offenses may apply under subsection (e) and shall be determined by the courts of the United States according to the principles of common law as they may be interpreted in the light of reason and experience. Concepts of justification and excuse applicable under this section may be developed in the light of reason and experience.

"(5) The term 'organization' means a legal entity, other than a government, established or organized for any purpose, and such term includes a corporation, company, association, firm, partnership, joint stock company, foundation, institution, trust, society, union, or any other association of persons.

"(6) The term 'serious bodily injury' means--

"(A) bodily injury which involves a substantial risk of death;

"(B) unconsciousness;

"(C) extreme physical pain;

"(D) protracted and obvious disfigurement; or

"(E) protracted loss or impairment of the function of a bodily member, organ, or mental faculty.

"(g) CIVIL PENALTY.—Any person who violates any requirement of this subtitle shall be liable to the United States for a civil penalty in an amount not to exceed $25,000 for each such violation. Each day of such violation shall, for purposes of this subsection, constitute a separate violation.

"RETENTION OF STATE AUTHORITY

"Sec. 3009. Upon the effective date of regulations under this subtitle no State or political subdivision may impose any requirements less stringent than those authorized under this subtitle respecting the same matter as governed by such regulations, except that if application of a regulation with respect to any matter under this subtitle is postponed or enjoined by the action of any court, no State or political subdivision shall be prohibited from acting with respect to the same aspect of such matter until such time as such regulation takes effect. Nothing in this title shall be construed to prohibit any State or political subdivision thereof from imposing any requirements, including those for site selection, which are more stringent than those imposed by such regulations.

"EFFECTIVE DATE

"Sec. 3010. (a) PRELIMINARY NOTIFICATION.—Not later than ninety days after promulgation of regulations under section 3001 identifying by its characteristics or listing any substance as hazardous waste subject to this subtitle, any person generating or transporting such substance or owning or operating a facility for treatment, storage, or disposal of such substance shall file with the Administrator (or with States having authorized hazardous waste permit programs under section 3006) a notification stating the location and general description of such activity and the identified or listed hazardous wastes handled by such person. In revising any regulation under section 3001 identifying additional characteristics of hazardous waste or listing any additional substance as hazardous waste subject to this subtitle, the Administrator may require any person referred to in the preceding sentence to file with the Administrator (or with States having authorized hazardous waste permit programs under section 3006) the notification described in the preceding sentence. Not more than one such notification shall be required to be filed with respect to the same substance. No identified or listed hazardous waste subject to this subtitle may be transported, treated, stored, or disposed of unless notification has been given as required under this subsection.

"(b) EFFECTIVE DATE OF REGULATION.—The regulations under this subtitle respecting requirements applicable to the generation, transportation, treatment, storage, or disposal of hazardous waste (including requirements respecting permits for such treatment, storage, or disposal) shall take effect on the date six months after the date of promulgation thereof (or six months after the date of revision in the case of any regulation which is revised after the date required for promulgation thereof).

"AUTHORIZATION OF ASSISTANCE TO STATES

"Sec. 3011. (a) AUTHORIZATION.—There is authorized to be appropriated $25,000,000 for each of the fiscal years 1978 and 1979, $20,000,000 for fiscal year 1980, $35,000,000 for fiscal year 1981, and $40,000,000 for fiscal year 1982 to be used to make grants to the States for purposes of assisting the States in the development and implementation of authorized State hazardous waste programs.

"(b) ALLOCATION.—Amounts authorized to be appropriated under subsection (a) shall be allocated among the States on the basis of regulations promulgated by the Administrator, after consultation with the States, which take into account, the extent to which hazardous waste is generated, transported, treated, stored, and disposed of within such State, the extent of exposure of human beings and the environment within such State to such waste, and such other factors as the Administrator deems appropriate.

"(c) ACTIVITIES INCLUDED.—State hazardous waste programs for which grants may be made under subsection (a) may include (but shall not be limited to) planning for hazardous waste treatment, storage and disposal facilities, and the development and execution of programs to protect health and the environment from inactive facilities which may contain hazardous waste.

[Editor's Note: The following Section 3012 is from the Used Oil Recycling Act of 1980. See additional Section 3012 following this section.]

"RESTRICTIONS ON RECYCLED OIL

"Sec. 3012. Not later than one year after the date of the enactment of this section, the Administrator shall promulgate regulations establishing such performance standards and other requirements as may be necessary to protect the public health and the environment from hazards associated with recycled oil. In developing such regulations, the Administrator shall conduct an analysis of the economic impact of the regulations on the oil recycling industry. The Administrator shall ensure that such regulations do not discourage the recovery or recycling of used oil.

[Editor's Note: The following Section 3012 is from the Solid Waste Disposal Act Amendments of 1980. See additional Section 3012 above.]

"HAZARDOUS WASTE SITE INVENTORY

"Sec. 3012. (a) STATE INVENTORY PROGRAMS.--Each State shall, as expeditiously as practicable, undertake a continuing program to compile, publish, and submit to the Administrator an inventory describing the location of each site within such State at which hazardous waste has at any time been stored or disposed of. Such inventory shall contain--

"(1) a description of the location of the sites at which any such storage or disposal has taken place before the date on which permits are required under section 3005 for such storage or disposal;

"(2) such information relating to the amount, nature, and toxicity of the hazardous waste at each such site as may be practicable to obtain and as may be necessary to determine the extent of any health hazard which may be associated with such site;

"(3) the name and address, or corporate headquarters of, the owner of each site, determined as of the date of preparation of the inventory;

"(4) an identification of the types or techniques of waste treatment or disposal which have been used at each such site; and

"(5) information concerning the current status of the site, including information respecting whether or not hazardous waste is currently being treated or disposed of at such site (and if not, the date on which such activity ceased) and information respecting the nature of any other activity currently carried out at such site.

For purposes of assisting the States in compiling information under this section, the Administrator shall make available to each State undertaking a program under this section such information as is available to him concerning the items specified in paragraphs (1) through (5) with respect to the sites within such State, including such information as the Administrator is able to obtain from other agencies or departments of the United States and from surveys and studies carried out by any committee or subcommittee of the Congress. Any State may exercise the authority of section 3007 for purposes of this section in the same manner and to the same extent as provided in such section in the case of States having an authorized hazardous waste program, and any State may by order require any person to submit such information as may be necessary to compile the data referred to in paragraphs (1) through (5).

"(b) ENVIRONMENTAL PROTECTION AGENCY PROGRAM.--If the Administrator determines that any State program under subsection (a) is not adequately providing information respecting the sites in such State referred to in subsection (a) the Administrator shall notify the State. If within ninety days following such notification, the State program has not been revised or amended in such manner as will adequately provide such information, the Administrator shall carry out the inventory program in such State. In any such case--

"(1) the Administrator shall have the authorities provided with respect to State programs under subsection (a);

"(2) the funds allocated under subsection (c) for grants to states under this section may be used by the Administrator for carrying out such program in such State; and

"(3) no further expenditure may be made for grants to such State under this section until such time as the Administrator determines that such State is carrying out, or will carry out, an inventory program which meets the requirements of this section.

"(c) GRANTS.--(1) Upon receipt of an application submitted by any State to carry out a program under this section, the Administrator may make grants to the States for purposes of carrying out such a program. Grants under this section shall be allocated among the several States by the Administrator based upon such regulations as he prescribes to carry out the purposes of this section. The Administrator may make grants to any State which has conducted an inventory program which effectively carried out the purposes of this section before the date of the enactment of the Solid Waste Disposal Act Amendments of 1980 to reimburse such State for all, or any portion of, the costs incurred by such State in conducting such program.

"(2) There are authorized to be appropriated to carry out this section $20,000,000.

"(d) NO IMPEDIMENT TO IMMEDIATE REMEDIAL ACTION.--Nothing in this section shall be construed to provide that the Administrator or any State should, pending completion of the inventory required under this section, postpone undertaking any enforcement or remedial action with respect to any site at which hazardous waste has been treated, stored, or disposed of.

"MONITORING, ANALYSIS, AND TESTING

"Sec. 3013. (a) AUTHORITY OF ADMINISTRATOR.--If the Administrator determines, upon receipt of any information, that—

"(1) the presence of any hazardous waste at a facility or site at which hazardous waste is, or has been, stored, treated, or disposed of, or

"(2) the release of any such waste from such facility or site may present a substantial hazard to human health or the environment, he may issue an order requiring the owner or operator of such facility or site to conduct such monitoring, testing, analysis, and reporting with respect to such facility or site as the Administrator deems reasonable to ascertain the nature and extent of such hazard.

"(b) PREVIOUS OWNERS AND OPERATORS.--In the case of any facility or site not in operation at the time a determination is made under subsection (a) with respect to the facility or site if the Administrator finds that the owner of such facility or site, could not reasonably be expected to have actual knowledge of the presence of hazardous waste at such facility or site and of its potential for release, he may issue an order requiring the most recent previous owner or operator of such facility or site who could reasonably be expected to have such actual knowledge to carry out the actions referred to in subsection (a).

"(c) PROPOSAL.--Any order under subsection (a) or (b) shall require the person to whom such order is issued to submit to the Administrator within 30 days from the issuance of such order a proposal for carrying out the required monitoring, testing, analysis, and reporting. The Administrator may, after providing such person with an opportunity to confer with the Administrator respecting such proposal, require such person to carry out such monitoring, testing, analysis, and reporting in accordance with such proposal, and such modifications in such proposal as the Administrator deems reasonable to ascertain the nature and extent of the hazard.

"(d) MONITORING, ETC., CARRIED OUT BY ADMINISTRATOR.--(1) If the Administrator determines that no owner or operator referred to in subsection (a) or (b) is able to conduct monitoring, testing, analysis, or reporting satisfactory to the Administrator, if the Administrator deems any such action carried out by an owner or operator to be unsatisfactory, or if the Administrator cannot initially determine that there is an owner or operator referred to in subsection (a) or (b) who is able to conduct such monitoring, testing, analysis, or reporting, he may—

"(A) conduct monitoring, testing, or analysis (or any combination thereof) which he deems reasonable to ascertain the nature and extent of the hazard associated with the site concerned, or

"(B) authorize a State or local authority or other person to carry out any such action,

and require, by order, the owner or operator referred to in subsection (a) or (b) to reimburse the Administrator or other authority or person for the costs of such activity.

"(2) No order may be issued under this subsection requiring reimbursement of the costs of any action carried out by the Administrator which confirms the results of an order issued under subsection (a) or (b).

"(3) For purposes of carrying out this subsection, the Administrator or any authority or other person authorized under paragraph (1) may exercise the authorities set forth in section 3007.

"(e) ENFORCEMENT.--The Administrator may commence a civil action against any person who fails or refuses to comply with any order issued under this section. Such action shall be brought in the United States district court in which the defendant is located, resides, or is doing business. Such court shall have jurisdiction to require compliance with such order and to assess a civil penalty of not to exceed $5,000 for each day during which such failure or refusal occurs.

"Subtitle D--State or Regional Solid Waste Plans

"OBJECTIVES OF SUBTITLE

"Sec. 4001. The objectives of this subtitle are to assist in developing and encouraging methods for the disposal of solid waste which are environmentally sound and which maximize the utilization of valuable resources including energy and materials which are recoverable from solid waste and to encourage resource conservation. Such objectives are to be accomplished through Federal technical and financial assistance to States or regional authorities for comprehensive planning pursuant to federal guidelines designed to foster cooperation among Federal, State, and local governments and private industry.

"FEDERAL GUIDELINES FOR PLANS

"Sec. 4002. (a) GUIDELINES FOR IDENTIFICATION OF REGIONS.--For purposes of encouraging and facilitating the development of regional planning for solid waste management, the Administrator, within one hundred and eighty days after the date of enactment of this section and after consultation with appropriate Federal, State, and local authorities, shall by regulation publish guidelines for the identification of those areas which have common solid waste management problems and are appropriate units for planning regional solid waste management services. Such guidelines shall consider--

"(1) the size and location of areas which should be included,

"(2) the volume of solid waste which should be included, and

"(3) the available means of coordinating regional planning with other related regional planning and for coordination of such regional planning into the State plan.

"(b) GUIDELINES FOR STATE PLANS.--Not later than eighteen months after the date of enactment of this section and after notice and hearing, the Administrator shall, after consultation with appropriate Federal, State, and local authorities, promulgate regulations containing guidelines to assist in the development and implementation of State solid waste management plans (hereinafter in this title referred to as 'State plans'). The guidelines shall contain methods for achieving the objectives specified in section 4001. Such guidelines shall be reviewed from time to time, but not less frequently than every three years, and revised as may be appropriate.

"(c) CONSIDERATIONS FOR STATE PLAN GUIDELINES.--The guidelines promulgated under subsection (b) shall consider--

"(1) the varying regional, geologic, hydrologic, climatic, and other circumstances under which different solid waste practices are required in order to insure the reasonable protection of the quality of the ground and surface waters from leachate contamination, the reasonable protection of the quality of the surface waters from surface runoff contamination, and the reasonable protection of ambient air quality;

"(2) characteristics and conditions of collection, storage, processing, and disposal operating methods, techniques and practices, and location of facilities where such operating methods, techniques, and practices are conducted, taking into account the nature of the material to be disposed;

"(3) methods for closing or upgrading open dumps for purposes of eliminating potential health hazards;

"(4) population density, distribution, and projected growth;

"(5) geographic, geologic, climatic, and hydrologic characteristics;

"(6) the type and location of transportation;

"(7) the profile of industries;

"(8) the constituents and generation rates of waste;

"(9) the political, economic, organizational, financial, and management problems affecting comprehensive solid waste management;

"(10) types of resource recovery facilities and resource conservation systems which are appropriate; and

"(11) available new and additional markets for recovered material and energy and energy resources recovered from solid waste as well as methods for conserving such materials and energy.

"REQUIREMENTS FOR APPROVAL OF PLANS

"Sec. 4003. (a) MINIMUM REQUIREMENTS.--In order to be approved under section 4007, each State plan must comply with the following minimum requirements--

"(1) The plan shall identify (in accordance with section 4006(b) (A) the responsibilities of State, local, and regional authorities in the implementation of the State plan, (B) the distribution of Federal funds to the authorities responsible for development and implementation of the State plan, and (C) the means for coordinating regional planning and implementation under the State plan.

"(2) The plan shall, in accordance with section 4004 (b) and 4005(a), prohibit the establishment of new open dumps within the State, and contain requirements that all solid waste (including solid waste originating in other States, but not including hazardous waste) shall be (A) utilized for resource recovery or (B) disposed of in sanitary landfills (within the meaning of section 4004 (a)) or otherwise disposed of in an environmentally sound manner.

"(3) The plan shall provide for the closing or upgrading of all existing open dumps with the State pursuant to the requirements of section 4005.

"(4) The plan shall provide for the establishment of such State regulatory powers as may be necessary to implement the plan.

"(5) The plan shall provide that no State or local government within the State shall be prohibited under State or local law from negotiating and entering into long-term contracts for the supply of solid waste to resource recovery facilities, from entering into long-term contracts for the operation of such facilities, or from securing long-term markets for material and energy recovered from such facilities or for conserving materials or energy by reducing the volume of waste.

"(6) The plan shall provide for such resource conservation or recovery and for the disposal of solid waste in sanitary landfills or any combination of practices so as may be necessary to use or dispose of such waste in a manner that is environmentally sound.

[Editor's Note: The following subsection (b) is from the Used Oil Recycling Act of 1980. See additional subsection (b) following the one below.]

"(b) DISCRETIONARY PLAN PROVISIONS RELATING TO RECYCLED OIL.- Any State plan submitted under this subtitle may include, at the option of the State, provisions to carry out each of the following:

"(1) Encouragement, to the maximum extent feasible and consistent with the protection of the public health and the environment, of the use of recycled oil in all appropriate areas of State and local government.

"(2) Encouragement of persons contracting with the State to use recycled oil to the maximum extent feasible, consistent with protection of the public health and the environment.

"(3) Informing the public of the uses of recycled oil.

"(4) Establishment and implementation of a program (including any necessary licensing of persons and including the use, where appropriate, of manifests) to assure that used oil is collected, transported, treated, stored, reused, and disposed of, in a manner which does not present a hazard to the public health or the environment.

Any plan submitted under this title before the date of the enactment of the Used Oil Recycling Act of 1980 may be amended, at the option of the State, at any time after such date to include any provision referred to in this subsection.

[Editor's Note: The following subsection (b) is from the Solid Waste Disposal Act Amendments of 1980. See additional subsection (b) above.]

"(b) ENERGY AND MATERIALS CONSERVATION AND RECOVERY FEASIBILITY PLANNING AND ASSISTANCE.—(1) A State which has a plan approved under this subtitle or which has submitted a plan for such approval shall be eligible for assistance under section 4008(a)(3) if the Administrator determines that under such plan the State will—

"(A) analyze and determine the economic and technical feasibility of facilities and programs to conserve resources which contribute to the waste stream or to recover energy and materials from municipal waste;

"(B) analyze the legal, institutional, and economic impediments to the development of systems and facilities for conservation of energy or materials which contribute to the waste stream or for the recovery of energy and materials from municipal waste and make recommendations to appropriate governmental authorities for overcoming such impediments;

"(C) assist municipalities within the State in developing plans, programs, and projects to conserve resources or recover energy and materials from municipal waste; and

"(D) coordinate the resource conservation and recovery planning under subparagraph (C).

"(2) The analysis referred to in paragraph (1)(A) shall include—

"(A) the evaluation of, and establishment of priorities among, market opportunities for industrial and commercial users of all types (including public utilities and industrial parks) to utilize energy and materials recovered from municipal waste;

"(B) comparisons of the relative costs of energy recovered from municipal waste in relation to the costs of energy derived from fossil fuels and other sources;

"(C) studies of the transportation and storage problems and other problems associated with the development of energy and materials recovery technology, including curbside source separation;

"(D) the evaluation and establishment of priorities among ways of conserving energy or materials which contribute to the waste stream;

"(E) comparison of the relative total costs between conserving resources snd disposing of or recovering such waste; and

"(F) studies of impediments to resource conservation or recovery, including business practices, transportation requirements, or storage difficulties.

Such studies and analyses shall also include studies of other sources of solid waste from which energy and materials may be recovered or minimized.

"CRITERIA FOR SANITARY LANDFILLS;
SANITARY LANDFILLS REQUIRED FOR ALL DISPOSAL

"Sec. 4004. (a) CRITERIA FOR SANITARY LANDFILLS.—Not later than one year after the date of enactment of this section, after consultation with the States, and after notice and public hearings, the Administrator shall promulgate regulations containing criteria for determining which facilities shall be classified as sanitary landfills and which shall be classified as open dumps within the meaning of this Act. At a minimum, such criteria shall provide that a facility may be classified as a sanitary landfill and not an open dump only if there is no reasonable probability of adverse effects on health or the environment from disposal of solid waste at such facility. Such regulations may provide for the classification of the types of sanitary landfills.

"(b) DISPOSAL REQUIRED TO BE IN SANITARY LANDFILLS, ETC.—For purposes of complying with section 4003(2) each State plan shall prohibit the establishment of open dumps and contain a requirement that disposal of all solid waste within the State shall be in compliance with such section 4003(2).

"(c) EFFECTIVE DATE.—The prohibition contained in subsection (b) shall take effect on the date six months after the date of promulgation of regulations under subsection (a) or on the date of approval of the State plan, whichever is later.

"UPGRADING OF OPEN DUMPS

"Sec. 4005. (a) CLOSING OR UPGRADING OF EXISTING OPEN DUMPS.—Upon promulgation of criteria under section 1008(a)(3), any solid waste management practice or disposal of solid waste or hazardous waste which constitutes the open dumping of solid waste or hazardous waste is prohibited, except in the case of any practice or disposal of solid waste under a timetable or schedule for compliance established under this section. For purposes of complying with section 4003(2) and 4003(3), each State plan shall contain a requirement that all existing disposal facilities or sites for solid waste in such State which are open dumps listed in the inventory under subsection (b) shall comply with such measures as may be promulgated by the Administrator to eliminate health hazards and minimize potential health hazards. Each such plan shall establish, for any entity which demonstrates that it has considered other public or private alternatives for solid waste management to comply with the prohibition on open dumping and is unable to utilize such alternatives to so comply, a timetable or schedule for compliance for such practice or disposal of solid waste which specifies a schedule of remedial measures, including an enforceable sequence of actions or operations, leading to compliance with the prohibition on open dumping of solid waste within a reasonable time (not to exceed 5 years from the date of publication of the criteria under section 1008(a)(3).

"(b) INVENTORY.--To assist the States in complying with section 4003(3), not later than one year after promulgation of regulations under section 4004, the Administrator, with the cooperation of the Bureau of the Census shall publish an inventory of all disposal facilities or sites in the United States which are open dumps within the meaning of this Act.

"PROCEDURE FOR DEVELOPMENT AND IMPLEMENTATION OF STATE PLAN

"Sec. 4006. (a) IDENTIFICATION OF REGIONS.--Within one hundred and eighty days after publication of guidelines under section 4002(a)(relating to identification of regions), the Governor of each State, after consultation with local elected officials, shall promulgate regulations based on such guidelines identifying the boundaries of each area within the State which, as a result of urban concentrations, geographic conditions, markets, and other factors, is appropriate for carrying out regional solid waste management. Such regulations may be modified from time to time (identifying additional or different regions) pursuant to such guidelines.

"(b) IDENTIFICATION OF STATE AND LOCAL AGENCIES AND RESPONSIBILITIES.--(1) Within one hundred and eighty days after the Governor promulgates regulations under subsection (a), for purposes of facilitating the development and implementation of a State plan which will meet the minimum requirements of section 4003, the State, together with appropriate elected officials of general purpose units of local government, shall jointly (A) identify an agency to develop the State plan and identify one or more agencies to implement such plan, and (B) identify which solid waste management activities will, under such State plan, be planned for and carried out by the State and which such management activities will, under such State plan, be planned for and carried out by a regional or local authority or a combination of regional or local and State authorities. If a multifunctional regional agency authorized by State law to conduct solid waste planning and management (the members of which are appointed by the Governor) is in existence on the date of enactment of this Act, the Governor shall identify such authority for purposes of carrying out within such region clause (A) of this paragraph. Where feasible, designation of the agency for the affected area designated nder section 208 of the Federal Water Pollution Control Act (86 Stat. 839) shall be considered. A State agency identified under this paragraph shall be established or designated by the Governor of such State. Local or regional agencies identified under this paragraph shall be composed of individuals at least a majority of whom are elected local officials.

"(2) If planning and implementation agencies are not identified and designated or established as required under paragraph (1) for any affected area, the governor shall, before the date two hundred and seventy days after promulgation of regulations under subsection (a), establish or designate a State agency to develop and implement the State plan for such area.

"(c) INTERSTATE REGIONS.--(1) In the case of any region which, pursuant to the guidelines published by the Administrator under section 4002(a) (relating to identification of regions), would be located in two or more States, the Governors of the respective States, after consultation with local elected officials, shall consult, cooperate, and enter into agreements identifying the boundaries of such region pursuant to subsection (a).

"(2) Within one hundred and eighty days after an interstate region is identified by agreement under paragraph (1), appropriate elected officials of general purpose units of local government within such region shall jointly establish or designate an agency to develop a plan for such region. If no such agency is established or designated within such period by such officials, the Governors of the respective States may, by agreement, establish or designate for such purpose a single representative organization including elected officials of general purpose units of local government within such region.

"(3) Implementation of interstate regional solid waste management plans shall be conducted by units of local government, for any portion of a region within their jurisdiction, or by multijurisdictional agencies or authorities designated in accordance with State law, including those designated by agreement by such units of local government for such purpose. If no such unit, agency, or authority is so designated, the respective Governors shall designate or establish a single interstate agency to implement such plan.

"(4) For purposes of this subtitle, so much of an interstate regional plan as is carried out within a particular State shall be deemed part of the State plan for such State.

"APPROVAL OF STATE PLAN; FEDERAL ASSISTANCE

"Sec. 4007. (a) PLAN APPROVAL.--The Administrator shall, within six months after a State plan has been submitted for approval, approve or disapprove the plan. The Administrator shall approve a plan if he determines that--

"(1) it meets the requirements of paragraphs (1), (2), (3), and (5) of section 4003; and

"(2) it contains provision for revision of such plan, after notice and public hearing, whenever the Administrator, by regulation determines--

"(A) that revised regulations respecting minimum requirements have been promulgated under paragraphs (1), (2), (3), and (5) of section 4003 with which the State plan is not in compliance;

"(B) that information has become available which demonstrates the inadequacy of the plan to effectuate the purposes of this subtitle; or

"(C) that such revision is otherwise necessary.

The Administrator shall review approved plans from time to time and if he determines that revision or corrections are necessary to bring such plan into compliance with the minimum requirements promulgated under section 4003 (including new or revised requirements), he shall, after notice and opportunity for public hearing, withdraw his approval of such plan. Such withdrawal of approval shall cease to be effective upon the Administrator's determination that such complies with such minimum requirements.

"(b) ELIGIBILITY OF STATES FOR FEDERAL FINANCIAL ASSISTANCE.--

"(1) The Administrator shall approve a State application for financial assistance under this subtitle, and make grants to such State, if such State and local and regional authorities within such State have complied with the requirements of section 4006 within the period required under such section and if such State has a State plan which has been approved by the Administrator under this subtitle.

"(2) The Administrator shall approve a State application for financial assistance under this subtitle, and make grants to such State, for fiscal years 1978 and 1979 if the Administrator determines that the State plan continues to be eligible for approval under subsection (a) and is being implemented by the State.

"(3) Upon withdrawal of approval of a State plan under subsection (a), the Administrator shall withhold Federal financial and technical assistance under this subtitle (other than such technical assistance as may be necessary to assist in obtaining the reinstatement of approval) until such time as such approval is reinstated.

"(c) EXISTING ACTIVITIES.--Nothing in this subtitle shall be construed to prevent or affect any activities respecting solid waste planning or management which are carried out by the State, regional, or local authorities unless such activities are inconsistent with a State plan approved by the Administrator under this subtitle.

"FEDERAL ASSISTANCE

"Sec. 4008. (a) AUTHORIZATION OF FEDERAL FINANCIAL ASSISTANCE.--(1) There are authorized to be appropriated $30,000,000 for the fiscal year 1978, $40,000,000 for fiscal year 1979, $20,000,000 for fiscal year 1980, $15,000,000 for fiscal year 1981, and $20,000,000 for fiscal year 1982 for purposes of financial assistance to States and local, regional, and interstate authorities for the development and implementation of plans approved by the Administrator under this subtitle (other than the provisions of such plans referred to in sec. 4003(b), relating to feasibility planning for municipal waste energy and materials conservation and recovery).

"(2)(A) The Administrator is authorized to provide financial assistance to States, counties, municipalities, and intermunicipal agencies and State and local public solid waste management authorities for implementation of programs to provide solid waste management, resource recovery, and resource conservation services and hazardous waste management. Such assistance shall include assistance for facility planning and feasibility studies; expert consultation; surveys and analyses of market needs; marketing of recovered resources; technology assessments; legal expenses; construction feasibility studies; source separation projects; and fiscal or economic investigations or studies; but such assistance shall not include any other element of construction, or any acquisition of land or interest in land, or any subsidy for the price of recovered resources. Agencies assisted under this subsection shall consider existing solid waste management and hazardous waste management services and facilities as well as facilities proposed for construction.

"(B) An applicant for financial assistance under this paragraph must agree to comply with respect to the project or program assisted with the applicable requirements of section 4005 and Subtitle C of this Act and apply applicable solid waste management practices, methods, and levels of control consistent with any guidelines published pursuant to section 1008 of this Act. Assistance under this paragraph shall be available only for programs certified by the State to be consistent with any applicable State or areawide solid waste management plan or program. Applicants for technical and financial assistance under this section shall not preclude or foreclose consideration of programs for the recovery of recyclable materials through source separation or other resource recovery techniques.

"(C) There are authorized to be appropriated $15,000,000 for each of the fiscal years 1978 and 1979 for the purposes of this section. There are authorized to be appropriated $10,000,000 for fiscal year 1980, $10,000,000 for fiscal year 1981, and $10,000,000 for fiscal year 1982 for purposes of this paragraph.

"(3)(A) There is authorized to be appropriated for the fiscal year beginning October 1, 1981, and for each fiscal year thereafter before October 1, 1986, $4,000,000 for purposes of making grants to States to carry out section 4003(b). No amount may be appropriated for such purposes for the fiscal year beginning on October 1, 1986, or for any fiscal year thereafter.

"(B) Assistance provided by the Administrator under this paragraph shall be used only for the purposes specified in section 4003(b). Such assistance may not be used for purposes of land acquisition, final facility design, equipment purchase, construction, startup or operation activities.

"(C) Where appropriate, any State receiving assistance under this paragraph may make all or any part of such assistance available to municipalities within the State to carry out the activities specified in section 4003(b)(1)(A) and (B).

"(b) STATE ALLOTMENT.--The sums appropriated in any fiscal year under subsection (a)(1) shall be allotted by the Administrator among all States, in the ratio that the population in each State bears to the population in all of the States, except that no State shall receive less than one-half of 1 per centum of the sums so allotted in any fiscal year. No State shall receive any grant under this section during any fiscal year when its expenditures of non-Federal funds for other than nonrecurrent expenditures for solid waste management control programs will be less than its expenditures were for such programs during fiscal year 1975, except that such funds may be reduced by an amount equal to their proportionate share of any general reduction of State spending ordered by the Governor or legislature of such State. No State shall receive any grant for solid waste management programs unless the Administrator is satisfied that such grant will be so used as to supplement and, to the extent practicable, increase the level of State, local, regional, or other non-Federal funds that would in the absence of such grant be made available for the maintenance of such programs.

"(c) DISTRIBUTION OF FEDERAL FINANCIAL ASSISTANCE WITHIN THE STATE.--The Federal assistance allotted to the States under subsection (b) shall be allocated by the State receiving such funds to State, local, regional, and interstate authorities carrying out planning and implementation of the State plan. Such allocation shall be based upon the responsibilities of the respective parties as determined pursuant to section 4006(b).

"(d) TECHNICAL ASSISTANCE.--(1) The Administrator may provide technical assistance to State and local governments for purposes of developing and implementing State plans. Technical assistance respecting resource recovery and conservation may be provided through resource recovery and conservation panels, established in the Environmental Protection Agency under subtitle B, to assist the State and local governments with respect to particular resource recovery and conservation projects under consideration and to evaluate their effect on the State plan.

[Editor's Note: The following subsection (2) is from the Used Oil Recycling Act of 1980. See additional subsection (2) following this subsection.]

"(2) In carrying out this subsection, the Administrator may, upon request, provide technical assistance to States to assist in the removal or modification of legal, institutional, economic, and other impediments to the recycling of used oil. Such impediments may include laws, regulations, and policies, including State procurement policies, which are not favorable to the recycling of used oil.

[Editor's Note: The following subsection (2) is from the Solid Waste Disposal Act Amendments of 1980. See additional subsection (2) above.]

"(2) In carrying out this subsection, the Administrator is authorized to provide technical assistance to States, municipalities, regional authorities, and intermunicipal agencies upon request, to assist in the removal or modification of legal, institutional, and economic impediments which have the effect of impeding the development of systems and facilities to recover energy and materials from municipal waste or to conserve energy or materials which contribute to the waste stream. Such impediments may include--

"(A) laws, regulations, and policies, including State and local procurement policies, which are not favorable to resource conservation and recovery policies, systems, and facilities.

"(B) impediments to the financing of facilities to conserve or recover energy and materials from municipal waste through the exercise of State and local authority to issue revenue bonds and the use of State and local credit assistance; and

"(C) impediments to institutional arrangements necessary to undertake projects for the conservation or recovery of energy and materials from municipal waste, including the creation of special districts, authorities, or corporations where necessary having the power to secure the supply of waste of a project, to conserve resources, to implement the project, and to undertake related activities.

"(e) SPECIAL COMMUNITIES.--(1) The Administrator, in cooperation with State and local officials, shall identify local governments within the United States (A) having a solid waste disposal facility (i) which is owned by the unit of local government, (ii) for which an order has been issued by the State to cease receiving solid waste for treatment, storage, or disposal, and (iii) which is subject to a State-approved end-use recreation plan;

"(B) which are located over an aquifer which is the source of drinking water for any person or public water system and which has serious environmental problems resulting from the disposal of such solid waste, including possible methane migration;

"(2) There is authorized to be appropriated to the Administrator $2,500,000 for the fiscal year 1980 and $1,500,000 for each of the fiscal years 1981 and 1982 to make grants to be used for the containment and stabilization of solid waste located at the disposal sites referred to in paragraph (1). Not more than one community in any State shall be eligible for grants under this paragraph and not more than one project in any State shall be eligible for such grants. No unit of local government shall be eligible for grants under this paragraph with respect to any site which exceeds 65 acres in size.

[Editor's Note: The following subsection (f) is from the Used Oil Recycling Act of 1980. See additional subsection (f) following this subsection.]

"(f) ASSISTANCE TO STATES FOR DISCRETIONARY PROGRAM FOR RECYCLED OIL.--(1) The Administrator may make grants to States, which have a State plan approved under section 4007, or which have submitted a State plan for approval under such section, if such plan includes the discretionary provisions described in section 4003(b). Grants under this subsection shall be for purposes of assisting the State in carrying out such discretionary provisions. No grant under this subsection may be used for construction or for the acquisition of land or equipment.

"(2) Grants under this subsection shall be allotted among the States in the same manner as provided in the first sentence of subsection (b).

"(3) No grant may be made under this subsection unless an application therefor is submitted to, and approved by, the Administrator. The application shall be in such form, be submitted in such manner, and contain such information as the Administrator may require.

"(4) For purposes of making grants under this subsection, there are authorized to be appropriated $5,000,000 for fiscal year 1982 and $5,000,000 for fiscal year 1983.

[Editor's Note: The following subsection (f) is from the Solid Waste Disposal Act Amendments of 1980. See additional subsection (f) above.]

"(f) ASSISTANCE TO MUNICIPALITIES FOR ENERGY AND MATERIALS CONSERVATION AND RECOVERY PLANNING ACTIVITIES.--(1) The Administrator is authorized to make grants to municipalities, regional authorities, and intermunicipal agencies to carry out activities described in subparagraphs (A) and (B) of section 4003(b)(1). Such grants may be made only pursuant to an application submitted to the Administrator by the municipality which application has been approved by the State and determined by the State to be consistent with any State plan approved or submitted under this subtitle or any other appropriate planning carried out by the State.

"(2) There is authorized to be appropriated for the fiscal year beginning October 1, 1981, and for each fiscal year thereafter before October 1, 1986, $8,000,000 for purposes of making grants to municipalities under this subsection. No amount may be appropriated for such purposes for the fiscal year beginning on October 1, 1986, or for any fiscal year thereafter.

"(3) Assistance provided by the Administrator under this subsection shall be used only for the purposes specified in paragraph (1). Such assistance may not be used for purposes of land acquisition, final facility design, equipment purchase, construction, startup or operation activities.

"RURAL COMMUNITIES ASSISTANCE

"Sec. 4009. (a) IN GENERAL.--The Administrator shall make grants to States to provide assistance to municipalities with a population of five thousand or less, or counties with a population of ten thousand or less or less than twenty persons per square mile and not within a metropolitan area, for solid waste management facilities (including equipment) necessary to meet the requirements of section 4005 of this Act or restrictions on open burning or other requirements arising under the Clean Air Act or the Federal Water Pollution Control Act. Such assistance shall only be available—

"(1) to any municipality or county which could not feasibly be included in a solid waste management system or facility serving an urbanized, multijurisdictional area because of its distance from such systems;

"(2) where existing or planned solid waste management services or facilities are unavailable or insufficient to comply with the requirements of section 4005 of this Act; and

"(3) for systems which are certified by the State to be consistent with any plans or programs established under any State or areawide planning process.

"(b) ALLOTMENT.--The Administrator shall allot the sums appropriated to carry out this section in any fiscal year among the States in accordance with regulations promulgated by him on the basis of the average of the ratio which the population of rural areas of each State bears to the total population of rural areas of all the States the ratio which the population of counties in each State having less than twenty persons per square mile bears to the total population of such counties in all the States, and the ratio which the population of such low-density counties in each State having 33 per centum or more of all families with incomes not in excess of 125 per centum of the poverty level bears to the total population of such counties in all of the States.

"(c) LIMIT.--The amount of any grant under this section shall not exceed 75 per centum of the costs of the project. No assistance under this section shall be available for the acquisition of land or interests in land.

"(d) APPROPRIATIONS.--There are authorized to be appropriated $25,000,000 for each of the fiscal years 1978 and 1979 to carry out this section. There are authorized to be appropriated $10,000,000 for the fiscal year 1980 and

$15,000,000 for each of the fiscal years 1981 and 1982 to carry out this section.

"Subtitle E--Duties of the Secretary of Commerce
in Resource and Recovery

"FUNCTIONS

"Sec. 5001. The Secretary of Commerce shall encourage greater commercialization of proven resource recovery technology by providing--

"(1) accurate specifications for recovered materials;

"(2) stimulation of development of markets for recovered materials;

"(3) promotion of proven technology; and

"(4) a forum for the exchange of technical and economic data relating to resource recovery facilities.

"DEVELOPMENT OF SPECIFICATIONS FOR SECONDARY MATERIALS

"Sec. 5002. The Secretary of Commerce, acting through the National Bureau of Standards, and in conjunction with national standards-setting organizations in resource recovery, shall, after public hearings, and not later than two years after September 1, 1979, publish guidelines for the development of specifications for the classification of materials recovered from waste which were destined for disposal. The specifications shall pertain to the physical and chemical properties and characteristics of such materials with regard to their use in replacing virgin materials in various industrial, commercial, and governmental uses. In establishing such guidelines the Secretary shall also, to the extent feasible, provide such information as may be necessary to assist Federal agencies with procurement of items containing recovered materials. The Secretary shall continue to cooperate with national standards-setting organizations, as may be necessary, to encourage the publication, promulgation and updating of standards for recovered materials and for the use of recovered materials in various industrial, commercial, and governmental uses.

"DEVELOPMENT OF MARKETS FOR RECOVERED MATERIALS

"Sec. 5003. The Secretary of Commerce shall within two years after September 1, 1979 take such actions as may be necessary to--

"(1) identify the geographical location of existing or potential markets for recovered materials;

"(2) identify the economic and technical barriers to the use of recovered materials; and

"(3) encourage the development of new uses for recovered materials.

"TECHNOLOGY PROMOTION

"Sec. 5004. The Secretary of Commerce is authorized to evaluate the commercial feasibility of resource recovery facilities and to publish the results of such evaluation, and to develop a data base for purposes of assisting persons in choosing such a system.

"NONDISCRIMINATION REQUIREMENT

"Sec. 5005. In establishing any policies which may affect the development of new markets for recovered materials and in making any determination concerning whether or not to impose monitoring or other controls on any marketing or transfer of recovered materials, the Secretary of Commerce may consider whether to establish the same or similar policies or impose the same or similar monitoring or other controls on virgin materials.

"AUTHORIZATION OF APPROPRIATIONS

"Sec. 5006. There are authorized to be appropriated to the Secretary of Commerce $5,000,000 for each of fiscal years 1980, 1981, and 1982 to carry out the purposes of this subtitle.

"Subtitle F—Federal Responsibilities

"APPLICATION OF FEDERAL, STATE, AND LOCAL LAW TO FEDERAL FACILITIES

"Sec. 6001. Each department, agency, and instrumentality of the executive, legislative, and judicial branches of the Federal Government (1) having jurisdiction over any solid waste management facility or disposal site, or (2) engaged in any activity resulting, or which may result, in the disposal or management of solid waste or hazardous waste shall be subject to and comply with, all Federal, State, interstate, and local requirements, both substantive and procedural (including any requirement for permits or reporting or any provisions for injunctive relief and such sanctions as may be imposed by a court to enforce such relief), respecting control and abatement of solid waste or hazardous waste disposal in the same manner, and to the same extent, as any person is subject to such requirements, including the payment of reasonable service charges. Neither the United States, nor any agent, employee, or officer thereof, shall be immune or exempt from any process or sanction of any State or Federal Court with respect to the enforcement of any such injunctive relief. The President may exempt any solid waste management facility of any department, agency, or instrumentality in the executive branch from compliance with such a requirement if he determines it to be in the paramount interest of the United States to do so. No such exemption shall be granted due to lack of appropriation unless the President shall have specifically requested such appropriation as a part of the budgetary process and the Congress shall have failed to make available such requested appropriation. Any exemption shall be for a period not in excess of one year, but additional exemptions may be granted for periods not to exceed one year upon the President's making a new determination. The President shall report each January to the Congress all exemptions from the requirements of this section granted during the preceding calendar year, together with his reason for granting each such exemption.

"FEDERAL PROCUREMENT

"Sec. 6002. (a) APPLICATION OF SECTION.—Except as provided in subsection (b), a procuring agency shall comply with the requirements set forth in this section and any regulations issued under this section, with respect to any purchase or acquisition of a procurement item where the purchase price of the item exceeds $10,000 or where the quantity of such items or of functionally equivalent items purchased or acquired in the course of the preceding fiscal year was $10,000 or more.

"(b) PROCUREMENT SUBJECT TO OTHER LAW.--Any procurement, by any procuring agency, which is subject to regulations of the Administrator under section 6004 (as promulgated before the date of enactment of this section under comparable provisions of prior law) shall not be subject to the requirements of this section to the extent that such requirements are inconsistent with such regulations.

"(c) REQUIREMENTS.--(1) After the date specified in applicable guidelines prepared pursuant to subsection (e) of this section, each procuring agency which procures any items designated in such guidelines shall procure such items composed of the highest percentage of recovered materials practicable, consistent with maintaining a satisfactory level of competition, considering such guidelines. The decision not to procure such items shall be based on a determination that such procurement items--

"(A) are not reasonably available within a reasonable period of time;

"(B) fail to meet the performance standards set forth in the applicable specifications or fail to meet the reasonable performance standards of the procuring agencies; or

"(C) are only available at an unreasonable price. Any determination under subparagraph (B) shall be made on the basis of the guidelines of the Bureau of Standards in any case in which such material is covered by such guidelines.

"(2) Agencies that generate heat, mechanical, or electrical energy from fossil fuel in systems that have the technical capacity of using energy or fuels derived from solid waste as a primary or supplementary fuel shall use such capability to the maximum extent practicable.

"(3) After the date specified in any applicable guidelines prepared pursuant to subsection (e) of this section, contracting officers shall require that vendors:

"(A) certify that the percentage of recovered materials to be used in the performance of the contract will be at least the amount required by applicable specifications or other contractual requirements and

"(B) estimate the percentage of the total material utilized for the performance of the contract which is recovered materials.

"(d) SPECIFICATIONS.--All Federal agencies that have the responsibility for drafting or reviewing specifications for procurement items procured by Federal agencies shall--

"(1) as expeditiously as possible but in any event no later than five years after the date of enactment of this Act, eliminate from such specifications--

"(A) any exclusion of recovered materials and

"(B) any requirement that items be manufactured from virgin materials; and

"(2) within one year after the date of publication of applicable guidelines under subsection (e), or as otherwise specified in such guidelines, assure that such specifications require the use of recovered materials to the maximum extent possible without jeopardizing the intended end use of the item.

"(e) GUIDELINES.--The Administrator, after consultation with the Administrator of General Services, the Secretary of Commerce (acting through the Bureau of Standards), and the Public Printer, shall prepare, and from time to time revise, guidelines for the use of procuring agencies in complying with the requirements of this section. Such guidelines shall--

"(1) designate those items which are or can be produced with recovered materials and whose procurement by procuring agencies will carry out the objectives of this section; and

"(2) set forth recommended practices with respect to the procurement of recovered materials and items containing such materials and with respect to certification by vendors of the percentage of recovered materials used, and shall provide information as to the availability, relative price, and performance of such materials and items and where appropriate shall recommend the level of recovered material to be contained in the procured product. The Administrator shall prepare final guidelines for at least three product categories, including paper, by May 1, 1981, and for two additional product categories, including construction materials, by September 30, 1982. In making the designation under paragraph (1), the Administrator shall consider, but is not limited in his considerations, to—

"(A) the availability of such items;

"(B) the impact of the procurement of such items by procuring agencies on the volume of solid waste which must be treated, stored or disposed of;

"(C) the economic and technological feasibility of producing and using other items; and

"(D) other uses for such recovered materials.

"(f) PROCUREMENT OF SERVICES.—A procuring agency shall, to the maximum extent practicable, manage or arrange for the procurement of solid waste management services in a manner which maximizes energy and resource recovery.

"(g) EXECUTIVE OFFICE.—The Office of Procurement Policy in the Executive Office of the President, in cooperation with the Administrator, shall implement the policy expressed in this section. It shall be the responsibility of the Office of Procurement Policy to coordinate this policy with other policies for Federal procurement, in such a way as to maximize the use of recovered resources, and to annually report to the Congress on actions taken by Federal agencies and the progress made in the implementation of such policy.

"COOPERATION WITH THE ENVIRONMENTAL PROTECTION AGENCY

"Sec. 6003. (a) GENERAL RULE.—All Federal agencies shall assist the Administrator in carrying out his functions under this Act and shall promptly make available all requested information concerning past or present Agency waste management practices and past or present Agency owned, leased, or operated solid or hazardous waste facilities. This information shall be provided in such format as may be determined by the Administrator.

"(b) INFORMATION RELATING TO ENERGY AND MATERIALS CONSERVATION AND RECOVERY.—The Administrator shall collect, maintain, and disseminate information concerning the market potential of energy and materials recovered from solid waste, including materials obtained through source separation, and information concerning the savings potential of conserving resources contributing to the waste stream. The Administrator shall identify the regions in which the increased substitution of such energy for energy derived from fossil fuels and other sources is most likely to be feasible, and provide information on the technical and economic aspects of developing integrated resource conservation or recovery systems which provide for the recovery of source-separated materials to be recycled or the conservation of resources. The Administrator shall utilize the authorities of subsection (a) in carrying out this subsection.

"APPLICABILITY OF SOLID WASTE DISPOSAL GUIDELINES TO EXECUTIVE AGENCIES

"Sec. 6004. (a) COMPLIANCE.—(1) If—

"(A) an Executive agency (as defined in section 105 of title 5, United States Code) or any unit of the legislative branch of the Federal Government has jurisdiction over any real property or facility the operation or administration of which involves such agency in solid waste management activities, or

"(B) such an agency enters into a contract with any person for the operation by such person of any Federal property or facility, and the performance of such contract involves such person in solid waste management activities,

then such an agency shall insure compliance with the guidelines recommended under section 1008 and the purposes of this Act in the operation or administration of such property or facility, or the performance of such contract, as the case may be.

"(2) Each Executive agency or any unit of the legislative branch of the Federal Government which conducts any activity--

"(A) which generates solid waste, and

"(B) which, if conducted by a person other than such agency, would require a permit or license from such agency in order to dispose of such solid waste,

shall insure compliance with such guidelines and the purposes of this Act in conducting such activity.

"(3) Each Executive agency which permits the use of Federal property for purposes of disposal of solid waste shall insure compliance with such guidelines and the purposes of this Act in the disposal of such waste.

"(4) The President or the Committee on House Administration of the House of Representatives and the Committee on Rules and Administration of the Senate with regard to any unit of the legislative branch of the Federal Government shall prescribe regulations to carry out this subsection.

"(b) LICENSES AND PERMITS.--Each Executive agency which issues any license or permit for disposal of solid waste shall, prior to the issuance of such license or permit, consult with the Administrator to insure compliance with guidelines recommended under section 1008 and the purposes of this Act.

"Subtitle G—Miscellaneous Provisions

"EMPLOYEE PROTECTION

"Sec. 7001. (a) GENERAL.--No person shall fire, or in any other way discriminate against, or cause to be fired or discriminated against, any employee or any authorized representative of employees by reason of the fact that such employee or representative has filed, instituted, or caused to be filed or instituted any proceeding under this Act or under any applicable implementation plan, or has testified or is about to testify in any proceeding resulting from the administration or enforcement of the provisions of this Act or of any applicable implementation plan.

"(b) REMEDY.--Any employee or a representative of employees who believes that he has been fired or otherwise discriminated against by any person in violation of subsection (a) of this section may, within thirty days after such alleged violation occurs, apply to the Secretary of Labor for a review of such firing or alleged discrimination. A copy of the application shall be sent to such person who shall be the respondent. Upon receipt of such application, the Secretary of Labor shall cause such investigation to be made as he deems appropriate. Such investigation shall provide an opportunity for a public hearing at the request of any party to such review to enable the parties to present information relating to such alleged violation. The parties shall be given written notice of the time and place of the hearing at least five days prior to the hearing. Any such hearing shall be of record and shall be subject to section 554 of title 5 of the United

States Code. Upon receiving the report of such investigation, the Secretary of Labor shall make findings of fact. If he finds that such violation did occur, he shall issue a decision, incorporating an order therein and his findings, requiring the party committing such violation to take such affirmative action to abate the violation as the Secretary of Labor deems appropriate, including, but not limited to, the rehiring or reinstatement of the employee or representative of employees to his former position with compensation. If he finds that there was no such violation, he shall issue an order denying the application. Such order issued by the Secretary of Labor under this subparagraph shall be subject to judicial review in the same manner as orders and decisions of the Administrator or subject to judicial review under this Act.

"(c) COSTS.--Whenever an order is issued under this section to abate such violation, at the request of the applicant, a sum equal to the aggregate amount of all costs and expenses (including the attorney's fees) as determined by the Secretary of Labor, to have been reasonably incurred by the applicant for, or in connection with, the institution and prosecution of such proceedings, shall be assessed against the person committing such violation.

"(d) EXCEPTION.--This section shall have no application to any employee who, acting without direction from his employer (or his agent) deliberately violates any requirement of this Act.

"(e) EMPLOYMENT SHIFTS AND LOSS.--The Administrator shall conduct continuing evaluations of potential loss or shifts of employment which may result from the administration or enforcement of the provisions of this Act and applicable inplementation plans, including where appropriate, investigating threatened plant closures or reductions in employment allegedly resulting from such administration or enforcement. Any employee who is discharged, or laid off, threatened with discharge or layoff, or otherwise discriminated against by any person because of the alleged results of such administration or enforcement, or any representative of such employee, may request the Administrator to conduct a full investigation of the matter. The Administrator shall thereupon investigate the matter and, at the request of any party, shall hold public hearings on not less than five days' notice, and shall at such hearings require the parties, including the employer involved, to present information relating to the actual or potential effect of such administration or enforcement on employment and on any alleged discharge, layoff, or other discrimination and the detailed reasons or justification therefor. Any such hearing shall be of record and shall be subject to section 554 of title 5 of the United States Code. Upon receiving the report of such investigation, the Administrator shall make findings of fact as to the effect of such administration or enforcement on employment and on the alleged discharge, layoff, or discrimination and shall make such recommendations as he deems appropriate. Such report, findings, and recommendations shall be available to the public. Nothing in this subsection shall be construed to require or authorize the Administrator or any State to modify or withdraw any standard, limitation, or any other requirement of this Act or any applicable implementation plan.

"(f) OCCUPATIONAL SAFETY AND HEALTH.--In order to assist the Secretary of Labor and the Director of the National Institute for Occupational Safety and Health in carrying out their duties under the Occupational Safety and Health Act of 1970, the Administrator shall--

"(1) provide the following information, as such information becomes available, to the Secretary and the Director:

"(A) the identity of any hazardous waste generation, treatment, storage, disposal facility or site where cleanup is planned or underway;

"(B) information identifying the hazards to which persons working at a hazardous waste generation, treatment, storage, disposal facility or site or otherwise handling hazardous waste may be exposed, the nature and extent of the exposure, and methods to protect workers from such hazards; and

"(C) incidents of worker injury or harm at a hazardous waste generation, treatment, storage or disposal facility or site; and

"(2) notify the Secretary and the Director of the Administrator's receipt of notifications under section 3010 or reports under sections 3002, 3003, and 3004 of this title and make such notifications and reports available to the Secretary and the Director.

"CITIZEN SUITS

"Sec. 7002. (a) IN GENERAL.--Except as provided in subsection (b) or (c) of this section, any person may commence a civil action on his own behalf--

"(1) against any person (including (a) the United States, and (b) any other governmental instrumentality or agency, to the extent permitted by the eleventh amendment to the Constitution) who is alleged to be in violation of any permit, standard, regulation, condition, requirement, or order which has become effective pursuant to this Act; or

"(2) against the Administrator where there is alleged a failure of the Administrator to perform any act or duty under this Act which is not discretionary with the Administrator.

Any action under paragraph (a) (1) of this subsection shall be brought in the district court for the district in which the alleged violation occurred. Any action brought under paragraph (a) (2) of this subsection may be brought in the district court for the district in which the alleged violation occurred or in the District Court of the District of Columbia. The district court shall have jurisdiction, without regard to the amount in controversy or the citizenship of the parties, to enforce such regulation or order, or to order the Administrator to perform such act or duty as the case may be.

"(b) ACTIONS PROHIBITED.--No action may be commenced under paragraph (a) (1) of this section--

"(1) prior to sixty days after the plaintiff has given notice of the violation (A) to the Administrator; (B) to the State in which the alleged violation occurs; and (C) to any alleged violator of such permit, standard, regulation, condition, requirement, or order; or

"(2) if the Administrator or State has commenced and is diligently prosecuting a civil or criminal action in a court of the United States or a State to require compliance with such permit, standard, regulation, condition, requirement, or order: PROVIDED, HOWEVER, That in any such action in a court of the United States any person may intervene as a matter of right.

"(c) NOTICE.--No action may be commenced under paragraph (a) (2) of this section prior to sixty days after the plaintiff has given notice to the Administrator that he will commence such action, except that such action may be brought immediately after such notification in the case of an action under this section respecting a violation of Subtitle C of this Act. Notice under this subsection shall be given in such manner as the Administrator shall prescribe by regulation. Any action respecting a violation under this Act may be brought under this section only in the judicial district in which such alleged violation occurs.

"(d) INTERVENTION.--In any action under this section the Administrator, if not a party, may intervene as a matter of right.

"(e) COSTS.--The court, in issuing any final order in any action brought pursuant to this section, may award costs of litigation (including reasonable attorney and expert witness fees) to any party, whenever the court determines such an award is appropriate. The court may, if a temporary restraining order or preliminary injunction is sought, require the filing of a bond or equivalent security in accordance with the Federal Rules of Civil Procedure.

"(f) OTHER RIGHTS PRESERVED.--Nothing in this section shall restrict any right which any person (or class of persons) may have under any statute or common law to seek enforcement of any standard or requirement relating to the management of solid waste or hazardous waste, or to seek any other relief (including relief against the Administrator or a State agency).

"IMMINENT HAZARD

"Sec. 7003. (a) AUTHORITY OF ADMINISTRATOR.--Notwithstanding any other provision of this Act, upon receipt of evidence that the handling, storage, treatment, transportation or disposal of any solid waste or hazardous waste may present an imminent and substantial endangerment to health or the environment, the Administrator may bring suit on behalf of the United States in the appropriate district court to immediately restrain any person contributing to such handling, storage, treatment, transportation or disposal to stop such handling, storage, treatment, transportation, or disposal or to take such other action as may be necessary. The Administrator shall provide notice to the affected State of any such suit. The Administrator may also, after notice to the affected State, take other action under this section including, but not limited to, issuing such orders as may be necessary to protect public health and the environment.

"(b) VIOLATIONS.--Any person who willfully violates, or fails or refuses to comply with, any order of the Administrator under subsection (a) may, in an action brought in the appropriate United States district court to enforce such order, be fined not more than $5,000 for each day in which such violation occurs or such failure to comply continues.

"PETITION FOR REGULATIONS; PUBLIC PARTICIPATION

"Sec. 7004. (a) PETITION.--Any person may petition the Administrator for the promulgation, amendment, or repeal of any regulation under this Act. Within a reasonable time following receipt of such petition, the Administrator shall take action with respect to such petition and shall publish notice of such action in the Federal Register, together with the reasons therefor.

"(b) PUBLIC PARTICIPATION.--(1) Public participation in the development, revision, implementation, and enforcement of any regulation, guideline, information, or program under this Act shall be provided for, encouraged, and assisted by the Administrator and the States. The Administrator, in cooperation with the States, shall develop and publish minimum guidelines for public participation in such processes.

"(2) Before the issuing of a permit to any person with any respect to any facility for the treatment, storage, or disposal of hazardous wastes under section 3005, the Administrator shall--

"(A) cause to be published in major local newspapers of general circulation and broadcast over local radio stations notice of the agency's intention to issue such permit, and

"(B) transmit in writing notice of the agency's intention to issue such permit to each unit of local government having jurisdiction over the area in which such facility is proposed to be located and to each State agency having any authority under State law with respect to the construction or operation of such facility.

If within 45 days the Administrator receives written notice of opposition to the agency's intention to issue such permit and a request for a hearing, or if the Administrator determines on his own initiative, he shall hold an informal public hearing (including an opportunity for presentation of written and oral views) on whether he should issue a permit for the proposed facility. Whenever possible the Administrator shall schedule such hearing at a location convenient to the nearest population center to such proposed facility and give notice in the aforementioned manner of the date, time, and subject matter of such hearing. No State program which provides for the issuance of permits referred to in this paragraph may be authorized by the Administrator under section 3006 unless such program provides for the notice and hearing required by the paragraph.

"SEPARABILITY

"Sec. 7005. If any provision of this Act, or the application of any provision of this Act to any person or circumstance, is held invalid, the application of such provision to other persons or circumstances, and the remainder of this Act, shall not be affected thereby.

"JUDICIAL REVIEW

"Sec. 7006. (a) REVIEW OF FINAL REGULATIONS AND CERTAIN PETITIONS.--Any judicial review of final regulations promulgated pursuant to this Act and the Administrator's denial of any petition for the promulgation, amendment, or repeal of any regulation under this Act shall be in accordance with sections 701 through 706 of title 5 of the United States Code, except that--

"(1) a petition for review of action of the Administrator in promulgating any regulation, or requirement under this Act or denying any petition for the promulgation, amendment or repeal of any regulation under this Act may be filed only in the United States Court of Appeals for the District of Columbia, and such petition shall be filed within ninety days from the date of such promulgation or denial, or after such date if such petition for review is based solely on grounds arising after such ninetieth day; action of the Administrator with respect to which review could have been obtained under this subsection shall not be subject to judicial review in civil or criminal proceedings for enforcement; and

"(2) in any judicial proceeding brought under this section in which review is sought of a determination under this Act required to be made on the record after notice and opportunity for hearing, if a party seeking review under this Act applied to the court for leave to adduce additional evidence, and shows to the satisfaction of the court that the information is material and that there were reasonable grounds for the failure to adduce such evidence in the proceeding before the Administrator, the court may order such additional evidence (and evidence in rebuttal thereof) to be taken before the Administrator, and to be adduced upon the hearing in such manner and upon such terms and conditions as the court may deem proper; the Administrator may modify his findings as to the facts, or make new findings, by reason of the additional evidence so taken, and he shall file with the court such modified or new findings and his recommendation, if any, for the modification or setting aside of his original order, with the return of such additional evidence.

"(b) REVIEW OF CERTAIN ACTIONS UNDER SECTIONS 3005 AND 3006.--Review of the Administrator's action (1) in issuing, denying, modifying, or revoking any permit under section 3005, or (2) in granting, denying, or withdrawing authorization or interim authorization under section 3006, may be had by any interested person in the Circuit Court of Appeals of the United States for the

Federal judicial district in which such person resides or transacts such business upon application by such person. Any such application shall be made within ninety days from the date of such issuance, denial, modification, revocation, grant, or withdrawal, or after such date only if such application is based solely on grounds which arose after such ninetieth day. Such review shall be in accordance with sections 701 through 706 of title 5 of the United States Code.

"GRANTS OR CONTRACTS FOR TRAINING PROJECTS

"Sec. 7007. (a) GENERAL AUTHORITY.--The Administrator is authorized to make grants to, and contracts with any eligible organization. For purposes of this section the term "eligible organization" means a State or interstate agency, a municipality, educational institution, and any other organization which is capable of effectively carrying out a project which may be funded by grant under subsection (b) of this section.

"(b) PURPOSES.--(1) Subject to the provisions of paragraph (2), grants or contracts may be made to pay all or a part of the costs, as may be determined by the Administrator, of any project operated or to be operated by an eligible organization, which is designed--

"(A) to develop, expand, or carry out a program (which may combine training, education, and employment) for training persons for occupations involving the management, supervision, design, operation, or maintenance of solid waste management and resource recovery equipment and facilities; or

"(B) to train instructors and supervisory personnel to train or supervise persons in occupations involving the design, operation, and maintenance of solid waste management and resource recovery equipment and facilities.

"(2) A grant or contract authorized by paragraph (1) of this subsection may be made only upon application to the Administrator at such time or times and containing such information as he may prescribe, except that no such application shall be approved unless it provides for the same procedures and reports (and access to such reports and to other records) as required by section 207(b) (4) and (5) (as in effect before the date of the enactment of Resource Conservation and Recovery Act of 1976) with respect to applications made under such section (as in effect before the date of the enactment of Resource Conservation and Recovery Act of 1976).

"(c) STUDY.--The Administrator shall make a complete investigation and study to determine--

"(1) the need for additional trained State and local personnel to carry out plans assisted under this Act and other solid waste and resource recovery programs;

"(2) means of using existing training programs to train such personnel; and

"(3) the extent and nature of obstacles to employment and occupational advancement in the solid waste management and resource recovery field which may limit either available manpower or the advancement of personnel in such field.

He shall report the results of such investigation and study, including his recommendations to the President and the Congress.

"PAYMENTS

"Sec. 7008. (a) GENERAL RULE.--Payments of grants under this Act may be made (after necessary adjustment on account of previously made underpayments or overpayments) in advance or by way of reimbursements, and in such installments and on such conditions as the Administrator may determine.

"(b) PROHIBITION.--No grant may be made under this Act to any private profitmaking organization.

"LABOR STANDARDS

"Sec. 7009. No grant for a project of construction under this Act shall be made unless the Administrator finds that the application contains or is supported by reasonable assurance that all laborers and mechanics employed by contractors or subcontractors on projects of the type covered by the Davis-Bacon Act, as amended (40 U.S.C. 276a-276a-5), will be paid wages at rates not less than those prevailing on similar work in the locality as determined by the Secretary of Labor in accordance with that Act; and the Secretary of Labor shall have with respect to the labor standards specified in this section the authority and functions set forth in Reorganization Plan Numbered 14 of 1950 (15 F.R. 3176; 5 U.S.C. 133z-5) and section 2 of the Act of June 13, 1934, as amended (40 U.S.C. 276c).

"Subtitle H—Research, Development, Demonstration, and Information

"RESEARCH, DEMONSTRATIONS, TRAINING, AND OTHER ACTIVITIES

"Sec. 8001. (a) GENERAL AUTHORITY.--The Administrator, alone or after consultation with the Administrator of the Federal Energy Administration, the Administrator of the Energy Research and Development Administration, or the Chairman of the Federal Power Commission shall conduct, and encourage, cooperate with, and render financial and other assistance to appropriate public (whether Federal, State, interstate, or local) authorities, agencies, and institutions, private agencies and institutions, and individuals in the conduct of, and promote the coordination of, research, investigations, experiments, training, demonstrations, surveys, public education programs, and studies relating to--

"(1) any adverse health and welfare effects of the release into the environment of material present in solid waste, and methods to eliminate such effects;

"(2) the operation and financing of solid waste management programs;

"(3) the planning, implementation, and operation of resource recovery and resource conservation systems and hazardous waste management systems, including the marketing of recovered resources;

"(4) the production of usable forms of recovered resources, including fuel, from solid waste;

"(5) the reduction of the amount of such waste and unsalvageable waste materials;

"(6) the development and application of new and improved methods of collecting and disposing of solid waste and processing and recovering materials and energy from solid wastes;

"(7) the identification of solid waste components and potential materials and energy recoverable from such waste components;

"(8) small scale and low technology solid waste management systems, including but not limited to, resource recovery source separation systems;

"(9) methods to improve the performance characteristics of resources recovered from solid waste and the relationship of such performance characteristics to available and potentially available markets for such resources;

"(10) improvements in land disposal practices for solid waste (including sludge) which may reduce the adverse environmental effects of such disposal and other aspects of solid waste disposal on land, including means for reducing the harmful environmental effects of earlier and existing landfills, means for restoring areas damaged by such earlier or existing landfills, means for rendering landfills safe for purposes of construction and other uses, and techniques of recovering materials and energy from landfills;

"(11) methods for the sound disposal of, or recovery of resources, including energy, from, sludge (including sludge from pollution control and treatment facilities, coal slurry pipelines, and other sources);

"(12) methods of hazardous waste management, including methods of rendering such waste environmentally safe; and

"(13) any adverse effects on air quality (particularly with regard to the emission of heavy metals) which result from solid waste which is burned (either alone or in conjunction with other substances) for purposes of treatment, disposal or energy recovery.

"(b) MANAGEMENT PROGRAM.—(1) (A) In carrying out his functions pursuant to this Act, and any other Federal legislation respecting solid waste or discarded material research, development, and demonstrations,the Administrator shall establish a management program or system to insure the coordination of all such activities and to facilitate and accelerate the process of development of sound new technology (or other discoveries) from the research phase, through development, and into the demonstration phase.

"(B) The Administrator shall (i) assist, on the basis of any research projects which are developed with assistance under this Act or without Federal assistance, the construction of pilot plant facilities for the purpose of investigating or testing the technological feasibility of any promising new fuel, energy, or resource recovery or resource conservation method or technology; and (ii) demonstrate each such method and technology that appears justified by an evaluation at such pilot plant stage or at a pilot plant stage developed without Federal assistance. Each such demonstration shall incorporate new or innovative technical advances or shall apply such advances to different circumstances and conditions, for the purpose of evaluating design concepts or to test the performance, efficiency, and economic feasibility of a particular method or technology under actual operating conditions. Each such demonstration shall be so planned and designed that, if successful, it can be expanded or utilized directly as a full-scale operational fuel, energy, or resource recovery or resource conservation facility.

"(2) Any energy-related research, development, or demonstration project for the conversion including bioconversion, of solid waste carried out by the Environmental Protection Agency or by the Energy Research and Development Administration pursuant to this or any other Act shall be administered in accordance with the May 7, 1976, Interagency Agreement between the Environmental Protection Agency and the Energy Research and Development Administration on the Development of Energy from Solid Wastes and specifically, that in accordance with this agreement, (A) for those energy-related projects of mutual interest, planning will be conducted jointly by the Environmental Protection Agency and the Energy Research and Development Administration, following which project responsibility will be assigned to one agency; (B) energy-related portions of projects for recovery of synthetic fuels or other forms of energy from solid waste shall be the responsibility of the Energy Research and Development Administration; (C) the Environmental Protection Agency shall retain responsibility for the environmental, economic, and institutional aspects of solid waste projects and for assurance that such projects are consistent with any applicable suggested guidelines published pursuant to section 1008, and any applicable State or regional solid waste management plan; and (D) any activities undertaken under provisions of sections 8002 and 8003 as related to energy; as related to energy or synthetic fuels recovery from waste; or as related to energy conservation shall be accomplished through coordination and consultation with the Energy Research and Development Administration.

"(c) AUTHORITIES.—(1) In carrying out subsection (a) of this section respecting solid waste research, studies, development, and demonstration, except as otherwise specifically provided in section 8004(d), the Administrator may make grants to or enter into contracts (including contracts for construction) with, public agencies and authorities or private persons.

"(2) Contracts for research, development, or demonstrations or for both (including contracts for construction) shall be made in accordance with and subject to the limitations provided with respect to research contracts of the military departments in title 10, United States Code, section 2353, except that the determination, approval, and certification required thereby shall be made by the Administrator.

"(3) Any invention made or conceived in the course of, or under, any contract under this Act shall be subject to section 9 of the Federal Nonnuclear Energy Research and Development Act of 1974 to the same extent and in the same manner as inventions made or conceived in the course of contracts under such Act, except that in applying such section, the Environmental Protection Agency shall be substituted for the Energy Research and Development Administration and the words 'solid waste' shall be substituted for the word 'energy' where appropriate.

"(4) For carrying out the purpose of this Act the Administrator may detail personnel of the Environmental Protection Agency to agencies eligible for assistance under this section.

"SPECIAL STUDIES; PLANS FOR RESEARCH, DEVELOPMENT, AND DEMONSTRATIONS

"Sec. 8002. (a) GLASS AND PLASTIC.--The Administrator shall undertake a study and publish a report on resource recovery from glass and plastic waste, including a scientific, technological, and economic investigation of potential solutions to implement such recovery.

"(b) COMPOSITION OF WASTE STREAM.--The Administrator shall undertake a systematic study of the composition of the solid waste stream and of anticipated future changes in the composition of such stream and shall publish a report containing the results of such study and quantitatively evaluating the potential utility of such components.

"(c) PRIORITIES STUDY.--For purposes of determining priorities for research on recovery of materials and energy from solid waste and developing materials and energy recovery research, development, and demonstration strategies, the Administrator shall review, and make a study of, the various existing and promising techniques of energy recovery from solid waste (including, but not limited to, waterwall furnace incinerators, dry shredded fuel systems, pyrolysis, densified refuse-derived fuel systems, anerobic digestion, and fuel and feedstock preparation systems). In carrying out such study the Administrator shall investigate with respect to each such technique--

"(1) the degree of public need for the potential results of such research, development, or demonstration,

"(2) the potential for research, development, and demonstration without Federal action, including the degree of restraint on such potential posed by risks involved, and

"(3) the magnitude of effort and period of time necessary to develop the technology to the point where Federal assistance can be ended.

"(d) SMALL-SCALE AND LOW TECHNOLOGY STUDY.--The Administrator shall undertake a comprehensive study and analysis of, and publish a report on, systems of small-scale and low technology solid waste management, including household resource recovery and resource recovery systems which have special application to multiple dwelling units and high density housing and office complexes. Such study and analysis shall include an investigation of the degree to which such systems could contribute to energy conservation.

"(e) FRONT-END SOURCE SEPARATION.—The Administrator shall undertake research and studies concerning the compatibility of front-end source separation systems with high technology resource recovery systems and shall publish a report continuing the results of such research and studies.

"(f) MINING WASTE.—The Administrator, in consultation with the Secretary of the Interior, shall conduct a detailed and comprehensive study on the adverse effects of solid wastes from active and abandoned surface and underground mines on the environment, including, but not limited to, the effects of such wastes on humans, water, air, health, welfare, and natural resources, and on the adequacy of means and measures currently employed by the mining industry, Government agencies, and others to dispose of and utilize such solid wastes and to prevent or substantially mitigate such adverse effects. Such study shall include an analysis of—

"(1) the sources and volume of discarded material generated per year from mining;

"(2) present disposal practices;

"(3) potential dangers to human health and the environment from surface runoff of leachate and air pollution by dust;

"(4) alternatives to current disposal methods;

"(5) the cost of those alternatives in terms of the impact on mine product costs; and

"(6) potential for use of discarded material as a secondary source of the mine product.

Not later than thirty-six months after the date of the enactment of the Solid Waste Disposal Act Amendments of 1980 the Administrator shall publish a report of such study and shall include appropriate findings and recommendations for Federal and non-Federal actions concerning such effects. Such report shall be submitted to the Committee on Environment and Public Works of the United States Senate and the Committee on Interstate and Foreign Commerce of the United States House of Representatives.

"(g) SLUDGE.—The Administrator shall undertake a comprehensive study and publish a report on sludge. Such study shall include an analysis of—

"(1) what types of solid waste (including but not limited to sewage and pollution treatment residues and other residues from industrial operations such as extraction of oil from shale, liquefaction and gasification of coal and coal slurry pipeline operations) shall be classified as sludge:

"(2) the effects of air and water pollution legislation on the creation of large volumes of sludge;

"(3) the amounts of sludge originating in each State and in each industry producing sludge;

"(4) methods of disposal of such sludge, including the cost, efficiency, and effectiveness of such methods;

"(5) alternative methods for the use of sludge, including agricultural applications of sludge and energy recovery from sludge; and

"(6) methods to reclaim areas which have been used for the disposal of sludge or which have been damaged by sludge.

"(h) TIRES.—The Administrator shall undertake a study and publish a report respecting discarded motor vehicle tires which shall include an analysis of the problems involved in the collection, recovery of resources including energy, and use of such tires.

"(i) RESOURCE RECOVERY FACILITIES.—The Administrator shall conduct research and report on the economics of, and impediments, to the effective functioning of resource recovery facilities.

"(j) RESOURCE CONSERVATION COMMITTEE.—(1) The Administrator shall serve as Chairman of a Committee composed of himself, the Secretary of Commerce, the Secretary of Labor, the Chairman of the Council on Environmental Quality, the Secretary of Treasury, the Secretary of the Interior, the Secretary of Energy, the Chairman of the Council of Economic Advisors, and a representative of the Office of Management and Budget, which shall conduct a full and complete investigation and study of all aspects of the economic, social, and environmental consequences of resource conservation with respect to—

"(A) the appropriateness of recommended incentives and disincentives to foster resource conservation;

"(B) the effect of existing public policies (including subsidies and economic incentives and disincentives, percentage depletion allowances, capital gains treatment and other tax incentives and disincentives) upon resource conservation, and the likely effect of the modification or elimination of such incentives and disincentives upon resource conservation;

"C) the appropriateness and feasibility of restricting the manufacture or use of categories of consumer products as a resource conservation strategy;

"(D) the appropriateness and feasibility of employing as a resource conservation strategy the imposition of solid waste management charges on consumer products, which charges would reflect the costs of solid waste management services, litter pickup, the value of recoverable components of such product, final disposal, and any social value associated with the nonrecycling or uncontrolled disposal of such product; and

"(E) the need for further research, development, and demonstration in the area of resource conservation.

"(2) The study required in paragraph (1)(D) may include pilot scale projects, and shall consider and evaluate alternative strategies with respect to—

"(A) the product categories on which such charges would be imposed;

"(B) the appropriate state in the production of such consumer product at which to levy such charge;

"(C) appropriate criteria for establishing such charges for each consumer product category;

"(D) methods for the adjustment of such charges to reflect actions such as recycling which would reduce the overall quantities of solid waste requiring disposal; and

"(E) procedures for amending, modifying, or revising such charges to reflect changing conditions.

"(3) The design for the study required in paragraph (1) of this subsection shall include timetables for the completion of the study. A preliminary report putting forth the study design shall be sent to the President and the Congress within six months following enactment of this section and followup reports shall be sent six months thereafter. Each recommendation resulting from the study shall include at least two alternatives to the proposed recommendation.

"(4) The results of such investigation and study, including recommendations, shall be reported to the President and the Congress not later than two years after enactment of this subsection.

"(5) There are authorized to be appropriated not to exceed $2,000,000 to carry out this subsection.

"(k) AIRPORT LANDFILLS.—The Administrator shall undertake a comprehensive study and analysis of and publish a report on systems to alleviate the hazards to aviation from birds congregating and feeding on landfills in the vicinity of airports.

"(l) COMPLETION OF RESEARCH AND STUDIES.—The Administrator shall complete the research and studies, and submit the reports, required under subsection (b), (c), (d), (e), (f), (g), and (k) not later than October 1, 1978. The Administrator shall complete the research and studies, and submit the reports, required under subsections (a), (h), and (i) not later than October 1, 1979. Upon completion, each study specified in subsections (a) through (k) of this section, the Administrator shall prepare a plan for research, development, and demonstration respecting the findings of the study and shall submit any legislative recommendations resulting from such study to appropriate committees of Congress.

"(m) DRILLING FLUIDS, PRODUCED WATERS, AND OTHER WASTES ASSOCIATED WITH THE EXPLORATION, DEVELOPMENT, OR PRODUCTION OF CRUDE OIL OR NATURAL GAS OR GEOTHERMAL ENERGY.—(1) The Administrator shall conduct a detailed and comprehensive study and submit a report on the adverse effects, if any, of drilling fluids, produced waters, and other wastes associated with the exploration, development, or production of crude oil or natural gas or geothermal energy on human health and the environment, including, but not limited to, the effects of such wastes on humans, water, air, health, welfare, and natural resources and on the adequacy of means and measures currently employed by the oil and gas and geothermal drilling and production industry, Government agencies, and others to dispose of and utilize such wastes and to prevent or substantially mitigate such adverse effects. Such study shall include an analysis of—

"(A) the sources and volume of discarded material generated per year from such wastes;

"(B) present disposal practices;

"(C) potential danger to human health and the environment from the surface runoff or leachate;

"(D) documented cases which prove or have caused danger to human health and the environment from surface runoff or leachate;

"(E) alternatives to current disposal methods;

"(F) the cost of such alternatives; and

"(G) the impact of those alternatives on the exploration for, and development and production of, crude oil and natural gas or geothermal energy.

In furtherance of this study, the Administrator shall, as he deems appropriate, review studies and other actions of other Federal agencies concerning such wastes with a view toward avoiding duplication of effort and the need to expedite such study. The Administrator shall publish a report of such study and shall include appropriate findings and recommendations for Federal and non-Federal actions concerning such effects.

"(2) The Administrator shall complete the research and study and submit the report required under paragraph (1) not later than twenty-four months from the date of enactment of the Solid Waste Disposal Act Amendments of 1980. Upon completion of the study, the Administrator shall prepare a summary of the findings of the study, a plan for research, development, and demonstration respecting the findings of the study, and shall submit the findings and the study, along with any recommendations resulting from such study, to the Committee on Environment and Public Works of the United States Senate and the Committee on Interstate and Foreign Commerce of the United States House of Representatives.

"(3) There are authorized to be appropriated not to exceed $1,000,000 to carry out the provisions of this subsection.

"(n) MATERIALS GENERATED FROM THE COMBUSTION OF COAL AND OTHER FOSSIL FUELS.—The Administrator shall conduct a detailed and comprehensive study and submit a report on the adverse effects on human health and the environment, if any, of the disposal and utilization of fly ash waste, bottom ash waste, slag waste, flue gas emission control waste, and other byproduct materials generated primarily from the combustion of coal or other fossil fuels. Such study shall include an analysis of—

"(1) the source and volumes of such material generated per year;

"(2) present disposal and utilization practices;

"(3) potential danger, if any, to human health and the environment from the disposal and reuse of such materials;

"(4) documented cases in which danger to human health or the environment from surface runoff or leachate has been proved;

"(5) alternatives to current disposal methods;

"(6) the costs of such alternatives;

"(7) the impact of those alternatives on the use of coal and other natural resources; and

"(8) The current and potential utilization of such materials.

In furtherance of this study, the Administrator shall, as he deems appropriate, review studies and other actions of other Federal and State agencies concerning such material and invite participation by other concerned parties, including industry and other Federal and State agencies, with a view toward avoiding duplication of effort. The Administrator shall publish a report on such study, which shall include appropriate findings, not later than twenty-four months after the enactment of the Solid Waste Disposal Act Amendments of 1980. Such study and findings shall be submitted to the Committee on Environment and Public Works of the United States Senate and the Committee on Interstate and Foreign Commerce of the United States House of Representatives.

"(o) CEMENT KILN DUST WASTE.--The Administrator shall conduct a detailed and comprehensive study of the adverse effects on human health and the environment, if any, of the disposal of cement kiln dust waste. Such study shall include an analysis of—

"(1) the source and volumes of such materials generated per year;

"(2) present disposal practices;

"(3) potential danger, if any, to human health and the environment from the disposal of such materials;

"(4) documented cases in which danger to human health or the environment has been proved;

"(5) alternatives to current disposal methods;

"(6) the costs of such alternatives;

"(7) the impact of those alternatives on the use of natural resources; and

"(8) the current and potential utilization of such materials.

In furtherance of this study, the Administrator shall, as he deems appropriate, review studies and other actions of other Federal and State agencies concerning such waste or materials and invite participation by other concerned parties, including industry and other Federal and State agencies, with a view toward avoiding duplication of effort. The Administrator shall publish a report of such study, which shall include appropriate findings, not later than thirty-six months after the date of enactment of the Solid Waste Disposal Act Amendments of 1980. Such report shall be submitted to the Committee on Environment and Public Works of the United States Senate and the Committee on Interstate and Foreign Commerce of the United States House of Representatives.

"(p) MATERIALS GENERATED FROM THE EXTRACTION, BENEFICIATION, AND PROCESSING OF ORES AND MINERALS, INCLUDING PHOSPHATE ROCK AND OVERBURDEN FROM URANIUM MINING.--The Administrator shall conduct a detailed and comprehensive study on the adverse effects on human health and the environment, if any, of the disposal and utilization of solid waste from the extraction, beneficiation, and processing of ores and minerals, including phosphate rock and overburden from uranium mining. Such study shall be conducted in conjunction with the study of mining wastes required by subsection (f) of this section and shall include an analysis of—

"(1) the source and volumes of such materials generated per year;
"(2) present disposal and utilization practices;
"(3) potential danger, if any, to human health and the environment from the disposal and reuse of such materials;
"(4) documented cases in which danger to human health or the environment has been proved;
"(5) alternatives to current disposal methods;
"(6) the costs of such alternatives;
"(7) the impact of those alternatives on the use of phosphate rock and uranium ore, and other natural resources; and
"(8) the current and potential utilization of such materials.

In furtherance of this study, the Administrator shall, as he deems appropriate, review studies and other actions of other Federal and State agencies concerning such waste or materials and invite participation by other concerned parties, including industry and other Federal and State agencies, with a view toward avoiding duplication of effort. The Administrator shall publish a report of such study, which shall include appropriate findings, in conjunction with the publication of the report of the study of mining wastes required to be conducted under subsection (f) of this section. Such report and findings shall be submitted to the Committee on Environment and Public Works of the United States Senate and the Committee on Interstate and Foreign Commerce of the United States House of Representatives.

"(q) AUTHORIZATION OF APPROPRIATIONS.—There are authorized to be appropriated not to exceed $8,000,000 for the fiscal years 1978 and 1979 to carry out this section other than subsection (j).

"COORDINATION, COLLECTION, AND DISSEMINATION OF INFORMATION

"Sec. 8003. (a) INFORMATION.—The Administrator shall develop, collect, evaluate, and coordinate information on—

"(1) methods and costs of the collection of solid waste;
"(2) solid waste management practices, including data on the different management methods and the cost, operation, and maintenance of such methods;
"(3) the amounts and percentages of resources (including energy) that can be recovered from solid waste by use of various solid waste management practices and various technologies;
"(4) methods available to reduce the amount of solid waste that is generated;
"(5) existing and developing technologies for the recovery of energy or materials from solid waste and the costs, reliability, and risks associated with such technologies;
"(6) hazardous solid waste, including incidents of damage resulting from the disposal of hazardous solid wastes; inherently and potentially hazardous solid wastes; methods of neutralizing or properly disposing of hazardous solid wastes; facilities that properly dispose of hazardous wastes;
"(7) methods of financing resource recovery facilities or, sanitary landfills, or hazardous solid waste treatment facilities, whichever is appropriate for the entity developing such facility or landfill (taking into account the amount of solid waste reasonably expected to be available to such entity);
"(8) the availability of markets for the purchase of resources, either materials or energy, recovered from solid waste; and
"(9) research and development projects respecting solid waste manage-

ment.

"(b) LIBRARY.--(1) The Administrator shall establish and maintain a central reference library for (A) the materials collected pursuant to subsection (a) of this section and (B) the actual performance and cost effectiveness records and other data and information with respect to—

"(i) the various methods of energy and resource recovery from solid waste,

"(ii) the various systems and means of resource conservation,

"(iii) the various systems and technologies for collection, transport, storage, treatment, and final disposition of solid waste, and

"(iv) other aspects of solid waste and hazardous solid waste management.

Such central reference library shall also contain, but not be limited to, the model codes and model accounting systems developed under this section, the information collected under subsection (d), and, subject to any applicable requirements of confidentiality, information respecting any aspect of solid waste provided by officers and employees of the Environmental Protection Agency which has been acquired by them in the conduct of their functions under this Act and which may be of value to Federal, State, and local authorities and other persons.

"(2) Information in the central reference library shall, to the extent practicable, be collated, analyzed, verified, and published and shall be made available to State and local governments and other persons at reasonable times and subject to such reasonable charges as may be necessary to defray expenses of making such information available.

"(c) MODEL ACCOUNTING SYSTEM.--In order to assist State and local governments in determining the cost and revenues associated with the collection and disposal of solid waste and with resource recovery operations, the Administrator shall develop and publish a recommended model cost and revenue accounting system applicable to the solid waste management functions of State and local governments. Such system shall be in accordance with generally accepted accounting principles. The Administrator shall periodically, but not less frequently than once every five years, review such accounting system and revise it as necessary.

"(d) MODEL CODES.--The Administrator is authorized, in cooperation with appropriate State and local agencies, to recommend model codes, ordinances, and statutes, providing for sound solid waste management.

"(e) INFORMATION PROGRAMS.--(1) The Administrator shall implement a program for the rapid dissemination of information on solid waste management, hazardous waste management, resource conservation, and methods of resource recovery from solid waste, including the results of any relevant research, investigations, experiments, surveys, studies, or other information which may be useful in the implementation of new or improved solid waste management practices and methods and information on any other technical, managerial, financial, or market aspect of resource conservation and recovery facilities.

"(2) The Administrator shall develop and implement educational programs to promote citizen understanding of the need for environmentally sound solid waste management practices.

"(f) COORDINATION.—In collecting and disseminating information under this section, the Administrator shall coordinate his actions and cooperate to the maximum extent possible with State and local authorities.

"(g) SPECIAL RESTRICTION.—Upon request, the full range of alternative technologies, programs or processes deemed feasible to meet the resource recovery or resource conservation needs of a jurisdiction shall be described in such a manner as to provide a sufficient evaluative basis from which the jurisdiction can make its decisions, but no officer or employee of the Environmental Protection

Agency shall, in an official capacity, lobby for or otherwise represent an agency position in favor of resource recovery or resource conservation, as a policy alternative for adoption into ordinances, codes, regulations, or law by any State or political subdivision thereof.

"FULL-SCALE DEMONSTRATION FACILITIES

"Sec. 8004. (a) AUTHORITY.—The Administrator may enter into contracts with public agencies or authorities or private persons for the construction and operation of a full-scale demonstration facility under this Act, or provide financial assistance in the form of grants to a full-scale demonstration facility under this Act only if the Administrator finds that—

"(1) such facility or proposed facility will demonstrate at full scale a new or significantly improved technology or process, a practical and significant improvement in solid waste management practice, or the technological feasibility and cost effectiveness of an existing, but unproven technology, process, or practice, and will not duplicate any other Federal, State, local, or commercial facility which has been constructed or with respect to which construction has begun (determined as of the date action is taken by the Administrator under this Act),

"(2) such contract or assistance meets the requirements of section 8001 and meets other applicable requirements of the Act,

"(3) such facility will be able to comply with the guidelines published under section 1008 and with other laws and regulations for the protection of health and the environment,

"(4) in the case of a contract for construction or operation, such facility is not likely to be constructed or operated by State, local, or private persons or in the case of an application for financial assistance, such facility is not likely to receive adequate financial assistance from other sources, and

"(5) any Federal interest in, or assistance to, such facility will be disposed of or terminated, with apropriate compensation, within such period of time as may be necessary to carry out the basic objectives of this Act.

"(b) TIME LIMITATION.—No obligation may be made by the Administrator for financial assistance under this subtitle for any full-scale demonstration facility after the date ten years after the enactment of this section. No expenditure of funds for any such full-scale demonstration facility under this subtitle may be made by the Administrator after the date fourteen years after such date of enactment.

"(c) COST SHARING.—Wherever practicable, in constructing, operating, or providing financial assistance under this subtitle to a full-scale demonstration facility, the Administrator shall endeavor to enter into agreements and make other arrangements for maximum practicable cost sharing with other Federal, State, and local agencies, private persons, or any combination thereof.

"(2) The Administrator shall enter into arrangements, wherever practicable and desirable, to provide monitoring of full-scale solid waste facilities (whether or not constructed or operated under this Act) for purposes of obtaining information concerning the performance, and other aspects, of such facilities. Where the Administrator provides only monitoring and evaluation instruments or personnel (or both) or funds for such instruments or personnel and provides no other financial assistance to a facility, notwithstanding section 8001(c)(3), title to any invention made or conceived of in the course of developing, constructing, or operating such facility shall not be required to vest in the United States and patents respecting such invention shall not be required to be issued to the United States.

"(d) PROHIBITION.—After the date of enactment of this section, the Administrator shall not construct or operate any full-scale facility (except by contract with public agencies or authorities or private persons).

"SPECIAL STUDY AND DEMONSTRATION PROJECTS ON RECOVERY OF USEFUL ENERGY AND MATERIALS

"Sec. 8005. (a) STUDIES.--The Administrator shall conduct studies and develop recommendations for administrative or legislative action on--

"(1) means of recovering materials and energy from solid waste, recommended uses of such materials and energy for national or international welfare, including identification of potential markets for such recovered resources, the impact of distribution of such resources on existing markets, and potentials for energy conservation through resource conservation and resource recovery;

"(2) actions to reduce waste generation which have been taken voluntarily or in response to governmental action, and those which practically could be taken in the future, and the economic, social, and environmental consequences of such actions;

"(3) methods of collection, separation, and containerization which will encourage efficient utilization of facilities and contribute to more effective programs of reduction, reuse, or disposal of wastes;

"(4) the use of Federal procurement to develop market demand for recovered resources;

"(5) recommended incentives (including Federal grants, loans and other assistance) and disincentives to accelerate the reclamation or recycling of materials from solid wastes, with special emphasis on motor vehicle hulks;

"(6) the effect of existing public policies, including subsidies and economic incentives and disincentives, percentage depletion allowances, capital gains treatment and other tax incentives and disincentives, upon the recycling and reuse of materials, and the likely effect of the modification or elimination of such incentives and disincentives upon the reuse, recycling and conservation of such materials;

"(7) the necessity and method of imposing disposal or other charges on packaging, containers, vehicles, and other manufactured goods, which charges would reflect the cost of final disposal, the value of recoverable components of the item, and any social costs associated with nonrecycling or uncontrolled disposal of such items; and

"(8) the legal constraints and institutional barriers to the acquisition of land needed for solid waste management, including land for facilities and disposal sites;

"(9) in consultation with the Secretary of Agriculture, agricultural waste management problems and practices, the extent of reuse and recovery of resources in such wastes, the prospects for improvement, Federal, State, and local regulations governing such practices, and the economic, social, and environmental consequences of such practices; and

"(10) in consultation with the Secretary of the Interior, mining waste management problems, and practices, including an assessment of existing authorities, technologies, and economics, and the environmental and public health consequences of such practices.

"(b) DEMONSTRATION.--The Administrator is also authorized to carry out demonstration projects to test and demonstrate methods and techniques developed pursuant to subsection (a).

"(c) APPLICATION OF OTHER SECTIONS.--Section 8001(b) and (c) shall be applicable to investigations, studies, and projects carried out under this section.

"GRANTS FOR RESOURCE RECOVERY SYSTEMS AND IMPROVED SOLID WASTE DISPOSAL FACILITIES

"Sec. 8006. AUTHORITY.-- The Administrator is authorized to make grants pursuant to this section to any State, municipal, or interstate or intermunicipal agency for the demonstration of resource recovery systems or for the construction of new or improved solid waste disposal facilities.

"(b) CONDITIONS.--(1) Any grant under this section for the demonstration of a resource recovery system may be made only if it (A) is consistent with any plans which meet the requiremente of subtitle D of this Act; (B) is consistent with the guidelines recommended pursuant to section 1008 of this Act; (C) is designed to provide area-wide resource recovery systems consistent with the purposes of this Act, as determined by the Administrator, pursuant to regulations promulgated under subsection (d) of this section; and (D) provides an equitable system for distributing the costs associated with construction, operation, and maintenance of any resource recovery system among the users of such system.

"(2) The Federal share for any project to which paragraph (1) applies shall not be more than 75 percent.

"(c) LIMITATIONS.--(1) A grant under this section for the construction of a new or improved solid waste disposal facility may be made only if—

"(A) a State or interstate plan for solid waste disposal has been adopted which applies to the area involved, and the facility to be constructed (i) is consistent with such plan, (ii) is included in a comprehensive plan for the area involved which is satisfactory to the Administrator for the purposes of this Act, and (iii) is consistent with the guidelines recommended under section 1008, and

"(B) the project advances the state of the art by applying new and improved techniques in reducing the environmental impact of solid waste disposal, in achieving recovery of energy or resources, or in recycling useful materials.

"(2) The Federal share for any project to which paragraph (1) applies shall not be more than 50 percent in the case of a project serving an area which includes only one municipality, and not more than 75 percent in any other case.

"(d) REGULATIONS.--(1) The Administrator shall promulgate regulations establishing a procedure for awarding grants under this section which—

"(A) provides that projects will be carried out in communities of varying sizes, under such conditions as will assist in solving the community waste problems of urban-industrial centers, metropolitan regions, and rural areas, under representative geographic and environmental conditions; and

"(B) provides deadlines for submission of, and action on, grant requests.

"(2) In taking action on applications for grants under this section, consideration shall be given by the Administrator (A) to the public benefits to be derived by the construction and the propriety of Federal aid in making such grant; (B) to the extent applicable, to the economic and commercial viability of the project (including contractual arrangements with the private sector to market any resources recovered); (C) to the potential of such project for general appplication to community solid waste disposal problems; and (D) to the use by the applicant of comprehensive regional or metropolitan area planning.

"(e) ADDITIONAL LIMITATIONS.--A grant under this section--

"(1) may be made only in the amount of the Federal share of (A) the estimated total design and construction costs, plus (B) in the case of a grant to which subsection (b)(1) applies, the first-year operation and maintenance costs;

"(2) may not be provided for land acquisition or (except as otherwise provided in paragraph (1) (B)) for operating or maintenance costs;

"(3) may not be made until the applicant has made provision satisfactory to the Administrator for proper and efficient operation and maintenance of the project (subject to paragraph (1) (B)); and

"(4) may be made subject to such conditions and requirements, in addition to those provided in this section, as the Administrator may require to properly carry out his functions pursuant to this Act.

For purposes of paragraph (1), the non-Federal share may be in any form, including, but not limited to, lands or interests therein needed for the project or personal property or services, the value of which shall be determined by the Administrator.

"(f) SINGLE STATE.--(1) Not more than 15 percent of the total of funds authorized to be appropriated for any fiscal year to carry out this section shall be granted under this section for projects in any one State.

"(2) The Administrator shall prescribe by regulation the manner in which this subsection shall apply to a grant under this section for a project in an area which includes all or part of more than one State.

"AUTHORIZATION OF APPROPRIATIONS

"Sec. 8007. There are authorized to be appropriated not to exceed $35,000,000 for the fiscal year 1978 to carry out the purposes of this subtitle (except for section 8002).

SOLID WASTE DISPOSAL ACT AMENDMENTS OF 1980

Sections that do not amend the Solid Waste Disposal Act
(Resource Conservation and Recovery Act of 1976)

Section 1. This Act may be cited as the "Solid Waste Disposal Act Amendments of 1980."

Sections 2 through 31 amend the Solid Waste Disposal Act (Resource Conservation and Recovery Act of 1976).

Section 3 [Repealed by PL 96-482]

Section 4 (a) In order to demonstrate effective means of dealing with contamination of public water supplies by leachate from abandoned or other landfills, the Administrator of the Environmental Protection Agency is authorized to provide technical and financial assistance for a research program to control leachate from the Llangollen Landfill in New Castle County, Delaware.

(b) The research program authorized by this section shall be designed by the New Castle County areawide waste treatment management program, in cooperation with the Environmental Protection Agency, to develop methods for controlling leachate contamination from abandoned and other landfills that may be applied at the Llangollen Landfill and other landfills throughout the Nation. Such research program shall investigate all alternative solutions or corrective actions, including--

(1) hydrogeologic isolation of the landfill combined with the collection and treatment of leachate;

(2) excavation of the refuse, followed by some type of incineration;

(3) excavation and transportation of the refuse to another landfill; and

(4) collection and treatment of contaminated leachate or ground water.

Such research program shall consider the economic, social, and environmental consequences of each such alternative.

(c) The Administrator of the Environmental Protection Agency shall make available personnel of the Agency, including those of the Solid and Hazardous Waste Research Laboratory (Cincinnati, Ohio), and shall arrange for other Federal personnel to be made available, to provide technical assistance and aid in such research. The Administrator may provide up to $250,000, of the sums appropriated under the Solid Waste Disposal Act, to the New Castle County areawide waste treatment management program to conduct such research, including obtaining consultant services.

(d) In order to prevent further damage to public water supplies during the period of this study, the Administrator of the Environmental Protection Agency shall provide up to $200,000 in each of fiscal years 1977 and 1978, of the sums appropriated under the Solid Waste Disposal Act for the operating costs of a counterpumping program to contain the leachate from the Llangollen Landfill.

Section 32. (a) ENERGY AND MATERIALS CONSERVATION AND RECOVERY. (a) The Congress finds that--

(1) significant savings could be realized by conserving materials in order to reduce the volume or quantity of material which ultimately becomes waste;

(2) solid waste contains valuable energy and material resources which can be recovered and used thereby conserving increasingly scarce and expensive fossil fuels and virgin materials;

(3) the recovery of energy and materials contributing to such waste streams, can have the effect of reducing the volume of the municipal waste stream and the burden of disposing of increasing volumes of solid waste;

(4) the technology to conserve resources exists and is commercially feasible to apply;

(5) the technology to recover energy and materials from solid waste is of demonstrated commercial feasibility; and

(6) various communities throughout the nation have different needs and different potentials for conserving resources and for utilizing techniques for the recovery of energy and materials from waste, and Federal assistance in planning and implementing such energy and materials conservation and recovery programs should be available to all communities on an equitable basis in relation to their needs and potential.

Sections 32 (b) through (g) amend the Solid Waste Disposal Act.

Section 33. NATIONAL ADVISORY COMMISSION ON RESOURCE CONSERVATION AND RECOVERY. (a)(1) There is hereby established in the executive branch of the United States the National Advisory Commission on Resource Conservation and Recovery, hereinafter in this section referred to as the "Commission".

(2) The Commission shall be composed of nine members to be appointed by the President. Such members shall be qualified by reason of their education, training, or experience to represent the view of consumer groups, industry associations, and environmental and other groups concerned with resource conservation and recovery and at least two shall be elected or appointed State or local officials. Members shall be appointed for the life of the Commission.

(3) A vacancy in the Commission shall be filled in the manner in which the

original appointment was made.

(4) Five members of the Commission shall constitute a quorum for transacting business of the Commission except that a lesser number may hold hearings and conduct information-gathering meetings.

(5) The Chairperson of the Commission shall be designated by the President from among the members.

(6) Upon the expiration of the two-year period beginning on (A) the date when all initial members of the Commission have been appointed or when (B) the date when initial funds become available to carry out this section, whichever is later, the Commission shall transmit to the President, and to each House of the Congress, a final report containing a detailed statement of the findings and conclusions of the Commission, together with such recommendations as it deems advisable.

(7) The Commission shall submit an interim report on February 15, 1982, and the Commission may also submit, for legislative and administrative actions relating to the Solid Waste Disposal Act, other interim reports prior to the submission to its final report.

(8) The Commission shall cease to exist 30 days after the submission of its final report.

(b) The Commission shall--

(1) after consultation with the appropriate Federal agencies, review budgetary priorities relating to resource conservation and recovery, determine to what extent program goals relating to resource conservation and recovery are being realized, and make recommendations concerning the appropriate program balance and priorities.

(2) review any existing or proposed resource conservation and recovery guidelines or regulations;

(3) determine the economic development or savings potential of resource conservation and recovery, including the availability of markets for recovered energy and materials, for economic materials savings through conservation, and make recommendations concerning the utilization of such potential;

(4) identify, and make recommendations addressing, institutional obstacles impeding the development of resource conservation and resource recovery; and

(5) evaluate the status of resource conservation and recovery technology and systems including both materials and energy recovery technologies, recycling methods, and other innovative methods for both conserving energy and materials extractable from solid waste.

The review referred to in paragraph (1) should include but not be limited to an assessment of the effectiveness of the technical assistance panels, the public participation program and other program activities under the Solid Waste Disposal Act.

(c)(1) Members of the Commission while serving on business of the Commission, shall be compensated at a rate not to exceed the rate specified at the time of such service for grade GS-16 of the General Schedule for each day they are engaged in the actual performance of Commission duties, including travel time; and while so serving away from their homes or regular places of business, all members of the Commission may be allowed travel expenses, including per diem in lieu of subsistence, as authorized by section 5703 of title 5, United States Code, for persons in Government service employed intermittently.

(2) Subject to such rules as may be adopted by the Commission, the Chairperson, without regard to the provisions of title 5, United States Code, governing appointments in the competitive service and without regard to the provisions of

chapter 51 and subchapter III of chapter 53 of such title relating to classification and General Schedule pay rates, shall have the power to—

(A) appoint a Director, who shall be paid at a rate not to exceed the rate of basic pay for level I, GS-16 of the General Schedule; and

(B) appoint and fix the compensation of not more than 5 additional staff personnel.

(3) This Commission is authorized to procure temporary and intermittent services of experts and consultants as are necessary to the extent authorized by section 3109 of title 5, United States Code, but at rates not to exceed the rate specified at the time of such service for grade GS-16 in section 5332 of such title. Experts and consultants may be employed without compensation if they agree to do so in advance.

(4) Upon request of the Commission, the head of any Federal agency is authorized to detail on a reimbursable or nonreimbursable basis any of the personnel of such agency to the Commission to assist the Commission in carrying out its duties under this section.

(5) The Commission is exempt from the requirements of sections 4301 through 4308 of title 5, United States Code.

(6) The Commission is authorized to enter into contracts with Federal and State agencies, private firms, institutions, and individuals for the conduct of research or surveys, the preparation of reports, and other activities necessary to the discharge of its duties and responsibilities.

(7) In order to expedite matters pertaining to the planning for, and work of, the Commission, the Commission is authorized to make purchases and contracts without regard to section 252 of title 41 of the United States Code, pertaining to advertising and competitive bidding, and may arrange for the printing of any material pertaining to the work of the Commission without regard to the Government Printing and Binding Regulations and any related laws or regulations.

(8) The Commission may use the United States mail in the same manner and under the same conditions as other departments and agencies of the United States.

(9) The Commission may secure directly from any department or agency of the United States information necessary to enable it to carry out its duties and functions. Upon request of the Chairperson, the head of any such Federal agency shall furnish such information to the Commission subject to applicable law.

(10) Financial and administrative services (including those related to budget and accounting, financial reporting, personnel, and procurement) shall be provided to the Commission by the General Services Administration for which payment shall be made in advance or by reimbursement, from funds of the Commission, in such amounts as may be agreed upon by the Chairperson of the Commission and the Administrator of General Services.

(d) In carrying out its duties under this section the Commission, or any duly authorized committee thereof, is authorized to hold such hearings and take testimony, with respect to matters to which it has a responsibility under this section as the Commission may deem advisable. The Chairperson of the Commission or any member authorized by him may administer oaths or affirmations to witnesses appearing before the Commission or before any committee thereof.

(e) From the amounts authorized to be appropriated under the Solid Waste Disposal Act for the fiscal years 1981 and 1982, not more than $1,000,000 may be used to carry our the provisions of this section.

USED OIL RECYCLING ACT OF 1980

Sections that did not amend the Solid Waste Disposal Act
(Resource Conservation and Recovery Act of 1976)

Section 1. This Act may be cited as the "Used Oil Recycling Act of 1980."

Section 2. FINDINGS. The Congress finds and declares that--

"(1) used oil is a valuable source of increasingly scarce energy and materials;

"(2) technology exists to re-refine, reprocess, reclaim, and otherwise recycle used oil;

"(3) used oil constitutes a threat to public health and the environment when reused or disposed of improperly; and

that, therefore, it is in the national interest to recycle used oil in a manner which does not constitute a threat to public health and the environment and which conserves energy and materials.

Sections 3, 4(a) and (b), and 5 through 7 amend the Solid Waste Disposal Act.

Section 4 (c). Before the effective date of the labeling standards required to be prescribed under section 383(d)(1)(A) of the Energy Policy and Conservation Act, no requirement of any rule or order of the Federal Trade Commission may apply, or remain applicable, to any container of recycled oil (as defined in section 383(b) of such Act) if such requirement provides that the container must bear any label referring to the fact that it has been derived from previously used oil. Nothing in this subsection shall be construed to affect any labeling requirement applicable to recycled oil under any authority of law to the extent such requirement relates to fitness for intended use or any other performance characteristic of such oil or to any characteristic of such oil other than that referred to in the preceding sentence.

Section 8. USED OIL AS A HAZARDOUS WASTE. Not later than ninety days after the date of the enactment of this Act, the Administrator of the Environmental Protection Agency shall—

(1) make a determination as to the applicability to used oil of the criteria and regulations promulgated under subsections (a) and (b) of section 3001 of the Solid Waste Disposal Act relating to characteristics of hazardous wastes, and

(2) report to the Congress the determination together with a detailed statement of the data and other information upon which the determination is based.

In making a determination under paragraph (1), the Administrator shall ensure that the recovery and reuse of used oil are not discouraged.

Section 9. STUDY. The Administrator of the Environmental Protection Agency, in cooperation with the Secretary of Energy, the Federal Trade Commission, and the Secretary of Commerce, shall conduct a study—

(1) assessing the environmental problems associated with the improper disposal or reuse of used oil;

(2) addressing the collection cycle of used oil prior to recycling;

(3) analyzing supply and demand in the used oil industry, including (A)

estimates of the future supply and quality of used oil feedstocks for purpose of re-fining and (B) estimates of the future supply of virgin crude oil available for refining for purposes of producing lubricating oil;

(4) comparing the energy savings associated with re-refining used oil and the energy savings associated with other uses of used oil; and

(5) recommending Federal, State, and local policies to encourage methods for environmentally sound and economically feasible recycling of used oil.

Where appropriate, for purposes of the study under this section, the Administrator may utilize and update information and data previously collected by the administrator and by other agencies, departments, and instrumentalities of the United States. The Administrator shall submit to Congress a report containing the results of the study under this section not later than one year after the date of the enactment of this Act.

SAFE DRINKING WATER ACT

as amended[1]

SHORT TITLE

SECTION 1. This Act may be cited as the "Safe Drinking Water Act".

PUBLIC WATER SYSTEMS

SEC. 2. (a) The Public Health Service Act is amended by inserting after title XIII the following new title:

TITLE XIV—SAFETY OF PUBLIC WATER SYSTEMS[1]

PART A—DEFINITIONS

DEFINITIONS

SEC. 1401. For purposes of this title:

(1) The term "primary drinking water regulation" means a regulation which—

(A) applies to public water systems;

(B) specifies contaminants which, in the judgment of the Administrator, may have any adverse effect on the health of persons;

(C) specifies for each such contaminant either—

(i) a maximum contaminant level, if, in the judgment of the Administrator, it is economically and technologically feasible to ascertain the level of such contaminant in water in public water systems, or

(ii) if, in the judgment of the Administrator, it is not economically or technologically feasible to so ascertain the level of such contaminant, each treatment technique known to the Administrator which leads to a reduction in the level of such contaminant sufficient to satisfy the requirements of section 1412; and

(D) contains criteria and procedures to assure a supply of drinking water which dependably complies with such maximum contaminant levels; including quality control and testing procedures to insure compliance with such levels and to insure proper operation and maintenance of the system, and requirements as to (i) the minimum quality of water which may be taken into the system and (ii) siting for new facilities for public water systems.

(2) The term "secondary drinking water regulation" means a regulation which applies to public water systems and which specifies the maximum contaminant levels which, in the judgment of the Administrator, are requisite to protect the public welfare. Such regulations may apply to any contaminant in drinking water (A) which may adversely affect the odor or

---

1 PL 93-523, December 16, 1974, as amended by PL 95-190, November 16, 1977; PL 96-63, September 6, 1979; and PL 96-502, December 5, 1980.

appearance of such water and consequently may cause a substantial number of the persons served by the public water system providing such water to discontinue its use, or (B) which may otherwise adversely affect the public welfare. Such regulations may vary according to geographic and other circumstances.

(3) The term "maximum contaminant level" means the maximum permissible level of a contaminant in water which is delivered to any user of a public water system.

(4) The term "public water system" means a system for the provision to the public of piped water for human consumption, if such system has at least fifteen service connections or regularly serves at least twenty-five individuals. Such term includes (A) any collection, treatment, storage, and distribution facilities under control of the operator of such system and used primarily in connection with such system, and (B) any collection or pretreatment storage facilities not under such control which are used primarily in connection with such system.

(5) The term "supplier of water" means any person who owns or operates a public water system.

(6) The term "contaminant" means any physical, chemical, biological, or radiological substance or matter in water.

(7) The term "Administrator" means the Administrator of the Environmental Protection Agency.

(8) The term "Agency" means the Environmental Protection Agency.

(9) The term "Council" means the National Drinking Water Advisory Council established under section 1446.

(10) The term "municipality" means a city, town, or other public body created by or pursuant to State law, or an Indian tribal organization authorized by law.

(11) The term "Federal agency" means any department, agency, or instrumentality of the United States.

(12) The term "person" means an individual, corporation, company, association, partnership, State, municipality, or Federal agency (and includes officers, employees, and agents of any corporation, company, association, State, municipality, or Federal agency).

(13) The term "State" includes, in addition to the several States, only the District of Columbia, Guam, the Commonwealth of Puerto Rico, the Northern Mariana Islands, the Virgin Islands, American Samoa, and the Trust Territory of the Pacific Islands.

Part B—Public Water Systems

COVERAGE

Sec. 1411. Subject to sections 1415 and 1416, national primary drinking water regulations under this part shall apply to each public water system in each State; except that such regulations shall not apply to a public water system—

(1) which consists only of distribution and storage facilities (and does not have any collection and treatment facilities);

(2) which obtains all of its water from, but is not owned or operated by, a public water system to which such regulations apply;

(3) which does not sell water to any person; and
(4) which is not a carrier which conveys passengers in interstate commerce.

NATIONAL DRINKING WATER REGULATIONS

SEC. 1412. (a)(1) The Administrator shall publish proposed national interim primary drinking water regulations within 90 days after the date of enactment of this title. Within 180 days after such date of enactment, he shall promulgate such regulations with such modifications as he deems appropriate. Regulations under this paragraph may be amended from time to time.

(2) National interim primary drinking water regulations promulgated under paragraph (1) shall protect health to the extent feasible, using technology, treatment techniques, and other means, which the Administrator determines are generally available (taking costs into consideration) on the date of enactment of this title.

(3) The interim primary regulations first promulgated under paragraph (1) shall take effect eighteen months after the date of their promulgation.

(b)(1)(A) Within 10 days of the date of the report on the study conducted pursuant to subsection (e) is submitted to Congress, the Administrator shall publish in the Federal Register, and provide opportunity for comment on, the—

(i) proposals in the report for recommended maximum contaminant levels for national primary drinking water regulations, and

(ii) list in the report of contaminants the levels of which in drinking water cannot be determined but which may have an adverse effect on the health of persons.

(B) Within 90 days after the date the Administrator makes the publication required by subparagraph (A), he shall by rule establish recommended maximum contaminant levels for each contaminant which, in his judgment based on the report on the study conducted pursuant to subsection (e), may have any adverse effect on the health of persons. Each such recommended maximum contaminant level shall be set at a level at which, in the Administrator's judgment based on such report, no known or anticipated adverse effects on the health of persons occur and which allows an adequate margin of safety. In addition, he shall, on the basis of the report on the study conducted pursuant to subsection (e), list in the rules under this subparagraph any contaminant the level of which cannot be accurately enough measured in drinking water to establish a recommended maximum contaminant level and which may have any adverse effect on the health of persons. Based on information available to him, the Administrator may by rule change recommended levels established under this subparagraph or change such list.

(2) On the date the Administrator establishes pursuant to paragraph (1)(B) recommended maximum contaminant levels he shall publish in the Federal Register proposed revised national primary drinking water regulations (meeting the requirements of paragraph (3)). Within 180 days after the date of such proposed regulations, he shall promulgate such revised drinking water regulations with such modifications as he deems appropriate.

(3) Revised national primary drinking water regulations promulgated under paragraph (2) of this subsection shall be primary drinking water regulations which specify a maximum contaminant level or require the use of treatment techniques for each contaminant for which a recommended maximum contaminant level is established or which is listed in a rule under paragraph (1)(B). The maximum contaminant level specified in a revised national primary drinking water regulation for a contaminant shall be as close to the recommended maximum contaminant level established under paragraph (1)(B) for such contaminant as is feasible. A required treatment technique for a contaminant for which a recommended maximum contaminant level has been established under paragraph (1)(B) shall reduce such contaminant to a level which is as close to the recommended maximum contaminant level for such contaminant as is feasible. A required treatment technique for a contaminant which is listed under paragraph (1)(B) shall require treatment necessary in the Administrator's judgment to prevent known or anticipated adverse effects on the health of persons to the extent feasible. For purposes of this paragraph, the term "feasible" means feasible with the use of the best technology, treatment techniques, and other means, which the Administrator finds are generally available (taking cost into consideration).

(4) Revised national primary drinking water regulations shall be amended whenever changes in technology, treatment techniques, and other means permit greater protection of the health of persons, but in any event such regulations shall be reviewed at least once every 3 years.

(5) Revised national primary drinking water regulations promulgated under this subsection (and amendments thereto) shall take effect eighteen months after the date of their promulgation. Regulations under subsection (a) shall be superseded by regulations under this subsection to the extent provided by the regulations under this subsection.

(6) No national primary drinking water regulation may require the addition of any substance for preventive health care purposes unrelated to contamination of drinking water.

(c) The Administrator shall publish proposed national secondary drinking water regulations within 270 days after the date of enactment of this title. Within 90 days after publication of any such regulation, he shall promulgate such regulation with such modifications as he deems appropriate. Regulations under this subsection may be amended from time to time.

(d) Regulations under this section shall be prescribed in accordance with section 553 of title 5, United States Code (relating to rulemaking), except that the Administrator shall provide opportunity for public hearing prior to promulgation of such regulations. In proposing and promulgating regulations under this section, the Administrator shall consult with the Secretary and the National Drinking Water Advisory Council.

(e)(1) The Administrator shall enter into appropriate arrangements with the National Academy of Sciences (or with another independent scientific organization if appropriate arrangements cannot be made with such Academy) to conduct a study to determine (A) the maximum contaminant levels which should be recommended under subsection (b)(2) in order to protect the health of persons from any known or anticipated adverse effects, and (B) the existence of ay contaminants the levels of which in drinking water cannot be determined but which may have an adverse effect on the health of persons.

(2) The result of the study shall be reported to Congress no later than 2 years after the date of enactment of this title, and revisions thereof reflecting new information which has become available since the most recent previous report shall be reported to the Congress each two years thereafter. The report shall contain (A) a summary and evaluation of relevant publications and unpublished studies; (B) a statement of methodologies and assumptions for estimating the levels at which adverse health effects may occur; (C) a statement of methodologies and assumptions for estimating the margin of safety which should be incorporated in the national primary drinking water regulations; (D) proposals for recommended maximum contaminant levels for national primary drinking water regulations, based on the methodologies, assumptions, and studies referred to in clauses (A), (B), and (C) and in paragraph (4); (E) a list of contaminants the level of which in drinking water cannot be determined but which may have an adverse effect on the health of persons; (F) recommended studies and test protocols for future research on the health effects of drinking water contaminants, including a list of the major research priorites and estimated costs necessary to conduct such priority research; (G) periodic assessments and evaluations of unregulated contaminants which may require continuous monitoring or regulation.

(3) In developing its proposals for recommended maximum contaminant levels unde paragraph (2)(D) the National Academy of Sciences (or other organization preparing the report) shall evaluate and explain (separately and in composite) the impact of the following considerations:

(A) The existence of groups or individuals in the population which are more susceptible to adverse effects than the normal healthy adult.

(B) The exposure to contaminants in other media than drinking water (including exposures in food, in the ambient air, and in occupational settings) and the resulting body burden of contaminants.

(C) Synergistic effects resulting from exposure to or interaction by two or more contaminants.

(D) The contaminant exposure and body burden levels which alter physiological function or structure in a manner reasonably suspected of increasing the risk of illness.

(4) In making the study under this subsection, the National Academy of Sciences (or other organization) shall collect and correlate (A) morbidity and mortality data and (B) monitored data on the quality of drinking water. Any conclusions based on such correlation shall be included in the report of the study.

(5) Neither the report of the study under this subsection nor any draft of such report shall be submitted to the Office of Management and Budget or to any other Federal agency (other than the Environmental Protection Agency prior to its submission to Congress.

(6) Of the funds authorized to be appropriated to the Administrator by this title, such amounts as may be required shall be available to

carry out the study and to make the report directed by paragraph (2) of this subsection.

STATE PRIMARY ENFORCEMENT RESPONSIBILITY

SEC. 1413. (a) For purposes of this title, a State has primary enforcement responsibility for public water systems during any period for which the Administrator determines (pursuant to regulations prescribed under subsection (b)) that such State—

(1) has adopted drinking water regulations which (A) in the case of the period beginning on the date the national interim primary drinking water regulations are promulgated under section 1412 and ending on the date such regulations take effect are no less stringent than such regulations, and (B) in the case of the period after such effective date are no less stringent than the interim and revised national primary drinking water regulations in effect under such section;

(2) has adopted and is implementing adequate procedures for the enforcement of such State regulations, including conducting such monitoring and making such inspections as the Administrator may require by regulation;

(3) will keep such records and make such reports with respect to its activities under paragraphs (1) and (2) as the Administrator may require by regulation;

(4) if it permits variances or exemptions, or both, from the requirements of its drinking water regulations which meet the requirements of paragraph (1), permits such variances and exemptions under conditions and in a manner which is not less stringent than the conditions under, and the manner in, which variances and exemptions may be granted under sections 1415 and 1416; and

(5) has adopted and can implement an adequate plan for the provision of safe drinking water under emergency circumstances.

(b)(1) The Administrator shall, by regulation (proposed within 180 days of the date of the enactment of this title), prescribe the manner in which a State may apply to the Administrator for a determination that the requirements of paragraphs (1), (2), (3), and (4) of subsection (a) are satisfied with respect to the State, the manner in which the determination is made, the period for which the determination will be effective, and the manner in which the Administrator may determine that such requirements are no longer met. Such regulations shall require that before a determination of the Administrator that such requirements are met or are no longer met with respect to a State may become effective, the Administrator shall notify such State of the determination and the reasons therefor and shall provide an opportunity for public hearing on the determination. Such regulations shall be promulgated (with such modifications as the Administrator deems appropriate) within 90 days of the publication of the proposed regulations in the Federal Register. The Administrator shall promptly notify in writing the chief executive officer of each State of the promulgation of regulations under this paragraph. Such notice shall contain a copy of the regulations and shall specify a State's authority under this title when it is determined to have primary enforcement responsibility for public water systems.

(2) When an application is submitted in accordance with the Administrator's regulations under paragraph (1), the Administrator shall within 90 days of the date on which such application is submitted (A) make the determination applied for, or (B) deny the application and notify the applicant in writing of the reasons for his denial.

FAILURE BY STATE TO ASSURE ENFORCEMENT OF DRINKING WATER REGULATIONS

SEC. 1414. (a)(1)(A) Whenever the Administrator finds during a period during which a State has primary enforcement responsibility for public water systems (within the meaning of section 1413(a)) that any public water system—

(i) for which a variance under section 1415 or an exemption under section 1416 is not in effect, does not comply with any national primary drinking water regulation in effect under section 1412, or

(ii) for which a variance under section 1415 or an exemption under section 1416 is in effect, does not comply with any schedule or other requirement imposed pursuant thereto,

he shall so notify the State and provide such advice and technical assistance to such State and public water system as may be appropriate to bring the system into compliance with such regulation or requirement by the earliest feasible time.

(B) If the Administrator finds such failure to comply extends beyond the thirtieth day after the date of the notice given pursuant to subparagraph (A), he shall give public notice of such finding and request the State to report within fifteen days from the date of such public notice as to the steps being taken to bring the system into compliance (including reasons for anticipated steps to be taken to bring the system into compliance and for any failure to take steps to bring the system into compliance). If—

(i) such failure to comply extends beyond the sixtieth day after the date of the notice given pursuant to subparagraph (A); and

(ii)(α) the State fails to submit the report requested by the Administrator within the time period prescribed by the preceding sentence; or

(β) the State submits such report within such period but the Administrator, after considering the report, determines that the State abused its discretion in carrying out primary enforcement responsibility for public water systems by both—

(I) failing to implement by such sixtieth day adequate procedures to bring the system into compliance by the earliest feasible time, and

(II) failing to assure by such day the provision through alternative means of safe drinking water by the earliest feasible time;

the Administrator may commence a civil action under subsection (b).

(2) Whenever, on the basis of information available to him, the Administrator finds during a period during which a State does not have primary enforcement responsibility for public water systems that a public water system in such State—

(A) for which a variance under section 1415(a)(2) or an exemption under section 1416(f) is not in effect, does not comply with any national primary drinking water regulation in effect under section 1412, or

(B) for which a variance under section 1415 (a)(2) or an exemption under section 1416(f) is in effect, does not comply with any schedule or other requirement imposed pursant thereto,

he may commence a civil action under subsection (b).

(b) The Administrator may bring a civil action in the appropriate United States district court to require compliance with a national primary drinking water regulation or with any schedule or other requirement imposed pursuant to a variance or exemption granted under section 1415 or 1416 if—

(1) authorized under paragraph (1) or (2) of subsection (a), or

(2) if requested by (A) the chief executive officer of the State in which is located the public water system which is not in compliance with such regulation or requirement, or (B) the agency of such State which has jurisdiction over compliance by public water systems in the State with national primary drinking water regulations or State drinking water regulations.

The court may enter, in an action brought under this subsection, such judgment as protection of public health may require, taking into consideration the time necessary to comply and the availability of alternative water supplies; and, if the court determines that there has been a willful violation of the regulation or schedule or other requirement with respect to which the action was brought, the court may, taking into account the seriousness of the violation, the population at risk, and other appropriate factors, impose on the violator a civil penalty of not to exceed $5,000 for each day in which such violation occurs.

(c) Each owner or operator of a public water system shall give notice to the persons served by it—

(1) of any failure on the part of the public water system to—

(A) comply with an applicable maximum contaminant level or treatment technique requirement of, or a testing procedure prescribed by, a national primary drinking water regulation, or

(B) perform monitoring required by section 1445(a), and

(2) if the public water system is subject to a variance granted under section 1415(a)(1)(A) or 1415(a)(2) for an inability to meet a maximum contaminant level requirement or is subject to an exemption granted under section 1416, of—

(A) the existence of such variance or exemption, and

(B) any failure to comply with the requirements of any schedule prescribed pursuant to the variance or exemption.

The Administrator shall by regulation prescribe the form, manner, and frequency for giving notice under this subsection. Notice under the first sentence of this subsection shall be given not less than once every 3 months, shall be given by publication in a newspaper of general circulation serving the area served by each such water system (as determined by the Administrator), shall be furnished to the other communications media serving such area, and shall be furnished to the communications media as soon as practicable after the discovery of the violation with respect to which the notice is required. If the water bills of a public water system are issued more often than once every 3 months such notice shall be included in at least one water bill of the system every 3 months, and if a public water system issues its water bills less often than once every 3 months, such notice shall be included in each of the water bills issued by the system. The Administrator may also require the owner or operator of a public water system to give notice to the persons served by it of contaminant levels of any unregulated contaminant required to be monitored under section 1445(a). Any person who willfully violates this subsection or regulations issued under this subsection shall be fined not more than $5,000.

(d) Whenever, on the basis of information available to him, the Administrator finds that within a reasonable time after national secondary drinking water regulations have been promulgated, one or more public water systems in a State do not comply with such secondary regulations, and that such noncompliance appears to result from a failure of such State to take reasonable action to assure that public water systems throughout such State meet such secondary regulations, he shall so notify the State.

(e) Nothing in this title shall diminish any authority of a State or political subdivision to adopt or enforce any law or regulation respecting drinking water regulations or public water systems, but no such law or regulation shall relieve any person of any requirement otherwise applicable under this title.

(f) If the Administrator makes a finding of noncompliance (described in subparagraph (A) or (B) of subsection (a)(1)) with respect to a public water system in a State which has primary enforcement responsibility, the Administrator may, for the purpose of assisting that State in carrying out such responsibility and upon the petition of such State or public water system or persons served by such system, hold, after appropriate notice, public hearings for the purpose of gathering information from technical or other experts, Federal, State, or other public officials, representatives of such public water system, persons served by such system, and other interested persons on—

(1) the ways in which such system can within the earliest feasible time be brought into compliance with the regulation or requirement with respect to which such finding was made, and

(2) the means for the maximum feasible protection of the public health during any period in which such system is not in compliance with a national primary drinking water regulation or requirement applicable to a variance or exemption.

On the basis of such hearings the Administrator shall issue recommendations which shall be sent to such State and public water system and shall be made available to the public and communications media.

VARIANCES

SEC. 1415. (a) Notwithstanding any other provision of this part, variances from national primary drinking water regulations may be granted as follows:

(1) (A) A State which has primary enforcement responsibility for public water systems may grant one or more variances from an applicable national primary drinking water regulation to one

or more public water systems within its jurisdiction which, because of characteristics of the raw water sources which are reasonably available to the systems, cannot meet the requirements respecting the maximum contaminant levels of such drinking water regulation despite application of the best technology, treatment techniques, or other means, which the Administrator finds are generally available (taking costs into consideration.) Before a State may grant a variance under this subparagraph, the State must find that the variance will not result in an unreasonable risk to health. If a State grants a public water system a variance under this subparagraph, the State shall prescribe within one year of the date the variance is granted, a schedule for—

(i) compliance (including increments of progress) by the public water system with each contaminant level requirement with respect to which the variance was granted, and

(ii) implementation by the public water system of such control measures as the State may require for each contaminant, subject to such contaminant level requirement, during the period ending on the date compliance with such requirement is required.

Before a schedule prescribed by a State pursuant to this subparagraph may take effect, the State shall provide notice and opportunity for a public hearing on the schedule. A notice given pursuant to the preceding sentence may cover the prescribing of more than one such schedule and hearing held pursuant to such notice shall include each of the schedules covered by the notice. A schedule prescribed pursuant to this subparagraph for a public water system granted a variance shall require compliance by the system with each contaminant level requirement with respect to which the variance was granted as expeditiously as practicable (as the State may reasonably determine).

(B) A State which has primary enforcement responsibility for public water systems may grant to one or more public water systems within its jurisdiction one or more variances from any provision of a national primary drinking water regulation which requires the use of a specified treatment technique with respect to a contaminant if the public water system applying for the variance demonstrates to the satisfaction of the State that such treatment technique is not necessary to protect the health of persons because of the nature of the raw water source of such system. A variance granted under this subparagraph shall be conditioned on such monitoring and other requirements as the Administrator may prescribe.

(C) Before a variance proposed to be granted by a State under subparagraph (A) or (B) may take effect, such State shall provide notice and opportunity for public hearing on the proposed variance. A notice given pursuant to the preceding sentence may cover the granting of more than one variance and a hearing held pursuant to such notice shall include each of the variances covered by the notice. The State shall promptly notify the Administrator of all variances granted by it. Such notification shall contain the reason for the variance (and in the case of a variance under subparagraph (A), the basis for the finding required by that subparagraph before the granting of the variance) and documentation of the need for the variance.

(D) Each public water system's variance granted by a State under subparagraph (A) shall be conditioned by the State upon compliance by the public water system with the schedule prescribed by the State pursuant to that subparagraph. The requirements of each schedule prescribed by a State pursuant to that subparagraph shall be enforceable by the State under its laws. Any requirement of a schedule on which a variance granted under that subparagraph is conditioned may be enforced under section 1414 as if such requirement was part of a national primary drinking water regulation.

(E) Each schedule prescribed by a State pursuant to subparagraph (A) shall be deemed approved by the Administrator unless the variance for which it was prescribed is revoked by the Administrator under such subparagraph.

(F) Not later than 18 months after the effective date of the interim national primary drinking water regulations the Administrator shall complete a comprehensive review of the variances granted under subparagraph (A) (and schedules prescribed pursuant thereto) and under subparagraph (B) by the States during the one-year period beginning on such effective date. The Administrator shall conduct such subsequent review of variances and schedules as he deems necessary to carry out the purposes of this title, but each subsequent review shall be completed within each 3-year period following the completion of the first review under this subparagraph. Before conducting any review under this subparagraph, the Administrator shall publish notice of the proposed review in the Federal Register. Such notice shall (i) provide information respecting the location of data and other information respecting the variances to be reviewed (including data and other information concerning new scientific matters bearing on such variances), and (ii) advise of the opportunity to submit comments on the variances reviewed and on the need for continuing them. Upon completion of any such review, the Administrator shall publish in the Federal Register the results of his review together with findings responsive to comments submitted in connection with such review.

(G)(i) If the Administrator finds that a State has, in a substantial number of instances, abused its discretion in granting variances under subparagraph (A) or (B) or that in a substantial number of cases the State has failed to prescribe schedules in accordance with subparagraph (A), the Administrator shall notify the State of his findings. In determining if a State has abused its discretion in granting variances in a substantial number of instances, the Administrator shall consider the number of persons who are affected by the variances and if the requirements applicable to the granting of the variances were complied with. A notice under this clause shall—

(I) identify each public water system with respect to which the finding was made,

(II) specify the reasons for the finding, and

(III) as appropriate, propose revocations of specific variances or propose revised schedules or other requirements for specific public water systems granted variances, or both.

(ii) The Administrator shall provide reasonable notice and public hearing on the provisions of each notice given pursuant to clause (i) of this subparagraph. After a hearing on a notice pursuant to such clause, the Administrator shall (I) rescind the finding for which the notice was given and promptly notify the State of such rescission, or (II) promulgate (with such modifications as he deems appropriate) such variance revocations and revised schedules or other requirements proposed in such notice as he deems appropriate. Not later than 180 days after the date a notice is given pursuant to clause (i) of this subparagraph, the Administrator shall complete the hearing on the notice and take the action required by the preceding sentence.

(iii) If a State is notified under clause (i) of this subparagraph of a finding of the Administrator made with respect to a variance granted a public water system within that State or to a schedule or other requirement for a variance and if, before a revocation of such variance or a revision of such schedule or other requirement promulgated by the Administrator takes effect, the State takes corrective action with respect to such variance or schedule or other requirement which the Administrator determines makes his finding inapplicable to such variance or schedule or other requirement, the Administrator shall rescind the application of his finding to that variance or schedule or other requirement. No variance revocation or revised schedule or other requirement may take effect before the expiration of 90 days following the date of the notice in which the revocation or revised schedule or other requirement was proposed.

(2) If a State does not have primary enforcement responsibility for public water systems, the Administrator shall have the same authority to grant variances in such State as the State would have under paragraph (1) if it had primary enforcement responsibility.

(3) The Administrator may grant a variance from any treatment technique requirement of a national primary drinking water regulation upon a showing by any person that an alternative treatment technique not included in such requirement is at least as efficient in lowering the level of the contaminant with respect to which such requirement was prescribed. A variance under this paragraph shall be conditioned on the use of the alternative treatment technique which is the basis of the variance.

(b) Any schedule or other requirement on which a variance granted under paragraph (1)(B) or (2) of subsection (a) is conditioned may be enforced under section 1414 as if such schedule or other requirement was part of a national primary drinking water regulation.

(c) If an application for a variance under subsection (a) is made, the State receiving the application or the Administrator, as the case may be, shall act upon such application within a reasonable period (as determined under regulations prescribed by the Administrator) after the date of its submission.

(d) For purposes of this section, the term "treatment technique requirement" means a requirement in a national primary drinking water regulation which specifies for a contaminant (in accordance with section 1401(1)(C)(ii)) each treatment technique known to the Administrator which leads to a reduction in the level of such contaminant sufficient to satisfy the requirements of section 1412(b)(3).

EXEMPTIONS

SEC. 1416. (a) A State which has primary enforcement responsibility may exempt any public water system within the State's jurisdiction from any requirement respecting a maximum contaminant level or any treatment technique requirement, or from both, of an applicable national primary drinking water regulation upon a finding that—

(1) due to compelling factors (which may include economic factors), the public water system is unable to comply with such contaminant level or treatment technique requirement,

(2) the public water system was in operation on the effective date of such contaminant level or treatment technique requirement **or, for a system that was not in operation by that date, only if no reasonable alternative source of drinking water is available to such new system,**

(3) the granting of the exemption will not result in an unreasonable risk to health.

(b)(1) If a State grants a public water system an exemption under subsection (a), the State shall prescribe, within one year of the date the exemption is granted, a schedule for—

(A) compliance (including increments of progress) by the public water system with each contaminant level requirement and treatment technique requirement with respect to which the exemption was granted, and

(B) implementation by the public water system of such control measures as the State may require for each contaminant, subject to such contaminant level requirement or treatment technique requirement, during the period ending on the date compliance with such requirement is required.

Before a schedule prescribed by a State pursuant to this subsection may take effect, the State shall provide notice and opportunity for a public hearing on the schedule. A notice given pursuant to the preceding sentence may cover the prescribing of more than one such schedule and a hearing held pursuant to such notice shall include each of the schedules covered by the notice.

(2)(A) A schedule prescribed pursuant to this subsection for a public water system granted an exemption under subsection (a) shall require compliance by the system with each contaminant level and treatment technique requirement with respect to which the exemption was granted as expeditiously as practicable (as the State may reasonably determine) but (except as provided in subparagraph (B))—

(i) in the case of an exemption granted with respect to a contaminant level or treatment technique requirement prescribed by the interim national primary drinking water regulations promulgated under section 1412(a), not later than January 1, **1984**.; and

(ii) in the case of an exemption granted with respect to a contaminant level or treatment technique requirement prescribed by revised national primary drinking water regulations, not later than seven years after the date such requirement takes effect.

(B) Notwithstanding clauses (i) and (ii) of subparagraph (A) of this paragraph, the final date for compliance prescribed in a schedule prescribed pursuant to this subsection for an exemption granted for a public water system which (as determined by the State granting the exemption) has entered into an enforceable agreement to become a part of a regional public water system shall—

(i) in the case of a schedule prescribed for an exemption granted with respect to a contaminant level or treatment technique requirement prescribed by interim national primary drinking water regulations, be not later than January 1, **1986**; and

(ii) in the case of a schedule prescribed for an exemption granted with respect to a contaminant level or treatment technique requirement prescribed by revised national primary drinking water regulations, be not later than nine years after such requirement takes effect.

(3) Each public water system's exemption granted by a State under subsection (a) shall be conditioned by the State upon compliance by the public water system with the schedule prescribed by the State pursuant to this subsection. The requirements of each schedule prescribed by a State pursuant to this subsection shall be enforceable by the State under its laws. Any requirement of a schedule on which an exemption granted under this section is conditioned may be enforced under section 1414 as if such requirement was part of a national primary drinking water regulation.

(4) Each schedule prescribed by a State pursuant to this subsection shall be deemed approved by the Administrator unless the exemption for which it was prescribed is revoked by the Administrator under subsection (d)(2) or the schedule is revised by the Administrator under such subsection.

(c) Each State which grants an exemption under subsection (a) shall promptly notify the Administrator of the granting of such exemption. Such notification shall contain the reasons for the exemption (including the basis for the finding required by subsection (a)(3) before the exemption may be granted) and document the need for the exemption.

(d)(1) Not later than 18 months after the effective date of the interim national primary drinking water regulations the Administrator shall complete a comprehensive review of the exemptions granted (and schedules prescribed pursuant thereto) by the States during the one-year period beginning on such effective date. The Administrator shall conduct such subsequent reviews of exemptions and schedules as he deems necessary to carry out the purposes of this title, but each subsequent review shall be completed within each 3-year period following the completion of the first review under this subparagraph. Before conducting any review under this subparagraph, the Administrator shall publish notice of the proposed review in the Federal Register. Such notice shall (A) provide information respecting the location of data and other information respecting the exemptions to be reviewed (including data and other information concerning new scientific matters bearing on such exemptions), and (B) advise of the opportunity to submit comments on the exemptions reviewed and on the need for continuing them. Upon completion of any such review, the Administrator shall publish in the Federal Register the results of his review together with findings responsive to comments submitted in connection with such review.

(2) (A) If the Administrator finds that a State has, in a substantial number of instances, abused its discretion in granting exemptions under subsection (a) or failed to prescribe schedules in accordance with subsection (b), the Administrator shall notify the State of his finding. In determining if a State has abused its discretion in granting exemptions in a substantial number of instances, the Administrator shall consider the number of persons who are affected by the exemptions and if the requirements applicable to the granting of the exemptions were complied with. A notice under this paragraph shall—

(i) identify each exempt public water system with respect to which the finding was made,

(ii) specify the reasons for the finding, and

(iii) as appropriate, propose revocations of specific exemptions or propose revised schedules for specific exempt public water systems, or both.

(B) The Administrator shall provide reasonable notice and public hearing on the provisions of each notice given pursuant to subparagraph (A). After a hearing on a notice pursuant to subparagraph (A), the Administrator shall (i) rescind the finding for which the notice was given and promptly notify the State of such rescission, or (ii) promulgate (with such modifications as he deems appropriate) such exemption revocations and revised schedules proposed in such notice as he deems appropriate. Not later than 180 days after the date a notice is given pursuant to subparagraph (A), the Administrator shall complete the hearing on the notice and take the action required by the preceding sentence.

(C) If a State is notified under subparagraph (A) of a finding of the Administrator made with respect to an exemption granted a public water system within that State or to a schedule prescribed pursuant to such an exemption and if before a revocation of such exemption or a revision of such schedule promulgated by the Administrator takes effect the State takes corrective action with respect to such exemption or schedule which the Administrator determines makes his finding inapplicable to such exemption or schedule, the Administrator shall rescind the application of his finding to that exemption or schedule. No exemption revocation or revised schedule may take effect before the expiration of 90 days following the date of the notice in which the revocation or revised schedule was proposed.

(e) For purposes of this section, the term "treatment technique requirement" means a requirement in a national primary drinking water regulation which specifies for a contaminant (in accordance with section 1401(1)(C)(ii)) each treatment technique known to the Administrator which leads to a reduction in the level of such contaminant sufficient to satisfy the requirements of section 1412(b)(3).

(f) If a State does not have primary enforcement responsibility for public water systems, the Administrator shall have the same authority to exempt public water systems in such State from maximum contaminant level requirements and treatment technique requirements under the same conditions and in the same manner as the State would be authorized to grant exemptions under this section if it had primary enforcement responsibility.

(g) If an application for an exemption under this section is made, the State receiving the application or the Administrator, as the case may be, shall act upon such application within a reasonable period (as determined under regulations prescribed by the Administrator) after the date of its submission.

Part C—Protection of Underground Sources of Drinking Water

REGULATIONS FOR STATE PROGRAMS

Sec. 1421. (a)(1) The Administrator shall publish proposed regulations for State underground injection control programs within 180 days after the date of enactment of this title. Within 180 days after publication of such proposed regulations, he shall promulgate such regulations with such modifications as he deems appropriate. Any regulation under this subsection may be amended from time to time.

(2) Any regulation under this section shall be proposed and promulgated in accordance with section 553 of title 5, United States Code (relating to rulemaking), except that the Administrator shall provide opportunity for public hearing prior to promulgation of such regulations. In proposing and promulgating regulations under this section, the Administrator shall consult with the Secretary, the National Drinking Water Advisory Council, and other appropriate Federal entities and with interested State entities.

(b)(1) Regulations under subsection (a) for State underground injection programs shall contain minimum requirements for effective programs to prevent underground injection which endangers drinking water sources within the meaning of subsection (d)(2). Such regulations shall require that a State program, in order to be approved under section 1422—

(A) shall prohibit,

effective on the date on which the applicable underground injection control program takes effect,

any underground injection in such State which is not authorized by a permit issued by the State (except that the regulations may permit a State to authorize underground injection by rule);

(B) shall require (i) in the case of a program which provides for authorization of underground injection by permit, that the applicant for the permit to inject must satisfy the State that the underground injection will not endanger drinking water sources, and (ii) in the case of a program which provides for such an authorization by rule, that no rule may be promulgated which authorizes any underground injection which endangers drinking water sources;

(C) shall include inspection, monitoring, recordkeeping, and reporting requirements; and

(D) shall apply (i) as prescribed by section 1447 (b), to underground injections by Federal agencies, and (ii) to underground injections by any other person whether or not occurring on property owned or leased by the United States.

(2) Regulations of the Administrator under this section for State underground injection control programs may not prescribe requirements which interfere with or impede—

(A) the underground injection of brine or other fluids which are brought to the surface in connection with oil or natural gas production, or

(B) any underground injection for the secondary or tertiary recovery of oil or natural gas,

unless such requirements are essential to assure that underground sources of drinking water will not be endangered by such injection.

(3)(A) The regulations of the Administrator under this section shall permit or provide for consideration of varying geologic, hydrological, or historical conditions in different States and in different areas within a State.

(B)(i) In prescribing regulations under this section the Administrator shall, to the extent feasible, avoid promulgation of requirements which would unnecessarily disrupt State underground injection control programs which are in effect and being enforced in a substantial number of States.

(ii) For the purpose of this subparagraph, a regulation prescribed by the Administrator under this section shall be deemed to disrupt a State underground injection control program only if it would be infeasible to comply with both such regulation and the State underground injection control program.

(iii) For the purpose of this subparagraph, a regulation prescribed by the Administrator under this section shall be deemed unnecessary only if, without such regulation, underground sources of drinking water will not be endangered by any underground injection.

(C) Nothing in this section shall be construed to alter or affect the duty to assure that underground sources of drinking water will not be endangered by any underground injection.

(c)(1) The Administrator may, upon application of the Governor of a State which authorizes underground injection by means of permits, authorize such State to issue (without regard to subsection (b)(1)(B)(i)) temporary permits for underground injection which may be effective until the expiration of four years after the date of enactment of this title, if—

(A) the Administrator finds that the State has demonstrated that it is unable and could not reasonably have been able to process all permit applications within the time available;

(B) the Administrator determines the adverse effect on the environment of such temporary permits is not unwarranted;

(C) such temporary permits will be issued only with respect to injection wells in operation on the date on which such State's permit program approved under this part first takes effect and for which there was inadequate time to process its permit application; and

(D) the Administrator determines the temporary permits require the use of adequate safeguards established by rules adopted by him.

(2) The Administrator may, upon application of the Governor of a State which authorizes underground injection by means of permits, authorize such State to issue (without regard to subsection (b)(1)(B)(i)), but after reasonable notice and hearing, one or more temporary permits each of which is applicable to a particular injection well and to the underground injection of a particular fluid and which may be effective until the expiration of four years after the date of enactment of this title, if the State finds, on the record of such hearing—

(A) that technology (or other means) to permit safe injection of the fluid in accordance with the applicable underground injection control program is not generally available (taking costs into consideration);

(B) that injection of the fluid would be less harmful to health than the use of other available means of disposing of waste or producing the desired product; and

(C) that available technology or other means have been employed (and will be employed) to reduce the volume and toxicity of the fluid and to minimize the potentially adverse effect of the injection on the public health.

(d) For purposes of this part:

(1) The term "underground injection" means the subsurface emplacement of fluids by well injection. **Such term does not include the underground injection of natural gas for purposes of storage.**

(2) Underground injection endangers drinking water sources if such injection may result in the presence in underground water which supplies or can reasonably be expected to supply any public water system of any contaminant, and if the presence of such contaminant may result in such system's not complying with any national primary drinking water regulation or may otherwise adversely affect the health of persons.

STATE PRIMARY ENFORCEMENT RESPONSIBILITY

SEC. 1422. (a) Within 180 days after the date of enactment of this title, the Administrator shall list in the Federal Register each State for which in his judgment a State underground injection control program may be necessary to assure that underground injection will not endanger drinking water sources. Such list may be amended from time to time.

(b)(1)(A) Each State listed under subsection (a) shall within 270 days after the date of promulgation of any regulation under section 1421 (or, if later, within 270 days after such State is first listed under subsection (a)) submit to the Administrator an application which contains a showing satisfactory to the Administrator that the State—

(i) has adopted after reasonable notice and public hearings, and will implement, an underground injection control program which meets the requirements of regulations in effect under section 1421; and

(ii) will keep such records and make such reports with respect to its activities under its underground injection control program as the Administrator may require by regulation.

The Administrator may, for good cause, extend the date for submission of an application by any State under this subparagraph for a period not to exceed an additional 270 days.

(B) Within 270 days of any amendment of a regulation under section 1421 revising or adding any requirement respecting State underground injection control programs, each State listed under subsection (a) shall submit (in such form and manner as the Administrator may require) a notice to the Administrator containing a showing satisfactory to him that the State underground injection control program meets the revised or added requirement.

(2) Within ninety days after the State's application under paragraph (1)(A) or notice under paragraph (1)(B) and after reasonable opportunity for presentation of views, the Administrator shall by

rule either approve, disapprove, or approve in part and disapprove in part, the State's underground injection control program.

(3) If the Administrator approves the State's program under paragraph (2), the State shall have primary enforcement responsibility for underground water sources until such time as the Administrator determines, by rule, that such State no longer meets the requirements of clause (i) or (ii) of paragraph (1)(A) of this subsection.

(4) Before promulgating any rule under paragraph (2) or (3) of this subsection, the Administrator shall provide opportunity for public hearing respecting such rule.

(c) If the Administrator disapproves a State's program (or part thereof) under subsection (b)(2), if the Administrator determines under subsection (b)(3) that a State no longer meets the requirements of clause (i) or (ii) of subsection (b)(1)(A), or if a State fails to submit an application or notice before the date of expiration of the period specified in subsection (b)(1), the Administrator shall by regulation within 90 days after the date of such disapproval, determination, or expiration (as the case may be) prescribe (and may from time to time by regulation revise) a program applicable to such State meeting the requirements of section 1421(b). Such program may not include requirements which interfere with or impede—

(1) the underground injection of brine or other fluids which are brought to the surface in connection with oil or natural gas production, or

(2) any underground injection for the secondary or tertiary recovery of oil or natural gas,

unless such requirements are essential to assure that underground sources of drinking water will not be endangered by such injection. Such program shall apply in such State to the extent that a program adopted by such State which the Administrator determines meets such requirements is not in effect. Before promulgating any regulation under this section, the Administrator shall provide opportunity for public hearing respecting such regulation.

(d) For purposes of this title, the term "applicable underground injection control program" with respect to a State means the program (or most recent amendment thereof) (1) which has been adopted by the State and which has been approved under subsection (b), or (2) which has been prescribed by the Adminstrator under subsection (c).

FAILURE OF STATE TO ASSURE ENFORCEMENT OF PROGRAM

SEC. 1423. (a)(1) Whenever the Administrator finds during a period during which a State has primary enforcement responsibility for underground water sources (within the meaning of section 1422(b)(3) **or section 1425(c))**
that any person who is subject to a requirement of an applicable underground injection control program in such State is violating such requirement, he shall so notify the State and the person violating such requirement. If the Administrator finds such failure to comply extends beyond the thirtieth day after the date of such notice, he shall give public notice of such finding and request the State to report within 15 days after the date of such public notice as to the steps being taken to bring such person into compliance with such requirement (including reasons for anticipated steps to be taken to bring such person into

compliance with such requirement and for any failure to take steps to bring such person into compliance with such requirement). If—

(A) such failure to comply extends beyond the sixtieth day after the date of the notice given pursuant to the first sentence of this paragraph, and

(B)(i) the State fails to submit the report requested by the Administrator within the time period prescribed by the preceding sentence, or

(ii) the State submits such report within such period but the Administrator, after considering the report, determines that by failing to take necessary steps to bring such person into compliance by such sixtieth day the State abused its discretion in carrying out primary enforcement responsibility for underground water sources,

the Administrator may commence a civil action under subsection (b)(1).

(2) Whenever the Administrator finds during a period during which a State does not have primary enforcement responsibility for underground water sources that any person subject to any requirement of any applicable underground injection control program in such State is violating such requirement, he may commence a civil action under subsection (b)(1).

(b)(1) When authorized by subsection (a), the Administrator may bring a civil action under this paragraph in the appropriate United States district court to require compliance with any requirement of an applicable underground injection control program. The court may enter such judgment as protection of public health may require, including, in the case of an action brought against a person who violates an applicable requirement of an underground injection control program and who is located in a State which has primary enforcement responsibility for underground water sources, the imposition of a civil penalty of not to exceed $5,000 for each day such person violates such requirement after the expiration of 60 days after receiving notice under subsection (a)(1).

(2) Any person who violates any requirement of an applicable underground injection control program to which he is subject during any period for which the State does not have primary enforcement responsibility for underground water sources (A) shall be subject to a civil penalty of not more than $5,000 for each day of such violation, or (B) if such violation is willful, such person may, in lieu of the civil penalty authorized by clause (B), be fined not more than $10,000 for each day of such violation.

(c) Nothing in this title shall diminish any authority of a State or political subdivision to adopt or enforce any law or regulation respecting underground injection but no such law or regulation shall relieve any person of any requirement otherwise applicable under this title.

INTERIM REGULATION OF UNDERGROUND INJECTIONS

SEC. 1424. (a)(1) Any person may petition the Administrator to have an area of a State (or States) designated as an area in which no new underground injection well may be operated during the period beginning on the date of the designation and ending on the date on which the applicable underground injection control program covering such area takes effect unless a permit for the operation of such well has been issued by the Administrator under subsection (b). The Administrator may so designate an area within a State if he finds that the area has one aquifer which is the sole or principal drinking water source for the area and which, if contaminated, would create a significant hazard to public health.

(2) Upon receipt of a petition under paragraph (1) of this subsection, the Administrator shall publish it in the Federal Register and shall provide an opportunity to interested persons to submit written data, views, or arguments thereon. Not later than the 30th day following the date of the publication of a petition under this paragraph in the Federal Register, the Administrator shall either make the designation for which the petition is submitted or deny the petition.

(b)(1) During the period beginning on the date an area is designated under subsection (a) and ending on the date the applicalbe underground injection control program covering such area takes effect, no new underground injection well may be operated in such area unless the Administrator has issued a permit for such operation.

(2) Any person may petition the Administrator for the issuance of a permit for the operation of such a well in such an area. A petition submitted under this paragraph shall be submitted in such manner and contain such information as the Administrator may require by regulation. Upon receipt of such a petition, the Administrator shall publish it in the Federal Register. The Administrator shall give notice of any proceeding on a petition and shall provide opportunity for agency hearing. The Administrator shall act upon such petition on the record of any hearing held pursuant to the preceding sentence respecting such petition. Within 120 days of the publication in the Federal Register of a petition submitted under this paragraph, the Administrator shall either issue the permit for which the petition was submitted or shall deny its issuance.

(3) The Administrator may issue a permit for the operation of a new underground injection well in an area designated under subsection (a) only if he finds that the operation of such well will not cause contamination of the aquifer of such area so as to create a significant hazard to public health. The Administrator may condition the issuance of such a permit upon the use of such control measures in connection with the operation of such well, for which the permit is to be issued, as he deems necessary to assure that the operation of the well will not contaminate the aquifer of the designated area in which the well is located so as to create a significant hazard to public health.

(c) Any person who operates a new underground injection well in violation of subsection (b), (1) shall be subject to a civil penalty of not more than $5,000 for each day in which such violation occurs, or (2) if such violation is willful, such person may, in lieu of the civil penalty authorized by clause (1), be fined not more than $10,000 for each day in which such violation occurs. If the Administrator has reason to believe that any person is violating or will violate subsection (b), he may petition the United States district court to issue a temporary restraining order or injunction (including a mandatory injunction) to enforce such subsection.

(d) For purposes of this section, the term "new underground injection well" means an underground injection well whose operation was not approved by appropriate State and Federal agencies before the date of the enactment of this title.

(e) If the Administrator determines, on his own initiative or upon petition, that an area has an aquifer which is the sole or principal drinking water source for the area and which, if contaminated, would create a significant hazard to public health, he shall publish notice of that determination in the Federal Register. After the publication of any such notice, no commitment for Federal financial assistance (through a grant, contract, loan guarantee, or otherwise) may be entered into for any project which the Administrator determines may contaminate such aquifer through a recharge zone so as to create a significant hazard to public health, but a commitment for Federal financial assistance may, if authorized under another provision of law, be entered into to plan or design the project to assure that it will not so contaminate the aquifer.

OPTIONAL DEMONSTRATION BY STATES RELATING TO OIL OR NATURAL GAS

SEC. 1425. (a) For purposes of the Administrator's approval or disapproval under section 1422 of that portion of any State underground injection control program which relates to—

(1) the underground injection of brine or other fluids which are brought to the surface in connection with oil or natural gas production, or

(2) any underground injection for the secondary or tertiary recovery of oil or natural gas,

in lieu of the showing required under subparagraph (A) of section 1422(b)(1) the State may demonstrate that such portion of the State program meets the requirements of subparagraphs (A) through (D) of section 1421(b)(1) and represents an effective program (including adequate recordkeeping and reporting) to prevent underground injection which endangers drinking water sources.

(b) If the Administrator revises or amends any requirement of a regulation under section 1421 relating to any aspect of the underground injection referred to in subsection (a), in the case of that portion of a State underground injection control program for which the demonstration referred to in subsection (a) has been made, in lieu of the showing required under section 1422(b)(1)(B) the State may demonstrate that, with respect to that aspect of such underground injection, the State program meets the requirements of subparagraphs (A) through (D) of section 1421(b)(1) and represents an effective program (including adequate recordkeeping and reporting) to prevent underground injection which endangers drinking water sources.

(c)(1) Section 1422(b)(3) shall not apply to that portion of any State underground injection control program approved by the Administrator pursuant to a demonstration under subsection (a) of this section (and under subsection (b) of this section where applicable).

(2) If pursuant to such a demonstration, the Administrator approves such portion of the State program, the State shall have primary enforcement responsibility with respect to that portion until such time as the Administrator determines, by rule, that such demonstration is no longer valid. Following such a determination, the Administrator may exercise the authority of subsection (c) of section 1422 in the same manner as provided in such subsection with respect to a determination described in such subsection.

(3) Before promulgating any rule under paragraph (2), the Administrator shall provide opportunity for public hearing respecting such rule.

Part D—Emergency Powers

EMERGENCY POWERS

Sec. 1431. (a) Notwithstanding any other provision of this title, the Administrator, upon receipt of information that a contaminant which is present in or is likely to enter a public water system may present an imminent and substantial endangerment to the health of persons, and that appropriate State and local authorities have not acted to protect the health of such persons, may take such actions as he may deem necessary in order to protect the health of such persons. To the extent he determines it to be practicable in light of such imminent endangerment, he shall consult with the State and local authorities in order to confirm the correctness of the information on which action proposed to be taken under this subsection is based and to ascertain the action which such authorities are or will be taking. The action which the Administrator may take may include (but shall not be limited to) (1) issuing such orders as may be necessary to protect the health of persons who are or may be users of such system (including travelers), and (2) commencing a civil action for appropriate relief, including a restraining order or permanent or temporary injunction.

(b) Any person who willfully violates or fails or refuses to comply with any order issued by the Administrator under subsection (a)(1) may, in an action brought in the appropriate United States district court to enforce such order, be fined no more than $5,000 for each day in which such violation occurs or failure to comply continues.

Part E—General Provisions

ASSURANCE OF AVAILABILITY OF ADEQUATE SUPPLIES OF CHEMICALS NECESSARY FOR TREATMENT OF WATER

Sec. 1441. (a) If any person who uses chlorine, activated carbon, lime, ammonia, soda ash, potassium permanganate, caustic soda, or other chemical or substance for the purpose of treating water in any public water system or in any public treatment works determines that the amount of such chemical or substance necessary to effectively treat such water is not reasonably available to him or will not be so available to him when required for the effective treatment of such water, such person may apply to the Administrator for a certification (hereinafter in this section referred to as a "certification of need") that the amount of such chemical or substance which such person requires to effectively treat such water is not reasonably available to him or will not be so available when required for the effective treatment of such water.

(b)(1) An application for a certification of need shall be in such form and submitted in such manner as the Administrator may require and shall (A) specify the persons the applicant determines are able to provide the chemical or substance with respect to which the application is submitted, (B) specify the persons from whom the applicant has sought such chemical or substance, and (C) contain such other information as the Administrator may require.

(2) Upon receipt of an application under this section, the Administrator shall (A) publish in the Federal Register a notice of the receipt of the application and a brief summary of it, (B) notify in writing each person whom the President or his delegate (after consultation with the Administrator) determines could be made subject to an order required to be issued upon the issuance of the certification of need applied for in such application, and (C) provide an opportunity for the submission of written comments on such application. The requirements of the preceding sentence of this paragraph shall not apply when the Administrator for good cause finds (and incorporates the finding with a brief statement of reasons therefor in the order issued) that waiver of such requirements is necessary in order to protect the public health.

(3) Within 30 days after—

(A) the date a notice is published under paragraph (2) in the Federal Register with respect to an application submitted under this section for the issuance of a certification of need, or

(B) the date on which such application is received if as authorized by the second sentence of such paragraph no notice is published with respect to such application,

the Administrator shall take action either to issue or deny the issuance of a certification of need.

(c)(1) If the Administrator finds that the amount of a chemical or substance necessary for an applicant under an application submitted under this section to effectively treat water in a public water system or in a public treatment works is not reasonably available to the applicant or will not be so available to him when required for the effective treatment of such water, the Administrator shall issue a certification of need. Not later than seven days following the issuance of such certification, the President or his delegate shall issue an order requiring the provision to such person of such amounts of such chemical or substance as the Administrator deems necessary in the certification of need issued for such person. Such order shall apply to such manufacturers, producers, processors, distributors, and repackagers of such chemical or substance as the President or his delegate deems necessary and appropriate, except that such order may not apply to any manufacturer, producer, or processor of such chemical or substance who manufactures, produces, or processes (as the case may be) such chemical or substance solely for its own use. Persons subject to an order issued under this section shall be given a reasonable opportunity to consult with the President or his delegate with respect to the implementation of the order.

(2) Orders which are to be issued under paragraph (1) to manufacturers, producers, and processors of a chemical or substance shall be equitably apportioned, as far as practicable, among all manufacturers, producers, and processors of such chemical or substance; and orders which are to be issued under paragraph (1) to distributors and repackagers of a chemical or substance shall be equitably apportioned, as far as practicable, among all distributors and repackagers of such chemical or substance. In apportioning orders issued under paragraph (1) to manufacturers, producers, processors, distributors, and repackagers of chlorine, the President or his delegate shall, in carrying out the requirements of the preceding sentence, consider—

(A) the geographical relationships and established commercial relationships between such manufacturers, producers, processors, distributors, and repackagers and the persons for whom the orders are issued;

(B) in the case of orders to be issued to producers of chlorine, the (i) amount of chlorine historically supplied by each such producer to treat water in public water systems and public treatment works, and (ii) share of each such producer of the total annual production of chlorine in the United States; and

(C) such other factors as the President or his delegate may determine are relevant to the apportionment of orders in accordance with the requirements of the preceding sentence.

(3) Subject to subsection (f), any person for whom a certification of need has been issued under this subsection may upon the expiration of the order issued under paragraph (1) upon such certification apply under this section for additional certifications.

(d) There shall be available as a defense to any action brought for breach of contract in a Federal or State court arising out of delay or failure to provide, sell, or offer for sale or exchange a chemical or substance subject to an order issued pursuant to subsection (c)(1), that such delay or failure was caused solely by compliance with such order.

(e)(1) Whoever knowingly fails to comply with any order issued pursuant to subsection (c)(1) shall be fined not more than $5,000 for each such failure to comply.

(2) Whoever fails to comply with any order issued pursuant to subsection (c)(1) shall be subject to a civil penalty of not more than $2,500 for each such failure to comply.

(3) Whenever the Administrator or the President or his delegate has reason to believe that any person is violating or will violate any order issued pursuant to subsection (c)(1), he may petition a United States district court to issue a temporary restraining order or preliminary or permanent injunction (including a mandatory injunction) to enforce the provisions of such order.

(f) No certification of need or order issued under this section may remain in effect—

(1) for more than one year, or

(2) after September 30, 1982;

whichever occurs first.

RESEARCH, TECHNICAL ASSISTANCE, INFORMATION, AND TRAINING OF PERSONNEL

SEC. 1442. (a) (1) The Administrator may conduct research, studies, and demonstrations relating to the causes, diagnosis, treatment, control, and prevention of physical and mental diseases and other impairments of man resulting directly or indirectly from contaminants in water, or to the provision of a dependably safe supply of drinking water, including—

(A) improved methods (i) to identify and measure the existence of contaminants in drinking water (including methods which may be used by State and local health and water officials), and (ii) to identify the source of such contaminants;

(B) improved methods to identify and measure the health effects of contaminants in drinking water;

(C) new methods of treating raw water to prepare it for drinking, so as to improve the efficiency of water treatment and to remove contaminants from water;

(D) improved methods for providing a dependably safe supply of drinking water, including improvements in water purification and distribution, and methods of assessing the health related hazards of drinking water; and

(E) improved methods of protecting underground water sources of public water systems from contamination.

(2) (A) The Administrator shall, to the maximum extent feasible, provide technical assistance to the States and municipalities in the establishment and administration of public water system supervision programs (as defined in section 1443(c)(1)).

(B) The Administrator is authorized to provide technical assistance and to make grants to States, or publicly owned water systems to assist in responding to and alleviating any emergency situation affecting public water systems (including sources of water for such systems) which the Administrator determines to present substantial danger to the public health. Grants provided under this subparagraph shall be used only to support those actions which (i) are necessary for preventing, limiting or mitigating danger to the public health in such emergency situation and (ii) would not, in the judgment of the Administrator, be taken without such emergency assistance. The Administrator may carry out the program authorized under this subparagraph as part of, and in accordance with the terms and conditions of, any other program of assistance for environmental emergencies which the Administrator is authorized to carry out under any other provision of law. No limitation on appropriations for any such other program shall apply to amounts appropriated under this subparagraph.

(3)(A) The Administrator shall conduct studies, and make periodic reports to Congress, on the costs of carrying out regulations prescribed under section 1412.

(B) Not later than eighteen months after the date of enactment of this subparagraph, the Administrator shall submit a report to Congress which identifies and analyzes—

(i) the anticipated costs of compliance with interim and revised national primary drinking water regulations and the anticipated costs to States and units of local governments in implementing such regulations;

(ii) alternative methods of (including alternative treatment techniques for) compliance with such regulations;

(iii) methods of paying the costs of compliance by public water systems with national primary drinking water regulations, including user charges, State or local taxes or subsidies, Federal grants (including planning or construction grants, or both), loans, and loan guarantees, and other methods of assisting in paying the costs of such compliance;

(iv) the advantages and disadvantages of each of the methods referred to in clauses (ii) and (iii);

(v) the sources of revenue presently available (and projected to be available) to public water systems to meet current and future expenses; and

(vi) the costs of drinking water paid by residential and industrial consumers in a sample of large, medium, and small public water systems and of individually owned wells, and the reasons for any differences in such costs.

The report required by this subparagraph shall identify and analyze the items required in clauses (i) through (v) separately with respect to public water systems serving small communities. The report required by this subparagraph shall include such recommendations as the Administrator deems appropriate.

(4) The Administrator shall conduct a survey and study of—

(A) disposal of waste (including residential waste) which may endanger underground water which supplies, or can reasonably be expected to supply, any public water systems, and

(B) means of control of such waste disposal.

Not later than one year after the date of enactment of this title, he shall transmit to the Congress the results of such survey and study, together with such recommendations as he deems appropriate.

(5) The Administrator shall carry out a study of methods of underground injection which do not result in the degradation of underground drinking water sources.

(6) The Administrator shall carry out a study of methods of preventing, detecting, and dealing with surface spills of contaminants which may degrade underground water sources for public water systems.

(7) The Administrator shall carry out a study of virus contamination of drinking water sources and means of control of such contamination.

(8) The Administrator shall carry out a study of the nature and extent of the impact on underground water which supplies or can reasonably be expected to supply public water systems of (A) abandoned injection or extraction wells; (B) intensive application of pesticides and fertilizers in underground water recharge areas; and (C) ponds, pools, lagoons, pits, or other surface disposal of contaminants in underground water recharge areas.

(9) The Administrator shall conduct a comprehensive study of public water supplies and drinking water sources to determine the nature, extent, sources of and means of control of contamination by chemicals or other substances suspected of being carcinogenic. Not later than six months after the date of enactment of this title, he shall transmit to the Congress the initial results of such study, together with such recommendations for further review and corrective action as he deems appropriate.

(10) The Administrator shall carry out a study of the reaction of chlorine and humic acids and the effects of the contaminants which result from such reaction on public health and on the safety of drinking water, including any carcinogenic effect.

(11) The Administrator shall carry out a study of polychlorinated biphenyl contamination of actual or potential sources of drinking water, contamination of such sources by other substances known or suspected to be harmful to public health, the effects of such contamination, and means of removing, treating, or otherwise controlling such contamination. To assist in carrying out this paragraph, the Administrator is authorized to make grants to public agencies and private nonprofit institutions.

(b) In carrying out this title, the Administrator is authorized to—

(1) collect and make available information pertaining to research, investigations, and demonstrations with respect to providing a dependably safe supply of drinking water together with appropriate recommendations in connection therewith;

(2) make available research facilities of the Agency to appropriate public authorities, institutions, and individuals engaged in studies and research relating to the purposes of this title;

(3) make grants to, and enter into contracts with, any public agency, educational institution, and any other organization, in accordance with procedures prescribed by the Administrator, under which he may pay all or a part of the costs (as may be determined by the Administrator) of any project or activity which is designed—

(A) to develop, expand, or carry out a program (which may combine training education and employment) for training persons for occupations involving the public health aspects of providing safe drinking water;

(B) to train inspectors and supervisory personnel to train or supervise persons in occupations involving the public health aspects of providing safe drinking water; or

(C) to develop and expand the capability of programs of States and municipalities to carry out the purposes of this title (other than by carrying out State programs of public water system supervision or underground water source protection (as defined in section 1443(c))).

(c) Not later than eighteen months after the date of enactment of this subsection, the Administrator shall submit a report to Congress on the present and projected future availability of an adequate and dependable supply of safe drinking water to meet present and projected future need. Such report shall include an analysis of the future demand for drinking water and other competing uses of water, the availability and use of methods to conserve water or reduce demand, the adequacy of present measures to assure adequate and dependable supplies of safe drinking water, and the problems (financial, legal, or other) which need to be resolved in order to assure the availability of such supplies for the future. Existing information and data compiled by the National Water Commission and others shall be utilized to the extent possible.

(d) The Administrator shall—

(1) provide training for, and make grants for training (including postgraduate training) of (A) personnel of State agencies which have primary enforcement responsibility and of agencies of units

of local government to which enforcement responsibilities have been delegated by the State, and (B) personnel who manage or operate public water systems, and

(2) make grants for postgraduate training of individuals (including grants to educational institutions for traineeships) for purposes of qualifying such individuals to work as personnel referred to in paragraph (1).

Reasonable fees may be charged for training provided under paragraph (1)(B) to persons other than personnel of State or local agencies but such training shall be provided to personnel of State or local agencies without charge.

(e) The Administrator is authorized to make grants to a public water system which is required, under State or local law, to meet standards relating to drinking water turbidity which are more stringent than the standards in effect pursuant to this title. Such grants shall be used by the public water system for the development and demonstration (including construction and installation) of any water filtration system which will demonstrate a new or improved method of meeting such more stringent standards.

(f) There are authorized to be appropriated to carry out the provisions of this section other than subsection (a)(2)(B) and provisions relating to research $15,000,000 for the fiscal year ending June 30, 1975; $25,000,000 for the fiscal year ending June 30, 1976; $35,000,000 for the fiscal year ending June 30, 1977; $17,000,000 for each of the fiscal years 1978 and 1979; $21,405,000 for the fiscal year ending September 30, 1980; $30,000,000 for the fiscal year ending September 30, 1981; and $35,000,000 for the fiscal year ending September 30, 1982. There are authorized to be appropriated to carry out subsection (a)(2)(B) $8,000,000 for each of the fiscal years 1978 through 1982.

GRANTS FOR STATE PROGRAMS

SEC. 1443. (a)(1) From allotments made pursuant to paragraph (4), the Administrator may make grants to States to carry out public water system supervision programs.

(2) No grant may be made under paragraph (1) unless an application therefor has been submitted to the Administrator in such form and manner as he may require. The Administrator may not approve an application of a State for its first grant under paragraph (1) unless he determines that the State—

(A) has established or will establish within one year from the date of such grant a public water system supervision program, and

(B) will, within that one year, assume primary enforcement responsibility for public water system within the State.

No grant may be made to a State under paragraph (1) for any period beginning more than one year after the date of the State's first grant unless the State has assumed and maintains primary enforcement responsibility for public water systems within the State.

(3) A grant under paragraph (1) shall be made to cover not more than 75 per centum of the grant recipient's costs (as determined under regulations of the Administrator) in carrying out, during the one-year period beginning on the date the grant is made, a public water system supervision program.

(4) In each fiscal year the Administrator shall, in accordance with regulations, allot the sums appropriated for such year under paragraph

(5) among the States on the basis of population, geographical area, number of public water systems, and other relevant factors. No State shall receive less than 1 per centum of the annual appropriation for grants under paragraph (1): *Provided*, That the Administrator may, by regulation, reduce such percentage in accordance with the criteria specified in this paragraph: *And provided further*, That such percentage shall not apply to grants allotted to Guam, American Samoa, or the Virgin Islands.

(5) The prohibition contained in the last sentence of paragraph (2) may be waived by the Administrator with respect to a grant to a State through fiscal year 1979 but such prohibition may only be waived if, in the judgment of the Administrator—

(A) the State is making a diligent effort to assume and maintain primary enforcement responsibility for public water systems within the State;

(B) the State has made significant progress toward assuming and maintaining such primary enforcement responsibility; and

(C) there is reason to believe the State will assume such primary enforcement responsibility by October 1, 1979.

The amount of any grant awarded for the fiscal years 1978 and 1979 pursuant to a waiver under this paragraph may not exceed 75 per centum of the allotment which the State would have received for such fiscal year if it had assumed and maintained such primary enforcement responsibility. The remaining 25 per centum of the amount allotted to such State for such fiscal year shall be retained by the Administrator, and the Administrator may award such amount to such State at such time as the State assumes such responsibility before the beginning of fiscal year 1980. At the beginning of each fiscal years 1979 and 1980 the amounts retained by the Administrator for any preceding fiscal year and not awarded by the beginning fiscal year 1979 or 1980 to the States to which such amounts were originally allotted may be removed from the original allotment and reallotted for fiscal year 1979 or 1980 (as the case may be) to States which have assumed primary enforcement responsibility by the beginning of such fiscal year.

(6) The Administrator shall notify the State of the approval or disapproval of any application for a grant under this section—

(A) within ninety days after receipt of such application, or

(B) not later than the first day of the fiscal year for which the grant application is made,

whichever is later.

(7) For the purposes of making grants under paragraph (1) there are authorized to be appropriated $15,000,000 for the fiscal year ending June 30, 1976, $25,000,000 for the fiscal year ending June 30, 1977, $35,000,000 for fiscal year 1978, $45,000,000 for fiscal year 1979, **, $29,450,000 for the fiscal year ending September 30, 1980, $32,000,000 for the fiscal year ending September 30, 1981, and $34,000,000 for the fiscal year ending September 30, 1982.**

(b)(1) From allotments made pursuant to paragraph (4), the Administrator may make grants to States to carry out underground water source protection programs.

(2) No grant may be made under paragraph (1) unless an application therefor has been submitted to the Administrator in such form and manner as he may require. **No grant may be made to any State under paragraph (1) unless the State has assumed primary enforcement responsibility within two years after the date the Administrator promulgates regulations for State underground injection control programs under section 1421.**

(3) A grant under paragraph (1) shall be made to cover not more than 75 per centum of the grant recipient's costs (as determined under regulations of the Administrator) in carrying out, during the one-year period beginning on the date the grant is made, an underground water source protection program.

(4) In each fiscal year the Administrator shall, in accordance with regulations, allot the sums appropriated for such year under paragraph (5) among the States on the basis of population, geographical area, and other relevant factors.

(5) For purposes of making grants under paragraph (1) there are authorized to be appropriated $5,000,000 for the fiscal year ending June 30, 1976, $7,500,000 for the fiscal year ending June 30, 1977, $10,000,000 for each of the fiscal years 1978 and 1979, **$7,795,000 for the fiscal year ending September 30, 1980, $18,000,000 for the fiscal year ending September 30, 1981, and $21,000,000 for the fiscal year ending September 30, 1982**.

(c) For purposes of this section:

(1) The term "public water system supervision program" means a program for the adoption and enforcement of drinking water regulations (with such variances and exemptions from such regulations under conditions and in a manner which is not less stringent than the conditions under, and the manner in, which variances and exemptions may be granted under sections 1415 and 1416) which are no less stringent than the national primary drinking water regulations under section 1412, and for keeping records and making reports required by section 1413(a)(3).

(2) The term "underground water source protection program" means a program for the adoption and enforcement of a program which meets the requirements of regulations under section 1421 and for keeping records and making reports required by section 1422(b)(1)(A)(ii). **Such term includes, where applicable, a program which meets the requirements of section 1425.**

SPECIAL STUDY AND DEMONSTRATION PROJECT GRANTS; GUARANTEED LOANS

SEC. 1444. (a) The Administrator may make grants to any person for the purposes of—

(1) assisting in the development and demonstration (including construction) of any project which will demonstrate a new or improved method, approach, or technology, for providing a dependably safe supply of drinking water to the public; and

(2) assisting in the development and demonstration (including construction) of any project which will investigate and demonstrate health implications involved in the reclamation, recycling, and reuse of waste waters for drinking and the processes and methods for the preparation of safe and acceptable drinking water.

(b) Grants made by the Administrator under this section shall be subject to the following limitations:

(1) Grants under this section shall not exceed 66⅔ per centum of the total cost of construction of any facility, and 75 per centum of any other costs, as determined by the Administrator.

(2) Grants under this section shall not be made for any project involving the construction or modification of any facilities for any public water system in a State unless such project has been approved by the State agency charged with the responsibility for safety of drinking water (or if there is no such agency in a State, by the State health authority).

(3) Grants under this section shall not be made for any project unless the Administrator determines, after consulting the National Drinking Water Advisory Council, that such project will serve a useful purpose relating to the development and demonstration of new or improved techniques, methods, or technologies for the provision of safe water to the public for drinking.

(4) Priority for grants under this section shall be given where there are known or potential public health hazards which require advanced technology for the removal of particles which are too small to be removed by ordinary treatment technology.

(c) For the purposes of making grants under subsections (a) and (b) of this section there are authorized to be appropriated $7,500,000 for the fiscal year ending June 30, 1975; and $7,500,000 for the fiscal year ending June 30, 1976; and $10,000,000 for the fiscal year ending June 30, 1977.

(d) The Administrator during the fiscal years ending June 30, 1975, and June 30, 1976, shall carry out a program of guaranteeing loans made by private lenders to small public water systems for the purpose of enabling such systems to meet national primary drinking water regulations (including interim regulations) prescribed under section 1412. No such guarantee may be made with respect to a system unless (1) such system cannot reasonably obtain financial assistance necessary to comply with such regulations from any other source, and (2) the Administrator determines that any facilities constructed with a loan guaranteed under this subsection is not likely to be made obsolete by subsequent changes in primary regulations. The aggregate amount of indebtedness guaranteed with respect to any system may not exceed $50,000. The aggregate amount of indebtedness guaranteed under this subsection may not exceed $50,000,000. The Administrator shall prescribe regulations to carry out this subsection.

RECORDS AND INSPECTIONS

SEC. 1445. (a) Every person who is a supplier of water, who is or may be otherwise subject to a primary drinking water regulation prescribed under section 1412 or to an applicable underground injection control program (as defined in section 1422(c)), who is or may be subject to the permit requirement of section 1424 or to an order issued under section 1441, or who is a grantee, shall establish and maintain such records, make such reports, conduct such monitoring, and provide such information as the Administrator may reasonably require by regulation to assist him in establishing regulations under this title, in determining whether such person has acted or is acting in compliance with this title, in administering any program of financial assistance under this title, in evaluating the health risks of unregulated contaminants, or in advising the public of such risks.

(b)(1) Except as provided in paragraph (2), the Administrator, or representatives of the Administrator duly designated by him, upon presenting appropriate credentials and a written notice to any supplier of water or other person subject to (A) a national primary drinking water regulation prescribed under section 1412, (B) and applicable underground injection control program, or (C) any requirement to monitor an unregulated contaminant pursuant to subsection (a), or person in charge of any of the property of such supplier or other person referred to in clause (A), (B), or (C), is authorized to enter any establishment, facility, or other property of such supplier or other person in order to determine whether such supplier or other person has acted or is acting in compliance with this title, including for this purpose, inspection, at reasonable times, of records, files, papers, processes, controls, and facilities, or in order to test any feature of a public water system, including its raw water source. The Administrator or the Comptroller General (or any representative designated by either) shall have access for the purpose of audit and examination to any records, reports, or information of a grantee which are required to be maintained under subsection (a) or which are pertinent to any financial assistance under this title.

(2) No entry may be made under the first sentence of paragraph (1) in an establishment, facility, or other property of a supplier of water or other person subject to a national primary drinking water regulation if the establishment, facility, or other property is located in a State which has primary enforcement responsibility for public water systems unless, before written notice of such entry is made, the Administrator (or his representative) notifies the State agency charged with responsibility for safe drinking water of the reasons for such entry. The Administrator shall, upon a showing by the State agency that such an entry will be detrimental to the administration of the State's program of primary enforcement responsibility, take such showing into consideration in determining whether to make such entry. No State agency which receives notice under this paragraph of an entry proposed to be made under paragraph (1) may use the information contained in the notice to inform the person whose property is proposed to be entered of the proposed entry; and if a State agency so uses such information, notice to the agency under this paragraph is not required until such time as the Administrator determines the agency has provided him satisfactory assurances that it will no longer so use information contained in a notice under this paragraph.

(c) Whoever fails or refuses to comply with any requirement of subsection (a) or to allow the Administrator, the Comptroller General, or representatives of either, to enter and conduct any audit or inspection authorized by subsection (b) may be fined not more that $5,000.

(d)(1) Subject to paragraph (2), upon a showing satisfactory to the Administrator by any person that any information required under this section from such person, if made public, would divulge trade secrets or secret processes of such person, the Administrator shall consider such information confidential in accordance with the purposes of section 1905 of title 18 of the United States Code. If the applicant fails to make a showing satisfactory to the Administrator, the Administrator shall give such applicant thirty days' notice before releasing the information to which the application relates (unless the public health or safety requires an earlier release of such information).

(2) Any information required under this section (A) may be disclosed to other officers, employees, or authorized representatives of the United States concerned with carrying out this title or to committees of the Congress, or when relevant in any proceeding under this title, and (B) shall be disclosed to the extent it deals with the level of contaminants in drinking water. For purposes of this subsection

the term "information required under this section" means any papers, books, documents, or information, or any particular part thereof, reported to or otherwise obtained by the Administrator under this section.

(e) For purposes of this section, (1) the term "grantee" means any person who applies for or receives financial assistance, by grant, contract, or loan guarantee under this title, and (2) the term "person" includes a Federal agency.

NATIONAL DRINKING WATER ADVISORY COUNCIL

Sec. 1446. (a) There is established a National Drinking Water Advisory Council which shall consist of fifteen members appointed by the Administrator after consultation with the Secretary. Five members shall be appointed from the general public; five members shall be appointed from appropriate State and local agencies concerned with water hygiene and public water supply; and five members shall be appointed from representatives of private organizations or groups demonstrating an active interest in the field of water hygiene and public water supply. Each member of the Council shall hold office for a term of three years, except that—

(1) any member appointed to fill a vacancy occurring prior to the expiration of the term for which his predecessor was appointed shall be appointed for the remainder of such term; and

(2) the terms of the members first taking office shall expire as follows: Five shall expire three years after the date of enactment of this title, five shall expire two years after such date, and five shall expire one year after such date, as designated by the Administrator at the time of appointment.

The members of the Council shall be eligible for reappointment.

(b) The Council shall advise, consult with, and make recommendations to, the Administrator on matters relating to activities, functions, and policies of the Agency under this title.

(c) Members of the Council appointed under this section shall, while attending meetings or conferences of the Council or otherwise engaged in business of the Council, receive compensation and allowances at the rate to be fixed by the Administrator, but not exceeding the daily equivalent of the annual rate of basic pay in effect for grade GS–18 of the General Schedule for each day (including travel time) during which they are engaged in the actual performance of duties vested in the Council. While away from their homes or regular places of business in the performance of services for the Council, members of the Council shall be allowed travel expenses, including per diem in lieu of subsistence, in the same manner as persons employed intermittently in the Government service are allowed expenses under section 5703(b) of title 5 of the United States Code.

(d) Section 14(a) of the Federal Advisory Committee Act (relating to termination) shall not apply to the Council.

FEDERAL AGENCIES

Sec. 1447. (a) Each Federal agency (1) having jurisdiction over any federally owned or maintained public water system or (2) engaged in any activity resulting, or which may result in, underground injection which endangers drinking water (within the meaning of section 1421(d)(2)) shall be subject to, and comply with, all Federal, State, and local requirements, administrative authorities, and process and sanctions respecting the provision of safe drinking water and respecting any underground injection program in the same manner, and to the same extent, as any nongovernmental entity. The preceding sentence shall apply (A) to any requirement whether substantive or procedural (including any recordkeeping or reporting requirement, any requirement respecting permits, and any other requirement whatsoever), (B) to the exercise of any Federal, State, or local administrative authority, and (C) to any process or sanction, whether enforced in Federal, State, or local courts or in any other manner. This subsection shall apply, notwithstanding any immunity of such agencies, under any law or rule of law. No officer, agent, or employee of the United States shall be personally liable for any civil penalty under this title with respect to any act or omission within the scope of his official duties.

(b) The Administrator shall waive compliance with subsection (a) upon request of the Secretary of Defense and upon a determination by the President that the requested waiver is necessary in the interest of national security. The Administrator shall maintain a written record of the basis upon which such waiver was granted and make such record available for in camera examination when relevant in a judicial proceeding under this title. Upon the issuance of such a waiver, the Administrator shall publish in the Federal Register a notice that the waiver was granted for national security purposes, unless, upon the request of the Secretary of Defense, the Administrator determines to omit such publication because the publication itself would be contrary to the interests of national security, in which event the Administrator shall submit notice to the Armed Services Committee of the Senate and House of Representatives.

(c)(1) Nothing in the Safe Drinking Water Amendments of 1977 shall be construed to alter or affect the status of American Indian lands or water rights nor to waive any sovereignty over Indian lands guaranteed by treaty or statute.

(2) For the purposes of this Act, the term "Federal agency" shall not be construed to refer to or include any American Indian tribe, nor to the Secretary of the Interior in his capacity as trustee of Indian lands.

JUDICIAL REVIEW

SEC. 1448. (a) A petition for review of—

(1) action of the Administrator in promulgating any national primary drinking water regulation under section 1412, any regulation under section 1413(b)(1), any regulation under section 1414(c), any regulation for State underground injection control programs under section 1421, or any general regulation for the administration of this title may be filed only in the United States Court of Appeals for the District of Columbia Circuit; and

(2) action of the Administrator in promulgating any other regulation under this title, issuing any order under this title,

or making any determination under this title may be filed only in the United States court of appeals for the appropriate circuit. Any such petition shall be filed within the 45-day period beginning on the date of the promulgation of the regulation or issuance of the order with respect to which review is sought or on the date of the determination with respect to which review is sought, and may be filed after the expiration of such 45-day period if the petition is based solely on grounds arising after the expiration of such period. Action of the Administrator with respect to which review could have been obtained under this subsection shall not be subject to judicial review in any civil or criminal proceeding for enforcement or in any civil action to enjoin enforcement.

(b) The United States district courts shall have jurisdiction of actions brought to review (1) the granting of, or the refusing to grant, a variance or exemption under section 1415 or 1416 or (2) the requirements of any schedule prescribed for a variance or exemption under such section or the failure to prescribe such a schedule. Such an action may only be brought upon a petition for review filed with the court within the 45-day period beginning on the date the action sought to be reviewed is taken or, in the case of a petition to review the refusal to grant a variance or exemption or the failure to prescribe a schedule, within the 45-day period beginning on the date action is required to be taken on the variance, exemption, or schedule, as the case may be. A petition for such review may be filed after the expiration of such period if the petition is based solely on grounds arising after the expiration of such period. Action with respect to which review could have been obtained under this subsection shall not be subject to judicial review in any civil or criminal proceeding for enforcement or in any civil action to enjoin enforcement.

(c) In any judicial proceeding in which review is sought of a determination under this title required to be made on the record after notice and opportunity for hearing, if any party applies to the court for leave to adduce additional evidence and shows to the satisfaction of the court that such additional evidence is material and that there were reasonable grounds for the failure to adduce such evidence in the proceeding before the Administrator, the court may order such additional evidence (and evidence in rebuttal thereof) to be taken before the Administrator, in such manner and upon such terms and conditions as the court may deem proper. The Administrator may modify his findings as to the facts, or make new findings, by reason of the additional evidence so taken, and he shall file such modified or new findings, and his recommendation, if any, for the modification or setting aside of his original determination, with the return of such additional evidence.

CITIZEN'S CIVIL ACTION

SEC. 1449. (a) Except as provided in subsection (b) of this section, any person may commence a civil action on his own behalf—

(1) against any person (including (A) the United States, and (B) any other governmental instrumentality or agency to the extent permitted by the eleventh amendment to the Constitution) who is alleged to be in violation of any requirement prescribed by or under this title, or

(2) against the Administrator where there is alleged a failure of the Administrator to perform any act or duty under this title which is not discretionary with the Administrator.

No action may be brought under paragraph (1) against a public water system for a violation of a requirement prescribed by or under this title which occurred within the 27-month period beginning on the first day of the month in which this title is enacted. The United States district courts shall have jurisdiction, without regard to the amount in controversy or the citizenship of the parties, to enforce in an action brought under this subsection any requirement prescribed by or under this title or to order the Administrator to perform an act, or duty described in paragraph (2), as the case may be.

(b) No civil action may be commenced—

(1) under subsection (a)(1) of this section respecting violation of a requirement prescribed by or under this title—

(A) prior to sixty days after the plaintiff has given notice of such violation (i) to the Administrator, (ii) to any alleged violator of such requirement and (iii) to the State in which the violation occurs, or

(B) if the Administrator, the Attorney General, or the State has commenced and is diligently prosecuting a civil action in a court of the United States to require compliance with such requirement, but in any such action in a court of the United States any person may intervene as a matter of right; or

(2) under subsection (a)(2) of this section prior to sixty days after the plaintiff has given notice of such action to the Administrator.

Notice required by this subsection shall be given in such manner as the Administrator shall prescribe by regulation. No person may commence a civil action under subsection (a) to require a State to prescribe a schedule under section 1415 or 1416 for a variance or exemption, unless such person shows to the satisfaction of the court that the State has in a substantial number of cases failed to prescribe such schedules.

(c) In any action under this section, the Administrator or the Attorney General, if not a party, may intervene as a matter of right.

(d) The court, in issuing any final order in any action brought under subsection (a) of this section, may award costs of litigation (including reasonable attorney and expert witness fees) to any party whenever the court determines such an award is appropriate. The court may, if a temporary restraining order or preliminary injunction is sought, require the filing of a bond or equivalent security in accordance with the Federal Rules of Civil Procedure.

(e) Nothing in this section shall restrict any right which any person (or class of persons) may have under any statute or common law to seek enforcement of any requirement prescribed by or under this title or to seek any other relief. Nothing in this section or in any other law of the United States shall be construed to prohibit, exclude, or restrict any State or local government from—

(1) bringing any action or obtaining any remedy or sanction in any State or local court, or

(2) bringing any administrative action or obtaining any administrative remedy or sanction,

against any agency of the United States under State or local law to enforce any requirement respecting the provision of safe drinking water or respecting any underground injection control program. Nothing in this section shall be construed to authorize judicial review of regulations or orders of the Administrator under this title, except as provided in section 1448. For provisions providing for application of certain requirements to such agencies in the same manner as to nongovernmental entities, see section 1447.

GENERAL PROVISIONS

SEC. 1450. (a)(1) The Administrator is authorized to prescribe such regulations as are necessary or appropriate to carry out his functions under this title.

(2) The Administrator may delegate any of his functions under this title (other than prescribing regulations) to any officer or employee of the Agency.

(b) The Administrator, with the consent of the head of any other agency of the United States, may utilize such officers and employees of such agency as he deems necessary to assist him in carrying out the purposes of this title.

(c) Upon the request of a State or interstate agency, the Administrator may assign personnel of the Agency to such State or interstate agency for the purposes of carrying out the provisions of this title.

(d)(1) The Administrator may make payments of grants under this title (after necessary adjustment on account of previously made underpayments or overpayments) in advance or by way of reimbursement, and in such installments and on such conditions as he may determine.

(2) Financial assistance may be made available in the form of grants only to individuals and nonprofit agencies or institutions. For purposes of this paragraph, the term "nonprofit agency or institution" means an agency or institution no part of the net earnings of which inure, or may lawfully inure, to the benefit of any private shareholder or individual.

(e) The Administrator shall take such action as may be necessary to assure compliance with provisions of the Act of March 3, 1931 (known as the Davis-Bacon Act; 40 U.S.C. 276a–276a(5)). The Secretary of Labor shall have, with respect to the labor standards specified in this subsection, the authority and functions set forth in Reorganization Plan Numbered 14 of 1950 (15 F.R. 3176; 64 Stat. 1267) and section 2 of the Act of June 13, 1934 (40 U.S.C. 276c).

(f) The Administrator shall request the Attorney General to appear and represent him in any civil action instituted under this title to which the Administrator is a party. Unless, within a reasonable time, the Attorney General notifies the Administrator that he will appear in such action, attorneys appointed by the Administrator shall appear and represent him.

(g) The provisions of this title shall not be construed as affecting any authority of the Administrator under part G of title III of this Act.

(h) Not later than April 1 of each year, the Administrator shall submit to the Committee on Commerce of the Senate and the Committee on Interstate and Foreign Commerce of the House of Representatives a report respecting the activities of the Agency under this title and containing such recommendations for legislation as he considers necessary. The report of the Administrator under this subsection which is due not later than April 1, 1975, and each subsequent report of the Administrator under this subsection shall include a statement on the actual and anticipated cost to public water systems in each State of compliance with the requirements of this title. The Office of Management and Budget may review any report required by this subsection before its submission to such committees of Congress, but the Office may not revise any such report, require any revision in any such report, or delay its submission beyond the day prescribed for its submission, and may submit to such committees of Congress its comments respecting any such report.

(i)(1) No employer may discharge any employee or otherwise discriminate against any employee with respect to his compensation, terms, conditions, or privileges of employment because the employee (or any person acting pursuant to a request of the employee) has—

(A) commenced, caused to be commenced, or is about to commence or cause to be commenced a proceeding under this title or a proceeding for the administration or enforcement of drinking water regulations or underground injection control programs of a State,

(B) testified or is about to testify in any such proceeding, or

(C) assisted or participated or is about to assist or participate in any manner in such a proceeding or in any other action to carry out the purposes of this title.

(2)(A) Any employee who believes that he has been discharged or otherwise discriminated against by any person in violation of paragraph (1) may, within 30 days after such violation occurs, file (or have any person file on his behalf) a complaint with the Secretary of Labor (hereinafter in this subsection referred to as the "Secretary") alleging such discharge or discrimination. Upon receipt of such a complaint, the Secretary shall notify the person named in the complaint of the filing of the complaint.

(B)(i) Upon receipt of a complaint filed under subparagraph (A), the Secretary shall conduct an investigation of the violation alleged in the complaint. Within 30 days of the receipt of such complaint, the Secretary shall complete such investigation and shall notify in writing the complainant (and any person acting in his behalf) and the person alleged to have committed such violation of the results of the investigation conducted pursuant to this subparagraph. Within 90 days of the receipt of such complaint the Secretary shall, unless the proceeding on the complaint is terminated by the Secretary on the basis of a settlement entered into by the Secretary and the person alleged to have committed such violation, issue an order either providing the relief prescribed by clause (ii) or denying the complaint. An order of the Secretary shall be made on the record after notice and opportunity for agency hearing. The Secretary may not enter into a settlement terminating a proceeding on a complaint without the participation and consent of the complainant.

(ii) If in response to a complaint filed under subparagraph (A) the Secretary determines that a violation of paragraph (1) has occurred, the Secretary shall order (I) the person who committed such violation to take affirmative action to abate the violation, (II) such person to reinstate the complainant to his former position together with the compensation (including back pay), terms, conditions, and privileges of his employment, (III) compensatory damages, and (IV) where appropriate, exemplary damages. If such an order is issued, the Secretary, at the request of the complainant, shall assess against the person against whom the order is issued a sum equal to the aggregate amount of all costs and expenses (including attorneys' fees) reasonably incurred, as determined by the Secretary, by the complainant for, or in connection with, the bringing of the complaint upon which the order was issued.

(3)(A) Any person adversely affected or aggrieved by an order issued under paragraph (2) may obtain review of the order in the United States Court of Appeals for the circuit in which the violation, with respect to which the order was issued, allegedly occurred. The petition for review must be filed within sixty days from the issuance of the Secretary's order. Review shall conform to chapter 7 of title 5 of the United States Code. The commencement of proceedings under this subparagraph shall not, unless ordered by the court, operate as a stay of the Secretary's order.

(B) An order of the Secretary with respect to which review could have been obtained under subparagraph (A) shall not be subject to judicial review in any criminal or other civil proceeding.

(4) Whenever a person has failed to comply with an order issued under paragraph (2)(B), the Secretary shall file a civil action in the United States District Court for the district in which the violation was found to occur to enforce such order. In actions brought under this paragraph, the district courts shall have jurisdiction to grant all appropriate relief including, but not limited to, injunctive relief, compensatory, and exemplary damages. Civil actions filed under this paragraph shall be heard and decided expeditiously.

(5) Any nondiscretionary duty imposed by this section is enforceable in mandamus proceeding brought under section 1361 of title 28 of the United States Code.

(6) Paragraph (1) shall not apply with respect to any employee who, acting without direction from his employer (or the employer's agent), deliberately causes a violation of any requirement of this title.

[NOTE: The following is not part of Title XIV, United States Code, The Public Health Service Act.]

(b) Section 2(f) of the Public Health Service Act is amended by inserting "(1)" after "except that" and by inserting before the semicolon at the end thereof the following: ", and (2) as used in title XIV such term includes Guam, American Samoa, and the Trust Territory of the Pacific Islands".

RURAL WATER SURVEY

SEC. 3. (a) The Administrator of the Environmental Protection Agency shall (after consultation with the Secretary of Agriculture and the several States) enter into arrangements with public or private entities as may be appropriate to conduct a survey of the quantity, quality, and availability of rural drinking water supplies. Such survey shall include, but not be limited to, the consideration of the number of residents in each rural area—

(1) presently being inadequately served by a public or private drinking water supply system, or by an individual home drinking water supply system;

(2) presently having limited or otherwise inadequate access to drinking water;

(3) who, due to the absence or inadequacy of a drinking water supply system, are exposed to an increased health hazard; and

(4) who have experienced incidents of chronic or acute illness, which may be attributed to the absence or inadequacy of a drinking water supply system.

(b) Such survey shall be completed within eighteen months of the date of enactment of this Act and a final report thereon submitted not later than six months after the completion of such survey, to the President and to the Congress. Such report shall include recommendations for improving rural water supplies.

(c) There are authorized to be appropriated to carry out the provisions of this section $1,000,000 for the fiscal year ending June 30, 1975; $2,000,000 for the fiscal year ending June 30, 1976; $1,000,000 for the fiscal year ending June 30, 1977; and $1,000,000 for each of fiscal years 1978 and 1979.

BOTTLED DRINKING WATER

SEC. 4. Chapter IV of the Federal Food, Drug, and Cosmetic Act is amended by adding after section 409 the following new section:

BOTTLED DRINKING WATER STANDARDS

SEC. 410. Whenever the Administrator of the Environmental Protection Agency prescribes interim or revised national primary drinking water regulations under section 1412 of the Public Health Service Act, the Secretary shall consult with the Administrator and within 180 days after the promulgation of such drinking water regulations either promulgate amendments to regulations under this chapter applicable to bottled drinking water or publish in the Federal Register his reasons for not making such amendments.

COMPREHENSIVE ENVIRONMENTAL RESPONSE, COMPENSATION, AND LIABILITY ACT OF 1980

as amended[1]

AN ACT

To provide for liability, compensation, cleanup, and emergency response for hazardous substances released into the environment and the cleanup of inactive hazardous waste disposal sites.

Be it enacted by the Senate and House of Representatives of the United States of American in Congress assembled, That this Act may be cited as the "Comprehensive Environmental Response, Compensation, and Liability Act of 1980".

TITLE I—HAZARDOUS SUBSTANCES RELEASES, LIABILITY, COMPENSATION

DEFINITIONS

SEC. 101. For purpose of this title, the term—

(1) "act of God" means an unanticipated grave natural disaster or other natural phenomenon of an exceptional, inevitable, and irresistible character, the effects of which could not have been prevented or avoided by the exercise of due care or foresight;

(2) "Administrator" means the Administrator of the United States Environmental Protection Agency;

(3) "barrel" means forty-two United States gallons at sixty degrees Fahrenheit;

(4) "claim" means a demand in writing for a sum certain;

(5) "claimant" means any person who presents a claim for compensation under this Act;

(6) "damages" means damages for injury or loss of natural resources as set forth in section 107(a) or 111(b) of this Act;

(7) "drinking water supply" means any raw or finished water source that is or may be used by a public water system (as defined in the Safe Drinking Water Act) or as drinking water by one or more individuals;

(8) "environment" means (A) the navigable waters, the waters of the contiguous zone, and the ocean waters of which the natural resources are under the exclusive management authority of the United States under the Fishery Conservation and Management Act of 1976, and (B) any other surface water, ground water, drinking water supply, land surface or subsurface strata, or ambient air within the United States or under the jurisdiction of the United States;

(9) "facility" means (A) any building, structure, installation, equipment, pipe or pipeline (including any pipe into a sewer or publicly owned treatment works), well, pit, pond, lagoon, impoundment, ditch, landfill, storage container, motor vehicle, rolling stock, or aircraft, or (B) any site or area where a hazardous substance has been deposited, stored, disposed of, or placed, or otherwise come to be located; but does not include any consumer product in consumer use or any vessel;

---

[1] PL 97-216, July 18, 1982; and PL 97-272, September 30, 1982.

(10) "federally permitted release" means (A) discharges in compliance with a permit under section 402 of the Federal Water Pollution Control Act, (B) discharges resulting from circumstances identified and reviewed and made part of the public record with respect to a permit issued or modified under section 402 of the Federal Water Pollution Control Act and subject to a condition of such permit, (C) continuous or anticipated intermittent discharges from a point source, identified in a permit or permit application under section 402 of the Federal Water Pollution Control Act, which are caused by events occurring within the scope of relevant operating or treatment systems, (D) discharges in compliance with a legally enforceable permit under section 404 of the Federal Water Pollution Control Act, (E) releases in compliance with a legally enforceable final permit issued pursuant to section 3005 (a) through (d) of the Solid Waste Disposal Act from a hazardous waste treatment, storage, or disposal facility when such permit specifically identifies the hazardous substances and makes such substances subject to a standard of practice, control procedure or bioassay limitation or condition, or other control on the hazardous substances in such releases, (F) any release in compliance with a legally enforceable permit issued under section 102 of section 103 of the Marine Protection, Research, and Sanctuaries Act of 1972, (G) any injection of fluids authorized under Federal underground injection control programs or State programs submitted for Federal approval (and not disapproved by the Administrator of the Environmental Protection Agency) pursuant to part C of the Safe Drinking Water Act, (H) any emission into the air subject to a permit or control regulation under section 111, section 112, title I part C, title I part D, or State implementation plans submitted in accordance with section 110 of the Clean Air Act (and not disapproved by the Administrator of the Environmental Protection Agency), including any schedule or waiver granted, promulgated, or approved under these sections, (I) any injection of fluids or other materials authorized under applicable State law (i) for the purpose of stimulating or treating wells for the production of crude oil, natural gas, or water, (ii) for the purpose of secondary, tertiary, or other enhanced recovery of crude oil or natural gas, or (iii) which are brought to the surface in conjunction with the production of crude oil or natural gas and which are reinjected, (J) the introduction of any pollutant into a publicly owned treatment works when such pollutant is specified in and in compliance with applicable pretreatment standards of section 307 (b) or (c) of the Clean Water Act and enforceable requirements in a pretreatment program submitted by a State or municipality for Federal approval under section 402 of such Act, and (K) any release of source, special nuclear, or byproduct material, as those terms are defined in the Atomic Energy Act of 1954, in compliance with a legally enforceable license, permit, regulation, or order issued pursuant to the Atomic Energy Act of 1954;

(11) "Fund" or "Trust Fund" means the Hazardous Substance Response Fund established by section 221 of this Act or, in the case of a hazardous waste disposal facility for which liability has been transferred under section 107(k) of this Act, the Post-closure Liability Fund established by section 232 of this Act;

(12) "ground water" means water in a saturated zone or stratum beneath the surface of land or water;

(13) "guarantor" means any person, other than the owner or operator, who provides evidence of financial responsibility for an owner or operator under this Act;

(14) "hazardous substance" means (A) any substance designated pursuant to section 311(b)(2)(A) of the Federal Water Pollution Control Act, (B) any element, compound, mixture, solution, or substance designated pursuant to section 102 of this Act, (C) any hazardous waste having the characteristics identified under or listed pursuant to section 3001 of the Solid Waste Disposal Act (but not including any waste the regulation of which under the Solid Waste Disposal Act has been suspended by Act of Congress), (D) any toxic pollutant listed under section 307(a) of the Federal Water Pollution Control Act, (E) any hazardous air pollutant listed under section 112 of the Clean Air Act, and (F) any imminently hazardous chemical substance or mixture with respect to which the Administrator has taken action pursuant to section 7 of the Toxic Substances Control Act. The term does not include petroleum, including crude oil or any fraction thereof which is not otherwise specifically listed or designated as a hazardous substance under subparagraphs (A) through (F) of this paragraph, and the term does not include natural gas, natural gas liquids, liquefied natural gas, or synthetic gas usable for fuel (or mixtures of natural gas and such synthetic gas);

(15) "navigable waters" or "navigable waters of the United States" means the waters of the United States, including the territorial seas;

(16) "natural resources" means land, fish, wildlife, biota, air, water, ground water, drinking water supplies, and other such resources belonging to, managed by, held in trust by, appertaining to, or otherwise controlled by the United States (including the resources of the fishery conservation zone established by the Fishery Conservation and Management Act of 1976), any State or local government, or any foreign government;

(17) "offshore facility" means any facility of any kind located in, on, or under, any of the navigable waters of the United States, and any facility of any kind which is subject to the jurisdiction of the United States and is located in, on, or under any other waters, other than a vessel or a public vessel;

(18) "onshore facility" means any facility (including, but not limited to, motor vehicles and rolling stock) of any kind located in, on, or under, any land or nonnavigable waters within the United States;

(19) "otherwise subject to the jurisdiction of the United States" means subject to the jurisdiction of the United States by virtue of United States citizenship, United States vessel documentation or numbering, or as provided by international agreement to which the United States is a party;

(20)(A) "owner or operator" means (i) in the case of a vessel, any person owning, operating, or chartering by demise, such vessel, (ii) in the case of an onshore facility or an offshore facility, any person owning or operating such facility, and (iii) in the case of any abandoned facility, any person who owned, operated, or otherwise controlled activities at such facility immediately prior to such abandonment. Such term does not include a person, who, without participating in the management of a vessel or facility, holds indicia of ownership primarily to protect his security interest in the vessel or facility;

(B) in the case of a hazardous substance which has been accepted for transportation by a common or contract carrier and except as provided in section 107(a) (3) or (4) of this Act, (i) the term "owner or operator" shall mean such common carrier or other bona fide for hire carrier acting as an independent contractor during such transportation, (ii) the shipper of such hazardous substance shall not be considered to have caused or contributed to any release during such transportation which resulted solely from circumstances or conditions beyond his control;

(C) in the case of a hazardous substance which has been delivered by a common or contract carrier to a disposal or treatment facility and except as provided in section 107(a) (3) or (4) (i) the term "owner or operator" shall not include such common or contract carrier, and (ii) such common or contract carrier shall not be considered to have caused or contributed to any release at such disposal or treatment facility resulting from circumstances or conditions beyond its control;

(21) "person" means an individual, firm, corporation, association, partnership, consortium, joint venture, commercial entity, United States Government, State, municipality, commission, political subdivision of a State, or any interstate body;

(22) "release" means any spilling, leaking, pumping, pouring, emitting, emptying, discharging, injecting, escaping, leaching, dumping, or disposing into the environment, but excludes (A) any release which results in exposure to persons solely within a workplace, with respect to a claim which such persons may assert against the employer of such persons, (B) emissions from the engine exhaust of a motor vehicle, rolling stock, aircraft, vessel, or pipeline pumping station engine, (C) release of source, byproduct, or special nuclear material from a nuclear incident, as those terms are defined in the Atomic Energy Act of 1954, if such release is subject to requirements with respect to financial protection established by the Nuclear Regulatory Commission under section 170 of such Act, or, for the purposes of section 104 of this title or any other response action, any release of source byproduct, or special nuclear material from any processing site designated under section 102(a)(1) or 302(a) of the Uranium Mill Tailings Radiation Control Act of 1978, and (D) the normal application of fertilizer;

(23) "remove" or "removal" means the cleanup or removal of released hazardous substances from the environment, such actions as may be necessary taken in the event of the threat of release of hazardous substances into the environment, such actions as may be necessary to monitor, assess, and evaluate the release or threat of release of hazardous substances, the disposal of removed material, or the taking of such other actions as may be necessary to prevent, minimize, or mitigate damage to the public health or welfare or to the environment, which may otherwise result from a release or threat of release. The term includes, in addition, without being limited to, security fencing or other measures to limit access, provision of alternative water supplies, temporary evacuation and housing of threatened individuals not otherwise provided for, action taken under section 104(b) of this Act, and any emergency assistance which may be provided under the Disaster Relief Act of 1974;

(24) "remedy" or "remedial action" means those actions consistent with permanent remedy taken instead of or in addition to removal actions in the event of a release or threatened release of

a hazardous substance into the environment, to prevent or minimize the release of hazardous substances so that they do not migrate to cause substantial danger to present or future public health or welfare or the environment. The term includes, but is not limited to, such actions at the location of the release as storage, confinement, perimeter protection using dikes, trenches, or ditches, clay cover, neutralization, cleanup of released hazardous substances or contaminated materials, recycling or reuse, diversion, destruction, segregation of reactive wastes, dredging or excavations, repair or replacement of leaking containers, collection of leachate and runoff, onsite treatment or incineration, provision of alternative water supplies, and any monitoring reasonably required to assure that such actions protect the public health and welfare and the environment. The term includes the costs of permanent relocation of residents and businesses and community facilities where the President determines that, alone or in combination with other measures, such relocation is more cost-effective than and environmentally preferable to the transportation, storage, treatment, destruction, or secure disposition offsite of hazardous substances, or may otherwise be necessary to protect the public health or welfare. The term does not include offsite transport of hazardous substances, or the storage, treatment, destruction, or secure disposition offsite of such hazardous substances or contaminated materials unless the President determines that such actions (A) are more cost-effective than other remedial actions, (B) will create new capacity to manage, in compliance with subtitle C of the Solid Waste Disposal Act, hazardous substances in addition to those located at the affected facility, or (C) are necessary to protect public health or welfare or the environment from a present or potential risk which may be created by further exposure to the continued presence of such substances or materials;

(25) "respond" or "response" means remove, removal, remedy, and remedial action;

(26) "transport" or "transportation" means the movement of a hazardous substance by any mode, including pipeline (as defined in the Pipeline Safety Act), and in the case of a hazardous substance which has been accepted for transportation by a common or contract carrier, the term "transport" or "transportation" shall include any stoppage in transit which is temporary, incidental to the transportation movement, and at the ordinary operating convenience of a common or contract carrier, and any such stoppage shall be considered as a continuity of movement and not as the storage of a hazardous substance;

(27) "United States" and "State" include the several States of the United States, the District of Columbia, the Commonwealth of Puerto Rico, Guam, American Samoa, the United States Virgin Islands, the Commonwealth of the Northern Marianas, and any other territory or possession over which the United States has jurisdiction;

(28) "vessel" means every description of watercraft or other artificial contrivance used, or capable of being used, as a means of transportation on water;

(29) "disposal", "hazardous waste", and "treatment" shall have the meaning provided in section 1004 of the Solid Waste Disposal Act;

(30) "territorial sea" and "contiguous zone" shall have the meaning provided in section 502 of the Federal Water Pollution Control Act.

(31) "national contingency plan" means the national contingency plan published under section 311(c) of the Federal Water Pollution Control Act or revised pursuant to section 105 of this Act; and

(32) "liable" or "liability" under this title shall be construed to be the standard of liability which obtains under section 311 of the Federal Water Pollution Control Act.

REPORTABLE QUANTITIES AND ADDITIONAL DESIGNATIONS

SEC. 102. (a) The Administrator shall promulgate and revise as may be appropriate, regulations designating as hazardous substances, in addition to those referred to in section 101(14) of this title, such elements, compounds, mixtures, solutions, and substances which, when released into the environment may present substantial danger to the public health or welfare or the environment, and shall promulgate regulations establishing that quantity of any hazardous substance the release of which shall be reported pursuant to section 103 of this title. The Administrator may determine that one single quantity shall be the reportable quantity for any hazardous substance, regardless of the medium into which the hazardous substance is released.

(b) Unless and until superseded by regulations establishing a reportable quantity under subsection (a) of this section for any hazardous substance as defined in section 101(14) of this title, (1) a quantity of one pound, or (2) for those hazardous substances for which reportable quantities have been established pursuant to section 311(b)(4) of the Federal Water Pollution Control Act, such reportable quantity, shall be deemed that quantity, the release of which requires notification pursuant to section 103 (a) or (b) of this title.

NOTICES, PENALTIES

SEC. 103. (a) Any person in charge of a vessel or an offshore or an onshore facility shall, as soon as he has knowledge of any release (other than a federally permitted release) of a hazardous substance from such vessel or facility in quantities equal to or greater than those determined pursuant to section 102 of this title, immediately notify the National Response Center established under the Clean Water Act of such release. The National Response Center shall convey the notification expeditiously to all appropriate Government agencies, including the Governor of any affected State.

(b) Any person—

(1) in charge of a vessel from which a hazardous substance is released, other than a federally permitted release, into or upon the navigable waters of the United States, adjoining shorelines, or into or upon the waters of the contiguous zone, or

(2) in charge of a vessel from which a hazardous substance is released, other than a federally permitted release, which may affect natural resources belonging to, appertaining to, or under the exclusive management authority of the United States (including resources under the Fishery Conservation and Management Act of 1976), and who is otherwise subject to the jurisdiction of the United States at the time of the release, or

(3) in charge of a facility from which a hazardous substance is released, other than a federally permitted release, in a quantity equal to or greater than that determined pursuant to section 102 of this title who fails to notify immediately the appropriate agency of the United States Government as soon as he has knowledge of such release shall, upon conviction, be fined not more than $10,000 or imprisoned for not more than one year, or both. Notification received pursuant to this paragraph or information obtained by the exploitation of such notification shall not be used against any such person in any criminal case, except a prosecution for perjury or for giving a false statement.

(c) Within one hundred and eighty days after the enactment of this Act, any person who owns or operates or who at the time of disposal owned or operated, or who accepted hazardous substances for transport and selected, a facility at which hazardous substances (as defined in section 101(14)(C) of this title) are or have been stored, treated, or disposed of shall, unless such facility has a permit issued under, or has been accorded interim status under, subtitle C of the Solid Waste Disposal Act, notify the Administrator of the Environmental Protection Agency of the existence of such facility, specifying the amount and type of any hazardous substance to be found there, and any known, suspected, or likely releases of such substances from such facility. The Administrator may prescribe in greater detail the manner and form of the notice and the information included. The Administrator shall notify the affected State agency, or any department designated by the Governor to receive such notice, of the existence of such facility. Any person who knowingly fails to notify the Administrator of the existence of any such facility shall, upon conviction, be fined not more than $10,000, or imprisoned for not more than one year, or both. In addition, any such person who knowingly fails to provide the notice required by this subsection shall not be entitled to any limitation of liability or to any defenses to liability set out in section 107 of this Act: *Provided, however,* That notification under this subsection is not required for any facility which would be reportable hereunder solely as a result of any stoppage in transit which is temporary, incidental to the transportation movement, or at the ordinary operating convenience of a common or contract carrier, and such stoppage shall be considered as a continuity of movement and not as the storage of a hazardous substance. Notification received pursuant to this subsection or information obtained by the exploitation of such notification shall not be used against any such person in any criminal case, except a prosecution for perjury or for giving a false statement.

(d)(1) The Administrator of the Environmental Protection Agency is authorized to promulgate rules and regulations specifying, with respect to—

(A) the location, title, or condition of a facility, and

(B) the identity, characteristics, quantity, origin, or condition (including containerization and previous treatment) of any hazardous substances contained or deposited in a facility;

the records which shall be retained by any person required to provide the notification of a facility set out in subsection (c) of this section. Such specification shall be in accordance with the provisions of this subsection.

(2) Beginning with the date of enactment of this Act, for fifty years thereafter or for fifty years after the date of establishment of a record (whichever is later), or at any such earlier time as a waiver if obtained under paragraph (3) of this subsection, it shall be unlawful for any

such person knowingly to destroy, mutilate, erase, dispose of, conceal, or otherwise render unavailable or unreadable or falsify any records identified in paragraph (1) of this subsection. Any person who violates this paragraph shall, upon conviction, be fined not more than $20,000, or imprisoned for not more than one year, or both.

(3) At any time prior to the date which occurs fifty years after the date of enactment of this Act, any person identified under paragraph (1) of this subsection may apply to the Administrator of the Environmental Protection Agency for a waiver of the provisions of the first sentence of paragraph (2) of this subsection. The Administrator is authorized to grant such waiver if, in his discretion, such waiver would not unreasonably interfere with the attainment of the purposes and provisions of this Act. The Administrator shall promulgate rules and regulations regarding such a waiver so as to inform parties of the proper application procedure and conditions for approval of such a waiver.

(4) Notwithstanding the provisions of this subsection, the Administrator of the Environmental Protection Agency may in his discretion require any such person to retain any record identified pursuant to paragraph (1) of this subsection for such a time period in excess of the period specified in paragraph (2) of this subsection as the Administrator determines to be necessary to protect the public health or welfare.

(e) This section shall not apply to the application of a pesticide product registered under the Federal Insecticide, Fungicide, and Rodenticide Act or to the handling and storage of such a pesticide product by an agricultural producer.

(f) No notification shall be required under subsection (a) or (b) of this section for any release of a hazardous substance—

(1) which is required to be reported (or specifically exempted from a requirement for reporting) under subtitle C of the Solid Waste Disposal Act or regulations thereunder and which has been reported to the National Response Center, or

(2) which is a continuous release, stable in quantity and rate, and is—

(A) from a facility for which notification has been given under subsection (c) of this section, or

(B) a release of which notification has been given under subsections (a) and (b) of this section for a period sufficient to establish the continuity, quantity, and regularity of such release:

Provided, That notification in accordance with subsections (a) and (b) of this paragraph shall be given for releases subject to this paragraph annually, or at such time as there is any statistically significant increase in the quantity of any hazardous substance or constituent thereof released, above that previously reported or occurring.

RESPONSE AUTHORITIES

SEC. 104. (a)(1) Whenever (A) any hazardous substance is released or there is a substantial threat of such a release into the environment, or (B) there is a release or substantial threat of release into the environment of any pollutant or contaminant which may present an imminent and substantial danger to the public health or welfare, the President is authorized to act, consistent with the national contingency plan, to remove or arrange for the removal of, and provide for remedial action relating to such hazardous substance, pollutant, or contaminant at any time (including its removal from any contaminated natural resource), or take any other response measure consistent with the national contingency plan which the President deems necessary to protect the public health or welfare or the environment, unless the President determines that such removal and remedial action will be done properly by the owner or operator of the vessel or facility from which the release or threat of release emanates, or by any other responsible party.

(2) For the purposes of this section, "pollutant or contaminant" shall include, but not be limited to, any element, substance, compound, or mixture, including disease-causing agents, which after release into the environment and upon exposure, ingestion, inhalation, or assimilation into any organism, either directly from the environment or indirectly by ingestion through food chains, will or may reasonably be anticipated to cause death, disease, behavioral abnormalities, cancer, genetic mutation, physiological malfunctions (including malfunctions in reproduction) or physical deformations, in such organisms or their offspring. The term does not include petroleum, including crude oil and any fraction thereof which is not otherwise specifically listed or designated as hazardous substances under section 101(14) (A) through (F) of this title, nor does it include natural gas, liquefied natural gas, or synthetic gas of pipeline quality (or mixtures of natural gas and such synthetic gas).

(b) Whenever the President is authorized to act pursuant to subsection (a) of this section, or whenever the President has reason to believe that a release has occurred or is about to occur, or that illness, disease, or complaints thereof may be attributable to exposure to a hazardous substance, pollutant, or contaminant and that a release may have occurred or be occurring, he may undertake such investigations, monitoring, surveys, testing, and other information gathering as he may deem necessary or appropriate to identify the existence and extent of the release or threat thereof, the source and nature of the hazardous substances, pollutants or contaminants involved, and the extent of danger to the public health or welfare or to the environment. In addition, the President may undertake such planning, legal, fiscal, economic, engineering, architectural, and other studies or investigations as he may deem necessary or appropriate to plan and direct response actions, to recover the costs thereof, and to enforce the provisions of this Act.

(c)(1) Unless (A) the President finds that (i) continued response actions are immediately required to prevent, limit, or mitigate an emergency, (ii) there is an immediate risk to public health or welfare or the environment, and (iii) such assistance will not otherwise be provided on a timely basis, or (B) the President has determined the appropriate remedial actions pursuant to paragraph (2) of this subsection and the State or States in which the source of the release is located have complied with the requirements of paragraph (3) of this subsection, obligations from the Fund, other than those authorized by subsection (b) of this section, shall not continue after $1,000,000 has been obligated for response actions or six months has elapsed from the date of initial response to a release or threatened release of hazardous substances.

(2) The President shall consult with the affected State or States before determining any appropriate remedial action to be taken pursuant to the authority granted under subsection (a) of this section.

(3) The President shall not provide any remedial actions pursuant to this section unless the State in which the release occurs first enters into a contract or cooperative agreement with the President providing assurances deemed adequate by the President that (A) the State

will assure all future maintenance of the removal and remedial actions provided for the expected life of such actions as determined by the President; (B) the State will assure the availability of a hazardous waste disposal facility acceptable to the President and in compliance with the requirements of subtitle C of the Solid Waste Disposal Act for any necessary offsite storage, destruction, treatment, or secure disposition of the hazardous substances; and (C) the State will pay or assure payment of (i) 10 per centum of the costs of the remedial action, including all future maintenance, or (ii) at least 50 per centum or such greater amount as the President may determine appropriate, taking into account the degree of responsibility of the State or political subdivision, of any sums expended in response to a release at a facility that was owned at the time of any disposal of hazardous substances therein by the State or a political subdivision thereof. The President shall grant the State a credit against the share of the costs for which it is responsible under this paragraph for any documented direct out-of-pocket non-Federal funds expended or obligated by the State or a political subdivision thereof after January 1, 1978, and before the date of enactment of this Act for cost-eligible response actions and claims for damages compensable under section 111 of this title relating to the specific release in question: *Provided, however,* That in no event shall the amount of the credit granted exceed the total response costs relating to the release.

(4) The President shall select appropriate remedial actions determined to be necessary to carry out this section which are to the extent practicable in accordance with the national contingency plan and which provide for that cost-effective response which provides a balance between the need for protection of public health and welfare and the environment at the facility under consideration, and the availability of amounts from the Fund established under title II of this Act to respond to other sites which present or may present a threat to public health or welfare or the environment, taking into consideration the need for immediate action.

(d)(1) Where the President determines that a State or political subdivision thereof has the capability to carry out any or all of the actions authorized in this section, the President may, in his discretion, enter into a contract or cooperative agreement with such State or political subdivision to take such actions in accordance with criteria and priorities established pursuant to section 105(8) of this title and to be reimbursed for the reasonable response costs thereof from the Fund. Any contract made hereunder shall be subject to the cost-sharing provisions of subsection (c) of this section.

(2) If the President enters into a cost-sharing agreement pursuant to subsection (c) of this section or a contract or cooperative agreement pursuant to this subsection, and the State or political subdivision thereof fails to comply with any requirements of the contract, the President may, after providing sixty days notice, seek in the appropriate Federal district court to enforce the contract or to recover any funds advanced or any costs incurred because of the breach of the contract by the State or political subdivision.

(3) Where a State or a political subdivision thereof is acting in behalf of the President, the President is authorized to provide technical and legal assistance in the administration and enforcement of any contract or subcontract in connection with response actions assisted under this title, and to intervene in any civil action involving the enforcement of such contract or subcontract.

(4) Where two or more noncontiguous facilities are reasonably related on the basis of geography, or on the basis of the threat, or

potential threat to the public health or welfare or the environment, the President may, in his discretion, treat these related facilities as one for purposes of this section.

(e)(1) For purposes of assisting in determining the need for response to a release under this title or enforcing the provisions of this title, any person who stores, treats, or disposes of, or, where necessary to ascertain facts not available at the facility where such hazardous substances are located, who generates, transports, or otherwise handles or has handled, hazardous substances shall, upon request of any officer, employee, or representative of the President, duly designated by the President, or upon request of any duly designated officer, employee, or representative of a State, where appropriate, furnish information relating to such substances and permit such person at all reasonable times to have access to, and to copy all records relating to such substances. For the purposes specified in the preceding sentence, such officers, employees, or representatives are authorized—

(A) to enter at reasonable times any establishment or other place where such hazardous substances are or have been generated, stored, treated, or disposed of, or transported from;

(B) to inspect and obtain samples from any person of any such substance and samples of any containers or labeling for such substances. Each such inspection shall be commenced and completed with reasonable promptness. If the officer, employee, or representative obtains any samples, prior to leaving the premises, he shall give to the owner, operator, or person in charge a receipt describing the sample obtained and if requested a portion of each such sample equal in volume of weight to the portion retained. If any analysis is made of such samples, a copy of the results of such analysis shall be furnished promptly to the owner, operator, or person in charge.

(2)(A) Any records, reports, or information obtained from any person under this section (including records, reports, or information obtained by representatives of the President) shall be available to the public, except that upon a showing satisfactory to the President (or the State, as the case may be) by any person that records, reports, or information, or particular part thereof (other than health or safety effects data), to which the President (or the State, as the case may be) or any officer, employee, or representative has access under this section if made public would divulge information entitled to protection under section 1905 of title 18 of the United States Code, such information or particular portion thereof shall be considered confidential in accordance with the purposes of that section, except that such record, report, document or information may be disclosed to other officers, employees, or authorized representatives of the United States concerned with carrying out this Act, or when relevant in any proceeding under this Act.

(B) Any person not subject to the provisions of section 1905 of title 18 of the United States Code who knowingly and willfully divulges or discloses any information entitled to protection under this subsection shall, upon conviction, be subject to a fine of not more than $5,000 or to imprisonment not to exceed one year, or both.

(C) In submitting data under this Act, a person required to provide such data may (i) designate the data which such person believes is entitled to protection under this subsection and (ii) submit such designated data separately from other data submitted under this Act. A designation under this paragraph shall be made in writing and in such manner as the President may prescribe by regulation.

(D) Notwithstanding any limitation contained in this section or any other provision of law, all information reported to or otherwise obtained by the President (or any representative of the President) under this Act shall be made available, upon written request of any duly authorized committee of the Congress, to such committee.

(f) In awarding contracts to any person engaged in response actions, the President or the State, in any case where it is awarding contracts pursuant to a contract entered into under subsection (d) of this section, shall require compliance with Federal health and safety standards established under section 301(f) of this Act by contractors and subcontractors as a condition of such contracts.

(g)(1) All laborers and mechanics employed by contractors or subcontractors in the performance of construction, repair, or alteration work funded in whole or in part under this section shall be paid wages at rates not less than those prevailing on projects of a character similar in the locality as determined by the Secretary of Labor in accordance with the Davis-Bacon Act. The President shall not approve any such funding without first obtaining adequate assurance that required labor standards will be maintained upon the construction work.

(2) The Secretary of Labor shall have, with respect to the labor standards specified in paragraph (1), the authority and functions set forth in Reorganization Plan Numbered 14 of 1950 (15 F.R. 3176; 64 Stat. 1267) and section 276c of title 40 of the United States Code.

(h) Notwithstanding any other provision of law, subject to the provisions of section 111 of this Act, the President may authorize the use of such emergency procurement powers as he deems necessary to effect the purpose of this Act. Upon determination that such procedures are necessary, the President shall promulgate regulations prescribing the circumstances under which such authority shall be used and the procedures governing the use of such authority.

(i) There is hereby established within the Public Health Service an agency, to be known as the Agency for Toxic Substances and Disease Registry, which shall report directly to the Surgeon General of the United States. The Administrator of said Agency shall, with the cooperation of the Administrator of the Environmental Protection Agency, the Commissioner of the Food and Drug Administration, the Directors of the National Institute of Medicine, National Institute of Environmental Health Sciences, National Institute of Occupational Safety and Health, Centers for Disease Control, the Administrator of the Occupational Safety and Health Administration, and the Administrator of the Social Security Administration, effectuate and implement the health related authorities of this Act. In addition, said Administrator shall—

(1) in cooperation with the States, establish and maintain a national registry of serious diseases and illnesses and a national registry of persons exposed to toxic substances;

(2) establish and maintain inventory of literature, research, and studies on the health effects of toxic substances;

(3) in cooperation with the States, and other agencies of the Federal Government, establish and maintain a complete listing of areas closed to the public or otherwise restricted in use because of toxic substance contamination;

(4) in cases of public health emergencies caused or believed to be caused by exposure to toxic substances, provide medical care and testing to exposed individuals, including but not limited to tissue sampling, chromosomal testing, epidemiological studies,

or any other assistance appropriate under the circumstances; and

(5) either independently or as part of other health status survey, conduct periodic survey and screening programs to determine relationships between exposure to toxic substances and illness. In cases of public health emergencies, exposed persons shall be eligible for admission to hospitals and other facilities and services operated or provided by the Public Health Service.

NATIONAL CONTINGENCY PLAN

SEC. 105. Within one hundred and eighty days after the enactment of this Act, the President shall, after notice and opportunity for public comments, revise and republish the national contingency plan for the removal of oil and hazardous substances, originally prepared and published pursuant to section 311 of the Federal Water Pollution Control Act, to reflect and effectuate the responsibilities and powers created by this Act, in addition to those matters specified in section 311(c)(2). Such revision shall include a section of the plan to be known as the national hazardous substance response plan which shall establish procedures and standards for responding to releases of hazardous substances, pollutants, and contaminants, which shall include at a minimum:

(1) methods for discovering and investigating facilities at which hazardous substances have been disposed of or otherwise come to be located;

(2) methods for evaluating, including analyses of relative cost, and remedying any releases or threats of releases from facilities which pose substantial danger to the public health or the environment;

(3) methods and criteria for determining the appropriate extent of removal, remedy, and other measures authorized by this Act;

(4) appropriate roles and responsibilities for the Federal, State, and local governments and for interstate and nongovernmental entities in effectuating the plan;

(5) provision for identification, procurement, maintenance, and storage of response equipment and supplies;

(6) a method for and assignment of responsibility for reporting the existence of such facilities which may be located on federally owned or controlled properties and any releases of hazardous substances from such facilities;

(7) means of assuring that remedial action measures are cost-effective over the period of potential exposure to the hazardous substances or contaminated materials;

(8)(A) criteria for determining priorities among releases or threatened releases throughout the United States for the purpose of taking remedial action and, to the extent practicable taking into account the potential urgency of such action, for the purpose of taking removal action. Criteria and priorities under this paragraph shall be based upon relative risk or danger to public health or welfare or the environment, in the judgment of the President, taking into account to the extent possible the population at risk, the hazard potential of the hazardous substances at such facilities, the potential for contamination of drinking water supplies, the potential for direct human contact, the potential for destruction of sensitive ecosystems, State preparedness to assume State costs and responsibilities, and other appropriate factors;

(B) based upon the criteria set forth in subparagraph (A) of this paragraph, the President shall list as part of the plan national priorities among the known releases or threatened releases throughout the United States and shall revise the list no less often than annually. Within one year after the date of enactment of this Act, and annually thereafter, each State shall establish and submit for consideration by the President priorities for remedial action among known releases and potential releases in that State based upon the criteria set forth in subparagraph (A) of this paragraph. In assembling or revising the national list, the President shall consider any priorities established by the States. To the extent practicable, at least four hundred of the highest priority facilities shall be designated individually and shall be referred to as the "top priority among known response targets", and, to the extent practicable, shall include among the one hundred highest priority facilities at least one such facility from each State which shall be the facility designated by the State as presenting the greatest danger to public health or welfare or the environment among the known facilities in such State. Other priority facilities or incidents may be listed singly or grouped for response priority purposes; and

(9) specified roles for private organizations and entities in preparation for response and in responding to releases of hazardous substances, including identification of appropriate qualifications and capacity therefor.

The plan shall specify procedures, techniques, materials, equipment, and methods to be employed in identifying, removing, or remedying releases of hazardous substances comparable to those required under section 311(c)(2) (F) and (G) and (j)(1) of the Federal Water Pollution Control Act. Following publication of the revised national contingency plan, the response to and actions to minimize damage from hazardous substances releases shall, to the greatest extent possible, be in accordance with the provisions of the plan. The President may, from time to time, revise and republish the national contingency plan.

ABATEMENT ACTION

SEC. 106. (a) In addition to any other action taken by a State or local government, when the President determines that there may be an imminent and substantial endangerment to the public health or welfare or the environment because of an actual or threatened release of a hazardous substance from a facility, he may require the Attorney General of the United States to secure such relief as may be necessary to abate such danger or threat, and the district court of the United States in the district in which the threat occurs shall have jurisdiction to grant such relief as the public interest and the equities of the case may require. The President may also, after notice to the affected State, take other action under this section including, but not limited to, issuing such orders as may be necessary to protect public health and welfare and the environment.

(b) Any person who willfully violates, or fails or refuses to comply with, any order of the President under subsection (a) may, in an action brought in the appropriate United States district court to enforce such order, be fined not more than $5,000 for each day in which such violation occurs or such failure to comply continues.

(c) Within one hundred and eighty days after enactment of this Act, the Administrator of the Environmental Protection Agency shall, after consultation with the Attorney General, establish and publish guidelines for using the imminent hazard, enforcement, and emergency response authorities of this section and other existing statutes administered by the Administrator of the Environmental Protection Agency to effectuate the responsibilities and powers created by this Act. Such guidelines shall to the extent practicable be consistent with the national hazardous substance response plan, and shall include, at a minimum, the assignment of responsibility for coordinating response actions with the issuance of administrative orders, enforcement of standards and permits, the gathering of information, and other imminent hazard and emergency powers authorized by (1) sections 311(c)(2), 308, 309, and 504(a) of the Federal Water Pollution Control Act, (2) sections 3007, 3008, 3013, and 7003 of the Solid Waste Disposal Act, (3) sections 1445 and 1431 of the Safe Drinking Water Act, (4) sections 113, 114, and 303 of the Clean Air Act, and (5) section 7 of the Toxic Substances Control Act.

LIABILITY

SEC. 107. (a) Notwithstanding any other provision or rule of law, and subject only to the defenses set forth in subsection (b) of this section—

(1) the owner and operator of a vessel (otherwise subject to the jurisdiction of the United States) or a facility,

(2) any person who at the time of disposal of any hazardous substance owned or operated any facility at which such hazardous substances were disposed of,

(3) any person who by contract, agreement, or otherwise arranged for disposal or treatment, or arranged with a transporter for transport for disposal or treatment, of hazardous substances owned or possessed by such person, by any other party or entity, at any facility owned or operated by another party or entity and containing such hazardous substances, and

(4) any person who accepts or accepted any hazardous substances for transport to disposal or treatment facilities or sites selected by such person, from which there is a release, or a threatened release which causes the incurrence of response costs, of a hazardous substance, shall be liable for—

(A) all costs of removal or remedial action incurred by the United States Government or a State not inconsistent with the national contingency plan;

(B) any other necessary costs of response incurred by any other person consistent with the national contingency plan; and

(C) damages for injury to, destruction of, or loss of natural resources, including the reasonable costs of assessing such injury, destruction, or loss resulting from such a release.

(b) There shall be no liability under subsection (a) of this section for a person otherwise liable who can establish by a preponderance of the evidence that the release or threat of release of a hazardous substance and the damages resulting therefrom were caused solely by—

(1) an act of God;

(2) an act of war;

(3) an act or omission of a third party other than an employee or agent of the defendant, or than one whose act or omission occurs in connection with a contractual relationship, existing

directly or indirectly, with the defendant (except where the sole contractual arrangement arises from a published tariff and acceptance for carriage by a common carrier by rail), if the defendant establishes by a preponderance of the evidence that (a) he exercised due care with respect to the hazardous substance concerned, taking into consideration the characteristics of such hazardous substance, in light of all relevant facts and circumstances, and (b) he took precautions against foreseeable acts or omissions of any such third party and the consequences that could foreseeably result from such acts or omissions; or

(4) any combination of the foregoing paragraphs.

(c)(1) Except as provided in paragraph (2) of this subsection, the liability under this section of an owner or operator or other responsible person for each release of a hazardous substance or incident involving release of a hazardous substance shall not exceed—

(A) for any vessel which carries any hazardous substance as cargo or residue, $300 per gross ton, or $5,000,000, whichever is greater;

(B) for any other vessel, $300 per gross ton, or $500,000, whichever is greater;

(C) for any motor vehicle, aircraft, pipeline (as defined in the Hazardous Liquid Pipeline Safety Act of 1979), or rolling stock, $50,000,000 or such lesser amount as the President shall establish by regulation, but in no event less than $5,000,000 (or, for releases of hazardous substances as defined in section 101(14)(A) of this title into the navigable waters, $8,000,000). Such regulations shall take into account the size, type, location, storage, and handling capacity and other matters relating to the likelihood of release in each such class and to the economic impact of such limits on each such class; or

(D) for any facility other than those specified in subparagraph (C) of this paragraph, the total of all costs of response plus $50,000,000 for any damages under this title.

(2) Notwithstanding the limitations in paragraph (1) of this subsection, the liability of an owner or operator or other responsible person under this section shall be the full and total costs of response and damages, if (A)(i) the release or threat of release of a hazardous substance was the result of willful misconduct or willful negligence within the privity or knowledge of such person, or (ii) the primary cause of the release was a violation (within the privity or knowledge of such person) of applicable safety, construction, or operating standards or regulations; or (B) such person fails or refuses to provide all reasonable cooperation and assistance requested by a responsible public official in connection with response activities under the national contingency plan with respect to regulated carriers subject to the provisions of title 49 of the United States Code or vessels subject to the provisions of title 33 or 46 of the United States Code, subparagraph (A)(ii) of this paragraph shall be deemed to refer to Federal standards or regulations.

(3) If any person who is liable for a release or threat of release of a hazardous substance fails without sufficient cause to properly provide removal or remedial action upon order of the President pursuant to section 104 or 106 of this Act, such person may be liable to the United States for punitive damages in an amount at least equal to, and not more than three times, the amount of any costs incurred by the Fund as a result of such failure to take proper action. The President is authorized to commence a civil action against any such person to recover the punitive damages, which shall be in addition to

any costs recovered from such person pursuant to section 112(c) of this Act. Any moneys received by the United States pursuant to this subsection shall be deposited in the Fund.

(d) No person shall be liable under this title for damages as a result of actions taken or omitted in the course of rendering care, assistance, or advice in accordance with the national contingency plan or at the direction of an onscene coordinator appointed under such plan, with respect to an incident creating a danger to public health or welfare or the environment as a result of any release of a hazardous substance or the threat thereof. This subsection shall not preclude liability for damages as the result of gross negligence or intentional misconduct on the part of such person. For the purposes of the preceding sentence, reckless, willful, or wanton misconduct shall constitute gross negligence.

(e)(1) No indemnification, hold harmless, or similar agreement or conveyance shall be effective to transfer from the owner or operator of any vessel or facility or from any person who may be liable for a release or threat of release under this section, to any other person the liability imposed under this section. Nothing in this subsection shall bar any agreement to insure, hold harmless, or indemnify a party to such agreement for any liability under this section.

(2) Nothing in this title, including the provisions of paragraph (1) of this subsection, shall bar a cause of action that an owner or operator or any other person subject to liability under this section, or a guarantor, has or would have, by reason of subrogation or otherwise against any person.

(f) In the case of an injury to, destruction of, or loss of natural resources under subparagraph (C) of subsection (a) liability shall be to the United States Government and to any State for natural resources within the State or belonging to, managed by, controlled by, or appertaining to such State: *Provided, however,* That no liability to the United States or State shall be imposed under subparagraph (C) of subsection (a), where the party sought to be charged has demonstrated that the damages to natural resources complained of were specifically identified as an irreversible and irretrievable commitment of natural resources in an environmental impact statement, or other comparable environment analysis, and the decision to grant a permit or license authorizes such commitment of natural resources, and the facility or project was otherwise operating within the terms of its permit or license. The President, or the authorized representative of any State, shall act on behalf of the public as trustee of such natural resources to recover for such damages. Sums recovered shall be available for use to restore, rehabilitate, or acquire the equivalent of such natural resources by the appropriate agencies of the Federal Government or the State government, but the measure of such damages shall not be limited by the sums which can be used to restore or replace such resources. There shall be no recovery under the authority of subparagraph (C) of subsection (a) where such damages and the release of a hazardous substance from which such damages resulted have occurred wholly before the enactment of this Act.

(g) Each department, agency, or instrumentality of the executive, legislative, and judicial branches of the Federal Government shall be subject to, and comply with, this Act in the same manner and to the same extent, both procedurally and substantively, as any nongovernmental entity, including liability under this section.

(h) The owner or operator of a vessel shall be liable in accordance with this section and as provided under section 114 of this Act notwithstanding any provision of the Act of March 3, 1851 (46 U.S.C. 183ff).

(i) No person (including the United States or any State) may recover under the authority of this section for any response costs or damages resulting from the application of a pesticide product registered under the Federal Insecticide, Fungicide, and Rodenticide Act. Nothing in this paragraph shall affect or modify in any way the obligations or liability of any person under any other provision of State or Federal law, including common law, for damages, injury, or loss resulting from a release of any hazardous substance or for removal or remedial action or the costs of removal or remedial action of such hazardous substance.

(j) Recovery by any person (including the United States or any State) for response costs or damages resulting from a federally permitted release shall be pursuant to existing law in lieu of this section. Nothing in this paragraph shall affect or modify in any way the obligations or liability of any person under any other provision of State or Federal law, including common law, for damages, injury, or loss resulting from a release of any hazardous substance or for removal or remedial action or the costs of removal or remedial action of such hazardous substance. In addition, costs of response incurred by the Federal Government in connection with a discharge specified in section 101(10) (B) or (C) shall be recoverable in an action brought under section 309(b) of the Clean Water Act.

(k)(1) The liability established by this section or any other law for the owner or operator of a hazardous waste disposal facility which has received a permit under subtitle C of the Solid Waste Disposal Act, shall be transferred to and assumed by the Post-closure Liability Fund established by section 232 of this Act when—

(A) such facility and the owner and operator thereof has complied with the requirements of subtitle C of the Solid Waste Disposal Act and regulations issued thereunder, which may affect the performance of such facility after closure; and

(B) such facility has been closed in accordance with such regulations and the conditions of such permit, and such facility and the surrounding area have been monitored as required by such regulations and permit conditions for a period not to exceed five years after closure to demonstrate that there is no substantial likelihood that any migration offsite or release from confinement of any hazardous substance or other risk to public health or welfare will occur.

(2) Such transfer of liability shall be effective ninety days after the owner or operator of such facility notifies the Administrator of the Environmental Protection Agency (and the State where it has an authorized program under section 3006(b) of the Solid Waste Disposal Act) that the conditions imposed by this subsection have been satisfied. If within such ninety-day period the Administrator of the Environmental Protection Agency or such State determines that any such facility has not complied with all the conditions imposed by this subsection or that insufficient information has been provided to demonstrate such compliance, the Administrator or such State shall so notify the owner and operator of such facility and the administrator of the Fund established by section 232 of this Act, and the owner and operator of such facility shall continue to be liable with respect to such facility under this section and other law until such time as the Administrator and such State determines that such facility has complied with all conditions imposed by this subsection. A determination by the Administrator or such State that a facility has not

complied with all conditions imposed by this subsection or that insufficient information has been supplied to demonstrate compliance, shall be a final administrative action for purposes of judicial review. A request for additional information shall state in specific terms the data required.

(3) In addition to the assumption of liability of owners and operators under paragraph (1) of this subsection, the Post-closure Liability Fund established by section 232 of this Act may be used to pay costs of monitoring and care and maintenance of a site incurred by other persons after the period of monitoring required by regulations under subtitle C of the Solid Waste Disposal Act for hazardous waste disposal facilities meeting the conditions of paragraph (1) of this subsection.

(4)(A) Not later than one year after the date of enactment of this Act, the Secretary of the Treasury shall conduct a study and shall submit a report thereon to the Congress on the feasibility of establishing or qualifying an optional system of private insurance for postclosure financial responsibility for hazardous waste disposal facilities to which this subsection applies. Such study shall include a specification of adequate and realistic minimum standards to assure that any such privately placed insurance will carry out the purposes of this subsection in a reliable, enforceable, and practical manner. Such a study shall include an examination of the public and private incentives, programs, and actions necessary to make privately placed insurance a practical and effective option to the financing system for the Post-closure Liability Fund provided in title II of this Act.

(B) Not later than eighteen months after the date of enactment of this Act and after a public hearing, the President shall by rule determine whether or not it is feasible to establish or qualify an optional system of private insurance for postclosure financial responsibility for hazardous waste disposal facilities to which this subsection applies. If the President determines the establishment or qualification of such a system would be infeasible, he shall promptly publish an explanation of the reasons for such a determination. If the President determines the establishment or qualification of such a system would be feasible, he shall promptly publish notice of such determination. Not later than six months after an affirmative determination under the preceding sentence and after a public hearing, the President shall by rule promulgate adequate and realistic minimum standards which must be met by any such privately placed insurance, taking into account the purposes of this Act and this subsection. Such rules shall also specify reasonably expeditious procedures by which privately placed insurance plans can qualify as meeting such minimum standards.

(C) In the event any privately placed insurance plan qualifies under subparagraph (B), any person enrolled in, and complying with the terms of, such plan shall be excluded from the provisions of paragraphs (1), (2), and (3) of this subsection and exempt from the requirements to pay any tax or fee to the Post-closure Liability Fund under title II of this Act.

(D) The President may issue such rules and take such other actions as are necessary to effectuate the purposes of this paragraph.

FINANCIAL RESPONSIBILITY

SEC. 108. (a)(1) The owner or operator of each vessel (except a non-self-propelled barge that does not carry hazardous substances as cargo) over three hundred gross tons that uses any port or place in the

United States or the navigable waters or any offshore facility, shall establish and maintain, in accordance with regulations promulgated by the President, evidence of financial responsibility of $300 per gross ton (or for a vessel carrying hazardous substances as cargo, or $5,000,000, whichever is greater). Financial responsibility may be established by any one, or any combination, of the following: insurance, guarantee, surety bond, or qualification as a self-insurer. Any bond filed shall be issued by a bonding company authorized to do business in the United States. In cases where an owner or operator owns, operates, or charters more than one vessel subject to this subsection, evidence of financial responsibility need be established only to meet the maximum liability applicable to the largest of such vessels.

(2) The Secretary of the Treasury shall withhold or revoke the clearance required by section 4197 of the Revised Statutes of the United States of any vessel subject to this subsection that does not have certification furnished by the President that the financial responsibility provisions of paragraph (1) of this subsection have been complied with.

(3) The Secretary of Transportation, in accordance with regulations issued by him, shall (A) deny entry to any port or place in the United States or navigable waters to, and (B) detain at the port or place in the United States from which it is about to depart for any other port or place in the United States, any vessel subject to this subsection that, upon request, does not produce certification furnished by the President that the financial responsibility provisions of paragraph (1) of this subsection have been complied with.

(b)(1) Beginning not earlier than five years after the date of enactment of this Act, the President shall promulgate requirements (for facilities in addition to those under subtitle C of the Solid Waste Disposal Act and other Federal law) that classes of facilities establish and maintain evidence of financial responsibility consistent with the degree and duration of risk associated with the production, transportation, treatment, storage, or disposal of hazardous substances. Not later than three years after the date of enactment of the Act, the President shall identify those classes for which requirements will be first developed and publish notice of such identification in the Federal Register. Priority in the development of such requirements shall be accorded to those classes of facilities, owners, and operators which the President determines present the highest level of risk of injury.

(2) The level of financial responsibility shall be initially established, and, when necessary, adjusted to protect against the level of risk which the President in his discretion believes is appropriate based on the payment experience of the Fund, commercial insurers, courts settlements and judgments, and voluntary claims satisfaction. To the maximum extent practicable, the President shall cooperate with and seek the advice of the commercial insurance industry in developing financial responsibility requirements.

(3) Regulations promulgated under this subsection shall incrementally impose financial responsibility requirements over a period of not less than three and no more than six years after the date of promulgation. Where possible, the level of financial responsibility which the President believes appropriate as a final requirement shall be achieved through incremental, annual increases in the requirements.

(4) Where a facility is owned or operated by more than one person, evidence of financial responsibility covering the facility may be

established and maintained by one of the owners or operators, or, in consolidated form, by or on behalf of two or more owners or operators. When evidence of financial responsibility is established in a consolidated form, the proportional share of each participant shall be shown. The evidence shall be accompanied by a statement authorizing the applicant to act for and in behalf of each participant in submitting and maintaining the evidence of financial responsibility.

(5) The requirements for evidence of financial responsibility for motor carriers covered by this Act shall be determined under section 30 of the Motor Carrier Act of 1980, Public Law 96-296.

(c) Any claim authorized by section 107 or 111 may be asserted directly against any guarantor providing evidence of financial responsibility as required under this section. In defending such a claim, the guarantor may invoke all rights and defenses which would be available to the owner or operator under this title. The guarantor may also invoke the defense that the incident was caused by the willful misconduct of the owner or operator, but such guarantor may not invoke any other defense that such guarantor might have been entitled to invoke in a proceeding brought by the owner or operator against him.

(d) Any guarantor acting in good faith against which claims under this Act are asserted as a guarantor shall be liable under section 107 or section 112(c) of this title only up to the monetary limits of the policy of insurance or indemnity contract such guarantor has undertaken or of the guaranty of other evidence of financial responsibility furnished under section 108 of this Act, and only to the extent that liability is not excluded by restrictive endorsement: *Provided,* That this subsection shall not alter the liability of any person under section 107 of this Act.

PENALTY

SEC. 109. Any person who, after notice and an opportunity for a hearing, is found to have failed to comply with the requirements of section 108, the regulations issued thereunder, or with any denial or detention order shall be liable to the United States for a civil penalty, not to exceed $10,000 for each day of violation.

EMPLOYEE PROTECTION

SEC. 110. (a) No person shall fire or in any other way discriminate against, or cause to be fired or discriminated against, any employee or any authorized representative of employees by reason of the fact that such employee or representative has provided information to a State or to the Federal Government, filed, instituted, or caused to be filed or instituted any proceeding under this Act, or has testified or is about to testify in any proceeding resulting from the administration or enforcement of the provisions of this Act.

(b) Any employee or a representative of employees who believes that he has been fired or otherwise discriminated against by any person in violation of subsection (a) of this section may, within thirty days after such alleged violation occurs, apply to the Secretary of Labor for a review of such firing or alleged discrimination. A copy of the application shall be sent to such person, who shall be the respondent. Upon receipt of such application, the Secretary of Labor shall cause such investigation to be made as he deems appropriate. Such investigation shall provide an opportunity for a public hearing at the request of any party to such review to enable the parties to present information relating to such alleged violation. The parties shall be given written notice of the time and place of the hearing at least five days prior to the hearing. Any such hearing shall be of record and shall be subject to section 554 of title 5, United States Code. Upon receiving the report of such investigation, the Secretary of Labor shall make findings of fact. If he finds that such violation did occur, he shall issue a decision, incorporating an order therein and his findings, requiring the party committing such violation to take such affirmative action to abate the violation as the Secretary of Labor deems appropriate, including, but not limited to, the rehiring or reinstatement of the employee or representative of employees to his former position with compensation. If he finds that there was no such violation, he shall issue an order denying the application. Such order issued by the Secretary of Labor under this subparagraph shall be subject to judicial review in the same manner as orders and decisions are subject to judicial review under this Act.

(c) Whenever an order is issued under this section to abate such violation, at the request of the applicant a sum equal to the aggregate amount of all costs and expenses (including the attorney's fees) determined by the Secretary of Labor to have been reasonably incurred by the applicant for, or in connection with, the institution and prosecution of such proceedings, shall be assessed against the person committing such violation.

(d) This section shall have no application to any employee who acting without discretion from his employer (or his agent) deliberately violates any requirement of this Act.

(e) The President shall conduct continuing evaluations of potential loss of shifts of employment which may result from the administration or enforcement of the provisions of this Act, including, where appropriate, investigating threatened plant closures or reductions in employment allegedly resulting from such administration or enforcement. Any employee who is discharged, or laid off, threatened with discharge or layoff, or otherwise discriminated against by any person because of the alleged results of such administration or enforcement, or any representative of such employee, may request the President to conduct a full investigation of the matter and, at the request of any party, shall hold public hearings, require the parties, including the employer involved, to present information relating to the actual or potential effect of such administration or enforcement on employment and any alleged discharge, layoff, or other discrimination, and the detailed reasons or justification therefore. Any such hearing shall be of record and shall be subject to section 554 of title 5, United States Code. Upon receiving the report of such investigation, the President shall make findings of fact as to the effect of such administration or enforcement on employment and on the alleged discharge, layoff, or discrimination and shall make such recommendations as he deems appropriate. Such report, findings, and recommendations shall be available to the public. Nothing in this subsection shall be construed to require or authorize the President or any State to modify or withdraw any action, standard, limitation, or any other requirement of this Act.

USES OF FUND

SEC. 111. (a) The President shall use the money in the Fund for the following purposes:

(1) payment of governmental response costs incurred pursuant to section 104 of this title, including costs incurred pursuant to the Intervention on the High Seas Act;

(2) payment of any claim for necessary response costs incurred by any other person as a result of carrying out the national contingency plan established under section 311(c) of the Clean Water Act and amended by section 105 of this title: *Provided, however,* That such costs must be approved under said plan and certified by the responsible Federal official;

(3) payment of any claim authorized by subsection (b) of this section and finally decided pursuant to section 112 of this title, including those costs set out in subsection 112(c)(3) of this title; and

(4) payment of costs specified under subsection (c) of this section.

The President shall not pay for any administrative costs or expenses out of the Fund unless such costs and expenses are reasonably necessary for and incidental to the implementation of this title.

(b) Claims asserted and compensable but unsatisfied under provisions of section 311 of the Clean Water Act, which are modified by section 304 of this Act may be asserted against the Fund under this title; and other claims resulting from a release or threat of release of a hazardous substance from a vessel or a facility may be asserted against the Fund under this title for injury to, or destruction or loss of, natural resources, including cost for damage assessment: *Provided, however,* That any such claim may be asserted only by the President, as trustee, for natural resources over which the United States has sovereign rights, or natural resources within the territory or the fishery conservation zone of the United States to the extent they are managed or protected by the United States, or by any State for natural resources within the boundary of that State belonging to, managed by, controlled by, or appertaining to the State.

(c) Uses of the Fund under subsection (a) of this section include—

(1) the costs of assessing both short-term and long-term injury to, destruction of, or loss of any natural resources resulting from a release of a hazardous substance;

(2) the costs of Federal or State efforts in the restoration, rehabilitation, or replacement or acquiring the equivalent of any natural resources injured, destroyed, or lost as a result of a release of a hazardous substance;

(3) subject to such amounts as are provided in appropriation Acts, the costs of a program to identify, investigate, and take enforcement and abatement action against releases of hazardous substances;

(4) the costs of epidemiologic studies, development and maintenance of a registry of persons exposed to hazardous substances to allow long-term health effect studies, and diagnostic services not otherwise available to determine whether persons in populations exposed to hazardous substances in connection with a release or a suspected release are suffering from long-latency diseases;

HAZARDOUS SUBSTANCE RESPONSE TRUST FUND *

Of the funds appropriated under this head in the Department of Housing and Urban Development-Independent Agencies Appropriation Act, 1982, $5,000,000 shall be made available to the Department of Health and Human Services, upon enactment, and up to an additional $2,000,000 may be made available by the Administrator to the Department for the performance of specific activities in accordance with section 111(c)(4) of Public Law 96–510, the Comprehensive Environmental Response, Compensation, and Liability Act of 1980. Management of all funds made available to the Department shall be consistent with the responsibilities of the trustee of the fund, as outlined in section 223(b) of the Act.

(5) subject to such amounts as are provided in appropriation Acts, the costs of providing equipment and similar overhead, related to the purposes of this Act and section 311 of the Clean Water Act, and needed to supplement equipment and services available through contractors or other non-Federal entities, and of establishing and maintaining damage assessment capability, for any Federal agency involved in strike forces, emergency task forces, or other response teams under the national contingency plan; and

(6) subject to such amounts as are provided in appropriation Acts, the costs of a program to protect the health and safety of employees involved in response to hazardous substance releases. Such program shall be developed jointly by the Environmental Protection Agency, the Occupational Safety and Health Administration, and the National Institute for Occupational Safety and Health and shall include, but not be limited to, measures for identifying and assessing hazards to which persons engaged in removal, remedy or other response to hazardous substances may be exposed, methods to protect workers from such hazards, and necessary regulatory and enforcement measures to assure adequate protection of such employees.

---

* This paragraph was provided by P.L. 97-216.

(d)(1) No money in the Fund may be used under subsection (c) (1) and (2) of this section, nor for the payment of any claim under subsection (b) of this section, where the injury, destruction, or loss of natural resources and the release of a hazardous substance from which such damages resulted have occurred wholly before the enactment of this Act.

(2) No money in the Fund may be used for the payment of any claim under subsection (b) of this section where such expenses are associated with injury or loss resulting from long-term exposure to ambient concentrations of air pollutants from multiple or diffuse sources.

(e)(1) Claims against or presented to the Fund shall not be valid or paid in excess of the total money in the Fund at any one time. Such claims become valid only when additional money is collected, appropriated, or otherwise added to the Fund. Should the total claims outstanding at any time exceed the current balance of the Fund, the President shall pay such claims, to the extent authorized under this section, in full in the order in which they were finally determined.

(2) In any fiscal year, 85 percent of the money credited to the Fund under title II of this Act shall be available only for the purposes specified in paragraphs (1), (2), and (4) of subsection (a) of this section.

(3) No money in the Fund shall be available for remedial action, other than actions specified in subsection (c) of this section, with respect to federally owned facilities.

(4) Paragraphs (1) and (4) of subsection (a) of this section shall in the aggregate be subject to such amounts as are provided in appropriation Acts.

(f) The President is authorized to promulgate regulations designating one or more Federal officials who may obligate money in the Fund in accordance with this section or portions thereof. The President is also authorized to delegate authority to obligate money in the Fund or to settle claims to officials of a State operating under a contract or cooperative agreement with the Federal Government pursuant to section 104(d) of this title.

(g) The President shall provide for the promulgation of rules and regulations with respect to the notice to be provided to potential injured parties by an owner and operator of any vessel, or facility from which a hazardous substance has been released. Such rules and regulations shall consider the scope and form of the notice which would be appropriate to carry out the purposes of this title. Upon promulgation of such rules and regulations, the owner and operator of any vessel or facility from which a hazardous substance has been released shall provide notice in accordance with such rules and regulations. With respect to releases from public vessels, the President shall provide such notification as is appropriate to potential injured parties. Until the promulgation of such rules and regulations, the owner and operator of any vessel or facility from which a hazardous substance has been released shall provide reasonable notice to potential injured parties by publication in local newspapers serving the affected area.

(h)(1) In accordance with regulations promulgated under section 301(c) of this Act, damages for injury to, destruction of, or loss of natural resources resulting from a release of a hazardous substance, for the purposes of this Act and section 311(f) (4) and (5) of the Federal Water Pollution Control Act, shall be assessed by Federal officials designated by the President under the national contingency plan published under section 105 of the Act, and such officials shall act for the President as trustee under this section and section 311(f)(5) of the Federal Water Pollution Control Act.

(2) Any determination or assessment of damages for injury to, destruction of, or loss of natural resources for the purposes of this Act and section 311(f) (4) and (5) of the Federal Water Pollution Control Act shall have the force and effect of a rebuttable presumption on behalf of any claimant (including a trustee under section 107 of this Act or a Federal agency) in any judicial or adjudicatory administrative proceeding under this Act or section 311 of the Federal Water Pollution Control Act.

(i) Except in a situation requiring action to avoid an irreversible loss of natural resources or to prevent or reduce any continuing danger to natural resources or similar need for emergency action, funds may not be used under this Act for the restoration, rehabilitation, or replacement or acquisition of the equivalent of any natural resources until a plan for the use of such funds for such purposes has been developed and adopted by affected Federal agencies and the Governor or Governors of any State having sustained damage to natural resources within its borders, belonging to, managed by or appertaining to such State, after adequate public notice and opportunity for hearing and consideration of all public comment.

(j) The President shall use the money in the Post-closure Liability Fund for any of the purposes specified in subsection (a) of this section with respect to a hazardous waste disposal facility for which liability has transferred to such fund under section 107(k) of this Act, and, in addition, for payment of any claim or appropriate request for costs of response, damages, or other compensation for injury or loss under section 107 of this Act or any other State or Federal law, resulting from a release of a hazardous substance from such a facility.

(k) The Inspector General of each department or agency to which responsibility to obligate money in the Fund is delegated shall provide an audit review team to audit all payments, obligations, reimbursements, or other uses of the Fund, to assure that the Fund is being properly administered and that claims are being appropriately and expeditiously considered. Each such Inspector General shall submit to the Congress an interim report one year after the establishment of the Fund and a final report two years after the establishment of the Fund. Each such Inspector General shall thereafter provide such auditing of the Fund as is appropriate. Each Federal agency shall cooperate with the Inspector General in carrying out this subsection.

(l) To the extent that the provisions of this Act permit, a foreign claimant may assert a claim to the same extent that a United States claimant may assert a claim if—

(1) the release of a hazardous substance occurred (A) in the navigable waters or (B) in or on the territorial sea or adjacent shoreline of a foreign country of which the claimant is a resident;

(2) the claimant is not otherwise compensated for his loss;

(3) the hazardous substance was released from a facility or from a vessel located adjacent to or within the navigable waters or was discharged in connection with activities conducted under the Outer Continental Shelf Lands Act, as amended (43 U.S.C. 1331 et seq.) or the Deepwater Port Act of 1974, as amended (33 U.S.C. 1501 et seq.); and

(4) recovery is authorized by a treaty or an executive agreement between the United States and foreign country involved, or if the Secretary of State, in consultation with the Attorney General and other appropriate officials, certifies that such country provides a comparable remedy for United States claimants.

CLAIMS PROCEDURE

SEC. 112. (a) All claims which may be asserted against the Fund pursuant to section 111 of this title shall be presented in the first instance to the owner, operator, or guarantor of the vessel or facility from which a hazardous substance has been released, if known to the claimant, and to any other person known to the claimant who may be liable under section 107 of this title. In any case where the claim has not been satisfied within sixty days of presentation in accordance with this subsection, the claimant may elect to commence an action in court against such owner, operator, guarantor, or other person or to present the claim to the Fund for payment.

(b)(1) The President shall prescribe appropriate forms and procedures for claims filed hereunder, which shall include a provision requiring the claimant to make a sworn verification of the claim to the best of his knowledge. Any person who knowingly gives or causes to be given any false information as a part of any such claim shall, upon conviction, be fined up to $5,000 or imprisoned for not more than one year, or both.

(2)(A) Upon receipt of any claim, the President shall as soon as practicable inform any known affected parties of the claim and shall attempt to promote and arrange a settlement between the claimant and any person who may be liable. If the claimant and alleged liable party or parties can agree upon a settlement, it shall be final and binding upon the parties thereto, who will be deemed to have waived all recourse against the Fund.

(B) Where a liable party is unknown or cannot be determined, the claimant and the President shall attempt to arrange settlement of any claim against the Fund. The President is authorized to award and make payment of such a settlement, subject to such proof and procedures as he may promulgate by regulation.

(C) Except as provided in subparagraph (D) of this paragraph, the President shall use the facilities and services of private insurance and claims adjusting organizations or State agencies in implementing this subsection and may contract to pay compensation for those facilities and services. Any contract made under the provisions of this paragraph may be made without regard to the provisions of section 3709 of the Revised Statutes, as amended (41 U.S.C. 5), upon a showing by the President that advertising is not reasonably practicable. When the services of a State agency are used hereunder, no payment may be made on a claim asserted on behalf of that State or any of its agencies or subdivisions unless the payment has been approved by the President.

(D) To the extent necessitated by extraordinary circumstances, where the services of such private organizations or State agencies are inadequate, the President may use Federal personnel to implement this subsection.

(3) If no settlement is reached within forty-five days of filing of a claim through negotiation pursuant to this section, the President may, if he is satisfied that the information developed during the processing of the claim warrants it, make and pay an award of the claim. If the claimant is dissatisfied with the award, he may appeal it in the manner provided for in subparagraph (G) of paragraph (4) of this subsection. If the President declines to make an award, he shall submit the claim for decision to a member of the Board of Arbitrators established pursuant to paragraph (4).

(4)(A) Within ninety days of the enactment of this Act, the President shall establish a Board of Arbitrators to implement this subsection. The Board shall consist of as many members as the President may determine will be necessary to implement this subsection expeditiously, and he may increase or decrease the size of the Board at any time in his discretion in order to enable it to respond to the demands of such implementation. Each member of the Board shall be selected through utilization of the procedures of the American Arbitration Association: *Provided, however,* That no regular employee of the President or any of the Federal departments, administrations, or agencies to whom he delegated responsibilities under this Act shall act as a member of the Board.

(B) Hearings conducted hereunder shall be public and shall be held in such place as may be agreed upon by the parties thereto, or, in the absence of such agreement, in such place as the President determines, in his discretion, will be most convenient for the parties thereto.

(C) Hearings before a member of the Board shall be informal, and the rules of evidence prevailing in judicial proceedings need not be required. Each member of the Board shall have the power to administer oaths and to subpena the attendance and testimony of witnesses and the production of books, records, and other evidence relative or pertinent to the issues presented to him for decision. Testimony may be taken by interrogatory or deposition. Each person appearing before a member of the Board shall have the right to counsel. Subpenas shall be issued and enforced in accordance with procedures in subsection (d) of section 555 of title 5, United States Code, and rules promulgated by the President. If a person fails or refuses to obey a subpena, the President may invoke the aid of the district court of the United States where the person is found, resides, or transacts business in requiring the attendance and testimony of the person and the production by him of books, papers, documents, or any tangible things.

(D) In any proceeding before a member of the Board, the claimant shall bear the burden of proving his claim. Should a member of the Board determine that further investigations, monitoring, surveys, testing, or other information gathering would be useful and necessary in deciding the claim, he may request the President in writing to undertake such activities pursuant to section 104(b) of this title. The President shall dispose of such a request in his sole discretion, taking into account various competing demands and the availability of the technical and financial capacity to conduct such studies, monitoring, and investigations. Should the President decide to undertake the requested actions, all time requirements for the processing and deciding of claims hereunder shall be suspended until the President reports the results thereof to the member of the Board.

(E) All costs and expenses approved by the President attributable to the employment of any member of the Board shall be payable from the Fund, including fees and mileage expenses for witnesses summoned by such members on the same basis and to the same extent as if such witnesses were summoned before a district court of the United States.

(F) All decisions rendered by members of the Board shall be in writing, with notification to all appropriate parties, and shall be rendered within ninety days of submission of a claim to a member, unless all the parties to the claim agree in writing to an extension or unless the President extends the time limit pursuant to subparagraph (I) of this subsection.

(G) All decisions rendered by members of the Board shall be final, and any party to the proceeding may appeal such a decision within thirty days of notification of the award or decision. Any such appeal shall be made to the Federal district court for the district where the arbitral hearing took place. In any such appeal, the award or decision of the member of the Board shall be considered binding and conclusive, and shall not be overturned except for arbitrary or capricious abuse of the member's discretion: *Provided, however,* That no such award or decision shall be admissible as evidence of any issue of fact or law in any proceeding brought under any other provision of this Act or under any other provision of law. Nor shall any prearbitral settlement reached pursuant to subsection (b)(2)(A) of this section be admissible as evidence in any such proceeding.

(H) Within twenty days of the expiration of the appeal period for any arbitral award or decision, or within twenty days of the final judicial determination of any appeal taken pursuant to this subsection, the President shall pay any such award from the Fund. The President shall determine the method, terms, and time of payment.

(I) If at any time the President determines that, because of a large number of claims arising from any incident or set of incidents, it is in the best interests of the parties concerned, he may extend the time for prearbitral negotiation or for rendering an arbitral decision pursuant to this subsection by a period not to exceed sixty days. He may also group such claims for submission to a member of the Board of Arbitrators.

(c)(1) Payment of any claim by the Fund under this section shall be subject to the United States Government acquiring by subrogation the rights of the claimant to recover those costs of removal or damages for which it has compensated the claimant from the person responsible or liable for such release.

(2) Any person, including the Fund, who pays compensation pursuant to this Act to any claimant for damages or costs resulting from a release of a hazardous substance shall be subrogated to all rights, claims, and causes of action for such damages and costs of removal that the claimant has under this Act or any other law.

(3) Upon request of the President, the Attorney General shall commence an action on behalf of the Fund to recover any compensation paid by the Fund to any claimant pursuant to this title, and, without regard to any limitation of liability, all interest, administrative and adjudicative costs, and attorney's fees incurred by the Fund by reason of the claim. Such an action may be commenced against any owner, operator, or guarantor, or against any other person who is

liable, pursuant to any law, to the compensated claimant or to the Fund, for the damages or costs for which compensation was paid.

(d) No claim may be presented, nor may an action be commenced for damages under this title, unless that claim is presented or action commenced within three years from the date of the discovery of the loss or the date of enactment of this Act, whichever is later: *Provided, however,* That the time limitations contained herein shall not begin to run against a minor until he reaches eighteen years of age or a legal representative is duly appointed for him, nor against an incompetent person until his incompetency ends or a legal representative is duly appointed for him.

(e) Regardless of any State statutory or common law to the contrary, no person who asserts a claim against the Fund pursuant to this title shall be deemed or held to have waived any other claim not covered or assertable against the Fund under this title arising from the same incident, transaction, or set of circumstances, nor to have split a cause of action. Further, no person asserting a claim against the Fund pursuant to this title shall as a result of any determination of a question of fact or law made in connection with that claim be deemed or held to be collaterally estopped from raising such question in connection with any other claim not covered or assertable against the Fund under this title arising from the same incident, transaction, or set of circumstances.

LITIGATION, JURISDICTION AND VENUE

SEC. 113. (a) Review of any regulation promulgated under this Act may be had upon application by any interested person only in the Circuit Court of Appeals of the United States for the District of Columbia. Any such application shall be made within ninety days from the date of promulgation of such regulations. Any matter with respect to which review could have been obtained under this subsection shall not be subject to judicial review in any civil or criminal proceeding for enforcement or to obtain damages or recovery of response costs.

(b) Except as provided in subsection (a) of this section, the United States district courts shall have exclusive original jurisdiction over all controversies arising under this Act, without regard to the citizenship of the parties or the amount in controversy. Venue shall lie in any district in which the release or damages occurred, or in which the defendant resides, may be found, or has his principal office. For the purposes of this section, the Fund shall reside in the District of Columbia.

(c) The provisions of subsections (a) and (b) of this section shall not apply to any controversy or other matter resulting from the assessment of collection of any tax, as provided by title II of this Act, or to the review of any regulation promulgated under the Internal Revenue Code of 1954.

(d) No provision of this Act shall be deemed or held to moot any litigation concerning any release of any hazardous substance, or any damages associated therewith, commenced prior to enactment of this Act.

RELATIONSHIP TO OTHER LAW

SEC. 114. (a) Nothing in this Act shall be construed or interpreted as preempting any State from imposing any additional liability or requirements with respect to the release of hazardous substances within such State.

(b) Any person who receives compensation for removal costs or damages or claims pursuant to this Act shall be precluded from recovering compensation for the same removal costs or damages or claims pursuant to any other State or Federal law. Any person who receives compensation for removal costs or damages or claims pursuant to any other Federal or State law shall be precluded from receiving compensation for the same removal costs or damages or claims as provided in this Act.

(c) Except as provided in this Act, no person may be required to contribute to any fund, the purpose of which is to pay compensation for claims for any costs of response or damages or claims which may be compensated under this title. Nothing in this section shall preclude any State from using general revenues for such a fund, or from imposing a tax or fee upon any person or upon any substance in order to finance the purchase or prepositioning of hazardous substance response equipment or other preparations for the response to a release of hazardous substances which affects such State.

(d) Except as provided in this title, no owner or operator of a vessel or facility who establishes and maintains evidence of financial responsibility in accordance with this title shall be required under any State or local law, rule, or regulation to establish or maintain any other evidence of financial responsibility in connection with liability for the release of a hazardous substance from such vessel or facility. Evidence of compliance with the financial responsibility requirements of this title shall be accepted by a State in lieu of any other requirement of financial responsibility imposed by such State in connection with liability for the release of a hazardous substance from such vessel or facility.

AUTHORITY TO DELEGATE, ISSUE REGULATIONS

SEC. 115. The President is authorized to delegate and assign any duties or powers imposed upon or assigned to him and to promulgate any regulations necessary to carry out the provisions of this title.

TITLE II—HAZARDOUS SUBSTANCE RESPONSE REVENUE ACT OF 1980

SEC. 201. SHORT TITLE; AMENDMENT OF 1954 CODE.

(a) SHORT TITLE.—This title may be cited as the "Hazardous Substance Response Revenue Act of 1980".

(b) AMENDMENT OF 1954 CODE.—Except as otherwise expressly provided, whenever in this title an amendment or repeal is expressed in terms of an amendment to, or repeal of, a section or other provision, the reference shall be considered to be made to a section or other provision of the Internal Revenue Code of 1954.

Subtitle A—Imposition of Taxes on Petroleum and Certain Chemicals

SEC. 211. IMPOSITION OF TAXES.

(a) GENERAL RULE.—Subtitle D (relating to miscellaneous excise taxes) is amended by inserting after chapter 37 the following new chapter:

"CHAPTER 38—ENVIRONMENTAL TAXES

"Subchapter A—Tax on Petroleum

"SEC. 4611. IMPOSITION OF TAX.

"(a) GENERAL RULE.—There is hereby imposed a tax of 0.79 cent a barrel on—

"(1) crude oil received at a United States refinery, and

"(2) petroleum products entered into the United States for consumption, use, or warehousing.

"(b) TAX ON CERTAIN USES AND EXPORTATION.—

"(1) IN GENERAL.—If—

"(A) any domestic crude oil is used in or exported from the United States, and

"(B) before such use or exportation, no tax was imposed on such crude oil under subsection (a),

then a tax of 0.79 cent a barrel is hereby imposed on such crude oil.

"(2) EXCEPTION FOR USE ON PREMISES WHERE PRODUCED.—Paragraph (1) shall not apply to any use of crude oil for extracting oil or natural gas on the premises where such crude oil was produced.

"(c) PERSONS LIABLE FOR TAX.—

"(1) CRUDE OIL RECEIVED AT REFINERY.—The tax imposed by subsection (a)(1) shall be paid by the operator of the United States refinery.

"(2) IMPORTED PETROLEUM PRODUCT.—The tax imposed by subsection (a)(2) shall be paid by the person entering the product for consumption, use, or warehousing.

"(3) TAX ON CERTAIN USES OR EXPORTS.—The tax imposed by subsection (b) shall be paid by the person using or exporting the crude oil, as the case may be.

"(d) TERMINATION.—The taxes imposed by this section shall not apply after September 30, 1985, except that if on September 30, 1983, or September 30, 1984—

"(1) the unobligated balance in the Hazardous Substance Response Trust Fund as of such date exceeds $900,000,000, and

"(2) the Secretary, after consultation with the Administrator of the Environmental Protection Agency, determines that such unobligated balance will exceed $500,000,000 on September 30 of the following year if no tax is imposed under section 4611 or 4661 during the calendar year following the date referred to above, then no tax shall be imposed by this section during the first calendar year beginning after the date referred to in paragraph (1).

"SEC. 4612. DEFINITIONS AND SPECIAL RULES.

"(a) DEFINITIONS.—For purposes of this subchapter—

"(1) CRUDE OIL.—The term 'crude oil' includes crude oil condensates and natural gasoline.

"(2) DOMESTIC CRUDE OIL.—The term 'domestic crude oil' means any crude oil produced from a well located in the United States.

"(3) PETROLEUM PRODUCT.—The term 'petroleum product' includes crude oil.

"(4) UNITED STATES.—

"(A) IN GENERAL.—The term 'United States' means the 50 States, the District of Columbia, the Commonwealth of Puerto Rico, any possession of the United States, the Commonwealth of the Northern Mariana Islands, and the Trust Territory of the Pacific Islands.

"(B) UNITED STATES INCLUDES CONTINENTAL SHELF AREAS.—The principles of section 638 shall apply for purposes of the term 'United States'.

"(C) UNITED STATES INCLUDES FOREIGN TRADE ZONES.—The term 'United States' includes any foreign trade zone of the United States.

"(5) UNITED STATES REFINERY.—The term 'United States refinery' means any facility in the United States at which crude oil is refined.

"(6) REFINERIES WHICH PRODUCE NATURAL GASOLINE.—In the case of any United States refinery which produces natural gasoline from natural gas, the gasoline so produced shall be treated as received at such refinery at the time so produced.

"(7) PREMISES.—The term 'premises' has the same meaning as when used for purposes of determining gross income from the property under section 613.

"(8) BARREL.—The term 'barrel' means 42 United States gallons.

"(9) FRACTIONAL PART OF BARREL.—In the case of a fraction of a barrel, the tax imposed by section 4611 shall be the same fraction of the amount of such tax imposed on a whole barrel.

"(b) ONLY 1 TAX IMPOSED WITH RESPECT TO ANY PRODUCT.—No tax shall be imposed by section 4611 with respect to any petroleum product if the person who would be liable for such tax establishes that a prior tax imposed by such section has been imposed with respect to such product.

"(c) DISPOSITION OF REVENUES FROM PUERTO RICO AND THE VIRGIN ISLANDS.—The provisions of subsections (a)(3) and (b)(3) of section 7652 shall not apply to any tax imposed by section 4611.

"Subchapter B—Tax on Certain Chemicals

"SEC. 4661. IMPOSITION OF TAX.

"(a) GENERAL RULE.—There is hereby imposed a tax on any taxable chemical sold by the manufacturer, producer, or importer thereof.

"(b) AMOUNT OF TAX.—The amount of the tax imposed by subsection (a) shall be determined in accordance with the following table:

"In the case of:	The tax is the following amount per ton
Acetylene	$4.87
Benzene	4.87
Butane	4.87
Butylene	4.87
Butadiene	4.87
Ethylene	4.87
Methane	3.44
Naphthalene	4.87
Propylene	4.87
Toluene	4.87
Xylene	4.87
Ammonia	2.64
Antimony	4.45
Antimony trioxide	3.75
Arsenic	4.45
Arsenic trioxide	3.41
Barium sulfide	2.30
Bromine	4.45
Cadmium	4.45
Chlorine	2.70
Chromium	4.45
Chromite	1.52
Potassium dichromate	1.69
Sodium dichromate	1.87
Cobalt	4.45
Cupric sulfate	1.87
Cupric oxide	3.59
Cuprous oxide	3.97
Hydrochloric acid	0.29
Hydrogen fluoride	4.23
Lead oxide	4.14
Mercury	4.45
Nickel	4.45
Phosphorus	4.45
Stannous chloride	2.85
Stannic chloride	2.12
Zinc chloride	2.22
Zinc sulfate	1.90
Potassium hydroxide	0.22
Sodium hydroxide	0.28
Sulfuric acid	0.26
Nitric acid	0.24

"(c) TERMINATION.—No tax shall be imposed under this section during any period during which no tax is imposed under section 4611(a).

"SEC. 4662. DEFINITIONS AND SPECIAL RULES.

"(a) DEFINITIONS.—For purposes of this subchapter—

"(1) TAXABLE CHEMICAL.—Except as provided in subsection (b), the term 'taxable chemical' means any substance—

"(A) which is listed in the table under section 4661(b), and

"(B) which is manufactured or produced in the United States or entered into the United States for consumption, use, or warehousing.

"(2) UNITED STATES.—The term 'United States' has the meaning given such term by section 4612(a)(4).

"(3) IMPORTER.—The term 'importer' means the person entering the taxable chemical for consumption, use, or warehousing.

"(4) TON.—The term 'ton' means 2,000 pounds. In the case of any taxable chemical which is a gas, the term 'ton' means the amount of such gas in cubic feet which is the equivalent of 2,000 pounds on a molecular weight basis.

"(5) FRACTIONAL PART OF TON.—In the case of a fraction of a ton, the tax imposed by section 4661 shall be the same fraction of the amount of such tax imposed on a whole ton.

"(b) EXCEPTIONS; OTHER SPECIAL RULES.—For purposes of this subchapter—

"(1) METHANE OR BUTANE USED AS A FUEL.—Under regulations prescribed by the Secretary, methane or butane shall be treated as a taxable chemical only if it is used otherwise than as a fuel (and, for purposes of section 4661(a), the person so using it shall be treated as the manufacturer thereof).

"(2) SUBSTANCES USED IN THE PRODUCTION OF FERTILIZER.—

"(A) IN GENERAL.—In the case of nitric acid, sulfuric acid, ammonia, or methane used to produce ammonia which is a qualified substance, no tax shall be imposed under section 4661(a).

"(B) QUALIFIED SUBSTANCE.—For purposes of this section, the term 'qualified substance' means any substance—

"(i) used in a qualified use by the manufacturer, producer, or importer,

"(ii) sold for use by the purchaser in a qualified use, or

"(iii) sold for resale by the purchaser to a second purchaser for use by such second purchaser in a qualified use.

"(C) QUALIFIED USE.—For purposes of this subsection, the term 'qualified use' means any use in the manufacture or production of a fertilizer.

"(3) SULFURIC ACID PRODUCED AS A BYPRODUCT OF AIR POLLUTION CONTROL.—In the case of sulfuric acid produced solely as a byproduct of and on the same site as air pollution control equipment, no tax shall be imposed under section 4661.

"(4) SUBSTANCES DERIVED FROM COAL.—For purposes of this subchapter, the term 'taxable chemical' shall not include any substance to the extent derived from coal.

"(c) USE BY MANUFACTURER, ETC., CONSIDERED SALE.—If any person manufactures, produces, or imports a taxable chemical and uses such chemical, then such person shall be liable for tax under section 4661 in the same manner as if such chemical were sold by such person.

"(d) REFUND OR CREDIT FOR CERTAIN USES.—

"(1) IN GENERAL.—Under regulations prescribed by the Secretary, if—

"(A) a tax under section 4661 was paid with respect to any taxable chemical, and

"(B) such chemical was used by any person in the manufacture or production of any other substance the sale of which by such person would be taxable under such section,

then an amount equal to the tax so paid shall be allowed as a credit or refund (without interest) to such person in the same manner as if it were an overpayment of tax imposed by such section. In any case to which this paragraph applies, the amount of any such credit or refund shall not exceed the amount of tax imposed by such section on the other substance manufactured or produced.

"(2) USE AS FERTILIZER.—Under regulations prescribed by the Secretary, if—

"(A) a tax under section 4661 was paid with respect to nitric acid, sulfuric acid, ammonia, or methane used to make ammonia without regard to subsection (b)(2), and

"(B) any person uses such substance, or sells such substance for use, as a qualified substance,

then an amount equal to the excess of the tax so paid over the tax determined with regard to subsection (b)(2) shall be allowed as a credit or refund (without interest) to such person in the same manner as if it were an overpayment of tax imposed by this section.

"(e) DISPOSITION OF REVENUES FROM PUERTO RICO AND THE VIRGIN ISLANDS.—The provisions of subsections (a)(3) and (b)(3) of section 7652 shall not apply to any tax imposed by section 4661.".

(b) CLERICAL AMENDMENT.—The table of chapters for subtitle D is amended by inserting after the item relating to chapter 37 the following new item:

"CHAPTER 38. Environmental taxes.".

(c) EFFECTIVE DATE.—The amendments made by this section shall take effect on April 1, 1981.

Subtitle B—Establishment of Hazardous Substance Response Trust Fund

SEC. 221. ESTABLISHMENT OF HAZARDOUS SUBSTANCE RESPONSE TRUST FUND.

(a) CREATION OF TRUST FUND.—There is established in the Treasury of the United States a trust fund to be known as the "Hazardous Substance Response Trust Fund" (hereinafter in this subtitle referred to as the "Response Trust Fund"), consisting of such amounts as may be appropriated or transferred to such Trust Fund as provided in this section.

(b) TRANSFERS TO RESPONSE TRUST FUND.—

(1) AMOUNTS EQUIVALENT TO CERTAIN TAXES, ETC.—There are hereby appropriated, out of any money in the Treasury not otherwise appropriated, to the Response Trust Fund amounts determined by the Secretary of the Treasury (hereinafter in this subtitle referred to as the "Secretary") to be equivalent to—

(A) the amounts received in the Treasury under section 4611 or 4661 of the Internal Revenue Code of 1954,

(B) the amounts recovered on behalf of the Response Trust Fund under this Act,

(C) all moneys recovered or collected under section 311(b)(6)(B) of the Clean Water Act,

(D) penalties assessed under title I of this Act, and

(E) punitive damages under section 107(c)(8) of this Act.

(2) AUTHORIZATION FOR APPROPRIATIONS.—There is authorized to be appropriated to the Emergency Response Trust Fund for fiscal year—

(A) 1981, $44,000,000,

(B) 1982, $44,000,000,

(C) 1983, $44,000,000,

(D) 1984, $44,000,000, and

(E) 1985, $44,000,000, plus an amount equal to so much of the aggregate amount authorized to be appropriated under subparagraphs (A), (B), (C), and (D) as has not been appropriated before October 1, 1984.

(3) TRANSFER OF FUNDS.—There shall be transferred to the Response Trust Fund—

(A) one-half of the unobligated balance remaining before the date of the enactment of this Act under the Fund in section 311 of the Clean Water Act, and

(B) the amounts appropriated under section 504(b) of the Clean Water Act during any fiscal year.

(c) EXPENDITURES FROM RESPONSE TRUST FUND.—

(1) IN GENERAL.—Amounts in the Response Trust Fund shall be available in connection with releases or threats of releases of hazardous substances into the environment only for purposes of making expenditures which are described in section 111 (other than subsection (j) thereof) of this Act, as in effect on the date of the enactment of this Act, including—

(A) response costs,

(B) claims asserted and compensable but unsatisfied under section 311 of the Clean Water Act,

(C) claims for injury to, or destruction or loss of, natural resources, and

(D) related costs described in section 111(c) of this Act.

(2) LIMITATIONS ON EXPENDITURES.—At least 85 percent of the amounts appropriated to the Response Trust Fund under subsection (b) (1)(A) and (2) shall be reserved—

(A) for the purposes specified in paragraphs (1), (2), and (4) of section 111(a) of this Act, and

(B) for the repayment of advances made under section 223(c), other than advances subject to the limitation of section 223(c)(2)(C).

PAYMENT TO THE HAZARDOUS SUBSTANCE RESPONSE TRUST FUND *

For payment to the Hazardous Substance Response Trust Fund as authorized by Public Law 96-510, $40,000,000.

HAZARDOUS SUBSTANCE RESPONSE TRUST FUND *

For necessary expenses to carry out the Comprehensive Environmental Response, Compensation, and Liability Act of 1980, including sections 111 (c)(3), (c)(5), (c)(6), and (e)(4), $210,000,000, to be derived from the Hazardous Substance Response Trust Fund, to remain available until expended: *Provided,* That not to exceed $37,380,000 shall be available for administrative expenses. Funds appropriated under this account may be allocated to other Federal agencies in accordance with section 111(a) of Public Law 96-510: *Provided further,* That of the funds appropriated under this head, $8,000,000 shall be made available to the Department of Health and Human Services, upon enactment, and up to an additional $2,000,000 may be made available by the Administrator to the Department for the performance of specific activities in accordance with section 111(c)(4) of Public Law 96-510, the Comprehensive Environmental Response, Compensation, and Liability Act of 1980: *Provided further,* That management of all funds made available to

---

* These paragraphs were provided by P.L. 97-272.

the Department shall be consistent with the responsibilities of the Trustee of the Fund, as outlined in section 223(b) of the Act: *Provided further,* That the administrative expenses contained in the first proviso are increased by $4,708,000: *Provided further,* That for purposes of carrying out section 3012 of the Resource Conservation and Recovery Act of 1976, as amended (42 U.S.C. 6933), as added by Public Law 96–482, $10,000,000, from the funds provided under this head, to remain available until September 30, 1984.

SEC. 222. LIABILITY OF UNITED STATES LIMITED TO AMOUNT IN TRUST FUND.

(a) GENERAL RULE.—Any claim filed against the Response Trust Fund may be paid only out of such Trust Fund. Nothing in this Act (or in any amendment made by this Act) shall authorize the payment by the United States Government of any additional amount with respect to any such claim out of any source other than the Response Trust Fund.

(b) ORDER IN WHICH UNPAID CLAIMS ARE TO BE PAID.—If at any time the Response Trust Fund is unable (by reason of subsection (a) or the limitation of section 221(c)(2)) to pay all of the claims payable out of such Trust Fund at such time, such claims shall, to the extent permitted under subsection (a), be paid in full in the order in which they were finally determined.

SEC. 223. ADMINISTRATIVE PROVISIONS.

(a) METHOD OF TRANSFER.—The amounts appropriated by section 221(b)(1) shall be transferred at least monthly from the general fund of the Treasury to the Response Trust Fund on the basis of estimates made by the Secretary of the amounts referred to in such section. Proper adjustments shall be made in the amount subsequently transferred to the extent prior estimates were in excess of or less than the amounts required to be transferred.

(b) MANAGEMENT OF TRUST FUND.—

(1) REPORT.—The Secretary shall be the trustee of the Response Trust Fund, and shall report to the Congress for each fiscal year ending on or after September 30, 1981, on the financial condition and the results of the operations of such Trust Fund during such fiscal year and on its expected condition and operations during the next 5 fiscal years. Such report shall be printed as a House document of the session of the Congress to which the report is made.

(2) INVESTMENT.—It shall be the duty of the Secretary to invest such portion of such Trust Fund as is not, in his judgment, required to meet current withdrawals. Such investments shall be in public debt securities with maturities suitable for the needs of such Trust Fund and bearing interest at rates determined by the Secretary, taking into consideration current market yields on outstanding marketable obligations of the United States of comparable maturities. The income on such investments shall be credited to and form a part of such Trust Fund.

(c) AUTHORITY TO BORROW.—

(1) IN GENERAL.—There are authorized to be appropriated to the Response Trust Fund, as repayable advances, such sums as may be necessary to carry out the purposes of such Trust Fund.

(2) LIMITATIONS ON ADVANCES TO RESPONSE TRUST FUND.—

(A) AGGREGATE ADVANCES.—The maximum aggregate amount of repayable advances to the Response Trust Fund which is outstanding at any one time shall not exceed an amount which the Secretary estimates will be equal to the sum of the amounts which will be appropriated or transferred to such Trust Fund under paragraph (1)(A) of section 221(b) of this Act for the following 12 months, and

(B) ADVANCES FOR PAYMENT OF RESPONSE COSTS.—No amount may be advanced after March 31, 1983, to the Response Trust Fund for the purpose of paying response costs described in section 111(a) (1), (2), or (4), unless such costs are incurred incident to any spill the effects of which the Secretary determines to be catastrophic.

(C) ADVANCES FOR OTHER COSTS.—The maximum aggregate amount advanced to the Response Trust Fund which is outstanding at any one time for the purpose of paying costs other than costs described in section 111(a) (1), (2), or (4) shall not exceed one-third of the amount of the estimate made under subparagraph (A).

(D) FINAL REPAYMENT.—No advance shall be made to the Response Trust Fund after September 30, 1985, and all advances to such Fund shall be repaid on or before such date.

(3) REPAYMENT OF ADVANCES.—Advances made pursuant to this subsection shall be repaid, and interest on such advances shall be paid, to the general fund of the Treasury when the Secretary determines that moneys are available for such purposes in the Trust Fund to which the advance was made. Such interest shall be at rates computed in the same manner as provided in subsection (b) and shall be compounded annually.

Subtitle C—Post-Closure Tax and Trust Fund

SEC. 231. IMPOSITION OF TAX.

(a) IN GENERAL.—Chapter 38, as added by section 211, is amended by adding at the end thereof the following new subchapter:

"Subchapter C—Tax on Hazardous Wastes

"SEC. 4681. IMPOSITION OF TAX.

"(a) GENERAL RULE.—There is hereby imposed a tax on the receipt of hazardous waste at a qualified hazardous waste disposal facility.

"(b) AMOUNT OF TAX.—The amount of the tax imposed by subsection (a) shall be equal to $2.13 per dry weight ton of hazardous waste.

"SEC. 4682. DEFINITIONS AND SPECIAL RULES.

"(a) DEFINITIONS.—For purposes of this subchapter—

"(1) HAZARDOUS WASTE.—The term 'hazardous waste' means any waste—

"(A) having the characteristics identified under section 3001 of the Solid Waste Disposal Act, as in effect on the date of the enactment of this Act (other than waste the regulation of which under such Act has been suspended by Act of Congress on that date), or

"(B) subject to the reporting or recordkeeping requirements of sections 3002 and 3004 of such Act, as so in effect.

"(2) QUALIFIED HAZARDOUS WASTE DISPOSAL FACILITY.—The term 'qualified hazardous waste disposal facility' means any facility which has received a permit or is accorded interim status under section 3005 of the Solid Waste Disposal Act.

"(b) TAX IMPOSED ON OWNER OR OPERATOR.—The tax imposed by section 4681 shall be imposed on the owner or operator of the qualified hazardous waste disposal facility.

"(c) TAX NOT TO APPLY TO CERTAIN WASTES.—The tax imposed by section 4681 shall not apply to any hazardous waste which will not remain at the qualified hazardous waste disposal facility after the facility is closed.

"(d) APPLICABILITY OF SECTION.—The tax imposed by section 4681 shall apply to the receipt of hazardous waste after September 30, 1983, except that if, as of September 30 of any subsequent calendar year, the unobligated balance of the Post-closure Liability Trust Fund exceeds $200,000,000, no tax shall be imposed under such section during the following calendar year.".

(b) CONFORMING AMENDMENT.—The table of subchapters for chapter 38 is amended by adding at the end thereof the following new item:

"SUBCHAPTER C—Tax on Hazardous Wastes.".

SEC. 232. POST-CLOSURE LIABILITY TRUST FUND.

(a) CREATION OF TRUST FUND.—There is established in the Treasury of the United States a trust fund to be known as the "Post-closure Liability Trust Fund", consisting of such amounts as may be appropriated, credited, or transferred to such Trust Fund.

(b) EXPENDITURES FROM POST-CLOSURE LIABILITY TRUST FUND.—Amounts in the Post-closure Liability Trust Fund shall be available only for the purposes described in sections 107(k) and 111(j) of this Act (as in effect on the date of the enactment of this Act).

(c) ADMINISTRATIVE PROVISIONS.—The provisions of sections 222 and 223 of this Act shall apply with respect to the Trust Fund established under this section, except that the amount of any repayable advances outstanding at any one time shall not exceed $200,000,000.

TITLE III—MISCELLANEOUS PROVISIONS

REPORTS AND STUDIES

SEC. 301. (a)(1) The President shall submit to the Congress, within four years after enactment of this Act, a comprehensive report on experience with the implementation of this Act, including, but not limited to—

(A) the extent to which the Act and Fund are effective in enabling Government to respond to and mitigate the effects of releases of hazardous substances;

(B) a summary of past receipts and disbursements from the Fund;

(C) a projection of any future funding needs remaining after the expiration of authority to collect taxes, and of the threat to public health, welfare, and the environment posed by the projected releases which create any such needs;

(D) the record and experience of the Fund in recovering Fund disbursements from liable parties;

(E) the record of State participation in the system of response, liability, and compensation established by this Act;

(F) the impact of the taxes imposed by title II of this Act on the Nation's balance of trade with other countries;

(G) an assessment of the feasibility and desirability of a schedule of taxes which would take into account one or more of the following: the likelihood of a release of a hazardous substance, the degree of hazard and risk of harm to public health, welfare, and the environment resulting from any such release, incentives to proper handling, recycling, incineration, and neutralization of hazardous wastes, and disincentives to improper or illegal handling or disposal of hazardous materials, administrative and reporting burdens on Government and industry, and the extent to which the tax burden falls on the substances and parties which create the problems addressed by this Act. In preparing the report, the President shall consult with appropriate Federal, State, and local agencies, affected industries and claimants, and such other interested parties as he may find useful. Based upon the analyses and consultation required by this subsection, the President shall also include in the report any recommendations for legislative changes he may deem necessary for the better effectuation of the purposes of this Act, including but not limited to recommendations concerning authorization levels, taxes, State participation, liability and liability limits, and financial responsibility provisions for the Response Trust Fund and the Post-closure Liability Trust Fund;

(H) an exemption from or an increase in the substances or the amount of taxes imposed by section 4661 of the Internal Revenue Code of 1954 for copper, lead, and zinc oxide, and for feedstocks when used in the manufacture and production of fertilizers, based upon the expenditure experience of the Response Trust Fund;

(I) the economic impact of taxing coal-derived substances and recycled metals.

(2) The Administrator of the Environmental Protection Agency (in consultation with the Secretary of the Treasury) shall submit to the Congress (i) within four years after enactment of this Act, a report identifying additional wastes designated by rule as hazardous after the effective date of this Act and pursuant to section 3001 of the Solid

Waste Disposal Act and recommendations on appropriate tax rates for such wastes for the Post-closure Liability Trust Fund. The report shall, in addition, recommend a tax rate, considering the quantity and potential danger to human health and the environment posed by the disposal of any wastes which the Administrator, pursuant to subsection 3001(b)(2)(B) and subsection 3001(b)(3)(A) of the Solid Waste Disposal Act of 1980, has determined should be subject to regulation under subtitle C of such Act, (ii) within three years after enactment of this Act, a report on the necessity for and the adequacy of the revenue raised, in relation to estimated future requirements, of the Post-closure Liability Trust Fund.

(b) The President shall conduct a study to determine (1) whether adequate private insurance protection is available on reasonable terms and conditions to the owners and operators of vessels and facilities subject to liability under section 107 of this Act, and (2) whether the market for such insurance is sufficiently competitive to assure purchasers of features such as a reasonable range of deductibles, coinsurance provisions, and exclusions. The President shall submit the results of his study, together with his recommendations, within two years of the date of enactment of this Act, and shall submit an interim report on his study within one year of the date of enactment of this Act.

(c)(1) The President, acting through Federal officials designated by the National Contingency Plan published under section 105 of this Act, shall study and, not later than two years after the enactment of this Act, shall promulgate regulations for the assessment of damages for injury to, destruction of, or loss of natural resources resulting from a release of oil or a hazardous substance for the purposes of this Act and section 311(f) (4) and (5) of the Federal Water Pollution Control Act.

(2) Such regulations shall specify (A) standard procedures for simplified assessments requiring minimal field observation, including establishing measures of damages based on units of discharge or release or units of affected area, and (B) alternative protocols for conducting assessments in individual cases to determine the type and extent of short- and long-term injury, destruction, or loss. Such regulations shall identify the best available procedures to determine such damages, including both direct and indirect injury, destruction, or loss and shall take into consideration factors including, but not limited to, replacement value, use value, and ability of the ecosystem or resource to recover.

(3) Such regulations shall be reviewed and revised as appropriate every two years.

(d) The Administrator of the Environmental Protection Agency shall, in consultation with other Federal agencies and appropriate representatives of State and local governments and nongovernmental agencies, conduct a study and report to the Congress within two years of the date of enactment of this Act on the issues, alternatives, and policy considerations involved in the selection of locations for hazardous waste treatment, storage, and disposal facilities. This study shall include—

(A) an assessment of current and projected treatment, storage, and disposal capacity needs and shortfalls for hazardous waste by management category on a State-by-State basis;

(B) an evaluation of the appropriateness of a regional approach to siting and designing hazardous waste management facilities and the identification of hazardous waste management regions, interstate or intrastate, or both, with similar hazardous waste management needs;

(C) solicitation and analysis of proposals for the construction and operation of hazardous waste management facilities by nongovernmental entities, except that no proposal solicited under terms of this subsection shall be analyzed if it involves cost to the United States Government or fails to comply with the requirements of subtitle C of the Solid Waste Disposal Act and other applicable provisions of law;

(D) recommendations on the appropriate balance between public and private sector involvement in the siting, design, and operation of new hazardous waste management facilities;

(E) documentation of the major reasons for public opposition to new hazardous waste management facilities; and

(F) an evaluation of the various options for overcoming obstacles to siting new facilities, including needed legislation for implementing the most suitable option or options.

(e)(1) In order to determine the adequacy of existing common law and statutory remedies in providing legal redress for harm to man and the environment caused by the release of hazardous substances into the environment, there shall be submitted to the Congress a study within twelve months of enactment of this Act.

(2) This study shall be conducted with the assistance of the American Bar Association, the American Law Institute, the Association of American Trial Lawyers, and the National Association of State Attorneys General with the President of each entity selecting three members from each organization to conduct the study. The study chairman and one reporter shall be elected from among the twelve members of the study group.

(3) As part of their review of the adequacy of existing common law and statutory remedies, the study group shall evaluate the following:

(A) the nature, adequacy, and availability of existing remedies under present law in compensating for harm to man from the release of hazardous substances;

(B) the nature of barriers to recovery (particularly with respect to burdens of going forward and of proof and relevancy) and the role such barriers play in the legal system;

(C) the scope of the evidentiary burdens placed on the plaintiff in proving harm from the release of hazardous substances, particularly in light of the scientific uncertainty over causation with respect to—

(i) carcinogens, mutagens, and teratogens, and

(ii) the human health effects of exposure to low doses of hazardous substances over long periods of time;

(D) the nature and adequacy of existing remedies under present law in providing compensation for damages to natural resources from the release of hazardous substances;

(E) the scope of liability under existing law and the consequences, particularly with respect to obtaining insurance, of any changes in such liability;

(F) barriers to recovery posed by existing statutes of limitations.

(4) The report shall be submitted to the Congress with appropriate recommendations. Such recommendations shall explicitly address—

(A) the need for revisions in existing statutory or common law, and

(B) whether such revisions should take the form of Federal statutes or the development of a model code which is recommended for adoption by the States.

(5) The Fund shall pay administrative expenses incurred for the study. No expenses shall be available to pay compensation, except expenses on a per diem basis for the one reporter, but in no case shall the total expenses of the study exceed $300,000.

(f) The President, acting through the Administrator of the Environmental Protection Agency, the Secretary of Transportation, the Administrator of the Occupational Safety and Health Administration, and the Director of the National Institute for Occupational Safety and Health shall study and, not later than two years after the enactment of this Act, shall modify the national contingency plan to provide for the protection of the health and safety of employees involved in response actions.

EFFECTIVE DATES, SAVINGS PROVISION

SEC. 302. (a) Unless otherwise provided, all provisions of this Act shall be effective on the date of enactment of this Act.

(b) Any regulation issued pursuant to any provisions of section 311 of the Clean Water Act which is repealed or superseded by this Act and which is in effect on the date immediately preceding the effective date of this Act shall be deemed to be a regulation issued pursuant to the authority of this Act and shall remain in full force and effect unless or until superseded by new regulations issued thereunder.

(c) Any regulation—

(1) respecting financial responsibility,

(2) issued pursuant to any provision of law repealed or superseded by this Act, and

(3) in effect on the date immediately preceding the effective date of this Act shall be deemed to be a regulation issued pursuant to the authority of this Act and shall remain in full force and effect unless or until superseded by new regulations issued thereunder.

(d) Nothing in this Act shall affect or modify in any way the obligations or liabilities of any person under other Federal or State law, including common law, with respect to releases of hazardous substances or other pollutants or contaminants. The provisions of this Act shall not be considered, interpreted, or construed in any way as reflecting a determination, in part or whole, of policy regarding the inapplicability of strict liability, or strict liability doctrines, to activities relating to hazardous substances, pollutants, or contaminants or other such activities.

EXPIRATION, SUNSET PROVISION

SEC. 303. Unless reauthorized by the Congress, the authority to collect taxes conferred by this Act shall terminate on September 30, 1985, or when the sum of the amounts received in the Treasury under section 4611 and under 4661 of the Internal Revenue Code of 1954 total $1,380,000,000, whichever occurs first. The Secretary of the Treasury shall estimate when this level of $1,380,000,000 will be reached and shall by regulation, provide procedures for the termination of the tax authorized by this Act and imposed under sections 4611 and 4661 of the Internal Revenue Code of 1954.

CONFORMING AMENDMENTS

SEC. 304. (a) Subsection (b) of section 504 of the Federal Water Pollution Control Act is hereby repealed.

(b) One-half of the unobligated balance remaining before the date of the enactment of this Act under subsection (k) of section 311 of the Federal Water Pollution Control Act and all sums appropriated under section 504(b) of the Federal Water Pollution Control Act shall be transferred to the Fund established under title II of this Act.

(c) In any case in which any provision of section 311 of the Federal Water Pollution Control Act is determined to be in conflict with any provisions of this Act, the provisions of this Act shall apply.

LEGISLATIVE VETO

SEC. 305. (a) Notwithstanding any other provision of law, simultaneously with promulgation or repromulgation of any rule or regulation under authority of title I of this Act, the head of the department, agency, or instrumentality promulgating such rule or regulation shall transmit a copy thereof to the Secretary of the Senate and the Clerk of the House of Representatives. Except as provided in subsection (b) of this section, the rule or regulation shall not become effective, if—

(1) within ninety calendar days of continuous session of Congress after the date of promulgation, both Houses of Congress adopt a concurrent resolution, the matter after the resolving clause of which is as follows: "That Congress disapproves the rule or regulation promulgated by the   dealing with the matter of   , which rule or regulation was transmitted to Congress on   .", the blank spaces therein being appropriately filled; or

(2) within sixty calendar days of continuous session of Congress after the date of promulgation, one House of Congress adopts such a concurrent resolution and transmits such resolution to the other House, and such resolution is not disapproved by such other House within thirty calendar days of continuous session of Congress after such transmittal.

(b) If, at the end of sixty calendar days of continuous session of Congress after the date of promulgation of a rule or regulation, no committee of either House of Congress has reported or been discharged from further consideration of a concurrent resolution disapproving the rule or regulation and neither House has adopted such a resolution, the rule or regulation may go into effect immediately. If, within such sixty calendar days, such a committee has reported or been discharged from further consideration of such a resolution, or either House has adopted such a resolution, the rule or regulation may go into effect not sooner than ninety calendar days of continuous session of Congress after such rule is prescribed unless disapproved as provided in subsection (a) of this section.

(c) For purposes of subsections (a) and (b) of this section—

(1) continuity of session is broken only by an adjournment of Congress sine die; and

(2) the days on which either House is not in session because of an adjournment of more than three days to a day certain are excluded in the computation of thirty, sixty, and ninety calendar days of continuous session of Congress.

(d) Congressional inaction on, or rejection of, a resolution of disapproval shall not be deemed an expression of approval of such rule or regulation.

TRANSPORTATION

SEC. 306. (a) Each hazardous substance which is listed or designated as provided in section 101(14) of this Act shall, within ninety days after the date of enactment of this Act or at the time of such listing or designation, whichever is later, be listed as a hazardous material under the Hazardous Materials Transportation Act.

(b) A common or contract carrier shall be liable under other law in lieu of section 107 of this Act for damages or remedial action resulting from the release of a hazardous substance during the course of transportation which commenced prior to the effective date of the listing of such substance as a hazardous material under the Hazardous Materials Transportation Act, or for substances listed pursuant to subsection (a) of this section, prior to the effective date of such listing: *Provided, however,* That this subsection shall not apply where such a carrier can demonstrate that he did not have actual knowledge of the identity or nature of the substance released.

(c) Section 11901 of title 49, United States Code, is amended by—

(1) redesignating subsection (h) as subsection (i);

(2) by inserting "and subsection (h)" after "subsection (g)" in subsection (i)(2) as so redesignated by paragraph (1) of this subsection; and

(3) by inserting the following new subsection (h):

"(h) A person subject to the jurisdiction of the Commission under subchapter II of chapter 105 of this title, or an officer, agent, or employee of that person, and who is required to comply with section 10921 of this title but does not so comply with respect to the transportation of hazardous wastes as defined by the Environmental Protection Agency pursuant to section 3001 of the Solid Waste Disposal Act (but not including any waste the regulation of which under the Solid Waste Disposal Act has been suspended by Congress) shall, in any action brought by the Commission, be liable to the United States for a civil penalty not to exceed $20,000 for each violation.".

ASSISTANT ADMINISTRATOR FOR SOLID WASTE

SEC. 307. (a) Section 2001 of the Solid Waste Disposal Act is amended by striking out "a Deputy Assistant" and inserting in lieu thereof "an Assistant".

(b) The Assistant Administrator of the Environmental Protection Agency appointed to head the Office of Solid Waste shall be in addition to the five Assistant Administrators of the Environmental Protection Agency provided for in section 1(d) of Reorganization Plan Numbered 3 of 1970 and the additional Assistant Administrator provided by the Toxic Substances Control Act, shall be appointed by the President by and with the advice and consent of the Senate, and shall be compensated at the rate provided for Level IV of the Executive Schedule pay rates under section 5315 of title 5, United States Code.

(c) The amendment made by subsection (a) shall become effective ninety days after the date of the enactment of this Act.

SEPARABILITY

Sec. 308. If any provision of this Act, or the application of any provision of this Act to any person or circumstance, is held invalid, the application of such provision to other persons or circumstances and the remainder of this Act shall not be affected thereby.

TOXIC SUBSTANCES CONTROL ACT
as amended[1]

SECTION 1. SHORT TITLE AND TABLE OF CONTENTS.

This Act may be cited as the "Toxic Substances Control Act".

TABLE OF CONTENTS

SEC. 2. FINDINGS, POLICY, AND INTENT.

(a) FINDINGS.—The Congress finds that—

(1) human beings and the environment are being exposed each year to a large number of chemical substances and mixtures;

(2) among the many chemical substances and mixtures which are constantly being developed and produced, there are some whose manufacture, processing, distribution in commerce, use, or disposal may present an unreasonable risk of injury to health or the environment; and

(3) the effective regulation of interstate commerce in such chemical substances and mixtures also necessitates the regulation of intrastate commerce in such chemical substances and mixtures.

---

[1] Amended by Public Law 97-129, December 29, 1981.

(b) Policy.—It is the policy of the United States that—

(1) adequate data should be developed with respect to the effect of chemical substances and mixtures on health and the environment and that the development of such data should be the responsibility of those who manufacture and those who process such chemical substances and mixtures;

(2) adequate authority should exist to regulate chemical substances and mixtures which present an unreasonable risk of injury to health or the environment, and to take action with respect to chemical substances and mixtures which are imminent hazards; and

(3) authority over chemical substances and mixtures should be exercised in such a manner as not to impede unduly or create unnecessary economic barriers to technological innovation while fulfilling the primary purpose of this Act to assure that such innovation and commerce in such chemical substances and mixtures do not present an unreasonable risk of injury to health or the environment.

(c) Intent of Congress.—It is the intent of Congress that the Administrator shall carry out this Act in a reasonable and prudent manner, and that the Administrator shall consider the environmental, economic, and social impact of any action the Administrator takes or proposes to take under this Act.

SEC. 3. DEFINITIONS.

As used in this Act:

(1) The term "Administrator" means the Administrator of the Environmental Protection Agency.

(2) (A) Except as provided in subparagraph (B), the term "chemical substance" means any organic or inorganic substance of a particular molecular identity, including—

(i) any combination of such substances occurring in whole or in part as a result of a chemical reaction or occurring in nature, and

(ii) any element or uncombined radical.

(B) Such term does not include—

(i) any mixture,

(ii) any pesticide (as defined in the Federal Insecticide, Fungicide, and Rodenticide Act) when manufactured, processed, or distributed in commerce for use as a pesticide,

(iii) tobacco or any tobacco product,

(iv) any source material, special nuclear material, or byproduct material (as such terms are defined in the Atomic Energy Act of 1954 and regulations issued under such Act),

(v) any article the sale of which is subject to the tax imposed by section 4181 of the Internal Revenue Code of 1954 (determined without regard to any exemptions from such tax provided by section 4182 or 4221 or any other provision of such Code), and

(vi) any food, food additive, drug, cosmetic, or device (as such terms are defined in section 201 of the Federal Food, Drug, and Cosmetic Act) when manufactured, processed, or distributed in commerce for use as a food, food additive, drug, cosmetic, or device.

The term "food" as used in clause (vi) of this subparagraph includes poultry and poultry products (as defined in sections 4(e) and 4(f) of the Poultry Products Inspection Act), meat and meat food products (as defined in section 1(j) of the Federal Meat Inspection Act), and eggs and egg products (as defined in section 4 of the Egg Products Inspection Act).

(3) The term "commerce" means trade, traffic, transportation, or other commerce (A) between a place in a State and any place outside of such State, or (B) which affects trade, traffic, transportation, or commerce described in clause (A).

(4) The terms "distribute in commerce" and "distribution in commerce" when used to describe an action taken with respect to a chemical substance or mixture or article containing a substance or mixture mean to sell, or the sale of, the substance, mixture, or article in commerce; to introduce or deliver for introduction into commerce, or the introduction or delivery for introduction into commerce of, the substance, mixture, or article; or to hold, or the holding of, the substance, mixture, or article after its introduction into commerce.

(5) The term "environment" includes water, air, and land and the interrelationship which exists among and between water, air, and land and all living things.

(6) The term "health and safety study" means any study of any effect of a chemical substance or mixture on health or the environment or on both, including underlying data and epidemiological studies, studies of occupational exposure to a chemical substance or mixture, toxicological, clinical, and ecological studies of a chemical substance or mixture, and any test performed pursuant to this Act.

(7) The term "manufacture" means to import into the customs territory of the United States (as defined in general headnote 2 of the Tariff Schedules of the United States), produce, or manufacture.

(8) The term "mixture" means any combination of two or more chemical substances if the combination does not occur in nature and is not, in whole or in part, the

result of a chemical reaction; except that such term does include any combination which occurs, in whole or in part, as a result of a chemical reaction if none of the chemical substances comprising the combination is a new chemical substance and if the combination could have been manufactured for commercial purposes without a chemical reaction at the time the chemical substances comprising the combination were combined.

(9) The term "new chemical substance" means any chemical substance which is not included in the chemical substance list compiled and published under section 8(b).

(10) The term "process" means the preparation of a chemical substance or mixture, after its manufacture, for distribution in commerce—

(A) in the same form or physical state as, or in a different form or physical state from, that in which it was received by the person so preparing such substance or mixture, or

(B) as part of an article containing the chemical substance or mixture.

(11) The term "processor" means any person who processes a chemical substance or mixture.

(12) The term "standards for the development of test data" means a prescription of—

(A) the—

(i) health and environmental effects, and

(ii) information relating to toxicity, persistence, and other characteristics which affect health and the environment,

for which test data for a chemical substance or mixture are to be developed and any analysis that is to be performed on such data, and

(B) to the extent necessary to assure that data respecting such effects and characteristics are reliable and adequate—

(i) the manner in which such data are to be developed,

(ii) the specification of any test protocol or methodology to be employed in the development of such data, and

(iii) such other requirements as are necessary to provide such assurance.

(13) The term "State" means any State of the United States, the District of Columbia, the Commonwealth of Puerto Rico, the Virgin Islands, Guam, the Canal Zone, American Samoa, the Northern Mariana Islands, or any other territory or possession of the United States.

(14) The term "United States", when used in the geographic sense, means all of the States.

SEC. 4. TESTING OF CHEMICAL SUBSTANCES AND MIXTURES.

(a) TESTING REQUIREMENTS.—If the Administrator finds that—

(1)(A)(i) the manufacture, distribution in commerce, processing, use, or disposal of a chemical substance or mixture, or that any combination of such activities, may present an unreasonable risk of injury to health or the environment,

(ii) there are insufficient data and experience upon which the effects of such manufacture, distribution in commerce, processing, use, or disposal of such substance or mixture or of any combination of such activities on health or the environment can reasonably be determined or predicted, and

(iii) testing of such substance or mixture with respect to such effects is necessary to develop such data; or

(B)(i) a chemical substance or mixture is or will be produced in substantial quantities, and (I) it enters or may reasonably be anticipated to enter the environment in substantial quantities or (II) there is or may be significant or substantial human exposure to such substance or mixture,

(ii) there are insufficient data and experience upon which the effects of the manufacture, distribution in commerce, processing, use, or disposal of such substance or mixture or of any combination of such activities on health or the environment can reasonably be determined or predicted, and

(iii) testing of such substance or mixture with respect to such effects is necessary to develop such data; and

(2) in the case of a mixture, the effects which the mixture's manufacture, distribution in commerce, processing, use, or disposal or any combination of such activities may have on health or the environment may not be reasonably and more efficiently determined or predicted by testing the chemical substances which comprise the mixture;

the Administrator shall by rule require that testing be conducted on such substance or mixture to develop data with respect to the health and environmental effects for which there is an insufficiency of data and experience and which are relevant to a determination that the manufacture, distribution in commerce, processing, use, or disposal of such substance or mixture, or that any combination of such activities, does or does not present an unreasonable risk of injury to health or the environment.

(b)(1) TESTING REQUIREMENT RULE.—A rule under subsection (a) shall include—

(A) identification of the chemical substance or mixture for which testing is required under the rule,

(B) standards for the development of test data for such substance or mixture, and

(C) with respect to chemical substances which are not new chemical substances and to mixtues, a specification of the period (which period may not be of unreasonable duration) within which the persons required to conduct the testing shall submit to the Administrator data developed in accordance with the standards referred to in subparagraph (B).

In determining the standards and period to be included, pursuant to subparagraphs (B) and (C), in a rule under subsection (a), the Administrator's considerations shall include the relative costs of the various test protocols and methodologies which may be required under the rule and the reasonably foreseeable availability of the facilities and personnel needed to perform the testing required under the rule. Any such rule may require the submission to the Administrator of preliminary data during the period prescribed under subparagraph (C).

(2)(A) The health and environmental effects for which standards for the development of test data may be prescribed include carcinogenesis, mutagenesis, teratogenesis, behavioral disorders, cumulative or synergistic effects, and any other effect which may present an unreasonable risk of injury to health or the environment. The characteristics of chemical substances and mixtures for which such standards may be prescribed include persistence, acute toxicity, subacute toxicity, chronic toxicity, and any other characteristic which may present such a risk. The methodologies that may be prescribed in such standards include epidemiologic studies, serial or hierarchical tests, in vitro tests, and whole animal tests, except that before prescribing epidemiologic studies of employees, the Administrator shall consult with the Director of the National Institute for Occupational Safety and Health.

(B) From time to time, but not less than once each 12 months, the Administrator shall review the adequacy of the standards for development of data prescribed in rules under subsection (a) and shall, if necessary, institute proceedings to make appropriate revisions of such standards.

(3)(A) A rule under subsection (a) respecting a chemical substance or mixture shall require the persons described in subparagraph (B) to conduct tests and submit data to the Administrator on such substance or mixture, except that the Administrator may permit two or more of such persons to designate one such person or a qualified third party to conduct such tests and submit such data on behalf of the persons making the designation.

(B) The following persons shall be required to conduct tests and submit data on a chemical substance or mixture subject to a rule under subsection (a):

(i) Each person who manufactures or intends to manufacture such substance or mixture if the Administrator makes a finding described in subsection (a)(1)(A)(ii) or (a)(1)(B)(ii) with respect to the manufacture of such substance or mixture.

(ii) Each person who processes or intends to process such substance or mixture if the Administrator makes a finding described in subsection (a)(1)(A)(ii) or (a)(1)(B)(ii) with respect to the processing of such substance or mixture.

(iii) Each person who manufactures or processes or intends to manufacture or process such substance or mixture if the Administrator makes a finding described in subsection (a)(1)(A)(ii) or (a)(1)(B)(ii) with respect to the distribution in commerce, use, or disposal of such substance or mixture.

(4) Any rule under subsection (a) requiring the testing of and submission of data for a particular chemical substance or mixture shall expire at the end of the reimbursement period (as defined in subsection (c)(3)(B)) which is applicable to test data for such substance or mixture unless the Administrator repeals the rule before such date; and a rule under subsection (a) requiring the testing of and submission of data for a category of chemical substances or mixtures shall expire with respect to a chemical substance or mixture included in the category at the end of the reimbursement period (as so defined) which is applicable to test data for such substance or mixture unless the Administrator before such date repeals the application of the rule to such substance or mixture or repeals the rule.

(5) Rules issued under subsection (a) (and any substantive amendment thereto or repeal thereof) shall be promulgated pursuant to section 553 of title 5, United States Code, except that (A) the Administrator shall give interested persons an opportunity for the oral presentation of data, views, or arguments, in addition to an opportunity to make written submission; (B) a transcript shall be made of any oral presentation; and (C) the Administrator shall make and publish with the rule the findings described in paragraph (1)(A) or (1)(B) of subsection (a) and, in the case of a rule respecting a mixture, the finding described in paragraph (2) of such subsection.

(c) EXEMPTION.—(1) Any person required by a rule under subsection (a) to conduct tests and submit data on a chemical substance or mixture may apply to the Administrator (in such form and manner as the Administrator shall prescribe) for an exemption from such requirement.

(2) If, upon receipt of an application under paragraph (1), the Administrator determines that—

(A) the chemical substance or mixture with respect to which such application was submitted is equivalent to a chemical substance or mixture for which data has been submitted to the Administrator in accordance with a rule under subsection (a) or for which data is being developed pursuant to such a rule, and

(B) submission of data by the applicant on such substance or mixture would be duplicative of data which has been submitted to the Administrator in accordance with such rule or which is being developed pursuant to such rule,

the Administrator shall exempt, in accordance with paragraph (3) or (4), the applicant from conducting tests and submitting data on such substance or mixture under the rule with respect to which such application was submitted.

(3)(A) If the exemption under paragraph (2) of any person from the requirement to conduct tests and submit test data on a chemical substance or mixture is granted on the basis of the existence of previously submitted test data and if such exemption is granted during the reimbursement period for such test data (as prescribed by subparagraph (B)), then (unless such person and the persons referred to in clauses (i) and (ii) agree on the amount and method of reimbursement) the Administrator shall order the person granted the exemption to provide fair and equitable reimbursement (in an amount determined under rules of the Administrator)—

(i) to the person who previously submitted such test data, for a portion of the costs incurred by such person in complying with the requirement to submit such data, and

(ii) to any other person who has been required under this subparagraph to contribute with respect to such costs, for a portion of the amount such person was required to contribute.

In promulgating rules for the determination of fair and equitable reimbursement to the persons described in clauses (i) and (ii) for costs incurred with respect to a chemical substance or mixture, the Administrator shall, after consultation with the Attorney General and the Federal Trade Commission, consider all relevant factors, including the effect on the competitive position of the person required to provide reimbursement in relation to the person to be reimbursed and the share of the market for such substance or mixture of the person required to provide reimbursement in relation to the share of such market of the persons to be reimbursed. An order under this subparagraph shall, for purposes of judicial review, be considered final agency action.

(B) For purposes of subparagraph (A), the reimbursement period for any test data for a chemical substance or mixture is a period—

(i) beginning on the date such data is submitted in accordance with a rule promulgated under subsection (a), and

(ii) ending—

(I) five years after the date referred to in clause (i), or

(II) at the expiration of a period which begins on the date referred to in clause (i) and which is equal to the period which the Administrator determines was necessary to develop such data,

whichever is later.

(4)(A) If the exemption under paragraph (2) of any person from the requirement to conduct tests and submit test data on a chemical substance or mixture is granted on the basis of the fact that test data is being developed by one or more persons pursuant to a rule promulgated under subsection (a), then (unless such person and the persons referred to in clauses (i) and (ii) agree on the amount and method of reimbursement) the Administrator shall order the person granted the exemption to provide fair and equitable reimbursement (in an amount determined under rules of the Administrator)—

(i) to each such person who is developing such test data, for a portion of the costs incurred by each such person in complying with such rule, and

(ii) to any other person who has been required under this subparagraph to contribute with respect to the costs of complying with such rule, for a portion of the amount such person was required to contribute.

In promulgating rules for the determination of fair and equitable reimbursement to the persons described in clauses (i) and (ii) for costs incurred with respect to a chemical substance or mixture, the Administrator shall, after consultation with the Attorney General and the Federal Trade Commission, consider the factors described in the second sentence of paragraph (3)(A). An order under this subparagraph shall, for purposes of judicial review, be considered final agency action.

(B) If any exemption is granted under paragraph (2) on the basis of the fact that one or more persons are developing test data pursuant to a rule promulgated under subsection (a) and if after such exemption is granted the Administrator determines that no such person has complied with such rule, the Administrator shall (i) after providing written notice to the person who holds such exemption and an opportunity for a hearing, by order terminate such exemption, and (ii) notify in writing such person of the requirements of the rule with respect to which such exemption was granted.

(d) NOTICE.—Upon the receipt of any test data pursuant to a rule under subsection (a), the Administrator shall publish a notice of the receipt of such data in the Federal Register within 15 days of its receipt. Subject to section 14, each such notice shall (1) identify the chemical substance or mixture for which data have been received; (2) list the uses or intended uses of such substance or mixture and the information required by the applicable standards for the development of test data; and (3) describe the nature of the test data developed. Except as otherwise provided in section 14, such data shall be made available by the Administrator for examination by any person.

(e) PRIORITY LIST.—(1)(A) There is established a committee to make recommendations to the Administrator respecting the chemical substances and mixtures to which the Administrator should give priority consideration for the promulgation of a rule under subsection (a). In making such a recommendation with respect to any chemical substance or mixture, the committee shall consider all relevant factors, including—

(i) the quantities in which the substance or mixture is or will be manufactured,

(ii) the quantities in which the substance or mixture enters or will enter the environment,

(iii) the number of individuals who are or will be exposed to the substance or mixture in their places of employment and the duration of such exposure,

(iv) the extent to which human beings are or will be exposed to the substance or mixture,

(v) the extent to which the substance or mixture is closely related to a chemical substance or mixture which is known to present an unreasonable risk of injury to health or the environment,

(vi) the existence of data concerning the effects of the substance or mixture on health or the environment,

(vii) the extent to which testing of the substance or mixture may result in the development of data upon which the effects of the substance or mixture on health or the environment can reasonably be determined or predicted, and

(viii) the reasonably foreseeable availability of facilities and personnel for performing testing on the substance or mixture.

The recommendations of the committee shall be in the form of a list of chemical substances and mixtures which shall be set forth, either by individual substance or mixture or by groups of substances or mixtures, in the order in which the committee determines the Administrator should take action under subsection (a) with repsect to the substances and mixtures. In establishing such list, the committee shall give priority attention to those chemical substances and mixtures which are known to cause or contribute to or which are suspected of causing or contributing to cancer, gene mutations, or birth defects. The committee shall designate chemical substances and mixtures on the list with respect to which the committee determines the Administrator should, within 12 months of the date on which such substances and mixtures are first designated, initiate a proceeding under subsection (a). The total number of chemical substances and mixtures on the list which are designated under the preceding sentence may not, at any time, exceed 50.

(B) As soon as practicable but not later than nine months after the effective date of this Act, the committee shall publish in the Federal Register and transmit to the Administrator the list and designations required by subparagraph (A) together with the reasons for the committee's inclusion of each chemical substance or mixture on the list. At least every six months after the date of the transmission to the Administrator of the list pursuant to the preceeding sentence, the committee shall make such revisions in the list as it determines to be necessary and shall transmit them to the Administrator together with the committee's reasons for the revisions. Upon receipt of any such revision, the Administrator shall publish in the Federal Register the list with such revision, the reasons for such revision, and the designations made under subparagraph (A). The Administrator shall provide reasonable opportunity to any interested person to file with the Administrator written comments on the committee's list, any revision of such list by the committee, and designations made by the committee, and shall make such comments available to the public. Within the 12-month period beginning on the date of the first inclusion on the list of a chemical substance or mixture designated by the committee under subparagraph (A) the Administrator shall with respect to such chemical substance or mixture either initiate a rulemaking proceeding under subsection (a) or if such a proceeding is not initiated within such period, publish in the Federal Register the Administrator's reason for not initiating such a proceeding.

(2)(A) The committee established by paragraph (1)(A) shall consist of eight members as follows:

(i) One member appointed by the Administrator from the Environmental Protection Agency.

(ii) One member appointed by the Secretary of Labor from officers or employees of the Department of Labor engaged in the Secretary's activities under the Occupational Safety and Health Act of 1970.

(iii) One member appointed by the Chairman of the Council on Environmental Quality from the Council or its officers or employees.

(iv) One member appointed by the Director of the National Institute for Occupational Safety and Health from officers or employees of the Institute.

(v) One member appointed by the Director of the National Institute of Environmental Health Sciences from officers or employees of the Institute.

(vi) One member appointed by the Director of the National Cancer Institute from officers or employees of the Institute.

(vii) One member appointed by the Director of the National Science Foundation from officers or employees of the Foundation.

(viii) One member appointed by the Secretary of Commerce from officers or employees of the Department of Commerce.

(B)(i) An appointed member may designate an individual to serve on the committee on the member's behalf. Such a designation may be made only with the approval of the applicable appointing authority and only if the individual is from the entity from which the member was appointed.

(ii) No individual may serve as a member of the committee for more than four years in the aggregate. If any member of the committee leaves the entity from which the member was appointed, such member may not continue as a member of the committee, and the member's position shall be considered to be vacant. A vacancy in the committee shall be filled in the same manner in which the original appointment was made.

(iii) Initial appointments to the committee shall be made not later than the 60th day after the effective date of this Act. Not later than the 90th day after such date the members of the committee shall hold a meeting for the selection of a chairperson from among their number.

(C)(i) No member of the committee, or designee of such member, shall accept employment or compensation from any person subject to any requirement of this Act or of any rule promulgated or order issued thereunder, for a period of at least 12 months after termination of service on the committee.

(ii) No person, while serving as a member of the committee, or designee of such member, may own any stocks or bonds, or have any pecuniary interest, of substantial value in any person engaged in the manufacture, processing, or distribution in commerce of any chemical substance or mixture subject to any requirement of this Act or of any rule promulgated or order issued thereunder.

(iii) The Administrator, acting through attorneys of the Environmental Protection Agency, or the Attorney General may bring an action in the appropriate district court of the United States to restrain any violation of this subparagraph.

(D) The Administrator shall provide the committee such administrative support services as may be necessary to enable the committee to carry out its function under this subsection.

(f) Required Actions.—Upon the receipt of—

(1) any test data required to be submitted under this Act, or

(2) any other information available to the Administrator,

which indicates to the Administrator that there may be a reasonable basis to conclude that a chemical substance or mixture presents or will present a significant risk of serious or widespread harm to human beings from cancer, gene mutations, or birth defects, the Administrator shall, within the 180-day period beginning on the date of the receipt of such data or information, initiate appropriate action under section 5, 6, or 7 to prevent or reduce to a sufficient extent such risk or publish in the Federal Register a finding that such risk is not unreasonable. For good cause shown the Administrator may extend such period for an additional period of not more than 90 days. The Administrator shall publish in the Federal Register notice of any such extension and the reasons therefor. A finding by the Administrator that a risk is not unreasonable shall be considered agency action for purposes of judicial review under chapter 7 of title 5, United States Code. This subsection shall not take effect until two years after the effective date of this Act.

(g) Petition for Standards for the Development of Test Data.—A person intending to manufacture or process a chemical substance for which notice is required under section 5(a) and who is not required under a rule under subsection (a) to conduct tests and submit data on such substance may petition the Administrator to prescribe standards for the development of test data for such substance. The Administrator shall by order either grant or deny any such petition within 60 days of its receipt. If the petition is granted, the Administrator shall prescribe such standards for such substance within 75 days of the date the petition is granted. If the petition is denied, the Administrator shall publish, subject to section 14, in the Federal Register the reasons for such denial.

SEC. 5. MANUFACTURING AND PROCESSING NOTICES.

(a) IN GENERAL.—(1) Except as provided in subsection (h), no person may—

(A) manufacture a new chemical substance on or after the 30th day after the date on which the Administrator first publishes the list required by section 8(b), or

(B) manufacture or process any chemical substance for a use with the Administrator has determined, in accordance with paragraph (2), is a significant new use,

unless such person submits to the Administrator, at least 90 days before such manufacture or processing, a notice, in accordance with subsection (d), of such person's intention to manufacture or process such substance and such person complies with any applicable requirement of subsection (b).

(2) A determination by the Administrator that a use of a chemical substance is a significant new use with respect to which notification is required under paragraph (1) shall be made by a rule promulgated after a consideration of all relevant factors, including—

(A) the projected volume of manufacturing and and processing of a chemical substance,

(B) the extent to which a use changes the type or form of exposure of human beings or the environment to a chemical substance,

(C) the extent to which a use increases the magnitude and duration of exposure of human beings or the environment to a chemical substance, and

(D) the reasonably anticipated manner and methods of manufacturing, processing, distribution in commerce, and disposal of a chemical substance.

(b) SUBMISSION OF TEST DATA.—(1)(A) If (i) a person is required by subsection (a)(1) to submit a notice to the Administrator before beginning the manufacture or processing of a chemical substance, and (ii) such person is required to submit test data for such substance pursuant to a rule promulgated under section 4 before the submission of such notice, such person shall submit to the Administrator such data in accordance with such rule at the time notice is submitted in accordance with subsection (a)(1).

(B) If—

(i) a person is required by subsection (a)(1) to submit a notice to the Administrator, and

(ii) such person has been granted an exemption under section 4(c) from the requirements of a rule promulgated under section 4 before the submission of such notice,

such person may not, before the expiration of the 90 day period which begins on the date of the submission in accordance with such rule of the test data the submission or development of which was the basis for the exemption, manufacture such substance if such person is subject to subsection (a)(1)(A) or manufacture or process such substance for a significant new use if the person is subject to subsection (a)(1)(B).

(2)(A) If a person—

(i) is required by subsection (a)(1) to submit a notice to the Administrator before beginning the manufacture or processing of a chemical substance listed under paragraph (4), and

(ii) is not required by a rule promulgated under section 4 before the submission of such notice to submit test data for such substance,

such person shall submit to the Administrator data prescribed by subparagraph (B) at the time notice is submitted in accordance with subsection (a)(1).

(B) Data submitted pursuant to subparagraph (A) shall be data which the person submitting the data believes show that—

(i) in the case of a substance with respect to which notice is required under subsection (a)(1)(A), the manufacture, processing, distribution in commerce, use, and disposal of the chemical substance or any combination of such activities will not present an unreasonable risk of injury to health or the environment, or

(ii) in the case of a chemical substance with respect to which notice is required under subsection (a)(1)(B), the intended significant new use of the chemical substance will not present an unreasonable risk of injury to health or the environment.

(3) Data submitted under paragraph (1) or (2) shall be made available, subject to section 14, for examination by interested persons.

(4)(A)(i) The Administrator may, by rule, compile and keep current a list of chemical substances with respect to which the Administrator finds that the manufacture, processing, distribution in commerce, use, or disposal, or any combination of such activities, presents or may present an unreasonable risk of injury to health or the environment.

(ii) In making a finding under clause (i) that the manufacture, processing, distribution in commerce, use, or disposal of a chemical substance or any combination of such activities presents or may present an unreasonable risk of injury to health or the environment, the Administrator shall consider all relevant factors, including—

(I) the effects of the chemical substance on health and the magnitude of human exposure to such substance; and

(II) the effects of the chemical substance on the environment and the magnitude of environmental exposure to such substance.

(B) The Administrator shall, in prescribing a rule under subparagraph (A) which lists any chemical substance, identify those uses, if any, which the Administrator determines, by rule under subsection (a)(2), would constitute a significant new use of such substance.

(C) Any rule under subparagraph (A), and any substantive amendment or repeal of such a rule, shall be promulgated pursuant to the procedures specified in section 553 of title 5, United States Code, except that (i) the Administrator shall give interested persons an opportunity for the oral presentation of data, views, or arguments, in addition to an opportunity to make written submissions, (ii) a transcript shall be kept of any oral presentation, and (iii) the Administrator shall make and publish with the rule the finding described in subparagraph (A).

(c) EXTENSION OF NOTICE PERIOD.—The Administrator may for good cause extend for additional periods (not to exceed in the aggregate 90 days) the period, prescribed by subsection (a) or (b) before which the manufacturing or processing of a chemical substance subject to such subsection may begin. Subject to section 14, such an extension and the reasons therefor shall be published in the Federal Register and shall constitute a final agency action subject to judicial review.

(d) CONTENT OF NOTICE; PUBLICATIONS IN THE FEDERAL REGISTER.—(1) The notice required by subsection (a) shall include—

(A) insofar as known to the person submitting the notice or insofar as reasonably ascertainable, the information described in subparagraphs (A), (B), (C), (D), (F), and (G) of section 8(a)(2), and

(B) in such form and manner as the Administrator may prescribe, any test data in the possession or control of the person giving such notice which are related to the effect of any manufacture, processing, distribution in commerce, use, or disposal of such substance or any article containing such substance, or of any combination of such activities, on health or the environment, and

(C) a description of any other data concerning the environmental and health effects of such substance, insofar as known to the person making the notice or insofar as reasonably ascertainable.

Such a notice shall be made available, subject to section 14, for examination by interested persons.

(2) Subject to section 14, not later than five days (excluding Saturdays, Sundays and legal holidays) after the date of the receipt of a notice under subsection (a)

or of data under subsection (b), the Administrator shall publish in the Federal Register a notice which—

(A) identifies the chemical substance for which notice or data has been received;

(B) lists the uses or intended uses of such substance; and

(C) in the case of the receipt of data under subsection (b), describes the nature of the tests performed on such substance and any data which was developed pursuant to subsection (b) or a rule under section 4.

A notice under this paragraph respecting a chemical substance shall identify the chemical substance by generic class unless the Administrator determines that more specific identification is required in the public interest.

(3) At the beginning of each month the Administrator shall publish a list in the Federal Register of (A) each chemical substance for which notice has been received under subsection (a) and for which the notification period prescribed by subsection (a), (b), or (c) has not expired, and (B) each chemical substance for which such notification period has expired since the last publication in the Federal Register of such list.

(e) Regulation Pending Development of Information.—(1) (A) If the Administrator determines that—

(i) the information available to the Administrator is insufficient to permit a reasoned evaluation of the health and environmental effects of a chemical substance with respect to which notice is required by subsection (a); and

(ii) (I) in the absence of sufficient information to permit the Administrator to make such an evaluation, the manufacture, processing, distribution in commerce, use, or disposal of such substance, or any combination of such activities, may present an unreasonable risk of injury to health or the environment, or

(II) such substance is or will be produced in substantial quantities, and such substance either enters or may reasonably be anticipated to enter the environment in substantial quantities or there is or may be significant or substantial human exposure to the substance,

the Administrator may issue a proposed order, to take effect on the expiration of the notification period applicable to the manufacturing or processing of such substance under subsection (a), (b), or (c), to prohibit or limit the manufacture, processing, distribution in commerce, use, or disposal of such substance or to prohibit or limit any combination of such activities.

(B) A proposed order may not be issued under subparagraph (A) respecting a chemical substance (i) later than 45 days before the expiration of the notification period applicable to the manufacture or processing of such substance under subsection (a), (b), or (c), and (ii) unless the Administrator has, on or before the issuance of the proposed order, notified, in writing, each manufacturer or processor, as the case may be, of such substance of the determination which underlies such order.

(C) If a manufacturer or processor of a chemical substance to be subject to a proposed order issued under subparagraph (A) files with the Administrator (within the 30-day period beginning on the date such manufacturer or processor received the notice required by subparagraph (B)(ii)) objections specifying with particularity the provisions of the order deemed objectionable and stating the grounds therefor, the proposed order shall not take effect.

(2)(A)(i) Except as provided in clause (ii), if with respect to a chemical substance with respect to which notice is required by subsection (a), the Administrator makes the determination described in paragraph (1)(A) and if—

(I) the Administrator does not issue a proposed order under paragraph (1) respecting such substance, or

(II) the Administrator issues such an order respecting such substance but such order does not take effect because objections were filed under paragraph (1)(C) with respect to it,

the Administrator, through attorneys of the Environmental Protection Agency, shall apply to the United States District Court for the District of Columbia or the United States district court for the judicial district in which the manufacturer or processor, as the case may be, of such substance is found, resides, or transacts business for an injunction to prohibit or limit the manufacture, processing, distribution in commerce, use, or disposal of such substance (or to prohibit or limit any combination of such activities).

(ii) If the Administrator issues a proposed order under paragraph (1)(A) respecting a chemical substance but such order does not take effect because objections have been filed under paragraph (1)(C) with respect to it, the Administrator is not required to apply for an injunction under clause (i) respecting such substance if the Administrator determines, on the basis of such objections, that the determinations under paragraph (1)(A) may not be made.

(B) A district court of the United States which receives an application under subparagraph (A)(i) for an injunction respecting a chemical substance shall issue such injunction if the court finds that—

(i) the information available to the Administrator is insufficient to permit a reasoned evaluation of the health and environmental effects of a chemical substance with respect to which notice is required by subsection (a); and

(ii)(I) in the absence of sufficient information to permit the Administrator to make such an evaluation, the manufacture, processing, distribution in commerce, use, or disposal of such substance, or any combination of such activities, may present an unreasonable risk of injury to health or the environment, or

(II) such substance is or will be produced in substantial quantities, and such substance either enters or may reasonably be anticipated to enter the environment in substantial quantities or there is or may be significant or substantial human exposure to the substance.

(C) Pending the completion of a proceeding for the issuance of an injunction under subparagraph (B) respecting a chemical substance, the court may, upon application of the Administrator made through attorneys of the Environmental Protection Agency, issue a temporary restraining order or a preliminary injunction to prohibit the manufacture, processing, distribution in commerce, use, or disposal of such a substance (or any combination of such activities) if the court finds that the notification period applicable under subsection (a), (b), or (c) to the manufacturing or processing of such substance may expire before such proceeding can be completed.

(D) After the submission to the Administrator of test data sufficient to evaluate the health and environmental effects of a chemical substance subject to an injunction issued under subparagraph (B) and the evaluation of such data by the Administrator, the district court of the United States which issued such injunction shall, upon petition, dissolve the injunction unless the Administrator has initiated a proceeding for the issuance of a rule under section 6(a) respecting the substance. If such a proceeding has been initiated, such court shall continue the injunction in effect until the effective date of the rule promulgated in such proceeding or, if such proceeding is terminated without the promulgation of a rule, upon the termination of the proceeding, whichever occurs first.

(f) PROTECTION AGAINST UNREASONABLE RISKS.—(1) If the Administrator finds that there is a reasonable basis to conclude that the manufacture, processing, distribution in commerce, use, or disposal of a chemical substance with respect to which notice is required by subsection (a), or that any combination of such activities, presents or will present an unreasonable risk of injury to health or environment before a rule promulgated under section 6 can protect against such risk, the Administrator shall, before the expiration of the notification period applicable under subsection (a), (b), or (c) to the manufacturing or processing of such substance, take the action authorized by paragraph (2) or (3) to the extent necessary to protect against such risk.

(2) The Administrator may issue a proposed rule under section 6(a) to apply to a chemical substance with respect to which a finding was made under paragraph (1)—

(A) a requirement limiting the amount of such substance which may be manufactured, processed, or distributed in commerce,

(B) a requirement described in paragraph (2), (3), (4), (5), (6), or (7) of section 6(a), or

(C) any combination of the requirements referred to in subparagraph (B).

Such a proposed rule shall be effective upon its publication in the Federal Register. Section 6(d)(2)(B) shall apply with respect to such rule.

(3)(A) The Administrator may—

(i) issue a proposed order to prohibit the manufacture, processing, or distribution in commerce of a substance with respect to which a finding was made under paragraph (1), or

(ii) apply, through attorneys of the Environmental Protection Agency, to the United States District Court for the District of Columbia or the United States district court for the judicial district in which the manufacturer, or processor, as the case may be, of such substance, is found, resides, or transacts business for an injunction to prohibit the manufacture, processing, or distribution in commerce of such substance.

A proposed order issued under clause (i) respecting a chemical substance shall take effect on the expiration of the notification period applicable under subsection (a), (b), or (c) to the manufacture or processing of such substance.

(B) If the district court of the United States to which an application has been made under subparagraph (A)(ii) finds that there is a reasonable basis to conclude that the manufacture, processing, distribution in commerce, use, or disposal of the chemical substance with respect to which such application was made, or that any combination of such activities, presents or will present an unreasonable risk of injury to health or the environment before a rule promulgated under section 6 can protect against such risk, the court shall issue an injunction to prohibit the manufacture, processing or distribution in commerce of such substance or to prohibit any combination of such activities.

(C) The provisions of subparagraphs (B) and (C) of subsection (e)(1) shall apply with respect to an order issued under clause (i) of subparagraph (A); and the provisions of subparagraph (C) of subsection (e)(2) shall apply with respect to an injunction issued under subparagraph (B).

(D) If the Administrator issues an order pursuant to subparagraph (A)(i) respecting a chemical substance and objections are filed in accordance with subsection (e)(1)(C), the Administrator shall seek an injunction under subparagraph (A)(ii) respecting such substance unless the Administrator determines, on the basis of such objections, that such substance does not or will not present an unreasonable risk of injury to health or the environment.

(g) STATEMENT OF REASONS FOR NOT TAKING ACTION.—If the Administrator has not initiated any action under this section or section 6 or 7 to prohibit or limit the manufacture, processing, distribution in commerce, use, or disposal of a chemical substance, with respect to which notification or data is required by subsection (a)(1)(B) or (b), before the expiration of the notification period applicable to the manufacturing or processing of such substance, the Administrator shall publish a statement of the Administrator's reasons for not initiating such action. Such a statement shall be published in the Federal Register before the expiration of such period. Publication of such statement in accordance with the preceding sentence is not a prerequisite to the manufacturing or processing of the substance with respect to which the statement is to be published.

(h) EXEMPTIONS.—(1) The Administrator may, upon application, exempt any person from any requirement of subsection (a) or (b) to permit such person to manufacture or process a chemical substance for test marketing purposes—

(A) upon a showing by such person satisfactory to the Administrator that the manufacture, processing, distribution in commerce, use, and disposal of such substance, and that any combination of such activities, for such purposes will not present any unreasonable risk of injury to health or the environment, and

(B) under such restrictions as the Administrator considers appropriate.

(2)(A) The Administrator may, upon application, exempt any person from the requirement of subsection (b)(2) to submit data for a chemical substance. If, upon receipt of an application under the preceding sentence, the Administrator determines that—

(i) the chemical substance with respect to which such application was submitted is equivalent to a chemical substance for which data has been submitted to the Administrator as required by subsection (b)(2), and

(ii) submission of data by the applicant on such substance would be duplicative of data which has been submitted to the Administrator in accordance with such subsection,

the Administrator shall exempt the applicant from the requirement to submit such data on such substance. No exemption which is granted under this subparagraph with respect to the submission of data for a chemical substance may take effect before the beginning of the reimbursement period applicable to such data.

(B) If the Administrator exempts any person, under subparagraph (A), from submitting data required under subsection (b)(2) for a chemical substance because of the existence of previously submitted data and if such exemption is granted during the reimbursement period for such data, then (unless such person and the persons referred to in clauses (i) and (ii) agree on the amount and method of reimbursement) the Administrator shall order the person granted the exemption to provide fair and equitable reimbursement (in an amount determined under rules of the Administrator)—

(i) to the person who previously submitted the data on which the exemption was based, for a portion of the costs incurred by such person in complying with the requirement under subsection (b)(2) to submit such data, and

(ii) to any other person who has been required under this subparagraph to contribute with respect to such costs, for a portion of the amount such person was required to contribute.

In promulgating rules for the determination of fair and equitable reimbursement to the persons described in clauses (i) and (ii) for costs incurred with respect to a chemical substance, the Administrator shall, after consultation with the Attorney General and the Federal Trade Commission, consider all relevant factors, including the effect on the competitive position of the person required to provide reimbursement in relation to the persons to be reimbursed and the share of the market for such substance of the person required to provide reimbursement in relation to the share of such market of the persons to be reimbursed. For purposes of judicial review, an order under this subparagraph shall be considered final agency action.

(C) For purposes of this paragraph, the reimbursement period for any previously submitted data for a chemical substance is a period—

(i) beginning on the date of the termination of the prohibition, imposed under this section, on the manufacture or processing of such substance by the person who submitted such data to the Administrator, and

(ii) ending—

(I) five years after the date referred to in clause (i), or

(II) at the expiration of a period which begins on the date referred to in clause (i) and is equal to the period which the Administrator determines was necessary to develop such data,

whichever is later.

(3) The requirements of subsections (a) and (b) do not apply with respect to the manufacturing or processing of any chemical substance which is manufactured or processed, or proposed to be manufactured or processed, only in small quantities (as defined by the Administrator by rule) solely for purposes of—

(A) scientific experimentation or analysis, or

(B) chemical research on, or analysis of such substance or another substance, including such research or analysis for the development of a product,

if all persons engaged in such experimentation, research, or analysis for a manufacturer or processor are notified (in such form and manner as the Administrator may prescribe) of any risk to health which the manufacturer, processor, or the Administrator has reason to believe may be associated with such chemical substance.

(4) The Administrator may, upon application and by rule, exempt the manufacturer of any new chemical substance from all or part of the requirements of this section if the Administrator determines that the manufacture, processing, distribution in commerce, use, or disposal of such chemical substance, or that any combination of such activities, will not present an unreasonable risk of injury to health or the environment. A rule promulgated under this paragraph (and any substantive amendment to, or repeal of, such a rule) shall be promulgated in accordance with paragraphs (2) and (3) of section 6(c).

(5) The Administrator may, upon application, make the requirements of subsections (a) and (b) inapplicable with respect to the manufacturing or processing of any chemical substance (A) which exists temporarily as a result of a chemical reaction in the manufacturing or processing of a mixture or another chemical substance, and (B) to which there is no, and will not be, human or environmental exposure.

(6) Immediately upon receipt of an application under paragraph (1) or (5) the Administrator shall publish in the Federal Register notice of the receipt of such application. The Administrator shall give interested persons an opportunity to comment upon any such application and shall, within 45 days of its receipt, either approve or deny the application. The Administrator

shall publish in the Federal Register notice of the approval or denial of such an application.

(i) DEFINITION.—For purposes of this section, the terms "manufacture" and "process" mean manufacturing or processing for commercial purposes.

SEC. 6. REGULATION OF HAZARDOUS CHEMICAL SUBSTANCES AND MIXTURES.

(a) SCOPE OF REGULATION.—If the Administrator finds that there is a reasonable basis to conclude that the manufacture, processing, distribution in commerce, use, or disposal of a chemical substance or mixture, or that any combination of such activities, presents, or will present an unreasonable risk of injury to health or the environment, the Administrator shall by rule apply one or more of the following requirements to such substance or mixture to the extent necessary to protect adequately against such risk using the least burdensome requirements:

(1) A requirement (A) prohibiting the manufacturing, processing, or distribution in commerce of such substance or mixture, or (B) limiting the amount of such substance or mixture which may be manufactured, processed, or distributed in commerce.

(2) A requirement—

(A) prohibiting the manufacture, processing, or distribution in commerce of such substance or mixture for (i) a particular use or (ii) a particular use in a concentration in excess of a level specified by the Administrator in the rule imposing the requirement, or

(B) limiting the amount of such substance or mixture which may be manufactured, processed, or distributed in commerce for (i) a particular use or (ii) a particular use in a concentration in excess of a level specified by the Administrator in the rule imposing the requirement.

(3) A requirement that such substance or mixture or any article containing such substance or mixture be marked with or accompanied by clear and adequate warnings and instructions with respect to its use, distribution in commerce, or disposal or with respect to any combination of such activities. The form and content of such warnings and instructions shall be prescribed by the Administrator.

(4) A requirement that manufacturers and processors of such substance or mixture make and retain records of the processes used to manufacture or process such substance or mixture and monitor or conduct tests which are reasonable and necessary to assure compliance with the requirements of any rule applicable under this subsection.

(5) A requirement prohibiting or otherwise regulating any manner or method of commercial use of such substance or mixture.

(6)(A) A requirement prohibiting or otherwise regulating any manner or method of disposal of such substance or mixture, or of any article containing such substance or mixture, by its manufacturer or processor or by any other person who uses, or disposes of, it for commercial purposes.

(B) A requirement under subparagraph (A) may not require any person to take any action which would be in violation of any law or requirement of, or in effect for, a State or political subdivision, and shall require each person subject to it to notify each State and political subdivision in which a required disposal may occur of such disposal.

(7) A requirement directing manufacturers or processors of such substance or mixture (A) to give notice of such unreasonable risk of injury to distributors in commerce of such substance or mixture and, to the extent reasonably ascertainable, to other persons in possession of such substance or mixture or exposed to such substance or mixture, (B) to give public notice of such risk of injury, and (C) to replace or repurchase such substance or mixture as elected by the person to which the requirement is directed.

Any requirement (or combination of requirements) imposed under this subsection may be limited in application to specified geographic areas.

(b) Quality Control.—If the Administrator has a reasonable basis to conclude that a particular manufacturer or processor is manufacturing or processing a chemical substance or mixture in a manner which unintentionally causes the chemical substance or mixture to present or which will cause it to present an unreasonable risk of injury to health or the environment—

(1) the Administrator may by order require such manufacturer or processor to submit a description of the relevant quality control procedures followed in the manufacturing or processing of such chemical substance or mixture; and

(2) if the Administrator determines—

(A) that such quality control procedures are inadequate to prevent the chemical substance or mixture from presenting such risk of injury, the Administrator may order the manufacturer or processor to revise such quality control procedures to the extent necessary to remedy such inadequacy; or

(B) that the use of such quality control procedures has resulted in the distribution in commerce of chemical substances or mixtures which present an unreasonable risk of injury to health or the environment, the Administrator may order the manufacturer or processor to (i) give notice of such risk to processors or distributors in commerce of any such substance or mixture, or to both, and, to the extent reasonably ascertainable, to any other person in possession of or exposed to any such substance, (ii) to give public notice of such risk, and (iii) to provide such replacement or repurchase of any such substance or mixture as is necessary to adequately protect health or the environment.

A determination under subparagraph (A) or (B) of paragraph (2) shall be made on the record after opportunity for hearing in accordance with section 554 of title 5, United States Code. Any manufacturer or processor subject to a requirement to replace or repurchase a chemical substance or mixture may elect either to replace or repurchase the substance or mixture and shall take either such action in the manner prescribed by the Administrator.

(c) PROMULGATION OF SUBSECTION (a) RULES.—(1) In promulgating any rule under subsection (a) with respect to a chemical substance or mixture, the Administrator shall consider and publish a statement with respect to—

(A) the effects of such substance or mixture on health and the magnitude of the exposure of human beings to such substance or mixture,

(B) the effects of such substance or mixture on the environment and the magnitude of the exposure of the environment to such substance or mixture,

(C) the benefits of such substance or mixture for various uses and the availability of substitutes for such uses, and

(D) the reasonably ascertainable economic consequences of the rule, after consideration of the effect on the national economy, small business, technological innovation, the environment, and public health.

If the Administrator determines that a risk of injury to health or the environment could be eliminated or reduced to a sufficient extent by actions taken under another Federal law (or laws) administered in whole or in part by the Administrator, the Administrator may not promulgate a rule under subsection (a) to protect against such risk of injury unless the Administrator finds, in the Administrator's discretion, that it is in the public interest to protect against such risk under this Act. In making such a finding the Administrator shall consider (i) all relevant aspects of the risk, as determined by the Administrator in the Administrator's discretion, (ii) a comparison of the estimated costs of complying with actions taken under this Act and under such law (or laws), and (iii) the relative efficiency of actions under this Act and under such law (or laws) to protect against such risk of injury.

(2) When prescribing a rule under subsection (a) the Administrator shall proceed in accordance with section 553 of title 5, United States Code (without regard to any reference in such section to sections 556 and 557 of such title), and shall also (A) publish a notice of proposed rulemaking stating with particularity the reason for the proposed rule; (B) allow interested persons to submit written data, views, and arguments, and make all such submissions publicly available; (C) provide an opportunity for an informal hearing in accordance with paragraph (3); (D) promulgate, if appropriate, a final rule based on the matter in the rulemaking record (as defined in section 19(a)), and (E) make and publish with the rule the finding described in subsection (a).

(3) Informal hearings required by paragraph (2)(C) shall be conducted by the Administrator in accordance with the following requirements:

(A) Subject to subparagraph (B), an interested person is entitled—

(i) to present such person's position orally or by documentary submissions (or both), and

(ii) if the Administrator determines that there are disputed issues of material fact it is necessary to resolve, to present such rebuttal submissions and to conduct (or have conducted under subparagraph (B)(ii)) such cross-examination of persons as the Administrator determines (I) to be appropriate, and (II) to be required for a full and true disclosure with respect to such issues.

(B) The Administrator may prescribe such rules and make such rulings concerning procedures in such hearings to avoid unnecessary costs or delay. Such rules or rulings may include (i) the imposition of reasonable time limits on each interested person's oral presentations, and (ii) requirements that any cross-examination to which a person may be entitled under subparagraph (A) be conducted by the Administrator on behalf of that person in such manner as the Administrator determines (I) to be appropriate, and (II) to be required for a full and true disclosure with respect to disputed issues of material fact.

(C)(i) Except as provided in clause (ii), if a group of persons each of whom under subparagraphs (A) and (B) would be entitled to conduct (or have conducted) cross-examination and who are determined by the Administrator to have the same or similar interests in the proceeding cannot agree upon a single representative of such interests for purposes of cross-examination, the Administrator may make rules and rulings (I) limiting the representation of such interest for such purposes, and (II) governing the manner in which such cross-examination shall be limited.

(ii) When any person who is a member of a group with respect to which the Administrator has made a determination under clause (i) is unable to agree upon group representation with the other members of the group, then such person shall not be denied under the authority of clause (i) the opportunity to conduct (or have conducted) cross-examination as to issues affecting the person's particular interests if (I) the person satisfies the Administrator that the person has made a reasonable and good faith effort to reach agreement upon group representation with the other members of the group and (II) the Administrator determines that there are substantial and relevant issues which are not adequately presented by the group representative.

(D) A verbatim transcript shall be taken of any oral presentation made, and cross-examination conducted in any informal hearing under this subsection. Such transcript shall be available to the public.

(4)(A) The Administrator may, pursuant to rules prescribed by the Administrator, provide compensation for reasonable attorneys' fees, expert witness fees, and other costs of participating in a rulemaking proceeding for the promulgation of a rule under subsection (a) to any person—

(i) who represents an interest which would substantially contribute to a fair determination of the issues to be resolved in the proceeding, and

(ii) if—

(I) the economic interest of such person is small in comparison to the costs of effective participation in the proceeding by such person, or

(II) such person demonstrates to the satisfaction of the Administrator that such person does not have sufficient resources adequately to participate in the proceeding without compensation under this subparagraph.

In determining for purposes of clause (i) if an interest will substantially contribute to a fair determination of the issues to be resoved in a proceeding, the Administrator shall take into account the number and complexity of such issues and the extent to which representation of such interest will contribute to widespread public participation in the proceeding and representation of a fair balance of interests for the resolution of such issues.

(B) In determining whether compensation should be provided to a person under subparagraph (A) and the amount of such compensation, the Administrator shall take into account the financial burden which will be incurred by such person in participating in the rulemaking proceeding. The Administrator shall take such action as may be necessary to ensure that the aggregate amount of compensation paid under this paragraph in any fiscal year to all persons who, in rulemaking proceedings in which they receive compensation, are persons who either—

(i) would be regulated by the proposed rule, or

(ii) represent persons who would be so regulated,

may not exceed 25 per centum of the aggregate amount paid as compensation under this paragraph to all persons in such fiscal year.

(5) Paragraphs (1), (2), (3), and (4) of this subsection apply to the promulgation of a rule repealing, or making a substantive amendment to, a rule promulgated under subsection (a).

(d) EFFECTIVE DATE.—(1) The Administrator shall specify in any rule under subsection (a) the date on which it shall take effect, which date shall be as soon as feasible.

(2)(A) The Administrator may declare a proposed rule under subsection (a) to be effective upon its publication in the Federal Register and until the effective date of final action taken, in accordance with subparagraph (B), respecting such rule if—

(i) the Administrator determines that—

(I) the manufacture, processing, distribution in commerce, use, or disposal of the chemical substance or mixture subject to such proposed rule or any combination of such activities is likely to result in an unreasonable risk of serious or widespread injury to health or the environment before such effective date; and

(II) making such proposed rule so effective is necessary to protect the public interest; and

(ii) in the case of a proposed rule to prohibit the manufacture, processing, or distribution of a chemical substance or mixture because of the risk determined under clause (i)(I), a court has in an action under section 7 granted relief with respect to such risk associated with such substance or mixture.

Such a proposed rule which is made so effective shall not, for purposes of judicial review, be considered final agency action.

(B) If the Administrator makes a proposed rule effective upon its publication in the Federal Register, the Administrator shall, as expeditiously as possible, give interested persons prompt notice of such action, provide reasonable opportunity, in accordance with paragraphs (2) and (3) of subsection (c), for a hearing on such rule, and either promulgate such rule (as proposed or with modifications) or revoke it; and if such a hearing is requested, the Administrator shall commence the hearing within five days from the date such request is made unless the Administrator and the person making the request agree upon a later date for the hearing to begin, and after the hearing is concluded the Administrator shall, within ten days of the conclusion of the hearing, either promulgate such rule (as proposed or with modifications) or revoke it.

(e) POLYCHLORINATED BIPHENYLS.—(1) Within six months after the effective date of this Act the Administrator shall promulgate rules to—

(A) prescribe methods for the disposal of polychlorinated biphenyls, and

(B) require polychlorinated biphenyls to be marked with clear and adequate warnings, and instructions with respect to their processing, distribution in commerce, use, or disposal or with respect to any combination of such activities.

Requirements prescribed by rules under this paragraph shall be consistent with the requirements of paragraphs (2) and (3).

(2)(A) Except as provided under subparagraph (B), effective one year after the effective date of this Act no person may manufacture, process, or distribute in commerce or use any polychlorinated biphenyl in any manner other than in a totally enclosed manner.

(B) The Administrator may by rule authorize the manufacture, processing, distribution in commerce or use (or any combination of such activities) of any polychlorinated biphenyl in a manner other than in a totally enclosed manner if the Administrator finds that such manufacture, processing, distribution in commerce, or use (or combination of such activities) will not present an unreasonable risk of injury to health or the environment.

(C) For the purposes of this paragraph, the term "totally enclosed manner" means any manner which will ensure that any exposure of human beings or the environment by the polychlorinated biphenyl will be insignificant as determined by the Administrator by rule.

(3)(A) Except as provided in subparagraphs (B) and (C)—

(i) no person may manufacture any polychlorinated biphenyl after two years after the effective date of this Act, and

(ii) no person may process or distribute in commerce any polychlorinated biphenyl after two and one-half years after such date.

(B) Any person may petition the Administrator for an exemption from the requirements of subparagagh

(A), and the Administrator may grant by rule such an exemption if the Administrator finds that—

(i) an unreasonable risk of injury to health or environment would not result, and

(ii) good faith efforts have been made to develop a chemical substance which does not present an unreasonable risk of injury to health or the environment and which may be substituted for such polychlorinated biphenyl.

An exemption granted under this subparagraph shall be subject to such terms and conditions as the Administrator may prescribe and shall be in effect for such period (but not more than one year from the date it is granted) as the Administrator may prescribe.

(C) Subparagraph (A) shall not apply to the distribution in commerce of any polychlorinated biphenyl if such polychlorinated biphenyl was sold for purposes other than resale before two and one half years after the date of enactment of this Act.

(4) Any rule under paragraph (1), (2)(B), or (3)(B) shall be promulgated in accordance with paragraphs (2), (3), and (4) of subsection (c).

(5) This subsection does not limit the authority of the Administrator, under any other provision of this Act or any other Federal law, to take action respecting any polychlorinated biphenyl.

SEC. 7. IMMINENT HAZARDS.

(a) Actions Authorized and Required.—(1) The Administrator may commence a civil action in an appropriate district court of the United States—

(A) for seizure of an imminently hazardous chemical substance or mixture or any article containing such a substance or mixture,

(B) for relief (as authorized by subsection (b)) against any person who manufactures, processes, distributes in commerce, or uses, or disposes of, an imminent hazardous chemical substance or mixture or any article containing such a substance or mixture, or

(C) for both such seizure and relief.

A civil action may be commenced under this paragraph notwithstanding the existence of a rule under section 4, 5, or 6 or an order under section 5, and notwithstanding the pendency of any administrative or judicial proceeding under any provision of this Act.

(2) If the Administrator has not made a rule under section 6(a) immediately effective (as authorized by subsection 6(d)(2)(A)(i)) with respect to an imminently hazardous chemical substance or mixture, the Administrator shall commence in a district court of the United States with respect to such substance or mixture or ar-

ticle containing such substance or mixture a civil action described in subparagraph (A), (B), or (C) of paragraph (1).

(b) RELIEF AUTHORIZED.—(1) The district court of the United States in which an action under subsection (a) is brought shall have jurisdiction to grant such temporary or permanent relief as may be necessary to protect health or the environment from the unreasonable risk associated with the chemical substance, mixture, or article involved in such action.

(2) In the case of an action under subsection (a) brought against a person who manufactures, processes, or distributes in commerce a chemical substance or mixture or an article containing a chemical substance or mixture, the relief authorized by paragraph (1) may include the issuance of a mandatory order requiring (A) in the case of purchasers of such substance, mixture, or article known to the defendant, notification to such purchasers of the risk associated with it; (B) public notice of such risk; (C) recall; (D) the replacement or repurchase of such substance, mixture, or article; or (E) any combination of the actions described in the preceding clauses.

(3) In the case of an action under subsection (a) against a chemical substance, mixture, or article, such substance, mixture, or article may be proceeded against by process of libel for its seizure and condemnation. Proceedings in such an action shall conform as nearly as possible to proceedings in rem in admiralty.

(c) VENUE AND CONSOLIDATION.—(1)(A) An action under subsection (a) against a person who manufactures, processes, or distributes a chemical substance or mixture or an article containing a chemical substance or mixture may be brought in the United States District Court for the District of Columbia or for any judicial district in which any of the defendants is found, resides, or transacts business; and process in such an action may be served on a defendant in any other district in which such defendant resides or may be found. An action under subsection (a) against a chemical substance, mixture, or article may be brought in any United States district court within the jurisdiction of which the substance, mixture, or article is found.

(B) In determining the judicial district in which an action may be brought under subsection (a) in instances in which such action may be brought in more than one judicial district, the Administrator shall take into account the convenience of the parties.

(C) Subpeonas requiring attendance of witnesses in an action brought under subsection (a) may be served in any judicial district.

(2) Whenever proceedings under subsection (a) involving identical chemical substances, mixtures, or arti-

cles are pending in courts in two or more judicial districts, they shall be consolidated for trial by order of any such court upon application reasonably made by any party in interest, upon notice to all parties in interest.

(d) Action Under Section 6.—Were appropriate, concurrently with the filing of an action under subsection (a) or as soon thereafter as may be practicable, the Administrator shall initiate a proceeding for the promulgation of a rule under section 6(a).

(e) Representation.—Notwithstanding any other provision of law, in any action under subsection (a), the Administrator may direct attorneys of the Environmental Protection Agency to appear and represent the Administrator in such an action.

(f) Definition.—For the purposes of subsection (a), the term "imminently hazardous chemical substance or mixture" means a chemical substance or mixture which presents an imminent and unreasonable risk of serious or widespread injury to health or the environment. Such a risk to health or the environment shall be considered imminent if it is shown that the manufacture, processing, distribution in commerce, use, or disposal of the chemical substance or mixture, or that any combination of such activities, is likely to result in such injury to health or the environment before a final rule under section 6 can protect against such risk.

SEC. 8. REPORTING AND RETENTION OF INFORMATION.

(a) Reports.—(1) The Administrator shall promulgate rules under which—

(A) each person (other than a small manufacturer or processor) who manufactures or processes or proposes to manufacture or process a chemical substance (other than a chemical substance described in subparagraph (B)(ii) shall maintain such records, and shall submit to the Administrator such reports, as the Administrator may reasonably require, and

(B) each person (other than a small manufacturer or processor) who manufactures or processes or proposes to manufacture or process—

(i) a mixture, or

(ii) a chemical substance in small quantities (as defined by the Administrator by rule) solely for purposes of scientific experimentation or analysis or chemical research on, or analysis of, such substance or another substance, including any such research or analysis for the development of a product,

shall maintain records and submit to the Administrator reports but only to the extent the Administrator determines the maintenance of records or submission of reports, or both, is necessary for the effective enforcement of this Act.

The Administrator may not require in a rule promulgated under this paragraph the maintenance of records or the submission of reports with respect to changes in the proportions of the components of a mixture unless the Administrator finds that the maintenance of such records or the submission of such reports, or both, is necessary for the effective enforcement of this Act. For purposes of the compilation of the list of chemical substances required under subsection (b), the Administrator shall promulgate rules pursuant to this subsection not later than 180 days after the effective date of this Act.

(2) The Administrator may require under paragraph (1) maintenance of records and reporting with respect to the following insofar as known to the person making the report or insofar as reasonably ascertainable:

(A) The common or trade name, the chemical identity, and molecular structure of each chemical substance or mixture for which such a report is required.

(B) The categories or proposed categories of use of each such substance or mixture.

(C) The total amount of each substance and mixture manufactured or processed, reasonable estimates of the total amount to be manufactured or processed, the amount manufactured or processed for each of its categories of use, and reasonable estimates of the amount to be manufactured or processed for each of its categories of use or proposed categories of use.

(D) A description of the byproducts resulting from the manufacture, processing, use, or disposal of each such substance or mixture.

(E) All existing data concerning the environmental and health effects of such substance or mixture.

(F) The number of individuals exposed, and reasonable estimates of the number who will be exposed, to such substance or mixture in their places of employment and the duration of such exposure.

(G) In the initial report under paragraph (1) on such substance or mixture, the manner or method of its disposal, and in any subsequent report on such substance or mixture, any change in such manner or method.

To the extent feasible, the Administrator shall not require under paragraph (1), any reporting which is unnecessary or duplicative.

(3)(A)(i) The Administrator may by rule require a small manufacturer or processor of a chemical substance to submit to the Administrator such information respecting the chemical substance as the Administrator may require for publication of the first list of chemical substances required by subsection (b).

(ii) The Administrator may by rule require a small manufacturer or processor of a chemical substance or mixture—

(I) subject to a rule proposed or promulgated under section 4, 5(b)(4), or 6, or an order in effect under section 5(e), or

(II) with respect to which relief has been granted pursuant to a civil action brought under section 5 or 7,

to maintain such records on such substance or mixture, and to submit to the Administrator such reports on such substance or mixture, as the Administrator may reasonably require. A rule under this clause requiring reporting may require reporting with respect to the matters referred to in paragraph (2).

(B) The Administrator, after consultation with the Administrator of the Small Business Administration, shall by rule prescribe standards for determining the manufacturers and processors which qualify as small manufacturers and processors for purposes of this paragraph and paragraph (1).

(b) INVENTORY.—(1) The Administrator shall compile, keep current, and publish a list of each chemical substance which is manufactured or processed in the United States. Such list shall at least include each chemical substance which any person reports, under section 5 or subsection (a) of this section, is manufactured or processed in the United States. Such list may not include any chemical substance which was not manufactured or processed in the United States within three years before the effective date of the rules promulgated pursuant to the last sentence of subsection (a)(1). In the case of a chemical substance for which a notice is submitted in accordance with section 5, such chemical substance shall be included in such list as of the earliest date (as determined by the Administrator) on which such substance was manufactured or processed in the United States. The Administrator shall first publish such a list not later than 315 days after the effective date of this Act. The Administrator shall not include in such list any chemical substance which is manufactured or processed only in small quantities (as defined by the Administrator by rule) solely for purposes of scientific experimentation or analysis or chemical research on, or analysis of, such substance or another substance, including such research or analysis for the development of a product.

(2) To the extent consistent with the purposes of this Act, the Administrator may, in lieu of listing, pursuant to paragraph (1), a chemical substance individually, list a category of chemical substances in which such substance is included.

(c) RECORDS.—Any person who manufactures, processes, or distributes in commerce any chemical substance or mixture shall maintain records of significant adverse reactions to health or the environment, as determined by the Administrator by rule, alleged to have been caused by the substance or mixture. Records of such adverse reactions to the health of employees shall be retained for a period of 30 years from the date such reactions were first reported to or known by the person maintaining such records. Any other record of such adverse reactions shall be retained for a period of five years from the date the information contained in the record was first reported to or known by the person maintaining the record. Records required to be maintained under this subsection shall include records of consumer allegations of personal injury or harm to health, reports of occupational disease or injury, and reports or complaints of injury to the environment submitted to the manufacturer, processor, or distributor in commerce from any source. Upon request of any duly designated representative of the Administrator, each person who is required to maintain records under this subsection shall permit the inspection of such records and shall submit copies of such records.

(d) HEALTH AND SAFETY STUDIES.—The Administrator shall promulgate rules under which the Administrator shall require any person who manufactures, processes, or distributes in commerce or who proposes to manufacture, process, or distribute in commerce any chemical substance or mixture (or with respect to paragraph (2), any person who has possession of a study) to submit to the Administrator—

(1) lists of health and safety studies (A) conducted or initiated by or for such person with respect to such substance or mixture at any time, (B) known to such person, or (C) reasonably ascertainable by such person, except that the Administrator may exclude certain types or categories of studies from the requirements of this subsection if the Administrator finds that submission of lists of such studies are unnecessary to carry out the purposes of this Act; and

(2) copies of any study contained on a list submitted pursuant to paragraph (1) or otherwise known by such person.

(e) NOTICE TO ADMINISTRATOR OF SUBSTANTIAL RISKS.—Any person who manufactures, processes, or distributes in commerce a chemical substance or mixture and who obtains information which reasonably supports the conclusion that such substance or mixture presents a substantial risk of injury to health or the environment shall immediately inform the Administrator of such information unless such person has actual knowledge that the

Administrator has been adequately informed of such information.

(f) DEFINITIONS.—For purposes of this section, the terms "manufacture" and "process" mean manufacture or process for commercial purposes.

SEC. 9. RELATIONSHIP TO OTHER FEDERAL LAWS.

(a) LAWS NOT ADMINISTERED BY THE ADMINISTRATOR.—(1) If the Administrator has reasonable basis to conclude that the manufacture, processing, distribution in commerce, use, or disposal of a chemical substance or mixture, or that any combination of such activities, presents or will present an unreasonable risk of injury to health or the environment and determines, in the Administrator's discretion, that such risk may be prevented or reduced to a sufficient extent by action taken under a Federal law not administered by the Administrator, the Administrator shall submit to the agency which administers such law a report which describes such risk and includes in such description a specification of the activity or combination of activities which the Administrator has reason to believe so presents such risk. Such report shall also request such agency—

(A)(i) to determine if the risk described in such report may be prevented or reduced to a sufficient extent by action taken under such law, and

(ii) if the agency determines that such risk may be so prevented or reduced, to issue an order declaring whether or not the activity or combination of activities specified in the description of such risk presents such risk; and

(B) to respond to the Administrator with respect to the matters described in subparagraph (A).

Any report of the Administrator shall include a detailed statement of the information on which it is based and shall be published in the Federal Register. The agency receiving a request under such a report shall make the requested determination, issue the requested order, and make the requested response within such time as the Administrator specifies in the request, but such time specified may not be less than 90 days from the date the request was made. The response of an agency shall be accompanied by a detailed statement of the findings and conclusions of the agency and shall be published in the Federal Register.

(2) If the Administrator makes a report under paragraph (1) with respect to a chemical substance or mixture and the agency to which such report was made either—

(A) issues an order declaring that the activity or combination of activities specified in the description of the risk described in the report does not present the risk described in the report, or

(B) initiates, within 90 days of the publication in the Federal Register of the response of the agency under paragraph (1), action under the law (or laws) administered by such agency to protect against such risk associated with such activity or combination of activities,

the Administrator may not take any action under section 6 or 7 with respect to such risk.

(3) If the Administrator has initiated action under section 6 or 7 with respect to a risk associated with a chemical substance or mixture which was the subject of a report made to an agency under paragraph (1), such agency shall before taking action under the law (or laws) administered by it to protect against such risk consult with the Administrator for the purpose of avoiding duplication of Federal action against such risk.

(b) LAWS ADMINISTERED BY THE ADMINISTRATOR.—The Administrator shall coordinate actions taken under this Act with actions taken under other Federal laws administered in whole or in part by the Administrator. If the Administrator determines that a risk to health or the environment associated with a chemical substance or mixture could be eliminated or reduced to a sufficient extent by actions taken under the authorities contained in such other Federal laws, the Administrator shall use such authorities to protect against such risk unless the Administrator determines, in the Administrator's discretion, that it is in the public interest to protect against such risk by actions taken under this Act. This subsection shall not be construed to relieve the Administrator of any requirement imposed on the Administrator by such other Federal laws.

(c) OCCUPATIONAL SAFETY AND HEALTH.—In exercising any authority under this Act, the Administrator shall not, for purposes of section 4(b)(1) of the Occupational Safety and Health Act of 1970, be deemed to be exercising statutory authority to prescribe or enforce standards or regulations affecting occupational safety and health.

(d) COORDINATION.—In administering this Act, the Administrator shall consult and coordinate with the Secretary of Health, Education, and Welfare and the heads of any other appropriate Federal executive department or agency, any relevant independent regulatory agency, and any other appropriate instrumentality of the Federal Government for the purpose of achieving the maximum enforcement of this Act while imposing the least burdens of duplicative requirements on those subject to the Act and for other purposes. The Administrator shall, in the report required by section 30, report annually to the Congress on actions taken to coordinate with such other Federal departments, agencies, or instrumentalities, and on actions taken to coordinate the authority under this Act with the authority granted under other Acts referred to in subsection (b).

SEC. 10. RESEARCH, DEVELOPMENT, COLLECTION, DISSEMINATION AND UTILIZATION OF DATA.

(a) AUTHORITY.—The Administrator shall, in consultation and cooperation with the Secretary of Health, Education, and Welfare and with other heads of appropriate departments and agencies, conduct such research, development, and monitoring as is necessary to carry out the purposes of this Act. The Administrator may enter into contracts and may make grants for research, development, and monitoring under this subsection. Contracts may be entered into under this subsection without regard to sections 3648 and 3709 of the Revised Statutes (31 U.S.C. 529, 14 U.S.C. 5).

(b) DATA SYSTEMS.—(1) The Administrator shall establish, administer, and be responsible for the continuing activities of an interagency committee which shall design, establish, and coordinate an efficient and effective system, within the Environmental Protection Agency, for the collection, dissemination to other Federal departments and agencies, and use of data submitted to the Administrator under this Act.

(2)(A) The Administrator shall, in consultation and cooperation with the Secretary of Health, Education, and Welfare and other heads of appropriate departments and agencies design, establish, and coordinate an efficient and effective system for the retrieval of toxicological and other scientific data which could be useful to the Administrator in carrying out the purposes of this Act. Systematized retrieval shall be developed for use by all Federal and other departments and agencies with responsibilities in the area of regulation or study of chemical substances and mixtures and their effect on health or the environment.

(B) The Administrator, in consultation and cooperation with the Secretary of Health, Education, and Welfare, may make grants and enter into contracts for the development of a data retrieval system described in subparagraph (A). Contracts may be entered into under this subparagraph without regard to sections 3648 and 3709 of the Revised Statutes (31 U.S.C. 529, 41 U.S.C. 5).

(c) SCREENING TECHNIQUES.—The Administrator shall coordinate, with the Assistant Secretary for Health of the Department of Health, Education, and Welfare, research undertaken by the Administrator and directed toward the development of rapid, reliable, and economical screening techniques for carcinogenic, mutagenic, teratogenic, and ecological effects of chemical substances and mixtures.

(d) MONITORING.—The Administrator shall, in consultation and cooperation with the Secretary of Health, Education, and Welfare, establish and be responsible for research aimed at the development, in cooperation with local, State, and Federal agencies, of monitoring techniques and instruments which may be used in the detection of toxic chemical susbtances and mixtures and which are reliable, economical, and capable of being implemented under a wide variety of conditions.

(e) BASIC RESEARCH.—The Administrator shall, in consultation and cooperation with the Secretary of Health, Education, and Welfare, establish research programs to develop the fundamental scientific basis of the screening and monitoring techniques described in subsections (c) and (d), the bounds of the reliability of such techniques, and the opportunities for their improvement.

(f) TRAINING.—The Administrator shall establish and promote programs and workshops to train or facilitate the training of Federal laboratory and technical personnel in existing or newly developed screening and monitoring techniques.

(g) EXCHANGE OF RESEARCH AND DEVELOPMENT RESULTS.—The Administrator shall, in consultation with the Secretary of Health, Education, and Welfare and other heads of appropriate departments and agencies, establish and coordinate a system for exchange among Federal, State, and local authorities of research and development results respecting toxic chemical substances and mixtures, including a system to facilitate and promote the development of standard data format and analysis and consistent testing procedures.

SEC. 11. INSPECTIONS AND SUBPOENAS.

(a) IN GENERAL.—For purposes of administering this Act, the Administrator, and any duly designated representative of the Administrator, may inspect any establishment, facility, or other premises in which chemical substances or mixtures are manufactured, processed, stored, or held before or after their distribution in commerce and any conveyance being used to transport chemical substances, mixtures, or such articles in connection with distribution in commerce. Such an inspection may only be made upon the presentation of appropriate credentials and of a written notice to the owner, operator, or agent in charge of the premises or conveyance to be inspected. A separate notice shall be given for each such inspection, but a notice shall not be required for each entry made during the period covered by the inspection. Each such inspection shall be commenced and completed with reasonable promptness and shall be conducted at reasonable times, within reasonable limits, and in a reasonable manner.

(b) Scope.—(1) Except as provided in paragraph (2), an inspection conducted under subsection (a) shall extend to all things within the premises or conveyance inspected (including records, files, papers, processes, controls, and facilities) bearing on whether the requirements of this Act applicable to the chemical substances or mixtures within such premises or conveyance have been complied with.

(2) No inspection under subsection (a) shall extend to—

(A) financial data,

(B) sales data (other than shipment data),

(C) pricing data,

(D) personnel data, or

(E) research data (other than data required by this Act or under a rule promulgated thereunder).

unless, the nature and extent of such data are described with reasonable specificity in the written notice required by subsection (a) for such inspection.

(c) Subpoenas.—In carrying out this Act, the Administrator may by subpoena require the attendance and testimony of witnesses and the production of reports, papers, documents, answers to questions, and other information that the Administrator deems necessary. Witnesses shall be paid the same fees and mileage that are paid witnesses in the courts of the United States. In the event of contumacy, failure, or refusal of any person to obey any such subpoena, any district court of the United States in which venue is proper shall have jurisdiction to order any such person to comply with such subpoena. Any failure to obey such an order of the court is punishable by the court as a contempt thereof.

SEC. 12. EXPORTS.

(a) In General.—(1) Except as provided in paragraph (2) and subsection (b), this Act (other than section 8) shall not apply to any chemical substance, mixture, or to an article containing a chemical substance or mixture, if—

(A) it can be shown that such substance, mixture, or article is being manufactured, processed, or distributed in commerce for export from the United States, unless such substance, mixture, or article was, in fact, manufactured, processed, or distributed in commerce, for use in the United States, and

(B) such substance, mixture, or article (when distributed in commerce), or any container in which it is enclosed (when so distributed), bears a stamp or label stating that such substance, mixture, or article is intended for export.

(2) Paragraph (1) shall not apply to any chemical substance, mixture, or article if the Administrator finds that the substance, mixture, or article will present an unreasonable risk of injury to health within the United States or to the environment of the United States. The Administrator may require, under section 4, testing of any chemical substance or mixture exempted from this Act by paragraph (1) for the purpose of determining whether or not such substance or mixture presents an unreasonable risk of injury to health within the United States or to the environment of the United States.

(b) NOTICE.—(1) If any person exports or intends to export to a foreign country a chemical substance or mixture for which the submission of data is required under section 4 or 5(b), such person shall notify the Administrator of such exportation or intent to export and the Administrator shall furnish to the government of such country notice of the availability of the data submitted to the Administrator under such section for such substance or mixture.

(2) If any person exports or intends to export to a foreign country a chemical substance or mixture for which an order has been issued under section 5 or a rule has been proposed or promulgated under section 5 or 6, or with respect to which an action is pending, or relief has been granted under section 5 or 7, such person shall notify the Administrator of such exportation or intent to export and the Administrator shall furnish to the government of such country notice of such rule, order, action, or relief.

SEC. 13. ENTRY INTO CUSTOMS TERRITORY OF THE UNITED STATES.

(a) IN GENERAL.—(1) The Secretary of the Treasury shall refuse entry into the customs territory of the United States (as defined in general headnote 2 to the Tariff Schedules of the United States) of any chemical substance, mixture, or article containing a chemical substance or mixture offered for such entry if—

(A) it fails to comply with any rule in effect under this Act, or

(B) it is offered for entry in violation of section 5 or 6, a rule or order under section 5 or 6, or an order issued in a civil action brought under section 5 or 7.

(2) If a chemical substance, mixture, or article is refused entry under paragraph (1), the Secretary of the Treasury shall notify the consignee of such entry refusal, shall not release it to the consignee, and shall cause its disposal or storage (under such rules as the Secretary of the Treasury may prescribe) if it has not been exported by the consignee within 90 days from the date of receipt of notice of such refusal, except that the Secretary of

the Treasury may, pending a review by the Administrator of the entry refusal, release to the consignee such substance, mixture, or article on execution of bond for the amount of the full invoice of such substance, mixture, or article (as such value is set forth in the customs entry), together with the duty thereon. On failure to return such substance, mixture, or article for any cause to the custody of the Secretary of the Treasury when demanded, such consignee shall be liable to the United States for liquidated damages equal to the full amount of such bond. All charges for storage, cartage, and labor on and for disposal of substances, mixtures, or articles which are refused entry or released under this section shall be paid by the owner or consignee, and in default of such payment shall constitute a lien against any future entry made by such owner or consignee.

(b) Rules.—The Secretary of the Treasury, after consultation with the Administrator, shall issue rules for the administration of subsection (a) of this section.

SEC. 14. DISCLOSURE OF DATA.

(a) In General.—Except as provided by subsection (b), any information reported to, or otherwise obtained by, the Administrator (or any representative of the Administrator) under this Act, which is exempt from disclosure pursuant to subsection (a) of section 552 of title 5, United States Code, by reason of subsection (b)(4) of such section, shall, notwithstanding the provisions of any other section of this Act, not be disclosed by the Administrator or by any officer or employee of the United States, except that such information—

(1) shall be disclosed to any officer or employee of the United States—

(A) in connection with the official duties of such officer or employee under any law for the protection of health or the environment, or

(B) for specific law enforcement purposes;

(2) shall be disclosed to contractors with the United States and employees of such contractors if in the opinion of the Administrator such disclosure is necessary for the satisfactory performance by the contractor of a contract with the United States entered into on or after the date of enactment of this Act for the performance of work in connection with this Act and under such conditions as the Administrator may specify;

(3) shall be disclosed if the Administrator determines it necessary to protect health or the environment against an unreasonable risk of injury to health or the environment; or

(4) may be disclosed when relevant in any proceeding under this Act, except that disclosure in

such a proceeding shall be made in such manner as to preserve confidentiality to the extent practicable without impairing the proceeding.

In any proceeding under section 552(a) of title 5, United States Code, to obtain information the disclosure of which has been denied because of the provisions of this subsection, the Administrator may not rely on section 552(b)(3) of such title to sustain the Administrator's action.

(b) Data From Health and Safety Studies.—(1) Subsection (a) does not prohibit the disclosure of—

(A) any health and safety study which is submitted under this Act with respect to—

(i) any chemical substance or mixture which, on the date on which such study is to be disclosed has been offered for commercial distribution, or

(ii) any chemical substance or mixture for which testing is required under section 4 or for which notification is required under section 5, and

(B) any data reported to, or otherwise obtained by, the Administrator from a health and safety study which relates to a chemical substance or mixture described in clause (i) or (ii) of subparagraph (A).

This paragraph does not authorize the release of any data which discloses processes used in the manufacturing or processing of a chemical substance or mixture or, in the case of a mixture, the release of data disclosing the portion of the mixture comprised by any of the chemical substances in the mixture.

(2) If a request is made to the Administrator under subsection (a) of section 552 of title 5, United States Code, for information which is described in the first sentence of paragraph (1) and which is not information described in the second sentence of such paragraph, the Administrator may not deny such request on the basis of subsection (b)(4) of such section.

(c) Designation and Release of Confidential Data.—(1) In submitting data under this Act, a manufacturer, processor, or distributor in commerce may (A) designate the data which such person believes is entitled to confidential treatment under subsection (a), and (B) submit such designated data separately from other data submitted under this Act. A designation under this paragraph shall be made in writing and in such manner as the Administrator may prescribe.

(2)(A) Except as provided by subparagraph (B), if the Administrator proposes to release for inspection data which has been designated under paragraph (1)(A), the

Administrator shall notify, in writing and by certified mail, the manufacturer, processor, or distributor in commerce who submitted such data of the intent to release such data. If the release of such data is to be made pursuant to a request made under section 552(a) of title 5, United States Code, such notice shall be given immediately upon approval of such request by the Administrator. The Administrator may not release such data until the expiration of 30 days after the manufacturer, processor, or distributor in commerce submitting such data has received the notice required by this subparagraph.

(B)(i) Subparagraph (A) shall not apply to the release of information under paragraph (1), (2), (3), or (4) of subsection (a), except that the Administrator may not release data under paragraph (3) of subsection (a) unless the Administrator has notified each manufacturer, processor, and distributor in commerce who submitted such data of such release. Such notice shall be made in writing by certified mail at least 15 days before the release of such data, except that if the Administrator determines that the release of such data is necessary to protect against an imminent, unreasonable risk of injury to health or the environment, such notice may be made by such means as the Administrator determines will provide notice at least 24 hours before such release is made.

(ii) Subparagraph (A) shall not apply to the release of information described in subsection (b)(1) other than information described in the second sentence of such subsection.

(d) Criminal Penalty for Wrongful Disclosure.—(1) Any officer or employee of the United States or former officer or employee of the United States, who by virtue of such employment or official position has obtained possession of, or has access to, material the disclosure of which is prohibited by subsection (a), and who knowing that disclosure of such material is prohibited by such subsection, willfully disclosures the material in any manner to any person not entitled to receive it, shall be guilty of a misdemeanor and fined not more than $5,000 or imprisoned for not more than one year, or both. Section 1905 of title 18, United States Code, does not apply with respect to the publishing, divulging, disclosure, or making known of, or making available, information reported or otherwise obtained under this Act.

(2) For the purposes of paragraph (1), any contractor with the United States who is furnished information as authorized by subsection (a)(2), and any employee of any such contractor, shall be considered to be an employee of the United States.

(e) Access by Congress.—Notwithstanding any limitation contained in this section or any other provision of law, all information reported to or otherwise obtained by the Administrator (or any representative of the Administrator) under this Act shall be made available, upon written request of any duly authorized committee of the Congress, to such committee.

SEC. 15. PROHIBITED ACTS.

It shall be unlawful for any person to—

(1) fail or refuse to comply with (A) any rule promulgated or order issued under section 4, (B) any requirement prescribed by section 5 or 6, or (C) any rule promulgated or order issued under section 5 or 6;

(2) use for commercial purposes a chemical substance or mixture which such person knew or had reason to know was manufactured, processed, or distributed in commerce in violation of section 5 or 6, a rule or order under section 5 or 6, or an order issued in action brought under section 5 or 7;

(3) fail or refuse to (A) establish or maintain records, (B) submit reports, notices, or other information, or (C) permit access to or copying of records, as required by this Act or a rule thereunder; or

(4) fail or refuse to permit entry or inspection as required by section 11.

SEC. 16. PENALTIES.

(a) Civil.—(1) Any person who violates a provision of section 15 shall be liable to the United States for a civil penalty in an amount not to exceed $25,000 for each such violation. Each day such a violation continues shall, for purposes of this subsection, constitute a separate violation of section 15.

(2)(A) A civil penalty for a violation of section 15 shall be assessed by the Administrator by an order made on the record after opportunity (provided in accordance with this subparagraph) for a hearing in accordance with section 554 of title 5, United States Code. Before issuing such an order, the Administrator shall give written notice to the person to be assessed a civil penalty under such order of the Administrator's proposal to issue such order and provide such person an opportunity to request, within 15 days of the date the notice is received by such person, such a hearing on the order.

(B) In determining the amount of a civil penalty, the Administrator shall take into account the nature, circumstances, extent, and gravity of the violation or violations and, with respect to the violator, ability to pay, effect on ability to continue to do business, any history of prior such violations, the degree of culpability, and such other matters as justice may require.

(C) The Administrator may compromise, modify, or remit, with or without conditions, any civil penalty which may be imposed under this subsection. The amount of such penalty, when finally determined, or the amount agreed upon in compromise, may be deducted from any sums owing by the United States to the person charged.

(3) Any person who requested in accordance with paragraph (2)(A) a hearing respecting the assessment of a civil penalty and who is aggrieved by an order assessing a civil penalty may file a petition for judicial review of such order with the United States Court of Appeals for the District of Columbia Circuit or for any other circuit in which such person resides or transacts business. Such a petition may only be filed within the 30-day period beginning on the date the order making such assessment was issued.

(4) If any person fails to pay an assessment of a civil penalty—

(A) after the order making the assessment has become a final order and if such person does not file a petition for judicial review of the order in accordance with paragraph (3), or

(B) after a court in an action brought under paragraph (3) has entered a final judgment in favor of the Administrator,

the Attorney General shall recover the amount assessed (plus interest at currently prevailing rates from the date of the expiration of the 30-day period referred to in paragraph (3) or the date of such final judgment, as the case may be) in an action brought in any appropriate district court of the United States. In such an action, the validity, amount, and appropriateness of such penalty shall not be subject to review.

(b) Criminal.—Any person who knowingly or willfully violates any provision of section 15 shall, in addition to or in lieu of any civil penalty which may be imposed under subsection (a) of this section for such violation, be subject, upon conviction, to a fine of not more than $25,000 for each day of violation, or to imprisonment for not more than one year, or both.

SEC. 17. SPECIFIC ENFORCEMENT AND SEIZURE.

(a) Specific Enforcement.—(1) The district courts of the United States shall have jurisdiction over civil actions to—

(A) restrain any violation of section 15,

(B) restrain any person from taking any action prohibited by section 5 or 6 or by a rule or order under section 5 or 6,

(C) compel the taking of any action required by or under this Act, or

(D) direct any manufacturer or processor of a chemical substance or mixture manufactured or processed in violation of section 5 or 6 or a rule or order under section 5 or 6 and distributed in commerce, (i) to give notice of such fact to distributors in commerce of such substance or mixture and, to the extent reasonably ascertainable, to other persons in possession of such substance or mixture or exposed to such substance or mixture, (ii) to give public notice of such risk of injury, and (iii) to either replace or repurchase such substance or mixture, whichever the person to which the requirement is directed elects.

(2) A civil action described in paragraph (1) may be brought—

(A) in the case of a civil action described in subparagraph (A) of such paragraph, in the United States district court for the judicial district wherein any act, omission, or transaction constituting a violation of section 15 occurred or wherein the defendant is found or transacts business, or

(B) in the case of any other civil action described in such paragraph, in the United States district court for the judicial district wherein the defendant is found or transacts business.

In any such civil action process may be served on a defendant in any judicial district in which a defendant resides or may be found. Subpoenas requiring attendance of witnesses in any such action may be served in any judicial district.

(b) Seizure.—Any chemical substance or mixture which was manufactured, processed, or distributed in commerce in violation of this Act or any rule promulgated or order issued under this Act or any article containing such a substance or mixture shall be liable to be proceeded against, by process of libel for the seizure and condemnation of such substance, mixture, or article, in any district court of the United States within the jurisdiction of which such substance, mixture, or article is found. Such proceeding shall conform as nearly as possible to proceedings in rem in admiralty.

SEC. 18. PREEMPTION.

(a) Effect on State Law.—(1) Except as provided in paragraph (2), nothing in this Act shall affect the authority of any State or political subdivision of a State to establish or continue in effect regulation of any chemical substance, mixture, or article containing a chemical substance or mixture.

(2) Except as provided in subsection (b)—

(A) if the Administrator requires by a rule promulgated under section 4 the testing of a chemical substance or mixture, no State or political subdivision may, after the effective date of such rule, establish or continue in effect a requirement for the testing of such substance or mixture for purposes similar to those for which testing is required under such rule; and

(B) if the Administrator prescribes a rule or order under section 5 or 6 (other than a rule imposing a requirement described in subsection (a)(6) of section 6) which is applicable to a chemical substance or mixture, and which is designed to protect against a risk of injury to health or the environment associated with such substance or mixture, no State or political subdivision of a State may, after the effective date of such requirement, establish or continue in effect, any requirement which is applicable to such substance or mixture, or an article containing such substance or mixture, and which is designed to protect against such risk unless such requirement (i) is identical to the requirement prescribed by the Administrator, (ii) is adopted under the authority of the Clean Air Act or any other Federal law, or (iii) prohibits the use of such substance or mixture in such State or political subdivision (other than its use in the manufacture or processing of other substances or mixtures).

(b) EXEMPTION.—Upon application of a State or political subdivision of a State the Administrator may by rule exempt from subsection (a)(2), under such conditions as may be prescribed in such rule, a requirement of such State or political subdivision designed to protect against a risk of injury to health or the environment associated with a chemical substance, mixture, or article containing a chemical substance or mixture if—

(1) compliance with the requirement would not cause the manufacturing, processing, distribution in commerce, or use of the substance, mixture, or article to be in violation of the applicable requirement under this Act described in subsection (a)(2), and

(2) the State or political subdivision requirement (A) provides a significantly higher degree of protection from such risk than the requirement under this Act described in subsection (a)(2) and (B) does not, through difficulties in marketing, distribution, or other factors, unduly burden interstate commerce.

SEC. 19. JUDICIAL REVIEW.

(a) IN GENERAL.—(1)(A) Not later than 60 days after the date of the promulgation of a rule under section 4(a), 5(a)(2), 5(b)(4), 6(a), 6(e), or 8, any person may file a petition for judicial review of such rule with the United States Court of Appeals for the District of Columbia Circuit or for the circuit in which such person resides or in which such person's principal place of business is located. Courts of appeals of the United States shall have exclusive jurisdiction of any action to obtain judicial review (other than in an enforcement proceeding) of such a rule if any district court of the United States would have had jurisdiction of such action but for this subparagraph.

(B) Courts of appeals of the United States shall have exclusive jurisdiction of any action to obtain judicial review (other than in an enforcement proceeding) of an order issued under subparagraph (A) or (B) of section 6(b)(1) if any district court of the United States would have had jurisdiction of such action but for this subparagraph.

(2) Copies of any petition filed under paragraph (1)(A) shall be transmitted forthwith to the Administrator and to the Attorney General by the clerk of the court with which such petition was filed. The provisions of section 2112 of title 28, United States Code, shall apply to the filing of the rulemaking record of proceedings on which the Administrator based the rule being reviewed under this section and to the transfer of proceedings between United States courts of appeals.

(3) For purposes of this section, the term "rulemaking record" means—

(A) the rule being reviewed under this section;

(B) in the case of a rule under section 4(a), the finding required by such section, in the case of a rule under section 5(b)(4), the finding required by such section, in the case of a rule under section 6(a) the finding required by section 5(f) or 6(a), as the case may be, in the case of a rule under section 6(a), the statement required by section 6(c)(1), and in the case of a rule under section 6(e), the findings required by paragraph (2)(B) or (3)(B) of such section, as the case may be;

(C) any transcript required to be made of oral presentations made in proceedings for the promulgation of such rule;

(D) any written submission of interested parties respecting the promulgation of such rule; and

(E) any other information which the Administrator considers to be relevant to such rule and which the Administrator identified, on or before the date of the promulgation of such rule, in a notice published in the Federal Register.

(b) ADDITIONAL SUBMISSIONS AND PRESENTATIONS; MODIFICATIONS.—If in an action under this section to review a rule the petitioner or the Administrator applies to the court for leave to make additional oral submissions or written presentations respecting such rule and shows to the satisfaction of the court that such submissions and presentations would be material and that there were reasonable grounds for the submissions and failure to make such submissions and presentations in the proceeding before the Administrator, the court may order the Administrator to provide additional opportunity to make such submissions and presentations. The Administrator may modify or set aside the rule being reviewed or make a new rule by reason of the additional submissions and presentations and shall file such modified or new rule with the return of such submissions and presentations. The court shall thereafter review such new or modified rule.

(c) STANDARD OF REVIEW.—(1)(A) Upon the filing of a petition under subsection (a)(1) for judicial review of a rule, the court shall have jurisdiction (i) to grant appropriate relief, including interim relief, as provided in chapter 7 of title 5, United States Code, and (ii) except as otherwise provided in subparagraph (B), to review such rule in accordance with chapter 7 of title 5, United States Code.

(B) Section 706 of title 5, United States Code, shall apply to review of a rule under this section, except that—

(i) in the case of review of a rule under section 4(a), 5(b)(4), 6(a), or 6(e), the standard for review prescribed by paragraph (2)(E) of such section 706 shall not apply and the court shall hold unlawful and set aside such rule if the court finds that the rule is not supported by substantial evidence in the rulemaking record (as defined in subsection (a)(3)) taken as a whole;

(ii) in the case of review of a rule under section 6(a), the court shall hold unlawful and set aside such rule if it finds that—

(I) a determination by the Administrator under section 6(c)(3) that the petitioner seeking review of such rule is not entitled to conduct (or have conducted) cross-examination or to present rebuttal submissions, or

(II) a rule of, or ruling by, the Administrator under section 6(c)(3) limiting such petitioner's cross-examination or oral presentations.

has precluded disclosure of disputed material facts which was necessary to a fair determination by the Administrator of the rulemaking proceeding taken as a whole; and section 706(2)(D) shall not apply with respect to a determination, rule, or ruling referred to in subclause (I) or (II); and

(iii) the court may not review the contents and adequacy of—

(I) any statement required to be made pursuant to section 6(c)(1), or

(II) any statement of basis and purpose required by section 553(c) of title 5, United States Code, to be incorporated in the rule

except as part of a review of the rulemaking record taken as a whole.

The term "evidence" as used in clause (i) means any matter in the rulemaking record.

(C) A determination, rule, or ruling of the Administrator described in subparagraph (B)(ii) may be reviewed only in an action under this section and only in accordance with such subparagraph.

(2) The judgment of the court affirming or setting aside, in whole or in part, any rule reviewed in accordance with this section shall be final, subject to review by the Supreme Court of the United States upon certiorari or certification, as provided in section 1254 of title 28, United States Code.

(d) FEES AND COSTS.—The decision of the court in an action commenced under subsection (a), or of the Supreme Court of the United States on review of such a decision, may include an award of costs of suit and reasonable fees for attorneys and expert witnesses if the court determines that such an award is appropriate.

(e) OTHER REMEDIES.—The remedies as provided in this section shall be in addition to and not in lieu of any other remedies provided by law.

SEC. 20. CITIZENS' CIVIL ACTIONS.

(a) IN GENERAL.—Except as provided in subsection (b), any person may commence a civil action—

(1) against any person (including (A) the United States, and (B) any other governmental instrumentality or agency to the extent permitted by the eleventh amendment to the Constitution) who is alleged to be in violation of this Act or any rule promulgated under section 4, 5, or 6 or order issued under section 5 to restrain such violation, or

(2) against the Administrator to compel the Administrator to perform any act or duty under this Act which is not discretionary.

Any civil action under paragraph (1) shall be brought in the United States district court for the district in which the alleged violation occurred or in which the defendant resides or in which the defendant's principal place of business is located. Any action brought under paragraph (2) shall be brought in the United States District Court for the District of Columbia, or the United States district court for the judicial district in which the plaintiff is domiciled. The district courts of the United States shall have jurisdiction over suits brought under this section, without regard to the amount in controversy or the citizenship of the parties. In any civil action under this subsection process may be served on a defendant in any judicial district in which the defendant resides or may be found and subpoenas for witnesses may be served in any judicial district.

(b) LIMITATION.—No civil action may be commenced—

(1) under subsection (a)(1) to restrain a violation of this Act or rule or order under this Act—

(A) before the expiration of 60 days after the plaintiff has given notice of such violation (i) to the Administrator, and (ii) to the person who is alleged to have committed such violation, or

(B) if the Administrator has commenced and is diligently prosecuting a proceeding for the issuance of an order under section 16(a)(2) to require compliance with this Act or with such rule or order or if the Attorney General has commenced and is diligently prosecuting a civil action in a court of the United States to require compliance with this Act or with such rule or order, but if such proceeding or civil action is commenced after the giving of notice, any person giving such notice may intervene as a matter of right in such proceeding or action; or

(2) under subsection (a)(2) before the expiration of 60 days after the plaintiff has given notice to the Administrator of the alleged failure of the Administrator to perform an act or duty which is the basis for such action or, in the case of an action under such subsection for the failure of the Administrator to file an action under section 7, before the expiration of ten days after such notification.

Notice under this subsection shall be given in such manner as the Administrator shall prescribe by rule.

(c) GENERAL.—(1) In any action under this section, the Administrator, if not a party, may intervene as a matter of right.

(2) The court, in issuing any final order in any action brought pursuant to subsection (a), may award costs of suit and reasonable fees for attorneys and expert witnesses if the court determines that such an award is appropriate. Any court, in issuing its decision in an action brought to review such an order, may award costs of suit and reasonable fees for attorneys if the court determines that such an award is appropriate.

(3) Nothing in this section shall restrict any right which any person (or class of persons) may have under

any statute or common law to seek enforcement of this Act or any rule or order under this Act or to seek any other relief.

(d) CONSOLIDATION.—When two or more civil actions brought under subsection (a) involving the same defendant and the same issues or violations are pending in two or more judicial districts, such pending actions, upon application of such defendants to such actions which is made to a court in which any such action is brought, may, if such court in its discretion so decides, be consolidated for trial by order (issued after giving all parties reasonable notice and opportunity to be heard) of such court and tried in—

(1) any district which is selected by such defendant and in which one of such actions is pending,

(2) a district which is agreed upon by stipulation between all the parties to such actions and in which one of such actions is pending, or

(3) a district which is selected by the court and in which one of such actions is pending.

The court issuing such an order shall give prompt notification of the order to the other courts in which the civil actions consolidated under the order are pending.

SEC. 21. CITIZENS' PETITIONS.

(a) IN GENERAL.—Any person may petition the Administrator to initiate a proceeding for the issuance, amendment, or repeal of a rule under section 4, 6, or 8 or an order under section 5(e) or (6)(b)(2).

(b) PROCEDURES.—(1) Such petition shall be filed in the principal office of the Administrator and shall set forth the facts which it is claimed establish that it is necessary to issue, amend, or repeal a rule under section 4, 6, or 8 or an order under section 5(e), 6(b)(1)(A), or 6(b)(1)(B).

(2) The Administrator may hold a public hearing or may conduct such investigation or proceeding as the Administrator deems appropriate in order to determine whether or not such petition should be granted.

(3) Within 90 days after filing of a petition described in paragraph (1), the Administrator shall either grant or deny the petition. If the Administrator grants such petition, the Administrator shall promptly commence an appropriate proceeding in accordance with section 4, 5, 6, or 8. If the Administrator denies such petition, the Administrator shall publish in the Federal Register the Administrator's reasons for such denial.

(4)(A) If the Administrator denies a petition filed under this section (or if the Administrator fails to grant or deny such petition within the 90-day period) the petitioner may commence a civil action in a district court of the United States to compel the Administrator to initiate a rulemaking proceeding as requested in the petition. Any such action shall be filed within 60 days after the Administrator's denial of the petition or, if the Administrator fails to grant or deny the petition within 90 days after filing the petition, within 60 days after the expiration of the 90-day period.

(B) In an action under subparagraph (A) respecting a petition to initiate a proceeding to issue a rule under section 4, 6, or 8 or an order under section 5(e) or 6(b)(2), the petitioner shall be provided an opportunity to have such petition considered by the court in a de novo proceeding. If the petitioner demonstrates to the satisfaction of the court by a preponderance of the evidence that—

(i) in the case of a petition to initiate a proceeding for the issuance of a rule under section 4 or an order under section 5(e)—

(I) information available to the Administrator is insufficient to permit a reasoned evaluation of the health and environmental effects of the chemical substance to be subject to such rule or order; and

(II) in the absence of such information, the substance may present an unreasonable risk to health or the environment, or the substance is or will be produced in substantial quantities and it enters or may reasonably be anticipated to enter the environment in substantial quantities or there is or may be significant or substantial human exposure to it; or

(ii) in the case of a petition to initiate a proceeding for the issuance of a rule under section 6 or 8 or an order under section 6(b)(2), there is a reasonable basis to conclude that the issuance of such a rule or order is necessary to protect health or the environment against an unreasonable risk of injury to health or the environment,

the court shall order the Administrator to initiate the action requested by the petitioner. If the court finds that the extent of the risk to health or the environment alleged by the petitioner is less than the extent of risks to health or the environment with respect to which the Administrator is taking action under this Act and there are insufficient resources available to the Administrator to take the action requested by the petitioner, the court may permit the Administrator to defer initiating the action requested by the petitioner until such time as the court prescribes.

(C) The court in issuing any final order in any action brought pursuant to subparagraph (A) may award costs of suit and reasonable fees for attorneys and expert witnesses if the court determines that such an award is appropriate. Any court, in issuing its decision in an action brought to review such an order, may award costs of suit and reasonable fees for attorneys if the court determines that such an award is appropriate.

(5) The remedies under this section shall be in addition to, and not in lieu of, other remedies provided by law.

SEC. 22. NATIONAL DEFENSE WAIVER.

The Administrator shall waive compliance with any provision of this Act upon a request and determination by the President that the requested waiver is necessary in the interest of national defense. The Administrator shall maintain a written record of the basis upon which such waiver was granted and make such record available for in camera examination when relevant in a judicial proceeding under this Act. Upon the issuance of such a waiver, the Administrator shall publish in the Federal Register a notice that the waiver was granted for national defense purposes, unless, upon the request of the President, the Administrator determines to omit such publication because the publication itself would be contrary to the interests of national defense, in which event the Administrator shall submit notice thereof to the Armed Services Committees of the Senate and the House of Representatives.

SEC. 23. EMPLOYEE PROTECTION.

(a) IN GENERAL.—No employer may discharge any employee or otherwise discriminate against any employee with respect to the employee's compensation, terms, conditions, or privileges of employment because the employee (or any person acting pursuant to a request of the employee) has—

(1) commenced, caused to be commenced, or is about to commence or cause to be commenced a proceeding under this Act;

(2) testified or is about to testify in any such proceeding; or

(3) assisted or participated or is about to assist or participate in any manner in such a proceeding or in any other action to carry out the purposes of this Act.

(b) REMEDY.—(1) Any employee who believes that the employee has been discharged or otherwise discriminated against by any person in violation of subsection (a) of this section may, within 30 days after such alleged violation occurs, file (or have any person file on the employee's behalf) a complaint with the Secretary of Labor (hereinafter in this section referred to as the "Secretary") alleging such discharge or discrimination. Upon receipt of such a complaint, the Secretary shall notify the person named in the complaint of the filing of the complaint.

(2) (A) Upon receipt of a complaint filed under paragraph (1), the Secretary shall conduct an investigation of the violation alleged in the complaint. Within 30 days of the receipt of such complaint, the Secretary shall complete such investigation and shall notify in writing the complainant (and any person acting on behalf of the complainant) and the person alleged to have committed such violation of the results of the investigation conducted pursuant to this paragraph. Within ninety days of the receipt of such complaint the Secretary shall, unless the proceeding on the complaint is terminated by the Secretary on the basis of a settlement entered into by the Secretary and the person alleged to have committed such violation, issue an order either providing the relief prescribed by subparagraph (B) or denying the complaint. An order of the Secretary shall be made on the record after notice and opportunity for agency hearing. The Secretary may not enter into a settlement terminating a proceeding on a complaint without the participation and consent of the complainant.

(B) If in response to a complaint filed under paragraph (1) the Secretary determines that a violation of subsection (a) of this section has occurred, the Secretary shall order (i) the person who committed such violation to take affirmative action to abate the violation, (ii) such person to reinstate the complainant to the complainant's former position together with the compensation (including back pay), terms, conditions, and privileges of the complainant's employment, (iii) compensatory damages, and (iv) where appropriate, exemplary damages. If such an order issued, the Secretary, at the request of the complainant, shall assess against the person against whom the order is issued a sum equal to the aggregate amount of all costs and expenses (including attorney's fees) reasonably incurred, as determined by the Secretary, by the complainant for, or in connection with, the bringing of the complaint upon which the order was issued.

(c) Review.—(1) Any employee or employer adversely affected or aggrieved by an order issued under subsection (b) may obtain review of the order in the United States Court of Appeals for the circuit in which the violation, with respect to which the order was issued, allegedly occurred. The petition for review must be filed within sixty days from the issuance of the Secretary's order. Review shall conform to chapter 7 of title 5 of the United States Code.

(2) An order of the Secretary, with respect to which review could have been obtained under paragraph (1), shall not be subject to judicial review in any criminal or other civil proceeding.

(d) Enforcement.—Whenever a person has failed to comply with an order issued under subsection (b)(2), the Secretary shall file a civil action in the United States district court for the district in which the violation was found to occur to enforce such order. In actions brought under this subsection, the district courts shall have jurisdiction to grant all appropriate relief, including injunctive relief and compensatory and exemplary damages. Civil actions brought under this subsection shall be heard and decided expeditiously.

(e) Exclusion.—Subsection (a) of this section shall not apply with respect to any employee who, acting without direction from the employee's employer (or any agent of the employer), deliberately causes a violation of any requirement of this Act.

SEC. 24. EMPLOYMENT EFFECTS.

(a) In General.—The Administrator shall evaluate on a continuuing basis the potential effects on employment (including reductions in employment or loss of employment from threatened plant closures) of—

(1) the issuance of a rule or order under section 4, 5, or 6, or

(2) a requirement of section 5 or 6.

(b)(1) Investigations.—Any employeee (or any representative of an employee) may request the Administrator to make an investigation of—

(A) a discharge or layoff or threatened discharge or layoff of the employee, or

(B) adverse or threatened adverse effects on the employee's employment,

allegedly resulting from a rule or order under section 4, 5, or 6 or a requirement of section 5 or 6. Any such request shall be made in writing, shall set forth with reasonable particularity the grounds for the request, and shall be signed by the employee, or representative of such employee, making the request.

(2)(A) Upon receipt of a request made in accordance with paragraph (1) the Administrator shall (i) conduct the investigation requested, and (ii) if requested by any interested person, hold public hearings on any matter involved in the investigation unless the Administrator, by order issued within 45 days of the date such hearings are requested, denies the request for the hearings because the Administrator determines there are no reasonable grounds for holding such hearings. If the Administrator makes such a determination, the Administrator shall notify in writing the person requesting the hearing of the determination and the reasons therefor and shall publish the determination and the reasons therefor in the Federal Register.

(B) If public hearings are to be held on any matter involved in an investigation conducted under this subsection—

(i) at least five days' notice shall be provided the person making the request for the investigation and any person identified in such request,

(ii) such hearings shall be held in accordance with section 6(c)(3), and

(iii) each employee who made or for whom was made a request for such hearings and the employer of such employee shall be required to present information respecting the applicable matter referred to in paragraph (1)(A) or (1)(B) together with the basis for such information.

(3) Upon completion of an investigation under paragraph (2), the Administrator shall make findings of fact, shall make such recommendations as the Administrator deems appropriate, and shall make available to the public such findings and recommendations.

(4) This section shall not be construed to require the Administrator to amend or repeal any rule or order in effect under this Act.

SEC. 25. STUDIES.

(a) Indemnification Study.—The Administrator shall conduct a study of all Federal laws administered by the Administrator for the purpose of determining whether and under what conditions, if any, indemnification should be accorded any person as a result of any action taken by the Administrator under any such law. The study shall—

(1) include an estimate of the probable cost of any indemnification programs which may be recommended;

(2) include an examination of all viable means of financing the cost of any recommended indemnification; and

(3) be completed and submitted to Congress within two years from the effective date of enactment of this Act.

The General Accounting Office shall review the adequacy of the study submitted to Congress pursuant to paragraph (3) and shall report the results of its review to the Congress within six months of the date such study is submitted to Congress.

(b) Classification, Storage, and Retrieval Study.—The Council on Environmental Quality, in consultation with the Administrator, the Secretary of Health, Education, and Welfare, the Secretary of Commerce, and the heads of other appropriate Federal departments or agencies, shall coordinate a study of the feasibility of establishing (1) a standard classification system for chemical substances and related substances, and (2) a standard means for storing and for obtaining rapid access to information respecting such substances. A report on such study shall be completed and submitted to Congress not later than 18 months after the effective date of enactment of this Act.

SEC. 26. ADMINISTRATION OF THE ACT.

(a) COOPERATION OF FEDERAL AGENCIES.—Upon request by the Administrator, each Federal department and agency is authorized—

(1) to make its services, personnel, and facilities available (with or without reimbursement) to the Administrator to assist the Administrator in the administration of this Act; and

(2) to furnish to the Administrator such information, data, estimates, and statistics, and to allow the Administrator access to all information in its possession as the Administrator may reasonably determine to be necessary for the administration of this Act.

(b) FEES.—(1) The Administrator may, by rule, require the payment of a reasonable fee from any person required to submit data under section 4 or 5 to defray the cost of administering this Act. Such rules shall not provide for any fee in excess of $2,500 or, in the case of a small business concern, any fee in excess of $100. In setting a fee under this paragraph, the Administrator shall take into account the ability to pay of the person required to submit the data and the cost to the Administrator of reviewing such data. Such rules may provide for sharing such a fee in any case in which the expenses of testing are shared under section 4 or 5.

(2) The Administrator, after consultation with the Administrator of the Small Business Administration, shall by rule prescribe standards for determining the persons which qualify as small business concerns for purposes of paragraph (1).

(c) ACTION WITH RESPECT TO CATEGORIES.—(1) Any action authorized or required to be taken by the Administrator under any provision of this Act with respect to a chemical substance or mixture may be taken by the Administrator in accordance with that provision with respect to a category of chemical substances or mixtures. Whenever the Administrator takes action under a provision of this Act with respect to a category of chemical substances or mixtures, any reference in this Act to a chemical substance or mixture (insofar as it relates to such action) shall be deemed to be a reference to each chemical substance or mixture in such category.

(2) For purposes of paragraph (1):

(A) The term "category of chemical substances" means a group of chemical substances the members of which are similar in molecular structure, in physical, chemical, or biological properties, in use, or in mode of entrance into the human body or into the environment, or the members of which are in some other way suitable for classification as such for purposes of this Act, except that such term does not mean a group of chemical substances which are grouped together solely on the basis of their being new chemical substances.

(B) The term "category of mixtures" means a group of mixtures the members of which are similar in molecular structure, in physical, chemical, or biological properties, in use, or in the mode of entrance into the human body or into the environment, or the members of which are in some other way suitable for classification as such for purposes of this Act.

(d) ASSISTANCE OFFICE.—The Administrator shall establish in the Environmental Protection Agency an identifiable office to provide technical and other nonfinancial assistance to manufacturers and processors of chemical substances and mixtures respecting the requirements of this Act applicable to such manufacturers and processors, the policy of the Agency respecting the application of such requirements to such manufacturers and processors, and the means and methods by which such manufacturers and processors may comply with such requirements.

(e) FINANCIAL DISCLOSURES.—(1) Except as provided under paragraph (3), each officer or employee of the Environmental Protection Agency and the Department of Health, Education, and Welfare who—

(A) performs any function or duty under this Act, and

(B) has any known financial interest (i) in any person subject to this Act or any rule or order in effect under this Act, or (ii) in any person who applies for or receives any grant or contract under this Act,

shall, on February 1, 1978, and on February 1 of each year thereafter, file with the Administrator or the Secretary of Health, Education, and Welfare (hereinafter in this subsection referred to as the "Secretary"), as appropriate, a written statement concerning all such interests held by such officer or employee during the preceding calendar year. Such statement shall be made available to the public.

(2) The Administrator and the Secretary shall—

(A) act within 90 days of the effective date of this Act—

(i) to define the term "known financial interests" for purposes of paragraph (1), and

(ii) to establish the methods by which the requirement to file written statements specified in paragraph (1) will be monitored and enforced, including appropriate provisions for review by the Administrator and the Secretary of such statements; and

(B) report to the Congress on June 1, 1978, and on June 1 of each year thereafter with respect to such statements and the actions taken in regard thereto during the preceding calendar year.

(3) The Administrator may by rule identify specific positions with the Environmental Protection Agency, and the Secretary may by rule identify specific positions with the Department of Health, Education, and Welfare, which are of a nonregulatory or nonpolicymaking nature, and the Administrator and the Secretary may by rule provide that officers or employees occupying such positions shall be exempt from the requirements of paragraph (1).

(4) This subsection does not supersede any requirement of chapter 11 of title 18, United States Code.

(5) Any officer or employee who is subject to, and knowingly violates, this subsection or any rule issued thereunder, shall be fined not more than $2,500 or imprisoned not more than one year, or both.

(f) STATEMENT OF BASIS AND PURPOSE.—Any final order issued under this Act shall be accompanied by a statement of its basis and purpose. The contents and adequacy of any such statement shall not be subject to judicial review in any respect.

(g) ASSISTANT ADMINISTRATOR.—(1) The President, by and with the advice and consent of the Senate, shall appoint an Assistant Administrator for Toxic Substances of the Environmental Protection Agency. Such Assistant Administrator shall be a qualified individual who is, by reason of background and experience, especially qualified to direct a program concerning the effects of chemicals on human health and the environment. Such Assistant Administrator shall be responsible for (A) the collection of data, (B) the preparation of studies, (C) the making of recommendations to the Administrator for regulatory and other actions to carry out the purposes and to facilitate the administration of this Act, and (D) such other functions as the Administrator may assign or delegate.

(2) The Assistant Administrator to be appointed under paragraph (1) shall (A) be in addition to the Assistant Administrators of the Environmental Protection Agency authorized by section 1(d) of Reorganization Plan No. 3 of 1970, and (B) be compensated at the rate of pay authorized for such Assistant Administrators.

SEC. 27. DEVELOPMENT AND EVALUATION OF TEST METHODS.

(a) IN GENERAL.—The Secretary of Health, Education, and Welfare in consultation with the Administrator and acting through the Assistant Secretary for Health, may conduct, and make grants to public and nonprofit private entities and enter into contracts with public and private entities for, projects for the development and evaluation of inexpensive and efficient methods (1) for determining and evaluating the health and environmental effects of chemical substances and mixtures, and their toxicity, persistence, and other characteristics which affect health and the environment, and (2) which may be used for the development of test data to meet the requirements of rules promulgated under section 4. The Administrator shall consider such methods in prescribing under section 4 standards for the development of test data.

(b) APPROVAL BY SECRETARY.—No grant may be made or contract entered into under subsection (a) unless an application therefor has been submitted to and approved by the Secretary. Such an application shall be submitted in such form and manner and contain such information as the Secretary may require. The Secretary may apply such conditions to grants and contracts under subsection (a) as the Secretary determines are necessary to carry out the purposes of such subsection. Contracts may be entered into under such subsection without regard to sections 3648 and 3709 of the Revised Statutes (31 U.S.C. 529; 41 U.S.C. 5).

(c) ANNUAL REPORTS.—(1) The Secretary shall prepare and submit to the President and the Congress on or before January 1 of each year a report of the number of grants made and contracts entered into under this section and the results of such grants and contracts.

(2) The Secretary shall periodically publish in the Federal Register reports describing the progress and results of any contract entered into or grant made under this section.

SEC. 28. STATE PROGRAMS.

(a) IN GENERAL.—For the purpose of complementing (but not reducing) the authority of, or actions taken by, the Administrator under this Act, the Administrator may make grants to States for the establishment and operation of programs to prevent or eliminate unreasonable risks within the States to health or the environment which are associated with a chemical substance or mixture and with respect to which the Administrator is unable or is not likely to take action under this Act for their prevention or elimination. The amount of a grant under this subsection shall be determined by the Administrator, except that no grant for any State program may exceed 75 per centum of the establishment and operation costs (as determined by the Administrator) of such program during the period for which the grant is made.

(b) Approval by Administrator.—(1) No grant may be made under subsection (a) unless an application therefor is submitted to and approved by the Administrator. Such an application shall be submitted in such form and manner as the Administrator may require and shall—

(A) set forth the need of the applicant for a grant under subsection (a),

(B) identify the agency or agencies of the State which shall establish or operate, or both, the program for which the application is submitted,

(C) describe the actions proposed to be taken under such program,

(D) contain or be supported by assurances satisfactory to the Administrator that such program shall, to the extent feasible, be integrated with other programs of the applicant for environmental and public health protection,

(E) provide for the making of such reports and evaluations as the Administrator may require, and

(F) contain such other information as the Administrator may prescribe.

(2) The Administrator may approve an application submitted in accordance with paragraph (1) only if the applicant has established to the satisfaction of the Administrator a priority need, as determined under rules of the Administrator, for the grant for which the application has been submitted. Such rules shall take into consideration the seriousness of the health effects in a State which are associated with chemical substances or mixtures, including cancer, birth defects, and gene mutations, the extent of the exposure in a State of human beings and the environment to chemical substances and mixtures, and the extent to which chemical substances and mixtures are manufactured, processed, used, and disposed of in a State.

(c) Annual Reports.—Not later than six months after the end of each of the fiscal years 1979, 1980, and 1981, the Administrator shall submit to the Congress a report respecting the programs assisted by grants under subsection (a) in the preceding fiscal year and the extent to which the Administrator has disseminated information respecting such programs.

(d) Authorization.—For the purpose of making grants under subsection (a) there are authorized to be appropriated $1,500,000 **each of the fiscal years 1982 and 1983.**

Sums appropriated under this subsection shall remain available until expended.

SEC. 29. AUTHORIZATION FOR APPROPRIATIONS.

There are authorized to be appropriated to the Administrator for purposes of carrying out this Act (other than sections 27 and 28 and subsections (a) and (c) through (g) of section 10 thereof) $58,646,000 for the fiscal year 1982 and $62,000,000 for the fiscal year 1983. No part of the funds appropriated under this section may be used to construct any research laboratories.

SEC. 30. ANNUAL REPORT.

The Administrator shall prepare and submit to the President and the Congress on or before January 1, 1978, and on or before January 1 of each succeeding year a comprehensive report on the administration of this Act during the preceding fiscal year. Such report shall include—

(1) a list of the testing required under section 4 during the year for which the report is made and an estimate of the costs incurred during such year by the persons required to perform such tests;

(2) the number of notices received during such year under section 5, the number of such notices received during such year under such section for chemical substances subject to a section 4 rule, and a summary of any action taken during such year under section 5(g);

(3) a list of rules issued during such year under section 6;

(4) a list, with a brief statement of the issues, of completed or pending judicial actions under this Act and administrative actions under section 16 during such year;

(5) a summary of major problems encountered in the administration of this Act; and

(6) such recommendations for additional legislation as the Administrator deems necessary to carry out the purposes of this Act.

SEC. 31. EFFECTIVE DATE.

Except as provided in section 4(f), this Act shall take effect on January 1, 1977.